"This is the book we've been waiting for. Anyone interested in the explosion of social movements in Latin America—and the complex interplay between those forces and the 'Pink Tide' governments—should inhale this book immediately. *Until the Rulers Obey* gives us country-specific context from a superb team of 'introducers,' who then step aside so we can hear a chorus of voices from some of the most inspiring grassroots organizations on the continent. This is a people's history in real time, bubbling up from below."
—Avi Lewis and Naomi Klein

"Latin America is the last region in the world that still has a vibrant Enlightenment left, which sets both the practical agenda in terms of policy and the horizon in terms of utopia. This wonderfully edited collection of analysis and first-person accounts shows why. It assembles people who are both activists and analysts, who see no difference between interpreting and changing the world. It deserves a wide audience."
—Greg Grandin, author of *Empire's Workshop* and *Fordlandia*

"A new world is dawning in Latin America from the bottom up. This book brings an all-star cast of scholar-activists together with social movement and community leaders from throughout the region. The reader will hear the clarion call for social justice from those who are on the front lines of grassroots resistance and popular struggles in this age of globalization, crisis, and transformation. These are the voices that too often are suppressed by the powerful and the means of communication they control. I cannot imagine a more important and timely volume for scholars and activists who wish to understand the transformations that are sweeping the subcontinent."
—William I. Robinson, professor of sociology, global studies, and Latin American studies, University of California at Santa Barbara, author of *Latin America and Global Capitalism*

D1040174

Until the Rulers Obey

Voices from Latin American
Social Movements

Edited by Clifton Ross and Marcy Rein

Until the Rulers Obey: Voices from Latin American Social Movements
Edited by Clifton Ross and Marcy Rein
© 2014 Clifton Ross and Marcy Rein, as well as the individual contributors
© 2014 PM Press

ISBN: 978–1–60486–794–7
LCCN: 2013911522

Cover by John Yates/www.stealworks.com. Top: Student march, Santiago de Chile, October 11, 2012. Photo © Jp Catepillan. Bottom: Demonstration by Confederation of Indigenous Nationalities of Ecuador (CONAIE), February 7, 2011. Photo © CONAIE, used by permission.
Interior design by briandesign

10 9 8 7 6 5 4 3 2 1

PM Press
PO Box 23912
Oakland, CA 94623
www.pmpress.org

Printed in the USA by the Employee Owners of Thomson-Shore in Dexter, Michigan.
www.thomsonshore.com

"We will resist until the rulers govern obediently."

—Zapatista National Liberation Army (EZLN),
Second Declaration of the Lacandon Jungle

University of Texas Libraries

Contents

Foreword by Raúl Zibechi   xi

Editors' Introduction   xv

Mexico

Introduction by Luis Ballesteros   3
Women in the Zapatista Movement   8
Voices from the Oaxaca uprising of 2006   13
Movement for National Renewal (MORENA)   20
#YoSoy132   26

Guatemala

Introduction by Phil Neff   33
Paula Barrios, Women Transforming the World (MTM)   38
Roberto Mendez, H.I.J.O.S. and CPR Urbana   44
Edwin E.A. Guevara, SITRAPETEN union organizer   50
Javier de León and Fernando Solís, anti-mining activists   53

Honduras

Introduction by Adrienne Pine   59
Nery Rodríguez, middle-school teacher   65
Leda Sánchez, Marina Pagoada, and Juana Buchanan, Nurses in
Resistance   69
Sara Hernández, Movimiento Unificado Campesino del Aguán
(MUCA)   73
Ricardo, gay activist, FNRP member   77

El Salvador

Introduction by J. Heyward 85
Miguel Rivera, community organizer 91
Lower Lempa River/Bay of Jiquilisco Coordinating Committee ... 96
Lilian Coto de Cuellar, FMLN National Secretariat for Women ... 101
Oswaldo Natarén and members of the University Front of
Roque Dalton 106

Nicaragua

Introduction by Clifton Ross 115
Andrea Morales Pérez, Sandinista Workers' Federation 120
Altagracia del Socorro Solís, Banana Workers' Encampment ... 125
Gloria Paniagua, Another World Is Possible 128
Victor Hugo Tinoco, Sandinista Renewal Movement 133
Luisa Molina, Civil Coordinating Committee 138
Yamilet Mejía, feminist lawyer and activist 143

Colombia

Introduction by Mario A. Murillo 151
Manuela Ruiz, ecologist 158
Luis Yonda, Regional Indigenous Council of Cauca 160
Antonio Navarro Wolff, governor of Nariño state, former M-19
guerrilla 164
Jesús Tuberquía, San José de Apartadó Peace Community 170

Venezuela

Introduction by Clifton Ross 179
Rosangela Orozco, El Panal 2021 Commune 186
J. Arturo Albarrán, National Socialist Council for Agroecology ... 191
María Vicenta Dávila, popular educator 196
Alexis Romero, indigenous activist 201
Orlando Chirino, CCURA (United Revolutionary Autonomous
Class Current), oil industry worker 204

Ecuador

Introduction by Marc Becker 211
Milton Chamorro, Itchimbía land occupation 216
Humberto Cholango, ECUARUNARI/CONAIE 221
Dioyenes Lucio, FENOCIN (National Federation of Indigenous,
Peasant, and Black Organizations) 226

Monica Chuji Gualinga, CONAIE, Constitutional Assembly   230
Luis Macas, Scientific Institute of Indigenous Cultures (ICCI)   236

Brazil

Introduction by Michael Fox   245
Ana Hanauer, Landless Workers' Movement (MST)   250
Nelsa Inês Fabian Nespolo, "We Will Overcome Cooperative of
United Seamstresses"   257
Ana Vanesca and Pedro Cardoso, City of Plastic and the
Urban Resistance Front   261
Eliana Sousa Silva, favela activist   266
Raimundo Belmiro, rubber tapper and environmental activist   268

Peru

Introduction by Raphael Hoetmer and Mar Daza   275
Hugo Blanco, writer and activist   281
Margarita Pérez Anchiraico, community organizer in National
Confederation of Peruvian Communities Affected by Mining
(CONACAMI)   286
Magdiel Carrión, Ayabaca Provincial Federation of Peasant
Communities, CONACAMI   290
Luzmila Chiricente and Sari Salinas Ponce, Regional Federation
of Ashaninka, Nomatsiguengas, and Kakintes Women from the
Central Jungle (FREMANK)   296
Veronica Ferrari, Homosexual Movement of Lima   298

Bolivia

Introduction by Ben Dangl   305
Pedro Portugal Mollinedo, editor of *Pukara*   311
Silvia Rivera Cusicanqui, scholar and activist   316
Julieta Ojeda, Mujeres Creando/Women Creating   319
Oscar Olivera, writer and activist   323

Paraguay

Introduction by Ben Dangl   331
Oscar Caceres, Secretariat of Information and Communication
for Development (SICOM)   338
Hipólito Acevei and Emiliano Vera, Coordination for the Self-
Determination of Indigenous Peoples (CAPI)   342
Jorge Galeano, Popular and Agrarian Movement (MAP)   348

Liz Becker, Social and Popular Front   351
Francisco Estigarribia, member of National Coordination of
Adolescent and Child Workers (CONNATs)   355
Marielle Palau, BASE Social Research   360

Uruguay
Introduction by Raúl Zibechi   367
Helios Sarthou, Frente Amplio/Broad Front   369
Gustavo, Pablo, and Noelia, Galpón de Corrales
community center   373

Argentina
Introduction by Marie Trigona   381
Diego Benegas Loyo, H.I.J.O.S. (Daughters and Sons for Identity
and Justice Against Forgetting and Silence)   388
Franco Basualdo, *Prensa de Frente*   393
Ernesto "Lalo" Paret, Movement of Recovered Companies   398
Claudia Acuña, Colectivo lavaca   403

Chile
Introduction by Marcy Rein   411
Edmundo Jiles, José Calderón Miranda Human Rights Committee 419
Iván Fuentes, Social Movement for Aysén   425
La Negra, feminist activist   428
José Ancalao, Federation of Mapuche Students   432
Marjory Cuello, Confederation of Chilean Students (CONFECH)   438

Contributors   443

Acknowledgments   450

Resources   454

Notes   455

Index   468

Foreword

In this book, those from below who are organized in movements speak—those who so often neither have a voice nor are heard; those who have to move in order to continue living because they have been displaced from their material and symbolic inherited space. The survival of those from below can't be maintained individually; they have to join with others like themselves, because they're the sort of people who, when they act alone, are disparaged or repressed.

Ten years ago I pointed out what seemed to me to be the common characteristics that distinguished the new movements of the region from the traditional union movements of the North. The new movements were born in the decade of the 1970s: the Mothers of the Plaza de Mayo (1977), the Landless Movement of Brazil (1979), and Ecuadorian indigenous organizations such as ECUARUNARI (1972). To that list we would have to add outstanding events such as the release of the Manifesto of Tiahuanaco (1973) by the Karista current in Bolivia, and the Indigenous Congress of San Cristóbal de las Casas in Chiapas (1974).

In these few years of intense history the subjects in the "subsoil," invisible and submerged in daily life, began to emerge at the same time that the union movement began its long, continuing decline as a transformative agent. These actors, born in harsh conditions under authoritarian regimes as a counterforce to hegemonic traditions, became the central actors on the social and political scene of the 1990s and played the main role in the great events that changed the relation of forces on a continental scale. The Zapatistas of Chiapas, the Landless Movement of Brazil, the indigenous movements, the Paraguayan *campesinos*, the Argentinian *piqueteros* are all descendants of this handful of organizations and events of the '70s.

With respect to the union struggle, the new generation of movements bore innovative traits such as territorial stability; an emphasis on identity, culture, and autonomy; an outstanding role for women and families; productive ventures in education and health; and the ability to form their own leaders and employ new modes of action. Thanks to these characteristics the popular movements have managed to create new lifestyles, woven from noncapitalist social relations in territories they've begun to control. What is clear is that in little time these movements won in two ways.

First, they overthrew neoliberal governments and imposed new power relations in the main countries of the region. Massive popular uprisings occurred in Venezuela (1989 and 2002), Ecuador (1997, 2000, and 2005), Argentina (2001), Bolivia (2000, 2003, 2005, and 2008), Paraguay (1999 and 2002), and Peru (2002), and large mobilizations also took place in Brazil, Mexico, and Colombia, all of which were led by these new protagonists.

Second, this new kind of movement became a sociopolitical reference point in the popular mind, displacing the union movement from that role. Currently, there are few who doubt that it has become the most influential actor on the scene.

Two fundamental characteristics differentiate these movements: occupying territory and reforming education.

First, people organized in these movements began by laying claim to their own territories, first the rural, and then the urban territories. This involved the occupation and recuperation of millions of hectares of farmland by those from below, either legally or illegally, but always by direct action of a collective-family-community nature. There are thousands of "self-organized islands," settlements of landless campesinos in Brazil, Paraguay, and Bolivia; small farmers who resist in their family agricultural territories, creating federations and cooperatives to sell their produce; and thousands of indigenous communities the length and breadth of the continent who have recuperated land and affirmed their autonomy. In some cases they have created truly autonomous territories, either explicitly or implicitly, in the most diverse ways. Although it isn't altogether common, but simply a tendency, sometimes other nonhierarchical powers arise in these territories, which elsewhere I have called "nonstate powers."

We can make out a panorama of a territory in intense struggle: On one side appear the uniform lands, centers of the vertically organized authority of big capital, characterized by a process of homogenization in which nature is disappeared and replaced by a kind of panoptical distribution of plants artificially modified in laboratories or chemical mining complexes. On the other side are the complex and diverse territories of people who can only exist by engaging with their environment, gatherings of socially heterogeneous relations that sometimes rise to become "emancipated territories," in the words of the Brazilian geographer Carlos Walter Porto Gonçalves.

In the periphery of the great cities, the homeless, the unemployed, and the poor in general build their housing and their neighborhoods, many times on illegally occupied lands which the state has to tolerate because it lacks the means to offer adequate housing. In the cities of Latin America, 50 percent of the housing is built by families or collectives and some part of collective facilities (sports, health, and education, as well as water and electrical services) have been built by the popular sectors organized in movements.

Second, social movements have taken in their hands the formation[1] of their members and the education of children from the families that are a part of them. At the beginning this was a way of compensating for the withdrawal of the national state from its social responsibilities such as education, health services, employment, housing, and other aspects related to the survival of popular sectors, activities that were degraded over the course of two decades of neoliberal policies. After having taken this step, the movements began to consider how they should confront the tasks that the state had previously fulfilled—whether they limited themselves to performing them better or whether through these experiences they might come across paths that would take them in different directions. In short, these ventures in health, education, and production might also be part of the process of emancipation. The issue of education in the movements has at least two dimensions. First, education is a form of movement-building that becomes an essential aspect of organizational life. Second, movements are building educational spaces in their territories where they decide how the schools are to operate, thus becoming a challenge to the national state in one of its key nuclei for the reproduction of the system.

There is yet a third dimension that is affecting nearly all the movements: The state has recuperated its capacity for action and is now implementing social policies that tend to dilute the power of the movements. The principal innovation of the new regional conjuncture where the so-called "progressive" governments stand out consists in the fact that the Washington Consensus has been delegitimized, but neoliberalism hasn't been defeated. On the contrary, accumulation through dispossession, anchored in the extractivist model, continues to deepen at this stage through transnational strip-mining, the monoculture of soy, cane and palm sugar, and tree farms for pulp. These ventures, always undertaken by the large multinationals, expropriate the common wealth—particularly land and water—to convert nature into merchandise (commodities) for export to the empire or to emerging countries like China and India.

When it's said that Latin America is a laboratory of resistance and the building of new worlds, it mustn't be forgotten that, in a parallel way, it's also the test bench for programs to undermine social insurgencies. The social programs have several problems: They install poverty as the problem and remove wealth from the visual field, avoiding structural changes, freezing inequality, and consolidating the power of the elites. Focusing on poverty obscures the incontestable fact that the central problem is the brutal accumulation of capital and power, because that is what destabilizes and destroys every element of society.

But the most serious problem with the state policies is that they tend to dissolve the self-organization of those from below. In this way they impede the consolidation of the autonomy of popular subjects built up in unfavorable circumstances over decades.

To this panorama it need only be added that the world crisis might change the regional reality, already changing and contradictory and suffering from attempts at destabilization through the foreign policy of the United States. The electoral triumph of Hugo Chávez in October 2012 could strengthen the South American regional independence from the North. But it will also consolidate the new presence of the state that often smothers the movements. In the final analysis these are contradictions in a permanently changing scenario. In this context, listening to the voices of those from below, hearing their dreams and hopes, is as necessary as it is stimulating.

Raúl Zibechi
Montevideo
October 2012

Introduction

"The ghosts of all the revolutions that have been strangled or betrayed through Latin America's tortured history emerge in the new experiments, as if the present had been foreseen and begotten by the contradictions of the past. History is a prophet who looks back: because of what was, and against what was, it announces what will be."

—Eduardo Galeano[1]

Pedro Portugal Mollinedo, Aymaran editor of the indigenous monthly Pukara, *had suggested we do our interview in the Plaza Abaroa, near downtown La Paz. As we talked, men in suits talking on cell phones walked past women in traditional chuluku bowler hats quietly chewing coca leaves (and often texting on their own cell phones); the Aymara language shared the air with Spanish and Kichwa.*

Even the most radical of the Euro-Left grounded itself in polarity, in contradictions, Portugal observed—Left versus Right, man versus nature. The problem, he argued, was Eurocentric colonialism in its entirety, Left and Right, and solutions for this new era of struggle could be found in the more synthetic, organic conception of life contained in the indigenous Andean cosmology.

"Andean ideology is also based on contradiction, but more so on complementarity," he said. "Rather than submitting ourselves to one of two oppositions, we feel a right to project our own political forms and try them out to see if they're effective. And we believe they are, because they're the ones we've used to survive thus far."

A wave of change rolled through Latin America at the turn of the twenty-first century, sweeping away neoliberal two-party governments, bringing calls to refound the states based on broad participation and democratically drafted constitutions. The power and motion of this wave, often referred to as the "Pink Tide," came from the social movements that had been gathering force for over a decade—rebuilding in spaces opened by the fall of U.S.-backed military dictatorships, rethinking in the spaces opened by the crumbling of the Soviet socialist models.

These movements galvanized long-silent—or silenced—sectors of society: indigenous people, campesinos, students, the LGBT community, the unemployed, and all those left out of the promised utopia of a globalized economy. They have deployed a wide array of strategies and actions to some common ends. They march against mines and agribusiness; they occupy physical spaces, rural and urban, and social space won through recognition of language, culture, and equal participation; they mobilize villages, towns, cities, and even nations for community and environmental survival. They are sloughing off the skin of the twentieth-century bipolar world, synthesizing old ways of working and finding new paths into an uncertain future.

Same story, different century

The Conquest of the Americas continues as an ongoing process of "primitive accumulation," that is, through brutal dispossession, only changed in detail. The looting, once only of gold and silver picked or shoveled from mines by slaves to satisfy the greed of conquistadores, has increased exponentially in recent decades to feed transnational capital. This behemoth has left behind the sword to devastate the region with an arsenal of new tools for plunder: strip-mining "megaprojects" with giant machines that dig for lithium, copper, and gold, laying waste to landscapes; countless drills for oil, poisoning rivers; dams for hydroelectric power that flood indigenous lands; battalions of tractors sowing industrial soy for cattle and biofuel, or cane for sugar and biofuel, or eucalyptus for paper mills, or other monocultures that raze entire ecosystems and steal peoples' ways of life.

And just as the tools for plunder have been "improved" for greater "efficiency," the instruments of domination have been refined to hide the brutality. The guns, alcohol, and disease borne by the Spaniards and Portuguese—and the torture tools of the Inquisition used by a coterie of priests to instill fear of hell in the natives—have turned into the IMF/World Bank armies of "economic advisors" and "democracy promotion," "stabilization," and "structural adjustment" programs, all part of the neoliberal mandate, backed by the big guns of Washington. Latin America continues to be "civilized" but no longer are the people slaughtered by sword, or burned alive at the stake, or set upon by the dogs of the conquistadores. Under the rule of transnational capital, populations in the millions are merely left to starve in slums or are murdered with pesticides in the margins of the miles-long GMO soy fields, or by the rivers poisoned by the new profiteers and minions of the empire.

The United States, of course, has played a major role in the modernization of the instruments of domination for plunder, only in recent years so "humanely" refined. During the more savage era of the Cold War, Washington fomented coups to dislodge nationalist and socialist governments across the continent—Árbenz in Guatemala, 1954; Goulart in Brazil, 1964; Allende in Chile, 1973—installing military dictatorships in their place. By the mid-1970s, most of Central and South America was under the rule of dictatorships armed, trained, directed, and financed by the United States. Hundreds of thousands were tortured, murdered, and disappeared, in some cases decapitating an entire generation of artists, writers, intellectuals, and activists.[2]

These dictatorships imposed a particularly virulent form of capitalism on the people of Latin America. Years before neoliberalism came to the United States and Europe, "the restructuring of the Latin American economies had begun in earnest when Pinochet invited the 'Chicago boys,' neoliberal academics from the USA, to run the dictatorship's economic policy. The socio-economic consequence for the majority in Latin America was catastrophic devastation."[3]

By the 1980s these military regimes had already begun to collapse and give way to democratic governments, beginning in Central America with the overthrow of Nicaragua's Somoza dictatorship by the Sandinistas (FSLN) in 1979, and in South America with the fall of Argentina's military dictatorship in 1983. Nevertheless, the dictatorships left behind massive debts, devastated economies, decimated social movements, traumatized societies, and neoliberal constitutions, some of which continue to direct national policies to this day.

New movements born from the ashes of the old

The 1989 collapse of the USSR set off a worldwide "crisis of the Left," which had dramatic repercussions in Latin America. Cuba underwent the "Special Period," its government forced to concern itself more with survival than with extending solidarity to international revolutionary struggles. In Nicaragua the Sandinistas lost power in elections in February 1990, after fighting what the International Court of Justice in 1986 ruled to be U.S. "terrorism" for several years. A little less than two years later, the FMLN in neighboring El Salvador was forced to negotiate a peace treaty with the U.S.-backed ARENA government. That was followed four years later by an agreement between rebels and the government of Guatemala. Within just a few years the guerrilla movements of Latin America had all but disappeared, leaving only Colombia's ELN (National Liberation Army) and FARC (Revolutionary Armed Forces of Colombia), the first and last of the Marxist-Leninist guerrilla battling the United States "hyperempire."

Meanwhile, even the labor unions and workers' movements, which had anchored the Left up to that moment, were struggling for survival, their leaders and membership still suffering from the blows of Operation Condor and other similar programs.[4] Neoliberal economics implemented under the dictatorships had gutted the state sector and manufacturing infrastructure. What Xavier Albo wrote of Bolivia in 1996 was true all over Latin America: "Neoliberal economic policies have dismantled mines and many factories, debilitating the once-powerful workers' movement."[5]

With the end of the Cold War there was a "shift from 'straight power concepts'" such as dictatorships, "to 'persuasion' . . . predicated on a new component in U.S. foreign policy: what policymakers call the 'promotion of democracy.'"[6] New democratic governments—often with "left" parties at the helm—obediently continued the policies of neoliberal austerity throughout the region. Union membership, activity, and power dropped significantly from 1991 to 2001, as governments pursued privatization, trade liberalization, and price stabilization, and the contingent workforce swelled.[7]

The neoliberal model, expressed as "TINA" ("There Is No Alternative") by British Prime Minister Margaret Thatcher, and affirmed by her U.S. counterparts, Ronald Reagan and George H.W. Bush, reigned supreme as opponents experienced "the collapse of the class-based model of the traditional Left."[8] However, despite this collapse, what a majority of Latin Americans envisioned in its place was another kind of "Left," since right-wing capitalist ideology has arguably been a minority perspective in Latin America, one governing the majority only tenuously by means of coercion and the North American Big Stick. Capitalism has never been, as it once was in the United States, a "popular" ideology advanced even by the working class.

Some form of socialism or communitarianism is embedded in the cultural matrix of the entire southern continent, in the indigenous concept of the "minga," "minka," or "cayapa," meaning "community work for the collective good without self-interest." (See the interview with Manuela Ruiz in the Colombia chapter.) The Roman Catholic Church—especially liberation theology—posed community as the way to redemption, unlike Protestantism, in which salvation has generally been considered an individual matter. When left to their own devices, Latin Americans have often chosen communal forms of mutual aid and populist, corporatist, or even socialist governments that advocated for the interests of the working majority. In any case, in the neoliberal globalizing world of TINA, Latin America seemed not to have gotten the memo that socialism was dead and capital was writing history's final chapter.

Even before the empire wrote that memo the situation was changing in Latin America, and not going well for its neoliberal governments of "democratic transition." Tens of thousands of Venezuelans took to the streets in February 1989, their tolerance for neoliberal policies pushed past the breaking point by an increase in transit fares. Police and military killed an unknown number in what later became known as the "Caracazo," but the event began a slow-moving transformation that would have profound consequences within a few years. In neighboring Ecuador, a little over a year later, in June of 1990, thousands of indigenous people rose up and marched on the capital under the banner, "Never again a nation without us," and small, local mobilizations that became national marches began in Bolivia, uniting lowlands indigenous people with the highland Aymara.

Meanwhile, indigenous people from all the Americas began to gear up for the Intercontinental Chaski for Self-Determination and other actions to protest five hundred years of genocide and celebrate five hundred years of resistance. Environmentalists began linking up with native peoples to protest everything from logging of virgin forests to mining on native lands. These bonds and a widening circle of concerns that incorporated new actors led to the founding of Via Campesina in 1993, bringing concerns for healthy, humane food production and food producers to public consciousness.

Remaining workers' movements and unions in the United States and Mexico began to organize against the imperial agenda behind "globalization" in the form of NAFTA (North American Free Trade Agreement) being pushed by then-president Bill Clinton. Their efforts failed, but as the treaty went into effect, precisely at midnight on January 1, 1994, the Zapatistas (EZLN, Zapatista National Liberation Army) emerged from the jungles of Chiapas, Mexico, to take five small towns and capture the left imagination by presenting a "counterpower" to what seemed an invincible unipolar empire in expansion.

The Zapatistas were a new kind of guerrilla, emerging out of the encounter between left (Maoist) and indigenous people in the backwoods of Southern Mexico, and they quickly began to occupy not only largely indigenous towns in Chiapas but also the newly created territory of cyberspace. The Zapatista spokesperson, Subcomandante Marcos, called for social movements from all over the world to gather in territory liberated by the EZLN for the First International Encuentro for Humanity and Against Neoliberalism in 1996, which became the basis of the later World Social Forum gatherings, beginning in 2001.

The antiglobalization movements, inspired by the Zapatistas and other emerging actors in what was to be the "autonomist" side of a new left movement, joined forces with labor, environmental groups, and an array of social justice organizations to battle the World Trade Organization, the World Bank, and other tools of domination used by international capital.

The rising "Pink Tide" and the new movements

Hugo Chávez and his Polo Patriótico movement won the Venezuelan election in 1998, setting the stage for the whole cast of new governments that came to power in the first decade of the new century, aided by the social movements that flourished again in the new context. With Luiz Inácio Lula da Silva, "Lula," as its candidate for the presidency, the Workers' Party took power in Brazil in 2002. Next door in Uruguay the left coalition, Frente Amplio (Broad Front), beat the traditional Red (Colorado) and White parties and won with their candidate, Tabaré Vazquez, in 2005. In early 2006 Evo Morales was inaugurated president in Bolivia, having been carried into office by a coalition of social movements, most of them indigenous. Later the same year Rafael Correa was elected president of Ecuador under the banner of the party he formed, Alianza PAIS. In 2008, Fernando Lugo, known as the "Red Bishop," won the presidency in Paraguay with the help of massive social mobilizations, although his term came to an abrupt end with a June 2012 impeachment, which many saw as a *golpe* (coup).

These governments of the "Pink Tide" surged to power on the backs of social movements—both the new activism that arose from the changed circumstances of the 1990s, and organizing like that of the Landless Workers' Movement of Brazil (MST) and other groups that dated back to the 1970s and had grown and adapted since. Many new left groups and grassroots community organizations began to occupy and flourish in the spaces vacated by the old left parties, swept away with the departing Soviet giant. These social movements have become a formidable enemy of the remaining giant, the Washington Consensus and its neoliberal client governments of the region.

At the core of these new movements is a diverse cross-section of the marginalized and the excluded: slum dwellers, the unemployed, indigenous people, disaffected urban youth, LGBT communities, women, Afrodescendants, students, and many more "invisibilized" new actors, now determined to take center stage in their world. While it would be impossible to generalize about such a varied collection of people, some common themes emerge in many of the movements in Latin America.

First, they often attempt to occupy a "territory." Facing displacement by the modern-day enclosures that come with the extractive economy, poor people, campesinos, and indigenous, stake claims to land for their very survival: Witness the Zapatistas in Chiapas, the MST across vast swaths of Brazil, indigenous defending ancestral and sacred lands, and slum dwellers throughout Latin America. In these liberated territories, protagonists redesign their society outside the control of capital, and promote a "dispersed" autonomy that facilitates a strengthened resistance.

As the members of the Galpón de Corrales tell us (in our Uruguay chapter) many of these territories organize horizontal relationships of power, often implementing a concept of "leadership as service." In this model, dramatically different from the democratic centralism of a vanguard organization, leadership arises from the base and is accountable to its base. It serves; it does not rule. This is consistent with the influential liberation theology that emerged in the 1970s in Latin America, as well as with indigenous ideas of leadership. As the Zapatistas put it, leaders are to "govern by obeying."

As they stake out their territories, these movements sink ideological roots in local wisdom and symbol systems. Heroes of history and myth reinvent themselves in the emerging millions who relive the old stories, determined to write a new ending to the master narrative of the Conquest. The new movements see themselves as part of a heritage stretching back through more than five hundred years of resistance. Tupac Amaru and Tupak Katari inspire the activists of Peru and Bolivia just as Rumiñahui is present in the struggle of indigenous Ecuadorians. Votan Zapata, an invention of the Zapatistas, blends Tzeltal Maya myth with the hero of the Mexican Revolution from Chiapas, Emiliano Zapata. Subcomandante Marcos seems to be as comfortable quoting the Mexican anarchist Ricardo Flores Magón as he does Marx, or more so, as do members of MORENA (see the Jesús Ramírez Cuevas interview in our Mexico chapter), not to mention those of Oaxaca, birthplace of Flores Magón, where the image of the martyred anarchist was resurrected as protective and inspirational symbol in the 2006 uprising (see the APPO interviews).

This phenomenon is regionwide, with Venezuelans referring back to Bolívar, the Honduran resistance to Francisco Morazán, and Nicaraguans to Augusto Sandino, etc. This isn't a new phenomenon, but in the absence of a dominant Communist Party and its hegemonic symbology, regional systems of thought and histories have emerged into the foreground. (For more on historical memory, see the interview with Silvia Rivera in the Bolivia chapter.)

The new social movements also value the work of formation and education. This is at the core of both the Zapatista struggle and the MST, but it plays a role in all the social movements. Not only do they emphasize the formation of their members, but they also carry political education into the community at large. This has been an important corrective to much of the old left approach that downplayed the "subjective" elements of struggle in favor of the "transformation of material conditions." Without taking the other extreme and focusing exclusively on the subjective and affective dimension of social change, the new movements work to transform individual subjectivities (through education) and objective conditions and social structures.

The new movements share a practice of unity in diversity. The urban social movements represent every corner in the margins of the city: LGBT, squatters, unemployed, the "contingent," and self-employed workers such as recyclers. (See Adrienne Pine's description of post-coup Honduras in the introduction to the Honduras chapter.) There are indigenous movements such as CONAIE and ECUARUNARI and other similar organizations that incorporate diverse tribes and peoples and make alliances across ethnicities. Those relegated to the margins realize that these alliances not only ensure strength in numbers, but they also facilitate dialogue, since there is no single, all-encompassing ("totalitarian") ideology that would exclude free thought and the right of minorities or individuals to question dominant ideas. The focus is put on solving specific practical problems in communities or locales so that political party affiliation becomes secondary or irrelevant. (See the interview with Iván Fuentes in the Chile chapter.)

Just as the new social movements have no single guiding ideology or single type of actor, neither do they work with a single form of organization or structure. While most movements tend to favor "horizontal" or non-hierarchical forms of organization, organizational models are extremely diverse.

Beyond binaries

Debate rages among social movement scholars over the most effective relations between movements and the state. For the most part, their opinions break down along the historic fault line in the Left between the anarchists, libertarian or "autonomist," and the socialists and communists who contest for state power. This is what some have called the "pseudodebate,"[9] but the problem is real, though it need not—and should not—be understood as a binary. William I. Robinson frames it better as a problem to be resolved when he writes, "At some point, the popular movements must work out how the vertical and horizontal intersect."[10] At present, as revealed in the interviews presented here, activists and movement intellectuals are generally conscious of this problem to which they take a pragmatic, nuanced approach, keeping a sober critique of capitalism and its power always in view.

Most analysts, and many activists, believe the movements must maintain autonomy from the state, and offer only conditional support (if any) to the progressive governments. They offer convincing arguments, based on analysis of the practices behind the discourse the governments offer, as well as the social movements' experience with previous regimes, often of self-styled "left" or "progressive" reformist varieties.[11]

Most of the nations represented in this book have "progressive" governments, but none are in a "revolutionary process" in which a vanguard party controls state power and the mass of social forces submit to its authority and integrate themselves into that "process." The states in the fifteen countries represented here range from quasimilitary "democracies" of the Right (Guatemala) to governments that say they are "on the road to socialism" but that are actually "reformist" at best.[12] They, and their political parties, also claim to represent "the people." But in fact, the interests of civil society, as organized in social movements, rarely converge with those of parties and states, because reformist states must respond to the pressures of international capital, local oligarchies, and other forces that directly oppose the interests of the majority.[13]

This situation often leads to deep contradictions and conflicts between even the most "progressive" governments and social movements. In this book, we offer the perspective of social movements on those conflicts, even if doing so casts a poor light on governments whose accomplishments we recognize and applaud and whose sovereignty we would defend.

The contradiction between the Pink Tide states' discourse and practice is most obvious in their economic model. Most of the leaders of these states, particularly Correa in Ecuador and Morales in Bolivia, have expressed concern for "Pachamama" (Mother Earth) and adopted the language of "the socialism of the twenty-first century" promoted by Hugo Chávez in Venezuela. But none of the Latin American governments are making a serious attempt to develop socialism. Instead, they are building welfare states, as designed by Robert McNamara when he served as president of the World Bank after his tenure as secretary of defense in the Johnson administration, where he helped design the genocide known as the "Vietnam War." There's little reason to believe that these social welfare programs are working any better now in Latin America than they did in the context where they were designed as counterinsurgency programs in the United States in the 1960s under the rubric of "the War on Poverty."[14]

As a matter of fact, poverty, inequality, and landlessness actually increased in Brazil under Lula, whose *Zero Fome* (Zero Hunger) and Bolsa Familia (Family Basket) programs were financed by taxing the middle class and stable workers, as were the social welfare payment plans in Argentina and Uruguay."[15] Despite these programs, in Brazil "poverty, inequality and landlessness actually increased during the Lula years."[16] None of the Pink Tide states have structurally challenged the roots of poverty, and their social programs, while certainly more helpful to the people than the austerity regimes of prior neoliberal governments, nevertheless serve to mask the real problem of wealth. "These programs ... tend to weaken autonomous mobilization from below by depoliticizing the question of poverty, turning inequality into an administrative problem, and creating a support base for the state independent of unions and social movements," Robinson writes.[17]

The solution, obviously, is not to withdraw support for the poor and marginalized, but to contend with the basic structural problem of wealth: The progressive governments operate in a system that is geared exclusively to accumulate wealth for the transnational capitalist class (TCC).[18] To maintain this process of capital accumulation for the TCC, Raúl Zibechi believes the progressive governments "install poverty as the problem and remove wealth from the visual field."[19] In the absence of powerful, critical and autonomous social movements, "the structural power of global capital can impose itself on direct state power and impose its project of global capitalism."[20]

As for the environmental policies of the "progressive" governments, there doesn't seem to be much improvement over their neoliberal predecessors. Despite talk of "the rights of Pachamama," the progressive governments are hostage to the resource exploitation practices of the TCC. This contradiction is sharpest in Bolivia, where the government of Evo Morales attempted to build a highway through the Isiboro-Sécure Indigenous Territory and National Park (Territorio Indígena y Parque Nacional Isiboro Sécure, or TIPNIS) that critics argue, would serve first and foremost Brazilian capital. Bolivian scholar and activist Silvia Rivera calls this another "discrepancy between discourse and practice, because [the Morales government] has talked about the Pachamama, this great Pachamama, as an enlightened position internationally, but internally what they want is a developmentalist policy with hydroelectric [dams] that would drown indigenous lands, forests and highways all for an alliance with Brazil. They're betting on serving the interests of Brazil. So it's a new colonialism." (See the interview in our Bolivia chapter.) Venezuela has nationalized gold "and given it to the multinational corporations, those same ones qualified as 'savage capitalists'" by the government, indigenous Pemón activist Alexis Romero observes. (See the Venezuela chapter.)

In Brazil, Paraguay, and Argentina vast swaths of the countryside are planted in cane and genetically modified soy for export, and transnationals are invading indigenous lands, destroying unique ecosystems to plant other crops for biofuels. Mining companies have exercised their muscle over governments, says Claudia Acuña of the lavaca collective. The mining companies "held a meeting at the Government House and forced the state in some kind of mining coup against the government, which we're now living through," Acuña told us. (See her interview in the Argentina chapter.)

Wherever they are pursued, development policies based on resource extraction not only destroy the environment, original cultures and peoples; they can also gut and corrupt social movements that let go of their ability to criticize and protest. Thus, the movements often see the need to maintain a critical, autonomous stance toward these governments to navigate the gap between the rhetoric of "democracy" and the actual practice—and to recognize the governments' tactics for subverting and co-opting the social and grassroots organizations.

Examples of the attempts of governments to co-opt the movements abound in the interviews in this book. Julieta Ojeda of Mujeres Creando talks of MAS (Movimiento al Socialismo, Evo Morales's party) having "penetrated certain organizations and divided them. They enter these social movement spaces and create divisions by forming their own parallel organizations." (See the Bolivia chapter.) Franco Basualdo of Argentina's Prensa de Frente talks about a "government claiming to have a new policy that is apparently encouraging participation but there is no opening, no room for political participation or discussion." (See the Argentina chapter.) Ecuadorian President Rafael Correa accused indigenous activist Monica Chuji of being an "infiltrator" after she spoke critically in the Constitutional Assembly. This showed Chuji that "the power is once again in the executive. Once again the citizens have no opportunity to say anything." (See the Ecuador chapter.) Arturo Albarrán and María Vicenta Dávila express concern that Hugo Chávez has generated new structures to serve as steppingstones to the "socialism of the twenty-first century" but ignored deep-rooted community organizations in the process. Orlando Chirino has an even harsher critique, contending that the "socialism of the twenty-first century" has been nothing more than a charade behind which to dismantle workers' organizations. (See the Venezuela chapter.)

And so these contradictions between discourse and practice have rightly warned the social movements to maintain a certain critical distance from the progressive states. Activists have also learned this lesson from painful historical experience. Those who have been through the tantalizing dance with power, people like Dioyenes Lucio and Humberto Cholango, will tell us it's crucial to work with "progressive" governments, but without losing autonomy. Lucio and Cholango point out that CONAIE and Pachakutik lost much of their credibility and their ability to organize resistance to President Lucio Gutiérrez's neoliberal policies when they entered into a power alliance with his government and he betrayed them. Even now, ten years later, those in organizations that were former collaborators with Gutiérrez are working very hard to regain the trust of their communities.[21]

FENOCIN learned from this, Lucio said. After Correa's election, "We worked out an arrangement where some of our people went to work in the government, but lower-profile people, not the leadership of the organization because that would weaken our organization, and weaken our ability to maintain a critical stance toward the government." (See the Ecuador chapter.)[22]

Autonomy and necessity

In times of acute social crisis—and in the permanent crisis that globalization has created for the poor and the working class—people have created alternative institutions, liberated spaces, simply to enable them to survive. Most famously, the Zapatistas set up their autonomous municipalities in the Lacandon jungle, claiming land for the long-dispossessed indigenous residents of Chiapas. When industrial agriculture began displacing thousands of rural families in Brazil, the Landless Workers' Movement (MST) started occupying fallow land as a way of acquiring it, and organized their liberated spaces along radically democratic lines. (See the interview with Ana Hanauer in the Brazil chapter.) City dwellers have done the same thing all over the continent, from Quito to Bahia. (See interviews with Milton Chamorro in the Ecuador chapter and Ana Vanesca and Pedro Cardoso in the Brazil chapter.) Argentina saw an explosion of organizing after the 2001 collapse. With the economy in shards, jobs and savings gone, people took over factories, schools, and clinics to keep basic services going, organizing their projects collectively, horizontally. (See the interview with Ernesto "Lalo" Paret in the Argentina chapter.)

Globalization will continue to make survival more difficult, as industrial agriculture snatches land from subsistence farmers and indigenous people (a major theme in the Paraguay chapter), trade agreements wreck local economies, and manufacturing migrates around the world in search of the most exploitable workforces. Some form of autonomous space will be an essential base from which to struggle.

But autonomy, creation of "counterpowers" as an exclusive strategy, poses problems of its own. Movements that choose to build autonomous zones under alternative "good governments" are still vulnerable to the whims of the official state; even a movement as large as the MST has had to contend with harassment from the Workers' Party government in Brazil. By withdrawing into autonomous zones, the movements may not only lose the ability to affect the larger political debate, as some argue the Zapatistas did, but they might lose even their autonomous spaces, as Occupy in the United States did in the fall of 2011.[23]

Autonomy, therefore, has to be carefully crafted to bring critical social movements into the center of the struggles with the state and not to further marginalize the forces built from marginalization. Only the combined power of autonomous social movements willing to engage with states and political powers beyond "liberated zones" can prevent, for example, a "progressive" FMLN government in El Salvador from giving in to the pressure of the TCC and granting concessions to Pacific Rim Mining Corporation to mine gold in its national territory. (See the interview with Miguel Rivera in the El Salvador chapter.) Building autonomous spaces to organize and experiment with alternatives is an important step toward building a movement that might challenge "progressive" governments to transform national structures in such a way that people's movements can gain footing in the larger struggle against the TCC.

Given the scope and sway of the TCC, even larger international structures will need to change to enable governments in Latin America to support the people's movements and sustain positions that defy corporate interests. President Chávez took steps to concretize this strategic vision for Latin America, with initiatives such as the Bolivarian Alternative for the Americas (ALBA), a socially oriented alternative to the Free Trade Area of the Americas; UNASUR, the Union of South American Nations, a network for economic and security cooperation modeled on the European Union; the proposed Banco del Sur, CELAC (Community of Latin American and Caribbean States), and other projects for regional union. Nevertheless, much more work in this area remains.

Latin American social movements have some leading-edge experience in successfully tackling the problem of the "horizontal-vertical intersect"—building autonomous spaces run with "servant leadership" and cooperative decision-making, while also organizing to make demands on the state. The Coordinadora del Bajo Lempa y Bahía de Jiquilisco in El Salvador is doing this, as is the MST in Brazil; the APPO (Asamblea Popular de los Pueblos de Oaxaca) ran the entire city in a horizontal fashion, while continuing to press for the removal of the state government—until the movement was crushed by federal troops. (See the interviews in the respective chapters.)

About the book

We live in a world more closely connected than ever by the maturing of transnational capitalism as "globalization" and the planetwide environmental crisis it has engendered. The Latin American social movements have been confronting this dire moment head-on, raising their voices to call for a new world that will include them. We have tried to select as broad a sampling of their experiences and perspectives as we could find, though we recognize that this collection has many omissions—and represents at best a series of snapshots over time.

In that sense, this book is the outcome of a journey we and others have made into that magical world of Latin America. That's why we've chosen to order it as a voyage that might be taken by any reader who picks it up to read (and we might well assume anyone wishing to read of societies in movement in Latin America must harbor somewhere a secret love of travel). Adventurous tourists from the north might start the trip with Mexico and travel from there into Guatemala, Honduras, El Salvador, and Nicaragua, perhaps skipping over Costa Rica, Belize, Panama, and the Guianas, as we have done. They might then take a boat to Colombia and travel west to Ecuador, or east to Venezuela, before traveling south to Peru, Bolivia, and Brazil. Eventually, either way, they would arrive in the Southern Cone, and could visit Uruguay and Paraguay before exploring the long reaches of Chile and Argentina, stretching through Patagonia to the Straits of Magellan.

That was our route, and it took some eight years to complete, although we visited a few countries numerous times in the process, like Venezuela, where one of us lived for a year and ended up making a second home. In the end, however, we had to recruit a whole community of people like ourselves to complete the project: translators, editors, writers, social movement and solidarity activists all, since no one else would agree to work for free or nearly free. We have credited them at the back of the book but can't acknowledge too many times how valuable their contributions have been to making this book come together.

As for our choice of interviewees, we did our homework, but, frankly, it sometimes was done by serendipity—like the meeting with Jorge Galeano, leader of the Popular Agrarian Movement of Paraguay who we'd been hoping to track down, only to find him our next-door neighbor one night in a hotel. We've also cast as wide a net as possible to include in this elusive, ambiguous, contended category of "social movements" a few ex-guerrilla politicians (notably Victor Hugo Tinoco and Antonio Navarro Wolff), as well as NGO activists such as Yamilet Mejía, whose work falls outside of a strict definition of "social movements." We have included their voices because, while not themselves social movement activists, their roles, work, and political positions, not to mention their sincere support of the movements, give them unique and valuable perspectives that we feel would be useful to readers.

As much as possible, we tried to relinquish our own preconceived notions and preferences in favor of creating a space for open debate, a space to wrestle with some of the more difficult, thorny issues. We hope the resulting book might help open up the possibilities for deeper and more productive relations of solidarity between North Americans and our Latin American counterparts struggling for justice in this world. The people assembled here have arrived at their conclusions through their own struggles. We have merely translated their words and helped them to sing in our language. We hope, like us, you will come to cherish their songs.

Clifton Ross and Marcy Rein
Berkeley, California

Mexico

University of Texas Libraries

Movements seek to renew the twentieth century's first revolution

By Luis Ballesteros

When we begin analyzing the social movements in Mexico, we must remember that this country generated the first revolution of the twentieth century anywhere in the world. Different social forces participated in the Revolution of 1910, represented by leaders like Emiliano Zapata, Francisco Villa, and the Flores Magón brothers, and many of the social movements that developed over the following decades drew their inspiration, ideas, and slogans from the 1910 uprising.

The end of the Mexican Revolution led to its institutionalization through the PNR (National Revolutionary Party) in 1928. In 1946 it changed its name to the Institutional Revolutionary Party (Partido Revolucionario Institucional, PRI). This party was the unifying and mediating force of Mexican society for seventy-two years, thanks to its clientelistic and sectoral control, and construction of infrastructure and institutions. It was, as poet Octavio Paz put it so aptly, "the political party as a philanthropic ogre"—an ogre without counterweights, utterly opposed to transparency and appropriating the symbols of the Revolution to perpetuate its own power.

The PRI's hold on the country eroded as it used its power more and more to favor a privileged minority. In 2000, it lost the federal elections to the National Action Party (PAN), a conservative party that had succeeded in garnering the support from the middle class. However, the PRI did not lose the power it had at the state level, and from there it paved the way to return to the presidency, oiling the machinery of clientelism and political operation.

Once in power, the PAN only coexisted with the same long-standing PRI apparatus and Mexico didn't experience a successful transition, but rather a continuity of the previous model—so much so that in July 2012 the PRI recaptured the presidency of the republic.

Generally speaking, it can be said that from 1930 to 1968, the PNR-PRI managed to keep the country cohesive and avoid major mishaps.

In 1968, a watershed for the progressive social movements in Mexico, young people started to break open the monolithic power of the Mexican government and even managed to wring some concessions from it. That was the year a student movement arose almost spontaneously in response to an antidemocratic system that concentrated power in a single party and, by extension, in only one person. But these youths were the victims of brutal repression by a system closed to dialogue. To this date it is not known how many young people were killed, beaten, or disappeared when the army and the political police attacked a massive demonstration in the Plaza de las Tres Culturas of Tlatelolco in October 1968. In 1971, a similar event occurred, which was known as the Corpus Christi Massacre.

From the second half of the 1960s to the first half of the 1970s, rural and urban guerrilla movements were present in Mexico, which was an unequivocal sign of a state that did not allow for a broad and democratic participation of the population, particularly of the youth.

Over the last twenty-five years, Mexico has suffered from a permanent crisis and mediocre economic growth, which has been reflected in the flow of emigrants, most headed to the United States. Contrary to common belief, a substantial number of those leaving were skilled workers, which caused a drain on Mexico's resources and contributed to a vicious cycle of economic erosion in Mexico and an unrecognized provision of labor capital—skilled and unskilled—to the United States. Mexican households raised and fed them, and Mexican schools educated them, all at Mexican taxpayers' expense. By the time they arrive in the United States, they are "work-ready" without any previous investment from U.S. taxpayers.

Mexico's various social movements operate in this context. Most are more or less localized, lacking a truly national scope.

In 1988, a splinter of the dominant state party (PRI) merged with the traditional Mexican Left and founded the FDN (National Democratic Front). In that year's elections, the government was forced to suspend vote counting because the results were going against the PRI. The explanation given was that "the system had crashed." This was true in more than one sense, since it was the beginning of the end of an eminently one-party or state-party system. Several of the left and center-left political currents active in the electoral arena grouped around the political lines of the PRD (Party of the Democratic Revolution). Their main bastion was, and still is, the Federal District, Mexico City.

Zapatistas raise debate on globalization

In 1994, the Zapatista Army of National Liberation (Ejército Zapatista de Liberación Nacional, EZLN) declared war on the Mexican state. It started as a movement that envisaged the possibility for change only through direct confrontation with the national government. Because the EZLN formed within a very reduced space—twenty-six communities in the state of Chiapas—the Mexican government was able to encapsulate it and thereby limit its activity and reach. The EZLN gained its greatest national prominence in 1994; since then, it has concentrated on building autonomy, mostly at a regional level.

The EZLN, through its eloquent and charismatic leader, Subcomandante Marcos, garnered nationwide and worldwide support. Leftist movements hungry for hope after the collapse of the Berlin Wall greeted it enthusiastically, seeing the advent of a new utopia, or at least a new revolutionary model. This support helped EZLN survive, as did the massive demonstration in Mexico City in 1994 that demanded that the Mexican government stop any attempts to repress the Zapatistas and adopt a negotiated solution to the conflict.

The EZLN cultivates participatory democracy in the indigenous communities and seeks the autonomy of its members vis-à-vis the national state, making it a deeply antisystemic movement. It also brings women into central roles and elevates them to leadership: Suffice it to recall the emblematic Comandante Ramona.

The EZLN identified the neoliberal model as the cause and precipitator of social dynamics of exclusion and worsening inequality. It also advanced an alternate cosmogony, rejecting the ideology globalization proclaims. In reframing the debate with neoliberalism at the center, EZLN was a precursor to movements that would spring up around the world fifteen years later—the "Occupy" and "We Are the 99 Percent" movements in Spain and the United States, for example.

Working people say "enough"

The "Barzón" (yoke-ring) as a social movement representative of debtors originated from the 1994 bank crisis. As it explains on its website, "It arose as a result of the crisis of insolvency, lack of liquidity and profitability of the production, economic and family units that led to their failure to meet their payment commitments with the financial institutions. Some want to characterize it as a debtors' organization, but it is actually an organization of productive sectors and working people affected by an exclusionary economic policy that pushed them into what in Mexico is known as 'past-due portfolio.'"

NAFTA aggravated the crisis, indiscriminately opening Mexico to the entry of cheaper agricultural products, often subsidized, while subsidies for the country's own products were being removed. The agricultural sector wasn't adequately prepared or financed to successfully face the effects of such an opening, which explains why the Barzón Movement initially had a stronger presence in the agricultural sector. The Barzón ended up joining forces with "El Campo No Aguanta Más" (The Countryside Can't Stand It Anymore). The convergence of both movements was the organized response from those affected by NAFTA and the ravages of neoliberalism on Mexican agriculture.

In Oaxaca in 2006, a vicious state police attack on a peaceful encampment of striking teachers galvanized a broad-based uprising. The Oaxaca teachers, members of a reform wing of the national teachers union, struck not over narrow wage-and-benefit issues but the damage done by neoliberalism to the education system—and their students' lives. Diverse Oaxacan social organizations came together after the police attack to form the Popular Assembly of the Peoples of Oaxaca (APPO). They shared the critique of neoliberalism, though their key immediate demand was the ouster of Oaxaca Governor Ulises Ruíz Ortíz, known for repressing social movements and violating human rights.

APPO brought together horizontal and vertical organizing forms, offering valuable lessons to other movements in Mexico and elsewhere. Nevertheless, the movement could be seen as a victim of the electoral fraud in the 2006 national elections, when the PAN apparently stole a second term in office: It's likely that the rightful winner of the election, Andrés Manuel López Obrador of the PRD, would have pressured the governor to negotiate rather than sending in federal troops. The final assault on the movement of Oaxaca came a month before PAN President Vicente Fox handed power over to his PAN successor, Felipe Calderón.

Social movements in Mexico have had to face their criminalization by the state, supported by the media and the aligned conservative groups. A clear example of this was the repression suffered by the Front of People in Defense of the Land, in San Salvador Atenco, State of Mexico. In 2002, the Front led the community's successful effort to keep the Fox government from seizing their farmland to build an international airport. In May 2006, police rampaged through a local market, beating and arresting people and killing two young boys. Three leaders of the Front—Ignacio del Valle Medina, Felipe Álvarez Hernández, and Héctor Galindo Gochicua—were arrested and sentenced to serve sixty-seven years in prison, which was seen as a clear attempt by the government to dissuade protest. The sentences were finally overturned, due to the national and international pressure, because the attacks on Atenco involved such widespread violations of human rights, including sexual abuse of Mexican and foreign women alike.

There is a large void in party or institutional representation among the Mexican population, which affords an opportunity for the organized action of diverse social movements.

The Movement for National Renewal (MORENA) arose in this context as a way of giving a coherent shape to the social discontent that followed the questionable elections of 2006. It drew diverse sectors of the Mexican population together around an electoral and postelectoral movement headed by Andrés Manuel López Obrador, who ran for the presidency of Mexico for the second time in 2012. Currently, it has more than four million members and a presence in all 2,500 municipalities of the country.

Internet organizing to counter the media duopoly
Social movement activists in Mexico must contend with the distortions made by the mass media, especially television. Two companies (Televisa and TV Azteca), often called a "duopoly," shape and lead the political opinions of a large part of the population. Their control also extends to the radio and the print media. Clearly, the democratization and opening of the media, and the opening of the radio waves to a greater public, must be one of the main strategic goals for the transformation of the country.

In response, new forms of organization are being developed on the Internet. Every website representative of a social movement has links and references to movements or like-minded organizations, which has a multiplying effect and counters the information monopoly.

Social media had a considerable impact in the 2012 election, even though it wasn't sufficient to obtain an electoral majority for López Obrador, who was unable to counter the lavish campaign expenditures of the PRI and its allied media apparatus, its electoral machine and its multiple alliances.

Perhaps the clearest media critique, and most effective use of social media in 2012, came from #YoSoy132. This movement was detonated by the visit of the former PRI candidate to the Ibero-American University, a private university attended by upper-middle and upper-class students. Students from all over the country joined in, mostly from the university level, from public and private schools alike. The movement brought into the spotlight television's power over the population and its clear preference and bias for the then-PRI candidate.

Widespread price hikes, unstoppable violence, and a growing war on drug trafficking[1] set the stage for the emergence or strengthening of other social movements of all kinds, such as the Movement for Peace with

Justice and Dignity, led by poet Javier Sicilia. This movement undertook an intense campaign and many actions around Mexico and also a caravan to the United States, thereby forcing the Mexican authorities and presidential candidates of the time to hear the voice of the victims.

The proximity to the United States holds a particular importance for Mexican social movements—and not only because the United States sees Mexico as a "part of its backyard" and doesn't hesitate to cooperate with the Mexican state to preserve the status quo. Social movements in the United States can be a great source of support and solidarity for those in Mexico. For example, U.S. unions and human rights groups first formed support networks for women maquiladora workers in the late 1970s; binational groups such as Frente Indígena de Organizaciones Binacionales (FIOB) advocate for their members' rights on both sides of the border. Ties between labor unions in the United States and Mexico go back more than a century. In the years since NAFTA, these relationships have been more organized, though still small-scale.[2]

There is still a long way to go, but there is great potential for social movements in the two neighboring countries to strengthen each other, given the close ties forged by immigration of Mexicans to the United States and the economic connections between the two countries. After all, the social movements in the two countries face the same economic model.

Women in the Zapatista Movement
"We have opened our eyes and opened our hearts"

Interviews and translation by Hilary Klein, 2001–2002

The Zapatista National Liberation Army (Ejército Zapatista de Liberación Nacional, EZLN) is a guerrilla army but also a broad social and political movement of indigenous people in Chiapas, Mexico. The EZLN captured the attention and imagination of the world on January 1, 1994, when it took over several municipal capitals in an armed uprising that lasted only twelve days.

Large landowners in the area fled after the uprising, leaving their ranches unoccupied and vulnerable. Throughout eastern Chiapas, the EZLN took over vast tracts of land that indigenous peasants had been working on for generations and which had historically belonged to their ancestors. Claudia and Débora, two of the women interviewed here, describe defending this land from the Mexican army and the judiciales, a federal police force. Each time the army or the police entered the village, the people took refuge in the mountains and then returned again once the attackers left.

Women gathered in front of the *Aguascalientes* of Morelia (now known as the *Caracol* of Morelia), 1998. Photo by Mariana Mora.

The village of Moisés Gandhi, where Claudia and Débora live, is now a thriving community of around a hundred indigenous families. The headquarters of its autonomous municipality, it has a regional school and health clinic. Brightly colored murals decorate the auditorium in the center of town, right next to the basketball court with "EZLN" painted on the basketball hoops.

Since 1994, the Zapatista movement has been engaged in a political struggle for basic demands, such as land and freedom (Tierra y Libertad was Emiliano Zapata's rallying cry during the Mexican Revolution) and is known as one of the first antiglobalization social movements. Since the late 1990s, it has also focused on the construction of indigenous autonomy within Zapatista communities.

Women have played an important role in the EZLN, as insurgents in the guerrilla army, as political leaders in the civilian support base communities, as health and education promoters in the construction of autonomous infrastructure, and as members of economic collectives in the development of local and regional economies. Women's participation in the EZLN has helped shape the Zapatista movement and this movement has, in turn, opened new spaces for women and led to dramatic changes in their lives.

The early years of the Zapatista movement

Victoria, a Zapatista authority from the Morelia region: Since I was little, my family suffered from sickness and hunger. We didn't have any money, and we didn't have fertile land to work on. My father would look for work on the coffee plantations to earn a little money and buy corn for us to eat. It was only enough for us to survive because we were thirteen brothers and sisters. Three of my brothers and sisters died of curable diseases. When I was a child, I saw my younger sister die in my mother's arms while she cried for her baby daughter.

In 1990 I was invited to a workshop about health. I decided to attend this workshop because of the problems I had seen in my own family, because there was never enough money to buy medicine and we didn't know about medicinal plants.

In 1991, the same man who invited me to the health workshop told me about an organization which fights against injustice and asked me what I thought. All the suffering I had seen had made me very angry, because so many poor people die, but people who have money don't die from curable diseases. So I decided to join the organization [the EZLN].[3] I started going to meetings and, when we got back, we would share the information with other people in our community.

One time I called all the women together; I wanted to share some information and discuss it with them, because as women our participation in the struggle is necessary too. One of the men didn't like this. He asked why the women were meeting separately, why we weren't meeting all together. He even told me that I shouldn't be working with the women. Some of the men who weren't very politically conscious used to criticize me. They said I was only there looking for a husband. The *priistas* [government supporters] also started rumors that I was having a secret affair. I didn't pay attention to them. I endured it all and I continue to put up with things like this.

In spite of the criticisms and rumors about me, I have always liked to participate. I always participated in everything that I could. When other villages joined the organization, I would visit them and give talks to the women, so they would organize more and know how to defend their rights as women. I am conscious in my work and I want to help my people.

Zapatista land takeovers

Débora, a Zapatista woman from the Morelia region: We made an agreement, everyone who came to live here, because we knew that this land had been taken away from our ancestors and we had the opportunity to make it ours again. This land was paid for with the blood of our fallen compañeros in January 1994. We decided to occupy this land in March 1994. Our authorities told us that we were going to reclaim some land, and that anyone who did not have any land could live there.

Zapatista women in the autonomous municipality of Vicente Guerrero distribute lettuce harvested from their collective vegetable garden, 2002. Photo by Hilary Klein.

Claudia, a Zapatista woman from the Morelia region: When we arrived here, we hung up a piece of plastic sheet as a roof and then little by little we started building our houses. We prepared our food in the open air, many times in the rain.

Débora: Staying here meant that we had to defend this land. Those of us who occupied the land knew that we had to be very determined and that it was going to be hard work, because they might come and try and kick us off the land at any moment. We had to pay attention, day and night. We had to be very careful. We took turns keeping watch. I didn't want them to show up when I was asleep.

When we first came here, we began to build our houses, and then the soldiers kicked us out. We were afraid, and we went back to the villages where we had lived before. We started coming back little by little. At first, just for a little while: for a day, then for a week, then for a month. When we left, we took all our things—our chickens, our tables, everything—because we didn't want the soldiers to take them. But our houses were still here. We stepped to one side, but we didn't leave altogether. We weren't going to abandon this community. We resisted the soldiers' pressure.

Claudia: Some people didn't want to come back because they were afraid of the soldiers. "Why are we going to go back there if the soldiers are there?" they said. [The soldiers] said they were going to kick us off the land, and that they were going to burn down our houses. But we forced ourselves to come back, and that's how we held onto this land.

Several times we had to flee, leaving our food on the table and the houses open. One day some of our compañeros came across a group of *judiciales* entering the community. They began threatening them with their pistols. Another day, we got the message to leave the community because the soldiers were coming in their Hummers. They came into the center of the village, right up to where the church is. They came together with the landowner.

We went through a lot to defend this little piece of land. One time we spent two days in the mountains. Many of the women didn't have time to bring any food with them and the children were very hungry. We had to drink dirty water. We only lasted two days in the mountains because we didn't have any food. We had grabbed some tostadas and that was all we had to eat.

Débora: The women held a sit-in for a whole day to demand that the soldiers not enter our community again. We went to demonstrate our strength as an organization. At the end of the day, the women left the sit-in and went back to their houses, and that's when we came back to stay.

The people who stayed, stayed; some other people who left, left. Back then, many of the women were pregnant or sick and even still, they did their work of defending this village. We don't want them to come back and try and kick us out again. They can't kick us out now. It's our right to be here and we will defend this land so that our children don't have to suffer the way we did.

Women in the Zapatista Movement

Segunda, a health promoter from La Garrucha region:[4] Before 1994, we had never seen a woman participating, or a woman who left her village to go anywhere else. In some communities, where the soldiers attacked us in '95, a lot of women protested; we spoke up and we organized against the soldiers. As women, we found the courage to defend ourselves and our communities. After that, women started to participate in other ways too, because we felt stronger.

Zapatista women from the Morelia region (collective testimony):[5] Thanks to our organization, we have opened our eyes and opened our hearts. Now we know that men and women have the same rights. Women who had already joined the EZLN came and gave us talks and explained to us that it's not just men who have rights, that women also have the right to participate in assemblies and be elected as authorities. For the women who were in the ranks of the EZLN, it's like the war woke us up, and we began to lose our fear. The women insurgents were a great example for us.

Now, as Zapatista women, we have the right to participate in the struggle as members of the support base, the militia, and as insurgents. We have the freedom to participate in meetings and gatherings. In community and regional assemblies we participate side by side with the men. We also have the right to hold any responsibility within our organization. There are women who are local and regional representatives, and there are coordinators of the collectives. We also participate in the areas of health and education, and in the Church.

Manuela, an education promoter from the Morelia region:[6] When we entered into the resistance and formed the autonomous education system, I was still studying with the government teachers. I didn't know much about the organization and my father came and explained it to me. He explained to me about politics, about the struggle, and he explained how important it is to find a good path in life. He encouraged me to participate, and he asked if I wanted to be a community educator with the organization. Once I understood how important the work of a community educator is, I accepted this responsibility. I was enthusiastic about the work because we live in a new community on occupied land and there was no school for the children. My community named me as a community educator. They told me there would be training workshops for the new community educators and my father said to me, "You should go because the workshops will help you and you will be better equipped to serve your community." So I began learning, and sharing what I was learning with the other men and women who make up our autonomous education system.

I am able to go to all the meetings and workshops for the community educators because my family is very supportive. After a while, the community organized itself better and began supporting me by paying the bus fare each time I go to a meeting; they pay for it with money from the collectives.

If it were not for the EZLN and autonomous education, I would be in a very different space. I give thanks to everyone who fought and died for us as part of this struggle.

Voices from Oaxaca 2006
"We don't want a government of murderers that represses the people"

Interviews by Clifton Ross and Patricia Luna, July 2006
Translation by Clifton Ross

The struggle of Oaxaca in 2006 calls into question the line between an uprising and a movement. Certainly the uprising had all the makings of a movement. The rebellion exploded after state and local police, sent in by PRI governor

Ulises Ruíz Ortíz, violently attacked a plantón *(occupation) by striking members of the educators' union in the center of the city of Oaxaca. Thousands of people from virtually every sector of the city and around the state came to the teachers' defense, and established the Popular Assembly of the Peoples of Oaxaca (Asamblea Popular de los Pueblos de Oaxaca, APPO). The people essentially ran the city for the next six months with a decentralized network of collective and cooperative processes. Increasingly, paramilitary forces began to terrorize the city and region and eventually federal troops were sent in to crush the rebellion. Nevertheless, the uprising continued to flare time and again over the following months. More than twenty people were killed, including U.S. independent journalist Brad Will. The governor was finally defeated at the polls in 2010.*

Rufino Gutiérrez Hernández, Section 22 of the National Education Workers Union (Sindicato Nacional de Trabajadores de la Educación, SNTE)

I'm Rufino Gutiérrez Hernández, assistant in Press and Propaganda for Section 22 of the SNTE. After twenty-six years of struggle, each year in May we have activities [in Oaxaca]. This year it was prolonged because there was no response to our written demands from the state government nor from the federal government. We waited for fifteen days from the time we turned in our demands and nothing, until May 22, which was when all these overwhelming activities began: blockades, the taking of public buildings, and the blocking highways.

It all started in keeping with the practices and tactics of the teacher's movement, beginning with a *plantón* (occupation) and an indefinite strike of the Oaxaca teachers. But as there was no response, an invitation went out to all the unions, all the independent organizations, not only in the state but at a national level. Gradually people began to arrive from all over, especially after this government, trying to politicize the situation, used the public forces to evict the employees and teachers who were occupying the plantón, something this state government should never have done.

That was the final straw, because from then on the teachers began to defend themselves, and rather than the government reaching its objective of evicting them, the plantón grew stronger. More people and groups arrived, and it grew into a people's assembly of the peoples of Oaxaca. Then the movement moved from being a democratic teachers' movement to a democratic people's social movement. Of course there were people trying to divert things to their own purposes so the popular assembly was prudent by making a call to the wisdom of the people's movement and urging two

Members of the teachers' union march in Oaxaca, 2003. Photo by Marcy Rein.

or three leaders to redirect their thoughts and political ideas away from divisions, because that's one of the tactics of the government that says if it divides, it rules.

So the popular assembly was very clear and precise calling on these compañero leaders to clear up what was a misunderstanding, and since then there's been a growing and strengthening unity. The teachers' union is determined not to take a step backward but continue forward until the state governor Ulises Ruíz Ortíz is removed from office.

Now with this broader support there is an ongoing dialogue about an alternative national project against neoliberalism. Those who are going to profit from the neoliberal activities are the rich. That's why they're interested in the privatization of all the national resources, that is, the water, the businesses, commerce, everything. And then to maintain the poor that way.

The organizations of the different communities continue to be repressed by these fascist governments and murderous oppressors who are unable to respond to the people. We base our demands on the law, the political Constitution of the United States of Mexico, which defines how the people are to conduct themselves, and how the federal, state, and city governments are to conduct themselves. We, the people, can't ignore this, but the state and federal governments on many occasions have broken that law, for which reason the people, from whatever state of the republic, have to show their unhappiness with the ineptitude of those in power. We have to organize in assemblies and move forward with determination, little by little, to overthrow this government. We have to put in a government that comes from the people, a form which we've already begun to implement here in Oaxaca with the popular assembly. We know it's not easy nor a short-term work but rather something that is going to take a lot of time but the people are already clear that this is the route we have to take, and that democracy in this country has to begin with one town, one state, and then move forward to another state, and then another to close like a pincer movement such that at a certain moment we'd be able to overthrow these worthless governors who offer no response. Let them open up a path for the people to name their own leaders.

Jordi Hernández, Santiago Caballero, and Angélica Domínguez Chávez, members of the central commission of the Popular Assembly of the Peoples of Oaxaca (APPO)

Jordi Hernández: Oaxaca is one of the poorest cities of the country in a state of enormous poverty, and rich in forests, natural resources, and biodiversity. Oaxaca needs to have its teachers organized. It has a community organization of indigenous people, of its original people and their communities, but there's also a development in the whole state of its natural organizations and natural leaders among campesinos, students, indigenous, and its urban popular movements. So the Popular Assembly of the Peoples of Oaxaca is the result of a historical process of organization and unity.

Santiago Caballero: Right now we've taken twenty-one *priista* towns [towns under control of the Institutional Revolutionary Party, PRI] in different parts of the state and we're not going to let them go until Ulises leaves. It's the end for the state governor who, in the dawn of June 14 (2006), attacked and evicted the teachers. We regathered our forces and retook the historic center. There were people killed, some wounded; one teacher was raped by the police and one lost an eye. Children were killed. As a result we've organized with the social movement organizations and held megamarches where something over a million people attended to protest the repressive state governor and to say we want a government that represents the people. For example, over there (pointing) is the ex-governor's palace, which he closed and turned into a museum without consulting the people. We think the governor's palace should be in the city center. So we'll have to open that by means of the assemblies, with the residents and everyone.

We've been very close to the teachers because they work in different marginalized communities and what they've done to the teachers leaves me speechless. This is a murderous, repressive government and we here in

Oaxaca don't want a government of murderers that represses the people. And it's not just the teachers. They've also imprisoned many leaders of social movements in different parts of the state; there are many political prisoners here. There are killings, disappearances, and other things, and we're not leaving here until Ulises leaves.

Angélica Chávez: The APPO is trying to save the state of Oaxaca. It's no longer just the teachers, but all the people who are against [Ulises]. The blinders have come off the eyes of the people, and there are only a few left with him. And why is that? Because they have relatives working with him and it's obvious that they have to support him. But no longer does the majority. The popular assembly has united with the state assembly of teachers and 385 organizations, and not only teachers' [organizations] but social, community, and indigenous organizations in the struggle. And now the task is to begin organizing assemblies in the neighborhoods, committees, APPO, but in the neighborhoods. And all the organizations are autonomous. They don't receive any money from anyone from any political party. We're not affiliated with any party, which is the main thing. We don't want any more political parties. And this is so we can gather signatures, which have now passed one million, signatures of all the people from the surrounding mountains. This is a government of thieves and what the people want now is to retake the palace, as they should, since it's the palace of the government and that's where it should be, because they just use it for parties. And where does that money go? It's all in their pockets.

We've had enough of such leaders. The next leader the APPO is going to elect. But we're not going to choose anyone from any party; that's what this is all about. That is, it's going to be different. We're going to get rid of the police and have community police, *topiles*, people's police, armed with nothing more than a baton. They'll be people who have a term of office and win that term in social service. They'll be groups of citizens that take care of the city of Oaxaca, and the whole state, just topiles: no police, nor ministers. That's what we're trying to bring about, so Oaxaca will be free. That's it with everything having to do with the state government. It's starting now and there will be civil disobedience because no one is going to pay their taxes. So, for instance, in the schools people have to pay a fee, right? Now it's going to be free. Why? Because it's said that the fee is voluntary, but if a person doesn't have 300 or 500 pesos ($30 or $50) their child isn't enrolled in kindergarten or primary school. And that money isn't for the teachers but supposedly for a committee of parents who have to share it with the government because the government is obliged to maintain the schools and pay the janitors and give material support even though the [state] government receives money from the federal government for all that. So people will no longer pay those fees.

Once Ulises leaves we'll take the rest of the town halls. This one remains to be taken. And the house of [state] representatives will be taken and all the government offices and we'll make rules and set up an autonomous state.

Flavio Sosa/APPO member
Interview by Hernán Ouviña, November 2006
Translation by Chuck Morse

Flavio Sosa was a member of the "provisional collective council" of the Popular Assembly of the Peoples of Oaxaca (APPO, in Spanish). Despite being one of APPO's most visible faces at the moment, he insisted on saying, "Ours is a movement of the grassroots, not leaders." What follows are some fragments of a much longer conversation that we had with him and other comrades in the tent city in the emblematic Santo Domingo Plaza, a bastion of communalist resistance in Oaxaca.

There is a long tradition of assemblies in Oaxaca that goes back to the pre-Hispanic era—the popular assembly is the ultimate authority in indigenous communities—and APPO was born with the goal of being an assembly of assemblies; one that would include the Zapotecos, the Mixtecos, the Mixes, the rest of the indigenous peoples, and black people. It arose as an exercise in democracy carried out by the various people, communities, and organizations that want to participate in the movement.

Community and neighborhood organizations participated from the very beginning, as well as unions, political fronts, civil society organizations, and even professional associations. Initially, APPO was a popular response to the aggression inflicted upon the teachers and a mechanism for reaching a common goal, which was the departure of Ulises Ruíz Ortíz. Later, the idea spread of working not only to topple Ulises Ruíz Ortíz but also to transform the conditions of life, to lay the foundations for a new relationship between society and government. In this context, there have been many interesting discussions about the reforms that Oaxaca needs and what direction the government we want should go. Intellectuals, academics, religious people, and members of other organizations have taken part. It's as if there's APPO on the one side and the street movement on the other, which is ultimately turning itself into a movement that is pacifist yet able to respond to attacks, such as those that we suffered at the hands of the Federal Preventive Police (PFP).

This movement was born as a response to a brutal aggression, but began to question everything: to question the media, which it seized and took over in some instances; to question the traditional ways of doing politics and attempt to articulate new methods of doing them; to question the political parties and stop any one from calling the shots; even to question the leadership itself and create a collective leadership; and also to question a bad government and try to remove it. This has made it an antisystemic movement that alarms the political class. "How can a protest movement challenge the status quo and how we do politics?" the politicians ask themselves.

The social fabric in Oaxaca has suffered terrible wounds: people have lost jobs, the teachers aren't teaching; there are problems in the communities; the health sector has shut down. Third parties have been affected, it has to be recognized. We're in an emergency situation and need to resolve local matters first. But in no way does that mean that we will disregard national issues. In fact, we think it's necessary to connect ourselves to the Other Campaign, the National Democratic Convention, and various additional organizations.

You're speaking to one of APPO's most visible faces right now. Suppose that I decide to make a deal with Ulises. In that case, they'd push me aside and the movement would continue. I don't make the decisions. I have a responsibility—to speak with the press and articulate a position—but I don't control APPO. Sometimes my opinions are received favorably in the assemblies and other times they say "this guy is crazy" and simply ignore me. This isn't a party-based movement. And you can't try to discipline it, because it isn't an army either. For example, yesterday it took the "provisional council" a great deal of effort to get something passed in a general assembly, despite the fact that we brought a proposal, agreed upon by consensus, arguing that the main highways should be cleared. We barely managed to get it passed. But it's going to take a lot of work to get the base to accept that agreement, even if we explain all the virtues of the proposal. That's something that no leader can pull off.

If you suggest to the university people that they remove the blockades around the Ciudad Universitaria, they'll tell you to go to hell. That's why I said that this movement doesn't depend on leaders. Here's another example: they have a committee that runs Radio Universidad, and on the day of the fighting I said, "Listen, give me a moment to send a message." They told me, "No, you can't go in. There's an emergency." I insisted, telling them that I only needed a minute, but the response was the same. That's why we say that this movement isn't homogeneous, but multidirectional.

It's the conventional view of politics that leads people to search for someone to be the leader, perhaps someone who is at the head of the demonstrations or appears most frequently on television. Actually, some guys here painted "if you create a leader, you create a tyrant" on a wall. They have good reasons to say that and we respect them. That's why it's important to understand that this movement is about all of society, trying to live together and move forward together. There are comrades that wear the hammer and sickle symbol and then there are the base church communities that come with the Virgin of Guadalupe. That's the great strength of our movement. That's why we always say, "It's not about the leaders." On one occasion, when this phrase began to circulate, someone made a sign saying, "This isn't a movement of leaders but the grassroots," and the group later signed it. Shortly afterward, some thoughtful young guys added underneath with a pen, "It's not about leaders... or even groups." That's the reality.

Jesús Ramírez Cuevas, editor of *Regeneración* and member of MORENA
"Only the people can save the people"

Interview by Clifton Ross and Luis Ballesteros, August 2011
Translation by Luis Ballesteros

Jesús Ramírez Cuevas is a journalist whose work has appeared frequently in Mexico's progressive daily newspaper, La Jornada, *and elsewhere. He edits* Regeneración, *the free newspaper of MORENA (Movement for National Renewal) and he was an advisor to Andrés Manuel López Obrador (AMLO), former mayor of Mexico City, and left candidate for*

Jesús Ramírez Cuevas of the Movement for National Renewal (MORENA). Photo by Clifton Ross.

the Party of the Democratic Revolution (PRD) in the elections of 2006 and 2012.

It's a rare treat to sit down with someone in the leadership of a left electoral party who frankly, and openly, admits to an early and ongoing fascination with anarchist thinkers like Ricardo Flores Magón. There was a time in Mexico when Flores Magón, murdered by the U.S. government in the federal penitentiary in Leavenworth, Kansas, was all but forgotten. Ramírez Cuevas brought the martyred revolutionary back onto the stage of Mexican politics in Regeneración, *envisioned in some way as a continuation of the Mexican political thought reaching back to a newspaper by the same name that Flores Magón edited.*

This interview was conducted in Mexico City in the Fine Arts Palace (Palacio de Bellas Artes) where Luis Ballesteros and I met Jesús one morning over a cup of coffee. It was a year before AMLO and MORENA lost the presidential election of 2012. In November of 2012, MORENA decided in its postelectoral national convention to reorganize as a political party for future elections.

MORENA is the end result of a process of organization, work, and unification of experiences and the maturation of certain long-lasting work processes of the Mexican Left that have been occurring for many years. Strictly speaking, it is not an organization but a movement that hinges on very strong leadership by Andrés Manuel López Obrador, but which at the same time has disseminated its connections, efforts, and links throughout the country.

MORENA is the recovery of the legacy of struggle of the Mexican people that can't be summarized in a concrete ideology but can be defined as an array of libertarian ideas that don't belong to a traditional leftist current. It has socialist, communist, anarchist, Maoist, Trotskyist members but also members without a political or ideological identity. All of them participate as citizens and active agents of change.

MORENA is building a horizontal grassroots work structure. It's seeking to reach sixty-five thousand committees nationwide. At present, thirty-four thousand have been formed and the committees encompass twenty-five hundred municipalities. It's essential to build a territorial structure to be able to transform the country with a broad organization to better tackle the crisis we live in, which is also a crisis of today's civilization.

It's the first time that we're in a position to really build a left-leaning citizens' movement with presence in all the municipalities of Mexico, not only in certain regions, which has been the case until now. The movement has two basic purposes: to gather the concrete demands of the people and to carry out the radical social, political, and economic transformation of Mexico in a peaceful way.

State of war

I think that we are in a completely unprecedented scenario. We are living a war with levels of violence and a death toll equal to the wars in Central America, not to mention Afghanistan and Iraq, because even though we're not at that level, we're in a low-intensity war that is a high-intensity war at the same time, because it targets the population. The challenge is to be able to build a political and peaceful proposal in a climate of war.

We're witnessing an acceleration of the destructive processes of the country that, together with the United States interventionism, take violence as a strategy. In my opinion, the war on drugs is not a natural fact but something injected, induced, worked, and planned from international agencies and by big capital. After all, if we see now that there are no moral hesitations to destroy a country with speculative financial attacks, then how can there be any moral hesitation to flood it with drugs and turn that into a profitable business or to fill it with weapons, no matter the death toll? Human trafficking is also part of the equation of big capital in Mexico.

Now the regime wants to instill fear and demobilize the people. In this context, the regime attempts to impose the PRI. That's the trick! They sacrificed the PRI in 2000 to try to maintain the economic model and the PAN had to resort to electoral fraud in 2006 to remain in power for another presidential term. It's out of the question that the PAN will retain the government, despite the allocation of money from the national budget to Televisa and the media trying to impose the PAN's candidate.

Crisis of economic model

The crisis affecting the world and, of course, Mexico, is a crisis of civilization and of an economic model. It's the crisis of a way of life, of a pattern of consumption that's ending life on the planet and taking with it the rights of the people and the possibility of future generations. Furthermore, the neoliberal domination of the past thirty years has resulted in the abduction of political and economic institutions, as well as the state institutions that should serve society. All are co-opted by the interests of large corporations.

Here in Mexico Walmart doesn't pay taxes. The Canadian and U.S. mining companies in Mexico don't pay a peso in taxes, something that doesn't happen anywhere in the world. Telephone and bank rates are among the highest in the world, even though there is no economic or market reason for that. They charge us those rates while the salaries of Mexicans are twelve times lower than in Europe and eight times lower than in the United States. Mexico is turning into a land of conquest and plunder.

The PRI and social control by any means necessary

Now it's no longer the police or the army that repress on the streets. The TV also plays a prominent role. They want to impose a candidate who could be Peña Nieto or whoever guarantees the continuation of the regime, the system, and the economic model, this model that's concentrated political and economic power in the same hands, the 1 percent of the population that holds almost 40 percent of the national wealth. They don't pay taxes and yet they receive from the public budgets, since the state is at the service of the corporate, industry, business, and private powers and evidently, which is more terrible, of the transnational powers.

MORENA is against this continuity or against the predominance of this system that leaves no option for people than migration or drug trafficking, because agricultural or industrial production can't meet the demand for jobs. MORENA is the proposal of sectors of the cultural, social, trade union, peasant, indigenous, university, and political Left, to construct an honest and politically viable and radical option in terms of its offers for change. Unfortunately, we've seen how the partisan political Left itself has become more and more corrupt, which is part of the game of neoliberalism.

The crisis we're living in is partly political. We come from an authoritarian and repressive seventy-year, quasi-single-party regime that wanted to use the same techniques and policies of Operation Condor.[7] Here we had more than one thousand disappearances for political reasons. The army and the public forces were used against social movements and that kept the PRI in power for more than seventy years.

Then there was a civic awakening combined with a growing social influence of the Left. This intersected with a break-up in the PRI. This would have led to the loss of the PRI's majority in Congress in 1988 for the first time but the party resorted to ballot-rigging to impose Carlos Salinas. They lost Mexico City, Morelos, etc. The Salinas presidential term was one of legalized plunder and of construction of a political and economic force to support the neoliberal model.

In 2006 it was thought that the vote by itself would make the change, but it was demonstrated that the oligarchy, the Right, wasn't willing to accept any change and would use any means to prevent it. Too much money and vested interests were in play, with the added problem that the United States openly took sides with the oligarchy and the continuity of the model in that election. In 2006, we had an electoral majority but were not socially or politically organized to defend that vote or even to be able to guarantee certain governance.

New media with old tools

It became clear that the electoral fraud was facilitated by the lack of representatives and observers at all the polling stations, and also that nowadays television is the main instrument to control the population, and that it was necessary to break the information blockade. That's when *Regeneración* newspaper appeared, i.e., an old weapon, a very old instrument such as the printing press, was suddenly fighting against technology.

It's very clear: Domination by thirty names in Mexico can perfectly describe the oligarchic system in which we live. The governing oligarchy owns the PRI and the PAN and, obviously, controls Televisa. The Board of Directors of Televisa is interesting because it lists the different economic and political interests in Mexico. With its power, Televisa has virtually become the Ministry of Information, but not only that, since it's the main source of social control. TV or radio spaces are very restricted and controlled here. Two companies control 92 percent of the television; nine groups control 88 percent of the radio. Most of the magazines belong to a handful of companies that, in a recent transaction involving Televisa, Time Warner, and others, formed a holding company that controls 80 percent of the magazines.

There are nothing but monopolies here, where the neoliberal model was imposed. But then again, there was never a free market or free play of forces and, therefore, medium and small producers and companies are subjected to the domination of monopolies. Another lesson from 2006 was that social mobilization started after the election.

Regeneración is a militant newspaper, not one that you can find in the newspaper stands. It's not a newspaper for public opinion but for the people, so it's distributed free of charge, house to house. This is the link of the movement with the people.

MORENA's platform represents a substantive change, an alternative project for the nation, an in-depth vision of radical transformation, but the electoral reform and the economic and political programs are more moderate. It doesn't foresee the expropriation of large companies or the transformation of the market economy but it does intend to create a counterweight and strengthen social economy, social ownership, and the agencies of the state to change the direction of the economy. Finally, it must be a decision of society how deep the change must be and to which extent, but it isn't the political decision beforehand from a vanguard that decides to impose a change, either socialist or closer to capitalism.

We believe that the Left must make a decision as to which side it is going to support. I hope the comrades of la Otra Campaña, other social movements, and even trade union members, understand that we must be united, that all social struggles must join forces, resorting to all the experience of the Left to strengthen a path that involves a change at the top of the state institutions, in the public offices, but with a mobilized and organized society, since no change will occur without it.

I believe that after the rise of the Zapatistas, the Left changed the way it constructs its discourse, which before used to be exclusively, or mostly, ideological. Marxism-Leninism or Maoism was the ultimate explanation of reality and the only alternative, and today we see that the contribution of the Zapatistas was to recover the national imaginary and the national history as the banners of struggle. After all, the national-popular component is what has transformed the country and its recovery is the central force for transformation. To achieve that, you have to use the underlying symbols, language, and collective imaginary in order to build a radical vision.

The Flores Magón brothers are a moral example in Mexico and also one of the most radical currents that has ever existed. The Flores Magóns went to the United States to help build trade unions and ended up being imprisoned. Ricardo Flores Magón was even killed in prison because he never conceded. He opposed the war, confronted imperialism, and never betrayed his ideal, regardless of the cost. It's a negated historical current, but that negated revolution, the revolution of the anarchists, has influenced the construction of the country's imaginary. The Flores Magón or the Mexican Liberal Party developed a highly interesting proposal for organization and struggle.

Around 1906, before the Mexican Revolution, they envisioned a radical but democratic, liberal, and justice-seeking program. They published one or several newspapers and against all odds and against any logic, challenged the iron-fist control exerted by the dictatorship of Porfirio Díaz. We are taking up their example by recovering the unbending historical moral example of endless struggle and their proposal for radical change that ended up as the banner of the Constitution of 1917. Despite their political-military defeat, their ideas permeated and remained.

Their phrase "only the people can save the people," which is used by Andrés Manuel López Obrador, belongs to Ricardo Flores Magón, which means that what is truly democratic in terms of the construction of citizenship depends on the participation of the people and not on constitutional or legal changes. It rather depends on the exercise of rights and the capacity of the people to make the popular will prevail.

I know that my anarchist friends take issue with the name *Regeneración* for the newspaper, because in their opinion this is a reformist, snobbish, and bourgeois democratic movement. But the idea is to recover the example of the Flores Magón brothers; the message behind *Regeneración* is to tell the people that we're facing the same situation we faced one hundred years ago.

And now MORENA is seeking the same deep social, political, economic, ecological, and ethical transformation of Mexico. It has a very strong leadership but also a more horizontal form of construction. It has its own contradictions and different levels of maturation from place to place but we need a left organized from the grassroots, producing the vaccines that would stave off corruption and recover the capacity to influence the social and political processes of Mexico.

#YoSoy132
"It's our turn"

Interview by Oscar Bustamante, June 2012
Translation by Clifton Ross

When then-presidential candidate for the PRI (Institutional Revolutionary Party) Enrique Peña Nieto held a campaign event at Ibero-American University in Mexico, he didn't expect to spark a student movement. During his visit, a large number of students expressed their anger over state repression of dissent and the potential return of the PRI system. Peña Nieto was the governor of the State of Mexico at the time of the repression in San Salvador Atenco, as a result of which two young men were killed: Javier Cortés Santiago and Ollin Alexis Benhumea Hernández, a student of the National University of Mexico (UNAM) who was also a dancer and a supporter of the EZLN and La Otra and who could very well be the precursor of #YoSoy132. (Note: See letter from Subcomandante Marcos on the occasion of Hernández's death: http:// milfuegos.blogspot.mx/2006/06/letter-from-subcomandante-marcos-to.html.)

The PRI tried to distort the protest of the students at the Ibero-American University, resorting to the monopolized media to make them appear like a bunch of manipulated young people and even questioning whether they were actually students of that university. In response to that, 131 students protested by uploading a video showing their Ibero-American University student IDs. The next day a demonstration was called against Televisa and hundreds more students arrived, claiming to be student number 132, using the hashtag à la Occupy, in the USA, and a movement was born. "#YoSoy132" is a collective, ongoing protest against the corrupt political system and the media monopoly that collaborates with it. This interview was posted at http://www.scribd.com/ doc/98149757/Entrevista-Yosoy-132-UAM-Xochimilco. The two young men, identified as Carlos Vega, student of economics, and Bob, student of sociology, are both students at the Autonomous Metropolitan University of Xochimilco.

Bob: We've worked intensely since this movement started in the Ibero-American University. We're organizing an International Gathering of Latin

YoSoy132: Concert in the Zócalo of Mexico City, June 2012. Photo licensed under Creative Commons by Mundo al Revés (www.mundoalreves.org).

American Public Universities (UPUAL) where Camila Vallejo will be the speaker.

Carlos: The same day of the events at the Ibero-American University, students from these other private universities began to organize and call for a demonstration in front of Televisa. It was well-organized and efficient, it must be said, because we avoided calling an assembly, but rather organized by social networking. A student coordinating committee was called, but the first march overwhelmed it because it became a massive event. Later a demonstration was held at the "Stele of Light" (*Estela de Luz*), which is seen as the greatest symbol of corruption here in the Federal District (DF), and here public and private university students, who had up to the time had been historically distant, met together. It was a milestone.

Bob: The first sign that things were wrong happened when students at a private university rebelled. Related to that, here in Mexico we've been fed up with things for seventy years. Seeing the students demonstrating, more joined and decided to get involved. This is my first action. With the demonstration at the Stele of Light and the University City (CU) assembly, it seems we've reached a key moment in this movement because we've begun to organize internal assemblies in the schools aimed at working in commissions within the CU. In other words, now the movement is beginning to take on a structure.

Carlos: I think that also this movement is responding to a specific historical process. Up to 2000, Mexico experienced a total party system, then began a series of progressive governments. What you'll find in Mexico, DF now, for instance, began with Cuauhtémoc Cárdenas (1997–1999), which opened up an ideological and cultural horizon. The process deepened with successive PRD governments in the city. For example, Aztec dancing was prohibited except outside of the churches or on days celebrating patron saints. But with Cárdenas this restriction ended, opening a whole spectrum of cultural demonstrations, and visiting artists from other parts of the world gave oxygen to this change. This cultural change began to have a multiplying effect, even if it was slow. This is partly attributable to the centralized nature of the country.

There's also the world context. The movement didn't arise while the rest of the world stayed the same. This movement took place in the context of the mobilizations in Arab countries, in Spain, in Chile, and with Occupy. There's a world context that is filtering through and on the news. That's the external situation. Inside, meanwhile, you have to study the national contexts. From 1982 on, Mexico strongly adopted neoliberalism, the doctrine of the total market. For those of us who are young, we lived through the crisis of 1994, the "tequila effect," [the sequel or aftershock of the crisis and devaluation occurring that year] and for us it's socially accepted that the PRI is synonymous with corruption and authoritarianism. But also it's a fact, as I was saying, that that there's been an opening toward more information. We now know more things about, for instance, the Tlatelolco massacre in 1968, the "halconazo" of 1971, [two repressive blows against student activists by government forces] adding to what our parents told us at home of the history of our country, and then suddenly a spark exploded in the Ibero and it was the moment we said, "It's our turn."

Bob: Here in Mexico we have a very paternalistic culture. When the youth rise up, the other sectors embrace the movement because they consider us the future. And I also think that in our case there's an artistic-cultural dimension. While it's true that this movement has bottom-line demands that are almost the same as those proposed by the students of 1968, there's a novelty in the way the call went out. At the moment, for example, we have adherents to the movement from nearly one hundred art schools and that's been a great support insofar as it adds a very attractive format to the demands. And these two things feed very nicely into each other.

Carlos: Before #132 the general discourse in the country was, "The youth are apathetic, submissive, indifferent, etc." The professors themselves were desperate when they saw that disinterested attitude. But there's another important element and that's that the few youth privileged enough to get into higher education, despite what I just said, already have a latent critical consciousness but we were not perhaps ready to get involved, because there was also a lack of interest in overly ideologized forms of political participation that weren't very attractive. The incident at Ibero and what happened afterward, then, were detonators that mobilized us and brought us into this movement on our own terms.

Bob: Democratization of the media means we must have our own means of communication. The social networks have become our own alternative media and the information monopoly of Televisa has really twisted information. It's also begun a "dirty war" against the student movement. They said, for instance, that for her trip to Mexico Camila Vallejo charged a million pesos. We're working to create our own media and in the case of the School of Communication of UAM, for example, they've created a project to start an independent television channel. All that [is] to say that for us access to information is fundamental.

Carlos: You have to understand also that in this neoliberal context, Televisa is like Coca-Cola for Mexicans: it's already on top of the structure of power, and from there it "educates." There's a monopolistic invasion of viewers and it becomes the only form of accessing information for millions of Mexicans, who interpret the world through the eyes of Televisa and TV Azteca. The television monopolies, as well as Carlos Slim, have a national project and in that sense the social networks, for some strange reason of capitalism, are open for other voices to also express themselves. And I think they'll be unstoppable in terms of the informational opening happening for millions who are using them. It's just the beginning and I think it'll be very difficult to set back. To the degree that more and more people have more and better connectivity, there'll be a broader horizon for our attack.

Guatemala

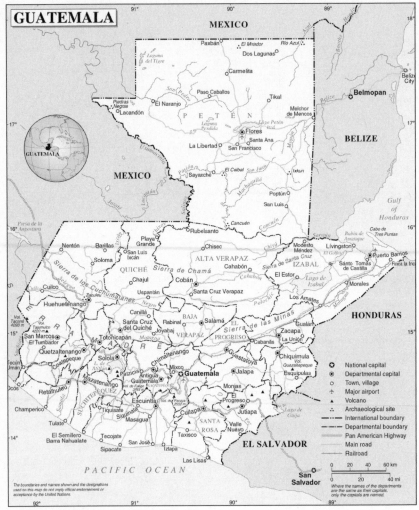

Deep-rooted movements defy violence to fight for a better way of life

By Phil Neff

Social movements are flourishing in today's Guatemala, drawing on rich traditions of indigenous and popular struggle for collective survival, self-determination, and emancipation. In the face of this power from below, the country's economic and political oligarchy has repeatedly used violence to repress challenges to its dominance and shape the state and economy to its benefit. The direct culprit of this violence is a military trained in the assassination and disappearance of "internal enemies," responsible for the elimination of generations of unionists, students, campesinos, and human rights defenders, culminating in the genocidal "scorched earth" campaigns of the 1980s in which hundreds of indigenous Maya communities were massacred. This historical pattern continued in 2012, under President Otto Pérez Molina, a retired general and veteran of counterinsurgency and military intelligence. Social movement analysts characterize the current model as "neoliberal militarism," combining formal democracy with authoritarian political processes, militarization, and unchecked exploitation by national and transnational capital.[1]

Guatemala's exceptional levels of violence and inequality can be traced to a regressive social structure based in extreme racism and the concentration of land and resources by first colonial, then national and global elites. The Spanish invasion in 1542 found in Central America both abundant natural riches and a large population of Maya city-states and communities, which were subjugated through disease, division, war, and enslavement. Indigenous people were displaced from their traditional territories into settlements under the feudal authority of colonial and religious administrators, eventually establishing a racially determined class system that endures to the present day.

The indigenous majority forms the base of the social hierarchy, with twenty-two Maya ethnolinguistic groups, as well as Xinca and Garifuna communities, composing up to 60 percent of the population,[2] while the mestizo lower and middle classes identify with a European-focused *ladino* culture that denies or trivializes its indigenous heritage. At the top is the *criollo* elite that claims "pure-blooded" European ancestry and maintains inherited control of land, capital, and political influence.[3]

The economic basis of the modern Guatemalan state was established in the 1871 "Liberal Reform," which intensified the economy's reliance on agricultural exports through the concentration of land in massive plantations of crops such as coffee, sugar, and cotton. Communal landholdings and traditional authorities were dismantled and indigenous people were further displaced into the highlands. Local elites partnered with multinational corporations such as the United Fruit Company, which appropriated vast tracts of land and held a monopoly over rail and port infrastructure.

At the outset of the twentieth century, the first unions had emerged among artisans and small-scale industry, with railroad, port, and brewery workers leading the first strikes and facing repression during the 1920s. Radical workers found allies among students at the public San Carlos University (USAC), where the Association of University Students (AEU) was a powerful motor of social protest throughout the twentieth century.[4] The incipient political and labor organizing of the 1920s was cut short by President Jorge Ubico in 1931, whose fascist-sympathizing, U.S.-compliant regime governed until 1944 and oversaw the militarization of public institutions and the abolition of unions and revolutionary political parties. Nevertheless, a general strike brought down Ubico in July 1944; his replacement was soon ousted in a revolution led by students and progressive military officers. The "October Revolution" installed a junta that called for the country's first democratic elections.

The successive presidencies of Juan José Arévalo and Jacobo Árbenz led to labor, educational, agrarian, and electoral reforms, as well as the proliferation of unions and political parties, including the communist Guatemalan Labor Party (PGT). Inspired by Christian socialism and Roosevelt's New Deal, the governments of Arévalo and Árbenz sought to independently modernize Guatemala within a capitalist framework. With the dominance of the local elite and the monopoly of the United Fruit Company threatened, and imbued with the anticommunist fervor of the Cold War, the U.S. State Department and CIA engineered a coup in 1954.[5]

Aided by CIA-supplied lists of individuals to be "disposed of,"[6] the Guatemalan military began a campaign of assassination, imprisonment, and exile against dissidents and supporters of the Arévalo and Árbenz governments. Representatives of the AFL-CIO "reorganized" the fractured union movement, and unions and political parties accused of communist sympathies were disbanded,[7] while government decrees reversed the gains of the agrarian reform. Survivors organized underground; many gravitated toward armed struggle, following the example of Cuban and other Latin American revolutionary movements.

The guerrilla movement focused on the highlands and other indigenous regions. The two main organizations, the Guerrilla Army of the Poor (EGP) and the Revolutionary Organization of the People in Arms (ORPA), formed a common front in 1982 under the Guatemalan National Revolutionary Unity (URNG).

Civil social movements as well as armed struggle threatened the economic basis of the state in the 1970s, with renewed industrial action on sugar plantations and among mine workers, the formation of campesino unions, and a cooperative movement that allowed communities to develop economic and political autonomy. The social teachings of the Catholic Action movement spurred consciousness-raising among both indigenous and ladino youth, and indigenous catechists trained in liberation theology promoted Maya identity. A massive earthquake in 1976 further exposed social inequalities.[8]

During this same period, the military government again sought to modernize the economy by granting mining and oil licenses to foreign investors and promoting development "megaprojects" in indigenous territories, including highways and dams. To make way for these projects, indigenous communities were displaced or massacred—as in the construction of the World Bank–financed Chixoy Dam, which exterminated and inundated the community of San José Río Negro.[9]

State terror reached its maximum during the regimes of Generals Romeo Lucas García (1978–82) and Efraín Ríos Montt (1982–83). Under Lucas García disappearances and assassinations in the cities increased, and a policy of wholesale massacre of indigenous communities was instituted in the countryside. Ríos Montt's government decreased urban repression while intensifying and institutionalizing rural violence through forced conscription of paramilitary "self-defense patrols" (PACs) and concentration of the indigenous population in "model villages" based on U.S. counterinsurgency tactics developed in Vietnam.[10] The military consolidated power independent of the state through the theft of land and collusion with organized crime, also solidifying alliances with the oligarchy through intermarriage and joint investments.[11] One hundred fifty thousand people became refugees in Mexico, and at least a million and a half were internally displaced. Though some Maya supported or joined the insurgency, the majority of those affected by the violence were civilians. Some of the internally displaced formed Communities of Population in Resistance (CPRs), which developed means of collective survival during twelve years in the jungle and mountains.[12]

In the face of extreme repression, widows and mothers of the disappeared and massacred broke the silence, organizing to search for their loved ones and publicly accusing the military of human rights abuses: "They were taken from us alive, we want them back alive." The Mutual Support Group (GAM) and National Coordination of Widows (CONAVIGUA) mobilized in parallel in the cities and countryside, while campesinos organized to resist paramilitary conscription and denounce rural violence and exploitation. In 1980 members of the Committee of Campesino Unity (CUC) and students occupied the Spanish embassy in Guatemala City; police and military responded by firebombing the building, killing thirty-six. Among the dead was the father of Rigoberta Menchú, whose testimony increased international awareness of the intensity of human rights violations in Guatemala.

Neither the transition to electoral democracy in 1986 nor the 1996 peace accords addressed the issues of inequality and racism underlying the armed conflict, which also left a tenacious legacy of impunity, violence, and official corruption. Though the military was initially reduced in size, former and current military officials remained involved in organized crime, and the 1998 murder of human rights advocate Bishop Juan Gerardi by intelligence operatives demonstrated that the military repressive apparatus was still in place.[13]

The URNG became a legal political party, and while the electoral Left has had success in local elections, offering coverage for nascent social movements and facilitating access to state institutions, at the national level left parties have not overcome division and have been unable to compete with the economic clout of the oligarchy. Although the 2007 election of President Álvaro Colom, a self-described "social democrat," proved that progressive messaging can attract votes and opened some state institutions to meaningful reform, structural inequality, militarization, and the neoliberal economic agenda remained unchallenged during the Colom administration.

Survivors of genocide and state terror have endured a long and incomplete process in search of justice and healing. Many displaced people and refugees were able to refound communities during the early 1990s, forming "victims' committees" to seek reparations. Bolstered by the findings of United Nations and Catholic Church-sponsored truth commissions, which established military and state responsibility for the vast majority of human rights violations, human rights organizations documented specific cases through survivor testimony and exhumations. The Association for Justice and Reconciliation (AJR) filed legal complaints for genocide in the Guatemalan courts against Lucas García and Ríos Montt in 1999 and 2000. After more than a decade of protracted legal battles, by 2012 Ríos Montt and members of his military high command were finally charged and currently await trial in Guatemala.[14]

By the end of the twentieth century, the families of the *criollo* oligarchy had merged with transnational capital and become corporate entities, founding powerful lobbying chambers and pursing neoliberal policies such as the privatization of state services, a free trade agreement with the United States, and legislation facilitating expropriation of land for projects considered to be of national interest.[15]

As agroindustry, extraction of natural resources, and energy projects demand the voracious accumulation of land and water, the government has ignored its obligation to consult indigenous communities regarding projects affecting their territory. Communities have responded by organizing popular referendums, or *consultas*, from the bottom up, working through municipal and indigenous authorities to satisfy the letter of both Guatemalan and international law. Following the early example of communities affected by Goldcorp's Marlin mine in San Marcos department, at least a million people in the more than sixty municipalities have participated in consultas to date, all resulting in near-unanimous rejection of megaprojects. Guatemala's Supreme Court, while recognizing the referendums as legal, has refused to consider them binding.

Resistance to megaprojects involves community organizing to educate the population about their harmful impacts and to organize consultas, public statements and protests, environmental monitoring, and direct action tactics such as blockades or the expulsion of unauthorized state or private presence in threatened territories. Broad-based territorial defense movements coordinate local communities, organizations, and authorities on behalf of indigenous self-determination and provide spaces for exchange of ideas and analysis as well as additional legal and political support at the regional level. Communities in resistance also receive support from environmental and human rights NGOs, campesino organizations, independent media, and progressive sectors of the Catholic Church. They face severe threats stemming from the division of communities and criminalization of protest; most interactions with the state take the form of petitions and manifestos which go unanswered, protracted dialogue without political will to reach settlements, or repression.[16]

Campesinos and organized labor have also been adversely impacted by state repression and the economic agenda of neoliberalism. The current rate of unionization, at 2 percent of the economically active population, compares to upward of 10 percent during the democratic opening of 1944–1954. Combative and densely organized unions exist in the public sector, particularly among teachers and health workers, fighting against underfunding, corruption, and top-down reform. Only 12 percent of unions are in the private sector, where industrial and agricultural workers are met with fraudulent factory closures, mass firings, and blacklists, as well as death threats and assassinations.[17]

In the countryside, campesino organizations struggle to win productive land for communities and to resolve land and labor conflicts. Families and workers occupying land—as both a political and survival tactic—suffer violent evictions and attacks at the hands of police, military, and private security forces.[18] Campesino organizations have also worked with state agrarian institutions and promoted legislation to address rural inequality and lack of access to land, despite a lack of political will to implement reforms for integral rural development. Instead, agroindustry encroachment and land markets have exacerbated rural poverty and conflict.[19]

Social conflict and repression are likely to increase in coming years, as political and economic actors show no intention of allowing their agendas to be compromised by demands from below. Social movements will remain a primary source of opposition and alternatives, each in its own way contributing toward the construction of a society based not on accumulation and domination, but on cultivation of *"el buen vivir"*—a better way of living grounded in common needs and respectful of mutual difference. A Guatemala and a world for the many, not for the few.

Paula Barrios, Women Transforming the World (MTM)
"To know that one is not alone"

Interview by Coordination of International Accompaniment in Guatemala (ACOGUATE), November 2012
Translation by Christy Rodgers

Guatemala's legacy of violence, exclusion, and impunity has reserved some of its most horrific manifestations for women. Patriarchy and machismo are perhaps even more deep-seated than racial and class hierarchies, a fact revealed by an ongoing epidemic of gender violence: In 2012, the United Nations found that Guatemala has the second greatest rate of femicide in the world, a pattern of murders of women that shows no distinction between social or economic categories. Violence against women is met by almost complete impunity for perpetrators, with sentences in less than 3 percent of reported cases.

As mothers and widows of the disappeared and massacred, women were the founders of, and have remained central to, Guatemala's human rights movement. However, women are also among the principal victims of the culture of silence inculcated through the combination of state terror and social stigma. While the UN's Historical Clarification Commission collected lower rates of women's testimony of direct human rights violations during the internal armed conflict, it found that women bore more impacts of forced displacement and that rape was a systematic component of massacres and detention of women.[20]

Through the dedicated work of feminists and social psychologists with survivors, the full extent of sexual violence by the military during the armed conflict has begun to emerge. In 2010, the National Union of Guatemalan Women (UNAMG), the Guatemalan Community Studies and Psychosocial Action Team (ECAP), the feminist newspaper La Cuerda, *and Women Transforming the World (MTM) organized a Tribunal of Conscience where women publicly related their testimonies in front of symbolic judges.[21] This action set the stage for formal legal complaints in 2012 by fifteen Maya-Q'eqchi' women who denounced sexual enslavement by soldiers over a period of months during 1982 at a military recreation base in Sepur Zarco, Izabal. Their testimony opens the first cases specifically seeking to hold the Guatemalan military responsible for sexual violence during the armed conflict.[22]*

The women are monolingual; they are elderly women in general, more than sixty years old, who live in conditions of extreme poverty. Several of the women are very ill. Some have cancer, others are losing their sight. In those vulnerable conditions, they are facing a whole military structure; and in communities that are very closed about this issue as well. If we are socially bad on this issue at the level of the country as a whole, at the community level machismo is even more reinforced. We've been on this road now with them for approximately three years, and we have gotten this far. But the social conditions are still very poor.

The main difficulty is that fear and insecurity are still present. The country doesn't provide the social and political conditions under which cases like this can be tried. We have a military government currently, and that's a big obstacle: That policy of pardoning and making the issue disappear, of not getting to the truth of what happened during the war. At the community level [we have] the issue of security. Women still live with the perpetrators in their communities.

Twelve years after the peace accords were signed, there have been no major social or political advances. The peace accords are there, but they have not been translated into public policies that permit each of the agreements to advance, above all [for] indigenous peoples. However, we can't continue to wait; we've been silent for too long.

But there's fear, because sexual violence in general is a taboo subject. And if not, it's because we provoked it, we consented to it or it's our responsibility. The clear example was recently with the Roosevelt case [in which a group of criminals were charged with at least fourteen cases of rape, among other crimes]. What did the secretary of the interior do? Put out a communiqué that women should not be out in the streets after 8:00 p.m., alone, wearing provocative clothing. They always focus on the woman's responsibility. Sexual violence isn't seen as a social problem and a problem of the patriarchal system.

All the advances made in terms of women's rights have been pushed back. Now there's no budget, shelters are being shut down, projects being terminated, resources are all channeled through the government. This government emphasizes economic policies, production, and things like women's cooperatives, and the problem of sexual violence gets pushed aside, and every day there are more cases of violence and deaths of women. So in that context it's very difficult.

Building the case, fact by fact

But we have to look into the details—how it was, in each area, with each individual person. We have to answer for each one of the victims: who, how, when, where? And that's what it means to be in the case together, because everyone was in the same place during the same period of time, suffering sexual violence, which was sexual slavery inside the base. Let's say that those are the details of the case. There's another case in a community in the Q'eqchi' region. Three young women from the community were taken to a house at the back of the community and raped in a grotesque way. They put rifles in their vaginas, in their anuses, they were hung from the house beams. So the cases are being classified [according to] where the incidents happened, who was responsible in each region. For example, in Chimaltenango, there are various women with children conceived in rape, who are now adults. So in each region, this was a pattern, and [one of] the few we've documented because the National Compensation Program also has hundreds of cases in all provinces and they are the ones who have to present these accusations to the Public Prosecutor's Office. The Public Prosecutor has, I think, three hundred accusations of rape already presented to the war unit.

We are just collaborating on the whole legal strategy. However, the impetus, the work, all comes from them, in addition to facing everything— a corrupt system, a corrupt judicial system in this country. Just the fact of taking on this search for justice, is an example for other cases to come, a motivation for other women to see that it's possible to take on these cases. And we are also collaborating on recent cases seeking justice for sexual violence. It's possible to imagine so many cases [of that] in this country. And with each one we have to break down all these barriers of impunity, in addition to confronting the patriarchal system. The law is in this patriarchal context where we say the victim has to prove she was raped, and not the other way around. From the start it's a challenge with women who in addition aren't socialized in this western legal system. However, we have worked hard precisely to make them agents in the process.

Visualizing the case

These women are illiterate, and they only speak their native language, Q'eqchi'. So we said fine, we'll use drawings that represent [the parties] in some way. The owl, for example, who listens and sees. So we said, fine, the owl is the judge. Sometimes there's one judge, sometimes there's three judges, depending on the stage of the trial. Butterflies, well, in feminism, since forever butterflies have been identified with the women's struggle, a symbol of November 25, the International Day for the Elimination of Violence against Women in honor of the assassination of the Mirabal sisters in the Dominican Republic. So we printed out some butterflies on the computer, and each woman painted her own butterfly. That represented her in the trial. And we are the bees, being somewhat like the butterflies. So the bees, and then came the public prosecutor, so we had to look for that. They are the ones who ask questions, interrogate, interview, so they talk a lot. So we represented them with parrots.

The lion is a big, strong animal we were confronting, that represented the perpetrators. And we have a banner that represents the road. We have two roads. One to reparations, and one to justice. So each step we take, we go further down the road. And at the stage we're working at, who intervenes? And so we keep placing the figures: Where will the owl be, where will the parrot be? We place ourselves, the bees, and the women who have been recording this whole process during the hearings, who are represented by the dove—the women themselves chose that—and the hummingbirds are the psychologists, who have also worked with them. And so we keep moving the figures around, depending on who intervenes [when]. But we are also really learning by doing.

We have proposed almost a mission impossible: to break all these barriers of impunity that are rooted in this system. It seemed almost impossible to bring one of these cases to justice, but today we can see it clearly. The case is so clear. All that took a huge amount of work, several years' work. Three years' work to collect the testimonies, the ideas, work with the victims. But it's a case that first off is creating precedents. Internally, in the national justice system, it's the first case, and we want to break down [the] barrier of impunity that is rooted in the justice system.

The biggest challenge was to succeed in getting and ordering the facts in a logical, coherent way. But we hope for a conviction. There's a long way still to go to get there. There's a whole chain of command—there are material perpetrators, there are intellectual perpetrators, and depending a little on how the case moves forward, any one of the convictions will not just be one alone but various convictions. That's what we hope. That is the example for other legal proceedings, other women who want to take this route.

It's not easy. But we didn't think it was possible to bring suit, and now we have. We didn't think it was possible to get testimonies and now they've been given. Little by little. Step by step. It's a collective effort of many organizations and an interdisciplinary team too. But in this same effort, every step the women take is a step closer to justice.

If it wasn't for this process, for this accusation by these women, we would never have been able to carry out the exhumation in the Tinajas plantation. The fifty mass graves would never have been exhumed. And that is what we talk about with women. They are the protagonists of those efforts, of achieving that. In the region everybody talks about the plantation where the community leaders, the husbands of the women who were asking for land were massacred, were disappeared. The exhumation was carried out and we succeeded—in this first step, because another remains to be made. And there are others in this area. It's an area that was hard hit by the war.

And conditions haven't changed in thirty years. We could practically say no time has passed. They are still enslaved, now by the transnationals, [working] monocrops in conditions of slavery, because there there are no other resources. To be able to go study, get a degree, you have to go to El Estor; to do that you have to cross two rivers, take several pickups, transport vehicles. This costs about 100 quetzales a day, maybe more. There's no access to anything there. There's no health care, no education. So what's left? Work for the plantation.

Barillas: Women from Santa Cruz de Barillas, Huehuetenango, protesting the state of siege imposed by the Guatemalan president and Congress in May 2012. The government sent hundreds of state forces to carry out arrests and search homes in Barillas following local resistance to a hydroelectric dam project owned by a Spanish company, **Hidro Santa Cruz.** Photo from Consejo de Pueblos del Occidente (Western People's Council).

Now it's African palm, more all the time. [They are] pushing people to the edges, to live in the mountains, without light, without water, but working on the plantation. Social security? None. So to work for justice living under these conditions is a challenge. But the impetus of the women is their own. [It's] their petition, their voice. We just join in with that effort. It's their case, and that's what makes the case legitimate. If it weren't for them, there'd be no legal proceedings.

And it's a group process. That's a very important part, to identify that the process is a group effort. Also to know that one is not alone. And that's what they've seen with the exhumations, others have come forward who are victims and want to tell their story and support these cases. They realize there are other women in other parts of the world. They've exchanged letters with women from Japan, in translation of course. But there was even one meeting on Skype with Japanese women. They've shared with women of other countries also seeking justice, in Peru, Rwanda. So it's been very important, symbolic from the beginning, to be able to show the world, to share with other women, to know they're not crazy, this isn't craziness, a whim, or foolishness. It's what happens all over the world, and keeps happening.

H.I.J.O.S. mural 2011: The mural reads, "No to mining. Respect the popular referenda. Liberty for political prisoners. Justice." More than sixty communities around Guatemala have held referenda on mining megaprojects, and voted overwhelmingly against them. Photo by Kevin Hayes.

Roberto Mendez, H.I.J.O.S. and CPR Urbana
"The same communities that suffered genocide are victims in this new era of dispossession"

Interview and translation by Courtney Martinez/NISGUA, November 2012

Founded in Argentina in 1995 through a reunion of children of martyred and disappeared university students and teachers, H.I.J.O.S. (Daughters and Sons for Identity and Justice against Forgetting and Silence) is a social movement of generations of young people born into social movements and state repression, into orphanhood, exile, loss, and struggle. The Guatemalan chapter formed in 1999, taking an uncompromising stance on behalf of judgment and punishment for military perpetrators of violence, and against militarization and economic exploitation. The tactics of H.I.J.O.S. Guatemala center on historical memory, illustrating the continuity of historical violence and class struggles, and defending the legacy of left and antiauthoritarian militancy using tools such as graffiti and murals, music, and independent media. Actions range from disruptions of the official June 30 celebrations of "Army Day"—renamed

*"Day of Heroes and Martyrs"—to support of indigenous territorial defense
and legal cases for human rights violations. Autonomous projects like the
CPR Urbana blog and the Internet broadcast Radio Guerrilla combine street
art, poetry, reportage, and commentary in a position of direct grassroots solidarity with popular movements, without any organizational intermediary.*[23]

I'm a member of H.I.J.O.S., the organization H.I.J.O.S., and I'm also part
of an alternative media project called CPR Urbana, which means Urban
Communities of Population in Resistance. The name hearkens back to the
war when there were communities in many places that called themselves
Communities of Population in Resistance. In some cases these communities
were places the army never entered. I chose the name CPR Urbana to try to
draw attention to the contribution that the CPRs made, how they resisted
all the army's attacks by living in the mountains, and also to pay tribute to
the effort of those who lived as refugees in the jungle. The project is closely
tied to the recovery of historic memory, which is the strategic method of
the organization H.I.J.O.S., not working from a focus that tries to evoke the
past separate from the present, but rather working in a way that focuses
on the current context with its historic roots. Moreover, this method is an
attempt to reassess the revolutionary process that unfolded during the war
here in Guatemala, a process that in the present has been made invisible
and intentionally denied.

All my work has been driven by the topic of memory as a result of
being a part of the organization H.I.J.O.S. [Looking at CPR Urbana,] the
photo-reports or the questions that we make on the media are in some way
a reflection of the collective construction of the group [H.I.J.O.S.] but it's also
a deconstruction. It's a deconstruction because the method we use helps
redefine the way we interpret history. H.I.J.O.S. is basically a collective or
an organization that works under various principles that break with the
traditional approach to organizing with survivors of the war. These principles are processes of self-management, volunteerism, consensus, and horizontality. Some of these principles are what keep people so connected to
H.I.J.O.S., and that in some way complements this alternative media project,
also very connected to H.I.J.O.S.

It's true; we do promote the idea of accompanying [survivors'] legal
processes and all. We also accompany processes in the present via alternative media and very particular processes of support—for example, related
to the defense of territory.[24] If you look closely, you'll see that many of the
same communities that suffered genocide [and are a part of the current
legal processes] are victims in this new era of dispossession.

We identify the signing of the peace accords as more than anything part of a counterinsurgency plan and not in keeping with the desire of the people here in Guatemala to address the structural problems that were [the] cause of the war. The accords were a way for economic power to continue the project of domination that is still an experience of many communities today. First they were dispossessed and displaced during the war and today once again they are subject to a new era of forced displacement but with a component of new forms of domination. Why? Because Guatemala has a long history of economic development projects that involved the dispossession of indigenous people and rural farmworkers, the current expansion requires more land. For example, many of the native people were forced west onto land that wasn't believed to be very rich. Now, it seems that many of these territories are where the great wealth of this country is concentrated. So this new era of capitalist accumulation will see the implementation of the same policies of displacement that previously resulted in thousands of deaths and disappearances.

Mario Payeras, from the Guerrilla Army of the Poor (EGP), said that economic power needs another class, or needed another class, and continues to need that class in order to drive all its economic plans. He said that the class of the mestizo or ladino people has a divided role. On the one hand, the class is oppressed by economic power and on the other hand it is an oppressor of the indigenous people who have an even more limited space of participation than the ladino or mestizo people.

The genocide that was carried out during the 1980s was possible, not thanks to the mestizo people directly, but it was the mestizo people who participated in some way with their silence, and this profound silence was due to various factors. Among these are the manipulation that exists in the corporate media, education in the hands of the economically powerful, and an image of indigenous people as historically backward. So the state configures itself in a racist way, keeping in mind that the mestizo class is oppressed by the dominant power but also serves the rulers to operate, for example, the economic project that was historically imposed.

We believe in the battle for memory

The media project [CPR Urbana] came about because we believe in, and want to make visible, what we call a battle for memory, which is a struggle between the dominant power and the power of the people, the legitimate power. In this dispute, the media plays a very important role. We know the limits of trying to make an impact on the mentality of the urban social imaginary. The origin of the language of racism, discrimination, what justifies the violence against the indigenous, it all comes from here, from the urban sphere. Keep in mind that we aren't an NGO; we criticize that traditional form of work because we think that it's a very subtle way of intervention from foreign countries by way of economic cooperation. We organize as a collective with a volunteer model and we try to open up our space for participation. In this case we promote it in the urban space. One way of promoting it is by entering into social networks as a type of alternative communication. But the fight of H.I.J.O.S. goes beyond just doing work in the networks. We think that even the social networks don't reach where they should. That's why we use other types of communication like street art, graffiti, and murals.

So, the blog started as part of this fight, or this battle. We think it's important to take it on in an ideological way. We want people to know their history but not in a passive way that tells of people who fought, were massacred, and tortured; instead, we want to try to bring to light the values that mobilized a whole group of people against the hegemonic power. That's one point. Another is that we praise these very values that motivated them, for example anti-imperialism, and think it's necessary to introduce them in the social imaginary and start there to make this ideological battle in the urban space.

The truth is that we were skeptical about using electronic media this way because social networks only reach 17 percent of the general population here in Guatemala, although in urban areas it's more. If you think about it, the sector is small, but it's usually those who have access to the networks who generate opinions, so we considered that. We've been using social networks for about three years and CPR Urbana has only been around for two.

H.I.J.O.S. is thirteen years old. Before, what was our strongest work, where we spent most of our time, was working in the street. We haven't retreated but we've decided to change our strategy for various reasons. One reason is that when H.I.J.O.S. started, it was 1999 and we started to work a lot with graffiti, painting, and murals but since we're not an NGO, since we're a collective, we all had to use our free time in the afternoons or on weekends. It became harder and harder to paint murals. Little by little we reduced our work painting in the street.

Unfortunately with this government, and previous ones, but particularly this one, we recognize painting a graffiti message, rather than evoking empathy, causes rejection on the part of the population because the idea of protecting private property is widely accepted in the city. Here you can kill someone in your neighborhood and that's more accepted than damaging someone's private property. So we've decided to change our method. Two years ago we started to use the blog more as a tool in and of itself. We used to spend more time working in the street and it's not that we don't do it at all anymore, just that we've changed our strategy a bit.

Changes since the peace accords in 1996

Since the peace accords some things have changed. One example is that in general there has apparently been a change in the attitude that allows for organization. I say "apparently" because even though it's been over fifteen years since the signing of the peace accords, this doesn't mean that there hasn't been a series of assassinations. I'm referring to San Marcos where there have recently been more than fifteen assassinations of people who fought against the transnational Unión Fenosa, a Spanish company that has exchanged assets and has sold capital to a British company. In San Juan Sacatepequez there have been around four assassinations. There are more or less thirty-two people linked to judicial processes with charges that range from terrorism, assassination, suspected intention to commit an offense, and more.

I think this year has been one of the most complicated since the peace accords were signed. Why? Because the return of this soldier [President Otto Pérez Molina] coincides with many things. One is the global economic crisis that capitalism is suffering. This global capital crisis has brought corporations and financial capital to search for places to invest. And throughout Latin America the issue of investing in mines, especially gold and silver, is a hot issue that's causing great conflicts all over Latin America, not just here in Guatemala.

At the national level, there's the current ideological dispute between power and official memory, on one hand, against the people and officially unrecognized memory on the other and this is seen in the rise to power of the current president coinciding with the advance of the judicial processes against the soldiers [Ríos Montt and his high command, being accused of genocide]. The other is the agroexport/mining project has been the main economic project since the signing of the peace accords. The agroexport/mining model situates Guatemala in the international chain of production as a provider of raw materials that are rapidly running out—so much so that it's making for a polarization of society and conflicts that in my mind could be very worrisome.

Why? Because even though peace was signed in Guatemala it was never debated, and there has never been a debate on the national level that attempts to reflect what the genocide was—a senseless act by the rulers against the people. There has never really been a dismantling of this counterinsurgency way of thinking. Now if we look at the whole international,

national, and regional stage, the situation tends to polarize even more because one side of the people already know or identify with the project that has continuity with economic policies and other interventionist policies and military policies. It's in large part the counterinsurgent soldiers who have become a part of transnational security forces and who are also driving all the economic projects.

So have there been changes? There have been some changes but this doesn't mean that, given what's happened in Honduras, the rulers won't turn to soldiers to guarantee the continuity of this project. I simply say Honduras because in some ways in Honduras the coup d'état against Zelaya was so violently experienced by the people who were trying to create a transformation. We're talking about an army that wasn't as strong as our own. I have no doubt that the rulers will turn to the army in the moment that they need to [to ensure their economic power].

So, there have been some changes. There have already been advances but part of the problem is that there haven't been structural changes in the least, in my opinion. There have been some changes that sometimes seem positive, but what of finding a solution to the agrarian problem, which was one of the structural roots that made for the war, since the distribution of land is heavily concentrated? The reconcentration of the land is an issue of the monocultures for example, or an issue of mining. This government has offered 798,000 hectares in oil concessions. This means that 7.31 percent of the territory will be handed over to foreign companies to freely extract oil.

They're identifying communities that are up for grabs for foreign manipulation. They see the people as ignorant or as being manipulated by "communists," and the fear among the rulers is evident in the reimplementation of this counterinsurgent discourse, a discourse that is being widely accepted by the media.

It's one of the risks of the current neoliberal economic model that the person no longer counts. That's why I feel it is so important to know history. But more than just knowing history as a tragic fact, arriving at the negative story of what happened, we need to discover this revolutionary project that once mobilized the people to join others to search for national alternatives to move forward in what we call constructing this process for a new economic independence. We believe in what Alfonso Bauer Paiz said, that it's necessary to work directly for this country to achieve its own true economic and political independence because, if not, the consequence will be tragic. Not only for the people but also for the planet itself because this model is based on the destruction of the earth. This is something we're not in favor of; we're opposed to it.

SITRAPETEN: When workers at Salvavidas water bottling plant got laid off for supporting the SITRAPETEN union, they occupied the street in front of the plant. When they got kicked out there, they set up camp in the park in front of the National Palace, 2011. Photo by NISGUA.

Edwin Enrique Álvarez Guevara, general secretary, Petén Distributors Employees' Union (SITRAPETEN)
"They wouldn't address our concerns, so we had to organize"

Interview by ACOGUATE, July 2008
Translation by Chuck Morse

Since well before the 1954 counterrevolution, the risks of daring to challenge the economic interests of the Guatemalan oligarchy and its monopolies have been brutally clear. Nevertheless, in 2007 workers at the Petén Distributors water bottling plant in Guatemala City became the latest generation to take on the Castillo family: owners of the Salvavidas brand of purified water and the national brewing industry, corporate partners with PepsiCo and powerful political and economic players. On their sixth attempt to legally inscribe their union, SITRAPETEN, the bottling plant declared bankruptcy four days before approval of the union and its workers were laid off—all but the union members were offered new employment at another plant. For the next four years the workers of SITRAPETEN lived in constant struggle. First they occupied the street in front of the plant, and faced intimidation by security guards.

Because of these threats, they relocated to the central park in front of the National Palace; police violently evicted them in December 2009. Undeterred, they rebuilt their protest tent and continued to demand reinstatement of their jobs in a lawsuit that demonstrated the bias of the Guatemalan courts against labor, with several favorable rulings overturned on appeal. In 2011 the Constitutional Court ruled that the union members had not been improperly fired, and had no right to regain their jobs.[25] The workers have since ended their occupation, reached an agreement to regain a portion of their lost wages, and some now work for their own water purification company, independently distributing water to loyal customers in Guatemala City.

We always worked on commission, and the company demanded a huge sales volume, so it could make more money, but we earned very little working on commission. They brought in a lot per jug, which is why they forced us to meet unrealistic quotas. There was a total of six hundred thirty-eight employees here in Guatemala and we had to organize because of the mistreatment that we endured. There were times when we came in late and, since we hadn't met the quota, they turned us back out to try to meet it again, and nothing was sold and we simply came back once more, when it was already late in the evening. We also needed to increase our salary; in practical terms, we were working double and sometimes triple shifts. But they wouldn't address our concerns, so we had to organize.

There were one hundred fourteen of us [organized] at first—of which thirteen formed the organizing committee—but the company applied pressure and gave them money, etc. So, most workers gave up, thus leaving us with nineteen. As a result of this, workers lodged six reports with the Labor Inspectorate, and the Ministry of Labor reacted by simply waiting for the company to present paperwork showing that the workers no longer wanted a union. And, meanwhile, the Ministry of Labor worked with the company in such a way as to gain time for them and gave them a chance to scare the workers. They issued a series of threats. They told people that they wouldn't get a job if they unionized, that there would never be a union, etc. Ultimately, people ended up giving up the union drive.

We hope that our organization can create a situation in which the company and workers share profits. We understand that the employer will always bring in more, but workers should at least receive just pay—something that has not occurred in this business. And we want job security too—we've never had this, because they always tell us to meet the quotas, that they'll fire us if we don't, and that they have thousands of students who are ready to work, whereas we've never been to college.

Organizing a union

The process began on February 4, 2007. Thirteen of us decided to deal with the conflict collectively, establishing the ADOP committee. We formalized this that day. Five days later, we went to the Labor Inspectorate, which reacted by immediately notifying the company, which, in turn, responded by firing the thirteen of us.

We didn't sign anything and explained to our coworkers that we were putting together a committee to look after all of our interests. Because of that, and given that the company didn't rehire us and because we had registered complaints legally, we decided to call a work stoppage three days later, on Tuesday, February 13. At around 6:00 p.m. that day, managers from the company said that they were going to reinstate us. However, after the agreement was signed that they were going to reinstate the thirteen workers, they issued a declaration saying that the disruption in business had cost the firm 400,000 quetzales and that we had to pay for it, because we were responsible for the loss.

Legalizing the union was a very slow process because, just as they've said, they have enough money to buy off all the Guatemalan authorities. Many believe that the people in the Ministry of Labor accepted money, because they used stalling tactics while dealing with paperwork formalizing the union, hoping that the workers would desist. The company has always been hostile, saying that there will never be a union in any of its many businesses and that we should give up.

All of our actions have been perfectly legal, but unfortunately it's easy for the rich to influence the Guatemalan legal system. Right now we're striking to hurt them politically—they boast that they create jobs in Guatemala, that they are the best employer, that they pay well, etc., but that's simply not true.

They've tried to intimidate us in different ways: things like death threats, saying they have enough to hire criminals to hurt us and buy their way out of any legal trouble. Supervisors have told us in person and over the phone that the company is powerful enough to pay murderers to come after us, and that we better stop organizing, because there will never be a union. And they've been working hard to undermine us. In fact, there are suspicions that a hospitalized comrade suffered his injuries at the hands of one of their thugs, and yet neither the Public Ministry nor other Guatemalan authorities have done anything to resolve the case. Complaints have been lodged, but they've sat on their hands. I think that it was one of their henchmen who did it because, after all, they've stated that they have people ready to attack. Actually, they called a day before the company shut down and threatened me in multiple ways, telling me that my family and I would pay if I didn't give up.

I've always said that this is not just our battle, but also one for unionism globally, for people everywhere who have to put up with threats when they organize. The battle is intense. Sometimes we have enough to eat, but sometimes we don't. We really haven't been able to provide for our families.

Javier de León, Maya Mam community leader, coordinator of the Association for the Integral Development of San Miguel Ixtahuacán (ADISMI)
Fernando Solís, editor of *El Observador*, alternative political economy journal
"Community consultations are one of the forms of resistance carried out in defense of our land"

Interview by ACOGUATE, November 2009
Translation by Christy Rodgers

Hundreds of indigenous communities across the Guatemalan highlands whose land is coveted by transnational corporations confront problems similar to those caused by Goldcorp's Marlin mine. Residents of the municipalities of San Miguel Ixtahuacán and Sipakapa in the department of San Marcos, where the Canadian-owned mine operates, have denounced the disappearance of water sources, failure of crops and deaths of livestock, debilitating ailments, and houses that have crumbled due to blasting and heavy equipment traffic. They assert that they were never consulted before the mine began operating in 2005, and locals opposed to the mine have faced constant intimidation, death threats, and assassination attempts. In response, the Association for the Integral Development of San Miguel Ixtahuacán (ADISMI) and allies have organized popular consultations, independent environmental and human rights monitoring, and legal defense for community members facing criminalization for acts of protest. In 2010 the Inter-American Commission for Human Rights ordered the suspension of mining operations, but later reversed its decision, despite a lack of meaningful compliance by the Guatemalan government. The Marlin mine continues to operate, generating millions in profits for investors and continued conflict and environmental threats for local communities.

Fernando: The end of the civil war led to the imposition of a particular model of government. When I speak of government, I'm not speaking of institutions *per se*, but rather a set of power relations that will produce the conditions under which Guatemala can join and be accepted into the company of democratic countries. Guatemala was considered an undemocratic country because of its military governments. Officially, there's democracy [now] and we're at peace. However, the reality is otherwise. The same conditions that gave rise to the conflict continue. The legal system never asked who'd been responsible for violating human rights and carrying out the counterinsurgency plan. The military officers are still around, and the rich who supported the war financially were never brought to justice.

The government created after the signing of the peace accords promoted tying the country to global capitalism, more globalized. All it produced was the legal conditions for allowing companies, in an officially capitalist liberal democracy, to come in and set themselves up to exploit our resources. Now this is done using a principle of expansion and acquisition of land (as in colonial times) and also basically through ideological subjection, or winning over people's minds. That's a kind of violence.

Javier: When the mining industry came in, we began comparing the development model we have with first world countries and the capitalist model. They are completely contradictory. The substrata, or the earth, for indigenous peoples, has a name. For example, in Mam it's called *Knan Chojch*. *Knan* means "our mother" and *Chojch* is "earth," so "our Mother Earth." That cultural element is broken when a transnational comes in for whom there's no such thing as Mother Earth. For a transnational company, the earth is the earth; it's there for the extraction of resources. The cultural meaning is broken by that, and that's where the conflict comes from, that's why they're not compatible.

Fernando: For extractive industries, development is a result of income and profit. The idea is that the earth, resources, water, forests, mountains, volcanoes, are merchandise that can be extracted and sold. Development for indigenous people is basically life reproducing itself in optimal conditions. The problem is not that the mining company should pay more for what it takes; the problem is what it takes, and the price of those resources outside the country. Some propose that the mines should pay 5 or 10 percent royalties. Even if they paid 100 percent of what they took, the fundamental problem is that they extract resources that are not renewable, affecting not only the environment in this way, but the local people's way of life.

Javier: In Guatemala, and in San Marcos in particular, in the Mam and Sipakapense communities, resistance and community organization are based in the local authorities. The community authorities, or traditional authorities, have carried out the functions of communication, education, orientation, and organization to build community consensus and

Anti-mining demo. Hundreds of representatives from more than fifty municipalities massed in front of the National Palace in March 2011 to repudiate the central government's initiative to regulate community consultations. Communities all over Guatemala have used these local referenda to organize opposition to large-scale development projects on their territory. Photo by Graham Hunt.

see whether or not they agree on the issue of resource extraction. That's where community consultations, as they're called, come from. They're one of the forms of resistance carried out in defense of our lands. This democratic process has been practiced for hundreds of years in the communities. They meet, talk, arrive at consensus, and write the agreements in a formal statement.

That's connected to the issue of the rights established by national and international law. Article 66 of the Guatemalan constitution states that people have the right to determine the kind of life they want, including the type of social organization. Elsewhere, the municipal code states that communities or their traditional authorities, in this case the community mayors, must be consulted. All of this is also supported in international law, such as the ILO's Convention 169, in Articles 6, 7, 8, and 15.

Although the government or the Constitutional Court may maintain that these consultations are not binding, they still are, because this is a legitimate and legal practice of the communities. A report by the Congressional National Commission for Transparency says that even if the consultations are taking place years later, this does not stop them being a legitimate right, because it's legally established.

Fernando: One fundamental problem is that the government denies the communities recourse to the laws that the system itself provides them with to defend their rights, like Convention 169. The first question is: what form should be used if the government itself refuses to apply the laws? In Convention 169, the fundamental principle is that communities have a right to free, prior, and informed consultation. That has not happened in any of these cases.

The second important problem is the criminalization of the struggle, the government using security forces against social protest. Demonstrations are met by the police and the army, using means they used during the war: violent harassment, extrajudicial executions, disappearances, direct attacks. So what are the ways to get rights to be respected in that context? You can't go to court, because the courts defend private interests. Here the whole structure of justice is based on bribery and serving the powerful. Whoever pays is in charge. Whoever has the money to pay off a representative of the justice system will come out on top at a trial.

Javier: One problem is the political division in the leadership. It's one of the elements of strategy that slows the growth of community movements. Then there's the issue of poverty and extreme poverty. People don't have much time to be thinking about what the movement's going to do to defend their land; instead they're thinking about how they're going to eat today. Then there's the issue of the political parties, who, far from trying to build community power to confront collective problems, destroy community unity. The struggle for leadership is a fatal problem in Guatemala. That explains why we haven't been able to win a government when we Maya are the majority here.

Fernando: It's important to be clear that the mining industry has had a lot of power here historically. The power of business, of transnationals and powerful groups goes centuries back. You have to understand that to challenge that power, it's necessary to create a new one. Now building this power doesn't come from a political party, or the government, because it's power against power. This means building a political project, and I don't mean a partisan one. The nation's bourgeoisie, the corporate family groups, are very clear about their political and economic projects. It's to get profits. The communities are clear that they don't want this; they want another kind of development. We have to build power that will be capable of holding up, of telling the transnationals that we don't want that.

Honduras

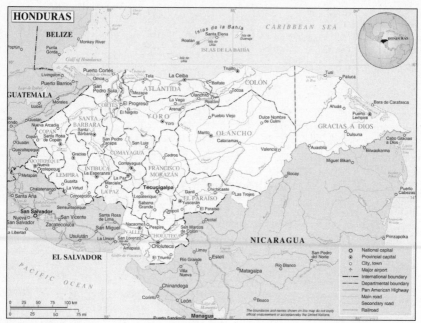

HONDURAS

United Nations Map No. 3856 Rev. 3, May 2004

INTRODUCTION
Blows forge a stronger movement

By Adrienne Pine

Honduras has a vibrant history of protest, but the state's response to opposition movements has largely relied on co-optation, coupled with more intermittent brutal repression by the military.

The June 28, 2009, coup that ousted the country's democratically elected President José Manuel Zelaya Rosales ignited a broad-based, massive oppositional movement for the first time since massive wildcat banana strikes roiled the country in 1954. But although the National People's Resistance Front (FNRP) drew on the 1954 struggle for symbolic inspiration, it owed more to the post-1954 model of labor organizing, and to the broad array of regional and identity-based movements that had been quietly building during the previous decades.

Bordered by Nicaragua, El Salvador, Guatemala, and the Atlantic Ocean, Honduras covers an area about the size of Ohio—and houses a rich diversity of peoples. These include the Afro-Caribbean Garifuna residents of the north Atlantic Coast, the indigenous Miskitu, Pech, and Lenca peoples in the eastern, central, and western parts of the country, along with Maya people and mestizos. By the late 1800s the banana export industry dominated the country's economy and, employing mercenaries and U.S. troops, laid a heavy hand on its politics through what became known as the "Banana Wars." The U.S.-based United Fruit Company alone controlled nearly 90 percent of the country's best agricultural lands by 1929.

In 1954, United Fruit Company workers went on strikes throughout the north coast of Honduras, demanding treatment in compliance with new labor laws implemented by former United Fruit lawyer-turned president of the republic, Juan Manuel Gálvez. Industrial workers soon joined them in what became a general strike, and they enjoyed nationwide (and international) support.

In response, United Fruit turned to its allies and investors in the U.S. government to help pacify the workers. Initially they did this by granting concessions. Over the following decades, they collaborated with the AFL-CIO on CIA-funded projects aimed at reining in the communist tendencies of the Honduran labor movement and integrating hierarchical trade unions into capitalist electoral politics. But as Dana Frank has chronicled, not all trade unions followed a conciliatory or U.S.-led path. Some received Soviet and even Chinese funds and training during the Cold War era; others remained more independent, and many, in particular women-led unions, have been leaders in radical organizing.

Because of the relatively low population density in Honduras, land struggles have only come to a head in recent decades, with the combination of population growth and the concentration of lands into a few oligarchic hands.

At midcentury, a tradition of communally held lands and a relatively amicable social contract between cattle ranchers and *milperos*—corn-based subsistence farmers—allowed for 90 percent of the population to survive as milperos.[1] This agricultural pattern held for most of the mestizo campesinos as well as the indigenous Lencas. Other indigenous and Afro-Caribbean groups had diets that were less dependent on corn, but also consisted of foods locally harvested by the communities themselves. The "extraordinary self-sufficiency of the Honduran peasant well into the 1950s" enabled most Hondurans to lead an existence with fewer violent impositions by state and industry than their neighbors, despite an impressive series of coup-installed governments and military dictatorships.[2]

Around 1960, encouraged by World Bank and private loans, Honduran cattle ranchers began carrying out often-violent enclosures of previously communal lands, causing a steep growth in the number of landless peasants and in hunger and malnutrition.

Milperos did not take this lying down. An early communist peasant union affiliated with the banana unions behind the 1954 strike was violently quashed by the Honduran military from 1960 to 1962. Following that, the National Association of Honduran Campesinos (ANACH) was formed with AFL-CIO ties and money. Another group, the National Peasant Union (UNC) formed with the support of the liberation theology-identified Latin American Christian Trade Union (CLASC). Despite their different allegiances, the tens of thousands of members of both groups worked together. Their land occupations forced the National Agrarian Institute (INA) to begin redistribution of land and ultimately resulted in comprehensive agrarian reform legislation.[3]

The success of the Honduran Agrarian Reform helped keep the revolutions in neighboring countries from taking hold in Honduras. Another contributing factor was the campaign of terror carried out by the CIA-trained death squad, Battalion 3–16, in Honduras in the 1980s, when the U.S. was using Honduras as a base of operations for its wars against El Salvador and Nicaragua. Death squad activity and accompanying virulently anticommunist rhetoric had a chilling effect on peasant movements and on land redistribution, which came to a virtual halt during that decade. By 1992, with the help of USAID, the Honduran Congress was able to pass the so-called Agricultural Modernization Law, which enabled the sale of agricultural reform lands to wealthy agribusiness investors.

In addition to peasant movements with their focus on land redistribution, village and urban neighborhood associations have organized over the years to demand basic utilities and resources from local governments (or organize and administer them themselves in the absence of the state), and in some cases to fight harmful development projects like hydroelectric dams, tourist developments, etc.

Militant indigenous and Afro-Caribbean organizations organized over the past three decades fight for the same survival rights, while at the same time fighting against their systematic and racist exclusion from the structures and history of the nation. As historian Darío Euraque has amply demonstrated, the Honduran state has carried out an intentional project of Mayanization over more than half a century, entailing the simultaneous creation of a false Maya history and the narrative erasure and real disenfranchisement of indigenous peoples (Maya and others) in Honduras.[4]

Two of the most prominent, militant indigenous and Afro-Caribbean organizations are the Garifuna organization OFRANEH and the Lenca group COPINH (Civic Council of Popular and Indigenous Organizations of Honduras).

OFRANEH, the Fraternal Black Organization of Honduras, was founded in 1978 and describes itself as having a "matrifocal" vision, reflecting anthropological labeling of Garifuna culture itself. Indeed, its presidents and leadership are predominantly women. Its organization is more horizontal that Honduran unions and student groups, and relies largely on local democratically organized assemblies for decision-making. One of its main struggles has been the fight to defend collectively held Garifuna coastal lands against takeover by international developers and agribusiness.

COPINH was officially founded in 1993. Like OFRANEH, the organization's overall strategy has combined locally focused community-building programs in health, education, and other arenas with direct action tactics taking aim at national and international privatization schemes and harmful outside development projects. COPINH successfully reappropriated a discourse of Lenca militancy that has been used for nefarious purposes by the Honduran state and applied it to movement-building to protect land, environment, and culture through militant anti-neoliberal struggle.[5] While it does not stake a claim to matrifocality, some of COPINH's most powerful leaders and a large percentage of its base are women.

Students also have a consistent history of organizing. Their political parties at the national university receive significant funding from the national parties with which they are allied, and often serve as training grounds for national politics. Left-wing student parties and organizations are primarily Marxist and vanguardist in their orientation, looking more to Russia of 1917 than Latin American models of revolution for their inspiration. As evidenced by some of the violence surrounding student organizing over the years—including the disappearance of numerous student leaders in the 1980s by Battalion 3–16, violent police crackdowns on high school and college student political actions and intermittent physical altercations (sometimes leading to murder) during student election time—elements of the Honduran state share the students' view that they pose a real threat to state power.

A final category of mobilization that must not be ignored is religious organization. Honduras is a very religious country, and churches—Catholic, Evangelical Protestant, Mormon, and others—have organized as much as any other group around issues of poverty and democracy. There is a long tradition of revolutionary liberation theology in Honduras shared by Catholic and Evangelical lay people and leaders, who have fought alongside campesino, student, feminist and LGBTQ, indigenous, community, and other groups. Pockets of liberation theology exist around the country, and have particularly thrived in places like Santa Rosa de Copán where progressive priests and bishops have held posts in the Catholic hierarchy. Many of the salient martyrs and heroes (past and present) of Honduran revolutionary lore have been priests.

Despite a rich history of feminism and LGBTQ activism in Honduras, groups dealing with gender and sexuality issues organized primarily around a nonprofit model in the 2000s, and often found themselves limited by the priorities of their funders. Much feminist work focused on documentation of and service to women victims of domestic violence, "empowerment," sexuality trainings, and other narrowly defined women's issues; LGBTQ organizations found themselves working primarily on antihomophobia and HIV/AIDS prevention educational outreach work.

Thus, prior to the 2009 coup in Honduras, the broad spectrum of progressive and radical organizations sometimes coordinated struggles, but more often worked separately. The coup was such a blow to the people that within hours, thousands of Hondurans who had never before been organized began mobilizing across the country to fight it. Within mere days those thousands—together with participants from the social movements— became hundreds of thousands, and ultimately, in one way or another, millions. In 2010, of approximately 4.6 million eligible voters, 1.3 million signed a petition promoted by the FNRP calling for a constituent assembly to rewrite the constitution.

Social movements unite after the coup

In the months following the coup, the interconnectedness of formerly separate struggles became clear, and the need for solidarity among radical movements became much more pressing. In part this stemmed from the greed of the coup perpetrators, as they usurped not just democracy and civil rights but natural and economic resources. And in part it arose in reaction to the violent repression by state security forces. Rather than suppressing resistance as it had done in the 1980s, the attacks created martyrs that galvanized the resistance movement to mobilize with even greater determination.

The emergent coalition of oppositional organizations and previously unorganized Hondurans called itself the FNRP. And in the months following the coup, while the FNRP's self-proclaimed leaders modeled the group after the more hierarchical organizations they came from, more horizontal forms emerged from the city streets that were the central battleground of the coup and enabled emergent forms of radical action. For the first time that anyone remembered, young urbanites started articulating their democratic aspirations in terms of anarchist ideals, looking internationally to Argentinean and Zapatista models (among others) and within Honduras, to more horizontal and consensus-based forms of organizing, like those present within radical Afro-Caribbean and indigenous groups.

People who—because of their identification with certain oppressed groups—had been excluded from revolutionary leadership in Honduras, now became powerful leaders. Walter Tróchez, a young gay man with years of experience as an HIV and antihomophobia educator, became widely recognized for his writings tying together neoliberalism, the violence of the coup, homophobia, fraudulent elections, and other broad-ranging themes, as well as his fearless advocacy on behalf of the victims of human rights abuses carried out by the regime.

Tróchez was assassinated December 13, 2009, but his martyrdom and the militant advocacy of other members of the LGBTTI community only served to catapult the centrality of homophobia to other forms of oppression to the forefront of the FNRP's agenda.[6] Similarly, Feminists in Resistance forced the movement to evaluate its own patriarchal assumptions, tying together violence against women, femicides, and the coup (which was supported by the most misogynist actors within the Honduran civil and religious hierarchies). Their popular slogans, including *"Ni golpes de estado, ni golpes a las mujeres"* (Neither coups d'état, nor blows against women) helped to bring these links into the realm of common sense for many members of the resistance movement.

Following the fraudulent election of President Porfirio "Pepe" Lobo in 2010, repression against resistance members continued and even increased, with certain sectors particularly targeted: journalists, members of the LGBTTI community and campesinos in the Aguán valley region chief among them. The FNRP has split into two broad camps: the *electoreros*, who favor participating in the 2014 presidential elections, and the *refundacionalistas*, who represent the more horizontally organized groups and argue that the constitution must be rewritten to ensure participatory democracy before the Front engages in electoral work.

As the 2014 presidential elections approach, many pin their hopes on the newly formed LIBRE party, whose candidates hail from the FNRP. But many Hondurans, inspired by the power of the resistance movement to challenge the legitimacy of the coup government (it took two years for Lobo's administration to be internationally recognized, despite mighty efforts on the part of the U.S. State Department), are also organizing in their communities with a more acute sense of the interconnectedness of their struggles against state-sponsored killings, institutionalized homophobia and sexism, neoliberal capitalism, and other forms of structural and political violence, and for land, water, food, health care, and other forms of justice, as part of refounding the nation so that Hondurans' future will be one with dignity and without fear.

Nery Rodríguez, middle-school teacher
"Zelaya promoted the people's interests more than any other president"

Interview by Clifton Ross, July 2009
Translation by Margi Clarke

Nery Augusto Rodríguez teaches social sciences at the Pedro Nufío Middle School. Nery and I met in a demonstration outside of the University of Honduras, Tegucigalpa, about a month after the coup. He invited me along to the border with Nicaragua where we—and hundreds of others—hoped to meet President Mel Zelaya and accompany him back to Tegucigalpa. But the president wasn't able to enter the country, and we were trapped on the border: We weren't allowed to return to Tegucigalpa or to go forward to Nicaragua.

Nery and I left with a small group and walked through the jungle and over the mountains that separated Honduras from Nicaragua. The twelve-hour trek was especially hard on Nery, because he had run out of heart medication and the walk was difficult and exhausting. I said goodbye to him in a refugee camp for Hondurans in Ocota, Nicaragua where he stayed for a few days before returning to Honduras—without the president.

The interview was taken in the midst of turmoil, but Nery nevertheless managed to take some time to offer some political background—and his eyewitness account of the assault at Tegucigalpa's Toncontín airport on July 5,

Nery Rodríguez. Photo by Clifton Ross.

when President Zelaya tried to fly back into the country, but his plane wasn't allowed to land. Soldiers and riot police attacked the peaceful throng that had gathered to welcome him home, leaving four people dead and many more injured.

As an educator, I belong to COPEMH [*Colegio de Profesores de Educación Media de Honduras*, Secondary School Teachers Association of Honduras]. Of course many teachers are aware of what is happening, and we decided to resist [right-wing oppression] with peaceful resistance, without any violence. But there are many people among those who are active who have financial problems. They're very upset, very hurt.

Many are also activists with the Liberal Party, including teachers who are are members of the Liberal Party, which was formed by the people, the masses. In response, the rich, the powerful, formed the National Party. They didn't want anything to change, because they had seized power and gained control of the country's wealth and resources. They were all wealthy people of the country, "the haves," we could say. And the truth is that when the National Party wins, it always benefits people with power.

But when the Liberal Party wins, it benefits the majority, because it's born from the people. The major reforms, the great social achievements of the country, have been created by the Liberal Party. Social Security, and many others social benefits like the right to unionize were also achievements of the Liberal Party.

President Zelaya played a huge leadership role, and still does. His leadership is so influential he has been able to unify the labor unions. The teachers have also joined to support the movement, as well as the indigenous and peasant organizations, all of whom are supporting Zelaya precisely because he's promoted the people's interests more than any other president.

He has had some ties to Hugo Chávez, with Evo Morales, president of Bolivia, and Rafael Correa of Ecuador. Together they are creating the bloc in South America which is called ALBA, the Bolivarian Alternative. This effort was created specifically to help the poor, needy people, and because Honduras is, like all Latin America countries, suffering extreme poverty. The whole country, our whole people are a forgotten people: nobody knows if you eat, nobody knows if you get an education, no one knows if you have a house, if you have clothes, nobody cares.

Politicians never remembered our people who live in extreme poverty. I wouldn't even call it extreme poverty, I would say extreme misery. Of the whole country, of the seven million people that we have, at least six million live in extreme poverty, another million are poor but not in extreme poverty,

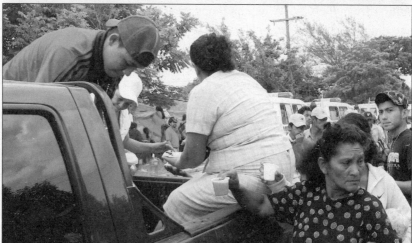

Supporters of ousted president Manuel "Mel" Zelaya trapped near the Nicaraguan border as they attempt to accompany their president back to Tegucigalpa, July 2009. Photos by Clifton Ross.

and a very small group enjoys all privileges and owns the major businesses. You see here are several chain stores. There is this one, there is another just over there, and they are across the country and always the same families are owners of these companies and are the only beneficiaries.

Zelaya wanted the people to get some of that profit that goes mostly to the wealthy, the rich. That was why Zelaya was called a communist who they had to get rid of at all costs. When Zelaya wanted to hold a plebescite, that became a big reason to get him out of the country, to oust him from power.

Yes, yes, I am liberal and I support him, and most of the people support him. There are eighteen departments or provinces nationwide. You go to any department and you'll see many people who support the president. All those who are coming out in the demonstrations in the streets, they're all supporting the president right now.

Assault at the airport

They say everything is normal here. The U.S. ambassador is watching all this, is seeing how human rights have been violated, is seeing the army suppress a demonstration with automatic rifles [at Toncontín airport]. Even the Honduran counsel responsible for human rights claimed they weren't real bullets, but were rubber bullets. Seeing the dead who fell there, he said only rubber bullets were used!

There was not only one, there were four who died. And many were injured, many injured. When the shooting began, the cameramen left until the shooting ended. They hid because they were just protecting themselves from bullets. Many people fell, badly wounded, and people got them up, took them to the cars to take them immediately to the hospital because some were already dying. Some died on the road, some died in the hospital. The only one left was just the boy, Isis Obed, he was there and he was the only one that the cameramen could take pictures of, because they went back in after the shooting ended.

But many people left precisely because they couldn't leave the people who were dying there, they had take them away immediately but they died on the way, on the way to hospital and a few others died in hospital. There were many were injured, at least eighteen people were injured. Later the prosecutors who went to the scene of the attack, they were able to confirm the caliber of the bullets that were fired.

Indeed, I was there, about fifteen feet from where there were some shots fired. I was lying on the grass and when the shooting started, I was about five meters where some bullets hit, but I ran in the other direction. I had to throw myself on the ground about three times, and I dropped when I felt the tear gas, I couldn't breathe. Then I ran and went to hide behind a statue that's south of the airport. I had to hide there and when it was all over the investigators came, and they were able to study and collect the shell casings; they collected about two hundred casings that were fired.

When I was there in the melee and saw people running. I saw that it was machine guns they were firing. Because rubber bullets are shot one by one, and machine guns sound very different. I listened very closely, that's why I was afraid and ran away to protect myself. I expected at any moment to be shot. At that time many people fell to the ground, many of us took the wounded, and only the boy was left there. He was alone.

Nurses in Resistance
"We collaborated on the human part, from the commitment we have to our vocation"

Interview and translation by Adrienne Pine, July 2010

After the coup that ousted President Zelaya, people who had previously identified with groups without explicit anti-neoliberal or radical agendas suddenly found themselves in an environment where neutrality was not imaginable. This was the case for professional nurses, licenciadas. *Unlike auxiliary nurses, they had not previously as a group drawn explicit links between policies of privatization, lack of democratic participation in governance, and their ability to care for their patients. When patients started pouring in by the dozens, bloodied and beaten by the neoliberal coup state, they immediately began to organize as Nurses in Resistance, a move they themselves framed as being necessary to be able to do their job as healers. At the time of the interview, Licenciada Leda Sánchez was president of the* Colegio de Profesionales de Enfermería de Honduras; *Licenciadas Marina Pagoada, Juana Buchanan, and Eda Hernández were members of the association's board.*

Licenciada Leda Sánchez: When we joined the Resistance, we did not even understand what was happening. It was something so huge, a coup d'état, and at that moment we reacted first and foremost to a situation that was not right: removing a Honduran, unarmed and with his hands up, and we didn't know what they were going to do with him. He was our president [Manuel "Mel" Zelaya] and at that moment, regardless of whether he had acted well or poorly, he was being judged by a group of the country's most powerful people.

Things got more intense every day, with people going out on the streets. We would go out and we wouldn't know what was going to happen. We would coordinate, the whole pueblo and the human rights and humanitarian organizations. We organized and it was so beautiful how by e-mail, through text messages, through phone calls, we would communicate. It was a network. I had ten people as contacts, those ten people would send the message to others, and that was how in a matter of seconds, minutes, we would all arrive in one place.

And as nurses we saw the need to be united. We had to look at things, to plan, we had someone in each strategic location, for example Licenciada

Marina Pagoada was in the Hospital Escuela in the Emergency Room and thank God she was there, because all the people who had been injured and attacked, or who had suffered whatever else arrived there, and she was our contact. She also had her people inside the hospital, registered nurses (RNs) as well as licensed vocational nurses (LVNs) and doctors who formed our network to protect people who came at that time.

I joined the medical brigades [going to El Paraíso, on the border of Honduras and Nicaragua, where people were hoping Zelaya would reenter the country] with Licenciada Marina Pagoada. The two of us nurses were the only brigade that arrived where all the people were gathered together at a military checkpoint and they weren't allowed to leave. We hired a Green Cross [Cruz Verde] ambulance and that was the only way we could get through.

Traveling to the border was quite an experience because at each roadblock they would stop us, and since our assistance was humanitarian, we would treat the soldiers who have digestive problems, or ophthalmological problems like conjunctivitis, all from being exposed to such long hours and being outside in the weather. Our labor in that squad was strategic. At no point were we worrying about the soldiers, but seeing the situation that they were also going through, we attended to them.

Let me tell you, the solidarity of the pueblo was so beautiful, they brought the medicines and food and that helped us have abundant food and medicine to distribute to people. We also brought soap, water, and personal hygiene items. This was one of the many things we did, but it is one that has given us great personal satisfaction, as nurses and as people.

Lic. Marina Pagoada: To add to what Leda has said, we were also subjected to a lot of fear. The same police and soldiers who were at the roadblocks searched us thoroughly. They took pictures of us and took down our RN license numbers. And they said, "What are you doing here? Let them die, don't worry about them." So we collaborated on the human part, the commitment we have to our vocation, which is a vocation committed to the dispossessed, to the neediest people. At that moment there were people who were beaten, imprisoned, and we coordinated with CPTRT, with Dr. Juan Almendares.

At that point we weren't on the executive board of the Nurses Association [Colegio de Profesionales de Enfermería de Honduras] that we were members of. Our association turned its back on us, and said we couldn't use our blue and white uniform. In the assembly they barred us from using the name of the Association and the uniform too.

On July 5 we had a planning meeting in Hospital Escuela with our colleagues and with the auxiliary nurses, because we had a feeling that something would happen during that march, because it was when Mel Zelaya was coming.

Around one in the afternoon when Isis Obed had already been shot [Isis was the first recognized martyr of the Resistance, killed in a nonviolent mass mobilization of Hondurans hoping to receive President Zelaya as he flew overhead at the Tegucigalpa airport], I received him along with another colleague in the adult emergency room, but he was dead on arrival. We had feared that something bad would happen and it did, but after that we took in ten more patients who had been beaten up at the same time and that was when we began to coordinate between our colleagues who were out on the streets and those of us who were in the hospital.

You get so much satisfaction from serving your pueblo, because we are part of this pueblo. And even though the police would come [to the hospital], I would keep doing my [resistance] work in secret. And I remember I would call Leda [and say] "Leda, I don't know how I can leave the hospital," because I felt afraid because the police were there.

But since nursing is a vocation in which we must not be afraid, I stopped being afraid. Just this morning there was a man hurting a woman [right outside]. We all went out to defend the woman, to call the police and call the human rights groups. That brute was throwing bottles at her feet and we were there close by and she was terrified and we told her, "Don't be afraid, we are here." [Our experience] has strengthened us a lot—we are not afraid at all, we can stand up to anyone.

Resistance brings change to Nurses' Association

Lic. Sánchez: In Honduras every two years we have elections, because the executive board [of the Nurses' Association] changes every two years. This year there had to be a change of the executive board in May, and it was when we started marching in the streets—because that was where our leadership began, in the streets—and we began to say among ourselves, "Let's do this."

From there we began to put together Slate #2—that is what it was called—and our slogan was "unity and change," because our objective was to unite nurses and also to create a change. Believe me that it wasn't easy, because the people who were in power were *golpista* and they denigrated us in every way possible. There are three or four black compañeras [on our slate/board] and they said that we were the "Black spot" slate. They were very rude. There were a lot of us who were LVNs first and later managed to get our *licenciatura* degree. And so they also said we were the LVN slate.

We had a number of strategies in putting together our slate. The majority of us are with the Resistance but what we did was seek equilibrium because we knew we'd be at a disadvantage if we did not include these compañeras, who ended up being more Resistance than us, militant like you can't imagine!

Lic. Juana Buchanan: We also included another person from Olancho on the slate, because in the previous slates there had only been people from here, from Tegucigalpa. So another strategy was to involve other people from other departments and areas within the association to ensure greater participation of association members.

The other thing that I think played an important role was the professional development of many members in building nursing resources, at the university level as well as through the Ministry of Health, with LVNs. Many people know us and that's important. There are people who believe in us, and not just because we were in a campaign, but because they already know who we are. And they told us that they had a lot of faith that we could make big changes in the association, for example in the area of training, opportunities for continuing education, grants, etc.

Lic. Sánchez: And another thing is previously the slates for the executive boards of the Nurses Association had been from hospitals, whereas in this slate we also included community health workers, which I am very happy to be representing.

The elections were on May 28. The other slate was *golpista*—I'll call them that because I can't think of another word to describe them.

It was the election with the highest voter turnout in the history of nursing. There are approximately 2,000 of us nationwide and approximately 1,000 voted in all. In other elections the most who ever came out to vote was 200, 150, at most.

[We won by] 75 percent, and that's after they annulled a lot of votes. They annulled forty-seven of ours, in total around sixty votes were annulled.

Lic. Eda Hernández: I also think that the pueblo has woken up, from the poorest person to the most . . . Starting on June 28, 2009 [the day of the coup], the people woke up. You won't find the same nation. We are prepared for anything to happen.

Lic. Pagoada: I believe that we here will achieve many things, because we came out of a struggle to support a democratic process.

Lic. Buchanan: In our country we have lost that right that we used to think we had, protection from the authorities, from the police. We thought that, according to the constitution, those people were there to protect us. But when you see in this movement that they are beating innocent people, it fills you with anger, you feel impotent. How can it be that someone who is armed to the teeth is going out there to beat up children, women, pregnant women, elderly people, and everyone else?

Lic. Pagoada: In the marches there were real community people ["people from the *pueblo pueblo*"] who took care of us. We are already well recognized and we even have an organized committee. We belong to an ALBA [Bolivarian Alternative for the Americas] project. Personally, I have always felt that we very much need to be in alliance with people in other countries who have their [nurses'] unions and that for us as nurses it is something we really need.

Lic. Buchanan: I believe it is important to apply those principles. This must not get lost—principles of solidarity, unity, empathy that we should maintain as part of who we are. Support, respect, all of these are things that have characterized the Resistance and there are many of us in the country.

And something that empowers us is knowing that we have been leaders. In a matter of seconds we drew together a brigade and it was the nurses who led it. The doctors said, "Leave that to the nurses because they are the leaders here." They recognized our place, "Let them do it, they know how to run things." In a matter of seconds we had a big room with a whole bunch of beds and we already had a unit set up. And it's improvised, because we already have the knowledge, but it's the ability to organize, and we are recognized for that, they recognize us as leaders in that regard.

Sara Hernández, Unified Campesino Movement of Aguán (Movimiento Unificado Campesino del Aguán, MUCA)
"They say we are guerrilleros, we have heavy weapons— but we are barely able to feed our children"

Interview and translation by Adrienne Pine, April 2012

The 1992 law that allowed agricultural reform lands to be sold to agribusiness investors forced thousands of newly landless families to migrate to the cities or out of the country. Others, in regions like the fertile Bajo Aguán on the country's Atlantic coast, had to battle predatory landholders—with private standing armies at their disposal—to keep their agrarian reform lands. The fight for land rights escalated after the coup that ousted President Zelaya. Since the fraud-tainted election of his successor, Pepe Lobo, around sixty campesinos have been killed.

We as women suffer in various ways, since the coup d'état in particular. Before the coup, with the government voucher, I paid only 80 [lempiras] that Mel gave us, for electricity. I didn't have any extra, just enough to pay the electricity. And since then, to my sorrow, instead of paying the 80 I was paying, my bill went up to 3,000 lempiras. And so I called the engineer and told him what was going on. And he told me to go to the office. So I went to the office and it was closed. I went to ENEE complain about my bill, and they said, "No, you can't make a complaint. Go pay."

These are obvious attacks. Robbery. They're all out there in broad daylight shamelessly robbing from you. Since the coup I have had no peace, so many bills, so many charges. And I said to my compañeras, "Women, let's organize ourselves, because we have to get ahead." In this struggle, like Christ, we will continue with this cross on our shoulders, because there's no other choice. Life is hard. So we organized. There are ninety of us women who are organized.

There are ninety of us from this village, and some from Tesorito, Silín, and Las Crucitas. It was just Marañones and the indigenous women who didn't want to join us. They're organized, but on their own, not with us. So we have meetings with women and with men. And this struggle is to the finish because we don't want to continue suffering from this coup d'état. The more time goes by, the more we are in crisis, and we women are the ones who suffer most.

We aren't able to find any food to put on the table for our children. If things go on like this, our children will not be able to study. There's no end in sight. As I was just saying now, when you got off the bus, life is sad. Look how high bus fare is today—everything is up in the clouds. And we will not be silent, no. Jesus said that if men don't speak, stones would speak. We won't wait for the stones to speak, we will shout out too, us too. We're all in this struggle and in the end now they're not just murdering men; they're also murdering children, women, and anyone who is in their way.

The effects of the coup

The coup is at the root of all the cost increases, because they have to get back the money they stole [*los tarantines*], the big shots, because they looted INPREMA [the national pension fund for teachers], they looted the Banco del Trabajador, so the worker was even worse off. Why? Because they stole all the money. They didn't tell the people.

The seven months that Micheletti [Roberto Micheletti, who stepped as interim president immediately following the coup] was in power were to sweep everything away that was left, so all of our crises come from there. We don't have any solution with regards to the economy because they want to take everything. And we won't stop fighting until the end.

They were the beneficiaries of everything, and the people just watched it happen. They are businessmen who have everything under their control. To this day, they are trying to privatize water, electricity, and public schools, and these are the only three things the people had left. They privatize those three things, and as poor people, we are screwed.

We won't be able to get water. We won't be able to put our children in school because it will be only for those who can pay. We won't have electricity because that will be privatized. If the rich man wants to give it to us he will; if not, he won't. If you don't pay, that's it.

We were in Guatemala, with a group of compañeras and compañeros from Polochic in Guatemala. We were in the hotel for two days sharing our experiences. We told them how things are for us here in Honduras and they told us how they live in their country too. It's the same situation that we have here. Our compañeros' houses have been burned, the same thing, their houses have been burned down there. All their crops have been destroyed. Those people have lost work, their humble homes, their compañeros have been killed. We watched videos that they showed us. Our struggle is also their struggle. The only part that is different is that they are in that country and we are in this one.

Operation Lightning and the paramilitaries

Last time a group entered a farm, it was a Sunday, I don't remember the date but it was a Sunday, and we went to Tocoa. The hitmen had staked out Corocito, they had an operation in place, here in Honduras Aguán, and in Quebrada [de Arena]. All of the paid private guards, they are all dressed as soldiers and with convoys in the street carrying out operations. So in other words they are the ones in charge here, not the humble people who live here.

Facussé [a powerful wealthy landholder in the region] has all the soldiers paid off, and whenever he feels like grabbing a campesino, they rig the trap; they put up roadblocks and you better be prepared [*póngase chiva*] because if they get you, they capture you, and who knows where you'll end up.[7]

They pay by the body. The same people who work there talk about it. And you know there are always people who will start talking without realizing that one is a campesino, and that's how they end up telling us about it.

The people [who work as hitmen are] from here, from a nearby town. They are poor people who go in search of work. In Trujillo I had just dropped off a patient and I was sitting outside talking with a man and another man came by, and he was one of Facussé's hitmen. He let out the story. He said, "This campesino so-and-so, these campesinos are lots of guaranteed money for us." Out of caution I didn't ask his name, so as to not let on that I was the investigating kind. So the story came out there and that's how one finds out about everything.

They don't think we are people who have our ears open, as they say. If you go by bus, they'll be right there talking about it and you have to remain mute and be careful. That's how you find out, it's always from their own mouths.

When they had us surrounded here, when they had us surrounded in the community, they attacked a youth who was taking pictures with a camera. The soldiers told him, "Hey you, drop the camera. If you don't, we'll come and take it from you along with your head." "Come and take it from me," said the youth. And I said to them, "Look, be very careful, because even if it's with sticks and stones, we will defend the young man."

And a month later, they trapped him, Juan Chinchilla. Perhaps they have told you the story of how it happened? We imagined it could happen, because they knew him well and took photographs of him. Look, it was a big action that we undertook in Trujillo, I assure you. We were prepared for them to kill us, to take us however they wanted.

When they called and told me they had taken the young man, that he was being tortured, I tell them, "Compañeros, it was the guards of Facussé who took him. It couldn't have been anyone else. It was the guards of Facussé and he's in El Tumbador."

And look, just as I had thought, and as we analyzed it, so it was. I told him, "Thank God, thank God who freed you from the hands of the assassins." They already had him in the place where they were going to kill him. But we rescued the boy. With God's help and Juan's intelligence, he came out okay.

I look at him again and again and it seems like a miracle of God, because as I say to him, they threatened him here and already had his photograph. So that's why I say, when something like that happens and I am safe, I think, "What if I had gone with Chavelo, I'd be in jail too, if I had gone with Chavelo." Can you imagine?

It's a crime to say you are a campesino here, because they don't believe you are a campesino but rather another guerrillero. I heard them say on Radio América, "Those leftists!" We're not leftists, we are defenders of everyone's rights. We're not leftists, we're not guerrilleros. If they call us guerrilleros it's because we defend our rights and those of everyone else.

The Hospital Salvador Paredes discriminates against us when we say we are from Guadalupe. I, as a midwife with certification, get angry and I frequently say to the nurse, "They don't like us here," and the nurse says, "Yes, it's true, I hear things. I tell you, I feel bad because when one brings patients there, they don't take good care of them and what I'd like is for them to be looked after well, because when one takes care of a patient one should do so out of love. One should approach them with sensitivity to help that person heal. No one should come out asking you whether you are from here or there."

So, as a midwife, I work at the clinic, and if I have to transport someone who is sick I don't take her to the hospital here. I go to Tocoa. Because in Tocoa, at the Hospital San Isidro, no matter where you are from, they will take care of you. They look after you well. It's a serious problem for those of us who live here.

And today when they say "They're guerrilleros, they're heavily armed," and that they're going to take away all the weapons—how long have they been going on like that? Since we arrived here. That we are guerrilleros, that we have weapons, that we have this and that. And meanwhile, we are barely able to feed our children. And that is the sad part of the story. How are we going to be able to afford an AR15, to buy an AK, to buy a heavy weapon?

And what do they gain by accusing us? If it's not one thing it's another. It's slander that we have had to live with from the start. When we were out in the streets for fifteen days, the Trujillo Chamber of Commerce told us they would come kick us out one way or another, but they didn't try it because there were always people who said, "They are campesinos who are demanding their rights." So there are always people who are on our side. So we don't complain about God's protection because God is always with us. God is with us at all times, so for me there is nothing more marvelous than the Lord. And I will say He has protected us to this day from the horrible criminality that is out there.

Ricardo, gay activist, FNRP member, now in exile
"The coup regime had not anticipated that the people would become united"

Interview and translation by members of Solidarity with Honduras, Manchester, UK: Dominic McCann, Juliette, Steve Sinacola, and Jo Haydock, March 2010[8]

Ricardo helped start the LGBT movement in Honduras in the mid-1980s. After the coup that ousted President Zelaya in 2009, LGBT activists found themselves working with people across the political spectrum, united by the desire to see the president—and constitutional order—return to the country. The post-coup repression fell particularly hard on their community, which lost nineteen people to assassination in 2009. At the time of this interview, Ricardo was being followed and receiving death threats. He ultimately fled the country.

Right now I am effectively without a home because of the events that happened last year with the coup d'état, when the gay movement joined the resistance. Persecution affected all members of the resistance and all those who were opposed to the coup. The LGBT movement experienced far greater repression and many individual cases of persecution. The gay community and gay movement in Honduras experienced nineteen deaths as a result of the coup d'état. Between June to December a total of nineteen homosexuals were assassinated, homosexuals, lesbians, and trans. The repression was such that our group practically disintegrated.

Of those nineteen, two were members of our organization. They assassinated the secretary and a leading member of the community. The first assassination took place almost immediately on the second day of the coup. The secretary of our organization, Walter Tróchez, who was openly part of the resistance, was assassinated on December 13. Because the repression was very severe, the group has practically disintegrated and the leaders such as myself are practically in exile in our own country. For example I am here as refugee because in my city in Tegucigalpa I am followed everywhere I go, and they come looking for to me. I am effectively homeless.

AIDS and the cold war

It has been a very hard struggle, because the culture here has been very chauvinistic. We experienced homophobia from the state, under its discriminatory laws, also; the LGBT community always has been a discriminated [against] community.

The gay movement appeared immediately after the appearance of HIV in Honduras; that was in 1985, when the first case of HIV occurred in Honduras. You have to remember that they were talking in terms of the gay plague, that it was gay cancer, that this was God's punishment for being homosexual; and because of this, repression against the gay community started at that time.

The 1980s were the years of the disappeared, the cold war in Honduras. Here we experienced a war that was not even ours. It was an internal war in neighboring Nicaragua and El Salvador. I began taking part in the social movements at that time; not in the gay movement, because that didn't exist in the '80s. I started out in revolutionary student groups. I experienced the repression of the '80s as well; I was one of the few survivors of that repression. In the '80s they tried to bury to me alive. When they quote unquote arrested us under the pretext of being communist, that was the term used by the Armed Forces at that time to repress the people who were opposing them. Soon after that, HIV appeared and a new wave of persecution against the gay community began. It was a witchhunt against the gay community.

Resistance and repression

Honduras can be divided into two periods: before and after the coup d'état. Before the coup d'état, yes, there were very strong popular organizations here in this country, but everyone fought their own separate battles; there was no unity of all the sectors. For example the teachers fought for education, the campesinos fought their battle on problems of land rights and the water, the agrarian reform, the workers each in their own area, the gay community as always working on HIV.

I believe that the coup regime had not anticipated that the people at certain moment of the coup would become united with all the sectors around a single issue. That was firstly the restitution of President Zelaya, but soon we began to see that it is not simply the presidency but the constitutional order in the country that was at stake. The government imposed the coup with curfews and with repression.

For us it was no longer enough to speak only about HIV, we are a strong community, we have a history of campaigning going back more than twenty years. Hence, we demanded to be included and participate in the resistance against the coup. So that is how we became united with the resistance.

But there was a period during the many curfews, curfews that lasted up to forty-eight [hours] when we were working in citizen participation and politics without stopping our work on HIV/AIDS because we have many friends infected by this disease. Hence through the curfews the population was a victim of the military coup, a silent victim.

The curfews and state of siege were intended to prevent the population from mobilizing. For example, Tegucigalpa is a city with two teaching hospitals, which not only treat people locally, but also treat people from other parts of the country. So during the curfews people who were receiving retroviral treatment were unable to travel to Tegucigalpa and receive medication. These are drugs that are required on a daily basis to keep people alive, but this didn't matter to [interim President Roberto] Micheletti and he imposed the curfews.

The people couldn't get out; I received phone calls from friends saying "Ricardo I haven't got any medicine for tomorrow, I can't get to Tegucigalpa; what am I going to do?" I spoke to people close to me and said, "Have you got surplus medication? There is a comrade who needs medication for tomorrow!" Across mountains we delivered medicine to people who needed it. These are people that I know, friends who have access to a cell phone. But there are people in villages and communities who weren't able to mobilize. I know of a friend from the Paraíso area, which was an area where repression and the curfews were most intense. This is the area where President Zelaya was trying to enter the country via Nicaragua. So there was an incredible curfew situation. The result was that in December he died through lack of medication. That is when I said to myself that I couldn't keep quiet any longer and began to participate in resistance marches rather than just working behind the scenes and keeping a low profile.

Friends such as Walter Tróchez were so committed, and he said, "I just can't keep quiet!" He was one of the people who was always visible in demos and marches. Ever since they initiated the marches in Tegucigalpa, he participated. Walter underwent three attacks. Almost from the beginning, as early as August or September, he began to undergo persecution. First they played a game of cat and mouse. Capturing him, releasing him, and as soon as he was released they would stop him again. In the second abduction, because they were not really arrests but more like abductions, in the second abduction they broke his nose.

Walter was planning to flee the country. It was just one week before he was due to leave. He was arrested on December 13, and I was with him at the last meeting he attended on the eleventh.

They kidnapped Walter, they tortured him first in a cell and simply took him to a public street in order to kill him.

The forensic [coroners] report from the state merely said "death through gunshot wound." When the body of Walter was given to us and we were preparing him [for funeral] with a journalist who is also a Spanish doctor, we discovered that Walter had three broken ribs and had no tongue.

This is a technique heavily used in Honduras as a punishment and as a message, "You're going to keep quiet and we will silence the movement." He wasn't the first person to have their tongue cut out.

On January 3, [2010] I experienced the first death threat.

[Afterward] a foreign journalist who is working with Tele-Sur arrived and I did an interview with him. That was the tenth of February, and on the eleventh I experienced the second assassination threat: The coup supporters were monitoring the opposition media outlets and television stations.

I went to COFADEH to give my testimony concerning these threats, my second testimony. Soon after that they assassinated a compañero from San Pedro Sula. The assassinations were happening all over the country, but we continued with our work despite this.

Three friends of mine took on the responsibility of . . . in the morning they came to fetch me at home. They came with me to work. I never walked alone. In the afternoon they would call me on my cell phone and say, "What time are you leaving work? We'll come and meet you." They really looked after me.

But on the fifteenth of February I was at home getting ready to have a bath. I got a call at 6:00 a.m. and one of these friends said to me, "Ricardo where are you?"

"At home. I'm coming down now," I reply. So they say, "Don't go out . . . no, because the grey van is . . ." In Tegucigalpa it is well known that the Police (CID) uses a grey van with blacked out windows and no number plates to carry out abductions. He said to me, "The van is in front of your house! Don't go out, hide! I'll keep you informed." But I said to myself, "If they are in front of my house, it's better to be killed in the street than at home, because at home there are children, there's my mum."

Then they call back and say, "Don't go out. Two men have got out of the truck and are coming toward to the house." There is a neighbor who has door that opens onto the street behind ours and my friend said I should get out that way.

But if they come to my house they are going to attack my family.

Then two more friends arrived and they began to play football in the street, kids joined in and the street filled up with people. In other words, now there were plenty of witnesses.

Because of all the friends or people in the street they backed off.

I went to work anyway and later I gave my testimony to COFADEH (Comité de Familiares de Detenidos Desaparecidos en Honduras/Committee of Families of Disappeared Detainees in Honduras). They said that I couldn't stay in Tegucigalpa. So since February 15 I have been on the run and I am in the process of trying to flee the country.

My friends who looked after me have told me that the same van came for them and that they were arrested. They were questioned about my location.

And COFADEH has been moving me around for security reasons. This is really unsettling because I am unable to stay in one place for any length of time.

El Salvador

United Nations Map No. 3903 Rev. 3, May 2004

INTRODUCTION
A people's victory at the polls amid growing U.S. militarism

By J. Heyward

El Salvador's historic presidential elections in 2009 signaled a new era of popular struggle in the country. Despite a multi-million-dollar corporate fear campaign that promised the people would suffer if they voted for the Left, the FMLN (Farabundo Martí National Liberation Front)—former guerrilla army turned political party in 1992—won the presidency for the first time. The ARENA (Nationalist Republican Alliance) party, founded by right-wing death squad architect Roberto D'Aubuisson, had held the presidency without interruption for the previous twenty years. The FMLN now governs over 50 percent of the population at the local level and has become the largest single force, or party, in the Legislative Assembly.

Throughout the sixteen-month-long electoral campaign, the Salvadoran social movement—teachers, students, public-sector unions, nurses, and human rights organizations—electrified the nation in door-to-door campaigns and public forums. Whole communities mobilized to defeat ARENA's attempts to bus more than forty thousand Nicaraguans, Guatemalans, and Hondurans into El Salvador to cast ballots against the FMLN. Twenty-four-hour public radio broadcasts by Radio Cadena Mi Gente and the FMLN Headquarters for Denunciations and Voter Irregularities circulated eyewitness reports of these attempts at fraud from rural border towns to the urban cores and back.

The historic victory could be considered El Salvador's first institutional break from 485 years of colonial rule. It took Spanish conquistadores three attempts to overwhelm indigenous resistance to their invasion of Cuzcatlán in 1524 and another fifteen years to dominate the social order of the Lenca (Pokomam Maya) and Pipil (Nahua Aztec) people. Prior to the mid-1970s armed revolt by campesinos, students, teachers, and shantytown dwellers that led to the country's twelve-year civil war, many uprisings broke out but were swiftly, brutally upended by regional armies and a revolving cast of military and civilian dictators trained and financed by Europe and the United States. El Salvador's long history of indigenous resistance and workers' revolts on coffee and indigo plantations are boldly reflected in land defense, environmental justice, labor, health care, and education struggles throughout the country today.

This said, enormous challenges remain. Much of El Salvador's economic, cultural and political life revolves around a cash economy, bankrupted by twenty years of right-wing corruption and neoliberal doctrine. The vast majority of land and infrastructure is owned by five families and many public services such as energy, public transport, and telecommunications are owned by private corporations. Today over 2.5 million people, or one-third of the Salvadoran population, live and work in the United States and remittances are the largest single source—nearly 20 percent—of the nation's GDP. With a tiny annual budget of $11 billion, a dollarized economy, and exorbitant international loan interest rates, it will be impossible for the Salvadoran government to guarantee basic services to the population while paying its full $39 million debt to the IMF/World Bank under the current economic model.

Perhaps most alarming is the U.S. State Department's growing security oversight in the country and throughout Central America in order to expand its political influence and control over land and resources in the region. The United States has established an FBI office and a regional police training academy called the ILEA (International Law Enforcement Academy) in San Salvador, ostensibly to professionalize the police and fight the war on drugs. In March 2011, President Obama announced an additional $200 million agreement called CARSI (Central American Regional Security Initiative), through which the United States will fund various components of a regional security plan. Similar military-policing partnerships in Colombia and Mexico have resulted in massive displacement, political assassinations, and forced disappearances.

FMLN gambles with reformism

For the first time in 2009, the FMLN decided to run a candidate from outside its ranks, popular journalist Mauricio Funes. The party felt that in order to win, they had to run a moderate candidate to avoid negative historical associations the Right had impressed upon mainstream voters in the failed 2004 presidential bid of former FMLN combatant Shafik Handal. Indeed, Funes's candidacy drew the interest of a solvent base of middle-class business owners, professionals, and undecided voters who had previously withheld their support from the FMLN.

Actions by the new Salvadoran government in its first three and a half years reveal the competing aspirations of the FMLN party and the Funes administration. On one hand, Funes gave space to appointees in Education, Labor, Health, and Agricultural Ministries to recover previously stolen and misallocated money and direct it toward new food and health initiatives in poor, rural communities; however, on transnational economic and security fronts, he proved compliant with the neoliberal model.

In defiance of FMLN doctrine, Funes has continued the neoliberal program to the letter by subsidizing big business with taxpayer money and accepting millions of dollars in new IMF/World Bank loans, and Millennium Challenge Corporation (MCC) funds for neocolonial efforts initiated by the United States and the right-wing Salvadoran oligarchy. MCC funds are dedicated to Plan Mesoamerica, a massive infrastructure project that spans the Central American Isthmus, from Panama to Puebla, Mexico, intended to augment a constellation of private hydroelectric dams, ports, gold mines, and tourist zone developments as part of North America and Europe's industrial design grid for expedited resource and labor extraction from the region.

Funes's positions on U.S. foreign policy in Central America also stand in stark contrast to the FMLN's. When it became clear that the U.S. State Department played a key role in engineering a coup d'état in Honduras in June 2009, Funes stayed silent, even as FMLN base committees mobilized solidarity efforts to the capital of Tegucigalpa to fortify popular resistance. In January 2010, Funes recognized the fraudulent election of Pepe Lobo and resumed normalized relations with Honduras, to the dismay of the Latin American Left.

It is not clear whether the radical leadership of the FMLN can counter Funes legislatively on macroeconomic and security fronts; nor is it clear which forces are motivating Funes beyond his financial connections and the very rational fear of another U.S.-engineered coup. In order to drive a national agenda, the FMLN needs a two-thirds legislative majority, or another twenty-one seats in Congress, a gain which seems unlikely in the near future. Though the four major right-wing parties are fractured beyond immediate repair, they still hold a collective majority in Congress.

The FMLN and the Salvadoran social movement have a problem on their hands, apart from Funes, and they know this problem well: A transnational capitalist regime headed by U.S. World Bank/IMF appointees is setting the near-absolute terms under which a centralized state can function, no matter who the government is.

The traditional base of the FMLN party (about 810,000 people) and most of its political leaders are much more radical than Funes. For example, over forty FMLN mayors are signed onto agreements with the Venezuela-led ALBA (Bolivarian Alternative for the Americas) and are engaged in various forms of interregional, cooperative trade with other Central and South American countries. Many FMLN mayors have encouraged the formation of community *consultas* (consultation bodies or committees) to develop social, environmental, and political curricula to lend to an informed, participatory process in budgeting and other forms of localized decision-making. Thus, leftist alternatives are already underway; the question is whether these can be extended to the entire country while current neoliberal policies, U.S. security oversight, and an entrenched Salvadoran right in economic, social, and government affairs are still dominant forces for exclusion and repression.

U.S. exporting police repression tactics

In order to understand the current *coyuntura* (political moment) in El Salvador, it is important to identify forces that were set in motion between the country's March 2006 midterm election—when what many call the "Leftist Tide" was beginning to turn in Latin America—and the 2009 presidential election when the FMLN party achieved victory, since this is essentially the situation the Salvadoran Left has inherited.

In March 2006 the ruling ARENA party lost the midterm election to the FMLN and faced massive opposition in the streets of the capital to cost-of-living increases and recurring police raids on street vendors in the Central Market. At the same time, rural communities mobilized to defend themselves from corporate attacks on water and the environment. That year, after a number of Salvadoran National Civilian Police (PNC) members had received training at the ILEA, state violence surged and police conducted dozens of raids.

In May 2006, Human Rights Ombudswoman Beatrice de Carrillo publicly denounced the reemergence of extermination groups, whom she believed to be connected to the highest reaches of power in El Salvador. A paramilitary force called *Sombra Negra* (Black Shadow) resurfaced for the first time since the civil war, terrorizing rural communities with death threats and imposing curfews. Dead bodies were suddenly appearing throughout the countryside with their hands tied behind their backs and eyes covered, reminiscent of death squad killings in the past.

Between July 2006 and September 2007, the PNC engaged in more unprovoked attacks on street vendors and community protests, culminating in the arrest of twenty-eight protestors who were charged with acts of

FMLN supporters in San Salvador celebrate the Front's 2009 election victory. Photo © Sean Hawkey.

terrorism under ARENA's new antiterrorist law, which criminalized protest. As part of ARENA's Mano Dura (Iron Fist) policy, the police were indiscriminately detaining youth and boarding crowded public buses to display photo albums of "wanted" gang members. In 2007 alone, the PNC were identified as the source of 67 percent of 2,779 formal public complaints made to the Human Rights Office on matters regarding public safety. Additionally, the force was implicated in eight political assassinations, two student disappearances, and forcible occupation of the National University.

These conflicts have by and large ceased since Funes was elected, indicating that ARENA's ouster at the executive level was the best thing that could happen in this political moment, despite Funes's capitulations to the United States. The FMLN has thus succeeded in providing a major opening for the social movement to proactively broaden its base through community education programs and participatory decision-making structures; however, repressive forces merely lie idle as a potential force for the United States and Salvadoran Right to activate if and when new land and resource disputes come into play and to prevent the FMLN from making further moves to the left.

Community resistance to neoliberalism

When the FMLN has not been able to resist neoliberal reforms within government, communities have fought their own battles against private, and mostly foreign, mining, ineffective waste management, poor health-care and construction corporations, and corrupt government officials. Many of the most organized semiautonomous communities were repopulated at the end of the war by ex-guerrillas who still mobilize in support and coordination with the FMLN and belong to broader social movement networks like the Frente Social por un Nuevo País (Social Front for a New Country), Concertación Popular por un País sin Hambre y Seguro (Popular Coalition for a Safe Country without Hunger), and Movimiento Patria para Todos (Homeland for Everyone Movement), and Asociación Amigos de San Isidro (Friends Association of San Isidro).

Within the last decade, communities in Trinidad and San Isidro, Cabañas, halted attempts by Canadian-based Pacific Rim Mining Corporation to open a gold mine and dump 720 tons of cyanide per year into the Río Lempa, El Salvador's main water supply. An agrarian community in Cutumay Camones held off attempts by their mayor and the Los Angeles company PreSys to build a massive garbage dump on a hill above their farm. Riot police violently and repeatedly raided the community, which nevertheless held its blockade for five months and effectively killed the project. In what were called the White Marches (because protestors wore their white lab coats), nurses, doctors and other health care professionals successfully mobilized to resist the government's attempt to occupy and privatize the public hospital of San Salvador. Threats to privatize water have also been thwarted by people who dared to resist and won.

The Salvadoran social movement is most directly charged with the task of challenging the economic model the United States and the Salvadoran Right have aggressively maintained, since few deterrent measures can be taken within the government at this time. This situation raises critical and important questions. For example, what can the FMLN do at the state level as a political party to end the country's participation in the neoliberal project while the president has shown his willingness to comply? If that's not enough, can community resistance prevail? These are the questions faced by organizers in El Salvador's social movement today, whose voices and analysis are presented in this chapter.

Marcelo Rivera was assassinated for his work in mobilizing resistance to mining in his Cabañas community. Here, his brother, Miguel, sits in front of a shrine to his memory. Photo by Clifton Ross.

Miguel Rivera, community organizer
"Water is more valuable than gold"

Interview and translation by Clifton Ross, August 2009

The mural on the San Isidro community center depicting the martyred Monsignor Oscar Romero and the recently murdered anti-mining and FMLN activist, Marcelo Rivera, had just been painted, something I knew from the bright colors of the paint and the fact that Rivera's body had only been dis-covered about a month before my arrival. The people of San Isidro, in the Department of Cabañas, were fighting efforts by the Canadian-owned Pacific Rim Mining Corporation to begin mining gold there. Marcelo had been active in efforts to stop the mining, and prevent Pacific Rim and its shills from steal-ing the local elections in January. One day he boarded a bus and that was the last anyone saw of him until his body, showing signs of torture, was found at the bottom of a well after days of searching.

Inside the community center a number of community members and friends were gathered. At one end of the large room was an altar for Marcelo, a large "FMLN" banner at the back, bouquets of flowers arcing out of the photo of Marcelo and, in red sand on the brown sand covering the floor was written, "Marcelo lives in our hearts."

It was the final feast celebrating Marcelo's life, an event that takes place, according to Salvadoran Catholic tradition, a month after burial. I was

invited to eat with the community, and I gratefully sat down at the table with
some twenty or thirty people. I kept glancing over at Marcelo's brother, Miguel,
and noticed the heaviness about him: he ate dutifully, but without evident
relish; he seemed dazed as he raised his napkin to his mouth; he hardly spoke,
except to whisper something in response to a neighbor's question or expres-
sion of condolences.

After the meal we went outside to do the interview and Miguel told of
starting to organize with his brother Marcelo when he was twelve and Marcelo
was eighteen. Their first project was gathering books from people in the town
to organize a community library. Eventually they got possession of a build-
ing that had been used as a morgue for those killed during the civil war, and
they converted the space into the community cultural center.

In 2005, there was work going on with the mining companies. People said
that the old river, or the San Isidro River, was being killed. There used to be
shrimp and other species of life, but today it's entirely dead, sterile.

We saw the mining and we thought it was going to bring development
to the country. But a friend, Antonio Pacheco, coming from a meeting of
a sister organization in Honduras, said, "Look, this is the worst curse that
could happen to a community." And he told us about the effects people in
Honduras were suffering from the mining going on there, and contacts were
formed and an exchange began. And then, just as people were beginning to
develop skin diseases, Pacific Rim bought the mining rights and imposed an
environmental impact study on the Ministry of the Environment in order
to take out permits for exploitation.

They brought in a North American mining engineer to offer an environmental impact report to the Ministry. He never touched on the issue of water,
which is the major issue that such businesses affect. Up to now they haven't
been able to address this issue of water. Yet nevertheless they want to be
given permission to mine; they're still petitioning the government for that.

We made a major effort to get out the information about the effects of
mining to the greatest number of people and to the social organizations,
particularly where most of the mining is taking place, in the north of El
Salvador. We started making more contacts there with other organizations,
and through this process a call went out to form an organization that is
known today as Mesa Nacional Frente a la Minería (National Roundtable
Against Mining).

Meanwhile, activities were being developed here to make members of
the community aware of their rights and the true environmental impact that
the mining would have on them. But allies were also being sought out, and

one of the allies to prevent the approval of the mines was Marcelo. He played an important role because he was a link between the social and the political in our anti-mining organization. So there was a backlash and the mining interests began to buy leaders. Among the latter were municipal mayors, and the mayor of San Isidro appeared as a promoter of the mining business.

Friction grew between Marcelo, as representative of the social movement, and others. And perhaps he was always the target. For instance, Francisco Piñeda works in the local environmental committee here in Cabañas, and he and a woman who is a cook were offered two thousand dollars by Pacific Rim to poison Marcelo's food. The woman, frightened and crying, told Francisco's father-in-law, "I can't do that. I couldn't kill anyone for money."

In nearby Trinidad, the compañeros who are working in anti-mining actions have been brought to court five times for filming the work of the corporations. People have gotten organized and pleaded with the companies to withdraw their machinery, because they're damaging the environment and the community. And the activity has stopped but the people live under the threat from the companies. The people invite the companies to debate the issue, and after the debates people are more clear about the fact that water is more valuable than gold. We can live without gold, but we can't live without water. This, in fact, has become one of the slogans of the anti-mining struggle.

And Pacific Rim has been losing ground here, so they made other plans.

Stealing elections

The mining companies not only pollute the environment, but also institutions: they buy leaders who should be working for the people. But at the same time there was increasing growth in the anti-mining association. It grew politically with the FMLN and became an immanent threat to mining activity. In fact, before going into the elections, Mauricio Funes wrote a letter in which he committed to no more permits for mining in the country.

But the mining interests have gone to such extremes in San Isidro as to buy an ex-leader of the FMLN, Wilber Serrano, who entered the CD (Democratic Center) party to join forces with ARENA here in San Isidro, where not only was the mayor's post at stake, but also all the municipal authorities overseeing the mining project. They bought a political party to unite forces and have twice the people at the table. They brought people in from elsewhere to vote, as usual, but now in greater numbers.

In response young people got together on a mission and said, "No, the same thing isn't going to happen again; here we're going to vote and we have to speak up for the future of San Isidro; we're not going to let people come in from outside to make our decisions." So there was a clear position on the part of the social organizations and a political growth of the FMLN, represented here by Marcelo. That happened this past January in the elections for mayor and the National Assembly.

This is the only place in the country where the results of the election were annulled. Here the elections were stopped and forced to be repeated. That's because we had people monitoring all areas of San Isidro, so we discovered the people from the outside being trucked in by a City Council member. The people [of San Isidro] boxed them in and forced them out. The people decided that the following day [Election Day], if there was a massive entrance of people from outside the town, they were going to shut down the election—and they did.

So a barrier was formed here. The news was explosive: It got out nationally and internationally that San Isidro was the eye of the hurricane for having stopped the elections for the mayor and National Assembly. Well, the rumor ran that Hector de Rio and Marcelo were going to be killed for having organized the ending of voter fraud here in San Isidro. And this rumor ran all over town.

The week after the elections the mayor, José Ignacio Bautista, brought three hundred *mareros* (gang members) into San Isidro. Some who were stopped by the police were carrying Molotov cocktails and shotguns, and they were intimidating the people and keeping them from voting. But they were also part of the coordination of a force to bring in a greater number of police and military to lay siege to the town and keep people from voting.

The following day it was as if we were in a military camp, all the way to the voting urns, the GRP (Grupo de Respuesta Policial, equivalent of SWAT teams) and all the known police forces of El Salvador were gathered in San Isidro. Even the Air Force planes were flying over the town. This terrified the people. And people were also sent out into the outlying communities and people from there later told us that people who weren't likely to vote ARENA were discouraged from going into town and were told, "Look, don't go into town because there are lots of mareros, fights and even people with guns. You could get killed in a confrontation." They were instilling fear in them, but the others, who they knew would vote for ARENA, were told they would be brought in, and they were.

The day after the rumor started that Hector and Marcelo were to be killed for having stopped the elections, all of us in the social organizations met at Hector's house and began trying to figure out what we could do.

It was already clear that they wanted to impose the elections on us, and if the ballot was cleaned up, they could lose the election. And here it wasn't just an election over the mayor's seat, but also the support for the mining project where a huge amount of money was in play. The company hopes to make $300 million from right here where we're sitting.

So we began to establish the mechanisms needed to prove and denounce the electoral fraud at a national level, knowing that locally it would be a waste of time, knowing the prosecutors and their intentions. So we did this, gathering evidence and people who could testify to the fraud and talk about how they had been paid twenty dollars and been brought in to vote. We gathered all these interviews.

When the opposition found out, they broke into the house, stole the computer, the USB memory drive, the video and photo cameras, everything that could contain evidence of the electoral process here in San Isidro. The compañero Hector even had the money he'd been paid for his work that month there, and they didn't take that. So it was clear they entered there with one objective, which was they couldn't allow these facts to emerge into the public light, especially at an international level. But that compañero they robbed but didn't kill.

[Miguel describes the disappearance of his brother and the eventual discovery of his body at the bottom of a well.]

The real tomb isn't the grave

Who was Marcelo? He was a person who had devoted his whole life to social and political work. We have no personal enemies. We've always been known to be people who help out in the community. But yes, we've affected economic interests of many by having opposed powerful people and defended the rights of the poorest among us and by having informed them about the true consequences of mining activity.

We're indignant about this death, but we're going to do everything we can to make sure that the people who tried to make Marcelo's struggle disappear will not succeed because, obviously, the problem they had wasn't a person, but what that person was doing. And we have to keep going with that project, now with even greater force and indignation.

For us the real tomb of a person isn't the grave; in the grave one simply leaves the body but not the mind nor the work that is done, and that work is the struggle that is ongoing. And that's why I was filled with joy even at the burial, the funeral of my brother, when I came to realize that the sadness was shared. A friend, Leonel Herrera, in a message from the national anti-mining group, [said] that it was one of the few burials where one didn't weep alone, nor just with a family, but with all those who attended, because the feelings and tenderness are shared and the weight of having lost someone is also shared. You can see that there are many people here, since the morning, since yesterday, since he disappeared, accompanying the struggle, all the activities from the vigil to the burial.

The day of the burial was memorable also because there was no space in the cemetery: it was a huge crowd, a sea of people from the town, from the different cantons of El Salvador and also people like you, from outside of the country who were in solidarity with us and our struggle and with the people of San Isidro. Here in San Isidro history is being made: the history of social and political struggle.

Members of the Coordinadora del Bajo Lempa y Bahía de Jiquilisco
"The opportunity has come for us to build a power with roots that neither the wind nor anything will be able to move or uproot"

Interview and translation by Clifton Ross, July 2009

The Coordinadora del Bajo Lempa y Bahía de Jiquilisco (Coordinating Committee for the Lower Lempa and Bay of Jiquilisco), known locally simply as "la Coordinadora," came together after the civil war ended in 1990, when the region experienced a new wave of settlement by FMLN guerrilla supporters returning from exile, as well as former members of the Armed Forces. Many of these people were given land, but the right-wing ARENA government never offered them services, and to this day the residents have had to rely on their own resources to maintain roads and infrastructure, and to develop emergency measures to protect the community from occasional floods from the Río Lempa. Out of that necessity emerged the Coordinadora, representing sixty-four communities and some 4,500 families.

In a country characterized by extreme violence from the "salvatruchas" and "maras," or gang members armed with guns left over from the civil war, the Coordinadora signed the "Declaration of the Local Peace Zone" in August 1998.[1] The Declaration was "conceived as a territory in which the inhabitants define with autonomy the conditions of life to which they aspire, participate collectively in reaching those ends and resort to alternative methods to violence to resolve their problems. The key principles of the Local Peace Zone are the strengthening of community organization and democratic participation in the spaces where decisions are made." To reach these goals, the Coordinadora works to reduce the "vulnerability of the population by means of the construction of productive, environmental, social and organizational alternatives."

The community is as committed to preserving the environment as it is to keeping peace: The area around Bajo Río Lempa is an internationally recognized biosphere reserve, so the Coordinadora is developing infrastructure that minimizes environmental impact.

Members of the Coordinadora met with me one hot July afternoon. The directors had gathered for the interview, but the first speakers who offered background on the Coordinadora failed to identify themselves.

Unidentified man: We began working on this process after the peace accords in an area where the communities were able to establish themselves. Here there were no highways or housing and the people arrived here from the armed conflict having to design a strategy for life. So the communities settled on the left side of the Lempa River, the largest river of the country.

The local population comes from two groups: the old Armed Forces and the Frente Farabundo Martí (FMLN). The government gave them both parcels of land, thinking they were giving it to people who were demobilized [after the civil war], but that with time it would return to the large landowners. That didn't happen because the [Coordinadora] was able to maintain an occupation of the zone even though the government wanted to declare the area "uninhabitable," even though it was "habitable" when it was previously in possession of the big landlords. The fact that we were poor meant we weren't to be allowed to live in the Bajo Lempa.

So people built their power, refused to leave and began demonstrating and presenting proposals to the government. If we hadn't been organized it would have been very difficult, because when the people aren't organized they arrive and are told lies and then quietly leave. But because we were organized, with this power, we stopped the evictions.

Little by little we're consolidating our energy toward building an area that will really be healthy. When we first came here with the hopes of forming an organization, it was an area in great conflict. There were misunderstandings, but also it was a high-crime area with lots of robberies and assaults. Everyone has contributed to making this an area where now there's great respect for visitors, security for the population, and a greater understanding on all parts, because both the old Armed Forces and the people of the FMLN are still living here, side by side. But now most of the work has been done and they're no longer seen as two sides [of a conflict] but as one population with a single mission: to improve the quality of life for everyone.

Because we have the river so nearby, there were opportunities for development here—but at the same time this made us vulnerable, because there were floods and it has neither floodgates nor any infrastructure that would contain the flow of water this river receives. [The Lempa] begins in Guatemala, passes through Honduras and all this water flows into the Lempa River. Also, there was no help to be had from the government, given the [political allegiances of] the people of the region.

Worse still, there is a hydroelectric dam on this river and the government workers open the dam indiscriminately, with no warning to [our] communities. This made for floods, year after year, floods that destroyed our crops and the birds we tended. That was the beginning of the communities, really, the organization we called the Coordinadora del Bajo Lempa. We began by identifying our alternatives for development and confronting these vulnerabilities, one of which was the flooding, and the other, drought. Our very geographical location put us in this complicated situation.

Our culture of production was based on monoculture of basic grains, which at that time were sesame and corn. And these aren't crops resistant to either floods or droughts. So the first thing we had to do was to work on a transformation of our culture in relation to agriculture. We recognized we needed to change these methods and think about the kind of region we had and to adapt our crops. That's when we began to work with a program of agricultural diversification. This has been the emphasis for us up until last year. The food security program and the organization have both been growing.

We also have an organizing program that's based on participation and the autonomy that the communities must have to make decisions in life. Of course we have a great political impact on government at the city and national levels, because we're clear that the problems are of a local but also national nature. If the structures aren't changed, no matter what you do at a community level, the changes won't be possible.

We're also working on the issue of infrastructure, doing all we can in our situation to find ways to carry out our projects. We're working on housing and on potable water, which is one of the most basic things. We've come a long way on this: 75 percent of the communities now have potable water. There's work on improving the kitchens.

There's also garbage, and with that we're working on campaigns and trainings on how to manage this issue. We're also working on the construction of composting toilets, which eliminates air and water pollution in the area. Moreover, these toilets also convert waste into organic fertilizer.

We've been able to obtain funds for the different programs we're undertaking. We aren't able by ourselves to manage each series of projects as an organization or as a social movement, so to do this work we've decided to create an administrative arm, the Mangrove Association. Now the Mangrove Association contracts technical help necessary for each one of the programs and does the management and administration of funds. But the supervision and follow-up on the projects is done by the organization, from each community.

Luis Ramos: The power we've attained here, practically speaking, is power we build as a zone. There are two kinds of power: local and national. We work more in the local and we're quite clear that to be able to reach that which we propose, we need to create power first. So, we're creating different forms of power, for example, like agricultural producers.

The team of facilitators in this program consists of Carmencita, Estela, and me. We facilitate the organizational project, but the group makes the decisions, not us. We facilitate. In that sense we're creating power in the people themselves. It's not like the power comes from the directors or the office telling people what to do, but rather the people in their locality, in their community where they review, and make decisions and agreements, and are responsible for the activities.

Unidentified man #2: We've always believed that the way to solve the problems of crime in the area is not by detaining a person or by using violence, but rather by educating a population as a preventative measure. So we work on specific problems, but also on developing consciousness. Detaining a person is a last resort. We prefer to let the person know and become conscious of the fact that his style of life isn't the best, and that there are other options.

So, for instance, we talk about delinquency but we could also talk about fishing with bombs. We could point out how much damage a bomb does to the sea and how it kills all the larvae and eggs, so instead of jailing someone we can make him aware that we've stopped fishing with bombs and we can build a pond where there will always be fish to catch if he decides to take care of it. The same with delinquency. Now we've been doing this for twelve years with some success, teaching a practical lifestyle and getting people involved in projects, which is better than locking them up.

José Amilcar: I work in the area of permaculture. That is, on our farm where we grow many different crops, we try to implement the principles of permaculture, because permaculture has various principles. "Permaculture" means permanent agriculture. So what we try to do is involve designs and use spaces in the best way possible. Traditionally, people only grow one crop—usually corn or sesame—on their parcels. By contrast, permaculture uses land to produce all a family needs to live and, of course, also includes the needs of nature, too. With permaculture there is an array of designs one might use, and in implementing one or another one attempts to break with the traditional model designed for the straight lines of the tractor. In permaculture you try to avoid using the tractor, and rather make circular or curved designs according to the existing landscape, or rose-shapes, or a diversity of shapes.

Carmencita: There are sixty-four communities making up the Coordinadora. We break that down into sections and right now we have seven local groups, each of which are made up of seven or eight communities. Each group has a group of directors that coordinate and facilitate the work of the organization, and sometimes works on some internal problem until it's resolved to everyone's satisfaction.

Not all communities have the same problematic: Each zone has its own special situation. For instance, the Bajo Lempa is a protected zone with eight communities. Our mission is the conservation of marine life and mangroves. Other communities with sandy soil do aquaculture with shrimp, and cleaner fishing, which is what we want to implement here, so people no longer fish with bombs but work with other small-fishing techniques. In other communities there's cattle ranching and there we're working to ensure that they get credits so they can develop and make a good living.

In the Coordinadora each community sends its representative to the meetings and we also have general assemblies with committee meetings, women's, and youth meetings. There are various spaces where the people have the opportunity to participate and explain their situation, and that's where we're expanding and broadening the organization.

We know that in the capitalist system power rules from above, but here as an organization we have twelve years working in the communities to help build their power and to ensure that power would come from the base, from below, and rise up; that it would rise up to build the power we've longed for. Now we have a left government and we're going to be able to build a power that moves toward socialism, which is what the people of Latin America have wanted. Today the opportunity has come for us to be able to work and build a solid power, a power with roots that neither the wind nor anything will be able to move or uproot. That's what we're doing as an organization in the communities of Bajo Lempa.

Lilian Coto de Cuellar. Photo by Clifton Ross.

Lilian Coto de Cuellar, coordinator, FMLN National Secretariat for Women
"Women of all political stripes are struggling for our right to participate"

Interview and translation by Clifton Ross, July 2009

Lilian Coto de Cuellar taught in El Salvador's public schools for thirty years, and began her movement activism as a member of the National Association of Salvadoran Educators, ANDES 21 de Junio. She took part in the great strikes of 1968 and 1971 that established basic labor rights for teachers, and in the twelve-day hunger strike in 1992 that preceded the signing of the peace treaty between the FMLN and the ARENA (Nationalist Republican Alliance) government. After the accord, the FMLN transformed itself from a guerrilla army to a political party. Coto served as an acting representative and then a full representative in El Salvador's Legislative Assembly before becoming a representative to the Central American Parliament. We sat down for this interview at the Parliament's offices in San Salvador.

El Salvador has had a unique experience, in which the different organizations struggling for rights had a direct relationship with the FMLN as an insurgent force of the country—but on signing the peace accords, the FMLN broke relations with the social movements. The idea was that the social movements would become now become autonomous, but it had the effect of weakening the movements. There was no longer any sense of direction without the FMLN. Perhaps also this debilitation came as a result of an atmosphere of peace, that people no longer felt a great need to struggle.

Reality brought the social movement to initiate a process of rebuilding itself. It became clear over twenty years with the ARENA Party in power that instead of enforcing the peace accords, which were to bring harmony and better living conditions for Salvadorans, [ARENA] began to implement an orthodox neoliberal economic model that began to destroy the living conditions of the people and exclude them completely from accessing the wealth we were producing as workers. The state began to undermine its own power and turn it over to the "free market," something that impacted Salvadoran families and Salvadorans in general. All this brought the social movement to reconstruct itself and take up the struggle again.

And of course the FMLN has been in a state of constant growth as a political party. In all these electoral processes in which we've participated, we've increased our participation in public office but we've also increased the recognition of our people who have accompanied us in this process. Ninety-six municipalities are now governed [by the FMLN] through municipal councils, in some parts in alliance with social sectors or in coalition with political parties. And of course the principal achievement is to have arrived in the executive branch, since it's in the executive branch where decisions are made and programs are undertaken that can have an impact on the living conditions of the Salvadoran people.

Meanwhile, the right wing is in the process of fortifying itself after losing executive power, and it's trying to take over the other spaces like the judicial branch, in this case, the Supreme Electoral Tribunal. This is part of a larger regional process of the right wing as it tries to set back the electoral processes of the Left taking place now. We see this happening in Guatemala as they try to depose President Colón, using a pack of lawyers who are trying to get him to renounce power. We see this more recently in the coup d'état in Honduras: It had been twenty-seven years since a coup had taken place in the region, and this is a real setback that shows the desperation on the part of the right wing to reinforce itself and regain hegemony in the region. They're not only trying to regain economic and political power, but also the power over the [political] parties, to be able to create conditions that would favor the power of a much smaller economic elite over the region. Members of the ARENA party even went so far as to threaten that here in El Salvador we should heed the example of Honduras, since something similar could happen here.

We hope that won't be the case here, since the FMLN has shown itself to have an adequate ability to move forward and take political space in Salvadoran society by means of dialogue and negotiation. The [FMLN] party has in its aim to strengthen the unaffiliated social organizations. That is, we already have a party structure, and the social movements and the general population are strengthening the social fabric through community organizations, which we in government believe are needed for different means and forms of participation.

Recently we've had a movement against the construction of hydroelectric dams in the country, a movement accompanied by priests, who the president of the republic, in searching for a solution to the problem, received and heard. There's also a great, unified force of churches, political parties, and social movements against mining. We're all agreed that the mining companies shouldn't be allowed to work in our country because they'll completely destroy the environment.

According to the United Nations there are no decent salaries [in El Salvador], which is to say that labor isn't being given its due. In recent years all the work has opened up in the textile industry, in the *maquilas* where 95 percent of the workers are women, and the poorest women, especially single mothers who are being exploited with hard work, low wages, and a complete denial of their rights. There's been a strong movement demanding that the rights of women in this sector be respected.

FMLN, women's organizations cooperate to effect change

The signing of the peace accords made it possible for women from different parties and different ideological tendencies to connect. One place that happens is in the Parliament of El Salvador. It also happens in the associations of city governments, like city councils, and in unions. In other words, women who participate in local governments find these pluralistic organizations where women of all political stripes are struggling to guarantee our right to participate as women in the field of politics. We've proposed a reform to the electoral code in the Legislative Assembly asking that all political parties integrate [women into] their internal structures as well as having candidates for public office be a minimum of 40 percent [women]. We've also asked for a reform of [sexist] language, because in the Supreme Electoral Tribunal they put down "assemblyman" even for women. In addition to these pluralistic spaces, we're organizing training and education sessions thematically to draw together women from different parties.

Women, especially during the war, began to organize themselves to defend their basic rights against the repression that was directed against families and communities. During the war single mothers were left in charge of their families, and after the peace accords different organizations were strengthened and given legal standing so the women could better struggle to guarantee their rights, and, of course, the social and economic rights of the entire Salvadoran family. In 1994, women proposed what was called "Platform '94": All the women's organizations presented a proposal to the presidential candidates that went toward resolving the economic and social problems as well as opening political spaces for the participation of Salvadoran women.

The FMLN is the only party that has in its statutes a quota for the participation of women and youth, two sectors that have traditionally been excluded from political participation. Even though we've not reached the minimal goal, it's still in our statutes and ours is the party with the greatest openness and greatest participation of women. In this assembly, women hold thirteen of the thirty-five seats we hold, while the other parties have four women among them all. Here in the Central American Parliament, women hold five of the eight FMLN seats. Women are represented in all the city councils. Unfortunately, there's less representation [among] mayors.

This government in its campaign made proposals to solve different problems of women. Chief among them were access to credit, but also training in business development or in the company where the credit would be used. There's also a need for specialized medical attention in centers for child development where children could stay when mothers are working. There's also a need for legal and psychological help for women who are the objects of family or criminal violence, big problems in our country. All this to say that organizations, and we in the Legislative Assembly, have been working hard on legislation favoring women since the FMLN came to power.

Many of the programs that have been announced have favored the family in general, but specifically the women [of the family], since in El Salvador as many as 35 percent of the homes have women as the sole support of the family. So, support for children in education, providing them with uniforms, shoes, school supplies, and so forth, is one program that will have an impact, because the government of this country has never given children the resources for really accessing a free, quality education.

There are also revisions to the legal code for the family. A new law was created and approved that deals with violence in the family. We've also reformed the work code so that pregnancy tests won't be required, because here companies require women who apply for work to take a pregnancy test to prove they aren't pregnant. This new law forbids this requirement for women applying for work.

So [the FMLN] is doing all this in cooperation with the women's movement because our party has more representatives in the Legislative Assembly. The compañeras have signed a protocol of understanding with the women's movement that allows us to elaborate legal proposals together and also to accompany the women's movement so they can have more impact in the Legislative Assembly.

Salvadoran women are generally quite conservative and very few participate or even vote, much less work as public functionaries—and when they have voted, they tend to vote for right-wing parties. For instance, in 2004 for the first time there were more women than men voting, because here nearly 52.7 percent of the population is women. So we made an effort at that time to increase women's participation. More women did vote in those elections, but there was an increase of participation across the board with Salvadorans who came together in the hope that change was possible in our country, and we were going to achieve it by everyone participating.

Now we're clear about the great challenge before us: We're holding power in public offices and internal party structures and strengthening the participation of women, but how do we develop among women the necessary skills for making their own decisions? The problem is that people in general, but particularly women, have been manipulated by right-wing parties through campaigns of fear, scaring them into maintaining a situation without any possible change.

Now that women have taken the power to change and the Salvadoran people have made changes this electoral period, challenges confront us. First, we need to guarantee the conditions for equal opportunities and treatment for men and women in El Salvador. Second, we need to see how we can guarantee that the Salvadoran families have access to the resources that would allow them to live with dignity, since the majority have never had that possibility. Then there there's the issue of the emigration of the majority, which leaves nearly 40 percent of Salvadoran homes with women as head of the house. And in some cases even if the man remains, it's the woman who is working, so either way it's always the woman who pays the highest cost to maintain the family. These are the situations that we need to change in the country, and these are the challenges we're taking up.

Oswaldo Natarén and members of the University Front of Roque Dalton (Frente Universitario Roque Dalton, FURD)
Voices from the leftist student movement in El Salvador

Interview by J. Heyward, November 2012

Oswaldo Natarén is an artist, activist, and cofounder of the University Front of Roque Dalton (FURD), a student group at the National University of El Salvador (UES). The FURD formed in 2002 to actively challenge the university's approach to administration, organization, admissions, and curriculum, as well as its overall role and participation in society.

In 2006, the right-wing National Republican Alliance (ARENA) government ordered the National Civilian Police (PNC) to invade the UES. The government then crafted a media campaign to brand FURD members terrorists and propagate

Stencil of Salvadoran revolutionary poet Roque Dalton, created by Oswaldo Natarén. Photo courtesy of J. Heyward.

false claims that students had been stockpiling weapons at the school. It was the first time the university had been attacked and occupied by state forces since June 1980, three months prior to the outbreak of the country's twelve-year civil war. Five years prior to that incursion, the Salvadoran military had assassinated three UES students and disappeared another sixteen.

Natarén is now a member of a Community Mental Health Team in Tonacatepeque, a densely populated town in the state of San Salvador. Community Mental Health Teams were created by the FMLN Administration's Health Ministry to deploy psychologists, nurses, social workers, and artists into low-income communities to strengthen awareness, recovery, and prevention of mental health issues. Tonacatepeque is known for high levels of interpersonal violence and a strong presence of street gangs. Natarén and two other members of the FURD, Jackie and Sonia, discuss their vision for radical reform within the National University, the legitimacy of a recent government-negotiated gang truce between the Mara Salvatrucha and 18th Street gangs—and claims that the truce has reduced homicides by 40 percent—as well as challenges confronting Salvadoran youth and social movements in this period of political transition.

Critical challenges to University curriculum and methodology

Jackie: The FURD was founded as a means to organize youth at the UES to transform its goals and purpose. We consider ourselves an autonomous organization. What interests us, as an organization, is the possibility of the university returning people to the path of commitment; to a society that really identifies the university as a place where people are developing new critiques and solutions. Our goal is to build an organization that engages young people who believe we can change society through our work at the UES.

One factor that's been forgotten is that the purpose of the university is not to merely create professionals. If one doesn't truly get involved here, they won't know or be able to be involved in what's happening in society. Colleges used to play a very important role in societal events, not only inside the university but outside too, nationally. It had a role in solving problems people were experiencing at the time.

Now the university creates professionals who go out and do nothing more but work. We need to reawaken the commitment we have to others—not only to ourselves. Many people have forgotten that we have to be interested in this country in its entirety, not just dependent upon the system for our own needs. Then we only live superficially and never create a more objective look into what's happening and consider, as young people, what we can truly give to society.

Exercising autonomy through leftist transition

Oswaldo: The FMLN has great influence within the UES, through its professors and administrative staff—the people who make decisions. And though these people have the freedom to act outside of party lines, they often don't. Some of the student organizations have demonstrated a certain independence from the party but many follow the FMLN's political agenda. That hasn't really helped the university. We can say that there are still many internal things that need to be worked on. The UES should generate proposals to the government and the FMLN should be receptive to those proposals, while the party maintains respect for the school's autonomy. Instead, UES officials consider themselves a part of the FMLN, so they aren't making any proposals. In many countries, universities play a very important societal role in the study and development of culture and science. It isn't like that here.

In El Salvador, we've been battling our own ghosts for some time now. There's a lack of leadership from the different sectors. The same old men are professors and student organizations tend not to form leadership. Because of this, no one is coming forth with larger proposals. The same is the case within social movement organizations. Many organizations have disappeared or lowered their profile and no longer take direct action because they don't want to challenge the FMLN, even though there are many areas in which they are not in agreement with the party's positions.

Sensationalized media portrayals of Salvadoran youth

Sonia: The media sensationalizes youth with tattoos and tries to convince people that the majority of us live violent lives or belong to the gangs. I recently heard about an eighteen-year-old who went to jail for killing someone. What is interesting is that this particular person was a rich kid, an artist. Much of the violent crime in El Salvador is committed by upper-class youth but the media doesn't explore this tendency. Many believe that poor people are to blame.

Jackie: There's no positive media representation of our communities, the barrios, the neighborhoods we come from. When they do come into our communities, they look down on us. They claim that our communities are saturated with violence, danger, and drugs. There's very little space for youth participation in the media. The Right controls media and access to forums of public debate. When there is a little space made for our participation, it's the result of our own efforts and demands.

Oswaldo: As politically conscious youth, we have a lot of distractions. We're bombarded with issues and are also victimized, criminalized, and faced with the threat of violence. There's a lot of insecurity that threatens us outside of the university. We can easily be killed. We carry a lot of fear when we're in the street or on the bus. Youth are the main victims of crime in El Salvador. At the same time we're thought of as criminals. Random young people without fault are often blamed for the deaths of compañero/as, friends, and gang members. This is a very complicated society and rarely does the media shed light on our situation.

The police harass youth directly. I work with a number of youth and they say they are harassed by the police and military just for being young. Every one of the kids I've worked with has been stopped and frisked by security forces—by police as well as soldiers. This means the repression of youth continues in a very significant way, above that of everyone else.

Numbers vs. reality: the legitimacy and effectiveness of the gang truce

Oswaldo: I have the same generalized perception that the majority of Salvadorans have, and that is that the situation remains unchanged. We must look at the sources of information and also consider the role the media is playing. Also, you have to know that this country lives under the constant influence of electoral propaganda. One election ends and another begins, then another. The electoral period never ends. Then the media plays its role of confusing the people about what's working and what is not working. Most of our information comes from the media. They tell us that the government and the gangs are negotiating but they also are telling us about the dead. There isn't a day that they don't fill news headlines with death statistics. The numbers that the ministry of security is giving are only numbers and we don't believe that this is real data. Our perception is that social violence hasn't decreased. In other words, bodies are still showing up in plastic bags and disappearances are still common.

Extortion has continued to go unabated and has now come to touch families that three or five years ago it didn't touch, like my family. We have a modest business that is in crisis because of the cost of flour. We have to pay a quota because of that. So sure, maybe the government is negotiating with the gangs and organized crime networks but we don't know what they are negotiating. And they are only negotiating to bring the level of homicides down, not to resolve the root causes of violence.

The government has been talking about a second phase of negotiations. What this means is that the first one is now over. This gives us the feeling that this specific approach to violence intervention is in vain. The people say that the only thing the government has done is to put gang leaders in privileged living conditions within the prisons. This is the generalized opinion. The government speaks of mediators and we know who they are, *Monseñor* Fabio Colindres and Raúl Mijango. But what about the negotiators? We know that the gangs are on one side of the table but who are the negotiators? It isn't civil society that is directly negotiating with the gangs, it is the government. But what are they negotiating? Is it acceptance? Are they negotiating control over certain territories in exchange for lower crime rates? As I mentioned earlier, the violence hasn't diminished.

The government speaks of giving gang members alternative opportunities for employment but there are millions of people who are unemployed and also need opportunities. So this is what the gangs win—legitimization by the government as a group capable of influencing society. Little by little, the gangs are being converted into a recognized structure and the problem is that the violence continues. People continue murdering. It could become a big problem for the country, above all because many gang members are involved in drug dealing and can control that market. I believe that if the social movement doesn't take a serious stance on this, it will be very difficult to change this dynamic.

I feel that the truce is just one more government project and that when Mauricio Funes's five years are up, this is going to become a project for another government to decide to continue or dismiss. There isn't a very clear plan for the future on the agenda and young people continue to join gangs.

The gangs are divided. They aren't all in agreement with these negotiations. Because there is no clarity or transparency, the truce will not advance beyond the government's stated intentions. And as I said, it isn't a problem of gang members. It isn't a problem of gang leaders. It is a much bigger problem, which is a general climate of poverty and violence. So as long as there isn't a more comprehensive focus given to these topics, the state will be doing nothing more than imprisoning more and more people.

We're going to arrive at a point at which territorial disputes will come into play because the gangs have real control in these communities. In my current job, as an art teacher and muralist, I go into these places. I teach kids in communities where the gangs have a presence, and they don't mess with our work. They've allowed us to work. So what's the function of the police? They exercise a certain level of pressure on the gangs but in the end, the police aren't in control there. Gang members are helping the children, mothers, and other family members in these communities.

What we want: FMLN resistance to free trade and colonization
Oswaldo: The FMLN must focus on reversing the social abandonment policies of previous governments. ARENA created a neoliberal system—a system that gives priority to individualism. The market gives priority to profit before anything else.

With the creation of laws that undermine our power and by signing commercial treaties like CAFTA and big contracts for private megaprojects, including U.S.-funded dams, mining projects, and the construction of a transnational highway (plans established through the Bush Administration's Millennium Challenge Corporation goals), ARENA violated El Salvador's sovereignty. They told us, rather than asked, what we want to develop in this country. So the new government must prioritize the social factor. It should be close to the people and respond to our interests.

At this point, the FMLN has said it will not consider breaking away from CAFTA or the U.S. dollar. I understand that this is an immediate strategy of the FMLN to accept real constraints of the existing power structure; however, we hope that future FMLN governments will continue to investigate the loss of benefits we've experienced as a result of free trade and privatization and soon determine another course. The party has to focus on educating people so that the people have the power.

We need to return to and revive the agricultural sector—agriculture being an essential element that can bring about the development of rural families and can also change the troubled course this country is on. ARENA completely abandoned this sector, even while poverty increased. Because of this neglect, the country isn't self-sufficient. We consume but do not produce. Through the agricultural sector, the FMLN government could guarantee food to the whole population while generating more jobs—and better jobs—so that people will no longer be forced to migrate.

We believe the need for change is great and that it will take some time for the FMLN to turn things around. But we also have immediate demands. We want to know that we will have protection and support when things go wrong. We want real social benefits, which to us are more than just political strategies. These basic expectations have been neglected by all of the previous governments. Now that the FMLN has an opportunity to lead, it must ensure our welfare; we believe that this will require, in addition to the things I've already mentioned, El Salvador's integration with other countries in Latin America that are also on a path of social change: Bolivia, Nicaragua, Venezuela, Ecuador, and Paraguay.

Nicaragua

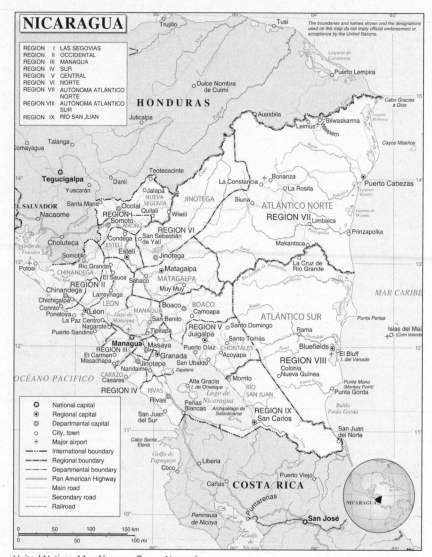

NICARAGUA

REGION	I	LAS SEGOVIAS
REGION	II	OCCIDENTAL
REGION	III	MANAGUA
REGION	IV	SUR
REGION	V	CENTRAL
REGION	VI	NORTE
REGION	VII	AUTÓNOMA ATLÁNTICO NORTE
REGION	VIII	AUTÓNOMA ATLÁNTICO SUR
REGION	IX	RÍO SAN JUAN

The boundaries and names shown and the designations used on this map do not imply official endorsement or acceptance by the United Nations.

HONDURAS

EL SALVADOR

Tegucigalpa

COSTA RICA

San José

MAR CARIBE

OCÉANO PACIFICO

○	National capital
◎	Regional capital
◉	Departmental capital
○	City, town
✈	Major airport
—··—··—	International boundary
—·—·—·	Regional boundary
—··—··—	Departmental boundary
———	Pan American Highway
———	Main road
———	Secondary road
┼┼┼┼	Railroad

NICARAGUA

United Nations Map No. 3932 Rev. 5, November 2011

Hope betrayed

By Clifton Ross

In the 1980s, hope had a name and an address for the worldwide Left: Sandinista Nicaragua. The victory of the Frente Sandinista Liberación Nacional (Sandinista National Liberation Front, FSLN) on July 19, 1979, was a high-water mark of the guerrilla struggles that shook the world as the Euro-American empires relinquished their direct control on colonies in the "Third World," even if only to control them more furtively and effectively by means of international financial instruments such as the IMF and World Bank. The decade-long rule in Nicaragua of the Junta of National Reconstruction under the direction of the FSLN opened great possibilities for a people newly liberated from a brutal dictatorship and it attracted hundreds of thousands of solidarity activists from around the world to join in the work of rebuilding the nation.

Nicaragua is the largest and poorest country of Central America and the second-poorest country of Latin America. It has an agricultural economy with a growing maquiladora sector. The country is divided culturally between the Caribbean and Pacific coasts, the former populated by English-speaking blacks and indigenous people, and the latter by the dominant Spanish-speaking mestizos.

The invasion by U.S. Marines in 1912 was the beginning of the longest and most brutal foreign occupation the country had endured, lasting until 1933. The Marines only left when they were driven out by a small guerrilla army of patriots, which took its name from its leader, Augusto Sandino.

Sandino was an anarcho-syndicalist and a theosophist who had worked briefly in the oil fields of Mexico where he'd been inspired by that nation's revolution, and the ideas of its most renowned anarchist, Ricardo Flores Magón, to return to liberate his own country. With a poorly armed guerrilla army organized mostly from the local peasantry, Sandino managed to drive out the U.S. Marines, but a few months later he was murdered by the head of the Nicaragua National Guard (notably trained by U.S. Marines before their exit) under orders of General Anastasio Somoza. Somoza eventually took power as the founder of a family dynasty that would rule the country for more than forty years.

The FSLN was founded in 1961 as one guerrilla organization among dozens that rose up to challenge the Somoza dictatorship. Inspired by the Cuban Revolution, they were Marxist-Leninists, a far cry from the early Sandinista Army that followed the "General of Free Men." But as the FSLN emerged as the single most powerful guerrilla army to challenge Anastasio Somoza, the son of Sandino's murderer, they began to incorporate new elements like liberation theology and Sandino's own nationalism into their ideology. By the time the FSLN came to power and formed the Junta of the Government of National Reconstruction in 1979, "Sandinismo" was becoming a distinct, if eclectic, political philosophy. While socialism was still a powerful guiding idea, the Sandinistas worked toward a mixed economy which included capitalist, cooperativist, and state-run enterprises.

Guerrillas build a "nation of poets"

Two among many exciting projects for the transformation of the nation were inspired by Catholic priests, brothers, who held ministerial positions in the new government. The literacy campaign of 1980, under newly appointed Minister of Education Fr. Fernando Cardenal and advised by Paulo Freire, mobilized nearly a hundred thousand volunteers. The effort reduced illiteracy in the country by more than 37 percent in six months, winning a UNESCO award. Fernando's brother, Minister of Culture Fr. Ernesto Cardenal, began organizing poetry workshops all over the country to create a "nation of poets." Every sector of society was invited to write out the grief and joy of the struggle that had engaged them, and some extraordinary work was produced by the most ordinary people: campesinos, housewives, policemen, militia recruits, children, prisoners.

Meanwhile, medical clinics, schools, daycare centers and food dispensaries were set up all over the country, much of the infrastructure financed by international solidarity. Solidarity brigades arrived from all directions to help the Nicaraguans reconstruct from an earlier earthquake (1972) and the destruction wrought by the struggle to overthrow the dictator. The possibilities seemed limitless, as one tourist pointed out, in this country where "campesinos now wore glasses and knew how to read and write poetry."

1984: In the early years after the Sandinista Revolution, students and workers from the city formed brigades to help get the coffee harvest in. Here, a woman releases two doves as *brigadistas* celebrate the end of the 1984 harvest. Photo by Clifton Ross.

But the incoming Reagan administration, characterized by a rigid Cold War ideology, wouldn't stand for a "communist beachhead" in its "backyard." The CIA began organizing mercenaries, ex-National Guardsmen and disaffected campesinos into a counterrevolutionary force, "*contrarevolucionarios*," known simply as the "Contras." They were trained and directed as a terrorist army to attack primarily civilian and infrastructure targets. The financing came from drug trafficking, arms sales to Iran, and the CIA's black budget after Congress cut off funds early on.[1]

The Contras murdered health-care workers, literacy workers, Christian "delegates of the word," cooperativists, farmers and occasionally, but rarely, engaged the Sandinista Army in direct battle. They mined the Nicaraguan harbors and eventually President Ronald Reagan managed to impose an economic embargo on the country. Food shortages grew, and so did the number of dead. In a country of 3.5 million, thirty thousand lost their lives in the Contra war. The Sandinista Revolution began to slip into reverse as the supermarket shelves grew empty and hunger and need became constant companions of Nicaraguans.

Through the course of the war, the Sandinistas demonstrated a remarkable, and perhaps naive, faith in democracy, despite the fact that they'd won power through armed insurrection. In the 1984 elections, Daniel Ortega of the FSLN *comandancia* won the presidency by a wide margin. Bolstered by that show of popular support, the FSLN held another round of elections in 1990, but under very different circumstances.

The war, shortages, and a leadership that was increasingly separated from the reality of the people weighed heavily on the voters. The new round of elections saw the floodgates of money from U.S. government institutions opened to pour over the opposition led by Violeta Chamorro.[2] Weeks before the election, Bush invaded Panama, ostensibly to "get" President Manuel Noriega, but also to send a message to Nicaraguan voters who now felt, as one reporter put it, that they were voting "with a gun held to their heads."

Despite polls showing the FSLN with a lead, Nicaraguan voters at last surrendered to the will of Washington in February 1990. As Fernando Cardenal later reflected, "People didn't vote between ideals. They voted between war and peace, life and death—not against the Revolution, but for life."[3]

To their credit, the Sandinistas and their president, Daniel Ortega, left power peacefully, determined to "govern from below" as an opposition party. But as they left power, Ortega and others in the comandancia divided up the assets of the country among themselves. This became known as the "Piñata" and it was a turning point for the revolutionary party of the FSLN. This was only the beginning of a process of division that would soon enter the party itself.

From revolutionary hope to politics as usual

Old divisions and tendencies that had been set aside with the victory in 1979 emerged with the process of reorganization after the electoral defeat.[4] The commanders of the FSLN had consciously worked for collective leadership and avoided the *caudillismo* so common in Latin America. But Daniel Ortega, having tasted presidential power, began to sideline any potential competitors for that position which he hoped to win back in the future. This led to a split in the FSLN in 1995 in which the Frente lost its best and brightest. Sergio Ramírez, a novelist and former FSLN vice president, Ernesto and Fernando Cardenal, Giaconda Belli, and many others left the party, some of them forming the Sandinista Renewal Movement (MRS).

In 1998 Daniel Ortega's stepdaughter, Zoilamérica Narvaez Murillo, accused him of rape and molestation. Ortega's forces went on the offensive, labeling her insane, a lesbian, and an agent of the CIA. Meanwhile, Ortega had been in secret meetings to arrange the infamous "Pacto" (pact) with Liberal Party *caudillo* and then-president of Nicaragua Arnoldo Alemán.[5]

The negotiations, hammered out over thirty secret meetings, were aimed at dividing power between the Liberal Party and the FSLN and excluding other actors from the political scene. The pact also appeared to be aimed at ensuring the two would be immune from prosecution for crimes: Ortega for rape and molestation, and Alemán for corruption.[6] The FSLN had come to power in 1979 in hopes of transforming the political landscape of Nicaragua, but within twenty years the political landscape had transformed the FSLN into just another political party.

Ortega ran for president three times before finally regaining power in 2006 and entering a "fourth stage of transformation." Ortega demonstrated in the runup to the election that he was willing to do anything to regain power. In addition to the previously made pact with Alemán to shut out competitors, he chose a former Contra commander, Jaime Morales Carazo, as his vice-presidential running mate. He reconciled with the Catholic Church hierarchy, in particular the old nemesis of the FSLN, and fierce anticommunist, Cardinal Obando y Bravo. Finally, in a peace offering to the Cardinal and the right wing, the FSLN joined with right-wing parties in Parliament to prohibit even "therapeutic" abortions, that is, those abortions done to save the life of the mother.[7]

Ortega's only real competition in the 2006 elections, given that the right-wing parties had split, had been Herty Lewites, another Sandinista who had proposed a primary race for presidential candidate within the FSLN. For this, "the party 'discharged' Lewites and some of his key support- ers, including disgruntled former FSLN leaders, while outside the conven- tion hall pro-Lewites demonstrators were met with a barrage of stones."[8] Herty then moved over to run as a candidate of the MRS, but Fortune smiled on Ortega: Lewites died of a heart attack just four months before the elec- tion, leaving the field wide open to Ortega.[9]

Since the 2006 victory, Ortega and his FSLN have clung to power, at least in part through electoral fraud. Both the mayoral elections of 2008 and Ortega's reelection in 2011 were tainted by fraud, vote-buying, and many irregularities.[10]

Oil from Venezuela also helps maintain the FSLN in power. To pay for the oil, the Chávez government gives Nicaragua low-interest loans, which will have to be paid back eventually.[11] Meantime, the proceeds from the sales of oil go into Ortega's personal bank account, and some funds flow out again to support social welfare programs like "Zero Hunger."

Nicaragua in the new century is a forgotten country. It no longer inspires the Left with hope nor the United States government with fear.[12] Some might argue that the current state of the FSLN under Daniel Ortega is the inevitable outcome of a Leninist democratic centralism. Certainly the historical development of the structure from military (guerrilla) command to governing junta made possible the ascendancy of a single, power-hungry individual such as Ortega. But "bourgeois democratic" structures have also certainly made it possible for "Ortega, who is maligned by 60 percent of the population but admired by a quarter of Nicaraguans" to come to power and take what increasingly appears to be near total control of the country.[13]

Not everyone sees Ortega's authoritarianism to be a problem. Indeed, a large majority (73 percent) "believed an 'authoritarian' president was necessary for their country." As for corruption, only 7 percent named it as a top problem, whereas "27 percent named 'poverty' as their country's main problem and 47 percent the closely related problem of 'unemployment.'"[14] Whatever else might be said of the "Danielista FSLN," it does have social programs for the poor, unlike the other parties that governed from 1990 to 2006, and some analysts, like Morris, see Ortega's concern for the poor as genuine and helpful.

Nevertheless, opinions on the meaning of the tale of the Sandinistas are as diverse and conflictive as the history of Nicaragua itself. The words one writer used to describe the present "Danielista" FSLN of today might just as well have been spoken of the Somoza regime: "a venal oligarchy run by a small elite satisfied to promote a form of what might be termed 'hacienda feudalism.'"[15] In such a context independent social movements and NGOs find their ability to operate, much less to take a political stance and criticize, severely limited. Most are presented with two options: operate under the patronage of the Danielista FSLN with absolute loyalty, or be shunned as "agents of imperialism." Nevertheless, much work still goes on in NGOs and progressive church groups, though most is cast in apolitical terms. Such is the case with Fernando Cardenal, now with Fe y Alegría, who maintains an optimistic tone, saying, "We are broken soldiers for an invincible cause."[16]

Andrea Morales Pérez, Central Sandinista de Trabajadores
"Toward a new type of unionism"

Interview conducted by Marcy Rein and Clifton Ross, July 2004
Translation by Clifton Ross

The Central Sandinista de Trabajadores (CST, Sandinista Workers' Central) lies on the edge of what was known as "Gringolandia" because it was where solidarity activists landed in the 1980s as they came to observe, or work with, the Sandinista Revolution. The hall in those years was always full and bus-tling with excitement, hope, and revolutionary discussions. In 2004 the hall looked pretty much the same as it did twenty years before, except that the paint was beginning to show signs of age and there were very few people to be seen. Even the cafés and outdoor food stands surrounding the hall, which used to do a relatively constant business, were now either closed or had just one or two customers. We wondered if we'd arrived at the wrong time of day and we weren't sure if we'd find Ms. Pérez in her office, but she was there and, fortunately, had the air conditioner on.

The Sandinista National Liberation Front (FSLN, referred to here as "the Front") hadn't yet changed its colors to pink from the earlier red and black colors under which the anarcho-syndicalist Augusto Sandino had launched his rebellion, colors adopted and used by the FSLN, and there were a few small FSLN flags in the office of the Women's section of the CST.

My name is Andrea Morales Pérez and I'm in charge of the Secretariat of Women of the CST José Benito Escobar where I've been working for four years. We have a union council for labor issues at a general level and the Secretariat of Women has a women's council comprised of fifty compañeras. We've been training the union women directors in specific areas, like gender, family violence, self-esteem and empowerment, and leadership. We've done this with the popular education methodology—not through seminars or forums, but rather through workshops where the participants are those who make the workshop itself. We aren't going to indoctrinate in these work-shops but we try to get participants to bring along their life experiences and their reality to build the workshop. This is how we build the study circles. We have plenary sessions where we have exchanges between different groups.

Right now we're in a new mode of work. We know we're in a country convulsed by a great economic crisis so people are actually psychologically sick; so in these workshops we also have tai chi exercises. This allows us to do relaxation, self-awareness, and personal growth exercises. This, in turn, allows women to bring a fresh leadership to the [CST] organization. Because it's not necessary to be young to have fresh leadership, but rather a leader-ship that facilitates collective work and effectively allows for a work done more horizontally, so that all of us feel that we're part of this process, and important parts, allowing us to transform reality. We have a slogan, "toward a new type of unionism," and we think that we women are helping to make that slogan a reality. We'll all benefit to the degree that women achieve a greater freedom, and to that degree the organization with also be more democratic, right?

This process is important to us because we're not only dealing with the worker or the member but this process allows us to reach the family, too. Because we women have more duties than the man because we're not only leaders and workers, we're also housewives, and in 26 percent of the families of Nicaragua, heads of families. So we're working not only with the women here but with families, since women are contributing not only to the economy but also to families, which is the fundamental unit. So we've gone out of the business to the community and the family.

Outreach beyond the workplace

Historically unions have been located in the businesses, but now we believe that with the new global processes there's a rotation among workers, there's no stability with them any longer, but there's no rotation in the family as you'll see in businesses where [workers] go from job to job. But the family doesn't "rotate" this way, so it's much more stable and working from that, in the community, allows new generations to get to know the role that unions play and understand that they're a bastion, a bastion of class solidarity. Women have this role that we have to play in the emancipation of the workers and of women.

I believe that the union is the ideal place to struggle for the emancipation of women because unionists can't be talking about liberation, respect, and integration and not allow women to be playing that role, or we'd be acting like demagogues. So this is where we can take the essential first steps into positions of power, get information—because we think knowledge gives you power—and this is how we can build a union movement that is more modern, participatory, and committed to civil society as a whole. Within that, we women play a very active role.

And so education and training are essential because we women are in the education committee; we're in the Commission for Education and members of the National Council of Education, in which we make sure that women are included and participate. One of the issues that we've also been struggling for and developing is the participation of youth, who are a major force in the economy. The economically active population of Nicaragua is very young and women [are a big part] because you're seeing women working in the maquiladora sector where 80 to 90 percent are women workers. So the issue of gender is critical for us, as well as youth, for the generational changing of the guard.

We now have a group of twelve women who we've prepared to train women in the Free Trade Zones in the neighborhoods. That's where we're working around themes, but also teaching tai chi, relaxation exercises,

FSLN graffiti in Managua, 2010. Photo by Clifton Ross.

and health maintenance, all of which enable them to return home and see things from another perspective. We train these women to do the training at the base. In other words, we have educators at different levels: the instructors train the facilitators, and the facilitators work at the base.

Women represent that sector of the population most beaten down because we have no opportunities. We have no quality work since we work in inhuman conditions: we have no place to leave our children; we have no social security, no access to doctors, nor the benefit of collective agreements that would help us maintain our homes. Another great blow is the limited access we have to education and if women can't study, it holds us back. So we are the most oppressed sector because we're often the only support for the home and the only work is in the Free Trade Zone, and there they only employ young women. I, for instance, wouldn't be able to get work in the Free Trade Zone. And a woman who works in the Free Trade Zone ten years may still be young, but she's physically old.

Relations with the FSLN

Historically we've been part of the Left, as you know. Most of our leaders, including me, are FSLN militants. We have respectful relations with the Front. When we make decisions, we don't consult the FSLN to see what's good or bad. We make our own decisions with the full weight of responsibility.

At the same time, this isn't to say that we don't recognize that the FSLN is one of, or the only, party that defends the rights of the poorest sectors of the country. We recently met with the FSLN about the maquiladoras, to talk about that kind of work, not to hear what they thought or what they thought we should think, but to tell them what we thought and what work we were doing in the maquiladoras.

I think the Front has somewhat changed its vision and strategy with regard to the social sectors. Before, the social sectors did nothing if the Front didn't tell them to do it. But now I think that each organization connected to the FSLN has begun to take a bit more autonomy, which has allowed them a bit more credibility.

Because whether or not those in our ranks are Sandinistas, our basic role is to struggle for the rights of workers, whoever they may be, and work for collective contracts with businesses. And we have cities with FSLN mayors and we rise up against them if they don't negotiate for a collective contract, even so far as to go on strike, and we do go on strike, because with the law what's good for the goose is good for the gander, and we fight for what's right. Obviously the relations are different because [Sandinista mayors] pay more attention and are a bit more open but that doesn't mean that just because they're more open we're going to do what they say. But that openness does effectively allow the possibility of opening cases and resolving them and not just forgetting them.

Elections of 1990 and the new left victories

Well, certainly we wanted the Front to win. The first defeat was for us, for me, a loss like that I felt losing my mother. So much energy and sacrifice went into making this Revolution and to lose that process, not the Revolution, but the process, was a terrible blow. [Now] we think the FSLN can improve things, but we don't believe that things will change radically because the process of globalization is powerful, as is big capital and we're still very weak.

[Those criticizing the FSLN] have to see both sides of a problem. It's often very difficult to criticize from the outside and often healthier to criticize from the inside. The FSLN has been learning and it's made mistakes, but I weigh things: On one side there are the errors, and on the other there are the assets. If the assets outweigh the errors, then I say one has to work on the errors to improve. You have to look at the context and see things in context. I wouldn't have told you that in the '80s because the context was completely different. But I think it can be a grave error to analyze out of context. These marvelous critics aren't connected to the Front, right? They're not on the Right. They're also not in the center. So where are they? You could ask that question and though they're not connected to any party, they continue to feel the Sandinista Front is theirs because it isn't a party of persons. We say that there's a leader, and for me that's Daniel [Ortega] but Daniel is the leader of a structure and I'm not of that structure. I'm Sandinista and whoever wants to take away my militancy, I say, I paid for it, and it cost me blood, sacrifice, my youth: I left it there.

Right now there's a process of discussion in the Front about the issue of women, so if they're called and don't come, then they should! If you have a voice, you need to raise it. And if you don't go where you're invited, then you aren't going to be heard. We're never going to take your criticism seriously if you don't make it in a constructive way, in the contexts within which you need to make it. That's my perspective, and my vision. I have great love and respect for them because they have a revolutionary vision and they're Sandinista women, and despite their resentment toward some leaders of the Front they play an aggressive role in society, and we're doing the same work in civil society. Outside of the Front? Yes. Outside of the structure of the Front there are a lot of people, but when it comes time to vote, they vote red and black.

Altagracia del Socorro Solís, Banana Workers' Encampment, Managua, Nicaragua
"Our demands are against the transnational corporations— but the government also has to do its part"

Interview by Clifton Ross, January 2010
Translation by Margot Pepper

You couldn't miss the banana workers' encampment, which occupied the land across the Avenida Simón Bolívar from the National Assembly and built around the monument to Pedro Joaquin Chamorro, the editor and journalist of La Prensa who was gunned down by the dictator Anastasio Somoza in January 1978. It was difficult to determine whether the workers had remained in permanent protest for so long out of determination, or despair, or simple physical exhaustion, or lack of alternatives—or all of the above. Plastic red and black FSLN flags waved over the plastic makeshift huts to express partisanship toward the only political force that had bothered to support them, even if only with beans and rice and lard. None of the previous neoliberal governments had even bothered to offer that much.

We, gathered here, make up the leadership, except for our vice president, who's having some problems and is in the hospital. We work in the western banana plantations where sixteen banana plantations service transnational

Banana workers' encampment, Managua, 2010. Photo by Clifton Ross.

corporations. Here, we don't find fault with anyone. Everyone's equal. Everyone's entitled to the same things. Lots of people have come here to distribute food and the only thing we ask for is order. We're not in the military; we're nothing like that, but we do need some kind of order, above all else.

First and foremost, we thank God. Secondly, we're grateful to the president [Daniel Ortega] who's given us this lodging, after sixteen years of struggle. We've marched one hundred forty kilometers (sixty-five miles). We've marched every six, eight months, through three administrations that never listened to a word [Violeta Chamarro, Enrique Bolaños, and Arnoldo Alemán]. They never heard a single word we had to say. That's why we're grateful to this new president who's given us these accommodations and who's helping us out with some food. It's not all positive, but we're grateful for the rice, beans, and oil he gives us. Though what we need here is money, everything, actually. A little more than just rice and beans: a little egg, some soup, whatever, or it's not really a meal. We're sick, malnourished. We're getting worse. We're dying.

They've sent in a doctor, but it's of little use because the banana plantation is making us chronically sick. They've been spraying with a PCB called Nemagon. We know its name because some of our members were foremen, bosses in the banana plantation and they know that the poison they sprayed stays in the ground one hundred and twenty years, so it was a deadly thing to do. We have a lot of sick people here with chronic diseases, people who have ovarian cancer, stomach cancer, whose hair is falling out, who are going blind. We have people who have skin cancer, cancer wracking their body. This cancer you see in my hand, we all have it. There are people who look just fine, but they have these tumors inside. Once they're operated on, you can tell they're in poor shape. You can tell they're just victims hanging onto their lives by a thread until God knows when.

We're taking part in this struggle so that the transnational corporations hear us, so that maybe they'll come here and see each case. We're open to talking with them. The last time we engaged in dialogue, three or four years ago, it was under a president we were able to unseat from this organization because he swindled us. He said he had connections to the transnationals, but he didn't. They swindled us, with all their lawyers. We don't need lawyers. What we need is the transnationals to meet us face to face, so they can see firsthand where we stand. We have enough proof to show them exactly how we're working, and what diseases we have. We want them to see for themselves. The president may have helped us out with some food and this place to stay, but he hasn't addressed any of our other concerns. We're left hanging out to dry. There are groups that have come here from the United States—university students.

We've written thousands of letters, letters to the president, demanding that he contact the transnationals and meet with us because everyone here is dying. Time is going by and we're getting old. I'm fifty-five years old. He's sixty. They're in their fifties. We're middle-aged cancer victims who will never see a single penny for all the diseases they've given us. What they did to us was deadly. They never offered us any protection. It was like they hit us with an atomic bomb that injured everyone. They exploded their bomb and then took off. Not a single company took responsibility for what occurred. There are seven corporations that are responsible. The worst are Standard Fruit Company, Dole, and Chiquita, but there are seven in all. And those seven are deaf to our demands. We don't want to pay a lawyer because, well, how can poor people pay a lawyer? So that's what's going on here.

The only thing that's keeping us going is the food the president sends our way. We don't have any other resources. Our children have grown tired of supporting us the last three years of our seventeen years in the struggle. And in those three years, we didn't achieve our goal because we've had to go back and forth and nothing has gotten resolved. So we're asking our government to help us make some ties with the U.S. government or with its companies. We're taking that position. Seventeen years, we've been on six marches. We've come on foot eleven, fourteen days. Now we can no longer make the journey on foot because we've grown sicker, because the reality is that now everyone's wasting away. If doctors were to evaluate us, they'd say we're not good for anything anymore, you know? I can no longer stand for very long because my back begins to ache so, my spine is swollen, and I have this cancerous hand. My compañeros also have chronic stomach problems. There are those that have what I have in my hand, in their spine. There are people here who are bedridden, who can't even get up anymore, and those in worse shape are in Chinandega. Some are really bad off in Chinandega.

Maybe you can't really see how sick I am. But if I were to take you to see my friends in Chinandega who are worse off and can't even walk anymore . . . . You know, there's a girl who's name was Antonia Leyton [Vásquez]. That girl had a tumor so big, she could no longer get up. It was choking her. So this girl died. I couldn't have her here because I had nothing healthy to feed her, much less medicine. But all this fell on deaf ears. We spent years and years marching. I think only crooks have their ear. At least in the United States, the government only seems to listen to crooks.

But as for us, there's not a single political party that will listen. Look, here we are in front of the assembly and house of deputies in vain. Frankly, come election time, they're out hugging everyone, and this and that, but as far as they're concerned, there's been no sign of us on the 24th of December, or the 31st. Never, though I've sent about twenty letters [for those occasions], and Mother's Day cards, because there are older stateswomen who might be motivated to open such a card on Mother's Day or on the 24th or 31st, but no one read [a single card]. It's a lie that they are working on this. They never work on anything like this. Our demands are against the transnational corporations. But the government also has to do its part, or else we're never going to reach any agreement.

Gloria Paniagua, Otro Mundo Es Posible (Another World Is Possible)
"We maintain autonomy to the degree that we keep ourselves on the margins of political parties"

Interview and translation by Clifton Ross, January 2010

The office of Otro Mundo Es Posible shared space with the gay, lesbian, and transgender movement in the Casa Giordando Bruno in Managua. The autonomous organization was working hard to maintain a space between the ruling FSLN on one side and the opposition, which includes old Contras and neoliberals, as well as members of MRS. It was a difficult balancing act but this mostly youth movement is doing its best to work in that small space and push for greater openness in Nicaragua.

"Another World Is Possible" is a movement that arose after 2001, initiated by solidarity between peoples, the war in Iraq, and also from looking toward the movement of the Zapatistas in Mexico and that resistance, as well as the resistance to the free trade agreements. The national movement in Nicaragua is composed of thirty-six organizations that do research and cultural work, and include environmental, indigenous, youth, and ecumenical organizations. While we like to talk about ourselves as being a national organization, most of us work in the Pacific and northern regions of the country.

We do lots of different work in solidarity with international struggles, but also here at home with our own members. We have two groups affected by agrochemicals: one is a group of former workers for the U.S. banana companies, and the other group is sugarcane workers. The latter worked in the San Antonio mill, which belongs to Pellas [a wealthy family, part of the Nicaraguan oligarchy].

As a regional and international movement we're anticapitalist and anti-patriarchal. It's the core of the matter in terms of economic, social, cultural, and environmental rights and how we see the effects of free trade agreements, and it also informs the way we organize meetings and activities as part of these international spaces. Our work doesn't just consist of showing solidarity, but also in promoting actions at the national and international levels. We work in international networks such as www.enlazandoalternativas.org, which is a bioregional network of Europe and Latin America. We also belong to the Hemispheric Social Alliance and we're the Nicaraguan founders of the Foro Mesoamericano de los Pueblos (The Central American Forum of the Peoples).

We've been developing themes for study or themes for action in a school for political education, now in its third year. We've developed research into free trade agreements in which we've focused on audiovisual media to educate people more easily, and we've also promoted permanent people's tribunals against European and U.S. multinationals.

We think of ourselves as an autonomous movement because, unfortunately, in our country there are social organizations that are tied to political parties. We're open in the sense that we see each other as equals and we have no [political] party affiliation. We believe that the autonomy of a social movement is maintained to the degree that we keep ourselves on the margins of political parties. At the same time we have to emphasize that we're political subjects because we're counting on a change in the system and we have to react to those changes.

[Those working in the Sandinista party] have shown that they don't have much political power to make those governing, the functionaries, change their minds; so this has been an obstacle in their organizations because they've been marginalized. They've been stuck helping processes of the government but they've not been able to make the kind of changes demanded by social organizations.

So for example, consumer organizations asked for an opening in the first year of [the Ortega] government and were ignored. So there was an opportunity and a moment for a possible opening to these social organizations and a validating of others that hadn't happened in sixteen years of neoliberal governments. It was an opportune moment but it passed, and we gained a certain clarity from it, because our analysis of the context when the Sandinista Front won was that we were changing governments, but not changing systems. This was very difficult, but it was clear that we needed to rely on the work in the social organizations without [regards to individual] interests, and work for the benefit of everyone. So we remained in the margins.

Some criticized us as right-wing and we had a very bitter experience of that in July 2008 when the Foro Mesoamericano de los Pueblos was held in Nicaragua. We invited those organizations that had formerly been in the social movement but had gone over to the [Sandinista] Front. They still had an affinity as NGOs toward the labor [issues] like all the other organizations of Mesoamericano so we thought it would be an opportunity to get together again, but it didn't happen like that. There were certain attacks from organizations [saying] that if we didn't involve the government from the convocation, they wouldn't participate; and we refused and were accused of being right-wing.

This was painful because the people, the representatives from outside, the foreign guests recognize our work, our position, our struggle, and that we know how to work and organize on a national and international level, so they weren't confused in this sense. But we'd also had experiences of working with the government on common causes such as the free trade agreements, in this case, with the European Union. And we've shared studies we'd done, like the Hemispheric Social Alliance which had a proposal for an alternative integration of peoples; we exchanged ideas and we had a forum exactly a year before in which social organizations and government representatives sat down to work at the same table.

When the Front (FSLN) lost the elections in 1990, there was a radical change as "progress" began, or at least that's what investors and the new government called it. They changed the streets, opened malls and this was going to generate work through Free Trade Zones and certain investment programs, but they were all cosmetic changes. None of this resolved the problems of poverty. The work was poorly paid and there were constant violations of the workers' rights. There was also constant pressure from the Chamber of Commerce, so you had to constantly be struggling for a minimum wage. This didn't help the situation.

Social movements face new challenges

Then the social struggles began: access to water; the rights of women; issues of the environment; and there were gains made by the social organizations prior to 2006, such as access to the law of information; the general law of water; the incorporation of some social organizations, which wasn't that great but there was an advance in that; the [struggle for] equal opportunities for women. And at that time it was much easier to protest those in power. Now it's a different situation, and it's like, "It's my party; I'm not going to protest." And those who protest are attacked by the base of the party.

We feel that it's hard to bring about internal changes in the government and the national situation, but when you're trying to make a democracy you have to be more willing to accept criticism. The process of making change with the neoliberal governments where we arrived with our demands and they received us has now changed; that process is closed off and it's more difficult. It's more difficult, for instance, to go out and march to ask that the government fulfill its electoral promises. That's more difficult.

For many social organizations it would have been encouraging if their party received their demands and there would have at least been the satisfaction that they were heard, even if it changed later. But that's not happening with the present government, and an example of that is that groups of evangelical [Christians] occupied the roundabouts of Managua as a way of taking them over. [The problem is the roundabouts] are the points of protest. There was also a process put in place so that when there was going to be a march the government brought out government workers and [Sandinista] members of the neighborhoods as shock forces against the marches. So there was a use of religion, with evangelicals out at the round-abouts for nearly a year, from July or August of last year to this July, with sound systems and permanent canopies and other resources, leading some to agree with reports that came out that the people were paid.

That's some of what happened last year and the Front has begun softening its tone but there's still an absence as regards democracy. There isn't much freedom of expression though we miraculously had a protest at the roundabout with people from the Front where there was no confrontation, because it was in solidarity with the Palestinian people about what had happened in 2008 in the Gaza Strip. It was the first time we found ourselves [with the Front] but I've never seen any other time that an organization managed to come out of such events unharmed.

And then there's the Coordinadora Civil (CC). We may be in disagreement with the Sandinista Front on some things and with it on others, but we continue struggling for our independence, to avoid party allegiance. But while we've not been able to be in complete agreement with the Front [Sandinista], neither do we express our disagreement by marching with the business sectors nor with the right-wing parties. In this, as a social movement, we must never be ideologically confused.

Over the course of the year [CC] has had two or three activities with political parties or business people, looking for points of agreement to push against this negativity toward democracy of the Sandinista Front, but we make this critique that we've had this political orientation to advocate for autonomy, not one side or another. I'm more or less in agreement with this, not completely, but I'm not willing to lose political focus. We're talking about political alliances, and they're necessary, but you have to have criteria for those alliances. It's sort of like trying to mix water and oil: I think there are some things better done together, but you have to be very careful about who you're making alliances with.

Spare change or real change?

There's been an increase of welfare [to the poor] compared to the previous governments of the 1990s. There have been improvements in education, in the area of health, and a certain investment in the family infrastructures of those with very little: housing, of housing for those with few resources, but that hasn't been adequate to make the deep changes that the country needs to improve. In that sense as a social movement we think that the funds coming from ALBA [the Venezuela-based Alternativa Bolivariana para las Américas] need to go into the state coffers and not to a growing bourgeoisie that is growing wealthy from that money.

This welfare approach is best seen around Christmas when little packages of food are handed out to the poor families. But this sort of thing would be better solved if they invested more in creating jobs, but not the sort of jobs where investors are invited to invest in the countryside with industrial parks. So there has to be a greater interest in generating employment, not of the kind that invites foreign investors, but rather of state jobs. I think there is where the Front has failed, because it could have reinvested the money from ALBA in this.

So that's how I see it: these are limitations, limitations for Nicaragua, limitations for the [FSLN] party, so it's difficult when you don't have control over the way that resources should enter [the country]. Because if they lose the elections, which is already very likely, there'll be nothing for the people. The wallet will close and there'll be nothing because then the party will have other concerns, no longer being in power.

Victor Hugo Tinoco, Sandinista Renewal Movement (Movimiento de Renovación Sandinista, MRS)
"We're talking about a recovery of the Sandinismo of the epoch of Sandino, the decade of the 1930s, and a recovery of the Sandinismo of the 1970s"

Interview and translation by Clifton Ross, January 2010

Victor Hugo Tinoco entered the FSLN in 1973 and soon became a commander of a guerrilla column. After the victory of the Revolution, he became Sandinista ambassador to the United Nations, then worked as chancellor in charge of many historic negotiations with the Contadora group, the United States, and the Contras. After the electoral defeat, he was elected political secretary of the FSLN. He was elected twice to terms in Parliament as an FSLN delegate (1996, 2002) and served in the national directorate of the FSLN until 2005. He went head-to-head with Daniel Ortega in the FSLN's 2001 internal presidential primary and narrowly lost. When he ran again in internal elections challenging Ortega in 2005, on a ticket with Herty Lewites, both he and Lewites were expelled from the party. He has served as a delegate to Parliament for the MRS since 2007. We met for this interview in Tinoco's office at the Nicaraguan Parliament.

Two theses have developed in the struggle within the FSLN since 1990. There were those who developed the opinion that the struggle for social justice wasn't compatible with civil liberties, so there had to be authoritarian thought married to the proposal of social transformation. And there were those who saw these [ideas] as complementary, that social justice can only be attained through a process that profoundly respects civil social and individual freedoms, and furthermore that social transformations are only sustainable over time if they are built and sustained on the basis of respect for civil rights and liberties.

In the 1970s there was a lot of debate. There were different positions and there were even three Sandinista fronts, divided a bit on the issue of freedom and citizens' rights, but more importantly on the method of struggle and what emphasis on methods of struggle: whether to prioritize the city, the countryside, or the workers.

Victor Hugo Tinoco, Sandinista Renewal Movement. Photo by Clifton Ross.

Then the Revolution won and almost immediately thereafter Reagan, who was the antithesis of the revolutionary movement, came to power [in the United States]. While revolutionary movements made gains in the Americas, in the United States the conservative movement advanced, so war began almost immediately. This in effect forced the ideological debate to another level, and [made] the implementation and development of a vertical, authoritarian practice justifiable by circumstances the whole world recognized. That was the '80s.

In the '90s, after the electoral defeat, the debate on democracy opened up at a new level. The opening that happened then began to grow in the processes of internal elections, internal debates, and discussions, leading to the problem of '95, and reached an equilibrium. This produced a schism in '95, the separation of the first group, who formed the MRS, from the original Sandinista Front. Other debates opened up inside the Sandinista Front after '95, but more than a debate, it was an argument of the deaf between those who pushed an authoritarian mentality and those of us who followed the line that respect for civil liberties wasn't in conflict with struggles for justice.

Then from '95, '96, and forward, the democratic spaces began to shrink in Sandinista thought. The authoritarian sector little by little began to close off the possibilities of party democracy, which shut in 2001. The final closing came as a result of the agreement Daniel Ortega made with the leader of the ultra-right, Arnoldo Alemán, the "pact" that gave power to the two of them. At this stage the Left, recently coming out of the opposition and returning to power, now governed with a program that really was of the absolute right: sanctioning free trade agreements at an international level, and trying to hide that with some social assistance projects and measures designed to help a small part of the population, but which have no implication for the social or economic transformation of the country in any real or deep terms.

By 2005 [Ortega] finished closing all possibilities of debate within the Front with the expulsion of the principal leaders of the party, the principal leaders of the current we could call civil liberties, [and in doing so] he expelled the most popular man in Nicaragua, Herty Lewites, the mayor of Managua. Why did he expel him? Because in internal elections [Lewites] would have won and Daniel Ortega knew he would lose. It had cost [Ortega] a lot to beat me when he accepted the only challenge [to his leadership] in 2001 as the result of strong pressure from the democratizing current in the Front. He'd beat me in 2001 by a relatively small margin, so when the internal primary elections came around again in 2005 for the 2006 election, we ran Herty, but [Ortega] would no longer accept challenges.

He did three things: First, the same day, he expelled Herty and me from the National Direction of the [FSLN] party. Second, he suspended internal elections. And third, he declared himself candidate. So he closed all possibilities and enthroned authoritarian control of the official apparatus of the Sandinista Front, forcing another group of people out of the [FSLN] to enter the ranks of the MRS. So the MRS, which was born in '95 as a weak challenge, was reinforced in 2005 and became a party with more weight and influence in [Nicaraguan] society.

Ortega went on to win the elections, not because he got more or less votes than earlier elections, but because the right-wing parties divided into 30 and 30 percent. Ortega in these last elections of 2006 got fewer votes than he did in 2001 and he won fewer votes in that election than he did in 1996. That is to say, in real terms, he hasn't advanced as a beloved leader of the population. What he has done is to control and manipulate the party apparatus and keep captive that percent of the population most firmly Sandinista, which represents about 30 percent, by proclaiming himself candidate and obliging them to vote for him, since he won't allow for any internal competition within Sandinismo.

The MRS is a political force that proposes social justice as necessarily united with the struggle for citizen's rights, and that the only social [program] possible, at least in Nicaragua, is one built alongside of struggle for civil liberties. You can't pretend to make profound social change permanent and stable simply [by] imposing yourself and forcing yourself on your ranks, but by winning the hearts and consciences of people. That, at root, is a political platform and at the same time an ethical program that comes into conflict with the authoritarian worldview that "power is power," and he who has it must exercise it.

The authoritarian politics of personal wealth
Since 2005 the deformation of "Orteguismo" has reached its maximum expression: It's no longer just the expression of authoritarian thought, but it now has become corrupt through tremendous enrichment. Large sums of money have begun to arrive from Venezuela without any monitoring by the state or any public institution.

The money from cooperation with Venezuela could have been managed by Ortega the way it was managed in El Salvador, or Guatemala or in Honduras. There the cooperation comes and enters the republic supervised by the institutions of state, but here they decided to privatize the aid. So the official state-to-state aid comes in the form of aid from a Venezuelan state business into a private Nicaraguan business, which is dominated by the Ortega family, [and] gives no information. There's no doubt that some part of this money goes to social projects, but just how much no one can say with any certainty.

Fraudulent elections
There's abundant proof of fraud [in the November, 2008 national municipal elections]. There were elections in one hundred fifty municipalities and [the FSLN] robbed the elections in fifty. In the other one hundred the results were more or less real, but in fifty, among them the most important, the capitals and the larger cities of the country, the elections were stolen and were fraudulent. That was revealed after the fact.

For example, here in Managua today, one and a half years later, they still haven't revealed the results of six hundred polling centers of a total of three thousand and these six hundred, according to the data from opposition groups, have been signed and the results changed. So there certainly was fraud, including fraud that was, in its original design, organized by Alemán, the most right-wing, corrupt leader in Nicaragua. But he didn't know the full extent of the fraud and thought it wouldn't be so enormous nor so evident.

So today there are six hundred polling stations without any data reported, none written or recorded, not on the Internet or anywhere else. Those results remain secret.

The alliance between Alemán and Daniel Ortega continues to be the main threat to democracy, civil liberties, and the way out of poverty. We'll never develop economically in this country as long as we live in constant political and armed crises. And this dual authoritarian threat of both the Right and the Left needs to be beaten, though right now the greater problem is Orteguismo, because that's what's in power. Right now [Ortega] has more money than the authoritarianism of the Right; he has more money from aid from [Hugo] Chávez. So both have to be stopped and that will only happen if there are free elections.

Daniel Ortega doesn't have the possibility of winning free elections. He's not the Chávez phenomenon: Daniel Ortega has less social backing as time goes on. His power rests in having co-opted and controlled the institutional apparatus of the FSLN. In historical experiences like ours—where the parties like the Sandinista Front aren't classical parties with a program but rather parties with an emotional draw, because they had to do with a war, with death—the bonds are much stronger. Ortega takes advantage of this sociological phenomenon of emotional adherence to the flag because, even though many people within Sandinismo don't agree with him, he knows they aren't going to leave this flag.

So a new Sandinismo is being built, and on the one hand, a lot of Sandinistas are seeing themselves reflected. On the other hand, there are many who were previously controlled by their political adherence to liberalism and they've also begun to see in the MRS an option that they could feel good about. For the latter they see in the MRS its complexity but also its power to attract other sectors of the Left, as well independents, and that part of the population that isn't Sandinista but who could opt for the MRS.

Recovering Sandinismo

The MRS is capable of attracting votes and you can see that in the statistical and demographical analysis, which shows that at this stage those attracted to the MRS are the young urban population. Remember that the Sandinista Revolution was basically young and urban: it wasn't a campesino revolution. So it's this same situation again, which is why I'm not concerned with the criticism that the MRS is a bunch of intellectuals with no strength in the countryside. We do have strength in the city. For example, in Matagalpa we got 2 percent of the vote but in Managua we got 20 percent, you see? [Our support] depends on the level of information and education and our support will grow because we have a very clear program.

First, we want to recover the proposal of unity and complementarity of social justice and social freedoms, civil liberties; that's the first priority. Second, we want to recover the issue of ethics, [deal with] issues of corruption and all the great problems that authoritarian thinking has unleashed.

The other great issue that the MRS is attempting to recover is the issue of democratic institutions, the importance of respect for those institutions and respect for the law, the constitution. Those are the three great issues we're working on and which are motivating us.

That's a recovery of Sandinismo, and we're talking about the Sandinismo of Sandino, the epoch of Sandino, the decade of the 1930s, and a recovery of the Sandinismo of the 1970s, that is, of the dictatorship of Somoza. Sandino never proposed an authoritarian model. Sandino came to propose a model of cooperativist participation in the fields of production. So we want to recover this focus of the historical Sandino but we also want to recover the historical thought of the Sandinista Front of the struggle against the dictatorship, which was a line of thought that was profoundly antidictatorial.

Generations were involved and died in the struggle against the dictator. They died not to substitute a dictator of the Right with a leftist dictator. No one would have died for that. Everyone would have just gone home. The people wanted to replace the dictator, who was the negation of civil liberties, the negation of individual rights, a criminal, a murderer; they wanted to replace him with a government of freedom with a social program. That was the Sandinismo that overthrew Somoza, the Sandinismo we want to recover. That's basically the idea that nourishes Sandinista thought, and that's why you'll find a good part of the historical leaders of Sandinismo in this movement.

Luisa Molina, Civil Coordinating Committee (Coordinadora Civil)
"We have to develop a strategic work of the mental transformation of Nicaraguans"

Interview and translation by Clifton Ross, January 2010

Rebuilding "civil society" after the turbulent 1980s has been a slow, complex process. Working to this end is the Coordinadora Civil, which Luisa Molina called "an open space for the organization of civil society." It's a heterogenous organization that has been criticized and attacked by the Left and the Right as it attempts to encourage the growth of critical, political subjectivity in a society that continues to be polarized.

Luisa Molina participated in the revolutionary struggle to overthrow the Somoza dictatorship and rebuild the country under the direction of the FSLN, but like many others she became increasingly critical of the Sandinistas under the direction of President Daniel Ortega, as she details here. For her criticism

Luisa Molina, standing next to a picture of Sandino, with the banner of her organization, Coordinadora Civil, in the background. Photo by Clifton Ross.

she has been physically attacked, threatened, and slandered in the press, but she continues to be an outspoken critic of the official parties, including the FSLN, and an advocate for citizen empowerment.

The Civil Coordinating Committee (CC) includes networks of women, youth, children, teachers, health workers, indigenous people, African descendants, regional networks, and other social movement organizations. Represented here are federations, territorial networks that work together in departments and cities of the country with some two thousand people and six hundred such organizations involving, at a political and organizational level, more than twenty thousand Nicaraguans.

The CC was founded in October 1998 with Hurricane Mitch. We became a space to watch over the social situation of our country and then we recognized that our role as an organization wasn't for emergency and reconstruction, because we weren't the government, so we constituted ourselves as a civil coordinator for intervention on public policies. Later we recognized that in addition to intervening on public policy, the center of our work had to be political, the transformation of subjects in the building of citizenship for changing Nicaraguans. We've been doing that now for twelve years.

Building citizens, not parties, is our purpose
The purpose of the CC is to function as an organizational space to find consensus on the development and strengthening of the citizen's role in

society, because in Nicaragua we've seen little of social movements or of an autonomous civil society. In general, until these last few years, civil society in Nicaragua has always responded to a political party's vision or a religious vision or a vision from powerful economic groups, so the CC has taken an autonomous role before those groups representing economic power, or a political or religious ideology.

The reason we take this stance as our philosophy is because these three elements or factors, the political, religious and economic, have polarized the country. Nicaragua is a very diverse country. Here we have more than thirty indigenous peoples, descendants of Africa; some of us are mestizos, others are Afro-descendant; others are diverse for their sexual preference; we have different religions, and some of us have no religion, while others have no party affiliation. There needs to be a space for civil society to come together on the principle of inclusivity and diversity; a representation of what Nicaragua is: that we are multiethnic, multicultural, pluricultural and, as we say here, multicolored (*variopintos*).

The option, the vision, the mission of the CC, is to work with citizens. We don't have, nor do we want to have, any particular party slant. The historical political culture of the political parties in Nicaragua is electoral and based on patronage and as such won't allow for democracy. They aren't the sorts of parties that allow for analysis, or to come to consensus in their assemblies. Rather, they're based on the leadership of caudillos; that's the culture in Nicaragua and today the Sandinista Front is called the "family's party" because the majority of Nicaraguans are clear that this isn't the Sandinista front that we once belonged to. This is the party of a family, [Daniel] Ortega–[Rosario] Murillo, and around that party with the "Sandinista Front" brand is a group with economic power. It's an electoral party, a party without a vision for the country nor even a vision of sensitivity toward the fact that this is a country needing to change its political culture.

The culture of these parties has been to maintain the subordination of their ranks, which they see as clients, subordinates, a mass, or militants, believers, or base, but not as people, as legal or political subjects, but as people to be subordinated to a misnamed "democratic centralism" or what they call a true democracy. These are the parties we've had for a hundred and fifty years in Nicaragua. They live on and never worry about changing. And we have hundreds of years of being educated to be servile—servants, vassals, not legal subjects.

We broke with this conception in 1979 when we made a revolution. The Sandinista Front had hundreds of thousands of militants, and I was one of them. It wasn't only the Sandinista Front that made the revolution, but the people, all Nicaraguans down to the children—thousands of children died in the revolution and the counterrevolution. And for that very reason we're working with the concept of citizenship, which, for Nicaraguans, is a new idea. But it has to be established as a basis for social power, and to get from here to where we want to go. The political parties have had 150 years to modernize, and that should be enough time for parties from the Left to the Right to modernize—and at present we have no left parties in Nicaragua; they're all right-wing.

It's this analysis that the CC has made and on which it's based its work over these past twelve years. We don't want to be a political party nor an opposition. What we want is a citizenry with a critical vision of those [parties] and the economic, political, social, and cultural history of our country. That's exactly why we keep our focus on the building of citizenship because the degree to which the diverse citizenry that lives here in Nicaragua changes its way of seeing things and its way of seeing political culture, is the degree to which we as people are going to press the parties to change. We don't believe we're going to change the parties, but if we can change people, the parties will change.

Democracy has to be built with information and with a conception based on culture but a culture has to be based on equality, in a culture of equity, and not in a culture of power and hierarchy from the family to the church. There has to be a collective construction on the basis of ethical principles.

So breaking with that authoritarian, patriarchal, *machista* culture, twisted by political parties, led by caudillos, this can't be done in a single year, nor by working inside the parties themselves. We have to develop a strategic work of the mental transformation of Nicaraguans, and that's what we're doing. We don't work situation by situation, but rather we work to change this entire conception.

Present government is not revolutionary

In fact the present government is a government with a traditional political party like any right-wing party. It's not a revolutionary party, nor could you call the people in it revolutionaries of the twenty-first century, nor revolutionaries like those thirty years ago. For instance, all the neoliberal governments of the past fifteen years here in Nicaragua have had an IMF economic policy and this government has fulfilled 100 percent, and more, all the policies of the IMF. So this government, and the earlier ones, all assume they're the owners of the country and they make decisions that commit the entire nation, every citizen, with policies of debt, for instance, and we're never consulted. The previous governments had no political or national vision which would include the diversity of who we as Nicaraguans are, but neither does this one. The previous governments did nothing about the extreme poverty and the extreme debt we Nicaraguans have with those in the countryside, and neither does this present government: the previous because they were right-wing neoliberal bourgeois governments and the same with this one, even though it says it's an ally of the poor.

Really, this government hasn't invested a single *córdoba* to reduce poverty in the countryside or the extreme poverty in the rural areas of the Caribbean coast. Currently more than 70 percent of Nicaraguans live on twenty córdobas [less than one U.S. dollar] a day. A pound of rice is six córdobas; a pound of beans, seven; a liter of milk, eleven and in a Nicaraguan family there are three, four or five people. A person can't live on a dollar a day, much less three people.

This government has made agreements with Venezuela and it receives $350 million petrodollars, and these $350 million are administered by the Ortega-Murillo family. This budget isn't reviewed by the National Assembly, and the people don't know what happens with this money. It builds a house and people in this country, with a culture of mendacity developed by the political parties, thank Mr. Daniel Ortega because he "gave" them a house. But it wasn't really Mr. Daniel Ortega but the people of Venezuela who are sharing their money, and I doubt that all the people of Venezuela know they're sharing $350 million with the Nicaraguans. That's the reality here in Nicaragua.

At the same time here in Nicaragua there are more than twenty-five thousand families that aren't taken into account, suffering hunger. This government came into power in 2007, now three years ago, and the problem of hunger isn't new. I can understand, even if it shames me, that the previous governments haven't had a policy to resolve the problem of hunger, even if one could easily be developed. After all, Nicaragua is the geographically largest country of Central America, with 138,000 square kilometers [50,446 square miles] and 5.3 million inhabitants, which is to say that there's plenty of land for each person, yet here is the problem of land, which they don't want to resolve because of many personal interests. There's a problem with the indigenous people who own lands, like in the reserve of Bosawas, they haven't the right to enforce their laws because this supposedly "revolutionary" government, which could have resolved the problem in the first year with political will, hasn't done so. So our country is unfortunately one of the poorest countries of the Americas despite it having the potential to be the wealthiest of Central America, due to its small population and enormous land base.

As a sociologist, I know what liberalism is, but I don't know what "revolutionary" means anymore because two years ago a law approving therapeutic abortions dating back to 1860 was overturned. The law had been approved to save the lives of thousands of women who live in the countryside and who get pregnant without realizing it, and this present government, through a pact with big capital and the upper hierarchy of the Catholic Church overturned this right women had from previous centuries. Neither has this government complied with the international Convention on the Rights of Children, where it says that childhood and adolescence must be the highest interest of the nation.

We of the CC are part of a regional social movement in Central America and through the World Social Forum we've shared different opinions and political positions on how to make a democratic revolution. We're trying to help build these new paradigms and the only thing we know for sure is that we have to build collective projects by consensus and maintain our autonomy. I think that's the challenge for civil society in Latin America: that political parties have come to consensus, but not social movements. We have so many restrictions, such as economic restrictions that don't allow us to have daily meetings or don't allow us to build a conceptual referential framework that would bring about an agreement on paradigms and which concept of what paradigm.

The autonomous spaces are very few and the majority are tied to political parties. I would say that the only autonomous space [in Nicaragua] is the Coordinadora Civil and that we don't really get any resources. On one hand we're accused of being right-wing, and others accuse us of being leftists. Really what we want is autonomy, and this has a political and an economic cost.

Yamilet Mejía, feminist lawyer and activist
"In terms of sexual rights and reproductive rights, there has been an incredible regression"

Interview by Marcy Rein and Clifton Ross, October 2012
Translation by Luis Ballesteros

When we first met Yamilet Mejía, we interviewed her at her workplace at the Network of Women against Violence in July 2004. The FSLN had yet to return to power, but the Ortega-Alemán Pact, accusations against Ortega for rape and molestation of his stepdaughter, and the lack of will among the Sandinistas to take a firm stand for women's rights, especially the right to choose to give birth or not, had all undermined women's support for the FSLN. Mejía has since moved on to independent legal consulting with a variety of women's groups. In 2007 she, along with Luisa Molina of the Coordinadora Civil and seven other women, came under attack by a right-wing human rights organization financed by the Catholic Church. They accompanied a nine-year-old girl, who was impregnated after being raped and whose life was at risk, to an abortion clinic.[17] *For this they faced prison on charges of "crimes against public administration," "concealment of rape," "conspiracy to commit a crime," and "incitement to commit a crime." All the charges were dropped in February 2010, but those charged were not notified until April 28, 2010.*

In Nicaragua the government remains in the 1980s, a decade when women weren't allowed to promote their real demands, such as the fight for abortion, the right to decide over their own bodies. This explains why many feminist women left the party and many were expelled once the Sandinista Front became a political party.

We're a coalition of that large movement of women who backed the accusation and still stand side by side with girls and women who have lived through sexual violence because their bodies have been used by and for men who perpetrate these types of violations against the rights of women.

In 1998 we backed the denunciation made by Zoilamérica Ortega of the repeated rape and various violations she had suffered from Daniel Ortega, and that let us see how the party colluded with him and did not proceed to condemn that violation of the human rights of one who at that time was a child, and then a woman when she decided to file the actual complaint.

By 2004–2006, we were already being subjected to political persecution by the Sandinista Front. They started to see us as enemies, no longer as allies. In due course, various expressions of this women's movement in Nicaragua opposed even the candidacy of Daniel Ortega because of his history of rape and abuse of his stepdaughter. We could not allow such a candidate. Still, the outcome is clear since the political pact between the Sandinista Front and the Liberal Party headed by Arnoldo Alemán. Now there's going to be an election in the country and there are no democratic conditions that would suggest transparent elections.

Attacks on the Autonomous Movement of Women

Women in this feminist movement have been victims of political persecution and nine of us, including me, have been brought up on charges. We have been victims of complaints aimed at demobilizing and demoralizing us, using institutions such as the attorney general's office to order searches against the Autonomous Movement of Women and, for example, Centro de Investigación de la Comunicación (CINCO, Center for the Investigation of Communication). The directors of this Center are journalist Carlos Fernando Chamorro and the feminist journalist Sofía Montenegro. They searched the premises together with the police, using excessive force, forced the doors open, and took away the computers, under the assumption that we were laundering money and moving it around illegally. They leveled other charges as well. We are not criminals, we are just social movements that defend the rights of men, women, and children in this country.

They wove a web of lies to fabricate crimes. In the end, they had to return everything they took from the Autonomous Movement of Women and CINCO. We publicly declared that no crime was proven, because we're not criminals. They label us "imperialists" to slander us as a part of their dirty tactics. They infiltrated the Coordinadora Civil to make up stories about embezzlement and slander them with lies.

Contradictions in the law on violence against women

Now, the issue of human rights has lagged behind in the Nicaraguan context, despite the existence of a law against violence toward women, which was passed last December and enacted as recently as June [2012]. This law already includes femicide and numberless crimes against women and even though it is true that the whole assembly approved it, it has no budget.

At least one or two million dollars are required to be able to set in motion this law on violence against women, which clearly deals also with sexual abuse. Then as a woman, are you going to file an accusation if the institutions don't have the means to act? If you don't allocate a budget to a law, then it isn't going to work. It's going to be a dead letter.

Here in Nicaragua there were two legal initiatives, one from the Supreme Court and another from the María Elena Cuadra Movement of Women. So the best part of each of the two legal initiatives was put together and it turned out to be a good law, on paper, but with many gaps that you identify when you assist the victims. Thus there would seem to be progress but there are also many steps backward. In terms of sexual rights and reproductive rights, there has been an incredible regression because of having repealed and penalized abortion and having also included it in that law of violence against women. They have included the crime of abortion, which entails a contradiction.

They have a "Zero Hunger" program that consists of giving animals to the people—poultry, pigs, or cows—but the people are very impoverished, and they need to incur expenses to feed the animals. Then, when they have to decide between feeding their children or a pig, they eat the pig.

A government that passes itself off as socialist, Christian, solidary, and the like, is committing a very serious sin by perpetuating poverty with its policies that only promote begging and have people stretching out their hands to receive charity, instead of policies to create decent jobs.

There have been critical mobilizations, and to counter them, the Sandinista Front has paid a lot of youngsters to go against those demonstrations and throw stones at us and attack us in many other ways ... sheer vandalism! Any social protest that takes the streets faces a demonstration promoted by the Sandinista Front and, besides, they use the national police to go against the people.

What is even crueler is that the police are a part of that revolution, and they know most of us who participate in the social movements protesting an oppressive system in Nicaragua where they're closing the spaces for participation, after having completely closed the state's institutional channels for participation.

We are in a dictatorship. We believe that we are in a dictatorship that we need to dismantle. Nicaragua doesn't deserve to be in a dictatorship again. We already had a forty-year dictatorship with Anastasio Somoza and this man [Ortega] can't do the same again.

About two months ago, a group of young people put a sign in front of the Supreme Electoral Council to protest. Then they were attacked by different groups related to the Sandinista Front and even made a woman abort. This is a sign that they are building something dirtier and Machiavellian, warning the population that they could be next if they go on the streets to protest.

I am still optimistic because I see that we in the social movements are doing the little we can here in Nicaragua, which is constant denunciation and promoting a different way to do things, using different means because we can no longer take to the streets without facing a counterdemonstration. In cyberspace we are helping to raise awareness through means of communication that are not progovernment, and we are doing door-to-door work. For example, we are working with the women in each territory of this country with our meager resources, and we continue to raise critical consciousness.

The social movements were probably active in the work of the revolution but the social movement of women was also active in the movement to fight for the social rights of women and for true equality and democracy in our country. We were promoting the right to abort, promoting sexual and reproductive rights, and speaking about violence against women and at least giving a name to it, which resulted in the expulsion of many women [from the FSLN]. Women like Sofía Montenegro, Patricia Orozco, and Martha Munguía were critics who identified violence and criticized the violence-prone attitudes of their male comrades of the Sandinista Front.

Situations like this led women to organize their own social movement to promote their own cause. At a personal level, I can say that the Left here or anywhere else has not defended the rights of women. It has not been a priority of this sector but only of us as a women's movement. Nationwide it is very difficult to coordinate with the state institutions. In the departments and municipalities it is an easier task, as 10 percent of the people are receptive to our political work regarding the treatment of women, at least in the area of violence against women. There is no chance to raise the issue of abortion as it is criminalized and this would be considered incitement to crime.

An NGO is a legal figure that can be used by social movements. NGOs cannot substitute for social movements, because the latter are the ones that create change in a society. But an NGO can be a legal instrument to assure that social movements can be supported in their ideas and activities.

The MRS (Sandinista Renewal Movement) was deprived of its legal status and they don't intend to give it back. The MRS filed a legal complaint with the Supreme Court of Justice and they have not received an answer yet, but they are generating a full-fledged social movement. They have not stood idly by after their legal status was taken away from them, and they continue to work with the people. To be able to hold some seats in the Legislative Assembly they made an alliance with the PLI (Independent Liberal Party).

They are working with the grassroots, visiting the departments, holding assemblies and doing a continuous review of the constitution. They are promoting a critical social consciousness with the population, doing the door-to-door work I told you about, in order to inform the people, who otherwise would not have access to information because of their extreme poverty.

I am still a member of the Autonomous Movement of Women. I am still in Petateras, in the Network of Women against Violence, which is where I acquired my critical consciousness to defend the rights of women, and I think I will continue to do that until the day I die.

Colombia

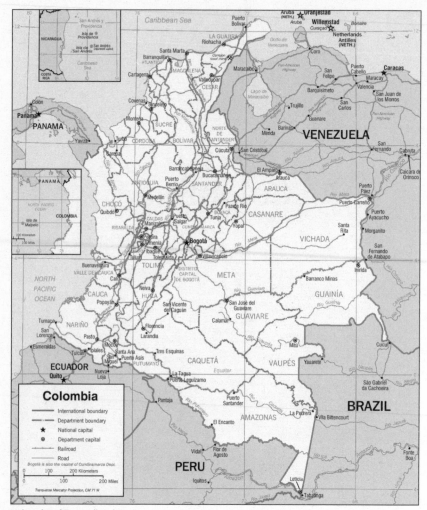

University of Texas Libraries

Colombia's countercurrent: Historical paradoxes of a democracy in crisis

By Mario A. Murillo

From the standpoint of broader Latin American political trends, Colombia serves up many interesting paradoxes for the historian, analyst, or activist, especially since its overall trajectory has so often gone against the prevailing currents of any particular moment in the hemisphere's history.

For example, when the nations of the South were dominated by military dictatorships from the 1960s through the 1980s, Colombia presented to the world an image of "democratic stability," characterized by the "peaceful" transfer of power between two dominant political parties who, for a generation, were embraced in a marriage of convenience known as the National Front, while truly oppositional forces were completely locked out of the electoral equation.[1] Later, as almost every Latin American country suffered the economic stagnation and the political repercussions caused by the trauma of the 1980s debt crisis, Colombia witnessed continued economic growth, buffered somewhat by the narcodollars that flooded just about every sector of the national economy, despite the drug war's negative impact on institutions of the state.[2]

And in recent years, while much of the hemisphere has lived under the elected leadership of a broad range of left-leaning governments, critical of the perpetual U.S. dominance of the strategic and development affairs of the region, Colombia has been governed by leaders who have had no compunctions about defending the interests of Washington as their own, whether manifested in further militarizing the drug war, or embarking on wide-ranging bilateral free trade agreements. This was especially the case under the eight-year presidency of Álvaro Uribe Vélez, who alienated regional leaders again and again because of his unflinching embrace of George W.

Bush's global war on terror. Current president Juan Manuel Santos, despite serving as Uribe's defense minister, has since distanced himself from many of Uribe's domestic and foreign policy initiatives, although he continues to represent a solid partner for Washington's broader interests, more so than any other government in the region.

Perpetual paradox

The Colombian establishment and its political leaders take pride in having one of the "oldest democracies in the Americas," yet the country has been tainted by an unprecedented two hundred years of extreme political violence that has gone on unabated, even to this day.[3] Colombia is rich in natural resources but continues to have one of the most uneven income distribution levels in the region, with almost 40 percent of its population of forty-six million living at or below the poverty line.[4] It is a multicultural, pluri-ethnic country of tremendous ethnic and regional diversity, yet its political class has been dominated by a predominantly white elite that has always identified itself first and foremost with its Spanish—that is, European—roots, institutionally marginalizing Colombians of African descent, indigenous peoples, and mestizo peasants of mixed ancestry.

To complicate the picture a bit further, there is another characteristic of contemporary Colombian society that makes it an exceptional case study, not quite fitting into any easy formulas or definitions. That is, notwithstanding the long history of systematic violence and intolerance directed at the country's most marginalized sectors, over the last forty years Colombia has developed a strong tradition of political and social dissent, with a dynamic civil society engaged in sophisticated campaigns of popular resistance, democratic participation, and community mobilization throughout the country.

From the alphabet soup that makes up the trade union movement to the disciplined militancy of peasant farmer associations, from the grassroots organizing of community mothers to consciousness-building campaigns of public university students, from the Afro-Colombian leaders fighting against state-sponsored racism and economic injustice to the many local, regional, and national organizations representing the country's over ninety officially recognized indigenous groups, Colombian civil society continues to challenge the profoundly undemocratic nature of the state, and its powerful benefactors who control the levers of both national and transnational private capital.

In raising their voices, these social movement activists have confronted extraordinary levels of unrepentant violence characterized by mass killings, forced displacement, and a wide array of egregious human rights abuses directed at them by the principal actors in the armed conflict: the military and national police, drug traffickers, right-wing paramilitaries, and left-wing guerrillas.

This consistent repression has led to the emergence of a vast network of independent, nongovernmental human rights organizations represent-ing the countless victims (and surviving family members) of torture, extra-judicial executions, forced disappearances, territorial displacement, kid-napping, and other crimes against humanity carried out in the country throughout its recent history. Colombian human rights workers continue to play an essential role as allies with the popular social movement in pro-moting transparency, fighting for justice for the victims of terror—state-sponsored and otherwise—and demanding their inclusion in any national dialogue designed to bring an end to the decades-long conflict.

These nonviolent popular struggles and campaigns of civil resistance have unfolded alongside seemingly endless leftist armed insurgencies that, with their primary roots in the peasant movements of the 1940s and '50s, have taken up arms to confront the institutions of the state. The largest group, the Revolutionary Armed Forces of Colombia (FARC) has evolved considerably since its emergence in 1964, and no longer garners much popular support from the vast majority of the Colombian people.[5]

There have been various attempts to bring an end to the conflict through dialogue and negotiation with FARC, although none of these efforts have yielded positive results. Peace talks with smaller groups, like the M-19, EPL, and the indigenous group Quintín Lame led to demobilization, but this had little effect on FARC, which is why today, as President Santos sits down with FARC leaders in direct peace talks, Colombians have their doubts about the potential for success in bringing an end to the war, especially if the popular social movements are not in one way or another included in the national dialogue.

Social movements amid an armed conflict

The internal armed conflict has left a permanent mark on the nature of Colombia's social movements, the manner in which they carry out their struggles, and how they are perceived both at home and abroad. It has made any effort at nonviolent popular resistance on a broad-based level extremely difficult to sustain, and to this day allows the entrenched political establish-ment to categorize diverse expressions of legal opposition as subversive or illegitimate, linked to guerrilla violence that in the current global context has been universally catalogued as "terrorist."

It would be a stretch to describe the above-mentioned popular sectors as a unified movement with shared goals and objectives operating in Colombia along a united front. Because of the decades-long conflict, and more specifically, the different movements' stated positions vis-à-vis the armed insurgency, most of these groups have been working independently, mobilizing primarily within specific constituencies, building strategic alliances on occasion, without projecting a central voice. When the Left did develop cohesive political leadership capable of challenging the permanent power duopoly of Colombian politics on an electoral level, as was the case of the Patriotic Union (UP) in the 1980s, the response of the Right was brutal and pervasive.[6]

The ten-year massacre of over three thousand UP members—from grassroots militants, to elected local officials, to its presidential candidates—set the stage for the consolidation of the paramilitary enterprise that rapidly spread throughout Colombia. These paramilitaries arose from the unholy alliance forged between powerful sectors of the landed aristocracy who were rabidly anticommunist, large-scale drug traffickers whose interests were threatened by guerrilla kidnappings, and the state security apparatus, which had been frustrated by its consistent failure to make any concrete gains militarily against FARC, as well as other, smaller insurgent groups.[7]

The dirty war against the UP also inevitably led to the further radicalization of FARC, as its leadership expanded its military program, thus putting aside its political agenda, considering it to be fruitless given the tragic example of the UP. Not coincidentally, this wave of violence against the UP picked up as peace talks were just getting started in 1984 between FARC and the Colombian government.

By the late 1990s and early 2000s, the paramilitaries, under the umbrella organization known as the United Self-Defense Forces of Colombia, AUC, carried out a war of terror throughout the countryside with the direct collaboration of the Colombian Armed Forces, killing thousands of people while intimidating their way to territorial and political control in municipality after municipality. Targeting primarily civilians in guerrilla strongholds, as well as trade union leaders, indigenous activists, human rights workers and other critics of the state, the AUC presented itself to the nation as a vigilante army whose work was justified because it was designed first and foremost to combat guerrilla violence. The paramilitaries' widespread intimidation in the countryside allowed them to gain considerable political influence at the national level, winning dozens of seats to the Colombian Senate and House of Representatives, as well as governorships. As the violence unfolded, with rare exception were the strategic and political motives of the AUC discussed and debated openly, their ideological foundations consistently examined, or their long-term political impact seriously addressed by political leaders and elected officials. To the victims of paramilitary terror, the so-called demobilization of the AUC under the government of President Uribe Vélez was a slap in the face of justice.

Ironically, the rapid expansion of the paramilitary project occurred subsequent to the rewriting of the Colombian constitution in 1991, a process of democratic opening resulting from widespread grassroots popular mobilization, and the peace agreements signed with the smaller insurgencies mentioned earlier. Because of the inherently undemocratic tendencies of Colombian politics, many of the nonviolent popular struggles focused much of their work on opening political spaces within official and institutional frameworks. The 1991 constitution was seen as a major breakthrough in this process. The judicial and political reforms included therein represented a broad array of protections for the typical Colombian, at least on paper, including for those most traditionally marginalized.

Paradoxically, these institutional gains on paper in some ways disempowered popular movements, first, by forcing them to focus on electoral politics as an end in and of itself, but also because they provided "evidence" of the existence of a democratic state based on the rule of law and responsive to the demands and rights of the citizenry, notwithstanding the consistent violations that continued to occur against the rights of the most marginalized sectors. Legitimate grievances were either written off as complaints by disgruntled constituents, or linked directly to FARC, that is, terrorist, manipulation.

The emergence of President Uribe as a transformative political figure with considerable popular appeal can only be understood within this context. The consolidation of the political program of the extreme right in Colombia was facilitated by this superficial fascination with so-called institutional reforms without structural and systemic changes. Reparations, accountability based on the search for truth, and countless demands for social justice have been compromised in the process.

During his eight years in office, Uribe's public discourse embraced the rule of law. He committed himself to strengthening the democratic institutions of the state, most prominently the military and police apparatus. This approach was at the heart of the U.S.-financed "Democratic Security Strategy," promoted incessantly by Uribe.

Uribe refused to acknowledge the existence of an "internal conflict" in Colombia, instead referring to FARC as nothing but a criminal gang that employed terrorism against civilians. He refused to accept government responsibility for human rights violations, and very often accused human rights workers and others of being guerrilla sympathizers whenever they made claims that state forces were guilty of carrying out attacks against civilians. By forcefully confronting the guerrillas on the battlefield, while at the same time embarking on a highly problematic "demobilization" process with the AUC, Uribe projected himself through the Colombian media as a thorough break with the military incompetence and political corruption of the past. He maintained high levels of public approval during his mandate, becoming the first president in recent Colombian history to be reelected.

Since taking office, President Santos has distanced himself from many of Uribe's positions, first and foremost by recognizing that there is indeed an internal conflict in Colombia that needs to be addressed politically. In jump-starting peace talks with FARC, however, he has not diminished the military offensive of his predecessor.

From the *minga* to the patriotic march

In recent years, we have seen a convergence of forces critical of the government that is drawing attention to the inherent contradictions that still exist within Colombia, and that in some instances have gotten worse. This convergence was evident in the fall of 2008, when Colombia's popular movement, spearheaded by the country's indigenous organizations, launched an unprecedented six-week mobilization to protest Uribe's policies related to economic development, national security, free trade, and relations with the United States.

The *minga indígena y popular*, as it was called, involved up to forty thousand people, demonstrating to the world the tremendous organizational capacity of the indigenous movement. It began in the southwestern department of Cauca, where Colombia's indigenous movement first emerged in the early 1970s, but it soon became a national mobilization that included representatives of the many diverse indigenous communities from every region of the country, as well as other sectors, including peasant farmers, sugarcane workers, trade union activists, and students.

The *minga popular* was described by the leadership as the beginning of a nationwide "conversation with the people," a popular uprising of sorts, designed to transform Colombian society and politics through coordinated, nonviolent mobilization. It received considerable support from within the Colombian population, as well as tremendous expressions of international solidarity. In essence, in bringing together so many diverse sectors, the popular movement was for the first time unifying along a platform of social and economic justice, on the one hand, and concrete reparations for the

Gathering of indigenous and Afro-Colombians to discuss water issues in Silvia, Cauca, Colombia, in 2008. Photo by Clifton Ross.

countless victims of state-sponsored violence, on the other. Their collective struggle is a multitiered battle in defense of a different way of seeing the world, what some have called a paradigm war.

In opposition to this collective struggle is a highly centralized system of power that under the cover of state institutions receives its legitimacy through superficial democratic practices of elections, competing political parties, and open "parliamentary debate," and is sustained by entrenched economic forces that have permanent and open access to those same institutions. This is why certain family names, usually with strong ties to domestic industrial and commercial capital, have dominated the political landscape for generations, making it almost impossible for truly independent actors to emerge as viable alternatives. Yes, there are intense rivalries among the dominant political class, but these rivalries revolve around the status quo set up by Colombia's elite.

This system of power is propped up by a state security and military apparatus that, as described above, has never in its history been successful at providing truly comprehensive security for the vast majority of the population, choosing instead to operate only for those same interests that have dominated Colombian politics for generations. This "security" apparatus—the Armed Forces, the National Police, the intelligence services—has been locked in a strategic stalemate with FARC that has rarely tilted in favor of one side over another, until now, thanks to the billions of dollars in military aid and training coming in from Washington since 2000 under Plan Colombia. Meanwhile, the political and military establishment is promoted and nourished by an incestuous mass media system operated by what on the surface appear to be independent actors, but who are undeniably cut out of the same narrow cloth of political, economic, and even racial privilege.

The hundreds of thousands of people that participate daily in Colombia's social movements stand in the way of the permanent consolidation of this system of power. They make up the other side of this paradigm war. This burgeoning popular movement is multifaceted, and by no means homogenous, although it generally shares the vision of indigenous leadership of the need to protect Mother Earth through comprehensive community projects based on the principles of sustainable development and civic participation. The indigenous movement and their allies have tried to carry this out through a complex process of grassroots communication and participation, keeping in mind the differences of perspectives that make up the collective will.

The voices featured in this text represent this other side of the paradigm war, a war that is coming to a head in Colombia. Their perspectives and experiences need to be heard in order to make sense of the reality that is Colombia today. They should be heard until the rulers obey.

Manuela Ruiz, ecologist

Interview and translation by Clifton Ross, July 2008

This brief interview was conducted at Manuela's house in Suesca, Colombia. Manuela works for the Wildlife Conservation Society, which offers the following bio for her at their website, www.wcscolombia.org: "Manuela is an ecologist from the Javeriana University in Bogotá. She has worked with the private natural reserves network of Colombia and in the National Natural Parks Office as part of the National Protected Area System (SINAP) coordination group where she mainly supported private conservation initiatives and their relation with SINAP. She joined the WCS Colombia program in 2010 and is currently coordinating activities in the Integrated Management of Indigenous Territories project with the Cofán People and supporting the consolidation of the Amazon program in Colombia." Here she talks about forms of organization that are at the core of the community life of traditional indigenous people.

The veredas

It's like a territorial and community base organization, you could say. First is the family, then a sort of village relationship because in many case a family settled a place and from that the village was generated. In many areas there are family relations with uncles, aunts, cousins, etc. There's a strong reference to family in a village, certainly at the traditional campesino level.

Much has been lost in many places but given that finally [the village] is like an extended family, then certainly that generates the dynamic of working in minga. The village exists as a space and the "minga" is a form of organization of work at the community level.

This is very common in many areas, but above all in the areas of the Andes and the Amazon. I'm not sure how far it extends, for instance, whether or not it extends to the coastal region. As I mentioned to you, one day, for example, everyone would come to my house to work, say, to plow, and I provide food. And a few days later this is done at a neighbor's house and we all go, each one carrying his or her tools. Occasionally the family has to look for tools and the whole family goes and it becomes a group project in which we all participate.

The village organizes the gatherings of community action where issues of fixing the road or some other work are decided among everyone.

So the gatherings of community action are organized within the villages, the groups of parents in the schools, the groups of village aqueducts, for paying the bills, who will collect funds, those checking whether or not the pipes are clean, etc. This is the first level of organization. After that comes the municipal level, of towns, with other groups, and later, at the regional level by department or geographical zone. For example, the Campesino Development Organization (ADC) functions this way. The ADC is the regional organization and it works in Nariño but at the same time it has groups of associated mingas that are village groups that work at the level of the family farm with the ecological integrated welfare concept of the family as developed by Max Neef. Max Neef has been there and followed the process of Nariño very closely, from production in the form of recycling nutrients, to recuperation of seeds, to distribution of the workload, and so forth.

The agricultural policy of the present government is focused on agro-industry [and ignores this form of organization].

Luis Yonda. Photo by Clifton Ross.

Luis Yonda, Regional Indigenous Council of Cauca (CRIC), Popayán, Colombia
"Through everything we've been murdered and suffered abuse, but the indigenous people have been persistent"

Interview and translation by Clifton Ross, July 2008

CRIC is one of the larger and more powerful indigenous councils of Colombia, with over forty years of work in the region of Cauca. They have training programs for indigenous agricultural methods, indigenous medicine, indigenous spirituality, and the list goes on. Their website is active and full of information: http://www.cric-colombia.org. I was introduced to Luis Yonda in the offices of the CRIC in Popayán. I know very little about Luis, other than what he told me in this interview. In the meeting we had with all members of the communications team, Luis said very little. At the time, Luis was working in communications for the organization.

I was one of those indigenous people who possibly lacked that sense of self-awareness, partly from formation, and partly from my family, but also from the self-awareness itself that comes from formal education. That is, in school, from kindergarten, through primary and secondary school, I was one of those victims of the disparagement of our culture because the educational system drives many young people and many of my generation have been driven into that space of rejecting their culture because it's granted no importance. So being disparaged for being indigenous, catalogued as the lowest [creatures] on the planet, being told others are better than us, has all resulted in our identity crisis. The cultural self-esteem has been so weak that today many of our youth don't see themselves as members of the original people. They don't want to speak their mother tongue. It pains them to say who they are, that they're indigenous, or the name of their people. In the same way, whole generations of relatives are no longer interested in teaching the youth their mother tongue. Previously, education was so homogenizing that to speak the mother tongue was forbidden. It was considered ugly, and it was demonized. Whoever spoke their native tongue was punished. This was something the Catholic Church practiced, and the Church, in agreement with the government, was in charge of education, specifically the nuns and priests, who fiercely punished our ancestors. My mother was one of those victims. She tells of being punished and tortured for having spoken her mother tongue. For that reason the elders today no longer teach the mother tongue, thinking that it could be the source of insults and social or cultural disparagement of their grandchildren.

I studied in high school, but I never got my diploma. In the end, I didn't want to study further because I told myself that if they were going to put me down, I wanted to do something else in another society that wouldn't put me down. So I went out in search of another identity and passed twelve years in the city. But those twelve years were hard on me because the city is even more discriminatory. There they don't discriminate against the indigenous, but against the socially poor, which is seen in marginalization, for instance. There people have to do as they're told. For example, people are paid what wages are imposed on them, and not the other way around. To have a more or less stable work, for example, I had to have my papers, my diplomas, recommendations . . . in the end, a whole lot of requirements. That was my experience in the city and to survive in it I had to be subject to this submission and that slavery. I lived in the city, away from home, outside of my land, denigrating my own identity, looking for another identity, which I never found in all that time, but rather in that time I lost my mother tongue which represented more than lost time, but rather a lost knowledge.

That made me begin to reflect again on trying to return to my community and recover my language. In the city people only speak one language, Spanish, and I saw the superiority of being able to speak two languages. This, the obstacles, the economic difficulties, and the discrimination in the big city were all a great learning experience, and I decided to return to my community.

When I returned to my community I was welcomed and experienced no rejection. The community was interested in my sharing with them the education, experience, and learning that I'd gained from that other space. And so I was called to be one of the directors of the organization. From that moment I entered this process.

I've been in the organizational process for nine or ten years now since, in my youth, I was never part of any organization. I would like to have been working here in the Regional Indigenous Council of Cauca (CRIC) from the age of twelve or thirteen, in the cabildos, which are the indigenous authorities, or in the local organizations that we've been building as part of our structure, but it didn't turn out that way. Unfortunately, I had to pass through other experiences to return to this space. This has meant that I've had a very important experience here in the regional organization of CRIC. I've learned a lot.

I think I've learned here so many things that the great academia doesn't teach. Academia makes all this ancestral knowledge of our communities invisible; it invisibilizes this cultural wealth, its values, its self-knowledge, which continues despite all the crisis of identity that I mentioned earlier. Basically, reflecting on this whole space of learning, I could say that learning contexts aren't only in academia nor in schools, but also in the context of everything relating to family, for instance. Cultural values like belonging to a tribe can give one the sense of living harmoniously in a collective and we indigenous people are clear that we all deserve to live on this planet, even the smallest microbe. All beings need to live and sustain themselves and so we have to live harmoniously with them. If the microbes didn't exist, the [larger] organism and the whole metabolism going on in our bodies and everywhere wouldn't function. Without that, there would be no life and this is what we understand from ancestral knowledge.

Celebrating Colombian independence

There are always these transcendental dates and national celebrations that the state and its institutions put in place. And so now we're preparing to celebrate July 20, a date that, according to history, independence from the Spanish regime was won. But we believe this to be at bottom a real lie because Colombia at this time is dependent on the United States. We know that Plan Colombia doesn't come free from the United States. The U.S. government has given some dollars, but it's awaiting payment with interest. The foreign debt [of Colombia] has grown from one government to another, and this debt is never paid but grows and grows. The developed world continues making loans to Colombia because it knows to whom it is lending. [In Colombia] there are natural resources, bioenergetics, forests, water, and mineral resources.

So where does the government come up with the idea that we're independent if we're depending on the developed countries? Worse than that, we're in hock, not because we want to be, but because the governments we put in power to defend all this patrimony that we have, rather than defending it, with the loans they take out to carry on their internal business, they're leaving Colombia in debt. Later on, what happened to Panama could happen to us, where the United States says "Panama is ours," and invaded with its armies saying it was the owner of that country and taking it over: that's where Colombia is headed. That's when one asks, "which independence?"

The reflection we make in CRIC is that we continue to be dependent. The capitalist sector has always kept us submitted to the structure of dependence. The release of resources for projects and infrastructure is made under their conditions without our having a say in the matter. The same is true as regards resources for education. The state continues to manage the resources for the indigenous people. As long as we continue to be dependent, independence will never come. Our search for independence implies observing the structure of governability but this independence doesn't imply going against the state itself but rather the strengthening of autonomy. And autonomy would mean that the institutions would have their autonomy for social and economic investment but that the social movement would also have its autonomy in economic, cultural, educational, and social terms.

Many of our demands have been won—they haven't been "given" to us by the government. Examples of this would be the transfer of resources, participation in the city governments, the municipal councils, seats in Congress. All that has been the fruit of a process of struggle and the mobilizations of the indigenous people of Colombia. Through everything we've been murdered and suffered abuse, but the indigenous people have been persistent. From the 1970s to the present the indigenous movement has spoken for itself and organized itself and distinguished itself as an indigenous movement. Before it was just part of the social sectors, for example, part of the working class or unions. There was no indigenous organization. Then in 1971 the leaders and youth decided to form an organization for indigenous people to make their own demands and do their own work. The fruit of this struggle has been the CRIC, which now has thirty-seven years of organized life. That's where we come from, with all the difficulties that implies, supporting the youth and the *cabildos*.

Each community has its territory or reservation with collective titles recognized here in Colombia. These reservations have their own recognized governments, chosen and structured as the people choose, and in harmony with, and responsive to, the community. Those governments, in turn, work with the national institutions, channeling resources and support projects for the benefit of the community. The [tribal governments] also are in charge of administering justice.

Each community is also working with its own education, in its own official mother tongue. Also, they're adopting a focus on preventative medicine based on good nutrition, and clean natural foods; caring for the environment and breathing clean air, and maintaining clean water so as to avoid intestinal infections. Related to all this is food produced with organic fertilizers.

We, the indigenous people, are asking for independence from the government but that it not drop constitutional responsibility it has to give us the guarantees for that independence. Independence implies that the government takes economic responsibility for us to be able to develop the system of life we're proposing. That's what the government hasn't wanted. In this sense, internally this independence has been completely derailed. Meanwhile, the government proclaims independence from other states, as if it didn't have a foreign debt or wasn't supported by other states or economic organizations. So there's the European Union, which has also invested quite a bit in Colombia, and with certain interests. We're not talking here of social investments in solidarity. That's not how capitalism works; rather, it's always looking to see what it can get, year after year.

So that's how it is in Colombia. That's how we see it from the perspective of the indigenous movement from Cauca and Colombia.

Antonio Navarro Wolff, governor of Nariño state, former M-19 guerrilla
"I like starting from the concept of democracy: economic democracy, political democracy, social democracy"

Interview and translation by Clifton Ross, July 2008

Antonio Navarro Wolff (sometimes spelled "Wolf") entered the M-19 guerrilla movement in 1974 at the age of sixteen and rose to second in command of the organization before it disarmed and entered legal political activity. He cofounded Colombia's main left political party, Alternative Democratic Pole,

Antonio Navarro Wolff. Photo by Clifton Ross.

and served as its secretary general, ran for president on its ticket before he became governor of his home state of Nariño where he continues to serve at the time this book went to press. Wolff was joined in power in 2011 by Gustavo Petro, the elected mayor of Bogotá and also a former M-19 guerrilla. Together, these and other left public officials, while still a minority, reveal the extraordinary complexity of Colombia and its political system. This interview was conducted in Wolff's office in Pasto, Nariño, Colombia.

I was studying in the university and had participated in student movements and that brought me into the April 19th Movement [M-19] in 1974, and I went to the mountains. I was taken prisoner; I was tortured; I left; I lost a leg and now have a prosthesis. So I did all that from the age of sixteen until 1990 when a process of negotiation which began the year before came to an end and we signed a peace treaty.

The decision to sign the treaty was the result of many different factors. It came out of a very intense internal discussion in the M-19, but also of an analysis of reality. There were insurgent groups, paramilitaries organized by the state, and this would continue to grow. There was the rearguard of the United States, which was backing the Colombian government with what seemed unlimited support. If there wasn't very clear and well-defined public support [for us] it made no sense to continue. There was public support for a few years, but it began to diminish, especially between the years of 1979 and

1984 or 1985. We had decided that armed struggle would take us nowhere. We weren't going to win, but neither would we likely lose, so we faced the prospect of staying in the mountains and likely dying natural deaths with no prospects.

You go into the insurgent struggle to transform society but the prospect of it becoming an illness that doesn't kill, nor win, nor lose, this makes no sense. We could maintain ourselves, but there were no social conditions for a victory. And in the end, a guerrilla victory isn't a victory of arms but a political victory. You can take up arms as a method, but victory comes through politics. And if the political [victory] wasn't possible that way, then another route had to be found. So we signed a peace agreement and became a political party. In the end, we came to an agreement alone, but then other armed organizations in Colombia began to sign on for peace: the Popular Liberation Army (EPL), the Quintín Lame Armed Movement (MAQL), and the Revolutionary Workers' Party (PRT). All these represented half the guerrillas there were at the time.

Neither the ELN (National Liberation Army) nor FARC (Revolutionary Armed Forces of Colombia), each for different reasons, wanted to sign on. The ELN was in a process of reorganization after having been nearly annihilated, so they didn't want to talk much about politics, being in an internal process. And FARC was drawn to the process but they came to the conclusion that they had other possibilities of victory. They were growing and, indeed, continued to grow. They grew until 1998, eight years after we'd signed the peace treaty, when they arrived at the peak of their military power and capacity for favorable results. Now it seems to me they're in irreversible decline. Today the political consensus is against the armed struggle, the consensus of the great majority of the population. So without this there are no prospects of victory. And the prospect is of going backward, little by little, which is what is happening to FARC.

I think that in Colombia there are doors open for a movement, a left party that could win elections. But the greatest gift to the right wing is the presence of a guerrilla confronting the nation. We continue to pay for that. It continues to be a problem for the Left because the guerrilla is also left. And despite all the difficulties of the electoral process at this point, it's the only route if you want to transform society.

The hard road of peace

We signed the peace treaty because we bet on the idea that if we made a complete break with armed struggle we'd have a certain level of guarantees, and we did, to a very high degree. Of course, some of our members were killed, but they didn't kill us all, nor even the majority. In general, we were respected. On the other hand, what happened with the Patriotic Union was that they had an element that worked against them, and that was the armed guerrilla on one hand, and people connected to the guerrilla doing electoral work. This in its time was called simultaneous combination of all forms of struggle, and it goes on in other countries, such as with the ETA and Batasuna in Spain or the IRA in its moment with Sinn Fein in Northern Ireland. And [those countries] didn't kill them, but rather imprisoned them. Here we have a more complicated society, and a state with fewer controls. And so they killed thousands of people.

We made a complete break with this scheme. Nothing—zero arms. Simply everyone acting within the law. In 1990 they killed Carlos Pizarro of the M-19, who was at that time the most important figure. But there didn't follow a systematic extermination of the rest of us. We had an enormous public outcry against the death of Pizarro. Thousands, millions of people reacted, condemning that. In the end we managed to maintain a level of respect for our process, and other organizations followed: the EPL, the PRT, and the MAQL were also respected.

It's been difficult. First, we were alone, although we had a great initial backing. I think that the first important result of the peace process was the new Colombian Constitution of 1991, in which we played a decisive role. We were able to elect by popular vote a third of the members of the Constitutional Assembly. Our participation was consequential; much of what was democratic and progressive in the constitution came from our work. It was a moment in which the country wanted to leave behind the backward ways and do something new, a moment that unfortunately didn't last too long. Still, from July of 1990 to July 1991 was a year of hope. But then to go into elections was very difficult. We knew nothing about that: we had no experience; we knew nothing; we had no money.

I think in the end the creation of the current Democratic Pole, which comprises essentially the entire Left, is the result of all that experience. We're all there: the old M-19, the other demobilized guerrilla organizations, people from the Communist Party, people from other sectors of the Left, the Maoists, the Liberal Party, and independents. This is the result of experience and the need for unity and confronting a very right-wing project such as exists today in Colombia. We've won the mayor's seat in Bogotá twice, and we're making new paths. The Alternative Democratic Pole (ADP) ranges from the "orthodox" Left to the center so there are people in the center, the center-left, and leftists. We're all there together, which is something that isn't very common in Latin America.

But there's been a move to the right [in Colombia] because of Uribe's victories over FARC, which feed into a right-wing concept: power, authority, and a firm hand are the way. These ideas have been gaining the upper hand in public opinion. This has been causing great problems for us because we've been opening a space in the center that didn't previously exist. Now, to the degree to which public opinion is moving to the right, there's an emptiness in the center we wanted to fill but now this emptiness means we need to move to the right for support, and that would be difficult for the Pole.

Subsidizing paternalistic poverty

[The ADP] had an idea of distributing subsidies not through intermediaries but in a direct way, like what is being done in Brazil. Whenever you use an intermediary, the money gets spent in the process and doesn't arrive to the people for whom it's intended. Still, I have to say that the policy of direct subsidies is one that should be reexamined. I don't think today I'd propose what I did two years ago because it seems to me that a policy of direct subsidies has many problems. It serves clientelism, which is used all over the world, and it has degenerated the value of ideas, proposals, and political lines because poor people end up voting for the subsidy, but also because welfare policies always turn out to be unsustainable in the long run, and they lead to no human transformation.

In all sincerity, in this government we've decided against all welfare programs. Nothing. And if we're going to give subsidies, they'll be subsidies in packages that require a commitment of people to pitch in, finance, and be an active part insofar as they're able. They have to make an effort or, I think, they become in some sense "beggars," conceptually speaking, receiving "manna from heaven."

On the other hand, we do give to productive projects. We subsidize a credit, but it's a credit that the people have to pay. They may not have to pay 100 percent, but they have to pay a percentage of it. But it's a credit and the people have to make an effort and put in their share. We're working with the idea that "everyone contributes," everyone, even if they're very poor. With the very poor, they have to do some work, like fixing the roads or contributing a day of work. They'll be fed, but they'll spend that day working on the highway, doing what they're able so that public money will be used to help that work, but not "I'll stay home and you send me a check."

Socialism of the twenty-first century

In 1989 the world quit talking about socialism, but now it's coming up again in Latin America: in Ecuador one version, another in Venezuela and, to a lesser degree, in Uruguay. Social democracy also talked about democratic socialism, right? I like starting from the concept of democracy: economic democracy, political democracy, social democracy. Because really, socialism has to be associated with democracy in every way. Democracy is the power of the majority, the option of the majority, the property of the majority, access to services for the majority. I prefer the concept of democracy, but I'm not opposed to talking about socialism as such. The M-19 took up arms to defend democracy and we define our beginnings in economic democracy, political democracy, social justice, or social democracy and national independence. Those were the basic principles of the M-19. The M-19 originated in response to an electoral fraud and so we developed the idea of democracy, a profound, direct democracy.

Here [in Narino province] one of the things we're doing is a participatory budget with a whole process for doing things by a series of rules, procedures, and commitments and we're doing it well. We're helping put together community businesses, working with campesinos and supporting indigenous people and Afro-Colombians. When there are struggles for land we favor the campesinos who have a right to land. I would say then that the concept of democracy allows for an application less subject to interpretations because it's clearer and more direct. So that's what we're doing in the role of the state.

We feel the state has a role in the economy: to support the weak, to support the smaller actors to resolve their problems with the economy a state is needed. It's out of style, isn't it, but the distribution of the means of production is a role of the state. In Nariño, 70 percent of the campesinos have land. That's an uncommonly high percentage for Colombia and Latin America. But they're very weak; they're very small and have very little land: a hectare [10,000 square meters] or a hectare and a half. So we're working on organized projects with them to resolve problems of economy of scale. The problems of an economy of scale involve financing, technology, and access to markets. How does a small campesino get into a market? If we can organize them in blocks and help them arrive at the market, eliminating the intermediaries, we can make the productive chain work to help the small producer. And the idea of democracy provides the framework for this.

Now where the campesinos have no land, agrarian reform is needed. That's democracy. But the agrarian reform has to be planned so as to give land to the campesinos and not in a scheme for forming semistate associations; this latter hasn't worked well. What has worked is making the campesino the owner of the land and then helping groups of those campesinos do other things: get technology, credits, and find better ways for selling their products. But with the campesino, they need to keep the land as owners. For the average mestizo campesino, land is best maintained by each family.

The scheme of cooperatives, where the land is collectively owned, that's functioned with the indigenous, and more or less with the Afro-Colombians, where there's been a collective culture. That we do support. We're working with the indigenous people—we've been in office six months and we've developed relations with the Consejo Regional Indígena del Cauca (CRIC), relations which didn't exist before. We also have an indigenous secretary of agriculture named Javier Pecta and they have a different concept of agricultural economy, which is the integral farm. They're working in food security, security of inventories, and also medicinal plants. That's part of our policy, working also in food security and encouraging campesinos to have a portion of their land planted in crops for their own consumption, even if it's the back yard. With the Afro communities on the Pacific Coast, we're supporting cacao as part of an integrated credit for a program we're calling ethno-development, working with the indigenous and Afro-descendents of the region.

This is all being done with the social movements. It's a public pact with the people, with all of society, and we're all in this together. Of course where we're going to be working there are the paramilitaries who don't want us to succeed. But we're going to do it anyway, if society, if the great majority, want it. Perhaps we'll open a path that [the paramilitaries] will bury. We'll have to see. I think it can work, but we'll need everyone with us. Accompaniment of the people will be critical.

Jesús Tuberquía, San José de Apartadó Peace Community
"We believe in the dignity of human life, against a worldwide system of death"

Interview by Clifton Ross, March 2011
Translation by Christy Rodgers

The peace communities have taken a stunningly courageous stand refusing to take sides in Colombia's fifty-year civil war or engage in any form of violence, even to defend themselves or their communities. The spiritual strength required for such a stance can only come from the close-knit community they develop and enjoy. Undoubtedly, they are a living witness to the power of nonviolent resistance to the system of death and an example to the world that it's possible to live with integrity and principle even in the most inhumane circumstances.

Jesús Tuberquía was on tour in the United States in the spring of 2011, and while he was in Berkeley we met, along with his host and guide, John

Lindsay-Poland, who also helped set up this interview. A little less than a year after this interview, Jesús was the victim of an attempted assassination by paramilitaries who shot at him near his home.

Since 1996 we've been living in San José de Apartadó, in the province of Antioquia, very close to the Caribbean. It's a very rich area: a banana-producing region, livestock-producing, access to the sea, very fertile lands, coal mines, a very large and rich oilfield. There are many economic interests. And that's also what makes it very strategic for the armed groups.

There's been an ongoing conflict in the area between guerrilla and government forces. The civilian population has been extremely affected by this, with two or three displacements sometimes in one year, as well as actions against the civilian population. The government has done nothing to help the civilian population. On the contrary, it has been a coercive force, massacring the villagers, destroying their crops, stealing everything they have, and burning their houses. There have been criminal kidnappings, forced disappearances, and rapes of the women, some of whom are members of the peace communities. There have been many illegal detentions by the public security forces, where they set people up, using false accusations, using people as witnesses and paying them several million pesos to testify against someone else, whoever it may be. It's caused a great deal of destruction.

The San José de Apartadó Peace Community came into being in the midst of the armed conflict, as a project for neutrality with that conflict, basing ourselves in international humanitarian law that mandates respect for civilians in war situations. This respect for civilian rights doesn't exist in reality. Not in Colombia, nor in the peace communities, nor in any country is it respected. Hopefully, the governments, states, and organizations that have ratified international human rights laws will fulfill them one day.

San José de Apartadó has a long history of being socially involved. In the area of [San Pedro de] Urabá in 1996, when the social movements, the unions, and the grassroots organizations were almost destroyed, the peace communities were established. This has cost us a lot: almost two hundred dead in these fourteen years—and on the fourteenth anniversary itself, an assassination by the paramilitaries, in coordination with the public security forces. For us it continues to be very complex and difficult because ours is a movement for life that has to proceed in the middle of a war. It's very easy to create an organization when I'm living in complete peace and freedom, and I have everything I need. But when I'm in the middle of a war, suffering all the blows—it's a very hard struggle to create life in the midst of that.

Jesús Tuberquía. Photo by Clifton Ross.

But thanks to the conscience of the people, the members of the Peace Community, solidarity from everyone, the organizing power, the power of conscience—that's what allows us to continue in spite of all the difficulties. That's why, when they burn our houses or our villages, and they displace us, and we're left in the margins, we come back to rebuild and we start again from nothing.

For us, there's a Supreme Being who always helps us, because as humans [alone] we wouldn't be able to stand against [this]. A Being who's watched over many of our days. Others too, who've fulfilled their mission at some point, and who are no longer with us physically—but all those who have fallen in this long process of the Peace Community are people who [still] walk with us. They have not died. They have been sown in the earth, but they have not died. And they will not die. We are always very clear about that.

We resist inside an unjust system

Within the community we keep alive the memory of all the compañeros who have fallen but are with us still. And that's why, thanks to the efforts of the compañeros who walk along with us in this difficult journey, we've shown the world that another world is possible. That's been the history of humanity: great empires of injustice, and small groups of human society resisting [them]. And the injustices haven't ceased for us, but neither have they been able to stop this idea of life, of a possible system, of another, different world, that we human beings really will be able to live in peace. But an unjust system doesn't permit that. Not because it's not *possible*, but because it's not *allowed*. And so our experience is this: a movement for life, in solidarity, where life is the most important thing. In the unjust system, life is what's worth the least. In the unjust system, everything is decided by money. A piece of paper determines life or death.

To be able to resist inside this [system], you have to be constantly focused. You can't lose sight of the goal, what you're seeking, and you have to have a very clear sense of it. That it's not a problem of the thousand of us, more or less, who are members of the Peace Community, but rather a problem for all humanity, for society. And that's how we understand it. And that's why, always, when a person is killed, we feel it deeply, because we human beings are a [single] thread, no matter what color, what race, we're a single thread. And that's why for us any death is a problem for all of human society. It's a crime against humanity.

The real mission of the community is respect for human life. Everything is centered on that. How I'm taking human life into account. We in the Peace Community are people who believe in life, the dignity of human life, against a worldwide system of death, a doctrine of death. This doctrine of death has all the economic power, the power to annihilate any human being, and with weapons, with the additional threat of weapons, because weapons exist to kill. If people don't die from the extreme poverty generated by this system—millions of people, human beings—then it's necessary to kill them. And that's why it's a system of death, opposed to a system, a way of thinking really, a movement for *life*.

Anyone who picks up a gun is someone who considers destroying life. Anyone who picks up a weapon to kill is completely wrong, and it doesn't matter what name you give them. And so in this system of death, in the doctrine of death, money and weapons go together. That's how you destroy human beings. As long as great wealth is concentrated, with many riches for a very few people, millions of people will die of hunger, of extreme poverty, of illnesses. All the destruction of nature, of the ecosystem, that's done with the ambition of having [pieces of] paper—because that's all wealth is, the concentration of wealth is all numbers on a piece of paper. In every way, it's a system of death. And that's why we do the opposite, generating a movement for life, which we will achieve.

This is the problem: The justification for any guerrilla group is systemic injustice, no? But the bad thing is when they fall into the same logic of death. They say they don't share the ideas of this system of death, but at the end of the day, they produce the same thing. So this is the problem, the struggle, no? In the countries where movements that are called revolutionary have happened, how many deaths have been counted? It's the same, a struggle for power.

So we don't struggle for power, but for life. For us it's not who's in charge, who's the one who gives the orders, but rather that here we're all in charge. We must respect, first of all, we must care for, life, in every way possible—because life is surrounded by all of nature itself. We have to care for the natural world, because it's [the] cycle of life inside of everything.

In the end, all of this has to do with the idea that in this society things are determined by a piece of paper. And for that piece of paper, wars are fought, all sorts of things are done. If you have to kill, you kill; if you have to destroy, you destroy. Because we've given more worth to this piece of paper than to a human being. So life in this system has no value. Those who take up arms, who go to war, fight over a piece of paper so that they get that, and life is unimportant. That's why it's written, you know, that the root of all human problems is the love of money.

When they destroy our villages, we return together and support one another, and we rebuild them. They destroy our crops, so we return together to replant them. They kill members of the community, so we go together to recover the bodies of our compañeros. And thus it's an ongoing practice. We have the ongoing work of education and human development in the community. It's a twenty-four-hour-a-day effort. That's why it requires us to reflect and to concentrate on what it is that we're doing. And thanks to this, the conscience of every person, the desire to show that we can live life differently within an unjust system, because of that, we've advanced a great deal. Fourteen years of struggle, of community life, recovering the land, buying land collectively for the people, for growing food, for having a place to live, a roof over their heads, doing this very carefully, in addition, that's to say, making use of the land, but in a very careful way. We have to protect nature at the same time and not use chemicals because these chemicals are poison, so we make organic fertilizers.

We're trying to be a model of a different world, to be such a small group, but one that's a model. We've learned it's possible to build an alternative, a model where life will be different. And not simply because one has the desire to do so, because we're not a theory written on paper, we're human beings who walk, live, and feel. We're not fables, because on paper you can put anything, theoretically I can invent anything, but reality can't be invented; it's made. And we, as an experience, we're a reality.

Many of the members of the Peace Community belong to different churches. Some are Protestants, some Catholics, but almost all of us have a vocation to be a bit more cultural-religious. So the community is ecumenical, and the name of your denomination really isn't that important. Because religious or political [parties] have been invented as part of this same unjust system. If you belong to such and such a church, and I belong to this one, it's just like the political [parties], the same unjust system has invented them. They've put that idea of society inside us. They've achieved their objective, and that's how they've divided the lower classes and kept themselves in power. If you can divide people, then they don't have the power to change things. We understand this perfectly because we always reflect on humanity, on the system, and [on] the solutions to them. So society would be much better off if there weren't those governments. I think all the people would be much better off, because it's the governments elected by the people, with these [parties] that they invented, that make all the evil that is done in this world. So a country can be much better off without a government, which is not to say that all the injustices that have built up over thousands of years would be ended overnight. But things would change if countries didn't have governments. There would be huge changes. Giant steps.

Venezuela

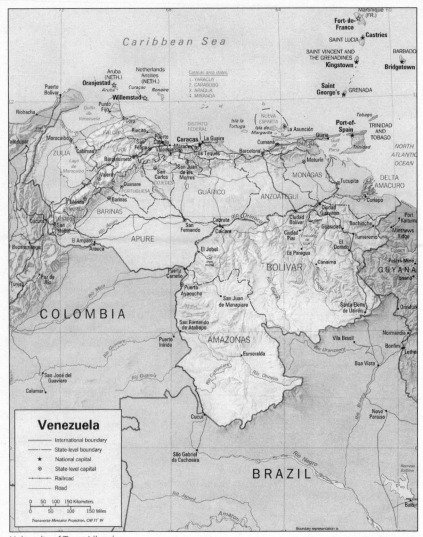

Venezuela

——— International boundary
·-·-·-· State-level boundary
★ National capital
⊕ State-level capital
⊢⊣⊢⊣ Railroad
——— Road

0   50   100   150 Kilometers
0   50   100   150 Miles

Transverse Mercator Projection, CM 71° W

Caribbean Sea

Caracas area states
1. YARACUY
2. CARABOBO
3. ARAGUA
4. MIRANDA

Martinique (FR.)
Fort-de-France
Castries
SAINT LUCIA
SAINT VINCENT AND THE GRENADINES
Kingstown
BARBADOS
Bridgetown
Saint George's
GRENADA

Tobago
TRINIDAD AND TOBAGO
Port-of-Spain
Trinidad

NORTH ATLANTIC OCEAN

Aruba (NETH.)
Oranjestad
Netherlands Antilles (NETH.)
Curaçao
Bonaire
Willemstad

Puerto Bolívar
Punto Fijo
Golfo de Venezuela
Ríohacha
Coro
Riecito

DISTRITO FEDERAL
Isla la Tortuga
NUEVA ESPARTA
Isla de Margarita
La Asunción
Cumaná
Güiria
Gulf of Paria

Valledupar
Maracaibo
Cabimas
FALCÓN
Puerto Cabello
San Felipe
Barquisimeto
Caracas
La Guaira
Maracay
Valencia
Los Teques
Barcelona
Maturín
SUCRE
MONAGAS
Tucupita
Curiapo
DELTA AMACURO
Port Kaituma

ZULIA
Lago de Maracaibo
LARA
Valera
Guanare
PORTUGUESA
San Carlos
COJEDES
San Juan de los Morros
GUÁRICO
ANZOATEGUI
Ciudad Guayana
Guasipati
Bochinche
Matthews Ridge

Mérida
Barinas
BARINAS
Cabruta
Ciudad Bolívar
Ciudad Piar
Tumeremo
Río Orinoco

Cúcuta
San Cristóbal
El Amparo
Arauca
APURE
San Fernando
Caicara
La Paragua
El Dorado
GUYANA
Issano

Bucaramanga
Río Apure
Puerto Carreño
El Jobal
iron mine
El Callao
Canaima
Santa Elena de Uairén
Uyuni
Peters Mine

Paz de Río
Río Meta
Puerto Ayacucho
San Juan de Manapiare
BOLÍVAR
Orinduik

Tunja
COLOMBIA
San Fernando de Atabapo
AMAZONAS
Vila Brasil
Normandia
Bonfim
Lethem

Río Guaviare
Puerto Inírida
Esmeralda
Boa Vista

San José del Guaviare
Calamar
Río Guainía
Río Orinoco
Río Uraricoera

Cucuí
Nova Paraíso

São Gabriel da Cachoeira
Río Negro

BRAZIL

Río Japurá
Amazon

Reprêsa Balbina
Balbina

Boundary representation is

University of Texas Libraries

INTRODUCTION
A nation at the crossroads

By Clifton Ross

For many in the Americas and beyond, Venezuela under President Hugo Chávez represented the most significant attempt in the new millennium to challenge the world capitalist system, under the rubric of the "socialism of the twenty-first century."

Chávez confronted U.S. hegemony in Latin America and undertook programs to build regional unity. His "Bolivarian Revolution" opened spaces for people to live, work, and even hope. As one foreigner visiting Venezuela recently told me, "I think Venezuela is the only country in the world where people still dream." As it directed efforts to eliminate extreme poverty, the Bolivarian Revolution has also tried to build new structures for popular participation through the community councils and the "communes."

Nevertheless, after nearly a decade directed toward building the "socialism of the twenty-first century," Venezuela remains very much a capitalist country. Although the "Missions" (social programs) have continued to redistribute some of the nation's vast oil wealth to the nation's poor, and have reduced misery and extreme poverty, they have also reinforced dependency and clientelism, and have done little to develop the country.[1] The "participatory, protagonistic democracy" that Chávez promised has also been largely directed to organizing for the "representative democracy" of elections. Many would argue that in Venezuela today more power resides in the command structure that Chávez left behind, the United Socialist Party of Venezuela (PSUV), than in the working people as a whole.

Chávez's death in March 2013 unleashed a series of crises, beginning in mid-April when his hand-picked candidate, Nicolás Maduro, won by a 1.5 percent margin in elections opponents claimed were fraudulent and illegal. Shortages of consumer goods, a shrinking supply of dollars for imports, a growing debt, and a dysfunctional economy are making life harder for Venezuela's 99 percent. A growing majority views the ruling party as illegitimate, incompetent, irresponsible, and corrupt. The future in which many around the world invested so much hope looks increasingly uncertain.

Fertile grounds for revolution

What became known as the Bolivarian Revolution unfolded in a country rich in natural and human resources. Venezuela displays a range of stunning landscapes—from Caribbean beaches in the north to Amazon jungles in the southeast, from rolling grasslands of the *llano* in the center to the Andes and their mist-hung high plains (the *páramo*) in the northwest. The country has vast swaths of fertile farmland and a year-round growing season in many areas. It also owns some of world's largest oil reserves, which have shaped its economy and politics.

Chávez consciously drew on the country's history for the name and the ideological framework of the social process he spearheaded. In 1811 Venezuela became the first Spanish colony of Latin America to declare independence. Under the leadership of Simón Bolívar, it won its freedom from Spain ten years later. Bolívar hoped to unite the northern republics of South America into "Gran Colombia," but power struggles ensued and engulfed much of the region in civil wars and power struggles that continued into the twentieth century.

Venezuela experienced intermittent periods of democratic rule between dictatorships before definitively entering civilian rule in 1958. The Punto Fijo Pact of that year allowed for a forty-year-long trade-off of power via the ballot box between the Social Christian Party (COPEI) and Democratic Action (AD, *Acción Democrática*).

The discovery of oil during the rule of General Juan Vicente Gómez (1908–1935) allowed his dictatorship to centralize state power and unite the country with highways built from the oil revenue, a process of infrastructure development continued and extended by President Marcos Pérez Jiménez, who ruled until 1958. From 1950 to 1980, Venezuela experienced an oil boom that made it the wealthiest country in Latin America, and its standard of living rivaled that of many European countries. These were years in which governments invested in food subsidies, transportation, health care, and education.

This era of social peace paid for in petrodollars, or at least the myth of social peace, was all too brief. With the collapse of oil prices in the 1980s, much of the social spending by the government began to be cut, and that process intensified as the neoliberal capitalist model was adopted.

Neoliberal policies aggravated inequality and led to the Caracazo of 1989. Hundreds of people were killed in this uprising, viewed by many as the turning point that led to Chávez's accession to power ten years later.

At the time of the Caracazo, Chávez was a Lieutenant Colonel in the Venezuelan Armed Forces, but he was also participating in MBR 200 (Bolivarian Revolutionary Movement 200), a left nationalist civic-military alliance that attempted a coup in 1992. Chávez was imprisoned for his leadership in that coup but was released on an amnesty a little over two years later, at which time he began campaigning for the presidency.

Chávez won the election of 1998 and immediately called for the writing of a new constitution upon which a new republic would be founded. The social movements had been active but not well-articulated for many years, and the writing of the constitution for the Fifth Republic brought together all the disparate actors of the country under the banner of the Bolivarian Revolution, although this was viewed by some as a ploy to circumvent the legislature and produce a document strengthening the executive where the "focus on [political] parties was replaced by a focus on the presidency."[2]

In any case, the document became the first constitution in the world to have been written not by a legislative body but by social movements and groups across the country, and it reflected the radical hopes of many sectors, among them ecologists, women's and indigenous organizations, and campesinos.

Chávez was reelected in 2000 as the first president of the new Bolivarian Republic and survived several U.S.-backed attempts to oust him, increasing his power with each blow. A coup removed him from the presidency on April 11, 2002, but he was back within two days. In December of that year, the management of the state oil company, Petróleos de Venezuela Sociedad Anónima (PDVSA), locked out the workers for two months. Once PDVSA was again under the control of the government, or "renationalized," Chávez began to direct its revenues to the building of his "Bolivarian Revolution," beginning with the Bolivarian universities. This was followed by dozens of social projects he dubbed "Missions," designed to gain him support in anticipation of the 2004 referendum vote that, as a result, failed to unseat him.[3] After that, he governed with relatively high approval ratings for the next nine years.

For several years the Venezuelan opposition fielded weak candidates with poor arguments for change. But as Chávez's health and the health of Venezuela's economy worsened, the opposition regrouped and made a fairly strong showing in the October 2012 presidential elections. Since Chávez's death in March 2013, support for an alternative has spread across

May Day parade in Caracas, 2006. Photo by Clifton Ross.

the political spectrum. The official Chavista narrative still brands the opposition as an "ultra-right-wing force directed by U.S. imperialism," but the
reality is far more complex. The Mesa de Unidad Democrática (Democratic
Unity Coalition, MUD) now incorporates sectors of the old left, disaffected
Chavistas, and social movement activists, as well business and right-wing
sectors.

Latin American unity

On the international front, the Bolivarian Revolution has arguably had a
more positive impact, especially on the region. President Chávez drew his
inspiration for international policy, particularly toward the other countries of Latin America, from Simón Bolívar's hope for the "Gran Colombia."
In this context, he has designed a series of international initiatives, often
in conjunction with other progressive governments of the region. Each of
these initiatives has sought to supplant the imperial projects of the United
States and strengthen regional unity.

The Bolivarian Alternative for the Americas, ALBA, is a trade and
aid alternative to U.S. free-trade treaties. Telesur is a television network
designed to challenge CNN's version of reality in Latin America. CELAC
(Community of Caribbean and Latin American States) is a regional organization backed by Venezuela which some see as a challenge to the U.S.-
dominated Organization of American States (OAS). UNASUR acts as a

mediator of conflicts (such as the right-wing uprising in Bolivia in 2008) but it also could be an umbrella for initiatives for a common passport, trade, military cooperation, a common currency, and a regional bank (Bancosur), the latter proposed by Venezuela as an alternative to the IMF and World Bank. Finally, Venezuela has used its vast oil resources to help the world's poorer regions develop and maintain themselves, particularly through instruments like PetroCaribe.

Taken together, these international initiatives have reignited a hope that international relations could be based on a socialist vision, rather than capitalist "free trade," on solidarity rather than international competition, and mutual, rather than mere national interests. In the wake of the collapse of the Soviet socialist bloc, the Bolivarian Revolution has proposed an anti-capitalist alternative in Latin America that is polycentric and pluralistic with a strong emphasis on solidarity and cooperation. But the initiatives have also been criticized by many Venezuelans who would prefer to see the funding for these projects used to shore up the nation's crumbling infrastructure and resolve problems closer to home.

Obstacles and challenges

The opposition isn't the only, or even most critical, enemy of the Bolivarian Revolution. A far more significant threat to the process that grew under Chávez is the so-called "internal enemy," or the "endogenous Right," those within the process who are either simply indifferent to the revolution, or actively working against it while using it to enrich themselves. This sector includes government bureaucrats and politicians who undermine reforms as well as the "Bolibourgeoisie," or "Boligarchy," a group of *nouveaux riches* who have gained wealth and power through their association with the process over the past decade.

Under their management—and mismanagement—the country's economy has declined dramatically. Devaluations, five in the past decade, including the 32 percent devaluation in February 2013, have slashed people's purchasing power, with the working class and the poor suffering the most. Basic industries nationalized under Chávez have seen production drop, in some cases, to a quarter of prenationalized levels, while the number of workers is often doubled.[4] The most troubling of the nationalized industries is PDVSA, the nation's oil company and main source of revenue, which is experiencing a 3 to 4 percent drop in production per year while expenses and maintenance leave the company only $4 in profit for every $100 of gross income, with fully 80 percent going to operating costs.[5] The company, once "considered one of the world's leading energy companies"[6] is now saddled with a debt some estimate to be U.S.$153 billion, at a time when oil prices are at historic highs.[7]

Undoubtedly, the most publicized problems discussed in Venezuela these days, besides scarcity of consumer products in the markets, are corruption, crime, and impunity. Corruption didn't arrive with the Bolivarian Revolution, but rather is endemic, as it is in most oil-producing economies. In 2012, Transparency International placed Venezuela near the bottom for corruption, ranking the country at 165 out of 176, just above Iraq.

Venezuela's legal system, with police and judicial corruption and an overcrowded and out-of-control prison system in which three-quarters of prisoners have been convicted of no crime, is by all accounts abysmal.[8] The country has among the world's highest murder rates, of which 96 percent go unpunished and nearly that many go uninvestigated. In the state of Aragua, over half of the 7,000 extrajudicial killings in 2000–2008 were carried out by the state police.[9] "Venezuela's murder rate quadrupled under Chávez, going from 4,550 homicides in 1999 to 16,047 in 2009 ... making Venezuela as unsafe as the Gaza Strip under Israeli offensives in 2009," according to Corrales and Penfold.[10] Despite promises of reform, very little has been done to transform the legal system and until such time, corruption and impunity will doubtlessly continue.

The Bolivarian government under Chávez and now under Maduro has also been seen as undermining the independence of the separate branches of government and politicizing them. This was an issue when the Chavista-packed National Electoral Commission refused to fully investigate many of the allegations of fraud and other illegal acts in the April 2013 elections. The judicial system has also been used politically to attack critics and perceived "enemies of the Bolivarian Revolution" but rarely "cronies" in or around the PSUV.[11]

Advocates for the Bolivarian Revolution believe the Missions are part of the building of a new *patria*, or homeland. Rooted in a long-standing tradition in Venezuela of governments distributing the wealth generated from oil revenues through social programs for the poor, the Missions certainly eliminated illiteracy and decreased extreme poverty. Misión Barrio Adentro (Mission in the Neighborhood) has brought health care to underserved, mostly urban, communities. Nevertheless, as Rafael Uzcategui and others have argued, the Missions compete with and undermine already existing state institutions. With the coming of Barrio Adentro, for instance, service in state hospitals has further collapsed as a result of defunding. Others question how long Venezuela, even with all its oil wealth, can continue to maintain and administer two parallel sets of state institutions, many with the same objectives.

Children of education workers in activities organized by Instituto de Previsión y Asistencia Social del Ministerio de Educación (IPASME), Ministry of Education's Institute for Oversight and Social Assistance, 2005. Photo by Clifton Ross.

A similar problem exists with the *consejos comunales* (community councils) and the *comunas* (communes), which city governments often see as competing with their authority. Advocates of these new forms of governance see in the emerging *consejos* the implementation of a "dual power" strategy: In contrast to the top-down structure of the PSUV,[12] the community councils and communes, they argue, are attempts to open spaces for participation at the local level, to bring management and control to the community. Even if the participation is limited and "conditioned,"[13] and despite all the complications involved in their organization, the community councils represent one of the most interesting and inspiring projects of the Bolivarian process.[14]

Nevertheless, the proliferation of new state institutions and actors to carry on social and community work has also posed problems for Venezuela's social movements. The new structures often sideline or eclipse the power of long-standing activists and community organizations. Organizers and their groups find they can't compete with well-funded, powerful state actors. Some have incorporated themselves in the government, believing it offers the best route to their goals. Others have risked being viewed with suspicion or rejected as opposition, "traitors" or "agents of imperialism" for questioning or challenging official policies.

In this chapter, we try to present a cross-section of views from those who want to see a revolutionary project develop in Venezuela. Some autonomous social movements see a "third way" between the Bolivarian government and the elite opposition. Indigenous movements, most notably among the Yukpa, Pemón, and Wayuu, independent workers' movements such as the current led by Orlando Chirino, and others have pointed to the need to form an independent, and in the latter case, left, opposition. The agroecology project in which Arturo Albarrán works and popular education projects and community organizing such as that represented by Albarrán and María Vicenta Dávila are part of a struggle that antedates the Bolivarian process and works alongside it. And some, like Rosangela Orozco, maintain the necessity of working within the Bolivarian process. We can only hope that the critical voices both inside and outside the process will be heard and respected so Venezuela will be able to pass through the many crises confronting it peacefully and consciously, respecting the many currents that make up the utopian dream of a better world for all Venezuelans.

Rosangela Orozco, El Panal 2021 Commune, Barrio 23 de Enero, Caracas
"Socialism is something you have to practice"

Interview and translation by Susan Spronk and Jeffery R. Webber, August 2012

Rosangela Orozco, who is affectionately known as "La Chiqui," is a young militant from the Caracas barrio 23 de Enero and a leading organizer with the Gran Polo Patriótico (Great Patriotic Pole, GPP). The GPP was created to prepare for the October 2012 elections and to deepen the Bolivarian process. The GPP builds on the legacy of the Polo Patriótico, a coalition of left political parties and social organizations that supported Chávez in electoral campaigns and referenda, which was replaced by the Partido Socialista Unido de Venezuela (United Socialist Party of Venezuela, PSUV), founded in 2007. Today, the GPP is conceived as an organization that aims to bring together diverse social movement militants and political party activists who support the revolutionary process but are not necessarily comfortable with the rigid organization of the PSUV. We caught up with Rosangela at a meeting of the Gran Polo Patriótico in Caracas.

I am a militant of a popular grassroots, communal movement that was named after a fallen compañero of the Coordinadora Simón Bolívar from a very popular neighborhood [where I live] in Caracas, the 23 de Enero. This Coordinadora brought together many youth and militants of different left tendencies in the parish of 23 de Enero in the 1990s. On April 11, 2002, Alexis Gonzalo was killed during the coup d'état [that tried to oust Chávez].

We took his name as our motto to remind ourselves that we need to dedicate our lives and everything we do to revolution, up to and including this interview.

I started as an activist in 1998 when Chávez came to power. I started with the social Missions, working at the grassroots on communal issues. We would participate in meetings where we would talk about politics, Marxism, feminism, Guevarism, social change, because this is the reality of what we are living in Venezuela; we have to wake up. But back then, Chávez was not yet talking about socialism. We in the barrios were talking about revolution while he was talking about a "government that includes everybody," the Third Way, etc.

But the representative democracy that Chávez stood for in the early years is an alternative to what we were living in the Fourth Republic [the pejorative phrase denominating the pacted two-party democracy that existed in Venezuela from 1958 until Chávez's election], and the political repression.

We in the 23 de Enero, for example, experienced violent state repression on February 27, 1989 [the Caracazo, the day when riots against IMF-imposed austerity were brutally suppressed by the military]. I was only nine years old then, but even then I could see how awful it was that arms were being used directly against our community. We didn't know what was happening or why. We were attacked simply because in our neighborhood there were popular organizations confronting the state. But we were not the only ones. The same thing happened in La Vega, Petare, in different parishes of Caracas, anywhere that people went to the streets to protest against the brutal neoliberal policies of the government.

Now I have been a militant left activist for ten years and am active in the Alexis Lives Foundation. We are a studious organization. We call ourselves Marxist-Leninists because we study Marxism, Leninism, and Bolivarianism. We believe in the doctrine of Bolívar, which we adopt for Latin America and also for the international proletariat. These are two very different bodies of thought, I realize.

But we are also Chavista, of course. We defend the binding force of Chávez and what he is building in Latin America and the world. He is an international leader. He is responsible for the fact that many countries that fly different flags have united under one philosophical, political, and economic program that confronts imperialism and globalization. And he is promoting another kind of exchange, based on an alternative logic of solidarity; this is scientific socialism.

This is what socialism looks like

We also believe in the commune that we are constructing, which will eventually exist at the national level. Our commune is called "Honeycomb 2021" *(El Panal* 2021). You are invited to come and visit. We have a lot of relations of exchange. Decisions are made in assembly where the maximum authority is the community, even down to the color of the walls. People decide upon their own rules of communal living. Due to the lack of popular planning mechanisms in previous governments, we are still dealing with the problems of delinquency and houses in poor condition. Of course, it is not perfect, but today at least we are organized. There are many projects that allow us to improve our material conditions such as the Missions, but the foundation of this process is popular participation.

We also have a community radio station, which provides an alternative source of information, and the users participate in the programming. They are not professionals, but locals who become journalists and report what is happening in their own communities. There are some professionals involved, of course, but they are also committed to the process. We do not allow advertising. The programming is basically educational. It is another way of producing information. We also have a newspaper that comes out once a month.

We believe in self-management instead of relying on the president [Chávez]. We also have our own factories—one that packages sugar, another that packages grains—which form part of a network of distribution among different popular neighborhoods in order to try to maintain the regulated price of basic foodstuffs and to make sure that the goods arrive. We do all this to make sure that in the event that there is another bosses' strike, they will not be able to pressure the public or the government by cutting off delivery of basic goods such as food. At the commune Honeycomb 2021, we want to help other organizations so that we can form a large network and create a platform, the Gran Polo Patriótico.

[Our name] is a metaphor, since a honeycomb is constructed by many worker bees. Each one contributes a little to the community and all benefit from what they have built. We are all part of this community, and we each take from it equally depending on what we need, which in turn, depends on our conditions. Everyone who is part of this commune has to be a worker bee to make sure that the commune has good services, tranquility, it stays clean, it is maintained, we have quality education, recreation, communal spaces. And we also say that we all benefit from the honey that this revolution produces—the benefits that come from the missions, the collective work. This is to say, the tranquility, the public health, the food policies, electricity, public spaces, the cleaning up of the streets; we all provide these benefits collectively.

We started building our commune at the end of 2006, beginning of 2007. It is one of the first communes that did not have a legal form, but rather popular legitimacy. Now there is a [commune] structure mandated by law.

The majority of the Venezuelan population identifies with Chávez, but they are not militants; they don't identify with terms like "socialism." This is the way we taught people about socialism, what exchange looks like in socialism, what a commune is, what an alternative economy looks like, what a popular economy looks like, what alternative community media looks like. The commune derives from political necessity.

Building a broad revolutionary current

The GPP is a necessary and vital instrument for the revolution. In Venezuela, we now have only one revolutionary party [the PSUV]. Before this party there were others. The party is just one way of doing politics as a revolutionary militant. There were many social movement organizations that were involved in revolutionary praxis in their large and small spaces, but were not party militants. Chávez, seeing this necessity, created the GPP. This is where the various social movements, from the ecologists to the intellectuals, campesinos, blue- and white-collar workers (*obreros y trabajodores*), communal movements, journalists, women, athletes, all of the movements in their diversity are brought together to militate in one organization for revolutionary socialism.

This is a space that permits the different organizations to recognize each other's struggles, to define who we are at the national level. Our goal is to create a large network, to be able to recognize our own weaknesses, to learn from each other. For example, I might learn a lot from the ecologists.

The elections are fundamental for the Polo Patriótico, but also for our allies. We Venezuelans who identify with this process want it to deepen. But we know that we need to reinvent our politics. Chávez is not a guarantor of this process. Only the people can guarantee that the process continues to move forward.

There is no [political] repression. In the previous era, there was repression. We were repressed for being poor. Even delinquency is treated differently now, a problem that is a historical problem. Because we had a government in a representative democracy and there were a lot of unmet needs. There were very large social problems: alcoholism, drug addiction, violence, and school dropouts. Things have changed. In my neighborhood, for example, now you can go to school for free from first grade to university. You pay nothing. And all the children have food to eat; they are given breakfast, lunch, and a snack.

Now the schools are better because together with the teachers the community is administering the education system. Now people are not scared of exercising their popular power. If the teacher does not show up for work, it is the community that holds them to account and gives the class instead. Of course, there is still a Ministry of Education, etc., but we now understand that the right to education is guaranteeing that the revolution continues. And that education is the only way to break that "genetic code" of individualism.

This is what we mean when we talk about co-responsibility. We cannot say that "Chávez is at fault," for all of us are responsible. This is why we believe in protagonist participation (*la participación protagónica*). Chávez gave us a constitution, political and legal support, but if the revolution does not advance it is because of us. We are not saying, "Go to the mountains with a gun." We are saying, "Study, organize, commune, Polo Patriótico, whatever you want, but express yourself."

We understand that Chávez and his team of ministers, embedded in the institutions of the state, are caught up in their own internal struggle about the form the state should take. It is not easy for them. We are also conscious of the fact that there are revolutionaries and socialists in these institutions, as members of the cabinet across various ministries—these people understand the logic of the popular movements. But these people are surrounded by others [who do not think the same way].

The popular movements themselves move at a rapid speed, doing politics, managing things. They are constructing communes, cleaning up their communities, building their own housing; the institutions of the state, by contrast, move at a much slower pace. There is still way too much bureaucracy.

This was one of the two primary motivations for creating the Gran Polo Patriótico: (1) to win the October elections, and (2) to deepen the revolution, to deepen socialist practice by overcoming all of this bureaucracy. This is what we are always saying in the movement: if there is no one who is talking about socialism, we will never have socialism. Socialism is not something that you only read about, it is something that you have to practice.

J. Arturo Albarrán. Photo by Marcy Rein.

J. Arturo Albarrán, Ministry of Agriculture and Land, and Consejo Socialista Nacional De Agroecología (COSONA, National Socialist Council for Agroecology)
"You have to walk hand in hand with the people"

Interview by Clifton Ross and Marcy Rein, January 2011
Translation by Clifton Ross

Arturo Albarrán works at the Ministry of Agriculture and Land (MAT) in the state of Mérida, acting as an intermediary between the government and campesinos in the region. In his spare time—between his responsibilities as a father, his work building his own home, his full-time job at the Ministry, and his work organizing conferences with campesinos interested in ecological agriculture—Arturo is a filmmaker. Even with his cheap "casero" (homemade) camcorder, and using the MAT's single Macintosh computer after hours, he has made probably a dozen short films in the last year. They're educational documentaries on such subjects as farming worms, growing organic vegetables, and conducting meetings of campesinos. He graduated from the University of the Andes in Mérida in cinema, but he's never quit studying, and even now he talks excitedly about different schools of filmmaking, especially documentary cinema.

Despite all these responsibilities, Arturo took time out to accompany us to Mucuchíes to meet with María Vicenta Dávila so we could talk to her about the popular education work she's done in the region, especially with campesinas. María Vicenta Dávila was one of the founders of the Popular Education Center (CEP) of Mixteque; Arturo became involved in the Center as an adolescent. The CEP has been a touchstone for both of them, and a standard by which to measure social projects. We interviewed Arturo on the bus on the way to Mucuchíes, with blaring beats of reggaeton competing for our attention.

María Vicenta Dávila has always worked to promote the dignity of the women farmers. She gathered around her women whose lives turned around their housework. They would arrive at her house to visit, hiding their faces, their heads down. Their lives revolved around taking care of their husbands and children, and nothing else. Now they're activists and organizers who are pushing forward an agenda for the dignity and respect for campesina and campesino organizations at a national level. Now they've become entrepreneurs. They have a center called CEPDIF, which is the Popular Education Center for Integrated Family Development, which comes out of the popular education centers. This organization has been going on for some thirty years. It wasn't born from this [Bolivarian Revolutionary] process, so it's more natural and legitimate.

Around this center has developed other women's businesses and organizations, such as the collective of women weavers and a project called Seven Steps, Seven Ideas. This group of women are promoting the textiles woven from wool from their sheep, and the improvement of local wool through better breeding of the sheep, resulting in finer work in the typical dress of the people of the *páramo*.

They also have a trout farm, and another organization has formed around this to develop the solidarity economy. They're also raising worms and developing a network of campesino guest-houses to foster agroecological tourism. They're busy with all sorts of things.

And then there's Asociación de Coordinadores de Ambiente por los Agricultores de Rangel (ACAR), a group of campesino women and men who have been dedicated to the recovery of springs of water. Up to now they've recovered more than two hundred springs [in the páramo]. These are springs that, due to the environmental impacts of the misuse of the land, have dried out. People were suffering from a lack of water.

Then one of the women from this whole process of the movement of popular education arrived and began an analysis on the origins of the problem. She came to the conclusion that it was a result of the misuse of the land, the use of agrochemical contamination, overpopulation of livestock trampling the earth, and deforestation.

She gathered the campesinos together and began a process of conscientization [consciousness-raising]. Coming out of this there were workdays organized for the recovery of water springs; two hundred or so campesinos would gather in the paramo. On these days they would do reforestation and indigenous rituals, and restore areas where there was once water. There were dry lakes that were completely dead, without a drop of water. They worked there, and now eight lakes have returned. There were also springs that were drying up which they've now restored, hundreds of these, which have been brought back to life.

Many of these campesinos who have gone through this process of popular education [organized by CEPDIF] have created organizations and formed a block of organizations that meets in a house they've rehabilitated called "Mucututuy," which means "place of gatherings." That's where all these groups meet and work in cooperation with each other: CEPDIF is there, ACAR (Associacion y Coordinacion de Agriculturas de Rangel), ACOPAMED which is a group that's producing medicinal plants, the women weavers, the Weavers of the Paramo, who also belong to the popular education movement that started twenty years before. That was the beginning of all this, and that [movement] was the great opening that gave rise to a number of other organizations and movements. That movement, in turn, was started with a movement for reforestation.

We began learning how to read and write through the process started by Paulo Freire. We started reading and writing through [uncovering] a problem in the community, through a problem experienced by the campesinos. Through a process of selecting a problem and focusing on it, we began reading and writing, which is the process as Paulo Freire conceived it. Through that process, all of these organizations began to emerge in the municipality of Rangel.

As of yet they've received very little from the government and they're very disappointed. This type of organization hasn't been taken into account by the Revolution, and they've received very little (funding). All these people who have been in the process for twenty, thirty years, we're all exhausted, and tired, because we haven't been backed up by the process that the country is going through, by the Revolution, by the government. Why is that? Because the system, Venezuelan revolutionary process, the government, has put forth its own organizational model and it hasn't favored, valued or respected this natural, legitimate form of organization.

The people in these organizations acknowledge the [Bolivarian revolutionary] process and the government, value the changes, and identify with the proposals of the president [Chávez] but they don't agree with its dysfunctional practices.

The laws governing the community councils are horizontalist, but a deeper analysis shows they aren't so horizontal. You have to meet certain standards imposed from above. It's like the Law of Participation: It's so very confusing and complicated and not at all like you go in, raise your hand and choose. It's something far more complicated. Similarly with the communes, they're imposing [from above]. Those that function best are those that have functioned a long time and have developed naturally and legitimately, born from the base, from the heart of the community. I'm in agreement with promoting the communes, but they should be built by respectfully accompanying the communities, hand in hand, not by forcing, pressuring, or imposing. It has to be self-organized.

Agroecology: seeds falling on stony ground

You have to arrive at the ministry (Ministry of Agriculture and Land, MAT) and keep quiet, shake hands, and not criticize anything, and then you can get your raises and maybe even be a director of something. But I've bothered people, I've disagreed, I've been very critical and I haven't kept quiet. And that doesn't matter to me since I do the work that I'm there to do. What's needed there is someone to tell the truth, criticize things that are bad, and be critical with the people. But at least I've managed to strengthen the space for agroecology, and work with people in other states on agroecology.

Everyone in the MAT was trained in the model of the Green Revolution, so they don't believe in agroecology. So in the ministry there are mafias that do business in the international importation of potato, garlic, and coffee seeds. Every time there's need for seed, these mafias in the upper spheres of the ministry do business. Just now a shipment of contaminated seeds arrived from Canada and many campesinos were smart enough to know that and they wouldn't accept them. Those that planted had damaged crops, or crops that didn't produce.

At one point [2008] there was a national plan [to implement agroecology] but nothing came of it. At that point there was more support [for agroecology] because there was a national plan imposed and a convergence of [government] funding agents, FONDAS, proposed funding agroecology. But the director at the time didn't believe in agroecology and didn't fund any of the 318 campesinos, many well established, who applied. The director of the state of Mérida in a meeting said that mass production for the country was needed and he didn't believe that it could be done through agroecology.

So the laws were made favoring agroecology at the executive and legislative level, but those put in charge to carry the program out didn't do so. What happens is that every director has a *padrino* at the national level, like a mafia, and they don't question them. It's better to keep quiet. That's why we've formed the Consejo Socialista Nacional de Agroecología (COSONA), because the directors at the state levels have blocked the work of agroecology.

The campesino movement here has managed to get three people for agroecology elected to the National Assembly. We've only managed to get three elected, but that's at least something of a voice for agroecology—one from the state of Portuguesa, one from Yaracuy and one from the state of Lara. They want to push forward on the proposals and discussions from COSONA and they'll carry them into the National Assembly, which is the sort of thing we've been working for.

So [in COSONA] there are these three representatives [to the National Assembly] and forty-eight organizations from all over the country, campesino cooperatives that have been around for twenty or thirty years like Cooperativa Alianza, which is also part of COSONA, organizations and groups from Yaracuy. It's an organization completely independent of the state. We want to affiliate with the state but under the control of the people, the campesinos.

The three representatives are part of the PSUV, but in the case of César Alejandro González, [the representative] from Portuguesa, he was proposed by the campesino base in the internal state elections and he competed against another candidate who was pushed by the inner circle of the [PSUV] party and had the support of the entire National Assembly, including Cilia Flores [PSUV president of the National Assembly] and [foreign minister] Nicolás Maduro. This candidate had already served a term but hadn't responded to his base, so César Alejandro was proposed by the people, and he began his campaign with nothing.

The other candidate had all the machinery of the party for his propaganda, a sound system, microphones, and everything. [Alejandro] didn't have even a bullhorn. He had nothing but went directly to talk to the campesinos—and he won! But there was a message for him. César Alejandro told me that later that when Cilia Flores had gathered the assembly together she took César and others [of the left opposition] aside and said, "There will be no debate here. The party lines have already been established, and the line of the Comandante [President Chávez] have been established."

Only César replied, "We're not here to just raise our hands. We've been elected by the community and the people to debate, and that's what we'll do." So you can't rule by decree. How can you oblige a candidate, a representative to follow a [party] line? That won't work.

I feel a lot of admiration for President Hugo Rafael Chávez as the only person in this government who believes in the creative power of the people. Still, like everyone, he's made mistakes, and one of those is that he's fallen into the same scheming politics and power struggles and he's let things slip. He's wanted to push at a pace beyond the dynamic of the people. I've always believed that you have to walk hand in hand with the people and not try to change things too radically or too quickly. So Chávez has had some great ideas for the country, but you can't impose them and expect changes overnight.

María Vicenta Dávila, popular educator
"I consider President Chávez to be a popular educator"

Interview by Marcy Rein and Clifton Ross, January 2011
Translation by Clifton Ross

Mucuchíes sits almost eight thousand feet up in the Andes, in the municipality of Rangel in the state of Mérida. To reach María Vicenta Dávila's house there, we walked up a long hill that seemed to have about a thirty-degree grade, under a bright blue sky with the peculiar clarity of high altitude. Arturo Albarrán, who was accompanying us, thoughtfully stopped to let us catch our breaths and pick exotic wild fruit growing along the side of the road.

María Vicenta cofounded the Centro de Educación Popular de Mixteque (CEP, Popular Education Center). The Center trained hundreds of women leaders who have built a whole web of projects in the area—including a cluster of houses for women who had no homes, built with their own hands, after they cleared the stones off the earth they were building on. Clearing the land gave María Vicenta the idea for a writing group. "All the stones in the area have stories," she said. The group brought together people from the community— housewives who had done little outside the home, farmers, and bricklayers. Working as a collective, they compiled a book of oral histories of the elders in the area, and illustrated it themselves.

María Vicenta's work has brought her to numerous national and international gatherings, where she made presentations on women, popular education, and development. Her first, Organización Popular para un Mejor Vivir (Grassroots Organizing for a Better Way of Life) was in 1995 in Caracas, around the time that the Fourth World Conference on Women met in Beijing. She attended the Segundo Encuentro de Pobladores de Montaña a Nivel

María Vicenta Dávila. Photo by Marcy Rein.

Mundial 2004 (Second Global Gathering of Mountain Peoples) in Quito, Ecuador, and the Second Encuentro de Mujeres Líderes Barriales (Second Gathering of Women Community Leaders) in Bolivia in 2005. She attends such conferences because, she said, we need "to have spaces where women can participate, because we saw before how the woman was the one who was in the house, washing, cooking, watching after husband and child and giving birth and giving birth… and never having space to participate."

I'm from Mucuchíes, specifically, the community of Mixteque. We have a great history of struggle here. When Inparques [Instituto Nacional de Parques] established the Parque Sierra Nevada, we protested in Mucuchíes so they would set up the park as the community proposed. When they didn't want to open more classrooms for the students, a group of mothers there in Mucuchíes protested.

I'm a popular educator and my formation has come through processes like the National Literacy Plan that started at the end of the 1970s. We began to structure the Center of Popular Education (CEP) of Mixteque and Mucumpate and I formed part of the coordinating group in agriculture. I was drawn into the agricultural aspects because that's where we have to guarantee the supply of food. The agricultural committee was the beginnings of what would later become the *cajas rurales*, the rural banks. The committee gave credits of fifty bolívares, and [back then] fifty bolívares was a lot of money. So, for example, we'd give Arturo the credit so he could buy his fertilizer and if he didn't pay it back, I wouldn't benefit, nor would anyone else. And we began to work.

Besides the agricultural committee there was the culture committee, which organized beautiful works of street theater in the community. It was part of a process of demands for community needs for housing, electricity, and public services. The structure of the CEP was lovely, like a daisy. The center was the coordination and the petals were all the committees.

It wasn't a single, exclusive project, which is why I would criticize the community councils of today. The community councils work in concrete, block by block: it's cement for the sidewalk, cement for the street, but no work done on forming people. In popular education we did a lot of work on formation, helping people grow, on the integrated growth of people in community. We had a lot of workshops, which is what popular education is all about: participation, community organization. And we popular educators will tell you that the national project of the president [Chávez] was a dream of many popular educators, many of whom are no longer with us.

All this grew and resulted in 144 popular education centers in the municipality of Rangel. And we joined with other popular education centers in Mucuchíes and from that emerged a proposal to create a municipal organization that would be called CEPZONAL Rangel, the Popular Educational Centers of Rangel Municipality. We met there the first Sunday of every month as representatives of each of the CEPs. It was really beautiful because we had exchanges, for instance, between the agricultural committees and the cultural committees.

There was an organizational structure at the national level in the CEP, made up of people from the nine states where there were CEPs, and they settled on an agreement with the [national] Ministry of the Family for the creation of the "multihome" daycare centers. But later problems developed with the "multihome" centers as they weren't fulfilling the objectives that we had in mind.

We ended participation in that project, turning the "multihomes," as well as projects of trout farming, textiles and worm farms over to cooperatives, so the people of the communities themselves could assume responsibility for the administration and direction of their own projects. You know the saying, "When you have children who marry, they want their own house" (*cuando ya se casan, el que se casa quiere casa*), well, that was the idea.

There was a hope that these organizations would become autonomous and carry out their own projects. Unfortunately, the communities continue to have a paternalistic attitude of dependence: do it for me, search for me, direct me. So in some ways these projects haven't advanced because of that.

Now as the Popular Education Center we've looked over our bylaws and rules and decided we've changed, so we've had to restructure. Now we call ourselves Popular Education Centers for the Integrated Development of the Family. We're no longer working directly in the community because, unfortunately, there isn't the support for that. I say that not wanting to offend anyone in the state, but the state is supporting the community councils. So there's no support for a grassroots organization that has been born without any great promotion, that has created its own laws and rules for itself, like the CEP.

If you look at the structure [of the community councils] you can see that it comes in part from the CEPs. This is something that the president [Chávez] has mentioned a lot, because it was an idea of Paulo Freire. The proposal of Paulo Freire was to generate a process of social justice from the most dispossessed. That's been the idea behind the organizations here in Mucuchíes. The majority of the community councils that have been successful and the people who've formed part of them at the municipal level, and there are a lot of them, all have a history of which we've been a part, and we all come from a process of popular education.

Community councils

The community councils have been founded on a lovely structure, but there's a problem. For example, it's obligatory to elect a culture committee and the people elect it and vote for someone, but that person doesn't have an idea of the role of a coordinator of culture nor of a cultural committee. Or there's a water committee, but what work needs to be done? There's no coherent plan for the training of these work committees that are part of the community councils. Those who have free time go, but they don't learn how to transmit this knowledge they gain to others.

On the other hand, in the popular education centers we form schools and train people and form leaders. We have a training plan, some done here, some in Caracas. How do we support it? We have raffles, house parties, and fundraisers. The community councils should be doing that and say, "Okay, we're going to make a plan for a workshop for the culture committee," "Well, the role of the culture committee is such and such, and we're going to start a school for three months, or six."

I think the president [Chávez] has a lot of dreams. I consider him to be a popular educator. He wants to work directly from top to bottom and also from bottom to top so there really would be horizontality, but the people with him don't get this process. And there are others at his side who are enemies and don't want to see this process realized.

I think that the plan of the community councils is really good but that this plan shouldn't blot out those solid, grassroots organizations that have grown up locally, like the CEPs, and the irrigation committees. The irrigation committee here in the municipality is a real solid organization that is working on water for agriculture and what happens? Right now it's being overruled by those in power, those who make the decisions, that is to say, the community council.

On the other hand, they're limiting resources to the community councils. For instance, the mayor's office is trying to intervene, or there are people in the bureaucracy there who are trying to intervene, in the community councils. So, for example, there's the problem of changing roofs because the roofs are made of asbestos, which, you know, is a carcinogenic material. Since last year they've been discussing this and there's 120 million [bolívares] available. They looked over the houses and later the housing committee from the community did a revision and there was an election for eight people. That was last September. Now [January] we've had a meeting of the community council and the money hasn't yet come to the community, because it's being held up at the mayor's office. So the technical committee is waiting for someone to release the funds. [The mayor's office] is holding up the national project of the president.

I'm Chavista and I believe in the national project of the president, but I don't believe in his ministers. And there's too much bureaucracy. The president says, "The bureaucracy has to be eliminated," that the community shouldn't have to do so much. They say one thing here and do something else there and if you argue with them, they say, "You aren't a Chavista, you aren't supporting the government."

I think this is all about the hunger for power, rather than a hunger for a real process of change in the people. Those who hunger for power and see us working to make a real process of change in the people, they want to limit us. So here when there was an election for mayor we fought for one person, and the officialists, the other "Chavismo," shall we say, were in power. They had all the machinery of power: the telephones, the cars, money for advertisements.

There was a dirty war against us, with verbal and physical abuse, and there were complaints lodged in writing and a tremendous violation with corruption, dividing up money, taking people's ID cards, and paying off voters. It was just like the Fourth Republic. We were told, "You're not Chavista, you're in the opposition," because we were supporting a comrade who was really clear in his process, a person we loved and who would do good work. They cut him off, and they cut us off such that many of us no longer go to the mayor's office because there isn't that support there.

So that's why I talk about the vices, and until they come to an end, the national project of Chávez won't be able to make the necessary changes. But I think there will be seeds of that project, and they will germinate, seeds of all these ideas that I've talked about.

Alexis Romero, Pemón in Resistance
"We should be the ones who exploit these resources"

Interview by Pepe el Toro, first published in *El Libertario*, Edition 69, April–May 2013.
Interview and introductory notes translated and edited by Clifton Ross.

In October 2011 and February 2013 indigenous Pemón of the Gran Sabana in Venezuela's Bolívar State surrounded, disarmed and detained columns of the Venezuelan Armed Forces to protest abuses and denounce the military's participation in illegal gold mining. El Libertario *talked with Alexis Romero, an indigenous Pemón imprisoned for his participation in these protests, about the motives for one of the most inspiring direct actions undertaken by local social movements in recent years.*

Romero explained to us that the whole Pemón community, including elders, women, and children, took part in the action against the military. After being detained for three days in the La Pica Penitentiary, he received a strange "presidential pardon," something only granted to convicted prisoners, even though he has not yet gone to trial. To complete the irregularity, despite the "pardon," he has to present himself biweekly to the courts and await a judgment against him. Romero is one more victim of the criminalization of protest by the Bolivarian government. As a Pemón spokesperson, he emphasized that the indigenous leadership is ready to take whatever action necessary to defend itself against further attacks on indigenous communities by the military.

The Venezuelan indigenous movement had a certain power and unity before the arrival of Chávez. Remember the campaign against laying the power lines in 1999 when we were at the front of the action? The Pemón people united with those in Amazonas and Zulia and carried forward the struggle. Then the president arrived with a pretty discourse that favored indigenous people. He managed to push the rights of indigenous people into the national constitution. All this brought our energy and our struggle down. We thought that the outlining and titling of our habitat and indigenous territories would happen without any pressure because they were

Indigenous Pemón of the Gran Sabana in Bolívar State surrounded, disarmed, and detained columns of the Venezuelan Armed Forces to protest abuses and denounce the military's participation in illegal gold mining, 2013. Photos courtesy of *Correo del Caroní.*

covered by the Magna Carta; the struggle of the indigenous movement became passive and declined.

We came to see that the government of President Chávez was more dangerous than the other governments because he'd set us back with his discourse, which we trusted that he would fulfill. Divisions grew in the indigenous movement of Bolívar, and the national movement now has parallel directing councils. We've had conflicts with the indigenous ministry. And this has all benefited the state that, in practice, doesn't want to concretize the rights it recognizes [on paper].

It's been difficult to carry the message to the Pemón people that the demarcation [of territory] and the title to our lands wasn't going to happen, in part because of the deposits of gold and other minerals we have here. The government isn't going to easily turn over this area. The only option [for us] will be to clarify our terms and take up the struggle again, no longer peacefully but with different [forms of] protest.

Communities resist military's abuse and extortion

I wasn't in the action [of taking the military captive]. When I arrived I saw there was no document that would explain the reasons for the action so we wrote up a resolution with a few indigenous leaders, and that's how we ended up here. And I mounted a defense, more than anything, verbal, as the military tried to force the protestors to submit.

I told them they were being abusive and that they themselves were involved in illegal mining, because the military itself was doing the mining. They were abusing the indigenous community, stripping women naked because they thought they might be hiding gold. That act, which took place in La Paragua where the indigenous people were ordinarily very passive, made people wake up. They were no longer willing to be humiliated by the military but were ready to respond. A group was gathering force, saying that there hadn't been concrete progress made on these rights. Now what's happening in Urimán is part of the continuity. Now the Chavista indigenous leaders are even more under siege and no longer have the same influence.

In Alto Paragua there was the direct participation of the military, especially in bribes and paying protection. So in Urimán a military captain charges every time he goes to the mines where the indigenous [work]; they say he takes two or three hundred grams or half a kilo of gold. He was taking some amount of gold for payment. The communities are under this control of paying to work. Then after what happened in Alto Paragua there was a change. They no longer were directly exploited, but they had to pay. [The military is] isolating the communities and only letting in two companies, charging 2,500 bolívares per person, 5,000 bolívares to come and go. And then the military began to enter the houses, not the mines, but where the equipment was in the houses. They asked for half a kilo of gold and if they weren't given half a kilo of gold, they would break the machines, the machines that weren't even being used but were in the houses.

The military came to get those who were detained. [In the deal] it was proposed that the zone be demilitarized. Our weakness was shown when some of our leaders moved forward and accepted [the agreement] before the negotiations were accepted by those most affected in Urimán. The people from Urimán said if the minister of defense or Vice President Nicolás Maduro himself didn't come they wouldn't free the soldiers. But the leaders from other communities began petitioning and accepted negotiations, as if the people from Urimán had accepted. Now, as to fulfilling this, they aren't going to keep the agreement. We'll have to strengthen this document since there are a lot of pitfalls, strengthen it and follow up on it.

There's a proposal for demilitarization with the idea that the Pemón people do their own security with their own indigenous militias from the community to deal with any possible problems of security. Right now there's a problem with the nonindigenous population since they weren't allowed [in the mines] in the original agreement. At first artisanal mining was allowed, but that was taken out in favor of just "mining," a dubious change since at the same time they weren't going to allow mining in the national park but the Urimán mines are inside the national park. And since these people feel excluded and blame it on the indigenous leaders, that group is under threat. One positive aspect of all this is that now the indigenous leadership is more united and ready to take any action necessary to ensure that the military stops violating the rights of the indigenous population.

You should know that the indigenous leadership has always been openly proenvironmentalist, defending Mother Nature, the earth, and the rivers. But it was precisely this discourse we believe in that led us to believe President Chávez's proposals would be fulfilled. But the as the situation presents itself now, gold has been nationalized so as to give it to the multinational corporations, those same ones the government calls "savage capitalists." So where is there consistency in the discourse? What should we do? Continue protecting our lands so someone else can come and exploit them, lands that they'll surely destroy in the process? They talk about mining royalties, but since when have the royalties come to the communities? Seeing the situation more clearly each time, we decided we should be the ones who exploit these resources, we who work and oversee the process, searching for ways to minimize the damage in doing so. That's where we are now. The communities themselves should be the ones who present a work plan, a living plan for those who want to exploit the mines. Already various communities have responded. I believe there are one hundred small communities in the Gran Sabana that are now living from mining.

Orlando Chirino, oil industry worker and member of United Revolutionary Autonomous Class Current
"Those who don't meet people like us, who are taking up a left political agenda, won't hear this version of history"

Interview and translation by Clifton Ross, May 2013

I first met Orlando Chirino in January 2006, when Marcy Rein and I were in Caracas for the Social Forum of the Americas. He had helped to found the National Workers' Union (UNT) as an alternative to the Venezuelan Workers Central (CTV), whose leadership opposed the Bolivarian process. Within the UNT, he was working with the United Revolutionary Autonomous Class Current (CCURA), which advocated union democracy and autonomy from political parties. CCURA looked likely to win the UNT elections in September 2006, but the government intervened. President Hugo Chávez declared that union autonomy was "a counterrevolutionary poison," and his action split the fledgling UNT. In 2007 Chirino was fired from his job at the state oil company, PDVSA, for publicly opposing the constitutional reform Chávez put forward. Though he won the right to return to work, PDVSA has refused to reinstate him.

The government has its official union, and it countersigns the most important contracts, which are resolved without discussion with the workers,

Orlando Chirino. Photo by Clifton Ross.

without assemblies. That's the main reason that today the union movement is divided and atomized: The collective bargaining agreements aren't
discussed. I'll give you an example. Central, state, and local government
public administration workers, as well as workers in autonomous institutes,
haven't discussed their contract framework since December 2004. This is
evidence of a government that calls itself socialist and pro-worker with its
words, but by its acts it is an anti-union, anti-worker government that violates union freedom, imprisons leaders who struggle, brings judicial proceedings against others, fires, and ignores orders to reinstate. This is the
real truth about this whole process that so many of us supported. I never
was a militant Chavista, nor claimed to be one, but we did accompany and
support this government in its early years.

After [Chávez] won the referendum of August 15, 2004, an intense
process of unity with Fidel began. [The Bolivarian government] formed
what we would call a bourgeois Stalinist regime that persecuted any sign
of autonomy in any social organizations of any type, be they worker movements, student movements, campesino movements. They entered them
and prostituted them with a policy of corrupting or co-opting the leaders.

So, for example, they control the elections for the community councils.
If they lose, the Ministry of Communes, where [new community councils]
have to register, doesn't register them unless they're Chavista. This is all part
of a process of decay. It might not be obvious to a foreigner who comes in
and doesn't find left union leaders, people like us, taking up a left agenda.

They won't hear this version of history but rather that Venezuela is undergoing a process of deep democratization in a socialist project, but that picture is completely false.

This isn't to deny that there are Missions and the constitution has important human rights elements. And they've fixed some bridges, but this government has done very little for the infrastructure of the country, especially if you compare what they did during the Pérez Jiménez dictatorship, and what was done under the Punto Fijo bourgeois democratic governments that ruled for forty years. You'll see how industry has shrunk, as well as infrastructure.

And you have to keep in mind that this government has enjoyed the highest price on oil, around $100 [per barrel], and managed to collect taxes as well as impose a value-added tax [sales tax], which is regressive and punishes even the unemployed. Add to that the fact that the loss of buying power is terrible. Here 70 percent of Venezuelan workers only make between minimum wage and double minimum wage, or two minimum-wage salaries. They're making under a living wage. The government itself says that the basic food basket is 4,400 or 4,500 bolívares but unofficial estimates are more like 8,000 or 9,000, which, as the father of a family, I can tell you is more like the actual cost, because inflation here is terrible.

The present crisis is an expression of a slow but sure process, a rupture that has begun and has expressed itself in the electoral arena. How else can you explain that between October and April [the Chavistas] have lost a million votes? Here there is an economically active population of thirteen million, three hundred thousand people, half of which are unemployed or employed in the informal economy. A million and a half are unemployed.

Collapse of basic industries, corruption of worker control

In Guayana the basic industries, some of which were in the hands of multinationals, have been nationalized. And now the majority of them are in the process of bankruptcy—and not just from the perspective of production—[the industries are only producing] 20 or 30 percent [of prenationalized levels]. Their workers have gone from being the best paid, from having great housing plans, cars, excellent quality of life, benefits paid by the companies, to losing absolutely all of that—and they've gone an average of four years without having discussed their collective bargaining agreements.

The entire experience of what they called "worker control" has been a big farce, because what the government tried to impose with "worker control" was controlled workers. In other words, this process had nothing to do with "popular power," or with the autonomy of union organizations, since real worker control has to be an initiative from below, from the base.

Since there's no autonomy allowed in the union movement, there is a direct, abusive and even gross interference of the state governor through a group of union leaders from the Bolivarian Socialist Workers' Central Union, founded by the government in 2010, a union which, as we say, is neither socialist nor Bolivarian and is directed by a clique of union leaders totally tied to the state.

On the other side, it's important to note that workers in some companies are engaged in a militant struggle for autonomy. The elections in Ferrominera [Orinoco] brought Rubén González to power as leader.[15] He's an icon of the worker's struggle. He was imprisoned and sentenced to seven and a half years; only a national workers' mobilization is keeping him out of jail now, since his case remains open and he has to report regularly to Caracas. His only "crime" was leading a couple of strikes the workers called because 80 percent of their contract had been violated or not fulfilled, and management refused to negotiate a new agreement.

Carbonorca and Bauxilum are directed by people from autonomous unions. In Bauxilum the company is using armed bands from a group called "Muralla Roja," from the construction [workers] armed shock brigades that nearly killed the old secretary general. They succeeded in making the employees vote in fraudulent elections by making themselves the majority of the union. But in Carbonorca Emilio Campos is an important leader, a real fighter, and there's Juan Gómez. Both are militant supporters of Capriles but at this time they're working in a process of unifying grassroots unions, like some movements coming out of Caracas to fight government policies, with an autonomy that we've questioned. For us, autonomy means autonomy from all government: an autonomous and independent union movement, not something that would be relinquished if Capriles wins. That's to return to the same thing.

So we have our differences, but they've done significant work even though their union authority hasn't been recognized and they can't get collective bargaining recognized. And when they turn in documents to the work inspectorates, which are appendages of the governing party [PSUV], they're audited because the government, above all in the strategic industries like electricity, oil, basic industries, is corporatizing the union movement, and forcing workers to submit through a union. In some cases the [government has] created "workers' councils." We're not opposed to workers' councils. We defend every kind of organization that the workers decide to build in an autonomous fashion, but we strongly oppose the government making these councils into tools by imposing hand-picked leaders who have nothing to do with the workers' aspirations.

And then there's the military. Imagine, CADAFE [the national electric company] is under Jesse Chacon, a military man from February 4;[16] [General] Carlos Osorio is at SIDOR [the nationalized steel company]; [Rafael] Ramírez isn't military but has his influence there, and he's in oil. [The military is in charge of] many businesses like cement and concrete, some in food. We're in a process of militarization because the government understands that given the condition workers are in, there are struggles coming, so they're preparing for repression.

Labor unity and independent political action

Venezuela isn't a socialist, but a capitalist country. It has nothing to do with socialism. But even in socialism we would have to defend the autonomy and independence of the union movement. As workers say, "If my union leader is the government, who is there to defend me?" Because when there are conflicts those union leaders side with the government, which is also the first boss to attack organizations or workers that engage in any struggle.

And now there's a strong polarization in the country, incarnated in Maduro and Capriles, the latter representing some sectors of the reformist Left. What stance do we have toward this? We believe two things. First, we've formed a legal organization called the Socialism and Freedom Party (PSL) and participated in the October elections, and received some five thousand votes. I ran as presidential candidate with the idea of defeating this perverse polarization the country is in, of which Chávez was the retaining wall.

Now Chávez is gone. Maduro's government is profoundly weak and facing a deep economic crisis. There's an enormous fiscal debt and much discontent, since they're not dealing with the immediate needs of people who are being squeezed by growing inflation and scarcity. So we think it's the right moment, from a union perspective, to unite. We're talking with the UNT and grassroots sectors of the CTV to propose a unity of action. Union organizations can have different politics but still come together on a concrete program [which would include] a general hike in wages and salaries, that the minimum wage be discussed with workers and not unilaterally imposed, an end to the criminalization and repression of protest, that collective bargaining be opened up now, that union autonomy be respected, that the value-added tax be rescinded and, finally, that we discuss the problem of dignified work in Venezuela.

Ecuador

"Never again without us": Indigenous movements shape the country

By Marc Becker

In June 1990, thousands of indigenous people took to the streets in Ecuador in protest of the government's economic, social, and political policies. Having a historically marginalized group dramatically insert themselves into political debates stunned the white elite of this small South American country. This uprising, subsequently called the *levantamiento indígena de Inti Raymi* because it took place just before the traditional June solstice "Sun Festival" celebrations, became a defining moment in that country's history. No longer could indigenous demands be ignored.

Ecuador is a small country on the Pacific coast of South America, and is divided into four geographic regions: the eastern Amazon forests, the high Andes mountains, the warm tropical coast, and the Galapagos archipelago located far from the coast in the Pacific Ocean. Historically these geographic divisions have been barriers to the creation of a unified national identity. Ecuador's largest city is the coastal port of Guayaquil, which traditionally had been seen as liberal, commercial, and outward-looking but now is the center for conservative neoliberal economic policies. In contrast, the capital Quito, located in the highlands, had a reputation as conservative, religious, and inward-looking but now is the home of leftist social movements.

About fourteen million people inhabit Ecuador. The wealthiest and most powerful people are the white descendants of the Spanish colonists. The largest part of the population are the mestizos, a mixture of European and indigenous cultures and peoples. About 10 percent of the population are Afro-Ecuadorians, descendants of escaped slaves who were brought to Ecuador during the colonial period. The percentage of people who trace their ancestry back to the original indigenous inhabitants is hotly contested. Census figures reveal that only 7 percent of the population wishes to identify as such, whereas indigenous organizations claim that they represent many more people, perhaps as much as 45 percent of the population.

Ecuador has long been plagued by issues of political instability. Since independence in 1830, about two hundred different people have held presidential power, competing with Bolivia for the record of the number and frequency of extraconstitutional changes in government. In 2008, the country adopted its twentieth constitution. During the twentieth century, Ecuador only had three periods during which power passed peacefully from one elected candidate to another. The first was during the 1910s and 1920s in the midst of a cacao boom, the second came in the 1950s with a banana boom, and the longest and most recent was in the 1980s and 1990s in the aftermath of an oil boom.

Politics was traditionally the realm of wealthy white males. In 1929, Ecuador was the first country in Latin America to give women the right to vote in federal elections. Although sometimes assumed to be a liberal reform, conservatives favored giving women the vote because of their association with tradition and religion, and an assumption that women would support conservative candidates. Although Ecuador was the first country in Latin America to give women the right to vote, it was one of the last to give indigenous peoples citizenship rights. Not until 1979 as part of constitutional reforms when Ecuador emerged out of its last military dictatorship did indigenous peoples gain the right to vote. Even with the broadening of the franchise, political and economic power still remained largely in the hands of the same elite classes.

Popular movements including labor unions and leftist political parties repeatedly challenged elite hegemonic control over the country. On several occasions, the Left has come close to gaining power only to have the conservative oligarchy reassert their domination. Often the Left has lost out to populist politicians who spouted rhetoric in support of the poor to gain electoral support, only to impose policies that benefited the oligarchy once they were elected. The most famous and successful of the populist politicians was José María Velasco Ibarra. From the 1930s to the 1970s, Velasco Ibarra won election five times but only was able to complete one of his terms, his third one in the 1950s in the midst of the banana boom that brought more political stability to the country. His last two terms in the 1960s and 1970s led to Ecuador's last two military dictatorships in 1963 and 1972. Populist politicians have undermined the ability of the Left to consolidate support for a movement to challenge Ecuador's exclusionary political and economic structures.

Ecuador has small but powerful leftist movements, divided at different points into socialist, communist, Maoist, Stalinist, and Cuban wings.

The first socialist party was founded in Quito in 1926, one year after a modernizing military government had brought an end to a sequence of liberal governments. The formation of the party came in the aftermath of a powerful anarchist general strike in Guayaquil. The police suppressed the strike with a terrible massacre on November 15, 1922, that resulted in the deaths of hundreds of workers. Observers said that Ecuador's labor movements had been born in a baptism of blood.

At the same time that leftists were organizing labor unions and political parties in the cities, rural activists were building strong movements in indigenous communities. Jesús Gualavisí and Dolores Cacuango mobilized their indigenous comrades in the rural district of Cayambe against neighboring haciendas. Similar to the 1990 indigenous uprising seventy years later, a 1931 rural strike shook the wealthy capitalist class to its core. A month later when indigenous activists in Cayambe called for a country-wide meeting to organize an indigenous federation to advance their interests, the military stepped in, arrested the leaders, and shut the meeting down. After the frustrated attempt in 1931 and another failed effort in 1935, indigenous activists with their leftist allies finally managed to create a national-level organization in 1944. For the next two decades, the Ecuadorian Federation of Indians (FEI) led struggles for land rights that eventually led to agrarian reform legislation in 1964 and 1973. Once they achieved their main demands, however, the Federation began to decline.

Under the influence of liberation theology, in the 1960s the Catholic Church helped organize new indigenous rights federations. They started with the Shuar Federation in the southeastern Amazon in 1961, and subsequently helped launch the National Federation of Peasant Organizations (FENOC) in 1965 and ECUARUNARI, an organization taking its name from the Kichwa phrase meaning the awakening of the Ecuadorian Indians, in 1972. All of these federations were meant to counteract the more radical FEI, but they also began to drift leftward in their political orientation.

In 1980, the Shuar Federation helped found the Confederation of Indigenous Nationalities of the Ecuadorian Amazon (CONFENIAE), and then together with ECUARUNARI the Confederation of Indigenous Nationalities of Ecuador (CONAIE) in 1986. CONAIE consciously structured their organization around the construction of some fourteen indigenous nationalities and eighteen indigenous pueblos (peoples). CONAIE attempted to present itself as the unified representative of all indigenous peoples in Ecuador, but FENOC (now known as the National Confederation of Peasant, Indigenous, and Black Organizations, FENOCIN) and the Ecuadorian Federation of Evangelical Indians (FEINE) contested that designation. Sometimes these organizations worked together for common goals, and at other times they fiercely competed with each other for grassroots support.

A long-running debate within indigenous organizations was whether activists should press for political changes as a social movement or as a political party. This ongoing dance between different organizing strategies led to the formation of Pachakutik in 1995 to contest for local office. Pachakutik achieved a fair level of success in placing their candidates in power in local races in indigenous communities, but were frustrated in their attempts to achieve broader political traction.

While Pachakutik contested for power at the ballot box, CONAIE continued with a policy of using street-level mobilizations to pull down neoliberal governments who ruled against their economic and political interests. In 1996, Abdalá Bucaram won election on a populist platform that, much like Velasco Ibarra before him, promised to aid the poor but once in office he proceeded to implement policies that benefited the oligarchy. After half a year, in February 1997, CONAIE mobilized large protests that forced Bucaram from office. But rather than CONAIE taking power, Fabian Alarcón, the president of the Congress, took over the presidency and continued with similar types of policies.

Four years later, once again CONAIE mobilized against the presidency of Jamil Mahuad that was implementing neoliberal economic policies that were particularly crushing for rural indigenous communities. In highly symbolic moves that struck against nationalist notions of sovereignty, he replaced the national currency, the sucre, with the U.S. dollar, and lent the Manta Air Base rent-free to the U.S. military for purposes of intervening in the drug and guerrilla wars in neighboring Colombia.

On January 21, 2000, in what some people called the last and shortest coup of the twentieth century, indigenous militants allied with lower-ranking members of the military to remove Mahuad from power. For a brief period of time, CONAIE president Antonio Vargas together with Colonel Lucio Gutiérrez held power in a Junta of National Salvation until an army general pulled rank on Gutiérrez and collapsed their provisional government. Gutiérrez emerged from this failed coup attempt as a political leader, and two years later won election to the country's highest office in alliance with the indigenous political movement, Pachakutik. At the time, some observers interpreted his actions as a repeat of those of his colleague Hugo Chávez in Venezuela, who initially led a failed military coup but then returned to win the presidency through the ballot box.

In a seeming repeat of previous populist politicians, Gutiérrez quickly allied with the capitalist and neoliberal interests that he had pledged to fight, and CONAIE and Pachakutik soon broke from his government. After two years of increasingly conservative policies, another popular uprising forced Gutiérrez from power. This time, instead of being led by indigenous activists, it was middle-class urban dwellers who pressed for his removal. In fact, the conservative evangelical indigenous federation FEINE which was now allied with Vargas came to his defense. Subsequently, evangelical indigenous communities as well as those in the Amazon would support Gutiérrez, drawing a significant amount of support away from Pachakutik.

In the lead up to the 2006 presidential elections, activists urged an alliance between Pachakutik and Rafael Correa who had gained reknown as minister of finance in the successor government to Gutiérrez. Some proponents dreamed of a joint ticket between Correa and a historic indigenous leader such as Luis Macas. In what many interpreted as an egotistical and perhaps racist move on Correa's part, he refused to play second fiddle to an indigenous leader with decades of experience leading political struggles. Nevertheless, Correa gained popular support and defeated banana magnate and Ecuador's richest man Álvaro Noboa to win the presidency.

Once in office, Correa quickly won a series of elections that deeply entrenched his hold on power. First he won a plebiscite to hold elections for a constituent assembly, then created a new political party that won the majority of seats in the assembly, then won approval for the new constitution that had been drafted under his guidance, and finally won reelection and a dominant presence in Congress under the new constitution. The decade before assuming office had been a particularly unstable one in Ecuador's history with about ten people moving through the presidential palace, but now Correa was positioned to remain in power for ten years.

Correa's ascendency came at the cost of social movements who felt that he had taken over their political issues and monopolized the spaces that they had previously enjoyed. In addition, indigenous communities repeatedly challenged Correa for his desire to build the economy on extractive industries, particularly petroleum and gold mining, which had especially harsh impacts on historically marginalized communities. Even though this resentment led to a falling out with leftist activists, Correa maintained a strong degree of popularity from the mestizo urban middle-classes and as a result retained dominant control over the country.

Milton Chamorro. Photo by Clifton Ross.

Milton Chamorro, mayor of Itchimbía, a successful land occupation in Quito

"We're building a popular, social power, a power where we can embrace each other and take each other's hands without fear"

Interview and translation by Clifton Ross, August 2008

Milton Chamorro brings a long history of working as a community organizer to his post as mayor of Itchimbía, a community that, as he describes in this interview, was won through a fifteen-year struggle with the city of Quito. He also participates in the media cooperative Minga Social and has a live, daily public affairs show on a community radio station, "Sounds and Voices of Our America."

I'm from the people, from the poor, as is everyone here. I never imagined being able to have a house here in Quito. I lived as a renter. This meant, in some sense or other, low self-esteem, living without possibilities, but with impotence, exploitation, discrimination, exclusion. That exclusion experienced by the lower classes causes you trauma and even mental, psychological problems. So you live depressed, downcast, half-heartbroken. So in this process [of struggle] the first thing we all reach is raising our self-esteem. We gain a greater sense of dignity.

This is the barrio of San Juan Bosco de Tito Cooperative, but we call it Itchimbía because the whole area is Itchimbía. In Kichwa "Itchimbía" means

"Overhead sun," or "the Cross of the Sun" (Sol Recto) because at midday the sun is directly overhead, in the center, up on the hill.

These condominium apartments that you see are the result of a struggle we began fifteen years ago. At the beginning we organized ourselves as an informal cooperative, then later we became a legal co-op. Later we began to look for sites in Quito for poor families. The fundamental objective, obviously, was housing for the members of this co-op. That's how we came to invade, and take by force, an ecological park named "Itchimbía."

At first we went around looking for land in Quito and we didn't find anything we could either buy or negotiate conditions to buy. There was nothing because, first, we didn't have the necessary resources and, second, as we were a cooperative of poor people we couldn't get credit. Given this, we made the decision to invade city lands.

We settled on Itchimbía, fifty-four hectares of land that the city had set aside for a park sixty years before, but had never done anything to make it a park. In fact, [the city] didn't want a park at all, but rather hoped to sell this space at a very low price to banks and real estate interests. When they were in the middle of this sale, we found out and made it known that instead of making a park they were selling it [to companies] that hoped to build a five-star, private hotel with swimming pools which would seal off access to the public.

The city, seeing its plans revealed and exposed, took a step back and began to negotiate with us. For our part, the first point of negotiation was that this fifty-four hectare space would be made into a park. The second point of negotiation was that a community would be allowed to live inside the park, and that community would be our cooperative.

September 23, 1996, was the day of the occupation. It happened that month because in the Andean cosmovision September is the month of planting and preparation of the earth. In keeping with this indigenous cosmovision we also thought of it as the month to prepare the land for our houses. It was the month of solidarity and fertility.

Sixty families initially took the land. Yet the following day, there were four hundred families. The first sixty families had already received political formation and education. It was difficult to receive so many families. Many of these latter families joined in on finding out about the occupation through the media as they were looking for housing. The fact that there were so many families ready to defend the occupation also made it more difficult to dislodge us. Yet as the process advanced, the number of families dropped since many of them believed that it was going to be a shorter, easier process. In fact, the fight was very difficult.

The next day [after the occupation], we were evicted by the police. But by this time we already had all the solidarity and international support, and media coverage. This happened over and over again. They evicted us and we returned and built again. Little by little we were winning.

How were we able to maintain ourselves there? We were only able to do it thanks to solidarity, because we were connected to the social movements. We'd asked for the support of the indigenous organizations: the Confederation of Indigenous Nationalities of Ecuador (CONAIE), the Confederation of the Peoples of the Nationality Kichwa of Ecuador (ECUARUNARI) and other organizations. At that time the Pachakutik movement, which is a political party of the indigenous people that also included mestizos, was growing, and they supported us. We asked for help from the Socialist Party and the People's Democratic Movement Party. In short, we asked for help from all sectors of the Left that seemed sympathetic. The Ecuadorian Front for Human Rights (FEDU) also supported us.

Also, we had friends in many foreign countries such as Spain, Italy, France, United States, Nicaragua, El Salvador, and so on. They sent letters to the city demanding that we not be evicted and calling for peaceful, political negotiations with us. For example, one day that [the city] planned to evict us, five hundred letters of solidarity [with us] arrived. This was a fundamental point for us in winning the fight.

Another fundamental point was that we were part of organizations. The five of us who began the land occupation as part of the cooperative had been part of a space that was called People's Coordinator of Quito (Coordinadora Popular de Quito), which was a coordination of a large number of groups of youth, women, base communities, neighborhood, and human rights organizations.

Six months later the most serious eviction happened. That's when we decided to chain ourselves to our houses and that stopped the eviction. Two years later there was another major attempt at an eviction, but seven of us buried ourselves and made an appeal to public opinion. In 1998 the photographs of our occupation and "burials" were considered some of the best photographs of the world. The foreign press came exclusively to cover this organizing process because it was unprecedented, in the first place because it dealt with the occupation of a public space located in a historic center where only the wealthy and powerful lived. We who were poor had no possibilities for anything there.

The previously mentioned acts pushed the city to begin offering concessions. We called for the naming of a commission for negotiations, a commission which would include the Church, representatives of human rights [organizations], the United Nations, authorities, senators, and the Red Cross. This commission served as a liaison between the two parties and it managed to get both sides to the negotiation table under equal conditions. The two sides were those of us representing people's power (citizens) and the state, in this case, the mayor's office or the city.

What the state proposed was that we go to another site to the south of the city, that is, into ugly, inhospitable corners in the cold and distant suburbs. [Editor's note: Traditionally in Latin America, the wealthier residents live in the city centers, and the poor are relegated to the suburbs.] Our response was to organize a plebiscite, a referendum, and consult with the people. We made ballots, formed an electoral tribunal, and invited human rights institutions, the Red Cross, ecology organizations, and all our organizations, and included the state; 99.9 percent of the participants in the occupation voted to remain here.

That was the process, a very important one. We had told [the government officials] that we could negotiate, but that any negotiation had to be done at Itchimbía, where we were.

There was a process of meetings and we accepted a proposal to come to this location. Since we'd now accepted [negotiations] we said we would need financing to build houses. The city facilitated that.

At first there were going to be individual houses, houses for each of us with a little piece of land, a lot, but there wasn't enough land for that because there are very fragile areas. So we settled on a single location where we'd build condominiums. That's why you can now see twenty-two condominiums. Some fifteen hundred of us live here, more or less two hundred and fifty families.

There are two hundred families who are partners, but since now the children have married and had their own families, there are more families. We have sewers, electricity, and water, and pavement down below. We built the bridge [over the highway] you see there [he points it out from the window] because there had been many accidents. We made our demand known and we went out and stopped traffic so they'd give us the bridge. We took the road and the police came, then the city [officials], and we asked them for the bridge and a month later we came back and began to build the bridge.

Women at the center

The women here have grown strong; they're very strong from the struggle. They're involved and they teach and work in forming the community. The previous president of the cooperative was a woman, and she was in power for ten years. I'm new; I've only been in power for three years. The role of women in this struggle has been fundamental because when they were trying to evict us, up above, when we were in the initial occupation, the women went out in front with their children and the men stood behind them. The women played a primary role. They're strong, tenacious; women have played a fundamental role in this organization. And there are also indigenous people. In general the indigenous movement has supported us. Humberto Cholango, president of ECUARUNARI, lives here. Also Lourdes Tibán, the woman in charge of Indigenous Affairs for the government, a secretary of state, she lives here.

Building our own power, and taking the power of the state

We have two perspectives [on power]: building power from below, what we call popular power, and also taking power so as to consolidate popular power. I believe those are the two perspectives we've taken on. In principle, in keeping with Marxist thought, you have to take power to modify conditions, but the road is very long for us. It's better to build power in the neighborhoods, citizen power, community power and from there to begin taking the other powers that we don't yet have.

In every mobilization, every struggle we, all members, have gone out into the streets and blocked the roads. Right now, at this moment, there are indications that big power is with us. That's as it should be. We agree that we should be in that power, when the poor, the common citizens, youth, women, campesinos, indigenous people are in the ministries [of the government]; when the common people have the possibility and the president doesn't do as he likes but rather governs in accord with the rule of the people. When that happens, that's when we'll be taking the other power.

So today I'd say I believe we have to take the two powers: building the one, our own, and taking the other, which is the power of the state. But it will have to be a different state, a socialist state, a human state, a state in solidarity.

So here [in Itchimbía] we've eliminated the big power and we're left to build a popular, social power, you could say, the power of solidarity, the power of dignity, a power where we can embrace each other, take each other's hand, without fear or any kind of problem. Because you don't convince people with speeches but with concrete things. You have to educate people, but with real things like housing, building houses, like health care, the building of a health-care center and work, the creation of microbusinesses. That's the kind of power we're building. And Itchimbía is an example of that kind of power.

Humberto Cholango. Photo by Clifton Ross.

Humberto Cholango, ECUARUNARI
"We're building an insurgency of ideas"

Interview and translation by Clifton Ross, August 2008

ECUARUNARI, also known as Ecuador Kichwa Llaktakunapak Jatun Tantanakui (Confederación de Pueblos de la Nacionalidad Kichwa del Ecuador or Confederation of the Kichwa Peoples of Ecuador) has its roots in the indigenous/post-Vatican II Catholic progressive awakening in the early 1970s. Gradually the organization drifted from the progressive Catholicism of the theology of liberation into a more general left position. ECUARUNARI, for instance, supported the guerrilla struggles of Central America in the 1980s and the Sandinista Revolution as it condemned the invasion of Grenada and the imperial development policies of the IMF and World Bank. It was a key organization in the May 1990 uprising of indigenous people of Ecuador to "defend life, the earth, justice, freedom against the corrupt governments, FTA... and water laws." (www.ecuarunari.org). The organization has been at every critical political juncture of Ecuador's recent history and acted as a major protagonist in CONAIE (Confederation of Indigenous Nationalities of Ecuador), representing the Kichwa peoples of the mountains.

Cholango is serious, direct, and he wastes no words. He's also very busy and has sandwiched this interview between two others. The Constituent

Assembly has just drafted the new constitution, and the result is controversial, at the very least. The indigenous people of Ecuador have spent ample time debating whether or not to support it, and now the media wants to know what the president of ECUARUNARI thinks about the final document. We're here for a more general discussion, and it's probably not a great time to "kick back and reflect" on what might be more "theoretical" problems. Cholango, however, takes on the task as we pursue a line of questions about democracy and power under the "progressive" presidency of Rafael Correa.

It is 2008. People in Ecuador are cautiously hopeful that Correa might bring some needed change to the country, but some, like Alberto Acosta, a respected intellectual and activist who many hope might one day be president, only consider the country to be entering into a "post-neoliberal capitalist capitalism." With such bleak prospects for those working for more radical change, Humberto Cholango reminds us of the need for greater patience. The indigenous people of our Americas have been waiting for their moment to return, the "pachakutik," for over five hundred years now.

Update: As of 2012, Humberto Cholango is now president of CONAIE.

We have to be very clear about this entire process of transformation that Latin America, and particularly South America, is undergoing, that it's all thanks to the work of the organized social movements: indigenous, campesinos, women, intellectuals, and journalists. Because Latin America, South America, has a higher level of sociopolitical consciousness and refuses to continue being used by multinational businesses or foreign powers or by a small group of people in each country. These struggles have come up over many years, and the path continues, the road continues, and it's a long road. We could say we've come along part of the road and we're continuing, with difficulty, even with those blocking our way, we're continuing to advance.

Here in Ecuador, for example, we have President Correa. We know he may be here ten years. He'll probably be reelected, right? But this road isn't only ten years long, but much longer. The people, the injustice, the discrimination, the redistribution of wealth and basic services, these [problems] aren't going to end.

So what is our strategy? It consists of social mobilization, obviously, but we also need a strategy not only of protest but also of proposals and alternatives. We have to work on something which we've discussed a lot with our compañeros from Bolivia, Peru, and elsewhere in Ecuador and that is, starting with the insurgency, the rebellion, but also beginning to build not only an insurgency, [usually] misunderstood as war, taking up arms, but here understood as an insurgency of ideas, an insurgency of the people and the masses who are in the process of transforming the consciousness of an entire people.

But after this transformation of consciousness, we can't allow anyone who might come along, like [former president Lucio] Gutiérrez, to take us away from our authentic project we're building, right? Including even Correa, in some areas. We can't say Correa is our friend, nor even our enemy: he's heading a government of transition with dramatic effects, but not under a [social] project. So it will depend a lot on the power, the consciousness of social forces, whether or not they'll allow Correa to continue on this path or, if not, whether they'll force him, by a mobilization of the people, to work in their interest.

In order for that to happen, two things are necessary: one, we have to advance today's resistance, today we have to advance. We're fighting the neoliberal model on this road, we're defeating that model, and we have to go much further. This is what we've called our compañeros to, to move from resistance to power, to build power, not to presidential power, but from resistance to building social, cultural, and intellectual power.

We need a new vision of South America. Because if we arrive, if we build from resistance to power and arrive in government but from there we have no intellectuals, no people, no culture, how are we going to change or influence anything? No matter what we do in Bolivia or here in Ecuador, if the rest of South America remains submerged in the free market and competition and all that, we're not going to move forward. So this resistance and building of power is essential, but so is globalizing this struggle and weaving alliances. We as an indigenous movement are conscious that the indigenous people of Bolivia or here in Ecuador, or Peru, alone and isolated, aren't going to be able to achieve this change we propose. We need to seek alliances, social alliances with workers, unions, women, intellectuals, academics, honest business people, patriots who love their country and aren't subjected to world business.

So this resistance, how will it be transformed? This struggle, this resistance, where will it transform itself? Precisely in defense of natural resources, in the defense of sovereignty, in the redistribution of wealth, and in the payment of the social debt. Up to now, what happened with the profits from oil, mining, [extraction of resources from] strategic areas? They've gone to pay the external debts; they've practically all gone to bail out banks. As in Argentina, here in Ecuador and elsewhere, they've gone bankrupt and that's where our money has been invested. Today we want to take back our natural resources from the hands of multinationals, and [have them] placed in the hands of the Ecuadorian state or the Bolivian state, but also we want to find a way of together generating a regional energy policy so we won't be blackmailed at any given moment by any business interest. This is what we need and I believe that's the struggle before us and we're moving forward with that.

If you look at power from a western perspective, it comes from above, but if you look at power from the Andean perspective, it's the people, the mass: There's not a single person who has much power, but rather it's the people, the community that is the power.

On the one hand, from a Western perspective, you could see a person with, say, political or economic power but if you want democracy, looking at power and democracy, it's critical that you're able to build the power of social forces. You could have left governments, progressive governments but if you don't have a social power, an accumulation of social power so as to turn the balance or to tip the scale to one side, you won't achieve what you want or be able to maintain it or keep people from leaving. You need that balance to guarantee the process and to avoid going off the road. That's the minimum necessary: it's not just in the new space, nor in the power of the president, but also the power of the people. The question is how to go about directing, educating, conscientizing, and training the rulers. Or in the case of Alan García in Peru, confronting governments to keep them from going off the deep end. How do we achieve this resistance?

Now, as for the vision of wanting to take the presidency of the republic or some other space, I think this is part, a small part, of the entire struggle in which we're engaged. If we have a presidency, from that space we might be able to help get things on track, but not necessarily be able to do things from there. That is, you could be in the presidency and quickly put together economic or energy policies in favor of the people, but then again, if you don't have a social force or power [behind you], you won't be able to build because an exclusively electoral social power composed only of votes, won't guarantee a long-term political project. We in Latin America know about votes: you come to power then the electorate suddenly doesn't want you and the people switch sides. Or the new generation comes up wanting more changes, recognizing greater need for change by the very necessity of human evolution. So we've recognized the need to work in this process of conscientization, training the base, the organizations.

Sometimes you say that one is in power, sometimes you say, "You're in the government," and it's not true; you're not. You're administering those spaces. You have a heavy bureaucracy, a clumsy bureaucracy, the mentality of which was formed in neoliberalism. First of all, you have no power, because you're a minister or director or something else and you become some sort of folklore. Obviously, you can make many decisions. You can, to the degree you're empowered, make decisions, but often you're there in a post, a position. Moreover, used, in that post, used by their neoliberal interests. Power turns to military, economic, political, and social uses and you have to be conscious of that and so the building up of the consciousness of the masses of people is fundamental.

The success of Evo Morales is his people, not just him alone. It's his people. That's true up to this moment and I'm sure that they'll win. Because the people are conscious, their project is conscious and that project isn't something Evo Morales has built in the last two elections. No, that project has been built over a long time, a very long time.

I think many social forces, many organized forces, aren't very often included in the governments nor are they on the [government's] agenda. For example, the Zapatistas weren't on the agenda of López Obrador. Nor, for example, in Peru, are the campesinos or local indigenous organizations on the agenda of Ollanta Humala. Nor, for example, here in Ecuador, is the CONAIE on the agenda of Correa. That is, the more tenacious activists, the clearer activists in the project [we're building] are left off the agenda. They're a force left out.

On one hand, there's a benefit because you maintain an absolute independence and call things as you see them, the good and the bad of a so-called progressive government, and you continue building your own struggle. The worst thing would be to be inserted into the [government] agenda and lose yourself in that wave. That would be the worst.

But it's important to affirm this. For example, the MST [Landless Workers' Movement of Brazil] isn't on Lula's agenda. So resistance and struggle might be joined, might be united [with the government] in certain ways, but they can also maintain their independence. That's fundamental for a new vision for South America. It's necessary there be at least minimal agreements between progressive governments and social movements, for example, against use of force or against the [U.S.] military bases. Fine, governments and social movements, we agree on that and advance together there, and also in undoing the privatization of strategic resources. Great. We can move forward by strengthening those points of agreement.

Dioyenes Lucio. Photo by Clifton Ross.

Dioyenes Lucio, FENOCIN (National Federation of Indigenous, Peasant, and Black Organizations)
"You need to preserve your organization and your power of protest"

Interview and translation by Clifton Ross, August 2008

FENOCIN is the acronym for the National Federation of Indigenous, Peasant, and Black Organizations. It was founded in 1965 as FETEP, Ecuadorian Federation of Agricultural Workers, an organization of the Catholic Church with a mission to reach out to campesinos and eventually undermine and take over the work of the Communist Party of Ecuador. As so often happens in such cases, the organization became radicalized and made a leftward turn, abandoning its relations with the Church for a more secular vision of struggle.

Dioyenes Lucio is FENOCIN's national director of juridical defense, and also directs its agroecology projects. He has held many positions in the organization over the years, and has as great a passion and willingness to talk about it as he does about his garden at home. Armando López of Minga Social introduced me to this wonderful man who took me to visit agroecological farms organized by FENOCIN to the south in the village of Píllaro and introduced me to campesinos connected to the Federation.

Our organization is intercultural, with indigenous and blacks and [mestizo] farmers all included. We demonstrate intercultural relations in practice.

We're working on [agroecology] on three fronts here in Ecuador. Of the twenty-four provinces of the country we have a presence in eighteen of them, with active projects in fourteen of those provinces.

We've created real variety, recapturing ancestral cultures of ecological production. We've saved varieties of local seeds and rejected the possibility of working with either hybrid or genetically modified seeds. And so we've been saving local seed varieties as well as the productive cultures of our ancestors.

We've formed teams of promoters and facilitators for this work with a methodology of farmer to farmer (*campesino a campesino*). This is another way of saying that in our program there's really no place for those famous agronomy engineers who are formed in a very elitist education and often think they know everything. They come to teach the "poor farmers," but that's all backward. We farmers teach the professors in the productive field.

Naturally, if we allow some expert to define the terms, they tell us it's easier to buy everything, but it's not true. It's important to value and use the resources of the piece of land itself, because on that parcel is everything necessary to produce, the fertilizers as well as pesticides. All that remains is to perfect these practices and technologies [of agroecology].

In the end, we don't want to destroy the microorganisms and that's what these agrochemicals do. They burn them up. But by carefully selecting plants and sowing them together, the plants themselves will control weeds and pests. None of this is taken into account by the professors. They don't take into account the economic investments involved, because, for example, whenever I use those agrochemicals, the land becomes each time more dependent on them, and each time needing more and more. On the other hand, with agroecology, it's completely the opposite: given land that's already suffered from these chemical treatments, at first it will need some investment, but as you build back these microorganisms, gradually you'll need to invest less and less.

Changing (agri)culture

We've come to see that those brought into the circle of the organization, those who are organized, are much more ready to understand agroecology and its advantages. Those not part of [social movement] organizations, those in the individualistic world-view, don't get it nor see the value in it and often even criticize [agroecology] as lazy and sloppy. Some of those come around out of curiosity and see the results and they're convinced, but those are few. It's through the process of entering the organization that many begin to assimilate and understand the importance of the need for change and transformation, or recovery of our culture.

There have also been advances [in terms of including women]. I recall when I was in the previous directorate there were women, but they sat there barely saying anything. But with this same process of conscientization, formation, and education all aimed at raising self-esteem, the women are beginning to open up. Now you'll see women talking and even debating and making proposals. And this affects everything. For example, you'll now see women going out into the public and doing the same, so there are advances, and you can really see them. I remember, again, in the previous directorate, we'd plead [with the women], "Please, take such and such a post or position," and nothing. It was really hard. Not now. Now there are even power struggles, and that's an advance. And you can see the same thing among youth, very competent, very respectful, and they learn the skills as they take positions of responsibility, not just protesting from below. Protests are fine, but people also need to be able to propose an alternative.

Agrarian revolution

The ideology of our organization [FENOCIN] is somewhat linked politically to the Socialist Party. But within the party we've begun to make our influence felt because all these parties have to change. They've got to transfer the protagonism to those very protagonists themselves. It has to change from the old top-down structure to a bottom-up structure, from the base, learning from those working in the field.

It's not easy, this transformation of society, and the way we see things, but all this in the twenty-first century has to start changing. Perhaps that's why we've been impacted and moved by the actions of our current government, because its aim is a healthy one, that of a social revolution in the country. We recognize that and are on board with it. That's why we're proposing an agrarian revolution in the country.

That implies free access of farmers to land; the democratization of access to water for irrigation; a real policy of access to preferential credits for farmers, because the small and medium-sized farmers produce about 64 percent of the country's food, while large agribusiness produces mainly for export, and not to feed the people; and a better quality of life in the countryside, which means better housing, access to education and health. All this is what we mean by an agrarian revolution in the country. With agrarian reforms of the past the farmers were given little pieces of land and left on their own. That's no way to build up massive production in the country. You have to really consider what's necessary to stimulate the farmers.

We like what [Correa] has done so far, but there's still much to be done. These are very slow processes, and society also has to participate. Sometimes people think the government has to do all this and that's not true. Society has to be an active participant in these processes. That's why we've participated in the Constituent Assembly [which wrote the constitution] with our president of FENOCIN (Pedro de la Cruz) participating as a member. We've been able to contribute to very important discussions and proposals, such as one on food sovereignty. We had to fight hard, even with the official bloc, to get people to understand the importance of food sovereignty. We also fought hard for the proposal on interculturality, which is the reality of our country. We also fought for issues of water, social security, and labor issues, especially decent work in rural areas.

We've also taken this same struggle for food sovereignty internationally, for instance to places like the last international meeting of the FAO in Brazil where we took a stand for food security and sovereignty. That's because FENOCIN is part of an international struggle and, as such, is a member of the Coordinadora Latinoamericana de Organizaciones Campesinas (CLOC, Latin American Coordinator of Farmer's Organizations) and Via Campesina (Farmers' Way), which are organizations that keep us informed and represented at the international level.

The struggle here in Ecuador against the Free Trade Agreement of the Americas (FTAA) came about precisely because of these international bonds that we developed because the information and evidence we needed came in from abroad about what was happening in other countries. That's why we were able to stop [FTAA] here in Ecuador. We used that information to make the Ecuadorian people aware so they could rise up and stop it. This is some of what we've been doing as an organization, yet we don't stop with just protests; we also propose policies. And agroecology is precisely an example of that. We don't want the technological packages because we want to remain free to explore, and to value, our own technologies.

Many from the social movements here in Ecuador have fallen into this trap [of believing they can change things by taking power at the top]. An example of this is CONAIE. CONAIE greeted the coming to power of Lucio Gutiérrez with a lot of fanfare and the best cadre went in to support the government. And they got burned.

I had the opportunity to be in Bolivia a few days after the inauguration of Evo Morales in a conference of indigenous campesinos and there, too, I found that the best cadre of the social movements had begun to collaborate with the government. Those who were left as spokespersons of their organizations didn't even know anything about their organization's own processes.

When I returned, Correa had just recently won the presidency and some in our executive council wanted to do the same thing. We had our own experiences to reflect on and also those of Bolivia, and we wouldn't let them fall into this error of letting our best people go into the government. We worked out an arrangement where some of our people went to work in the government, but lower-profile people, not the leadership of the organization because that would weaken our organization, and weaken our ability to maintain a critical stance toward the government. That's why it was agreed that none of the national directorate would take public office, despite the temptations.

On the other hand, the proposal to run as members of the Constituent Assembly was quite different. There we agreed to, because it involved a popular election to a specific and concrete task: to write a new constitution. And we reached our objectives. Because we were active, especially in food sovereignty, new, practical laws are being debated and proposed on this issue coming out of our work on the new constitution.

So it really isn't a simple matter of taking state power when you end up disarming your organization and burning out your best activists and automatically losing the critical, orienting power of your organization. Because the aim of all these right-wing, neoliberal governments is to scuttle the social movements, buy off the leaders and weaken the organizations. But [FENOCIN] has resisted this. We've been around for forty years, this year (2008), and we've lived through many processes. We've survived dictatorships and right-wing, neoliberal governments, and now we have a government which sort of embodies some of our ideals so we'll go with it, but without committing ourselves to it and endangering our organization. You have to maintain your organization intact to maintain the sovereign interests of the popular classes, because the aim isn't to get control of some ministry or governorship or other and, in the process, lose your power of protest.

Monica Chuji Gualinga, CONAIE activist and Constitutional Assembly member
"This constitution is a beginning … in the end the people will define their own destiny"

Interview and translation by Clifton Ross, August 2008

I first saw Monica Chuji in the gathering called by CONAIE and other indigenous groups after the ending of the Constitutional Assembly. They were debating whether or not to support the new constitution, which had been redacted, at the very last minute, by "editors" from the government of President Rafael Correa. Some of the edits were made for legal clarification, others to avoid

Monica Chuji. Photo by Clifton Ross.

ambiguities of meaning. Yet others, some maintained, were part of an attempt by the president to weaken provisions for the rights of indigenous peoples and Pachamama. Monica spoke rarely during the conference, but when she did speak everyone gave her their complete attention. During her time in the Constitutional Assembly she became recognized for her clarity, focus, and uncompromising, principled stances and actions. Armando López, who had accompanied me to the gathering, wanted to introduce me to Monica after the event. That proved impossible, but a few days later Armando and I went to her house for an interview. Inside the urban apartment, the walls were decorated with spears and other indigenous artifacts and art. The constant song of many caged birds gave me a slightly disorienting sense of being in the wild.

I'm Kichwa from the Amazon, a combination of two nationalities. On my father's side I'm Shuar and on my mother's I'm Kichwa, but I identify as Kichwa. I was born in the 1970s in the heart of the community. I became actively involved at the age of twelve, because I was a catechist in my community, and for us the presence of the Carmelite mission was a very important element in terms of [community] organization. Later I became a health promoter, involving a lot of preventative medicine, and that involving sexuality was the area where I was chosen to work in my community. Since then I've been involved in militant marches and uprisings and participated in meetings, assemblies, and congresses.

I belong to CONAIE (Confederación de Nacionalidades Indígenas del Ecuador, Confederation of Indigenous Nationalities of Ecuador), the largest [indigenous] confederation in Ecuador, an organization that integrates about 80 percent of the indigenous peoples and nations. I've gone through a process of formation, first through the organizational life, and I also have an academic formation. I've worked at a grassroots level, but also at a national and international level with COICA (Coordinadora de las Organizaciones Indigenas de la Cuenca Amazonica, Coordinator of Indigenous Organizations of the Amazon River Basin), which is an organization that includes all nine nations of the peoples of the Amazon basin.

From the government to the Constitutional Assembly

I became part of [Correa's] government at the beginning of his first six-year term, [working] in the Secretariat of Communication. In the government you have a very limited margin of action. I was working as a spokesperson in what was the area of a new form of intercultural communication, but there was no opportunity for more because the changes needed are structural and institutional. That's why I quit and decided to run as a candidate [for the Assembly] in Acuerdo País. I worked on plans with other candidates and we won.

I presided in the Assembly over the committee (mesa) on natural resources and biodiversity, one of the most controversial of all the issues that we dealt with, since it included the issues of oil, water, mining, and all of the environment. In addition to that, we pushed to make this issue a central axis of the new constitution. That was a space where we had eight months of the great presence of actors outside of organizations, which was important for giving the political support to those who were there defending the work. So my public political life has been very short, just a year and a half, but I'm aware and clear that the way of doing politics has to change. There has to be more honesty, transparency, more democracy, more dialogue without political gaming.

For me it could have been so simple to go to the Assembly and keep quiet and do everything Correa said and in that way be assured of a [post in a] ministry; I would have been assured of my next candidacy in the next election or whatever bureaucratic post. This is what a lot of people did but that doesn't seem to me to be the way politics should be. In my case, and in many cases, I don't think it's been like that. We've been very confrontational with the government, very critical, and I was in the ranks of the official party. But being critical isn't to be in opposition. Criticism is very important, especially for the very process the president is trying to lead, because when you

Encuentro 2010. In June 2010, 250 representatives from sixteen countries gathered for the Continental Encounter of the Original Nationalities and Peoples of Abya Yala to commemorate the twentieth anniversary of the "First Continental Conference on Five Hundred Years of Indigenous Resistance," an Indigenous meeting in Quito that advanced movements toward hemispheric unity. The Confederation of Indigenous Nationalities of Ecuador (CONAIE) anchored the organizing for the conference. Photo by Marc Becker.

aren't critical things get worse and you have no one to tell you what's really happening. Being oppositional is different; the opposition is made without arguments, without content, but blind opposition.

Power and the constitution

In the first six months everyone had proposals with articles from the social movements. They debated and it was really great, because the whole world could see what this or that organization was proposing: what the blacks, for example, were proposing, what the indigenous were proposing and were there similarities or not, or how did they complement each other? That was the dynamic.

The last two months were frustrating. We met and the chief of the political bureau or the political ministry would arrive and say, "This is our criteria," but when he said, "it is our criteria" it meant, "This is what you're going to do." But we in the assembly were elected by the people not to obey the thesis of a president who, with all respect, had the right to participate, but not to impose. These are some of the things that I crtiticized a lot and now, certainly, I'm on the list as one of the "infiltrators."

After all the debates we had a certain number of days, with a very tight schedule. At the final hour, given that we had such large documents to read, a team was created that began to change the texts. This was a team that came in from Quito as part of the political bureau of Rafael Correa. Moreover, this team wasn't of the same tendency [as Acuerdo País] but rather right-wing, and obviously there was great distrust. There was a lot of discomfort within the [Acuerdo] País bloc, lots of questions and of all the changes [they made], we would consider only those valid that were debated and approved in plenary.

And so we have all these beautiful principles about human rights, the rights of the environment and institutionality and it's very good—but power hasn't changed in the least. The power is once again in the executive. Once again the citizens have no opportunity to say anything. This is an issue that I don't think has been resolved. So I've said I'm going to vote "yes" [for the approval of the constitution] because I think it's an advance, that it's opening up a new path but it's not the solution and it isn't the end, as such, but rather a mechanism that enables us to continue opening. I always say the text doesn't make the context, but rather it's the context that makes the text.

For me, power, in political terms, in terms of the state, is your ability to generate consensus and process dissent with people. Power has to be exercised by being mutually shared with the citizens who elected you: There has to be a correspondence.

Now is the time to invent and create other mechanisms for real participation, for sharing power. For example, in the Assembly, the indigenous movement proposed that Congress has to have a balance of representation. Here there are peoples and nations: There are Afro-Ecuadorians, Montubios, and other sectors who have to be represented there. We lost because we always ended up being a minority within the official bloc. Worse, I and two other compañeros, but finally I alone, had to fight with the president of the republic to try to find middle ground, but we always ended up being a minority.

Power and the plurinational state

The plurinational state isn't the recognition that there are Indians living in this country: That's just a historical reality that no one can deny. Whether it's in the constitution or not, we'll go on living and so they're have to recognize us, but that's not the spirit of a plurinational state.

For me it's a new way of administering the state, that the state would be at the service of its citizens, and not the citizens at the service of [the state]. Another consciousness needs to be generated. The children need to learn that this is a diverse country; that the fact of being Kichwa or Shuar or black isn't synonomous with being inferior to the white-mestizo culture; that interculturality is the possibility of mutual esteem and equilibrium. That's the meaning of the plurinational state. I tell you honestly that up to now it's just a word [*membrete*, lit. "letterhead"] because within the institution itself it's not reflected in what we call the "character of the state."

And so I say this [constitution] is a beginning; I think it's a base, that it has shown the way so we can later begin building and all things are perfectable and nothing written in stone and in the end it's the people who will define their own destiny.

The power of dialogue

I think [people] have learned a lot in the whole process starting in the '90s until the present, there's been a process of "intereducation." The proposals of the indigenous movement at the beginning were only for the indigenous movement itself, reclaiming its lands and territories. Little by little we've been adding forces; the campesinos have been included, the people in the markets and the people in marginal neighborhoods of cities have added to the numbers.

What have we been learning? First, that we have common needs: this has been the starting point for mutual relearning. We have exclusion in common. I think, for instance, that Indians and blacks have become conscious of our common humanity and also of our rights and finally both have become conscious that it's true we were both here before 1830, to put it in a very general context. People have begun to learn that consensus is built by dialogue. And so when the call has gone out to various sectors, including union activists, they've come to meet with indigenous compañeros, with the leadership, to find common agreement and discuss points in common, that's the focus, even with all our differences, but we still can build together.

I think dialogue is one of the particular points that are important to me, the point of public debate. I think this is useful for socializing. So is, at another level, ancestral wisdom in the area of agriculture and traditional medicine. There's a great interest in ancestral medicine among mestizos. It's in great demand and you'll find in the villages people preparing medicines and buying them and proving that they work. There are so many things we're learning from each other—and we've learned in that process that we don't quit being indigenous. I've not stopped being Kichwa.

Indigenous poverty, indigenous wealth

Where there's a greater indigenous population, there's greater poverty. Look at Bolivia, with a 70 percent indigenous population. It's one of the poorest countries of the continent, a fact confirmed by research. [Here in Ecuador] Chimborazo, a province in the center of the country with a majority population of indigenous, is one of the poorest, like [the province of] Bolívar. These situations are part of a historical legacy, and it takes a long time to even begin to recognize the real economic, social, cultural, and political situation of our country.

In the end poverty has a political element, because the political decisions are those which are made as power is organized. But I'd like to see in the future, in the provinces especially where there is the larger indigenous population, that they would have their language be relevant and respected, and that it would be the language of the people, of their nationality. That wouldn't end poverty, but then all poverty is relative and dependent on how you see it. If you visit the communities you'll find those who'll tell you "I have no money to go to school, but I have my little piece of land where I grow potatoes and guinea pigs; I have chickens and something to eat." So I think that poverty can be overcome to the degree that all the rights are slowly sustained: the issue of housing, that of education, health, and culture. But you're really poor if you've lost your culture.

Luis Macas, Instituto Científico de Culturas Indígenas (Scientific Institute of Indigenous Cultures, ICCI)
"The key point for me is how to combine the indigenous struggle and the class struggle"

Interview and translation by Jeffery R. Webber, July 2010

Luis Macas, arguably the most renowned indigenous leader in Ecuador, was born in 1951 in Saraguro, in the Province of Loja. After three years of elementary school in the community, his father sent him to an urban school so he could learn Spanish—an experience he found "dehumanizing."[1] *After finishing secondary school, he returned to Saraguro and became the community's teacher.*

At the "First Educational Gathering of Mother Languages and Bilingual Education," in Quito, Macas had his first chance to talk with indigenous people from other parts of the country—and met a radical priest, Hernán Malo, who arranged a university scholarship for him. He studied the anthropology of languages and taught Kichwa for a while before taking a law degree from Central University. He credits the professors there with teaching him about dialectical and historical materialism.

Macas is an ex-president of the Confederation of Indigenous Nationalities of Ecuador (CONAIE), and former congressional deputy (in the late 1990s) and

Luis Macas. Photo by Marc Becker.

presidential candidate (in 2006) for the Movimiento Pachakutik (Pachakutik Movement, MP) party. We met in Macas's office at ICCI, where he serves as executive director.

I learned most of what's guided me for the better part of my life in the community where I was born and raised, Saraguro, in the Province of Loja. My father was a leader in the community at various points. He participated a great deal in the collective leadership of the community. There was no single leadership in the community, no type of *caudillismo* (big man leadership), but rather collective leadership. There are various people, men and women, who lead a process of organization, of unity in the community.

I really began to be integrated into this collective life when I was about eight years old. My father brought me along for the communitarian work of our people, what we call the *minga*. This is not a case of discriminatory, exploitative work as some like to think in the cities. It's a responsibility that the community asks of everyone—the children, teenagers, even the elderly, that they do their work in the community. This is how to ensure that none of the social sectors of the community are excluded.

I'll give you an example. My job when I was eight was to bring food to the workplace. Families in the community would prepare food for those who were working, and I would transport it to the workplace. So I would bring food, and drinks, for example *opaib*, from my house to the work site. This was the work we did, myself along with my eight other siblings. This was the kind of work children did, not physically demanding, not the kind of hard labor that the adults were engaged in. But, in any case, we had this responsibility to the community.

This tradition of communitarian obligation has diminished since that time in many communities, even disappearing in some, because obviously the system in which we are living is so powerful that it is destroying this fabric, this conduct, this way of thinking in the community.

When I finished high school I returned to my community once again. The community saw me as a bit of a rare bird. A high school diploma didn't mean much back in the community. What was it good for? Clearly, I had learned things. But my father said, "Good then, did you learn how to improve the cultivation of the earth, or what?"

I said no, that I had learned other things. "What did you learn," he asked slightly indignantly. "Did you learn how to take care of the animals that we have here in the countryside?" I said no. "Why did you go, then?" he said. There was a bit of recrimination on the part of my father, like what was the point of me having gone.

But it was my good fortune that the community said to me, "Did you know that we need a teacher? You could be the teacher."

I said, "Teacher?" I was unsure, you know, because I didn't have the training to be a teacher. But I said, "Good, then it's something that I can do." But I was afraid at the prospect of assuming this responsibility, this difficult work, which when it comes down to it, is preparing human beings—teaching children who need to learn how to become young adults.

In the end, I did it for a little more than one year. What I accomplished I don't know (laughing). But I learned a lot from the kids. The simplicity and innocence of children is a beautiful world.

The indigenous movement and the struggle for structural change

Reclaiming our identities is important for the reproduction of our histori-cal cultures as peoples—for example, the struggle for land is a vital element, because without land there can be neither our culture nor identity, abso-lutely nothing—but the constant of the indigenous movement has been what I call the global struggle, a proposal of an alternative to the entire system.

It doesn't bother me exactly, but it makes me pause, when I hear today that the indigenous movement is simply about the recovery of identity, that the indigenous movement is thinking only of its own community. No, no, no. The indigenous movement has always thought of the country, of the general society. And, above all, it has struggled for profound changes, structural changes.

The whole process of learning I've described has been important for me—my experience in the university, my experience in academia. But my formation was in the community.

The key point for me is how to combine two central struggles: the indigenous struggle—the struggle for identity, the historical struggle of the indigenous peoples—and the class struggle. This is what we need to do so that neither struggle is isolated. Because here it's not the case that we declare ourselves socialists and that's it—there's a diversity of social processes, of historical political processes.

The production of these political processes has to be the basis of a new society, a plural society—what we call here plurinationality. This is a project that did not simply emerge from the indigenous movement, but from the peasants, from intellectuals, from ecologists, workers, and so on. For me, plurinationality as such is a proposal for struggle. It's a proposal for radical change.

There are two conditions of struggle in my way of thinking. One is to make visible and to transcend coloniality. Coloniality is still very much alive in Ecuador, Peru, and Bolivia, and in all parts of Latin America—the coloniality of power; the coloniality of knowledge; the coloniality of being. This is one major component of what has to be overcome through political struggle.

But, there's another arm of struggle, which has to do with the condition of this economic model, the capitalist model. If we don't destroy both, one is going to remain.

Ecuador under Correa

I think that the political scenarios are basically the same as they have been for the last ten or twenty years. The people are living through a difficult time, where the different social and popular sectors of our country are dispersed and fragmented. Why? Because the government has facilitated this process.

The people are still here of course, the indigenous and the workers. But the government started out their process of disarticulation with the workers, with the elimination of collective contracts.

The objective is to dismantle the unions. It is not, as Correa's discourse suggests, an effort to get rid of undue privileges of bureaucratic unions. From my point of view, it is necessary to change the bureaucratic structures and privileges of the labor movement, the perks that the unions have given themselves at the expense of the rest of the workers. That would be good. But the way in which Correa is trying to dismantle popular workers' organizations is diabolical.

There's a political motivation for the government's assault on the indigenous movement. The objective is to liquidate the indigenous movement in this country, to dismantle and destroy this movement, because the indigenous movement is the principal social and political actor in the country that has struggled against the economic model, against neoliberalism. Correa wants to have a green light to do as he pleases. And his project of development is rooted in the exploitation of natural resources. We in the indigenous movement, which has an emphatically different conceptualization of Mother Nature, are saying no.

The weakness of the Left in this country is that in these crucial and difficult times we have not been able to respond. The priority, from my point of view, is to reclaim our agenda, and rearticulate the social and popular movement in this country—because the objective of this government is precisely to disarticulate this entire process of struggle.

For example, the criminalization of social struggle in this country is completely perverse. This is not a government of the Left, but a government of the Right, because these are popular social struggles that are being criminalized.

Let's take a look at the proposed Water Law, especially as it has to do with the development of hydroelectric projects. This is being challenged by the indigenous movement because it does not challenge the preexisting privatization of the access to water flows in this country. One percent of the population captures 80 percent of the water. What kind of revolutionary government, what kind of government of change, proposes a Water Law that doesn't challenge this scenario? Everything would remain intact with the new Water Law.

A revolution has to start with the people. The protagonist of change, in whatever part of the world, is the people. It's the people who make it, led by a government perhaps. But this is not what is happening here. The government is trying to get rid of the struggles of the people.

What's happened to the oligarchy under Correa? They certainly haven't been liquidated. The dispute for power at the moment is between the old oligarchy and the new one that is presently occupying the state. The government says that it has liquidated the old oligarchy. But the power of the banks remains intact. Agroindustry remains in the hands of the traditional oligarchy. This power is there, nothing has happened, it remains intact. This power is quiet at the moment, it's sleeping, but it hasn't been destroyed. If this were a government of the Left, a government of and for the people, this oligarchy would be liquidated.

Ecuador and the regional "left turn"

These new styles of governments have emerged in the region because the peoples of the Americas woke up, rose up, and made their presence felt. And the people want changes—at a minimum, a turn away from the existing order, this is what the people want—the peoples of Venezuela, Ecuador, Bolivia, Paraguay, and so on.

But I believe that the political and economic project of the region has not changed much. Because the conception of development based in the exploitation of natural resources, has not changed. The leaderships of these new political developments continue to have as their objective the "improvement" of economic development along these lines.

The new projects call for the end to imperialism, as we have called for. They have taken control of the natural resources away from the hands of imperialism in some cases, with a discourse of creating a new redistributive economy. But there hasn't been much redistribution.

The regional projects of economic integration have no clear vision of change. I, for one, doubt that the new models emerging respond authentically to the interests of the peoples of these countries.

I want to be absolutely frank and say that this vision of development is backward. The project of Integración de la Infraestructura Regional Suramericana (Integration of South American Regional Infrastructure, IIRSA), for example, is not some little or simple thing. Its purpose is to take advantage of all the natural resources of our country. The construction of this famous inter-Amazonian superhighway starting in Manta-Manaus, Brazil, will have as a consequence the expulsion of our natural resources to these other markets. The governments behind it can call themselves socialists of the twenty-first century, of the twenty-second century if they want, but they are not responding to the interests of our peoples.

Projects like IIRSA will destroy the indigenous communities at the heart of these popular anti-imperialist struggles; it will destroy them physically and spiritually, by destroying their territories.

This is the same sort of project that imperialism has in mind. Those managing the geopolitics will have changed, from the North to the South, but the project will remain the same.

There are these two conditions that we have to analyze with absolute responsibility inside the popular movements, and inside academia too. The first is the condition of coloniality, this entire schema of thought, the idea that we have to continue following the same path of development, at the same rate, and so on—the kind of "development" that was invented in the 1950s. There is still this idea that we have to continue with this kind of development! It doesn't matter who dies, how many human beings it pushes under, we have to develop ourselves!

This conception of development, this conception of welfare, this conception of economic growth that continues to drive everything, is a Eurocentric one. It's also an anthropocentric vision. We're stuck in this thinking that enriches a few, and so we can't break out of this development model. The other condition that we have to struggle against and to overcome, as I have said, is this capitalist economic model. The two conditions together—coloniality and capitalism—have to be fought simultaneously.

There are two civilizational models that are confronting one another in the current moment—two distinct paradigms, a Western paradigm, and a paradigm from here. But the paradigm from here has everything to lose because no one values it whatsoever. It's those Indians again, trying to recover their notion of *buen vivir*, living well. But this doesn't exist anymore, they say, because we're living in a period of *bienestar* or a Western conception of welfare. The paradigms of the original peoples, which are not the same paradigm as capitalist development, are being trodden upon, these paradigms of "living well," of harmony between humankind and nature. It's from these indigenous paradigms that, in part, an alternative must emerge.

And this platform has been raised here in a practical way. This is what the struggle for a plurinational state in Ecuador has been about, for example. It's been about communities taking care of nature, of life. Because your life does not depend only on you. It depends on this totality.

Lots of people say that we need to change things in this world, but we continue our assault on nature. We're killing ourselves in the process. The death of nature is the death of humanity. This is what we have to think about and reflect on.

Brazil

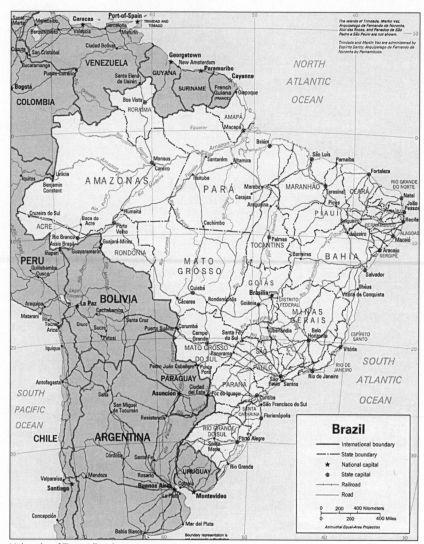

University of Texas Libraries

INTRODUCTION
Redefining democracy in South America's largest country

By Michael Fox

Since the fall of Brazil's last military dictatorship in 1984, "democracy" in Latin America's largest country has been a word in constant redefinition. Whether through cooperatives, social movements, or local government programs such as Participatory Budgeting, it is being redefined and reinvented in new ways, stretching beyond the hegemonic representative model of politics into grassroots direct participation. But the road has been long, and promises to be much longer still.

Brazil is one of the most breathtakingly beautiful, painfully heartbreaking, and bureaucratically nerve-racking places in the world. It's the world's fifth largest country, and home to over 193 million people, just under the total population of all of South America's Spanish-speaking nations combined. Brazil is diverse—composed of more than two hundred indigenous tribes; the African culture of Bahia; and the German, Italian, Japanese, and Eastern European descendents in the South. It is also a land of stark inequalities. In many major cities, the poor slums, or *favelas*, cover the hillsides overlooking glamorous neighborhoods or elite residential high-rises guarded by thick walls and expensive security. The country is home to the pristine white beaches of the Northeast, the Guaraní Aquifer—one of the largest freshwater aquifers in the world—and the "lungs of the planet" in the rainforests of the Amazon.

And while Brazil is bordered by more than half a dozen neighbors, it is cut off from the rest of South America by not only the natural boundaries, but also a language barrier. Brazilians speak mostly Portuguese, rather than Spanish, so the country has developed its own complicated and distinct culture separate from even its closest neighbors. This may be part of the reason that in Brazil, more than most places, you have to understand the past to understand the present.

In 1808, just before Simón Bolívar was liberating most of northern South America from Spanish rule, the Portuguese royal family was taking up residence in Rio de Janeiro—fleeing from the French army that had invaded their tiny Iberian country. The move intricately tied the Brazilian oligarchy to Portugal. In 1822, Portuguese Prince Pedro I declared Brazil's independence and crowned himself emperor of Brazil. When the monarchy was finally dethroned on November 15, 1889, it wasn't through a revolutionary struggle, but by Brazilian Emperor Pedro II's tacit acceptance of a minor military coup, backed by former slave owners who were upset with the abolition of slavery the previous year.

The new republic set up a constitution, and waded its way through subsequent dictatorships, coups d'état, populist governments, and pseudodemocracy, in which the right to vote was strictly controlled by the National Guard through a system that would come to be known as *coronelismo* ("Coronelism"), in which high-ranking members of the military acquired enough land and power to control local political, electoral, and judicial decisions. Those who didn't agree were dealt with accordingly.

By the late 1950s, Brazilians pushed to take control of their own lives. Inspired by the 1959 Cuban Revolution, students stepped up their organizing. The political ground shifted in late 1960 with the election of Brazilian president Jânio Quadros. Although Quadros was a member of the center-right National Democratic Union, he reestablished Brazilian relations with the Socialist bloc, embraced the Non-Aligned Movement, and criticized U.S. attempts to isolate Cuba. Only eight months into his term, however, Quadros resigned after backlash in Congress from his international policy shift, and the leftist Vice President João Goulart of the Brazilian Labor Party (PTB) assumed the presidency.

In 1963–64, Goulart launched a series of radical economic and social reforms, which propelled agrarian reform, initiated a Paulo Freire–inspired literacy campaign, capped excessive profits for foreign investors, and facilitated land and business expropriations by the state. By April 1, 1964, the military and the Right had had enough. Just two and a half weeks after Goulart announced his SUPRA decree—expropriating land which he said would be used for a first phase of agrarian reform—he was overthrown in a U.S.-backed coup d'état.

The putsch installed a two-decade-long repressive military dictatorship, which within a few short years would abolish the Congress and legalize torture. Armed urban guerrilla groups rebelled against the repression, but were squashed in a witch-hunt for "subversives." The military regime would soon unite with the U.S.-backed dictatorships in Paraguay, Bolivia, Uruguay, Chile, and Argentina to share intelligence in order to crack down on the dissidence through the U.S.-supported Operation Condor.

But in 1979, the ground began to crumble underneath the dictatorship. That year, a young metalworker by the name of Luiz Inácio Lula da Silva led a number of massive strikes against the junta, which signaled for many the beginning of the end. The following year, Lula and his metalworkers formed the Brazilian Workers' Party (PT), which inspired struggles for democracy across the region.

The Brazilian dictatorship formally fell in 1984. Quickly, Brazil began to readjust itself to democracy. The constitution was rewritten in 1988, guaranteeing many freedoms abolished or swept under the rug over the previous decades.

The PT continued to organize and by 1989 Lula was running for president on a radical platform of workers' rights and agrarian reform, and was running strong in the polls. Lula narrowly lost the runoff election—partially because of a well-oiled elite-backed media machine that rallied against his presidency. Nevertheless, the previous year, thirty-six PT mayors had been elected across the country, including three in state capitals—São Paulo, Porto Alegre, and Vitória. In Porto Alegre, Rio Grande do Sul, the office of the new PT mayor, Olívio Dutra, was willing to take chances and it embarked on a project whereby city residents would have a direct say in the allocation of city funds and public works projects. The new process, known as Participatory Budgeting, garnered international attention by allowing the direct participation of city residents in the local government.

On the national scene, subsequent Brazilian presidencies rose and fell through waves of corruption, the Real Plan (which stabilized the Brazilian currency), and IMF-backed neoliberal policies that, like neighbors Uruguay and Argentina, launched Brazil down the road toward financial crisis. Meanwhile the PT was growing. By 2000, PT mayors held offices in 187 cities and Lula was consolidating the lessons he had learned about winning office. In 2002, in his fourth and final attempt at the presidency, Lula spiced up his image; dropped the socialist red star from campaign propaganda; and joined in a coalition with several parties, including the center-right Partido do Movimento Democrático Brasileiro (PMDB, Brazilian Democratic Movement Party). He was finally elected president on October 27, 2002.

For the first time, Brazil's social movements, workers, students, and political Left saw a true hope for change at the presidential level. But it didn't last long. Lula promised to continue paying Brazil's international debt. He appointed fiscally conservative Antonio Palocci to the Finance Ministry and selected Henrique Meirelles, the former president of the International Bank of Boston, to head the Central Bank. Only a year and a half later, progressives had had enough. A bloc split from the PT and formed the Socialism and Liberty Party (PSOL).

Nevertheless, by 2010, most would argue that Lula's two presidential terms had been a success. By the end of his presidency Lula had an impressive approval rating of over 80 percent. He had lowered unemployment, made gains with social policies, and decreased poverty and malnutrition with programs like Fome Zero (Zero Hunger) and Bolsa Familia (Family Stipend). That said, most of these improvements were made through reforms and welfare-style programs, and not the transformative social change that many expected of a Lula presidency.

Current president Dilma Rousseff—Lula's former chief-of-staff—was elected in late 2010. She has continued, and expanded, Lula's poverty-alleviation programs, but she has also supported large multinational corporations and, according to public employees, been slow to respond to demands for increased wages and better career prospects. In May 2012, Brazilian teachers went on strike demanding higher pay. Other state employees quickly followed, and within a few months half the total public workforce—four hundred thousand federal employees from roughly thirty departments and agencies—had been protesting and holding strikes.

The Landless Workers' Movement (MST) continues to battle daily for the agrarian reform they had expected under the PT governments, while genetically modified crops are legalized and the powerful U.S.-backed Brazilian agroindustry only continues to grow.

The MST has made many strides in the Brazilian countryside, acquiring thirty-five million acres of land from 1984 through 2009 by occupying fallow land to force agrarian reform. Nevertheless, the inequality of Brazilian land ownership had changed little. In 2009, according to the MST, nearly half of the Brazilian territory was still in the hands of less than 2 percent of the population.

Meanwhile, little has been done to uproot the highly institutionalized system of violence and impunity that Brazil inherited from the colonizers. The system of *coronelismo* is very much alive today. With their vast landholdings, powerful interests, and local henchmen, the *coroneis*, or local oligarchs, hold near absolute power over local towns and regions, particularly in the interior of the country.

Impunity is systemic. As Human Rights Watch declared in its 2008 report, violations against human rights in Brazil are rarely brought to justice.

It cited the impunity of police crimes, forced worker camps, inhuman prison conditions, and the lack of justice for crimes under the dictatorship as major human rights concerns in Brazil.

By the end of the Brazilian dictatorship in 1984, roughly thirty thousand people are said to have been tortured and hundreds disappeared and murdered. While some of Brazil's closest neighbors have begun to try extorturers for crimes committed under their dictatorships, no Brazilian officials have been brought to justice.

"The Brazilian dictatorship set us back in history. It threw a lot of people in to poverty, and they are there until today. A power structure was installed. It pretended to leave, but it didn't. They are still there hiding. Hiding the crimes that they committed against human rights, and that's our struggle," said Diego Begolin, an actor with Porto Alegre's radical street theater group, Atuadores Ói Nóis Aqui Traveiz, in 2008.

This does not mean that Brazil has not had a rich history of social movements, mass mobilizations, and radical democracy.

From the moment the Portuguese set foot on the Brazilian shore, until Brazil's independence and its abolition of slavery in 1888, millions of Africans were enslaved, chained, and sent across the Atlantic to work in the inhuman sugarcane plantations of northeastern Brazil. Revolts were common, as were runaways, many of whom set up their own autonomous villages—known as *quilombos*—in the jungles. While the quilombos were often hunted down and destroyed by the Brazilian military, many lasted for decades, and hundreds have survived until today. According to the National Coordinator of Articulation of Rural Black Quilombo Communities (CONAQ, Coordenação Nacional de Articulação das Comunidades Negras Rurais Quilombolas), as of 2009, close to five thousand quilombos still existed in Brazil, and of those fifteen hundred were in the process of acquiring the legal titles to their land through the Brazilian Land Institute, INCRA. However, this push was, and continues to be, countered by political parties, traditional land elites, agribusiness, and mainstream media.

The largest and most emblematic quilombo, Palmares, was formed near the border of the present-day Brazilian states of Pernambuco and Alagoas in the late 1620s. It grew to twenty thousand residents before it was destroyed in 1695 by military forces.

A little more than fifty years later, the Spanish-Portuguese Treaty of Madrid turned the present-day southern Brazilian state of Rio Grande do Sul over to the Portuguese. The region of São Gabriel became the heart of the native Guaraní resistance. In 1756, joint Spanish and Portuguese forces killed Guaraní leader Sepé Tiaraju and fifteen hundred of his followers when they refused to leave their native lands. The Portuguese distributed the territory among the rich. Even today, "the large landowners have complete economic, territorial and political control over the whole western region of Rio Grande do Sul," says Ana Hanauer, a state MST leader.

In the 1920s, Captain Luís Carlos Prestes led an insurgency of 1,500 military officers on a 25,000 km march around the country, which came to be known as the Prestes Column. Although they did not defeat the Brazilian government they inspired hope for change. The *seringueiros*, or Amazonian rubber tappers, fought to preserve their forests against powerful cattle ranchers and local elites. Their struggle was immortalized by the death of their charismatic leader Chico Mendes in 1988 at the hands of hired assassins. The student struggle under the latest dictatorship left indelible marks on Brazil's society.

Nevertheless, because of Brazil's highly developed soap-opera media, the country's immense size, and the lack of accountability for corruption, killings, and human rights violations, powerful interests have often been successful at isolating movements for equality, social justice, and human rights. But not always.

Since the fall of the last Brazilian dictatorship, Brazil's social movements whether they are the MST, the quilombos, the indigenous movements, the National Movement for the Freedom of Housing (MNLM), local cooperatives, community media, and many others, have built off their rich and diverse history, redefining democracy and autonomy, and struggling in ways that have forced changes across Brazilian society.

Ana Hanauer, Landless Workers' Movement (MST)
"Included in our struggle for agrarian reform is also the need to develop the human being who has been excluded from everything"

Interview and translation by Michael Fox, December 2008

Brazil's twenty-year-long military dictatorship of the 1960s and 1970s exacerbated the country's traditional inequality. Policies bent on industrialization—both in the city and the fields—kicked millions of small farmers off their land.

In the late 1970s, the landless farmers began to organize. They joined forces with small farmers already united by farmers' unions and the Pastoral Land Commissions (CPT). The farmers began to occupy fallow land as a means of acquiring it. Local Catholic priests with ties to liberation theology came out to support them. In 1979, landless farmers began to camp on the side

Sao Gabriel: MST had just recently occupied this land in Sao Gabriel. Families were still sleeping in tents made of black tarps, 2009. Photo by Michael Fox.

of the Natalina crossroads in the northern part of Rio Grande do Sul, Brazil's southernmost state. Within a few months, hundreds more joined them and the population of the encampment grew to over two thousand families.

The military moved in and tried repression, oppression, and psychological operations to get the occupiers to leave, but most stood strong. Within a decade most of those at the camp would win their own land.

In the dying days of Brazil's military dictatorship, in late January 1984, nearly a hundred landless farmers from across Brazil met in Cascavel, Paraná to debate the founding of a movement for agrarian reform that would unite landless campesinos and farm workers from around the country.

Nearly three decades later, the tiny Landless Workers' Movement (MST) has grown into a formidable force. According to MST cofounder João Pedro Stédile, by 2009 the movement had forced the expropriation of 35 million acres of land—an area larger than the country of Uruguay. MST numbers show that by the same year, 370,000 families had acquired their own land in MST settlements, and 100,000 families were in encampments waiting for land. The movement has built hundreds of public schools and taught tens of thousands of its members to read and write. MST members have formed four hundred associations and cooperatives to collectively produce their food.

But it is the democracy within the movement that has held it together, observed João Amaral, a local MST member in Rio Grande do Sul.

"Everything is discussed. There is no voting," Amaral said. "Discussions tend to be by consensus. Perhaps that's one of the secrets of the unity of the MST—that we have not been divided over every issue where you have to make a decision."

The MST is now organized in twenty-four of Brazil's twenty-five states, and is one of the most highly regarded social movements on the planet.

At twenty-eight years old, Ana Hanauer is already a seasoned organizer with MST in Rio Grande do Sul, and a popular educator in the movement.

I'm the daughter of small farmers. My dad had twelve acres of land. My dad is descended from Germans, and my mom from blacks. Neither one of them had had land. They worked a lot to buy twelve acres. My mom died when I was two years old, and I remember when I was a child, we were able to produce everything that we ate. The only things we needed to buy were clothes. We had a tiny school in the community, so I studied through fourth grade and stopped, like everyone else. I'm the youngest of the children that my dad had with my mom. And so my brothers grew up and there wasn't space in that tiny place.

My oldest brother went to an MST camp in 1988 or '89, when he was sixteen. My dad was against it, so my brother ran away from home.

My brother's encampment had seven thousand people living there. It was really large. It was marvelous. One day we went to visit the encampment. I was just a child but I remember that my dad had a lot of questions for them. Is it safe? What is this MST? What is agrarian reform? Does it really work? Can you really acquire land?

My brother was settled and formed a cooperative that produced organic produce, and my dad saw that it worked. We were having a lot of problems in the community where we lived. All my brothers had left home. I was the youngest and I wanted to study, but there was no place for me to study. My dad decided to camp with another brother of mine, who was a little older than I. Less than a year after he went to camp, they were settled in the Municipality of Joya, and we began to organize. I was thirteen, and I liked it a lot. It was really fun. There were a bunch of children and youth.

My dad got married again and had more children, so that tiny piece of land had to be for them, and there wasn't room there for me. But I was clear about something. I didn't want to go to the city, because we had always lived in the country and I liked it.

At that time I had a partner, who is with me today. He was also the child of MST settlers, so we decided to camp with the movement. We camped for almost two years, and we won our land eight years ago. We were settled in the Carlos Marighella settlement in the Santa Maria Municipality in Rio Grande do Sul. When we got the taste for this collective coexistence, for the struggle, we weren't able to stop. We began to understand that our struggle isn't just our movement. It's for all of the campesinos, it's for the metalworkers, the proletariat from the city. This is a class struggle.

The movement gives us jobs to be done, but at the same time it is pure happiness, because it is through this companionship, this struggle, that we become complete. For me, this fight is essential for us to be happy. If not, it doesn't make any sense to win some land and confront the police.

Organization and participation

The organization of the movement is the same in every state, in all of the encampments and settlements across all of Brazil. We begin with one important principle, which is participation. Included in our struggle for agrarian reform—which is our most immediate objective—is also the need to develop the human being who has been excluded from everything. The people who struggle for agrarian reform are people who were excluded from all of the basic rights and all of the material needs, and also from self-esteem, from a feeling that they have potential in our society. We are always concerned about this, and we take care of this through participation.

In both the encampments and the settlements, we organize the people in base nuclei made up of twenty to thirty families each. The coordination of the encampments and settlements is made up of the coordinators of the base nuclei. All of the decisions that the movement is going to make are discussed in the base nuclei. You always have to hear the opinion of the nuclei, because that's the space everyone has to give their opinions, to participate. It's a philosophy: People are only subjects in the history of their movement, and their own history, if they participate, if they give their opinion.

We participate in the movement, in the struggles or the work. Some people take care of the food, the water, others take care of the tents in the encampment next door, others work with the security of the encampment. These are our collective duties. In our struggle, as well in our collective work, we divide up the chores, so there is no way that you don't change.

This way of doing things influences people's relationships, and it helps you to get over some of the values of individualism, and the collective values become more important, solidarity and sharing. The concern for "me and my family" turns into concern for "the families," the collective. It is the way we have to struggle, because it is impossible to acquire land alone. We need each other. It's not possible to confront the police alone. But together, that's something else. We learn this as we go along, and this changes the values and brings other values in to focus.

Agrarian reform is the immediate objective of the movement, but our central theme is the Brazilian revolution—socialism. So our struggle for agrarian reform now needs to project socialist values, including the form of organizing, practicing how socialism is going to be. We don't necessarily talk about this with the people, but they are doing it without knowing it, and if they feel good they are going to stay with the movement, and if they are going to stay in the movement, they are committed to our struggle.

The Brazilian government under Lula

The MST and the Brazilian working class in general had very high expectations that the Lula government would take large steps forward in agrarian reform. But in order to become president of the republic, Lula had to make some concessions to the Right, and one of those concessions was the agricultural program. Our analysis at the present time is that the Lula government opted for an agricultural project focused on agroindustry, agriculture, and monoculture for export. And the government has invested a lot of public money in this.

This agricultural policy of the Lula government excludes the workers and the small farmers, and it also doesn't do agrarian reform. At the same time it strengthens the large landowners, and it strengthens the monocultures, and even more so with the reconfiguration of the *latifundios*, which leaves the out-of-touch landowners behind as the transnational corporations enter on the scene.

The Lula government has thrown in a lot of money to save the paper pulp companies, the soy companies, the meat and bird producers. The majority of this production is genetically modified, and this is part of this model.

Our movement is ending the struggle against the leftover landowners and beginning to struggle against corporate capital, because the multinationals have also imposed this agroindustrial model on the Brazilian state. It is an imposition by Lula and his cabinet, but also an international imposition. In the international division of labor, Brazil has the job of producing raw material. So the Brazilian state has to create the conditions to produce this raw material—the case of the paper pulp, the meat, the soy, the ethanol, the biofuels.

Hope for the future of the MST

I hope we are able to unify the other workers—the workers in the city, the students, the machine operators, those that don't have work, the workers in the fields—not just the landless, but the small farmers. I hope that we are able to unite large struggles and involve the participation of women and youth, because they particularly deserve extra attention. We are at a moment where it is possible to fight small battles against large capital to support the processes in Latin America, as well as carry out the Brazilian revolution. If not, nothing that we are doing here makes any sense. Doing agrarian reform, just to do agrarian reform, isn't possible in capitalism. For us, it is important to be able to accumulate power for the class struggle.

The role of women in the MST

In the MST, we are in an important process of discussion and understanding of feminism in agrarian reform and in the class struggle. Capitalism needs women to remain much more submissive, oppressed, and exploited than men, because women produce the most valuable piece of the capitalist system: the workforce. This system needs them to continue to be oppressed in the private domestic sphere, so that they continue to be exploited, and do this work for free.

Within this context, we understand we need to treat women with intentionality. Women need to stop being oppressed. They need to stop being exploited. Private domestic work needs to be divided with men, because we want another society. This means that fighting against the oppression or exploitation of women means fighting against capitalism.

And even more, if we look at it, the day of the revolution, we are going to destroy capitalism, but the patriarchy came long before capitalism, so we're going to have another struggle to fight within socialism, which is patriarchy. For centuries women have borne the chore of birthing the children for the system, and we aren't willing to do that any longer. So we're going to have to discuss this within the movement and the class, and take action. That's why we have done women-only actions in the MST and Via Campesina, as in the case of March 8 [International Women's Day]. And there are a lot of women in the movement leadership who have given quality to the struggle and to the development of the movement.

State threats to the MST

In the last few years, the state has stepped up its response to our demonstrations. The confrontation manifests itself in police repression, but behind this is a completely articulated action by the state, the judiciary, the *latifundio*, and the multinationals. You see the police that come to repress, but we understand that behind this is this web of forces that are going to try and defeat the movement.

MST 25th Anniversary celebration. Brazil's Landless Workers' Movement celebrated its 25th anniversary in January 2009 at the MST Anonni settlement in the state of Rio Grande do Sul. Annoni, site of one of the first MST land occupations, was home to nearly 420 families at the time of the anniversary. Photo by Silvia Leindecker.

And in July 2008, the [Rio Grande do Sul] public ministry decided to make the MST illegal. They say that we don't really want agrarian reform, that we are just disputing for power, and that we are guerrillas. They try to make the connection between the MST and FARC in Colombia. Of course, this is not true, but this is the offensive against the movement. What's important is that our families confronted this moment of repression very united and ready to struggle.

Across the country in every state, the Left came together to defend the movement—Via Campesina, workers' unions in all parts of the city, students, and professors. We stopped debating over whether or not to support the Lula government, and began to debate over the model, asking, "This capitalist system doesn't work? Then what do we need?"

At the same time, it was a moment of many internal challenges for the movement, and for the Left. And we are still in the middle of it. Apparently the repression has subsided, but it hasn't, because many companions were accused of crimes and have trials pending, and many are in preventative detention. We believe that a lot of repression is yet to come, because our struggle took on another dimension. So we have to prepare for this, but what's important is that the families have carried the flag of agrarian reform and the movement ever higher.

Nelsa Inês Fabian Nespolo, the "We Will Overcome Cooperative of United Seamstresses" and the Solidarity Economy

"Feeling empowered is only possible by experiencing that things are possible"

Interview and translation by Michael Fox, March 2009

Cooperatives in Brazil, as in most Latin American countries, have a history that goes back to the beginning of the twentieth century. Partially in reaction to the disastrous neoliberal policies of the 1990s, the renewed democracy debate in Brazil over the last two decades has also carried with it new ideas and experiments in economic democracy for local communities in need. In 2005, according to figures from MERCOSUR's Specialized Reunion of Cooperatives, there were 6,700,192 co-op associate members out of 7,491 cooperatives in Brazil, which generated approximately 6 percent of Brazil's GDP.

The solidarity economy sector has grown along with local worker cooperatives.[1] Dozens of solidarity economy fairs take place each year across Brazil, where local producers can sell their products. Unisol Brasil is a cooperative federation formed in São Paulo in 2000, which has opened its doors to cooperatives and solidarity businesses across the country.[2] Unisol coordinators say their federation stands in stark contrast to Brazil's enormous Organization of Brazilian Cooperatives (OCB), because the Unisol representatives all remain grassroots workers in their co-ops or small solidarity businesses.

One of them is Nelsa Inês Fabian Nespolo, one of the founders of Univens (The "We Will Overcome Cooperative of United Seamstresses") who is also at the heart of Justa Trama (Just Threads). Univens was formed seventeen years ago among three dozen women in Porto Alegre's poor, working-class neighborhood, Sarandon. In 2005, Univens members coordinated three dozen cooperatives and small solidarity economy businesses that produced fifty thousand organic bags for Porto Alegre's World Social Forum. By 2009 the co-op had its own headquarters, and was making thirteen thousand pieces of clothing per month.

Today Univens has twenty-six members, and we're opening it up for two more because we're not able to fulfill all of the demand. And the co-op is taking on its own shape. We are doing a specific Univens product line talking about passion for the city, participation, citizenry, and themes that have been important during this period in the city. We've done fashion shows in the Public Market, and in the cultural area, and it was very important for the cooperative.

Justa Trama

Before 2005, we were already discussing in Unisol, the CUT (Central Única dos Trabalhadores, Unified Workers' Central) development agency and the Brazilian forum, that it was important to try to bring together the cooperatives that make the thread and the cloth with the farmers who plant cotton, because we could do what we did during the World Social Forum. We had always worked with various cooperatives, but what we did was join together various cooperatives and buy the cloth from the large capitalist business that would sell us the cloth at the lowest price. That was already good, but we weren't making big change, because we were still in the hand of someone that had a lot of power. And we said, "Man, we could really flip this thing on its head, and take out the intermediaries." Imagine an experience in solidarity economy if we could bring everyone together and eliminate all the intermediaries that could be getting rich off of our work.

So today, Justa Trama has the farmers in the Sertão of Ceará. We began with one hundred fifty farmers and today we have more than three hundred small farmers that plant organic cotton in nine municipalities of the Sertao, where it rains very little. But it needs to rain when the cotton is planted, which is in this period now, February and March, and afterward cotton doesn't need a lot of rain. The less rain the better. And the cotton there has a long fiber, which is of higher quality than the fiber that is produced here in southern or southwestern Brazil.

The cotton producers from these nine municipalities join together in this association called Adeqi. And the farmers make more than double for planting this cotton—they plant one row of cotton, a row of corn, a row of sesame, and a row of other foods which are planted there, beans or something. And this is good because if they lose the cotton, they are still going to have their corn, or their beans. Also because the pests often get confused with this type of planting, you also end up preserving the harvest and the environment. So this is really important for us.

From there, this cotton goes to São Paulo, where Aconis, which is a recuperated business with more than three hundred workers, makes the cotton into thread. And then we have the Fio Nobre, which today has transformed into a cooperative; when we started Justa Trama, it was a family solidarity economy small business. But today it's a cooperative and it makes the handmade cloth for Justa Trama from the thread. And we have the Univens cooperative here.

To produce all of this, we couldn't put on a plastic button. We also had to put on natural buttons. So we have an Açai cooperative in Rondonia of more than thirty artisans who make the natural buttons to put on the pieces

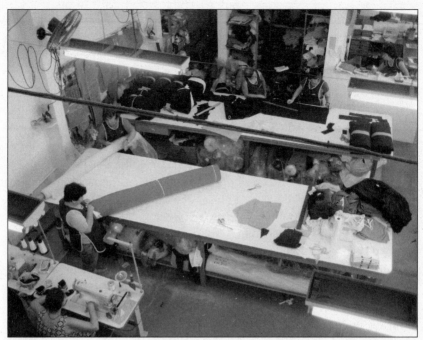

Univens: Members of the "We Will Overcome United Seamstresses Cooperative" (Univens) at work. Photo by Michael Fox.

of clothing. Today, this chain involves more than seven hundred workers. It is coordinated by one representative from each area. We meet two or three times a year. We share all of our information and decisions over the telephone and e-mail. Today our market is domestic, in the fairs. We are opening up a very important front in Italy. And our products have already gone to France, and also to Spain for fairs there.

Univens's impact in the community

Making Univens successful proves that it's possible to economically organize in another way, and that people can live on this. And this makes tremendous change in the local community, because everyone who works here, lives here. It helps the money stay in the community, because if I work in the center of the city, I go by a store and I buy something there. I pass by a fruit stand and I buy fruit there and then go home. So I strengthen the market that's here, because I am always here. It's also a way to organize the economy within our own community. So, just that is marvelous.

If you look at all the women who are here, what would they hope for economically? Some of them, because of their age, would no longer be working, and the cooperative gives them a good feeling about their lives.

We talk about our lives here, we talk about work, and we get together. We all know about each other. Our children study together. Now, on top of this, we are part of a production chain that isn't polluting the environment, especially when you stop to realize that cotton is the most polluting product on the planet, because 25 percent of all agrotoxins that go on the planet, go on cotton. There is no product that absorbs as much agrotoxins as cotton.

And so to have a product about which you can say, "No, this wasn't made like that," is marvelous. On top of this we have a productive chain in which everyone makes more for their work. Imagine, a seamstress sits at the machine and does the same thing to make the same piece of clothing that's in the market, and here she makes double. Double! That, for us, is the real meaning of distributing resources for social justice. It's not just benefiting one of us, but all of us. It has to be worth it for everyone, that's integration. We can give the consumer a product that was totally cooperated, and a product that preserved the environment, and a product that isn't more expensive than they are going to buy with another brand.

Sharing decisions

Univens has assemblies every month, on the twenty-third. Everyone stops. We discuss everything. It goes through everyone. No one has the right to make any changes that don't go through the assembly—changes that could interfere with the decisions that were made in assembly.

Rather than working with the concept of a president, we always try to work with the concept of a council. As incredible as it may seem, I've been in the presidency since the co-op began. Even if we have a decision that doesn't require everyone to get together, we bring together the council and say, "Well, what do you think about this idea?"

For other decisions, even small decisions, we bring everyone together. And since this is a cooperative, we can say, "At 9:00 a.m., let's have everyone stop, and come together for just ten minutes for us to talk about something." Sometimes it's just important that everyone is aware of what is going on. So we don't have any problem, at any time, any minute, stopping and asking for opinions. Or sometimes a new and different product arrives, and we need to decide together how we are going to work with it, or if we are going to take it on, so we all need to meet. It is not a sickness of assembly. I think this is really living democratically. It's not just about majority rules. People are participating and they feel like this is theirs.

We are not producing more because we have a decision that Univens will never grow to more than thirty workers. We'll strengthen other co-ops by giving them work instead. With thirty people you're able to have meetings and make decisions where everyone participates. We don't want a co-op where, within a little bit, it will be this or that council that decides in the name of everyone.

Empowerment

For me, this is the biggest change we have had. Feeling empowered is only possible by experiencing that things are possible. In a regular job, you think, "What am I going to do tomorrow? Well, a new machine might come and I won't be needed any longer. Or I might have a falling out with my boss and he might fire me. Or who knows, a crisis might come and they're going to boot us out, as is happening with a lot of workers right now in Brazil." To know that this isn't going to happen to you, and you can stay here always, because if the market has a problem, we can sell somewhere else, right? This is ours. It's not one person's. No one is going to have power over you, and over this.

And on top of this you are doing something you like. So to also be in a job that makes you happy is really good. To work as a team. I think that's a change that gives you meaning for your life. Things happen here that are just amazing, and they don't happen in other cooperatives. Like, a woman who works here hurt her leg last week. She went to the emergency room and they wrapped it up. After Sunday, she took the bandage off and she came to work. You only do that when you really feel like this is yours.

It's a change. You see that your life is better. People are changing things inside their home. They're seeing their children graduate as a result of all of this. They are passing their training courses. We've had experiences of women here who have sent their partners away because they were treating them badly. You can only make a decision like that if you are in a safe place. I think there are many changes that end up happening as a result of all of this.

Ana Vanesca and Pedro Cardoso, City of Plastic and the Urban Resistance Front
"The countryside is in the hands of agribusiness, which is driving family agriculture out"

Interviews by Raul Zibechi, January 2010
Translation by Luis Ballesteros

Palm trees and luxury hotels line the ocean shore of Salvador, capital of the state of Bahia—but on the outskirts of town, thousands of people live in impro-vised houses of plastic, wood, cardboard, and metal.

Brazil suffers from a severe housing shortage; monthly rents that exceed the minimum wage have exacerbated the problem for the country's poor.[3]

The Movimento Sem Teto (Homeless Movement) organizes people to occupy vacant buildings and land in order to pressure the government—and to build stable communities. The movement takes various forms around the country. The largest organization is the Movimento dos Trabalhadores Sem Teto (MTST, Homeless Workers' Movement), organized by the MST in 1997. Other groups, such as the Movimento Sem Teto Bahia (MSTB), have different origins but similar goals and praxis.

Nearly five thousand people live in MSTB camps. Seventeen of the camps are in Salvador, and five are scattered around the state. Cidade de Plástico (City of Plastic), the most emblematic of the MSTB settlements, houses two hundred twenty-eight families.

Ana Vanesca, a teacher, works with MSTB and cofounded the Urban Resistance Front; Pedro Cardoso became involved in the resistance to Brazil's dictatorship in 1979 through the Catholic base communities; he is now one of the coordinators of the MSTB.

Pedro: In the 1970s there was a movement for the defense of the slum dwellers but it did not organize occupations. In the 1980s, Salvador had more than five hundred occupations, generally spontaneous and individual, or collective but unplanned. Salvador had a high growth in the 1980s and '90s and those slums are now barrios, but unorganized ones. In 2003 we started in Salvador and we are now in the city and in municipalities of the metropolitan area.

At the beginning of an occupation, the barrio residents discriminate against the occupiers. We call it occupation, but many call it invasion. However, in the course of time relations improve, as they see that we are hard-working people. The neighbors are also slum dwellers. The entire area of the outskirts is dotted with occupations.

Before the occupation, the people form nuclei with families that pay rent or, many live in the same house and the nuclei start looking around for spaces to occupy, while researching the situation of the targeted land.

Cidade de Plástico has 228 families in twenty thousand square meters. Every household has an average of six to seven members, with an average family income of 300 reais [about $150] per month. *Bolsa Familia* [the "Family Stipend" provided by the government] covers only 10 percent of the inhabitants.

Ana: In the Guerreiras de Zeferina cooperative [which operates a communal dining hall], there are three men and four women, but twenty people are involved altogether. One hundred people have their meals every day for two reais.

Women are the protagonists in housing movements. The movement has succeeded in making the role of women visible in everyday life, to such an extent they hold the leading positions.

Pedro: The seventeen settlements of Salvador plus the five of Bahia are coordinated. We hold local assemblies that are the plenary sessions of the occupations, and then we organize the brigades, but we do not have brigades in all the camps.

The brigades do the daily management of the camps. If the occupation has fifty families, it has ten-person brigades. People rotate their tasks on a weekly basis: cleaning, hygiene, coordination of assemblies. There is no set rule. At the beginning there are daily assemblies; then these are spaced out as the camp becomes consolidated. They carry out community work.

Local assemblies draw 150–200 people, depending on the subject. These are also the political education nucleus of the movement.

The nucleus of women in Cidade de Plástico is divided into health and education areas, depending on each camp. The movement began six years ago and we are now working the popular education aspect.

There are occupations that do not belong to the movement, like the one we will visit up on the hill.

Quilombo of Escada

We call these communities quilombos, because we recognize part of the struggle of the black people. Escada is a three-year occupation inhabited by four hundred families, in a space smaller than Cidade de Plástico. It is the densest occupation of the movement.

Here the organization is very advanced. There is no cooperative yet, but we want to bring it here. Look, she is the coordinator; she is fifty-one years old and has four children. Somebody was selling the plots of land, and they were forced out of the movement.

Electricity has been connected illegally. One person made the whole installation of electricity and water. At the time of the first occupations, the power company used to cut off the power and people used candles for lighting, but this caused some fires. After a large demonstration we occupied the power company and forced them to let us have power.

They grow sugarcane, papaya, and banana. Papaya, for instance, grows in six months. The land is very uneven, filled with small ravines, and everything is too crowded. Somebody picked up all kinds of things from the garbage and made a colorful house with them—like an artist.

Quilombo do Paraiso

This is the newest camp and it has more space. The occupation started two years ago. This plot of land belonged to Votorantim, a cement company.

People were pressing the state to build, but they are learning that the state does not give anything, so they started to build.

They don't have electricity or water and all the connections are illegal. The social composition is the same in all of the camps: garbage pickers, cardboard pickers, and all kinds of informal and marginal activities.

Drug trafficking

Ana: The worker who used to work in a factory is now impoverished or unemployed and has gone to live on the outskirts as a homeless person. This is a trend. We are abandoning our young people because the countryside is more and more in the hands of agribusiness, which is driving family agriculture out.

My concern is the absence of policies designed for the youth. There is an increasing consumption of crack; each rock is worth fifty cents . . . a real life-endangering situation. A movement has to find alternatives, because kids have no other choices or points of reference. In the occupation that we will visit almost all of the young people are engaged in drug trafficking, which is the only reason for the large flows of money.

Pedro: Drug trafficking is present in all the camps. Where the spaces are closed, this is more difficult, but when the occupation is open, there is drug trafficking. The method we use [to deal with it] is related to the issue of coexistence. We tell them that it is necessary to make a pact of coexistence, because they live here and when they engage in drug trafficking, they put the whole camp at risk, since there could be police raids.

Also, drug dealers often have close links with the police. The pact is that they should not do anything to criminalize the camp. We try to convince them not to do that, but we have to be careful because they will not hesitate to get rid of you. Thus, we need to avoid falling into situations of violence. Unlike other sites, until now they have not killed any leader here, but there have been situations of extreme violence with families of the movement.

Ana: We have a female comrade who had to leave for São Paulo due to a situation of violence. She was a coordinator who decided to confront them. They stormed the camp and nearly killed her.

Pedro: The relationship between the drug dealers and the community is strange. With them, robberies decline because they do not want the police to come, and they want to avoid any problems that may jeopardize trafficking. Now the community experiences fewer robberies than before. But the [traffickers'] relations with women are very bad and riddled with violence.

Organizing the urban resistance

Ana: Now we are forming the Frente de Resistencia Urbana (Urban Resistance Front, FRU) with movements for housing, the black and hip-hop movements, people fighting against state violence and racial discrimination, and the indigenous people's movement. We started in 2006 with a meeting of unemployed workers in São Paulo at a farm. By then, there were many urban movements and all the attendees at the conference were dissatisfied with the Lula government. The FRU took root mainly in São Paulo, Rio de Janeiro, and Minas, with a small presence in the north and northeast. In Bahia the homeless movement promoted it.

The FRU is characterized by its autonomy, construction of popular power, class unity, and socialist orientation. It has a horizontal organization, and focuses on four points of action: urban reform, housing, and fights against poverty and for decent jobs.

We base our action on consensus and this is time-consuming. The FRU was only established last year, after a debate among fourteen movements from all over Brazil, since it is essential to gain a level of confidence. Each movement keeps its own banners and autonomy, and so we gradually build the FRU. It is a very open construction under a coordinating body, but in real life day-to-day events are more important. Coordination involves representatives of each movement, but here in Bahia things are less complicated and more dynamic, as there is a culture of horizontality. This is more in tune with the culture of urban youngsters than with the culture of trade unions.

Movements here already have principles such as popular power and horizontality, which made it possible to build the FRU. We were already similar in our ways of working, which explains why there is no fight for hegemony either. MTST is the only movement with a national scope.

This construction requires a great deal of patience. We are now deciding to support the creation of a new trade union association. Popular movements distrust trade union organizations because these have been always used by the system, as is the case with the CUT, which is now an arm of the government. There are no political parties because we are autonomous, but there always people who belong to parties. I am a member of the PSOL [Socialism and Liberty Party], specifically, within the Socialist Articulation current.

Eliana Sousa Silva, human rights activist
in Rio de Janeiro's favelas
"Police actions in the favelas follow a 'logic of war'"

Interview conducted by Fabíola Ortiz for Inter Press Service, September 2012. Translation by Fabíola Ortiz

Eliana Sousa Silva has lived nearly three decades in the Complexo da Maré in Rio de Janeiro, and has witnessed extensive violence and human rights abuses. A social worker by profession, she has founded two nongovernmental organizations, Observatório das Favelas and Redes da Maré. She has recently published the book Testemunhos da Maré *(Testimonies from Maré), which reflects life in the city's most populous shantytown complex. Here she gives her testimony about how the pacification of favelas can become a real public policy.*

The "pacification" of the favelas in Rio de Janeiro aims to drive out armed groups and fight drug trafficking. It begins when elite police squads are sent in to crack down on drug-trafficking gangs. Once the drug mafias have been run out of the favela, the government installs permanent "Police Pacification Units" (UPPs) to carry out community policing, and increases investments in health, education, sports, and income-generating activities for local residents.

Wave of changes in Rio de Janeiro's favelas

The Police Pacification Units (UPPs) are a response from the state, based on a project designed by the government's secretariat of security. They are part of an ongoing action that has a positive side: They are attempting to disarm the armed groups.

But at the same time, the strategy leaves something to be desired. It must take a step forward in order to become a real public policy. And an important aspect is missing: understanding the population of the favelas and how they relate differently to the police.

Progress will come when the people start to see that the arrival of the state, through the police, is designed to guarantee their right to security and not to victimize local people.

The residents must be included in the process of pacification. They must become active participants.

Until the 1980s, Complexo da Maré was made up of six favelas. Today there are over sixteen. These communities have become part of Maré as a result of a housing policy based on the government-financed construction of low-income apartment blocks.

That might explain aspects of Maré, which has become a huge favela, the biggest in the city of Rio de Janeiro in terms of population. Figures from

Eliana Sousa Silva. Photo by Elisângela Leite/Redes da Maré.

the Brazilian Institute of Geography and Statistics indicate that the complex is home to 129,400 people—a larger population than that of 80 percent of the cities in this country.

It is a complex of favelas but with a population of a medium-sized city, and with structural problems of urbanization, sanitation, rainwater drainage networks, conservation, environmental problems, lack of leisure spaces for art and culture, and the quality of its sixteen public schools.

Because Maré is near (the heavily polluted) Guanabara Bay and major freeways like Linha Vermelha and Avenida Brasil, the air we breathe is the worst in the city. There is a set of problems arising from the way the favelas emerged in the first place: the arrival of the population without the necessary infrastructure.

The arrival of the Police Pacification Units

The residents of Maré have mixed feelings, between anxiety and fear. The UPP could have positive aspects, but the lack of clarity about how the process will play out has caused uncertainty among the local people. The police have not changed their attitude. The arrival of the police is expected to be very violent.

I wrote the book *Testemunhos da Maré* in August 2012 to better understand the violence of the state expressed through the police—something I have wanted to get a grasp on since I was just a girl. I saw it and at that time I did not understand why it happened.

My community activism in Maré is aimed at improving the quality of life. I helped in the foundation of the Observatório das Favelas (Favelas Observatory) and Redes da Maré (Maré Networks) to have an impact on the social reality there.

But the issues of violence and security had to be addressed in order for activities on the social front to have an effect. Understanding public security became a question of utmost importance.

In the favelas, it is important to work on understanding security as a right, similar to health care or education, because local people there do not have any notion of their right to security.

In terms of designing public policies, the idea of the right to security must be taken into account. Police actions in the favelas follow a "logic of war." I mention the example of the Nazi state to help people understand the gravity of the situation. Even though it is unacceptable, in that context [the reality of Maré] there is a command and an order that naturalizes violence or makes drug trafficking seem justified. Even I, who was disturbed and bewildered by this phenomenon, had a way of looking at things that was influenced by these acts of violence.

I wanted to understand on one hand how the police felt, who are important protagonists of the process; on the other hand, how the people felt, who are supposed to receive that public service; and what things are like in the terrain of illegal activity.

I saw a vacuum and found a lack of dialogue among the three protagonists. And I found as well a deeply embedded preconception about the people living in favelas on the part of the security agents, which leads to a distorted vision of what kind of people live there, as if the entire community were involved in illegal activities.

Raimundo Francisco Belmiro Dos Santos, Riozinho do Anfrísio Extractive Reserve Association
"How come people who fight for the conservation of nature lose their lives?"

Interview conducted by Fabíola Ortiz for Inter Press Service, August 2011
Translation by Fabíola Ortiz

Raimundo Belmiro requested urgent protection from the Brazilian authorities in August 2011, reporting that landowners in the northern state of Pará had offered a $50,000 contract for his death and hired gunmen to pursue him.

Belmiro is a forty-six-year-old seringueiro *(rubber tapper) and the leader of the Riozinho do Anfrísio Extractive Reserve Association, which is resisting the destruction of the heart of the Amazon, the world's biggest rainforest, which fills 5.5 million square kilometers. He is one of many activists threatened with death for their work in defense of the Amazon jungle.*

The Riozinho do Anfrísio Extractive Reserve is a 736,000-hectare area located in the region of Terra do Meio between the Xingu River and its tributary, the Iriri River, in the southwest portion of the state of Pará.

Extractive reserves are areas in Brazil dedicated to the regulated use of natural resources in such a way that ecological balance is not affected. The idea came from environmental activist and seringueiro *leader Chico Mendes, whose 1988 murder shocked the world. The year the Riozinho reserve was created, Belmiro received the government's Human Rights Award.*

Belmiro dos Santos, who was born and raised in Riozinho, says his grandfather came to the area from the northeast state of Ceará during the rubber boom in the first half of the twentieth century. But when Brazil lost its global market dominance in natural latex, the local population started to shrink. Nowadays they have no basic public services, labor protections or social entitlements, and are constantly exposed to the predatory activities of the grileiros, *land-grabbers who invade and seize public property or private land belonging to others, using forged documents or, simply, intimidation and violence. This practice of taking illegal possession of the land to sell it to large landowners or agribusiness interests, known as* grilagem, *is carried out on a large scale in the Amazon rainforest.*

In Riozinho do Anfrísio there are many interests in play, ranging from land speculation to the sale of natural resources to money laundering. The families of Riozinho play an important role fighting deforestation and environmental destruction. But the situation is especially complex in that area due to the construction of the Belo Monte hydropower dam on the Xingu River. The dam would generate a real estate boom in the jungle and would lead to major expansion of the local market. Nevertheless, the authorities do not consider the reserves vulnerable to the environmental impact of the enormous construction projects.

My life is really complicated today because they have put a price on my head and say that I will be killed before the end of the year. Since 2004 I have been threatened, and landholders, loggers, and ranchers have invaded our lands, cutting down our wood illegally.

I have lived my entire life here in the Amazon. I am fighting to defend life, the jungle, nature, and I cannot live without protection anymore. Some time ago landowners wanted to buy my small plot of land so as to push me away, but I refused.

Riozinho do Anfrísio is an Extractive Reserve located in the region of *Terra do Meio* between the Xingu River and Iriri River in Pará, one of the biggest Brazilian states. It takes at least six days to reach the reserve by river from the nearest city Altamira, which is 800 km away from Belém, the capital of the state of Pará.

The reserve is a land full of chestnut and açaí (a typical Amazonian fruit) and rich in wood such as andiroba, opaiba, balsam, mogno, and mahogany. The wealth of our land awakens the ambition of outsiders.

The threats [against me] began in 2004, some time before the government of Luiz Inácio Lula da Silva created the Riozinho do Anfrísio Extractive Reserve on November 8. At that time I was the president of the local association at the reserve. One killer who had been hired to murder me was arrested and stayed two years in prison.

Some strangers used to come by and personally warn, "If you do not sell your land, we will end your life. If you do not accept what we want, you shall not stay here anymore." Gunmen often used to stop by my house and say, "You will be banished from here." Some anonymous caller told me once on the telephone, "They are going to the reserve to kill you. If I were you, I wouldn't go back." They think that eliminating people is the best way to get the land. But I cannot accept that. It is wrong.

Due to the increasing threats in 2004, my uncle Herculano and I had to leave the jungle by helicopter, escorted by the army. We headed to Brasília, the capital, and started to fight for the creation of the reserve by the federal government.

After one month in Brasília, we went back to Altamira and on November 8 we received the news that the Riozinho do Anfrísio reserve had been declared. It was such good news, and such a relief. Over the next ten months the army and the federal police stayed in the reserve in order to avoid invasion and keep us safe. But since they left, the threats have started all over again. We do not have any protection. The loggers are invading the area and there is no one to protect us. For a year we have been frightened and living in danger.

Landowners are offering 80,000 reais ($50,000) for my murder. It is said that by the end of the year, I will be killed. We are trying to ask for more protection but it has to be permanent. It is not enough to get some protection for a couple of days or months.

I am forty-six years old and was born and grew up in Riozinho do Anfrísio. My father was a rubber tapper and I used to help him when I was a child. At the age of twelve, I learned how to do it myself, and worked as a rubber tapper until I reached thirty-nine. I have been working as a community leader since then. I have six brothers and two sisters. I am now married and have nine children—six boys and three young ladies. They all live with me in the reserve. I am not scared of what might happen to me, but I am afraid for the lives of my family, of my children and the others who live in the reserve.

How come people who fight for the conservation of nature lose their lives? I do not want that my death shall be in vain. The situation is becoming more difficult as time goes by. There are many people interested in destroying the Amazon and we are trying to preserve it. In Riozinho do Anfrísio there are only fifty-eight families, no more than six hundred people living in a 736,000-hectare reserve. Measures should be taken before something even worse happens.

Peru

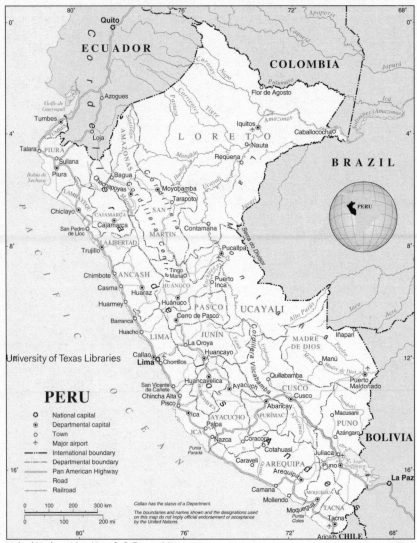

PERU

- ⚙ National capital
- ◉ Departmental capital
- ○ Town
- ✈ Major airport
- —·—·— International boundary
- –·–·– Departmental boundary
- ——— Pan American Highway
- ——— Road
- ——— Railroad

| 0 | 100 | 200 | 300 km |

| 0 | 100 | 200 mi |

Callao has the status of a Department.

The boundaries and names shown and the designations used on this map do not imply official endorsement or acceptance by the United Nations.

University of Texas Libraries

United Nations Map No. 3838, Rev. 3, May 2004

INTRODUCTION

Disputed bodies, territories, and imaginaries—social movements of Peru

By Raphael Hoetmer and Mar Daza

Peru is one of the most diverse countries in the world, both in natural and cultural terms. The country's geography includes the enormous Amazon basin, the Cotahausi and Colca canyons (the two deepest in the world), the Misti and Chachani volcanoes, the precious Urubamba, Mantaro, and Huaylas valleys, the mangrove swamps in Thumbe, the beaches of Piura, the Ballestas Isles, Lake Titicaca (at the highest elevation of any lake in the world), the cloud forests of the north, the glaciers and high peaks like Apu Ausangate (which the Andean people view as sacred living beings), and many other natural wonders.

A wide variety of peoples, nations, and civilizations have lived and interacted with these places. Major civilizations like the Moche, the Nasca, the Tiwanaku, and the Inkas have left their marks in the country, while in contemporary Peru more than fifty different peoples continue to live, including the Quechuas and Aymaras in the Andes, and the Shipiboo, Awajun, and Ashaninkas in the Amazon region. They share Peruvian society with Afro-descendants, Andean and Amazonian migrants in the bigger coastal cities, mestizo populations, and the descendants from European and Asian migrants (colonizers in the first case). Within these groups, and their daily intercultural interactions, live multiple dreams, desires, and plans for the future of the country, inspired by individual and collective subjectivities based on gender, class, ethnicity, culture, and historical memories, which include suffering and happiness, domination and struggle, despair and hope.

In spite of the richness of this diversity, and the obvious presence of a wide variety of knowledge and practices of development within society, development as economic growth based on the endless exploitation of the country's natural resources (and of the popular classes, women and nonwhite populations) has dominated public policies and debates during colonial and republican history. This hegemonic discourse has effectively categorized other visions of development as "backward and ignorant" and naturalized the incorporation of Peru into the world economy as an exporter of its primary resources up to this day.

At the same time, the Peruvian peoples have continuously sought another place in history. Perhaps the most well known episode of resistance was the uprising against the colonial regime led by Tupac Amaru and originating in the land of the old Inkan empire. The brutal repression of the uprising is an example of the particularly violent and genocidal way the territories now known as Peru were incorporated into the imperial, colonial, capitalist, patriarchal modernity. The independence struggle didn't break with this approach to power since it essentially transferred power from the Spanish Empire to the local elite of Lima.

The composition of contemporary Peruvian society

The decades of the 1960s and '70s were moments of great mobilizations that profoundly transformed the country. The taking of land in different parts of the nation inspired one of the most radical agrarian reforms of the continent, decreed and formalized by the military government of Velasco Alvarado, the man who dismantled the *latifundios* in the Peruvian countryside. Urban popular mobilizations, including union struggles, expanded labor and social rights and contributed to the overthrow of the military government. These processes of struggle spurred the formation of national social organizations, along with left parties that became among the strongest and most influential of the continent.

On the Left, in most, but not all, cases, a vanguardist and authoritarian culture predominated that generally privileged the struggle for central state power over other strategies. This culture impeded the consolidation of a single democratizing project and inspired armed movements like the Communist Party of Peru–Sendero Luminoso (Shining Path) and the Tupac Amaru Revolutionary Movement (MRTA) to rise up in the '80s, after the return to democracy.

The internal war cost the lives of approximately seventy thousand Peruvians, according to the Truth and Reconciliation Commission, and had the greatest impact on the Quechua and Asháninkas, both victims of a systematic violation of human rights by both the armed movements (specifically Shining Path) and government forces. The armed conflict also dramatically affected the democratic Left and the social movements, since dozens of social movement leaders were killed or disappeared. At the same time, a very aggressively anti-Left, anti-movement stigmatizing discourse was installed, which didn't distinguish between the social movements and armed groups, and which still continues.

The armed internal conflict and the economic and social crisis of the first government of Alan García Pérez (1985–1990) created the conditions for the Fujimori regime, which in turn reinforced a clientelistic, authoritarian political culture of patronage and institutionalized corruption, and a policy of violent repression against social movements and protest. This was the same regime that imposed the neoliberal model through economic "shock" (with the flexibilization of labor, among other measures), and the social and territorial reorganization of the country to favor the global capitalist market. Thereby it secured Peru's role as producer and exporter of prime materials in the global market.

The fall of the Fujimori regime and the return to democracy was brought about by social mobilizations throughout the country between 1998 and 2001, mobilizations which, in contrast with other countries of the region, did not reject the neoliberal model as such, but focused criticism on corruption and authoritarianism. These concerns were channeled electorally by the center-right party, Possible Peru (Perú Posible), led by Alejandro Toledo. The governments that followed, those of Toledo, Alan García, and Ollanta Humala, consolidated the neoliberal extractivist capitalist project installed by Fujimori, and continued his measures of criminalizing social protest.

The eco-territorial turn of social struggles

Since the new return to democracy, protests have emerged in growing numbers and with increasing intensity. Notable examples are the actions initiated by the teachers' union in 2004, 2008, and 2012; the mobilizations of coca growers; and the protests against the privatization of local energy companies in Arequipa (2002). Over the past decade the conflicts relating to the common goods came to represent half of the conflicts registered by the Office of the Ombudsman (Defensoría del Pueblo). These disputes are rooted in the struggle over what place different territories and people have in Peruvian society, and represent far more than simple "conflicts of interest."

The demands of the organizational and social mobilizations around extractive processes range from giving local people greater access to the jobs or profits generated by a given mining project, to providing reparations for damage to human health or quality and quantity of water available, to keeping the mining projects out altogether. In the latter cases they have begun to dispute the future of specific territories, paralyzing megaprojects through a great capacity for local organization, counterprojects with lives of their own, and territorial control under local social movement actors. This has happened in diverse places like Ayavaca, Cajamarca, Tambogrande, and Islay, where local communities and populations have defended their way of living based on community life and small-scale agriculture (in the first two cases), or based on medium-scale export-based agriculture (the last two cases). Particularly in Ayavaca and Cajamarca these struggles reinforced autonomous and communitarian practices of social and territorial control exercised by the so-called Peasant Circles.[1]

The eco-territorial struggles have expanded notably in Peru and the impact on society has grown, given the great size of the projects and their contested business promoters, the expansion of the conflicts through the country, the persistence over time of the organization and mobilization in them, and their growing political consequences (in the Humala government a cabinet has fallen for the first time as the result of a mining conflict). The resistance in the regions of Piura, Cajamarca, Arequipa, and Puno prevented (up to this writing in late 2012) the realization of million-dollar mining projects, raising incipient questions about extractivism and giving birth to new critical discourses like that of "*buen vivir*" (the good life) and "post-extractivism," and the recovery and reconstruction of different relations between humanity and nature.

Disputed bodies, imaginaries and territories

Aside from these territorial movements that dispute the future of certain concrete territories, we recognize movements by sectors and (counter-) cultures in Peruvian society.

The sectoral movements operate by reclaiming specific rights or benefits for specific sectors of society, like the people's kitchens (*comedores populares*[2]), teachers, and transport drivers. These often have the ability to mobilize large numbers but their agendas tend to be limited to their own specific interests and their strategies are principally aimed at gaining direct negotiating space with the government.

The (counter-) cultural movements seek to expand rights, deepen democracy, and constitute a culture and lifestyle different from the hegemonic. These include those in the struggle for memory and reparation for the victims of the internal war; those for sexual dissidence; those for gender justice, the recognition of, and respect for, cultural identity and cosmovision proper to the Afro-Peruvian or indigenous; and those for respect of human rights in general and what is now called the rights of nature, that is, those struggling for a more sustainable and equitable society in ecological terms.

The discourses of the defense and recovery of "our territories" from exploitation and endless merchandising—whether those territories be our bodies, sexualities, desires, minds, subjectivities, feelings, our community or place—seek to facilitate processes of liberation and generate other types of social well-being in balance with the welfare of nature. They are transforming into synthetic discourses and agendas through exchanges among different sectoral struggles or countercultures, and at the same time becoming bridges that reinforce and empower those syntheses.

Movement beyond national organizations

In Peru these movements are no longer channeled by national social organizations. National forms have lost representation and organic power due to the difficulty of reinventing themselves in the present context and of creating their agendas and decisions from below, building collective leadership, and entering into and sustaining local struggles. Although the contributions of national organizations to local struggles vary case by case, they've infrequently been the determining factors for the final results of struggles, with the principal exception of AIDESEP in the case of the Amazonian people's struggle (more on this struggle below).[3]

As a result we have a very fragmented and dispersed social movement, but by no means a weak one. The local struggles are not orphans or islands: They link up with others through discourse and imaginaries, support networks (of NGOs and collectives), actual people, meetings of leaders, streams of communication, and alternative media. Sometimes the strategies of the government itself bring them together. More than anything else, they are united by their shared desires and histories. In these ways they have expanded beyond just national organizations, and also from time to time the very territories of origin over the past decade.

One clearly outstanding struggle was that of the Amazon in 2009–2010 against a series of legislative decrees that sought to weaken legal protection and recognition of indigenous territories. Simultaneously in different areas of the Amazon native people rose up under the coordination of AIDESEP. They marched, blocked highways and rivers, undertook public and political campaigns over a period of months, and the response of the government was violent repression in the Bagua area, which cost the lives of thirty-four people, among them police. That resulted in massive solidarity mobilizations and campaigns around the country on behalf of the Amazonian struggle, all of which forced the government to overturn its infamous decrees.

A second moment occurred when the daughter of the ex-dictator Fujimori made it into the second round of presidential elections. A "No to Keiko" campaign arose (2011) that embodied a movement of movements for human rights, mobilizing the whole country, impacting the electoral results decisively and stimulating a political debate in the markets, public transport, taxis, high schools, and on the streets, about the future of the country.

Finally, the resistance to the Conga mining megaproject, moved forward by peasant groups and Fronts in Defense of Cajamarca, gave birth to the National March for Water (2012) that mobilized thousands of people on its way. There were solidarity protests from Iquitos to Espinar, and it culminated in an enormous and unusual march in the capital of Lima, a march in which the national and union organizations had small presence, but the campesino groups, communal leaders, and farmers from all over the country took the center of the capital.

A preliminary assessment

Making an assessment of the real impact on society of these movements, we recognize distinct levels. The processes of organization and social mobilization contend for the future of concrete territories in more and more spaces of the country. Here the protagonists begin to make de facto decisions from below that impede the expansion of the hegemonic development model. These local struggles have prepared the way for new political initiatives. The Ministry of the Environment and the implementation of certain recommendations from the Truth and Reconciliation Commission or proposals from the women's movement are all consequences of these persistent struggles. So, too, were the condemnation of Fujimori and Montesinos[4] and the justice and truth that only a minority of the victims of the internal war have found.

The Peruvian social movements have also managed to impact and enter continuously into the public debate, confronting the majority of the conservative media and also the conservative imaginary that predominates in society. No one can deny that the agendas of the human rights, environmentalist, feminist, indigenous, and sexual dissident movements have continued to provoke discussions and continuous transgressions against the status quo in the last decade. From these situations have arisen new discourses, practices, imaginaries, and proposals that enrich the discussions over the type of society that we want to be. From the discourse of the *buen vivir* as an alternative to "development" to the demands for the right to pleasure, the notions of rights, freedoms and possible lives continue to broaden.

In the processes of organization and social mobilization one can see new political practices and institutional innovations that respond to problems neither the central state nor the capitalist market resolve, and which, at the same time, prefigure other public policies. This is the case with the neighborhood consultations on the mining projects that have been undertaken throughout the country, and also the communitarian defenders, who work to control violence against women and children in the countryside.[5]

Finally, the processes of social organization have configured other social relations, as evidenced by the attention urban sectors are now paying to the native population as a result of the Amazonian mobilizations as well as the greater visibility and acceptance of the LGBT population in the country. As a consequence, there are greater possibilities for more people in Peru to choose different lives, rejecting situations of violence or discrimination and affirming their own identities and ways of life.

These organizational processes and social mobilizations have affected the correlations of power, but haven't transformed them. To the contrary, many of the advances have met new challenges or limits imposed by the factual powers and conservative norms. Such is the case with the Law of Previous Consultation, the final version of which is very far from that proposed by indigenous organizations and civil society. And if some mining megaprojects have been paralyzed or brought to an end, there is still no policy to adequately limit or regulate mining activity. There is also the step backward in the implementation of the law on "therapeutic" abortion, owing to the lack of a protocol that would give national hospitals a clear orientation on how to apply the law, and oblige them to do so. Nevertheless, the different processes described here have constituted a discursive, political, legal, social, and subjective space for transformation in the country. Without being too idealistic, we believe these multiple processes are real disputes in both public and private spheres of the future development of Peruvian society seeking social, ecological, cultural, and gender justice, equity, and democracy.

Hugo Blanco, writer and activist
"'The indigenous movements are building the new society"

Interview by Raúl Zibechi, June 2010
Translation by Luis Ballesteros

Hugo Blanco started out his political life in student strikes in Peru before traveling to Argentina, where he joined a Trotskyist party. He returned to his native Peru to work in the Quechua community, leading an armed uprising in

Hugo Blanco. Photo courtesy of PDTG.

1962 for which he was nearly executed. He became a leader in the Campesino Confederation of Peru (CCP) and he's seen as a link between the Quechua and Spanish-speaking communities of Peru, which perhaps explains his sympathy for the Zapatista cause in Mexico and indigenous causes throughout the Americas. He has served in the Peruvian Senate, been candidate for president, and continues to be active as director of the Cuzco newspaper Lucha Indígena *(Indigenous Struggle) and in regional struggles against mining, deforestation, oil extraction, and other causes that link environmentalism, indigenous, and anticapitalist struggles.*

The struggle for land was a struggle against the agrarian reform made by Velasco [Juan Velasco Alvarado]. It was a fight against Alan García, against the SAIS[6] and Sendero [Luminoso], since the latter said that all of us who said there were other forms of struggle other than the armed struggle were traitors. However, as a result of our struggle we recovered 1.25 million hectares for the communities in the first government of Alan García.

Most of the sixty thousand dead are indigenous people that were killed by the army and also by Sendero. This caused a serious setback because until then the CCP had bases all over the country and this meant its demise.

The oppression of the peasantry by the state and bureaucrats was such that they ended up supporting Sendero. When the people saw that the latter killed policemen, mayors, and officers, they rejoiced. It was a reaction to a very strong oppression and a tightly closed political system.

The internal strife was brutal but the movements were fragile and couldn't find their place. The Left moved to the parliamentary struggle and work at a grassroots level was weakened thereby, a situation Sendero capitalized on. The Left became elitist and turned into something resembling an ivory tower. A certain paternalism toward the grassroots prevailed. On one occasion, the Congress of the Steel and Iron Workers was suspended because the parties hadn't reached an agreement. The CCP was PUM[7]; the teachers were Red Fatherland.[8] Everything was divided at the top but without having the grassroots.

There were people aware of these problems. I was in Parliament and didn't play a role. It was my mistake. I should have refused to be a candidate from Lima because there was an underlying electoral criterion in 1980 to attract more votes. I should have been a parliamentarian for Cuzco and stayed there, close to the grassroots and obeyed their orders, to be the speaker of the movement before the institutions, because in my position as a Parliament member for Lima there were many neighborhoods to serve. When I was a Parliament member was the time I was most attacked. First, I was a member of the Constitutional Assembly; from 1980 to 1985, I was a congressman; from 1985 to 1990, I was out of the Parliament and, finally, I was a senator until the self-coup d'état.[9] In Lima, during the demonstration of street sellers, the water demonstration from the South [in 2002], I was hit hard on the head; that is why I wear a hat now. However, there was no possibility to have a closer relation with grassroots because Lima is very large.

In 1985 I was not appointed to any position because we were in Izquierda Unida. I became the leader of the CCP and went to live in Puno where there was a major recovery of lands. I was not a leader but I was at the service of the comrades from Puno. I was the organization secretary of the CCP and I requested to be assigned to Puno because that is where the fights were taking place. Then I went north to Piura to learn the experience of the peasant rounds and later on to Pucallpa, where I almost got killed.

The SAIS organized by Velasco had good proposals, but in reality these were for the bureaucrats. That's why a struggle was underway to recover the land. The Confederación Nacional Agraria Rumimaki agreed with the SAIS but we, the communities, wanted the land to return to the communities. Cooperatives were something completely alien to the peasant. North of Puno, first we had a demonstration, surrounding the land that we were going to occupy; it was a way of heating up the environment. What impressed me the most was the Buenavista occupancy, an SAIS between

Puno and Juliaca. There were six districts, and six columns arrived, taking the land and the premises. I was assigned the task of preparing self-defense because of my experience in [the province of] La Convención. Actually, it was not self-defense because it wasn't an armed act. If the army were to come, there was nothing to do. The peasantry wasn't conscious of the need to be armed.

There were many peasant theatrical activities, and Puno had several theater groups, which we invited to the occupation. They put on a play in which people first went to the procession and then, being already more conscious, they went to fight, because the play said that the procession was useless. At the end of the play I asked the peasants what they had understood, and they responded that it was necessary to be in the procession and in the struggle. Actually, they were right because we were waiting for a repression that didn't come. Instead, a priest arrived to say mass and while preaching he said, "Let's pray to God that your leaders lead you well, so that the government accepts your demands." At the time of the blessing, while sprinkling holy water upon the faithful, he said, "Brothers, we'll be with you now and at the time of repression, amen." With this type of priests it was impossible to tell the difference between struggle and religion. The priests from Puno were progressive, unlike those of the Opus Dei.

Indigenous movement becoming more important

Latin American reality and now even the Fourth Socialist International says that we, the indigenous people, are the avant-garde. But there is something that they don't recognize: This is a fight of five hundred years that has been strengthened by neoliberalism and that the fight is not only for the defense of nature but also for their collectivist form of organization, which is the key to defend nature. So it's no coincidence that Salinas de Gortari in Mexico and Fujimori in Peru, almost at the same time, enacted laws against the communities and that Alan García attacks nature and community at the same time. Europeans have yet to realize that. They want to define themselves as socialists, but they fail to see that in Chile and Ecuador they were repressed by socialism. How can they be socialists? And the word "ecology" does not tell anything to the indigenous people because they live in an ecological manner.

There was a generation of fights after Fujimori, such as the Arequipazo,[10] and then the protest in Moquegua, struggles that I think are marking out a path. I decided to publish the newspaper [*Lucha Indígena, Indigenous Struggle*] because I see that the indigenous movement will gain increasing importance and since the CCP is not indigenist, it's necessary to emphasize the indigenous component there. The CCP is of trade union origin, but this is becoming less evident over time. The proposal of the indigenous was received very skeptically but is taking a deeper and deeper root. Only a few have been open to this, for example Rodrigo Montoya and CONACAMI (National Confederation of Peruvian Communities Affected by Mining). The latter organization takes an indigenous approach but in my opinion it's a very bureaucratic organization that's too dependent on NGOs, although they do some positive things. I attended the meetings in Puno, then ECUARUNARI, CONAMAQ, and CONACAMI. The last three are in order of importance. CONACAMI has very few people, only in some communities in Pasco. The fact that they pay for the transportation of the people to help them mobilize does not mean that they have anything organized in the rank and file.

This is a process through which people who fight must coordinate among themselves, regardless of their central or coordination. Between three and five of us are involved in *Indigenous Struggle*: Enrique, Roberto Ojeda, and me. My goal is that the people have other ways to become informed. The three countries with left-leaning governments have problems with the indigenous people and the three countries also have the same problem with the mining industry.

Twenty-first-century socialism and the state

I think that socialism of the twenty-first century is very important chiefly because of its anti-imperialist character. It has a very interesting force at the bottom but with weaknesses at the top. I think that these are transition governments that we must strongly support against imperialism and the Right. We fully agree on this point. But when it comes to their confrontation with the indigenous people because of extractivism, I support the indigenous people. For that reason, I think that these are intermediate governments that we have to support sometimes and fight against them other times.

I don't agree with state socialism. I think of socialism from the communities, but the communities are not aware that they are building socialism. Furthermore, this is a democratic struggle because it tries to keep communal properties in the hands of the communities.

I back the idea of a plurinational state but I feel that these are still intermediate steps because there will be a phase when a construction from below will make the state unnecessary. Even Lenin said that the state must disappear. So, all of this is a transitory process toward something new.

If we think of a world without a state, the indigenous reference will be decisive. Now the indigenous movements are building the new society, creating the nuclei of what is to come and this is something that will go beyond the indigenous people. In this regard, I am very optimistic about the recovered factories of Argentina and other movements, but we can't overlook the fact that the community is the nucleus of that society of the future.

That's why we say that Peru will be an *ayllu* of *ayllus* (community of communities). Why? In the first place, because of their organizational criterion; the idea that the public officer is there to serve, not to be served and because the community is the least corruptible, and because it can do without many things of modernity. Even more so, the Amazonian indigenous people are the least corrupted by progress and modernity. I don't think that we need to go back to the life of the Amazonian indigenous but if we take them as a reference, we can think of which things we can do without in our society to avoid the extinction of humankind.

Amazonian people are today the most advanced and the least domesticated by the system. Now the CONAIE elected Marlon Santi, one from Sarayacu, a very combative community, to lead them. The people from the mountain area are more domesticated and influenced by capitalism and modernity.

There is no doubt that the next president [of Peru] will be a servant of multinationals because we are very far from processes like those of Ecuador and Bolivia. This is due to the twenty years of internal war, because there were seventy thousand deaths, most of them of indigenous people. Many people at the forefront of social struggles were massacred, mainly by the army, and to a lesser extent, by paramilitaries, and Sendero. This dismantled organizations, which means that we now are just rising from these ashes.

Margarita Pérez Anchiraico, community organizer in San Mateo Mayoc and member of National Confederation of Peruvian Communities Affected by Mining (CONACAMI)
"Progress for me would be enhancing livestock development and agriculture, and not sowing cement"

Excerpts of an interview published in *Minería y Territorio en el Perú* (Lima: PDGT, 2009), translation by Margi Clarke

Mayoc's main tourist attraction was the forest until the mining industry was privatized in the region in 1998, when the state mining agency CENTROMIN-Peru sold their land to a large mining company, Lizandro Proaño, S.A., which built a toxic waste dump and tried to take over lands around the village of San Mateo Mayoc. Villagers resisted and the conflict began.

In January 1999, Proaño's cranes and dump trucks came in to demolish the homes of Mayoc villagers. Margarita reported the abuse to the authorities of San Mateo, who banned the entry of the mining company's machines. But the company proceeded to clandestinely enter the forest lands acquired from CENTROMIN and deposited the toxic waste.

The town government of San Mateo recognized the seriousness of the matter, and denounced Proaño for possible environmental damage. The public health agency (General Directorate for Health/DIGESA) conducted tests of Mayoc villagers and found their blood contaminated with heavy metals. At that point the energy minister for Peru came to San Mateo to do an inspection and it coincided exactly with the mining company coming in and depositing more loads of toxic waste. The minister ordered a freeze on the mining company's operations on that land in 2002. That initiated the second stage of the struggle, to get the toxic tailings removed.

Before mining became so huge here, we were devoted to agriculture and livestock ranching. There was always some mining, but not on the scale and the damage it does today. There were mining outfits near here like Miqotin and Payococha. They were better connected with us and knew how to share mining profits with the community, but still didn't meet environmental standards. When the big mining companies arrived, some residents began to work for them, receiving weekly or monthly pay. It was supposed to lead to a better life. Those workers, and of course the companies, didn't think about the consequences for the people and the land when the mining is finished.

Before, the people were united and we advocated for our rights. Now things have changed a lot, many have forgotten our common cause and it is regrettable. The mining economy has also affected our identity and culture, because since the mines were installed, our customs have changed, our way of life and how we educate our children. This has caused a conflict of identity, because people imitate each other and now many no longer retain the customs of our people, and our culture has changed for the worse.

We are organized by neighborhood, by village, and by regional district. At each level we have representatives and with them we do consciousness-raising among the residents. So when we prepared to take action we had a great deal more strength. Many people identified with us and each area joined in under their own banner. By then, the municipality was heading the fight and unified everyone. We had meetings, trainings, and workshops. We knew we had to claim our rights.

We also built strong alliances which helped us be more powerful. For example, we sought out some of the nongovernemental organizations

(NGOs) and others approached us to offer help. For example, ISAT, APRODEH, Manos Unidas, OXFAM. Support from the national organization CONACAMI was also important. These organizations brought professionals to give us training and legal advice. Without them San Mateo wouldn't even have been registered as a town.

How the mining companies divided the people

The mining companies came in promising jobs. They sent groups to talk to the communities, and slowly tried to convince them that the companies meant progress. They also handed out gifts and hospitality, so people would believe them more than us, when it is we who are really defending our rights and our land. This is how people sold out to the company's interests.

Here in Mayoc, for example, the San Juan Mining Company bought them all off. They made them into brood hens and cooked them good. The company purchased several plots of land. Their plan was to disappear the Mayoc people; they had a clear vision with a twenty-year plan to take control of the area. The mining industry comes and says what needs to be done and people do it. At that point there is no response from the people.

Women come forward

As a woman, I value the opportunities I have had a lot, because I have gotten to a level of leadership and I have gone places I never thought I'd be. But many men still believe that women do not have the capacity and are not supposed to get involved in these things. They always think we have to be at a lower level than the men, but they are wrong. For example, as I took up this fight, many women followed me. They gained courage, opened their minds, and began to organize. The women joined a community council and voted in a woman president and a woman spokesperson. Before this struggle there were no women participating in the councils.

Land and development

Territory means a lot to me. Can you imagine what it is like to have your land stolen from you, your land so abused, illegally? It's like someone cut off a part of your body. I have here a house, a little farm and they come and take it, leaving me with nothing. Our land is very valuable—it is everything to us.

On the other hand, many people in San Mateo think, and this is regrettable, that mining brings development. But they shouldn't affect the agricultural zone, or the grazing areas. But it does affect us and it doesn't improve our lives. Progress for me would be to enhance livestock development and agriculture, and not the sowing of cement.

The same applies to the word "democracy," because the mining companies don't practice democracy. They dictate their terms. They say, you have to do this, I'll pay so much, and you can do nothing to stop me. So where is the democracy? I understand democracy to be collecting different opinions and reaching consensus.

Mining shreds the social fabric

First came the metal contamination, now the pollution is social. Because today there is no trust; we don't have the stability and cohesion we once had. All that reigns in the town of San Mateo is selfishness and envy, and the same is happening in the village of Mayoc. Many people are organized, but mining representatives go into every town and offer things, and through the village leaders, the mining companies buy off the opposition. These kinds of leaders only serve to benefit the mining interests. They don't want the development of their people.

I have suffered marginalization, humiliation, and isolation in this struggle. Many people don't value what we accomplished, what they accomplished themselves. And the ironic thing is that after all our struggle, in the end when the San Juan Mining had to pay compensation for what they had done, it was them giving gifts again, which is part of what we had been fighting to end.

We must be loyal to our people, so I maintain my position and keep fighting. It is impossible for me to be convinced that mining is good. But on the personal level, I have neglected my family, my children, myself. This work is constant, and sometimes people get tired. First a lot of people accompany you, then sometimes you get one or two, or you have to cope alone. For me it has been nine years of struggle. I've only been able to work a little and continue my studies. It has been hard to work for the future of my children, so many years that I've given to the work. At this point I feel helpless. At any time I may be attacked and I will have to defend myself alone.

The mining has to stop. This area is agriculture and livestock. We can live from our own efforts, with no need to go to a work camp or a mining site to cook for the workers or wash clothes for the miners. I don't believe in that kind of life. But this is the approach they offer people. Here we live by working our fish farms, organic gardens, small animal husbandry, that is our goal. Because we know the real challenge is that mining is not forever. It will end and the companies will not return and they will leave the area worse off.

Now Mayoc is silent, deserted. I honor Mayoc as a historic place, for our fight to stop the toxic dumping. Someday I imagine it will be healthy with green lands, a nature center, a place for relaxation, an example for the communities. I hope someday we will achieve that. I also envisioned San Mateo like that but the new mayor has sold out to the mining interests. If the tailings are piled up where they are, the river will be contaminated. Is this going to be ecological? They should move the waste into an empty mine. We have proposed that, but they don't want to pay for it. They want to do everything the easy way.

They harass us. In our community we get along well, we greet each other, but as you see I'm here all alone. While I'm alive, the miners will not enter Mayoc. If people sell out it's their problem. I know I'm in danger and that by myself I can do nothing but I keep on. For example, the companies organize a meeting, and I go alone, and those who work for the company speak out against me. The mining companies want to see me dead. If my complaint were not at the Inter-American Court,[11] I would be gone by now.

Magdiel Carrión, president of Ayabaca Provincial Federation of Peasant Communities and national leader of CONACAMI
"Our job is to make sure that the community's right to ownership of territory is respected"

Excerpts of an interview published in *Minería y Territorio en el Perú* (Lima: PDGT, 2009), translation by Margi Clarke

Magdiel Carrión is resident of the Yanta community in Ayabaca, in the Piura region north of Lima, home to one of the last intact ecosystems in the country. The Ayabaca forest generates water for three watersheds benefiting the coast, the Andes, and the jungle. This water supply has made Ayabaca a highly productive agricultural area. The Ayabaca area is south of Ecuador, near the border crossings at Chucuate, Río Blanco, and Macará. There are twenty-one communities across the region, located wherever there are natural springs, which in turn form large rivers. Most communities are located in the foothills or the mountains. Since 1997, they have been fighting the efforts of the Majaz mining company (now owned by a Chinese consortium) to dig a massive open-pit copper mine in this ecologically sensitive area.

There have been peasant organizations for many years in the region, which have changed form as the laws and regulations changed. We've organized ourselves from the times of the plantation owners who took the land from the original indigenous inhabitants and began to call them peasants instead of native communities.

Magdiel Carrión of the Confederation of Peruvian Communities Affected by Mining (center, with striped scarf), leading a five-day March of Sacrifice from Ayavaca to the regional capital of Piura, 2007. Photo by Raphael Hoetmer/Programa Democracia y Transformación Global (PDTG).

In this area we are mainly engaged in agricultural production, according to the season and local climate. Some are dedicated to crops and others to livestock. These are the livelihoods of the villagers and each community its own ways of organizing itself. Each community is registered in the public record, recognized in terms of how much land they have and how many families are in each village.

As leaders we can say that our form of organization is rooted in the traditions and culture of our area. Our model really has nothing to do with modernity. Here we all participate alike, men and women, children and adults. We've been present here for thousands of years as an indigenous people. Evidence of this are the various archaeological remains we have in the area. In addition, the community is known for being deeply religious, and every year in the month of October many people come from different parts of the country and the continent to make the pilgrimage to the shrine of Captive Lord of Ayabaca.

Our area is characterized as a peaceful community. We have no problems with anyone. We have lived for a very long time in peace and quiet, in a harmonious coexistence between people, earth, water, and nature.

Mining companies sneak in

In 1997, following permission from the Ministry of Energy and Mines, mining companies were given a concession for part of the land of the community of Yanta. They acted deceptively and bought off the president of the community, without talking to the general assembly, which would have been normal. All this was not known in the community.

When we began to see strange people in the community, we investigated and learned what was happening. We asked for information and we were told that there was a company that wanted to be in Yanta but their operations were actually happening in the neighboring province of Huancabamba. Following this, on January 10, 2004, we held a general assembly in Yanta, where even the company was present, as well as people from the Ministry of Energy and Mines. They wanted the assembly to discuss the situation in their presence, but that was rejected by the community and they had to leave.

The community of Yanta has 20,800 hectares of land. There is an area called Black Mountain, where there are more than one hundred fifty lakes. As a community we have always had great respect for this area as the source of several major river basins in the north. This Quiroz River basin in turn generates the Aranza, Tomayaco, and Parcochaca rivers on one side of the range, and on the other side is the gorge of the Gallo and Río Blanco River, which in turn flows to the Chinchipe which feeds the Marañón River and then to the Amazon. All these watersheds begin in Black Mountain in the community of Yanta.

Upon learning of the company's operations nearby, we formed a committee of seventy-six people to survey and verify the boundaries of our land. We went to the area and concluded that the land involved in the concession was within our Ayabaca province and in the community of Yanta, not in Huancabamba province.

At that point the conflict began. The company began to infiltrate our community with their people, at first sending in sons of families living in the regional capital city of Piura to offer trainings saying that the mine was good. Since we respected the decision of the community assembly to oppose the mining, we had to stop these trainings. At some points there were confrontations between parents and children, and between brothers. The reality was that the company paid these young people very well, and paid some community leaders, who challenged the Community Council but we kept firm in our position, though we were denounced by these mine supporters.

In addition to our struggle and the resistance we put up, three other communities joined us: the rural communities of Aranza, Santa Rosa de Pacaipampa, and Andurco. Together we four organized a strong resistance and began to deny entry to strangers. We even had to confront the police because the company wanted the police to back them. Peace ends when a mining coming comes into a community. Before there were some problems with petty thieves, but that was the worst trouble that we had faced in our communities before the presence of mining companies.

I am a villager from Yanta, that is why I was involved from the beginning in the conflict. With my brother George and some community members, I made a written request for clarification to the president of the community in December 2003. Then in 2004 we started to engage much more. We started organizing meetings at all the levels—village, county, and regional—where we tried to inform people and put forth these question for discussion. I want to note we got a lot of support from Professor Mario Tabra who came to Yanta and volunteered with research support and brought us a lot of information.

Turning points

Besides that point in January 2004 when we met in assembly to challenge the possibility that the mining company could come into the community, there were two important marches we led to the mining camp, one in 2004 which resulted in a confrontation with police who were providing security at the mine together with a private security company called FORZA 3. In that incident one villager died, others were kidnapped and thirty-two villagers were tortured.

In September 2007 we organized a local referendum, in which 94 percent of the population of the provinces of Ayabaca, Huancabamba, the districts of Carmen de la Frontera and Pacaipampa said "no" to mining. The government refused to recognize the plebescite as binding, so we performed a Sacrifice March from Ayabaca to the headquarters of the regional government in the city of Piura.

We're fighting against the encroachment of the Majaz mining company. All their efforts have been supported by the state and its laws, which only work to the benefit of transnational corporations rather than the farmers who live there. Our sole aim is that the company leave our land alone, and that they not pollute the waters that are the foundation of such highly productive agriculture throughout the region.

Since this conflict has emerged, the Church has been increasingly involved in environmental protection issues, and this has been key for us.

Strategies

We've developed different strategies, each depending on the particular situation and the changing context of the work. On one hand we have been trying to put pressure on state bodies, and at the same time doing work in the communities, especially putting out information to the residents.

Early in the process, when we faced the constant presence of miners in the area, we decided to install "gates" or checkpoints. This gave security to our communities, and allowed us to know who entered. Then we started using marches as a pressure mechanism. We also started participating in roundtables, especially those that guaranteed equal standing among participants. We will not accept being treated with arrogance or pedantry by others who do not want us to speak as equals. Another place where we have strengthened our thinking and developed strategies has been at the General Assembly of Communities [Affected by Mining].

From the private capital sector, one of the groups that has been very public, giving speeches on behalf of the mining industry has been the Romero 7 Group. They fund radio spots which air constantly and manipulate the public discourse, claiming that mining means development. The company also has support in the newspapers which constantly attack the leaders and divide the population with a messianic discourse of mining as the savior of the world. They have even pushed this position into church sermons.

The most common way that mining companies try to influence the communities is through gifts of money to defray costs of cultural and religious festivities. And they never stop trying to buy off the leaders. Very few leaders have been won over, but there have been very isolated cases.

Building at the base

The major partnerships we have built have been with grassroots organizations, such as local defense committees, among which is the Front for the Sustainable Development of the Northern Border. We are also allied with women's organizations, community assemblies, and, above all, with the campesino associations.

We have maintained relations with the state at two levels. The first is through government-sponsored roundtable discussions, where we reaffirm our willingness to partcipate, debate and talk to them, but each time we attend these we only hear pronouncements and arrogant positions from their representatives. We stated a condition that to continue in the roundtables, we must work from a relationship of equals. And since this is not how the state sees things, the roundtable meetings haven't continued.

The second relationship has been through the Front for the Sustainable Development of the Northern Border. This organization includes district mayors and provincial officials. The main objective of these partnerships is to work together in finding solutions through legal means, and to develop technically sound proposals for sustainable development strategies. We organize local roundtables and above all we show that we have proactive positive proposals and that we are nonviolent, despite what the government calls us.

When referring to sustainable development we not only speak of economic projects, but also cultural and intellectual growth, what we call human development. Democracy for us is not only casting a vote for an elected official. Democracy is full participation in decision-making at all levels, which is why we carried out the public referendum as an expression of true democracy. We know that there are laws and regulations that recognize individual human rights, but for us, we also value collective rights. What we value most is our land; what we appreciate most is our Mother Earth, who gives us food, life.

Our proposal is for sustainable development, based on agriculture and cattle ranching. We also support and plan to enhance the tourist economy based on the archaeological wealth we have in the area. Ecotourism could also be a central activity, thanks to the great biodiversity and water resources we possess. We plan to create a regional livestock market, but according to our customs, not imposed, but with a healthy balance of market forces, solidarity, and justice.

Fear and trauma

Being part of this process, we as leaders also have the burden of addressing intimidation by the mining company and the Peruvian state itself. Every time we leave our homes, we are victims of persecution, and along with other leaders we are facing legal suits in different courts. I'm personally currently embroiled in eighteen legal cases for different reasons. We have also been individually traumatized and our organization heavily affected by the abduction and torture of thirty-two fellow activists taken by the National Police and by security guards employed by the mining company after a peaceful march to the mining camp. This on top of the death of two comrades, Reemberto Herrera Racho and Melanio Garcia Gonzales, also due to repressive actions carried out by the police in conjunction with the private security company.

The work ahead

Our job is to make sure that the community's right to ownership of their territory is respected, that we gain respect for our right to choose our way of life and our development path, and that the government respects our decisions on this. Our work will not be done until the Majaz mining company with-draws from all of our territories.

So the main challenge that we set as communities and organizations is to achieve community power to enforce our rights. At the core of all our efforts is to lift up and recognize leadership of the community members and be able to promote and seek to constantly strengthen their abilities. And that each one believes that he can grow, and learn to govern. The main qualities of this kind of leadership are to be guided by values of solidarity, to show integrity in speaking and especially integrity in our actions. Leaders must withstand accusations and threats and, above all, honor the agree-ments we make with the community.

Our process has been long. It isn't over; the struggle continues. We must have courage to face the challenges. We have to resist the blows and the impositions. We must give ourselves to what we believe is right and just. Our fight is not just for Ayabaca, but for the world at large, for the conserva-tion of an ecosystem that produces water and generates life throughout the north of the country. I call for international solidarity to join and continue to support us on our journey.

Luzmila Chiricente and Sari Salinas Ponce, Regional Federation of Ashaninka, Nomatsiguengas, and Kakintes Women from the Central Jungle (FREMANK)
"We're the only ones who feel our environment as part of our feet, our hands, our heads"

From the Flora Tristan Peruvian Women's Center and published in *La Amazonía Rebelde: Peru 2009* (Buenos Aires: CLASCO, 2009), translation by Clifton Ross

The indigenous women of the central jungle region assume as their own the struggles undertaken by their brothers and sisters of the Amazon who came demanding respect for their collective rights, violated by the laws approved by the legislature in June 2008 and passed by the executive branch to fit the norms required by implementation of the free trade agreement signed with the United States.

Luzmila Chiricente Mahuanca, president of FREMANK
We're very worried and sad about what's happened. We want peace and tranquility and for them to suspend the laws the government has passed for at least six months so there can be a consultation, as guaranteed by Accord

Amazonians protest against laws that sought to privatize communal territories. Photo courtesy of AIDESEP.

169 of the ILO and the constitution. We join in solidarity with our brothers and sisters of the Amazon because the people of the Amazon are one people. We defend our lands and environment for the generations to come because from this they will feed themselves and build their houses and gather their medicine and craft their arts.

The logging companies cut the big and the little trees, ruining the environment not only for the indigenous people but also for all Peru. The oil company doesn't act like this is its country: It throws its waste out and kills the fish and poisons the water. When the land is contaminated we can no longer grow our produce, which we grow ecologically.

As women we've never benefited from the agreements the government has made with the logging or oil companies. They only come and try to buy us off with cooking pans or notebooks, which is an insult to our indigenous communities. For us our territory is the lungs of our generation because our parents, grandparents, and great-grandparents have died defending these lands, our mother, our blood.

Sari Salinas Ponce, health secretary of FREMANK
We're very angry. The indigenous people haven't been taken into account as the only humans who take care of nature, which is the source of our lives. That's where we find our natural medicines, our food, our market:

Everything is there. Taking care of the environment we use everything natural. We don't need anything else, since it would contaminate our gardens, so we keep it out. It's said we're lazy and not using our lands but it's not true that we're lazy or not using our lands. It's not out of laziness but because we don't want to further damage nature.

They say they're investing in the jungle, and generally what you see is the sowing of cement, but in the big cities. To the native communities nothing comes, and if it does, it comes on papers. They show us participatory budgets in which we don't participate for the most part, since we don't understand them because we aren't taken into account. We're not included because of the language difference and they come speaking technical words and don't ask if we really understand everything. In the end we don't benefit from any business. It's always those who have the most who are made wealthy, and they don't think of us.

The only thing we want now is to be left alone and that they don't come to take away the only thing we have, which is our nature, which we consider to be a part of our very lives. That's why they don't understand that if they hurt nature, they are hurting us, since we're the only ones who feel our environment as part of our feet, our hands, our heads.

Veronica Ferrari, Homosexual Movement of Lima
"We're completely without legal protection"

Interview by Katherine Alva Martínez, November 2012
Translation by Clifton Ross

The Homosexual Movement of Lima began in 1982 and is the oldest gay-lesbian organization anywhere in Latin America. Celebrating the group's thirty years of existence its executive director, Veronica Ferrari, welcomed us in for an interview.

The Homosexual Movement of Lima (HMOL) has a series of tasks before it, to generate laws that protect and guarantee our lives. That's the political work we have to undertake with the state. We meet with authorities and decision-makers to ensure that they include us in public plans, programs, and policies. We also provide a meeting space for equals for the entire LGBT community where everyone can feel comfortable. To this end we hold workshops, present a day of films and organize activities and meetings. That's how we strengthen LGBT organizations in all regions and educate LGBT leaders so they might be the new voices we need. Beyond this, HMOL was

Gay movement: Members of the Homosexual Movement of Lima (MHOL), the oldest LGBT organization in South America, march for Pride. Photo courtesy of MHOL.

founded to radicalize democracy, so that this democracy that doesn't represent everyone might be fully realized and lived.

Gays and lesbians before the movement

[Before the LGBT movement] it was almost impossible to come out, and more so for those in the provinces. The majority of lesbians twenty or thirty years ago had to get married or become nuns to escape oppressive family circles. The other possibility was death. In the case of [gay] men economic independence enabled them to get away but women were practically condemned and very few managed to escape that fate.

The only person in power who has shown any sincere interest in the LGBT community was Susana Villarán [mayor of Lima] who is now fighting a recall, organized by open homophobes who are supported by thousands of evangelicals opposed to our rights. The anti-LGBT discrimination ordinance that the City of Lima was preparing to bring forward, as Susana Villarán promised during her campaign, never appeared for fear of the recall and so as not to increase the dissatisfaction with her office. Still, people can't be ruled by fear, either.

The history of our movement is one of a series of lost legal battles, since all of our initiatives were blocked by the powerful forces of the Catholic and

Evangelical churches, the armed forces, conservative media, conservative parties and the sloth of the state. On the other hand, our movement is one of the most visible. During the AIDS crisis when many gay and trans lives were lost, the HMOL was there before the state itself and for many years we offered services that the state refused to offer due to its deep homophobia.

Not even the epoch of terrorism was able to destroy us, despite the fact that Sendero Luminoso (Shining Path) and the MRTA (Tupac Amaru Revolutionary Movement) had a policy of social "cleansing" toward homosexuals, along with prostitutes, common criminals, and drug addicts. To them we were the worst scum. And I don't think the armed forces thought differently, despite being their ideological polar opposites.

Then later, under Fujimori, the social movements were broken up and the leaders and proposals from civil society were generally depoliticized, but that didn't bring our movement to an end either, despite the state homophobia being manifested in the dismissal of 117 diplomats accusing them of having "dubious sexual practices." We survived, but in the shadows, and we think of that as the lost generation. The demonstration, "Kisses against Homophobia," where the police brutally beat us, showed us that a new generation of activists had arrived, very young people who confronted this violence, youth with a desire to struggle for their rights, and that gave us a lot of hope.

We've managed to make our existence known in other ways, outside of the stereotype, which is how we're portrayed in the media: the super-scandalous gay and the violent lesbian. What we've tried to do is push to the fore the diversity of LGBT people. We've managed to make ourselves a political subject with a definite agency. We've managed to show HMOL to be an organization for all it represents, but we've been unable to make any legal headway. We've been unable to make the conservative forces of Lima take a step back and allow us any sort of protection. We're completely without any protection.

And the ones facing greatest discrimination are the transsexual prostitutes. With Villarán there was an attempt at dialogue that didn't happen with [Mayor] Castañeda. During his term they were beaten and arrested daily and even robbed. They were the most abused as seen by the fact that they can't get ID cards, which means that they can't complete even the simplest paperwork, so they avoid it.[12] Moreover, they're always exposed to violence and expulsion from schools; they aren't accepted at the university and they find no place in the work force. They die young, many before the age of thirty-five, and those who do sexual work are exposed to even more violence.

During the term of Castañeda he gave orders that forbade demonstrations in the center of Lima, which they didn't apply to Coca-Cola, or to the
flash mobs. Yet when we did the "Kisses against Homophobia" we were brutally attacked by the police. Obviously it was provocative, but if we don't
provoke them, what will we gain? We women got access to education, to
politics, thanks to those who left their husbands and children and went out
to provoke. The same with Afro-descendants. To believe our kisses show a
lack of respect for anyone comes from the belief that we're sick, disgusting,
and perverted, that we have no right to kiss anywhere, or that we can only
kiss on Jupiter to please those who hate us.

We have every right in the world to go out and express our feelings
because we're not disrespecting anyone by kissing. For me it's a lack of
respect that this state isn't secular, that so much power is given the Church,
whose cathedral was built with the work of indigenous slaves who were
practically exterminated, and that the development of women has always
been opposed and LGBT rights are blocked with a discourse of hate toward
us; that they would impose a misogynous, macho, homophobic, discriminatory religion, full of fundamentalist prejudices, all with the approval of
the state.

Heterosexuality isn't a sexual orientation; it's a system of regulation

[Laws protecting LGBT rights] won't change people's minds about us, but
at least there would be some sort of protection. Racism isn't going to end
because there's a law prohibiting you from being racist, nor will homophobia end because of a law prohibiting it. There has to be some cultural shift
through education, which has to begin at home with instruction in respect,
a peaceful culture, and sexual diversity. But they say that children shouldn't
be taught that because it will cause gender confusion.

In fact, the least confused about their sexual orientation are the children. The majority of us are clear we're gay or lesbian by the time we're six
or seven. Thinking that [teaching sexual diversity] will affect children is to
invisibilize the fact that there are many gay, lesbian, and transsexual children who have no opportunity to develop a positive self-image. They hide
their lives out of fear of the violence they'll receive from their family, neighbors, and at school, their fellow students and teachers.

For me heterosexuality isn't a sexual orientation: It's a system of reg-
ulation, norming, controlling, and disciplining subjects, and organizing
unequal social relations. We're formed that way from birth until death and
obliged to be heterosexuals. Who does it? The family, the state, the church,

the media, the school, etc. So the degree to which there's a strong social mediation, we can't speak of "sexual preferences" as if they were natural inclinations. Heterosexuality has been carefully imposed: everything in accord with heterosexuality has been reinforced and everything that challenges it is punished. Taking a critical look at heterosexuality is a difficult but necessary process. If you evade this norm you'll be socially punished; you won't be able to realize your life's projects; you'll experience injustice or be raped or murdered.

The more that people feel outraged about an unjust situation, the more possibilities exist that material conditions will be generated to make life as it should be. Few people dare to show their faces and tell it like it is, but we hope that all the injustices we live and will continue to live will in some way make the next generations indignant and lead them someday to transform our society.

Bolivia

Bolivia

International boundary
★ National capital
┼─┼─┼─┼ Railroad
Road

0   50   100 150 Kilometers
0   50   100   150 Miles
Transverse Mercator Projection, CM 64°W

PERU

BRAZIL

BRAZIL

SOUTH
PACIFIC
OCEAN

CHILE

PARAGUAY

ARGENTINA

Bôca do Acre
Pôrto Velho
Abunã
Ariquemes
Rio Branco
Assis Brasil
Brasiléia
Cobija
Iñapari
Guayaramerín
Guajará-Mirim
Riberalta
Presidente Médici
BRAZIL
Puerto Maldonado
Puerto Ustarez
Costa Marques
Vilhena
Santa Ana de Yacuma
Magdalena
Rurrenabaque
Trinidad
Barra do Bugres
Pontes e Lacerda
Juliaca
Lago Titicaca
Caranavi
Puno
Copacabana
Desaguadero
★ La Paz
Guaqui
Vacha
Cáceres
San Mattas
Moquegua
Toquepala
Charaña
Cochabamba
Yapacani
San Ignacio de Velasco
Ilo
Tacna
Oruro
Santa Cruz
Montero
Arica
Uncia
Challapata
Aiquile
San José de Chiquitos
Roboré
Puerto Suárez
Corumbá
Zapiga
Lago Poopó
Sucre
Tarabuco
Potosí
Iquique
Salar de Uyuni
Uyuni
Camiri
Capitán Pablo Lagerenza
Ollagüe
Tupiza
Tarija
Villamontes
General Eugenio Garay
Fuerte Olimpo
Pôrto Murtinho
Tocopilla
Villazón
Yacuiba
Fortín Infante Rivarola
La Quiaca
Mariscal Estigarribia
Filadelfia
Calama
Tartagal
Mejillones
San Pedro de Atacama
San Ramón de la Nueva Orán
Antofagasta
Pozo Colorado
Concepción
Socompa
San Salvador de Jujuy
San Pedro
Salta
Las Lomitas

University of Texas Libraries

INTRODUCTION

Tupak Katari's promise lives on

By Ben Dangl

In 1781, the indigenous rebel leader Tupak Katari laid siege to colonial La Paz for over three months. As Katari and his army held their ground in what is now El Alto, on the rim of the valley that cradles La Paz, the Spanish below were helpless. The rebellion rocked the Andes for both its political and symbolic impact. Spain's colonization of the Andes, and indeed, of much of Latin America, depended on the subjugation and enslavement of the indigenous people in the silver mines and the estates. At the same time, the Spanish were vastly outnumbered by indigenous people, so the threat of an indigenous uprising constantly haunted the colonizers. Katari made that threat a reality, and his cry for justice and a return to indigenous rule resonated across the Andes, and into modern-day Bolivia. Before the Spanish, empowered by reinforcements, captured and quartered Katari, the rebel promised, "I will return, and I will be millions."[1]

This promise is present in the streets of El Alto today, where the largely indigenous, working-class population has risen up time and time again against neoliberal governments and foreign corporations—Latin America's new colonizers—laying siege to La Paz in acts of protest reminiscent of Katari and his army. The long-postponed dream of indigenous self-rule took on a new dimension with the 2005 election of Evo Morales as president. Upon taking office, Morales, a former llama herder, coca farmer, and union leader, promised to refound the nation and state in a way that was oriented by the country's many indigenous groups. But the road to self-rule has been rockier than many expected when Morales became the country's first indigenous president.

Before Morales's election, the social movements played a very active role in shaping the country's politics. As Morales himself said in late 2008,

"It is the experience and the effort of the social movements that is causing democracy to address the issues that really concern poor and needy people. Democracy is much more than a routine election every four years."[2] Indeed, democracy for many Bolivians in the years leading up to Morales's election in 2005 was full of insurrections, and nearly constant protests, strikes, and road blockades.[3]

In the mid-1980s, a neoliberal plan proposed by U.S. economist Jeffrey Sachs led to the privatization and closure of many Bolivian mines—work spaces which formed the backbone of the country's radical workers' unions. Faced with unemployment, thousands of mining families migrated to the Chapare to grow coca to survive, while others moved to El Alto, the working-class city outside of La Paz. The embers of the mining movement spread, sparking radical fires across the country. While movements in the Chapare and El Alto went on to transform the political landscape of the country, political actors and organizations in Santa Cruz emerged as a right-wing force, pushing for neoliberal policies and repression against working-class movements.[4]

The coca growers' (*cocalero*) movement led directly to the creation of the MAS party [Movimiento al Socialismo]. The coca leaf in Bolivia has been used for centuries in the Andes as a medicine to alleviate the pain of farming and mining work, and plays an important role in indigenous customs. The leaf is chewed and consumed in tea across the country within this wide, legal market. Over time, coca leaves and the unions that defended their production became symbols of anti-imperialism in a defense of indigenous and Bolivian culture. The U.S.-led war on drugs targeted the production of the leaf ostensibly to curtail drug production, but also to break one of the most formidable social movements—and eventually political parties—in the country.[5]

The Bolivian coca growers' movement fought U.S. militarization of land and communities in the war on drugs for decades, building up a fierce union that eventually grew into the MAS party. Working through this political instrument to transform the country from positions in the government, coca growers fought to legalize coca production, organized within their communities, and eventually played a key role in the Cochabamba Water War.

In 2000, the people of Cochabamba rose up against the multinational Bechtel corporation's privatization of their water. After weeks of protests, the company was kicked out of the city and the water went back into public hands. In February 2003, police, students, public workers, and regular citizens across the country rose up against an IMF-backed plan to cut wages and increase income taxes on a poverty-stricken population. The revolt forced the government and International Monetary Fund to surrender to movement demands and rescind the public wage and tax policies, ushering in a new period of unity and solidarity among movements as civil dissatisfaction gathered heat, reaching a boiling point during what came to be called the Gas War.[6]

The Gas War, which took place in September and October 2003, was a national uprising that emerged among diverse sectors of society against a plan to export Bolivian natural gas via Chile to the United States for $0.18 per thousand cubic feet, only to be sold in the United States for approximately $4.00 per thousand cubic feet. In a move that was all too familiar to citizens in a country famous for its cheap raw materials, the right-wing government in power worked with private companies to design a plan in which Chilean and U.S. businesses would benefit more from Bolivia's natural wealth than Bolivian citizens themselves.

Bolivians united across class lines in massive protests, strikes, and road blockades against the exportation plan. They demanded that the gas be nationalized and industrialized in Bolivia, so that the profits from the industry could go to government development projects and social programs. Neighborhood councils (FEJUVEs) in the city of El Alto, many of them with formerly unionized miners as members, banded together, blocking roads in their city located strategically above La Paz. The government fought back, shooting civilians from helicopters with semiautomatic weapons, pushing movements in the city into a fury that emboldened their resistance.[7]

By mid-October, the people successfully ousted the repressive neoliberal President Gonzalo Sánchez de Lozada, and rejected the exportation plan, pointing the way toward nationalization. Shortly after this series of conflicts, Evo Morales emerged as a serious contender in the 2005 presidential elections. By riding this wave of national discontent and running an adept campaign, Morales was elected president of the country on a platform that reflected the demands of the social movements. His electoral promises focused on land reform, gas nationalization, and the convocation of an assembly to rewrite the country's constitution. In varying degrees, he followed through on all of these central campaign promises.

The road to a new constitution proved far rockier than MAS promised. The constituent assembly convened to rewrite the document brought together representatives from around the country and across the political spectrum. The many interests of the divided nation—from the landowners in the wealthy province of Santa Cruz, to the radical social movements of El Alto—clashed dramatically.

Demonstration in La Paz: Crowd in La Paz protesting the massacre of campesinos by paramilitaries linked to the prefect of the department of Pando, and efforts by the wealthy "Media Luna" region to separate from the rest of Bolivia, September 2008. Photo by Clifton Ross.

The MAS tried to govern this assembly, using its clout as the nation's largest and most influential political party, but often failed to create peace or help the various constituents reach a consensus. Violent street conflicts flared up in Sucre, and fights broke out among representatives inside the theater where the constituent assembly was held. The struggle revealed the political tensions bubbling beneath this reconstruction of the country's political framework, exposing the racism of the right wing and the challenges for Bolivia's poor and indigenous majority.

More than two long years after the assembly began, it finally passed the new constitution—though not without concessions to the Right. Massive land holdings, for example, would not be broken up by the government and redistributed to landless farmers. But the document upheld the rights of indigenous people, the power of the government to provide public services to the poor, and the nation's sovereignty in the face of U.S. imperialism.

However, securing political approval for the document was a far cry from actually applying those changes on paper to the reality in the streets, homes, and institutions of Bolivia. Not only was it difficult or even impossible to reverse years of colonialism, poverty, and marginalization through government policy, there were other deep-seated problems in society in areas of corruption and racism.

In 2008, the right-wing political parties and social organizations in Santa Cruz and other eastern provinces rose up against indigenous people, attacking them in the street, burning and looting human rights offices and MAS headquarters, and even massacring dozens of unarmed indigenous men and women in the province of Pando. In 2009, Santos Ramírez, a MAS icon and the president of the much-touted state-run gas company YFPB, was arrested on corruption charges. Such setbacks on Bolivia's road to decolonization threatened to derail the MAS agenda and hegemony entirely.[8]

But rather than growing weaker, the MAS has secured its hold over the political landscape of Bolivia, dominating the right-wing opposition and absorbing other parties under its vast umbrella. The MAS has broad support in the countryside and in key highland cities, such as Oruro and La Paz. Its nationalized gas and oil industry has been a financial goldmine for the cash-strapped government, and the administration's alliances with Hugo Chávez in Venezuela and other left-leaning leaders in the region have proven to be financially as well as diplomatically helpful; Venezuela regularly gives Bolivia no-strings-attached loans, and pressure from regional leaders during the 2008 right-wing destabilization attempt helped squash the Right's momentum.

Yet where there were high hopes with Morales's election in 2006, one will now often find disillusionment. On the campaign trail and even today in political speeches, Morales promises to refound the nation, right five centuries of wrongs, end racism, decolonize the state, and put Bolivia on a track of sustainable, socialist development that places the marginalized at the center of political power. Certainly some of these promises have been fulfilled to a historic degree, speaking of the political will of the Morales administration against terrific odds. But, as Morales himself often says, everything can't be changed overnight.

Indeed, many of those interviewed here will explain that the pace of change is too slow, or that the government itself is undermining projects that align with the MAS's own radical promises. Indigenous rights have been upheld for some communities, but not all. The state-run extractivist agenda may reap profits from nationalized oil, gas, and mining projects for social programs, but the environment and local communities suffer the consequences. And while Morales touts solutions to climate change abroad, Bolivians criticize the MAS's own environmental policy at home.

And many of the social movements that were so instrumental in shaping the destiny of the country with such revolts as the Water War in

2000 and the Gas War in 2003 are now pushed aside by the MAS or co-opted. The radical agenda put forth by a wave of protests from 2000 to 2005 truly paved the way to Morales's election, making space for this president from below to win at the ballot box. Many of Morales's own platforms and policies simply institutionalized victories that had already been won by social movements in the streets. This social movement momentum has been divided, demobilized, and repressed by the MAS government in an attempt to expand the party's own hegemony over the country, silence critics from the Left, and translate the energy and capacity of movement organizing into the electoral and political machine of the party.

Such a dynamic came to the forefront in the case of the Isiboro-Sécure Indigenous Territory and National Park (Territorio Indígena y Parque Nacional Isiboro Sécure, or TIPNIS), an area where the MAS government pledged to build a massive highway connecting Brazil to Bolivia. Touted as a development project, the road would have displaced thousands of indigenous people from their own territory. The issue seemed to embody a central contradiction in the MAS: development at the expense of the environment, and indigenous rights for some people, while others, such as those in the TIPNIS, were disregarded as soon as they came into conflict with government policy.

The TIPNIS issues catalyzed simmering anger toward the government. A wide array of activists joined protests, including some on the right who sought to capitalize on the MAS's unpopularity. Thousands took part in national marches against the highway, often facing violent suppression from the government.[9]

The interviews you will find here come from the left side of this debate. Not a doctrinaire Left, or one that adheres to a party or union, but a Left dispersed among various social movements that seek to build a better world outside the political umbrella of the MAS. Many of them may have looked hopefully on Morales's election, only to realize that a truly emancipatory route could be found outside of the ballot box, and in the vibrant social movements, autonomy and forms of everyday resistance that characterized the period of upheaval from 2000 to 2005 and before. In these revolts, the logic of the political party died, and a new vision for Bolivia came into focus. This vision put the collective power of the community over the power of the president and the state itself. From the neighborhood assemblies in El Alto to the promise of Tupak Katari, this dream is still very much alive in Bolivia.

Pedro Portugal Mollinedo. Photo by Clifton Ross.

Pedro Portugal Mollinedo, editor of *Pukara*, an independent indigenous monthly
"In Andean ideology there are oppositions but also complementarity"

Interview and translation by Clifton Ross, April 2006

Not long after Evo Morales was inaugurated president of Bolivia with much fanfare, the indigenous monthly Pukara *published sharp criticisms of the first indigenous man to lead the country. This was enough to make me want to seek out the editor, Pedro Portugal Mollinedo, for an interview. We sat down to talk in a corner of the Plaza Abaroa, near downtown La Paz.*

Pukara deals primarily with the original peoples, their cultures, politics, and economics. We do this publication because for a long time we've worked together with indigenous organizations and supported them. Personally, I was a councilman in a rural municipality and saw the need to be able to get out the indigenous perspective so our needs could be taken into account. We take the side of the indigenous people and their organizations such as we understand it.

Here in Bolivia the majority of the population is indigenous, but that majority still isn't represented, that is, Bolivia continues as before, as if there'd been no change. You can see for yourself that things continue as "normal." Inside the country you don't sense this rupture that some see from outside, as if Bolivia had had an earthquake and we were living some sort of great mutation at the level of the recuperation of cultural values or the winning of indigenous rights.

Of course it's all a process, but in this process it seems to us that it would be worthwhile to speak out to keep things from going the opposite direction from that which would be in favor of the indigenous population. That's the reason for our critical stance.

We believe that there's a national question: There can't be a country where its indigenous majority lives out problems of racist exclusion and is unable to freely live out its politics. This majority has brought Evo Morales to power and that's why he's famous abroad, because he's considered an indigenous president, but this is a fiction. He's an indigenous president with an indigenous face who won and has an entire state apparatus that is the same as before.

A real change has to affect everything. So what do we want? We want not just a president with an indigenous face, but that the rest of society, the rest of power would really legitimately represent the indigenous majority.

It's an advance, we need to be clear, the fact that an indigenous has been elected president for the first time is certainly a great advance. But that doesn't mean paradise has arrived. It means that possibly something has begun that can be deepened, and that alternatives might be offered.

The Constitutional Assembly has raised expectations in some sectors, not only among the indigenous, but also among workers in political sectors. The progressive sectors are starry-eyed for Evo Morales because some way or another he represents them. But there are two ways of having a Constituent [Assembly]: either as something new or as the traditional way of doing politics. The traditional way is to fight in the elections and the most skillful, the one who best knows how to win votes, does what he wants.

The new way, on the other hand, is to give voice to those who never had a voice: to give those who have always suffered from events and never had the power of decision over events, the opportunity to define the future. So the majority thought the Constituent Assembly would be something new, first, at the level of those who would be brought in to participate. There have been many Constituent Assemblies in Bolivia and they've always excluded the workers, the indigenous. And now all these sectors have been drawn together around Evo Morales and the MAS.

There's recently been a rupture because [indigenous and workers] were hoping that representatives in the Constituent Assembly would come from the sectors that really want their rights recognized: not only the indigenous, but also the disabled and other minorities who have been excluded. Despite their having signed an agreement with MAS, MAS has chosen the traditional ways of doing politics.

And so we have to ask: Is this how a new nation is going to be built? If this goes on and is consolidated, it's going to continue being an unfinished obligation. If members of the Constituent Assembly are named in this scheme, nothing will change in Bolivia because they'll be people who speak in the name of others. We can't promise a new society with the same old mechanisms.

A very disturbing statement came out in the press a few weeks back. Vice President García Linera said there was no problem with indigenous people going to the Constituent Assembly [responding to those from reactionary sectors who don't think that the indigenous people should be allowed in the Assembly]. He said that it didn't matter if they didn't know how to read or write because there would be five or six lawyers who were going to edit the constitution, which is the same scheme that all the parties have used: bring along those who can't speak, grab any leader, and put him there to represent the indigenous people and they [the parties], with their lawyers, are the ones who define what is going to be the new republic.

And so the most advanced elements of the indigenous movements, the intellectuals, the political leaders, the representatives of the communities like CONAMAQ (Consejo Nacional de Ayllus y Markas del Qullasuyu, or National Council of Ayllus and Markas of Qullasuyu) aren't participating. In fact they've been the object of ridicule by Evo Morales; he promised to include them in the list and in the final moment he didn't but rather put others, in keeping with politics as usual.

Up to the present the Left has been a colonial Left, a Left of a nation that oppresses indigenous people. There isn't a Left that has broken with this colonial scheme. The majority of the Left in Bolivia is an "elegant" Left. It comes down to a negative colonial issue because as long as political alternatives remain in the hands of an elite that continues to dominate power, there will never be a serious transformation.

The political discussion has to include the majority and the political alternatives have to be taken to the base, to the indigenous population. But this is being impeded, as we're seeing now in the Constituent Assembly. So there's a danger that this colonial scheme will be maintained behind a cloak of legitimacy, saying, "We're progressives, we're pushing history forward," and they're opposing the advance of history.

Andean cosmology and politics

The indigenous world operates on the basis of oppositions, but not only Left and Right; they could be up and down, inside and out, right? The Left-Right opposition has been ideologized a lot, and perhaps the Andean ideology could help us get past this issue and keep us from being trapped in that particular opposition. We've seen that there can sometimes be contradictions that don't change things in favor of indigenous people, but instead they get caught in the crossfire between the Right and Left and become the principal victims. This happened recently to the CRIC (Consejo Regional Indígena de Cauca) in Colombia, and also with the Miskitus when they had problems in Nicaragua.

So now the West has an idea of a Left and a Right which are totally contradictory and antagonistic, even though when the Right comes to power it takes steps to the left and the Left, on taking power, sometimes is right-wing—and we see this globally.

I noticed that Evo Morales, proclaiming himself leftist, went off in his sweater to China, one of the remaining Communist countries. And there he was with the Central Committee of the Communist Party of China, and they were all dressed like businessmen with their neckties, and they're industrializing and building capital. So the division into Left and Right seems to be purely ideological, but in practice it offers us surprises.

Those of us who want deep changes might look to Andean ideology because here there are oppositions but also complementarity, and we don't just submit ourselves to the existing oppositions. It's as if the indigenous would have to say, "Well, we're friends of the Right or the Left," and to be friends in these conditions would mean to be simply an instrument in the struggle between these two sectors.

We believe that the indigenous people have the right to project their political aspirations and try them out to see if they are real and effective and, in any case, if they're going to be effective for their society, because they've been the basis for survival up to now.

The Andean vision is based on work: Production is intimately linked to ethics and interpersonal conduct. Individual relationships generate economic processes. Economy isn't separate; it isn't a set of laws or rules by which human conduct is set in motion, but the other way around. Human conduct is very closely tied to the production process, to the process of exchange and this naturally creates societies of solidarity.

Solidarity in the Western world has come to mean a kind of escape from poverty. So where there's poverty, a radio [station], for example, might make a campaign, calling on the world to give children Christmas presents.

Or else it has come to have some sort of ideological value, that is, a type of conclusion from some sort of mental lucubrations on the laws of history or some sort of opposition between social classes.

In the Andean world solidarity is simply the logical consequence of the economic life. The fiesta, the organizations are all organized for such a conclusion. This solidarity doesn't exclude economic development, like, for example, the adoption of forms of technology or productive forms or even forms of thought, all of which it actively integrates into the interaction of the extended family, which would be the community. And in the extension of that nucleus, it makes one's own the larger societies. This is the model we want. It was the model for the great Inkan society, as well as the Aymaras, and it's the model that has enabled indigenous societies to survive up to now.

It's possible that this model, contrasting with, and confronting the present situations could perhaps bring elements that might help resolve some common problems. But this would imply trying to legitimate a different point of view. And the Left isn't very open to this because it comes too close to certain ideas about solidarity, about which it's very negative since its sense of solidarity is ideologized.

Ideology in the West is a form of escape, and even the word "ideology" has bad connotations for many, like for Marx himself, as it overvalues "science." The indigenous don't criticize the Left for its sensitivity, but because we have many things in common with the Right which the Left can't see due to its own internal contradictions. Marx himself said that for the Indian, capitalism was good since it took the Indian out of backward forms of production and in the end made it possible for the rise of the proletariat and a world revolution.

Sometimes the Left has been more radical in destructive ways, such as in relation to nature. If you study the iconography of the socialist movement at its peak, with socialist countries, it's very interesting. What was on their shields? Factories. How was liberation portrayed? With a gun in one hand and a tool for production in the other, and in the background, gears. In other words, the blind transformation of nature has been stronger in the socialist models than in capitalist models. So the Left hasn't yet done a deep analysis of a model of civilization. But it's also not true to say that this civilization is no good. That would be absurd.

The Andean world is very permeable, and it is very open to everything around it and there may be practical ideas that could help the indigenous world. But now we see two sides. While there may be ideas that could help make the indigenous world adopt a more practical approach, in the daily life of our people the debate over ideas and experiences relate to another reality, Left or Right, that becomes a force for colonialism.

All interest in others is good, as is all curiosity. What's important is that while one becomes enriched by seeing distant issues, sometimes the key to the solution exists right where one is. I would suggest that one shouldn't be too ideological, but rather go to the concrete realities that change relationships between people so as to generate more profound and more radical changes in the system. Because if we consider it ideologically, we live like the system we're fighting and justify ourselves as thinking differently, and this is an aberration. Then we're just putting on a verbal facade, in a nice office, hanging out with beautiful people, living the culture of oppression while speaking a discourse of liberation. And that's where it all ends.

Silvia Rivera Cusicanqui, scholar and activist
"To do micropolitics is to act for ourselves"

Interview by Ben Dangl, May 2012
Translation by Clifton Ross

Silvia Rivera Cusicanqui is a sociologist and world-renowned intellectual. In her book Oppressed but Not Defeated: Peasant Struggles among the Aymara and Quechua in Bolivia, 1900–1980, *she elaborates on the role of popular memory in indigenous and campesino movements. Central to this book is the concept of long memory, where movements recall and interpret events such as Tupak Katari's 1781 siege of colonial La Paz, and short memory, where the history of Bolivia's 1952 National Revolution, for example, is recalled and understood in terms of an event that orients and inspires more contemporary movements. I interviewed Rivera in La Paz at the space where the anarchist organization Colectivo 2 has a garden and plans educational and political activist meetings.*

I think that the sense of history depends on the present conjuncture. If there's a moment of elevated consciousness of struggle in the people, it gives another sense to history and expands memory. When there was an uprising in 2003 in El Alto, people recalled the Siege of Tupak Katari. The theme of the siege was explicit and became the siege of La Paz in 2003 and that memory fit well [with the situation]. But now we're in a moment of the ebbing of the [social movement] struggles, except in the world of the lowlands where its own historical memory is at work. The Andean world is in an ebbing process due to the co-optation of the leadership, above all of the unions, by the government. The highland peoples have supported the struggle of the lowlands people because of their ecological consciousness and also because they know that if the door of the TIPNIS is opened to the miners all the transnational corporations will come in to plunder.

So historical memory continues to be important in these indigenous organizations, but the union organizations are caught in a process of collective amnesia. They don't even remember the Katari struggles of the '70s.[10] They're on the ladder of success, entrenched in power as functionaries or in government service and they've lost their autonomy. And so today there's an ebb in memory and history no longer has any importance for them, or it just becomes a cultural adornment. In that sense there's a very deteriorated and shortened memory, so short that they don't remember the '70s. And they've adopted a developmentalist discourse and been funded by the state so they've lost their autonomy. But this only happened with the leaders. At the base there's a lot of discontentment.

In El Alto there's a strong presence of the demands related to the Agenda of October,[11] and the "nationalization" is now being unmasked. As it turns out, the "nationalization" was simply a changing of the terms of the contract reference but it wasn't a "nationalization."[12] So there is a disenchantment with the government, which allows for the recuperation of a critique, and within this critique October is an important landmark.

The relationship between social movements and the MAS government

MAS isn't co-opting the social movements, but rather the movement's leaders. [The leaders'] task now is to demobilize the masses. They're demobilizing the people. When they have the people wait on directives of the state, they essentially put them into the service of the state. This is a co-optation that leaves the movements discontented, but the movements have lost their ability to organize themselves because they have lost their leaders. This sort of co-optation has happened before under the MNR [Movimiento Nacionalista Revolucionario] where the campesino leaders were completely subordinated to the party. Before, the MAS wasn't a party, but just a coalition of social organizations. Now it's a party, not a democratic party, but a populist party based on one man who directs it and a clique that makes all the decisions without consulting the people.

There are still struggles, very dispersed and even contradictory. The fact that we've survived two months without doctors shows that the doctors don't help the people.[13] Rather than cure them they are now distributors of pills from the transnational pharmacies, nothing more. The system of medicine is atrocious and worse, it's wrong because it doesn't recognize natural medicines or anything, and that's one struggle.

Another struggle is the valuable struggle of communities against mining. There are various coalitions because mining is a difficult struggle to take on. The mining sector is linked to narcotrafficking and taking contraband out through the border with Chile, which is an area very negatively affected by mines. Another region affected by mines is the TIPNIS. So on one side there's an agenda and on the other there's unemployment, the problem of salaries, so the workers are active, and the issue of ecology has had an impact. So there are still diverse, and dispersed, struggles going on.

Coca and the cocalero president

[The coca leaf] has been a revolutionary symbol in its moment, and a very important one, but the leap forward should have started with the goal of industrializing coca, promoting ecological coca. Instead the government has talked about coca as sacred and all, while behind the scenes it links up with narcotrafficking, which is what the cocaleros of Chapare are. They're a power very close and very supportive of MAS and now the cocaleros are turning against the larger society: They're against the doctors; they're against the indigenous and want the highway cut through TIPNIS because they've been seduced by the developmentalist discourse. They're business people. They have aspirations to be small businessmen and to accumulate, consume, and spend all that money from coca.

And so it's been cowardly on the part of the government to not undertake a radical restructuring of the coca market, privileging organic coca for legal ends, for thousands of industries. We could have bakeries, pasta, pizzas, pastries, crepes, everything with coca flour. This issue shows the cowardice and lack of political vision because [the government of Evo Morales] hasn't fought for legal coca but has kept to the discourse of "Pachamama" and gone along with the habitual illegal practices. Narcotrafficking has grown in Bolivia over these last few years and the worst of it is that it has corrupted people in the communities, in many rural areas where coca is processed. I think this also has to do with Evo's alliance with the military. The military are those who handle all this and are in charge of all these projects, so they're the ones who want the highway through TIPNIS widened so they can gain control there.

And this is another deviation in his practice or discrepancy between discourse and practice, because [the Morales government] has talked about the Pachamama, this great Pachamama, as an enlightened position internationally but internally what they want is a developmentalist policy with hydroelectric [dams] that would drown indigenous lands, forests, and highways, all for an alliance with Brazil. They're betting on serving the interests of Brazil. So it's a new colonialism.

The anarchists of Bolivia

The young anarcho-ecologists and anarcho-feminists like us have been very active in the issue of TIPNIS. There are many [anarchist] groups, mostly young, in alternative culture, in communities in different parts of Bolivia, but it's still not a high-profile political movement. It's more a cultural movement for changing daily life. And the beauty of it is that it's the youth and they don't believe in the parties because one of the explicit ideas is "enough of political parties."

What we're trying to do is simply put into practice what everyone is talking about, here where there's such a divorce between practice and discourse. The idea is to open a space with a low profile of micropolitics. To do micropolitics is to act for ourselves, for the body, for the food, making clothes, and everything. It's building and making things and with that offering a response to other youths who want to do politics another way. To be autonomous and self-organized is a very political way of working. You aren't asking anyone for money because we make our own money and that frees us so we can define ourselves and be a good example. There's a neighborhood here where we work with the schools to put on workshops making things with recycled materials like weaving with bags, and everything. We do urban agriculture and have a project this year to do activism in the streets with the urban gardens, because the city government has put in beautiful gardens but that land could be producing potatoes for the people of the neighborhood. So we have campaigns like this, but we don't neglect academic, theoretical, and political discussion and we intervene in public opinion with our publications, whether they be magazines, books, videos or cassettes. We now have a little capital accumulated in intellectual production that has a message that isn't apolitical.

Julieta Ojeda, Mujeres Creando
"We're just a little rock in the shoe"

Interview by Ben Dangl and April Howard, May 2012
Translation by Clifton Ross

Julieta Ojeda is a part of Mujeres Creando, *an anarchist/feminist organization that has been a radical voice for women's rights before and throughout Morales's time in office. We interviewed her in La Paz, in the midst of various*

Julieta Ojeda of Mujeres Creando at La Virgen de los Deseos, May 2012.
Photo by Ben Dangl.

social protests against the MAS government. Among the most prominent of
these was a strike of doctors and health professionals to protest increasing
the length of their workday. Another involved a proposed highway to be cut
through the San Isiboro Sécure National Park (TIPNIS), a protected nature
reserve and home to indigenous "lowland" tribes.

The Evo Morales government has made many big mistakes. For instance, I
think the way the new constitutional text was brought forward was a big
mistake. The "gasolinazo" was another. And the unwillingness to discuss,
debate, and negotiate with the indigenous peoples of the Amazon seems
to me another great error of the Evo Morales government. Why? Because
in principle Evo is a symbol of an indigenous man who has come to power,
has taken the powerful role of president, and the very fact of his being
indigenous one assumes he would defend the indigenous. But the relation
he's assumed with the thirty-four different indigenous nationalities reveal
that he isn't a man who identifies with this image. They say he's indigenous,
right? And yes, he is, but he identifies primarily with the cocaleros. In one
sense he's not indigenous but a cocalero, and he responds to that sector.

    And there's another issue. There are first [class] indigenous and indig-
enous of the second [class]. So there are different levels and another issue is

that of Aymara-centrism and the indigenous people who have value in this government are in the west and not the others, those of the lowlands. This is made clear to us, and also that [Evo] isn't going to be a man who respects nature, that is, who respects "Pachamama" as he's proposed in his discourse.

His government has a developmentalist project, a bad developmentalist project if you will, because the lowland indigenous people have their own forms of rational exploitation, or sustainable management of their resources. So for instance the hunting of lizards can only be done when the lizard is old and not in its reproductive phase. This is an approach taken by certain indigenous communities, which is not to say that there aren't exceptions, but in general, the social organizations of the lowlands peoples try to manage this type of exploitation in a rational manner. So there is a vision of development, but a development that doesn't destroy nature. And the government of Evo Morales is completely with that other vision.

Co-opting the social movements

[Evo's MAS] has penetrated certain organizations and divided them. They enter these social movement spaces and create divisions by forming their own parallel organizations. This is a common social movement or opposition group practice; MAS didn't invent it. The difference now is that those in the government occupy another space on the political stage. They're no longer a social movement but they continue functioning like a union, or a movement, and continue working at this level of wanting to infiltrate organizations and divide them.

It's a difficult thing to deal with, but the divisions created in the indigenous movement from the lowlands, they've done it. They did this after the eighth march [against the highway through TIPNIS], as it was ending. There had been unity up to then; obviously there were disagreements and all, but they'd preferred to put their differences aside to show unity. But starting with the ending of the eighth march, [MAS] began to co-opt the leaders and the communities inside of the lowlands organizations. It's the same thing they do with other social conflicts, such as the recent one with the doctors, when they signed an agreement with the health administrators but not with the doctors. So it becomes a long struggle, already at least two months of conflict. They sign an agreement with one sector, and not with the other; it's what they do with the miners, and what they do in regional conflicts, creating factions opposed to those who are moving mobilizations forward. So this is a permanent practice of the MAS to generate parallel groups to oppose the others.

With the doctors, because they don't want to work eight hours, but rather to maintain their six-hour work schedule, the government proposed

Women in a demonstration calling for the arrest of the Prefect of Pando, Leopoldo Fernández, for his role in the Pando massacre, 2008. Photo by Clifton Ross.

a summit in July and told them they would suspend the law until then. But what the government wants is to see if, in the next two or three months, it can buy off certain groups or leaders of the doctors' organization and the people connected to health so as to divide them and legitimize the policies its want approved.

The role of Mujeres Creando under the Morales government

We've managed to consolidate spaces, like this house itself, a space in this house and also a certain degree of social legitimacy and political relevance. That's to say, Mujeres Creando has a place and a space within society, but that's also very relative. Because it's true for some things and not for others. We've always been opening a space in radio, and also very persistent in our political project.

Nevertheless, we've also publicly taken a position with respect to the policies of Evo Morales, in the case of TIPNIS and the eighth march, which we joined and supported with all our resources. And so we've been very critical of certain leaders and in defense of this territory and against the proposed highway that would cross that territory, because that's playing with the future. And we've also criticized the machismo of the president on various occasions, the machismo of the government in its various manifestations. For instance, the attempts to organize the Miss Universe Pageant here in Bolivia—and all this we do not with writing letters but rather in public actions.

We're trying to generate a broader, more open debate [on abortion]. The Church is opposed and it's brought out all its weapons to bring discussion to an end. In this case the government of Evo Morales has been very lukewarm. This is a very conservative government as far as gay rights and abortion or anything having to do with women or women's rights. They talk about what they've done, like the mother's bonus, an allowance for mothers, but you have to be a mother to get it. So once again it reinforces the idea that women are only of value as mothers.

This government doesn't really see us as an enemy, but rather we're like a little rock in the shoe, a constant irritation. But neither have they decided to do anything to us, because when the government decides that someone is an enemy, it's terribly vengeful. With dissidents they try to bury them politically. But we're just a little rock in the shoe, and we don't really focus too much on the government's policies since we have our own political project, and that's only part of what we do.

And so right now in Santa Cruz we're going to do an action to denounce the machismo of the mayor, a right-wing macho misogynist who has groped women on camera, his secretaries and collaborators. So for me it's a matter of exploring other veins of criticism, oppositional, if you will, with respect to this government, but a stance that calls on other resources, and other perspectives on women.

Oscar Olivera, writer and activist
"Transnationals use the states as vehicles to continue plundering"

Interview and translation by Peter Lackowski and Sharyl Green, January 2012

Oscar Olivera is an activist, thinker, and writer based in Cochabamba, Bolivia. He was a leader during the uprising in 2000 in Cochabamba in which the people of the city threw out Bechtel, the multinational corporation that had privatized all the water in the city—even the rain that people collected. He reflected on that experience in ¡Cochabamba! Water War in Bolivia, a book written in collaboration with Tom Lewis and published by South End Press in 2004.

The government of Evo Morales did not come from above. It didn't come from propaganda or electoral competition. It has risen from the base, from a process of popular struggles of indigenous people. It took its legal form through a popular vote.

Evo Morales came to the government with two mandates. One is a substantial change in the economic model, the model of development that has been imposed for many years. The historical model was established in Potosí, development that was simply looting, without benefiting our people. This history of plunder and expropriation of our natural resources was forcefully rejected by our people in the Water War of 2000 and the Gas War of 2003. So the mandate is clear: We want another model and we want a model fundamentally based on respect and complete harmony with nature. This is a clear mandate of the people, simple but very profound. We are going from a model where everything—trees, animals, water—is converted into merchandise or commodities to another model where these things belong to everyone.

The other clear mandate is that we don't believe in a democracy of parties, where just a few leaders make all the decisions. We want a democracy of participation, a democracy where the people can make decisions about their own future. In 2005 the government of Morales came to power with those two main ideas.

I believe that these two mandates have not been accomplished by the government. We have an economic model that is continuing with the extractivist model that hands over our territory to transnationals, a model of plunder—a model that has absolutely not changed. We cannot deny that the government has been able to negotiate better terms, especially with the oil companies; the Bolivian state gets better royalties. But what happened on May 1, 2006, was in no way a real nationalization or taking over by the state of our hydrocarbons. And it is the same with the government's discourse about respecting the rights of Mother Earth and harmony with nature.

A pathetic example of the process of plundering and destruction of the natural environment of Bolivia is San Cristobal mine near the salt flats of Uyuni. The Japanese enterprise running that mine is taking out over a billion dollars per year, and it just pays a few million in taxes—it's nothing. That mine consumes as much water as all of Cochabamba. They mine silver and lead—the biggest open face mine in the world. And more recently there is the highway through the TIPNIS national park, destroying a natural area and an indigenous territory simply because Brazilian transnationals want it. We could go on with many more examples.

As to the other subject, a more participatory democracy, an institutional model that would allow us to have real participation in making decisions in this country, that doesn't exist either. Even though a new constitution was put in place three years ago, this constitution was not made in the way people wanted to write it. What people wanted was a new form for living together in this country for the next fifty years without political parties,

Oscar Olivera. Photo from Casa de America (CreativeCommons).

without the monopoly of the political parties. But that is not what happened. The convocation for the constituent assembly that wrote the constitution was decided upon by four people, and the final result was determined by the chiefs of the four parliamentary parties.

There are two other things. One is an attitude of the MAS that goes from the president down to the last functionary of the state, an arrogant attitude of defamation, criminalization, of any criticism from civil society.

The other issue is the narcotrafficking. At this time in Bolivia we are living with a tremendous level of narcotrafficking. It is observed and tolerated by the state structure, the government knows about this expansive activity, the production as well as the traffic. I think this force of narcotrafficking will exert a lot of pressure, not just distorting the economy of the country but also making itself felt in the content of the government's decisions.

So, the conditions of life for the people, particularly in the city, have not changed much, they have gotten worse in many sectors. However, in rural areas the situation has changed. Government policies have led to improvements in people's lives. But from the perspective of promoting productive communitarian processes that have long-term sustainability? There have been services—water systems, schools, hospitals. But there has been little done to promote productivity in rural areas.

Thus, people feel disenchanted, they expected things from the government, but they see that the situation doesn't change. I think that a year ago people were afraid to talk about what they were feeling about what was happening, but now there are more sectors of Bolivian society that are speaking up more bravely and firmly. There is in Bolivia a very vigorous and hopeful process of articulation to recapture those two agendas that were so important in 2000 and 2003.

So these are things that provoke conflicts with the people. There is the discourse of the government and a reality that is very different. There is an external image, but it does not correspond to the concrete reality.

Searching for new political forms

Bolivia is in a very profound process of questioning all that is going on, as is the world in general. In the United States, in Spain, in Egypt a year ago [2011], generally in Arab countries, in Europe, in Greece. It is series of popular uprisings that is not so spontaneous but rather organized, the product of a kind of suffering of the population from economic policies of the authoritarian governments all over. Here it happened in 2000 and 2003. The policies of the World Bank, the International Monetary Fund, authoritarian governments, privatization—exactly like what is happening now in Europe.

People want to construct something different: What we were proposing in 2000 and 2003, a new kind of economy, a way to recover politics for the people. I think that people in Europe and the United States and here in 2000 and 2003 did not fight for a political party. They fought to get back politics—not understood as a form in which someone rules over other people, but politics as a form to establish a type of relationship, a way of living together. A new way of living together not based on competition, individualism, but rather on solidarity, equality, complementarity.

Political parties or caudillos like Morales, like Correa, like the Peronists in Argentina, that are governments that are the result of an upsurge of a social movement, like in Egypt today, for example, these caudillos and the system they are part of have the remarkable ability to expropriate that social force, that constructive energy. They are very good at taking up this new discourse while the people are once again left waiting with just their hope. Curiously, in every society after any big change there are two institutions that survive no matter what: political parties and religions. So in Egypt the Muslims have taken 75 percent of the state apparatus, of the Egyptian Congress, and the other quarter are from Mubarak's party.

So here people don't want to make any party. I think that in Egypt and in Europe and the United States it's the same: The same people who don't want to form a party don't want to be part of a church either. We are looking for what we want that form to be, so we won't be a political party that doesn't last long, followed by the comeback, and so they go on cheating the people and all that. Nor do people want a religion, a church like in the old days.

So I think the great challenge today is what form of political organization gives us the means to change our conditions of life. Parties don't work and neither do religions. Now what?

Bolivia is an extensive territory in permanent deliberation. People are always waiting to see what's going on, and I think that's a big problem for any government. This is not a subordinate, submissive people; it's not a people who are indifferent to what is going on. You go to a beauty shop, stand in line at the market, people are talking politics, about what's going on. So I think the good thing is that people are searching here in Bolivia, and in the world, I would say: What do we want to be? I think that the great challenge is, as the compañeros here say, to be in the opposition. I think it is a process of structuring a social base that is looking for what to do in the long term. Not only for elections. Elections can be a step, but I think people have gone beyond this kind of democracy that doesn't work.

Breakdown of the state

Look, I believe that in the whole world there is a kind of breakdown of the connection between the social base—the population—and the state apparatus. Why don't people see a response from their state, from their government, from state organizations in general? Because the states have given up acting as such. How shall we say this? It is no longer a struggle as in the past, that perhaps very simple analysis that was made between the workers and the bosses, between the bourgeoisie and the proletariat, as we say. These are not the contradictions in themselves.

The contradictions are hardly between the peoples and the governments. Like here, with Evo, no? It's not a problem between the people and Evo because Evo wants to construct a highway though the TIPNIS [the Isiboro-Sécure Indigenous Territory and National Park]. I would say rather that in the whole world a conglomeration of social organizations, a social framework stands against the policies of a group of transnationals that use the states as vehicles to continue plundering.

So it is not a struggle between parties or leaders. Who defines the economic policies of Greece? Not the Greek government. It's the bankers, the transnationals. And here, who defines where the highway goes through the TIPNIS? Evo Morales? The government? No, it is the Brazilian transnationals who are interested in having a route for exporting iron to China. So the states have left off being nation states as such.

It is this group of transnationals who already have everything and their plan of plunder and destruction versus the people who are organizing a platform to confront these powers. So there are the movements of the *indignados* [indignant ones], like here in 2000 when the people came out against the sale of gas to Chile. It is these policies of the transnationals that start a rapid process of articulation of society to confront these policies of plunder and destruction and of ignoring that people exist. Because for these guys, people don't exist, that is, we don't exist. That fact, that attitude of considering that you don't exist, and making all the decisions—"Here is where the highway will go, or we'll construct a tunnel or build a dam," as if the people didn't exist—it's this that produces, I would say, a process of articulation of indignation. That is what is happening in the world, facing the destruction.

Rebuilding the social base

I think that the social fabric, the social base that was so strong and autonomous, and that brought Evo Morales into the government, does not exist today. Rather, they are following a process of confrontation: They have policies that are totally discriminatory between sectors. In other words, there is a disintegration of the social fabric that we constructed so laboriously starting in 2000, here in Bolivia. So I think that many people are starting over what we started twenty, thirty, forty, fifty years ago. We're doing it again. We are in a process of organization, gaining space from meeting, analysis, proposals, so as to see farther than the parties, farther than the state. That is to say, we are gathering our forces. We are informing people about what is happening—confronting the discourse of the government with what is really going on.

For example, we have got together a group of people, some of whom were in the MAS government, people who supported the MAS electoral process, people who have maintained their autonomy. We have worked in different ways. We've written articles that sometimes turn into books, in magazines of every type, answering the false policies of the government and also informing the population about what is really happening.

I have an absolute confidence in the people who paid for this process with so much sacrifice and without knowing how to do it. I believe that it would be very difficult for the rightists to return, or a military coup. I think that the people are not going to defend Evo Morales, either.

The important thing is to think beyond Evo Morales, beyond an electoral process. That is, how are we going to maintain this process that cost the people so much, and how will we press on? What a big thing it is to do!

Paraguay

PARAGUAY

BOLIVIA

BRAZIL

Capitán Pablo Lagerenza

Puerto Bahía Negra

ALTO PARAGUAY

Gral. Eugenio A. Garay

Fuerte Olimpo

Puerto Guarani

Fortín Infante Rivarola

BOQUERÓN

Mariscal Estigarribia

Minas Cué Km 160

Bella Vista

Doctor Pedro P. Peña

Filadelfia

Puerto Casado
Puerto Pinasco

San Lázaro

San Carlos

Pedro Juan Caballero

CONCEPCIÓN

Yby Yaú

Capitán Bado

Concepción

Horqueta

Fortín Ávalos Sánchez

Pozo Colorado

PRESIDENTE

HAYES

Tacuatí

SAN PEDRO

San Pedro

Itanara

Salto del Guairá

Fortín Gral. Díaz

Monte Lindo

Rosario

Curuguaty

San Estanislao

ALTO PARANÁ

Benjamín Aceval

Yhú

Villa Hayes

CORDILLERA

CAAGUAZÚ

Cnel. Oviedo

Hernandarias

Asunción

Caacupé

CENTRAL

Ciudad del Este

Villarrica

Santa Rita

Paraguarí

GUAIRÁ

Abaí

PARAGUARÍ

Caazapá

CAAZAPÁ

Alto Verá

San Juan Bautista

MISIONES

San Ygnacio

ITAPÚA

Capitán Meza

ÑEEMBUCÚ

Cnel. Bogado

Encarnación

Pilar

Isla Yacyretá
Isla Talavera

ARGENTINA

Paraná

Uruguay

ARGENTINA

BRAZIL

○ National capital
◉ Departmental capital
○ Town, village
✈ Major airport
– International boundary
– Departmental boundary
— Pan American Highway
— Main road
+ Railroad

| 0 | 50 | 100 | 150 km |
| 0 | 50 | 100 mi |

The boundaries and names shown and the designations used on this map do not imply official endorsement or acceptance by the United Nations.

United Nations Map No. 3760, Rev. 3, June 2004

INTRODUCTION
Land of utopian dreams

By Ben Dangl

The Tupí Guaraní who populated the region known today as Paraguay and Brazil were known as a wandering tribe on a search for the "Land without Evil," or "*Yvymara'eÿ*" in Guaraní. The language has become one of the two officially adopted in Paraguay, along with Spanish, but the hope represented by the utopian search of the Guaraní is the unofficial undercurrent that has long taken subterranean channels in this nation marked by decades of dictatorships.

It seems fitting that the first dictatorship was itself of a peculiarly utopian character. When Paraguay declared independence from Spain in May 1811, Brazilian historian Julio José Chiavenato wrote that it was "the only republic of Latin America that didn't suffer the presence of caudillos nor endure the presence of revolutions and coups." José Gaspar Rodríguez de Francia rose to power as the "Supreme" ruler of the country, a role he carried out until his death in 1840. Influenced by the French Encyclopedists and the ideas of Jean-Jacques Rousseau, de Francia set about to build a self-sufficient utopia, given the hostilities of neighboring countries that made access to the sea impossible for the land-locked nation.

De Francia eliminated, exiled, or imprisoned the old colonial elite and carried out a land reform that was previously unknown in Latin America. Peasants were encouraged to work the land in collectives as their Guaraní ancestors had, with distribution of resources and foreign exports carried out by the state. When the storehouses of the state had excess, and only then, it was exported. Not only were peasants ordinarily skilled in two or three trades, but the population had access to natural medicine pharmacies and schools. In fact, as many visitors to Paraguay noted, in 1840 when de Francia died, there was no illiteracy in the country—nor did Paraguay have a foreign debt.

The country continued to develop a self-sufficient industrial infrastructure under de Francia's nephew, Carlos Antonio López, who also began to
gradually open the borders that had been sealed off. Nevertheless, Brazil
hoped to expand its borders, as did Argentina. The two drafted Uruguay
into a war, financed by Britain, which resented Paraguayan independence
from its plans for globalization, and the War of the Triple Alliance began.
The besieged republic managed to fight off the combined forces of the three
countries for five years, manufacturing its own weapons and ammunition
and getting no help from the outside world. At the end of South America's
bloodiest war, Paraguay had lost 96.5 percent of its male population and one
hundred forty thousand square kilometers, nearly half of its territory, most of
which was sold to foreign capitalists in New York, London, and Amsterdam.

By blood and gore Paraguay had been dragged into the "global
economy," but another catastrophe awaited it in the twentieth century in
the form of the Chaco War with its also landlocked neighbor, Bolivia. The
dispute centered on the Chaco region that the two countries shared, and the
nations were pushed into the war by competing oil companies: Standard
(backing Bolivia) and Shell (backing Paraguay). Paraguay "won" that war,
securing some twenty thousand square kilometers of land, even as it lost
forty thousand soldiers in the fighting.

The Colorado Party's long shadow

Much of the current political landscape of Paraguay was shaped by the thirty-
five-year dictatorial rule of General Alfredo Stroessner, who maintained
power through a mixture of brutal repression, corruption, and cronyism.
After sixty-one years, the Colorado Party, which Stroessner was a part of, has
had the longest continuous run in power of any political party in the world.[1]

Stroessner's reign dominated the second half of the last century in
Paraguay, and casts a dark shadow into this one. Originally elected in 1954 to
fill a vacancy, Stroessner was "reelected" seven times through a state-of-siege
law in the constitution and with the aid of the military and the Colorado
Party. The Colorado Party had already ruled Paraguay from 1947 until 1962,
as a one-party state in which all other political parties were illegal.[2] Under
Stroessner, it served as one of the "twin pillars" supporting the regime, the
military being the other.[3]

The Colorado Party's vast system of clientelism—offering public jobs
to people to gain political support—relies entirely on state programs and
public services. The country's high unemployment rate makes this effective: One of citizens' few prospects for work is through the Colorado Party,
whether in such positions as a road construction worker, teacher, or mayor.

Though many citizens view the party as corrupt and ineffective, supporting it often means receiving a salary. The political machine of the Colorado Party remains intact and strong; as of 2007, it employed roughly two hundred thousand people.[4]

Stroessner collaborated with Chilean dictator Augusto Pinochet and the military junta in Argentina to orchestrate a regional crackdown on political opponents through a mixture of kidnapping, torture, and murder. Some four hundred people were disappeared under his rule, and another eighteen thousand tortured.[5]

Social movements organize against the odds

Under Stroessner, one of the only places for Paraguayans to organize without fear of repression was in the Catholic Church. It was there that the Christian Agrarian Leagues began to form in the late 1950s. Under the auspices of the Church they miraculously survived into the 1970s, despite ongoing attacks by security forces. The Leagues managed to keep alive a utopian Christian hope for justice among campesinos through the dark years of the dictatorship; they were formative antecedents of liberation theology and were also credited with having inspired the Landless Workers' Movement (MST) of Brazil.

Other movements stood up to the Stroessner regime, but met harsh repression. A general strike and wave of workers' protests from 1958 to 1959 resulted in a brutal crackdown on union leaders and dissidents; in an attempt to crush the workers' movement, the Colorado Party put the country's largest labor organization, the Central Paraguaya de Trabajadores (CPT), under state control. Inspired in part by the Cuban Revolution, leftist sectors launched various failed guerrilla attempts to overthrow Stroessner from 1959 to 1965. These guerrilla movements were crushed in the 1960s, as were the Christian Peasant Leagues in the 1970s.

Throughout the 1980s, new leftist labor and agrarian organizations grew under the waning shadow of the dictatorship, including the large Movimiento Campesino Paraguayo (MCP), which was founded in 1980. Unlike other nations in the region under dictatorship, Stroessner's reign did not end due to popular protest, but because of a military takeover led by General Andrés Rodríguez and Stroessner opponents within the Colorado Party itself. Such a transition ensured that while democracy would shortly return to Paraguay, the Colorado Party's stranglehold on Paraguayan politics would remain.[6]

With the end of the dictatorship in 1989 social movements began to emerge from clandestinity, but it took several years before they were able

Ycua Bolaños: Demonstration in support of the victims of the 2004 fire in the Asunción supermarket Ycua Bolaños. Nearly four hundred people died inside the market when the owners allegedly sealed the doors to prevent looting. The banner is striped like the Paraguayan flag and bears images of the dead. Photo by Clifton Ross.

to gain strength in a nation still suffering from the trauma of the Stroessner years. Throughout the 1990s in Paraguay, as in other Latin American nations, an uptick in neoliberal economic policies weakened the workers' movement, raised unemployment, and worsened working conditions. The privatization of state-run industries and companies and the financial crisis of 1995 hit the Paraguayan working class hard. During this time there was a boom in the development of maquiladoras in the textile and electronic industries, where cheap labor, terrible working conditions, and no workers' rights were the norm.[7]

After the return to democracy under the 1992 constitution, other movements and organizations, such as Servicio, Paz y Justicia (SERPAJ) were organizing against militarization in Paraguay, and particularly against obligatory military service. Within this movement, young people from ages seventeen to twenty-five organized within the Movimiento de Objeccion de Conciencia (MOC) both in rural and urban areas.[8]

The anti-militarization movement in Paraguay remained important as the years went by, and as a new threat to peace loomed in postdictatorial Paraguay: the militarization and paramilitarization of the countryside. This violence went hand in hand with the expansion of large agroindustries. As the century came to a close, the most dynamic movements in Paraguay became increasingly centered on agrarian issues. Indigenous and campesino organizations grew in size and influence, as their constituencies suffered from the encroaching soy production on traditional and collective lands and the drifting clouds of herbicides that were beginning to impact rural communities.

Land conflicts and soy production in Paraguay

Rural eastern Paraguay used to be full of jungle, small farms, schools and wildlife. Now it is a green sea of soybeans. The families, trees, and birds are gone. The schools are empty. The air is filled with the toxic stench of the pesticides like paraquat and 2,4-D used to protect the soy crops.

Unlike its resource-rich neighbors in Bolivia and Brazil, Paraguay has few mineral resources, and so most of its economy is focused on agriculture, predominantly soy. Soy production in Paraguay has increased exponentially in recent years due to rising demand worldwide for meat and cattle feed, as well as the booming biodiesel industry. Paraguay is the fourth-largest producer of soy in the world, and soy makes up 40 percent of Paraguayan exports and 10 percent of the country's GDP.[9]

As soy production expands, small farmers are losing their land and their health. Thirty million acres of land in Paraguay are now devoted to soy cultivation, according to sociologist Javiera Rulli.[10] This aggravates the inequality that marks the country: 83 percent of Paraguayan campesinos own only 6 percent of the country's land, while 351 landowners hold 40 percent of all the land.[11] In this country of 6.4 million people, 60 percent live in poverty. And 40 percent of the population own just 11.5 percent of the wealth, while the wealthiest 10 percent own 40.9 percent.

Since the first soy boom, the industry has evicted almost one hundred thousand small farmers from their homes and fields and forced the relocation of countless indigenous communities. Farmers have been bullied into growing soy with pesticides, at the cost of their food crops and subsequently their farms. An estimated twenty million liters of agrochemicals are sprayed across Paraguay each year.[12] The vast majority of Paraguayan farmers have been poisoned off their land either intentionally or as a side effect of the hazardous pesticides dumped by soy cultivation.

Managing the gargantuan agroindustry in South America are transnational seed and agrochemical companies including Monsanto, Pioneer, Syngenta, Dupont, Cargill, Archer Daniels Midland (ADM), and Bunge. International financial institutions and development banks have promoted and bankrolled the agroexport business of monoculture crops—much of Paraguayan soy goes to feed animals in Europe. The profits have united political and corporate entities from Brazil, the United States, and Paraguay, and increased the importance of Paraguay's cooperation with international businesses.

While more than a hundred campesino leaders have been assassinated, only one of the cases was investigated with results leading to the conviction of the killer. In the same period, more than two thousand other campesinos have faced trumped-up charges for their objections to the industry.

On September 24, 2008, when Paraguayan president Fernando Lugo spoke at the United Nations for first time, he denounced the soy industry as a type of "terrorism which in my country affects the children who are dying from pesticides."[13] But during Lugo's first two years in office, soy cultivation increased by 10 percent.[14] According to sociologist Marielle Palau, of the 105 campesino activists that were killed in land conflicts, ten of those assassinations took place during Lugo's time in office.

Lugo: hope and dilemmas

"Fireworks can still be heard in the distance where thousands of people are in the streets of downtown Asuncion sharing, embracing, reveling, hugging, smothering each other in kisses, and dancing until the early morning," reported Michael Fox from Asunción, Paraguay, upon the election of Fernando Lugo in April 2008. One reveler told Fox, "For the first time in our lives, we have hope, we have possibilities. We are a new nation!"[15]

The hope had largely to do with the political trajectory of a man who started out as a grassroots leader. Fernando Lugo was born in 1951 and as a young man taught in a rural school district. In 1977, Lugo was ordained as a Catholic priest and worked as a missionary in Ecuadorian indigenous communities until 1982. He then spent ten years studying at the Vatican, at which time he was appointed head of the Society of the Divine Word in Paraguay.

In 1994, Lugo became the bishop of the Paraguayan diocese of San Pedro. Though he was frequently away from Paraguay, he did not avoid the repercussions of the Stroessner dictatorship. In fact, three of his brothers were exiled, and the conservative Catholic hierarchy pressured him to resign as bishop due to his support for landless families' settlements on large estates owned by absent elites. He resisted this pressure until his name began to circulate as a presidential candidate. Old Paraguayan laws, stemming from anti-Jesuit legislation passed hundreds of years ago, forbid members of the clergy from running for president. In 2007, Lugo's resignation as bishop allowed him to realize his ambitions as a presidential contender.[16]

Once he took office, however, grim reality soon took hold. His party, the Patriotic Alliance for Change (APC), did not obtain a majority of seats in either house of the Paraguayan Congress. The right-wing opposition ended up controlling 82 percent of the Senate and the lower house,[17] so Lugo's reforms were regularly blocked by the opposition, including the Colorado Party.[18] The media immediately starting attacking the president, and he alienated his grassroots base by not moving fast enough on campaign promises. He demonstrated a lack of political will to confront the powerful industries, political sectors, and business elites that were gaining the most from the vast inequality in the country.

While much of the government remained in the hands of the Right, a significant amount of Lugo's party's base lay with the popular sectors of the country. Yet the administration all but squandered any chance of a productive relationship with them. Many landless and small farmers around the country demanded that the government conduct a new land survey to assess which lands were seized by Stroessner and illegally given to friends of the dictatorship, and which could therefore be legally redistributed to landless farmers. The rural movements' other main demand has been to stop the massive destruction of the environment and the campesino way of life through the use of paramilitary actions and poisonous pesticides on the soy crops of industrial farms.[19]

Under Lugo, the economic inequality, deficit in democracy, and marginalization of movements and dissenting voices were maintained, albeit with a president who represented more of a "populist" veneer than his predecessors. This contradiction aided the Right and confused and aggravated Lugo's voter base. "It's good for the oligarchy if Lugo stays in power and does nothing," said Paraguayan activist Leticia Galeano, referring to the fact that the Right and the elite benefited from Lugo's time in office, while the work of grassroots movements in the country was ignored or repressed under his watch.

A coup against hope

On June 22, 2012, the right-wing Federico Franco became president in what has been deemed a parliamentary coup against Lugo. Franco was Lugo's own vice president—Lugo himself had to form a pact with Franco's Liberal Party in order to garner enough support to win the election. Following a conflict over land in Curuguaty which left seventeen dead, Lugo's political opponents teamed up to levy impeachment charges against him.[20]

The process began on June 21, 2012, and within twenty-four hours the Senate gathered and officially initiated the trial, granting Lugo only two hours to defend himself. The next day, Lugo was removed from office in a 39–4 vote. He was accused of encouraging landless farmers' occupations, performing poorly as president, and failing to bring about social harmony in the country. Lugo stepped down and vice president and Liberal Party leader Federico Franco took his place.

Shortly after assuming office, the Franco administration fast-tracked controversial deals with Monsanto to allow for GMO cotton seeds in the country, and sped up negotiations with the mining company Rio Tinto Alcan for an aluminum smelter critics charged would pollute the environment.[21] Meanwhile, the government has cracked down on critics, democracy activists, and workers.[22]

For many Paraguayan activists, the coup showed conclusively that the country's power structure—feudal, repressive, elitist, and conservative as it is—stayed in power even after the dictatorship was gone. In the months after Lugo's ouster, calls began for a national Constitutional Assembly began to circulate. "There is an urgent need to develop stronger mechanisms which guarantee that the rights of the citizens are not violated," said Gabriela Schvartzman Muñoz, the spokeswoman for Movimiento Kuña Pyrenda, a socialist and feminist political organization. "We are moving toward this, we're discussing a new paradigm."

Oscar Caceres, ex–secretary general, Secretariat of Information and Communication for Development (SICOM)
"The Guaraní utopia is the construction of the unity of the people built from the inside"

Interview and translation by Clifton Ross, August 2008

I met Oscar at a gathering of social communications activists who were working in the Social and Popular Front (Frente Social y Popular, FSP) to support Lugo as rumors of a coup d'état were circulating around Asunción in the first days after the inauguration. Oscar, like many in the FSP, had been active in the Tekojojá Popular Movement, a group formed out of the social movements to confront neoliberal policies in the country and propose a democratic socialist alternative. Oscar had run for representative under that banner in the city government of Asunción in the elections that brought Fernando Lugo to power. At the time of this interview, he was working in the government's new Secretariat for Information and Communication for Development (SICOM). The interview took place in his modest office there.

Oscar Caceres. Photo by Clifton Ross.

In March 2006, a big mobilization of a dozen or so parties and social move-ments was called and led by Fernando Lugo, who was then a bishop. Everyone believed that it was going to be just another gathering, but forty thousand people joined in, making it the largest [gathering] in recent times. From that point political leaders said that we needed to support and make sure Lugo coordinated and led a political front. There was another social sector called Citizen Resistance, a fundamental actor among social sectors and left parties. All this came together under the name of Concertación Nacional (National United Front), and [Lugo] left his office as bishop and ran for president.

On December 17, 2006, a popular congress was held and out of it came the popular movement Tekojojá. Tekojojá began an interesting form of par-ticipation, a strategy of participation that it called *ñe mongeta guasu* (great dialogue). Fernando Lugo, along with the leaders of Tekojojá, went out to all parts [of the country] and Fernando took note of the problems and ill-nesses of the people, after which that [information] was systematized. After that, a second stage of ñe mongeta guasu began, in which the people made their proposals. Some four hundred meetings with the people [were held]. In this way Fernando Lugo became a phenomenon to mobilize all [sectors] of Paraguayan society, from the least to the sectors always mobilized. That's, briefly, how Tekojojá began, and now it's in the process of becoming a politi-cal party.

The Popular Social Bloc is a space primarily for the social movements and the left parties. So the Bloc, along with the left parties that came from the Concertación, signed the Pact of August 27 last year to become the Patriotic Alliance for Change (APC). The Bloc later watered down its platform when it began working on electoral issues. There was no agreement between the various political parties, so each left party ran its own candidates. The Bloc shrank quite a bit. Today there's hardly any talk about the Social Bloc as such; there's only the Patriotic Alliance for Change.

There was another process begun, which is possibly the continuation of the Bloc, or maybe a continuation of what came out of ñe mongueta guasú, and that was on May 12 of this year (2008) which was called the Frente Social y Popular (Social and Popular Front). The social organizations and the political organizations such as the Patriotic Socialist Alliance, the Tekojojá Popular Movement, the Communero's Popular Party, a party in formation, all these in some way gave birth to the FSP. And today the FSP is building a social structure in nearly all the departments [of the country].

Seeds of the present struggle: the Christian Agrarian Leagues

In the 1960s a sociopolitical project called the Agrarian Campesino Leagues (sometimes called Christian Agrarian Leagues) arose, a project with great vision and Christian inspiration related to liberation theology and Christian base communities and such. These were communities that were very much self-organized. They developed mutual cooperatives, collective work, their own production, forms of commerce with great autonomy. At the same time, [they had] a social, political, ideological, and spiritual development, the latter because the Catholic Church was involved. The [Leagues] were also a constituted as a strong movement of opposition, not only to the Stroessner regime but to the sociopolitical economic system [as a whole]. This movement had a lifespan of more or less twenty years. It was repressed and its leaders were taken to jail. Recently a report was issued saying that there were three hundred disappeared and nearly one hundred murdered.

So that's rising up again today, and being transformed in parties, movements, that thinking, that fraternity and equality, solidarity and building of horizontal structures; the autonomy, self-management, patriotism and endogenous growth: All that's being taken up again today, and what the FSP is building on, inspired by the objectives of the Leagues, especially in the theme of equality, fraternity and the Guaraní utopia of Yvymara'eỹ (land without evil).

It seems to me that in the collective unconscious there remains a line of thought in which we see translated the utopia of the Guaraní people and the "Yvymara'eỹ" and, in the case of Dr. Francia, becomes not so much a land, but the search for equality, equity as a first experience of socialism that lasted some twenty years, more or less. Then the Guaraní utopia is the construction of a society from itself, from my own self, the endogenous construction of a people, a unity of a people built from the inside. So this history turns around the Guaraní utopia, Dr. Francia and then other Colorado thinkers who, for example, have some relation to this line of thought, something that I think would be well worth studying. I think it could explain how many things have developed [in Paraguay].

Barrett himself, Rafael Barrett, in 1904, 1907, a Spaniard who lived in Paraguay quite a while, wrote what could be called [an early version of] *Open Veins of Latin America* by Eduardo Galeano. He wrote in those years of many situations in Paraguay and at an international level denounced the semifeudal, near slavery system called the "Mensú." Those were downtrodden people brought from different places to work in the yerba maté fields, where they had to work day and night. They weren't allowed to leave because they accumulated debts with the bosses and as they weren't able to pay, they couldn't leave. It was a very difficult situation, the last known instance of slavery in Paraguay, the Mensú. So the singers and poets inspired by the life of the Mensú once again looked to the land without evil, and the search for the land without evil as a slave seeks freedom. There's a permanent search and reference to the theme of this land without evil.

I think this continues to be a valuable inspiration. We have to explore this more deeply today. So, for instance, there's a new theological current that's called "Indian theology." Indian theology is a theology that by means of practice and reflection between indigenous and nonindigenous, there is a search for the presence of God, the presence of a God without fear of borders. In this fusion of indigenous, campesino, and urban cultures there is a new search for the "land without evil." It's very interesting, this Indian theology which arose in 1991, with its years of reflection. Nowadays [it] is recognized as a powerful force and form of life within Catholicism. And it's not only found in Catholicism, but in the Methodist and other non-Catholic churches and among indigenous people, among shamans and religious leaders.

I think there's another way, the deeper current that is discovered through the person, nature, a superior being, energies. I think this way is more profound, the way of the utopias, wherein we encounter the symbolic world, the ancestors, the present. We encounter a utopia of Saint Francis of Assisi who proposed the great cosmic brother and sisterhood. And so what

I do to the plant, I do to myself or I affect others. And so we speak of sister rain, sister illness, and sister plant. [Saint Francis] proposed a cosmovision, a utopia, and in Latin America we see this. In Bolivia with Pachamama or, for example, the indigenous name for Latin America as Abya Yala. The indigenous of Panama called the American continent by this name, and it meant "great continent" or "great land." Indian theology considered Abya Yala in [another] conference of bishops and in the formation of a movement of anthropological spirituality, deeper than the social organizations themselves. If we could come to [develop] this it might be a very good thing, no? It would be ethnic power and the indigenous people say that they have the solutions for the problems humanity faces today.

And what is that solution? Respect for nature; leaving behind modernity and its technologies without leaving them per se, but rather no longer being their instrument and being consumed by them. So the indigenous people say this, that they have the solution for the world; they say, "our way of life is the solution for the world." But we punish them and call them beggars, and we marginalize them.

Hipólito Acevei and Emiliano Vera, Coordination for the Self-Determination of Indigenous Peoples (CAPI)
"For indigenous people power is collective, it's constructive and something that benefits everyone equally"

Interview and translation by Clifton Ross, August 2008

It's a hot afternoon in Asunción and I arrive on time for a meeting with Hipólito Acevei and Emiliano Vera to find the two men quietly sipping tereré *from* guampas *(cups) made of palo santo wood, which gives the maté herb a slight but distinctive flavor. After brief introductions, we sit down to talk as I furtively wipe the sweat from my face.*

Both men sit quietly and wait for me to introduce myself and begin. I immediately recognize that these two men, though polite and even friendly, are not given to small talk, so we quickly begin the interview. Hipólito Acevei is president of CAPI and Emiliano Vera is one of the directors of CAPI and the Association of Ava Guaraní Communities of Alto Paraná (ACIGAP), a department on the border with Brazil.

The interview was conducted in September of 2008, in the first weeks of Fernando Lugo's presidency. The two men were hopeful that Lugo would act on behalf of the social movements, in particular, to rectify the injustices indigenous people have suffered for centuries.

Hipólito Acevei. Photo by Clifton Ross.   **Emiliano Vera.** Photo by Clifton Ross.

Hipólito: Eight years ago there arose an interesting meeting between indigenous peoples and organizations through community leaders in Chaco and the eastern regions. CAPI arose then, struggling for our rights, but not fighting. We didn't come to Asunción to fight but to struggle for our rights as indigenous people. We continue this work, coming to Asunción for meetings and to exchange experiences. Right now we're closely working with the struggle of indigenous people in their regions. We have, for example, a commitment to defend the brothers and sisters who still live in the wild, in what is commonly known as voluntary isolation. There's the Ayoreo in the Paraguayan Chaco, and the Ondurá people in the southern part of the country, in the area of the San Rafael Hill, where our indigenous brothers and sisters live in the wild, with its food and natural resources like water, wind, humidity, wild animals, and all.

There are big projects coming from outside that are affecting these brothers and sisters and pushing them out while empowering the big livestock businesses and agribusiness, [both of which result in] great deforestation; these [people] go in there and take indigenous land. So we're accompanying [our indigenous brothers and sisters] in this work. And we're consolidating this force that we have as directors coming from the grassroots in our communities to speak to the authorities. It's also an important issue for our side that we have the ability to make an indigenous government before a Paraguayan government, an indigenous government that would struggle and not submit to state powers but rather freely demand, respond, and make appeals. That's what we're seeking as a right. And at this very moment we're coming to this by means of the opening presented to us with these state powers.

We have a situation in Paraguay with the secretary of the environment who often, instead of protecting the environment, destroys it. We believe that the secretary of the environment should understand that we as indigenous people need to protect the reserves, the few wild areas that have left. That's our position.

Recently we were talking with some compañeros from the east because starting in 1960 the large dam of Itaipú was built and it destroyed a huge part of indigenous territory. It took everything away and dispersed everyone and families were removed involuntarily, kilometers and kilometers away from ancestral lands. Now the Paraguayan government and the new directors of Itaipú are preparing a document for the territorial recuperation of that which was taken. And we're talking and accompanying with a deep assessment and respectful content that soon we'll send to Itaipú and the national government. We're sending this information not so they'll give us a gift or something, but rather as a demand for the recuperation of territory taken from us, those invaded and flooded lands because millions and millions of indigenous lands are under water due to the construction.

And in the Paraguayan Chaco we're facing an important challenge from multilateral entities, in this case the Inter-American Development Bank, which signed an agreement with a foundation from the Paraguayan Chaco on a large, high level project, as they themselves call it, "Patrimony for Recuperation," conservation of the natural patrimony of the Paraguayan Chaco. And I'm from the Chaco and neither I nor anyone there know the content, the mechanism, how it's being prepared, how it must be implemented, where or when the diagnostic was done so as to make a firm basis for the contract. We know none of this.

Now we're demanding that the Inter-American Development Bank give us the pertinent information: When was the plan drafted, and who is the person who did the diagnostic? How did it aid the bank and this "From Chaco" foundation, as it's called, to be in the Chaco? How did it form this data to be a base for signing contracts for thousands and thousands of dollars for that work about which we still know nothing? But we remain concerned because they're talking about a reordering of territory where they show us, "Here it is, indigenous communities in the Chaco," and they'll call it "territory." This isn't "territory"; it's small communities that live in the Chaco. So within this plan of the natural patrimony of the Paraguayan Chaco they won't speak of [indigenous] territory, but yes, territories for thousands and thousands of cows; territories to be deforested, thousands and thousands of acres; they talk of territories where they'll plant pasture for livestock animals, but they'll never talk of indigenous territory. So this is a great concern for us.

CAPI is forced to become more organized, more united to take in this information and discuss, analyze, come to agreement on some sort of position on these plans underway in Paraguay. We're working, thinking, always thinking about what's happening and how to find a good point of struggle.

Emiliano: We have thirty-two community areas of indigenous associates. I represent five thousand indigenous people from Alto Paraná. We're looking for a way to confront the government, to develop ideas for reclaiming our rights, which we must defend. Usually the government pays more attention to its wallet than it does to us. So rather than giving us our due, it takes from us things that have belonged to us for a long time, things like land, jungle, water, everything. And we need all this as indigenous people because we've been here I don't know how long.

Our ancestors are now dead, but we have to keep struggling with our families in mind. Because if we don't struggle, our grandchildren will hold us accountable and ask why we didn't defend them. So for them we are struggling, in solidarity with each other, working to reclaim our rights and nothing more: to defend our territory, the jungle and the water, all of which is our wealth. Because we lived better before because we had a lot of forest, a lot of wild fruit, wild animals and we lived peacefully with few diseases. It's not like that now. Now there are many gullies and [the land] is drying up because there's no more jungle due to deforestation, and many animals have disappeared, many wild animals have gone extinct, and the fruits we ate [are gone]. All this worries us, but, as I said, on the other hand, we're happy: We've continued working and we're motivated to work, and that's our advantage. Because if we remained sitting, no one would defend anything.

There in the Alto Parana, for example, there's the dam called Itaipú and it has hurt us very, very much. Our grandparents were demanding that it be done elsewhere. They remembered that place, how they fished, and lived on the fish and now that's prohibited. It's difficult to get there. It's now property of the state. So there are many difficulties and we're trying to get some of that land back.

The indigenous movement here in Paraguay is relatively new compared to those of other countries that already had a long history of struggle, presence, and articulation. In Paraguay we're just beginning. The population is dispersed: one here, one there. It's a policy of the government to have one group living here and another one farther away, with no communication between. This is a very negative factor for us being able to put all our demands together.

We began this new struggle in 2000, and we're seeing that the indigenous movements aren't having an influence on the Left but rather that the Left exerts its influence on the indigenous movements, suddenly creating situations that are confusing for indigenous people. So we're struggling to understand the role of the indigenous movement toward the Left and how it might change things within the cosmovision, the vision and the understanding of the knowledge of the indigenous. There are various left-wing political parties forming in Paraguay and they're visiting communities in the indigenous movement and bringing another mentality. This is worrisome for us, but we've begun talking about it. It's a challenge for us to understand what they're doing and for the leaders to talk with our people.

These are not very favorable conditions for us, in the sense that we first have to consolidate and centralize the unity of indigenous people. We have to be well along in a sustained dialogue between indigenous people to be as well prepared as those on the left. I do think the strengthening and consolidation of the unity of these indigenous peoples can work well with a Left in solidarity with those without protection. But for this there first has to be consolidation and unity of indigenous people.

We've defined three central, profound themes because previous governments have always done that when they make public policies speaking of quality of life: They talk of education, health, and development. So we as indigenous people respond in kind, to talk about all they discuss, so there are three fundamental victories for indigenous people that must be assured. When there is finally a positive recognition of our territorial [rights] then we need to talk of conservation. We, ourselves, have to conserve this territory, guard, care for, and manage the animals and live in harmony there. Then there's a third strategic theme, once territory and conservation of the environment or nature are assured: then we can talk about quality of life. Conservation of nature and the environment, and then quality of life. This public policy for indigenous people needs to be written and the government has to put it in practice.

Indigenous democracy

Democracy for us means precisely that a leader transmits all that he or she is delegated to transmit; that the leader communicate all prior consensus on information, content and decisions so that the group of leaders can understand well and be able to decide. The communities are characterized by collectivity as a form of communitarian life. So a group of families elect a leader to represent the community, the same with each community. So we have here thirty-two heads, who gather and, in this case, elect a leader for the whole organization, and these [organizational leaders] meet with other organizations. So the issue isn't that you're from a locale (pueblo: people, town) but that there be a common cause for discussion, a dialogue, interchange of experiences, of what to do or what information we might have. So there are certain levels for [making] requests but when the requests open up it doesn't mean that the leaders submit to the least but that the least also has rights toward the group of leaders. In that sense we have another way of deciding, speaking, and discussing among us.

So if there's something left undone it might have been accidental, so the family corrects the problem. If there's a second incident, it's provocative. Then the family has to change things, there's a change of leadership, and the [leader] changes roles.

For us, power [in the usual sense] is individualistic, personalistic and very destructive and also monopolistic. But for indigenous people power is collective, it's constructive and something that benefits everyone equally. And this is exactly the kind of power we always exert outside on the government, demanding that our rights be respected. That is, for us, power.

To rule obeying, yes, that's it. That is also the culture [of indigenous people] here in Paraguay. As president of CAPI, for example, I am not the one who demands or imposes but rather what a member tells me to do I have to fulfill. I have to be beneath the level of the leaders. The Zapatistas are very good in this. "He who rules, obeys." And he obeys, ruling. So there's a rotation and there's no one who goes behind but we all make a wheel; there is no difference. That's also our culture here.

We sometimes worry because a leader, entering into the government becomes a functionary [of that government]. So we have to think this through, and we think about this a lot as indigenous people, that we make of ourselves a strong organization, consolidate ourselves and work alongside the government without submitting to that government so then we can have more freedom. And our organization is called "coordination for self-determination," and this means not to be submitted to a government but to be at its side. We see CAPI and indigenous people working beside the government: separate, but visible, so the government might offer its hand to the proposal of the indigenous people.

Jorge Galeano. Photo by Clifton Ross.

Jorge Galeano, president of Movimiento agrario y popular (Popular and Agrarian Movement, MAP)

"That person who works to produce food in a social fashion… is a subversive in the neoliberal economic system"

Interview and translation by Clifton Ross, August 2008

I'd nearly given up getting an interview with Jorge Galeano, since he was so busy he rarely answered my calls. Then it turned out one night I returned to my hotel and the white-haired Uruguayan manager with the big mustache met me as I walked to my room. "We have a new guest in the hotel, and he wants to talk to you," he said. "He's staying in the room next to yours. His name is Jorge Galeano." Jorge and I sat in the lobby and did the interview. He was red-eyed and exhausted, but he nevertheless articulately laid out a few of the considerable problems of Paraguay's campesinos as they confront soy agribusiness.

Ours is a union organization that includes small producers and landless campesinos, men and women field workers and also some indigenous communities. Our main activities are carried out in the departments of Caaguazú, Alto Paraná, and Canindeyú, in what are the three regions of Eastern Paraguay. We're also part of the Frente Social y Popular at a national level.

Our primary struggle is at the level of recuperating misallocated or poorly allocated land, as well as taking up the issue of family agriculture as a way of life and as a way of living in harmony with nature, respecting, above all, the environment. And so these struggles bring us into confrontation with the big soy and other large scale monocultural producers that are financed by international capital, the multinational corporations, which have done so much damage to our country, especially to people in the countryside where the model has had such negative social, economic, cultural, and environmental consequences.

Culturally, [this model] is destroying community, the community way of life of the campesinos. The production [under this model] creates food, not for people in the countryside but rather for the big cattle business in the north, and it drives our farmers out of their natural habitat. It's the destruction of a way of life, a culture of work, production, and community spirit. The traditional campesino is rooted in the form of production, the way of life in community. We call it campesino community because the people interact and thrive together as neighbors and develop their own culture in the schools, temples, sports centers, the little spaces of community sports and recreation. Their way of working collectively, their ways of producing and their ways of sharing community life are all the essence of the campesino. And for us, these values are irreplaceable, and this community life that encompasses these fundamental human rights is being threatened, trampled, and violated by this model that concentrates land and wealth and doesn't take life into account. For us, defense of life is fundamental, the defense of life in community.

It began in 1999 and 2000 when the model of GMO soy was advanced, a model of production that we could call criminal, because it depreciates life and substitutes it with machines, pushing aside the campesino workforce itself and generating poverty, expulsions, and misery throughout the cities of Paraguay. It's a model that develops wealth, but only for the few, not for the poorest of the country.

We began our struggle for the campesino communities and for public state lands that were being turned over to business interests in 1999–2000, years of the greatest advance [of privatizations] in the country. We rose up as an organization at that time, struggling for the community life of campesinos and the recuperation of state lands that had been illegally, unconstitutionally, and illicitly turned over to [private], and mostly foreign, interests who aren't subject to agrarian reform. In this context we proposed, in first place, formation and training of our people, community production, the cooperativization of production, and the return of all land illegally distributed. [We proposed] recuperating land as a way of life, as a means of production, and not as a market commodity, as the political and economic system of the country proposes.

For us the earth isn't a market good, but a good that generates and reproduces life and a good on which many of our campesinos depend. And we're speaking of agrarian reform not only in the area of production, but also as encompassing other values and instruments that could aid development, like education, health, infrastructure, and all that's related to real development. Generally speaking, the peoples of Latin America have historically struggled to realize an integrated agrarian reform, which has never gotten very far, neither in Paraguay nor elsewhere in Latin America.

In that sense, we support the political process that has begun, not only starting on the fifteenth [with the inauguration of President Lugo], but a change in government that could contribute to changing living conditions, balance and address inequalities in this country which has had seventy years of government under one party, which has left a deep impression and held the country back.

I think one of our greatest riches is our language, Guaraní, against which there has been a great battle. Capitalism has used every means in trying to destroy our language, but without success. Even now, upward of 80 percent of people in the countryside speak Guaraní and we're proud that a majority of the population speaks Guaraní, since it's our valuable patrimony and encompasses many things. Not only are we connected through the word, but our culture is also expressed in Guaraní, through music, dance, and through the harp. Guaraní is intrinsic to many aspects of our life. The Guaraní indigenous, as a people, have their communities, even up to the present, and with great sacrifice they've maintained them in a collective form with collective work. And the resistance is for life itself, for their culture and their country, and I believe we owe a historical debt to these original people. Many don't understand why we've lost connection with, and drifted away from, the rich origins of the Guaraní people. But in some sense in our organizations we're reclaiming this [tradition] of what it is to be Guaraní, as a people, as a race with a history. This is manifested in some way in the collective work of "minga" among the campesinos. It's a form of solidarity work where one not only shares work, but also all that is meant by community in work: the plans, ideas, thoughts, and many other really beautiful things.

I think there have been advances and retreats. There have been advances in terms of interpreting the changes in the region and Paraguay couldn't remain outside of this process. We think Fernando Lugo is the result of a political process that fell into an enormous contradiction which the traditional parties strengthened and could no longer control. Not even the hegemonic powers and states were any longer able to control or sustain power. This is not only true in this country, but in the region, where the majority of the traditional parties are wrapped in a generalized corruption and have lost the faith and credibility of the people. One of the great contradictions generated by this situation is the generalized poverty of the people of Latin America and the way [the poor] have come to see [that] the wealth doesn't come from anywhere else but from the people themselves. They saw that now had come the time to recuperate the fundamental values in the political life of the people and that these values weren't external, but rather in the people themselves.

As social leaders we have an enormous political responsibility in the life of our country. We have to recover those values that make a nation and struggle for the strengthening of those values to build, and not destroy. And in this our struggle is inspired by community life as well as by the social and political life. For us socialism up to now has been a utopia, a utopia that to some degree becomes a reality, incredibly, in the poorest communities precisely because there you have to help out and get along. And it's expressed in the form of production, the way of sharing. That person who works to produce food in a social fashion and not simply to buy it in a supermarket is a subversive in the neoliberal economic system.

Liz Becker, Social and Popular Front (Frente Social y Popular, FSP)
"The social struggles have been intensely criminalized"

Interview and translation by Clifton Ross, August 2008

Liz Becker was a member of the leadership team of the short-lived Frente Social y Popular (FSP). Seeing a possible political opening with Fernando Lugo's election in 2008, the FSP tried to organize Paraguay's fragmented social movements and sectoral organizations to press for their common agendas at a national level. Liz talked about the obstacles to achieving that unity, and about the key challenges facing Paraguyan women.

Paraguay has always had an authoritarian state or authoritarian governments that monopolized all powers. The Colorado Party has inserted itself in the unions and its own campesino organizations that are accountable to it. That has a great effect in terms of fragmentation and division, but particularly in terms of the ability to take a critical position before the government.

It becomes very difficult to disagree, to think critically and take a critical stance as a social movement, and to maintain autonomy. And when the social movements attempted to be autonomous, they were repressed and criminalized. Here, when something is won directly from the state, these organizations, these social movements lose their autonomy, their critical capacity, their ability to form proposals.

In the epoch of the dictatorship the social organizations, even though they weren't communist, were accused of that by the dictator so that the repression could be unleashed and leaders could be pressured. In the transition to democracy, leaders were co-opted. Leaders were bought, supposedly given "resources" but this did nothing but create corruption among social leaders. We have a whole history of clientelism in this country, of asking favors of the rulers, of asking for a favor in return for loyalty. It's a historical practice with deep roots in the social movements and organizations.

The social movements here are also very hierarchical and the leaders are installed as commanders (*comandantes*), as rulers and only to the degree that organizations open a debate on how to make a participatory process, an organic process from the base of the social movements, can this verticalism be broken, or so I believe. But it's very difficult because, for example, the homeless movement, is managed by leaders as bosses (*jefes*), and it's going to be very difficult to break that [model]. Only by building a popular base and problematizing the building of these organizations will we possibly see [change].

Many of us in the FSP believe in the process of political debate, confronting ideas and building, and elaborating on, proposals that respond to social problems. But it's a great challenge because this practice only comes through leadership that confronts even the social leaders themselves and their sectarian ideas. This debate is what will open the country because talking about social problems in this country is difficult: people here don't want to talk about social problems.

I think this is part of what neoliberalism has brought, and is bringing about here, so that social inequality is something [viewed as] normal, natural, a personal problem having to do with personal abilities, and it's not that way. Social inequality has a lot to do with the contradiction between powerful economic groups, like the livestock, soy or forestry mafias that control entire territories and the poverty resulting from this. And so the social reality of the country has to be problematized.

We have a neoliberal state that applies those sorts of policies, for example, in fighting poverty. One such policy is monetary transfers to poor campesino families and it's neoliberal in the sense that it hasn't really

Liz Becker. Photo by Clifton Ross.

fought poverty but rather reproduced it and, furthermore, formed clients for the Colorado Party. The issue of health care is left for the community itself to resolve its own problems, a neoliberal policy.

The social struggles have been intensely criminalized. Right now there are three thousand campesino leaders who are in judicial proceedings as a result of their struggle for lands, for land occupation against *latifundios*, big soy producers. They're also in proceedings for their struggle against agrotoxics, which are a byproduct of this soy production because as these soy producers advance on campesino communities they surround them and with their spraying and create enormous health problems [for campesinos]. For example, in the south of the country where soy production is most intense, we have children born with deformities, the greatest number of [spontaneous] abortions, of women with problematic pregnancies and births, and a prevalence of cancers, precisely because it's in a zone dominated by soy production. The state needs to put limits on soy and cattle production, but it doesn't. One form of fighting social inequality in this country is this: putting limits on private [business] sectors and applying policies of redistribution [of wealth].

Women face violence, lack of reproductive choice

Paraguay has one among the highest mortality rates among women for causes related to clandestine abortions, poorly done abortions. Here abortion is a crime but only the woman is punished. So we've proposed decriminalization of abortion and the reduction of maternal deaths from this cause. This is among the sexual and reproductive proposals for women, which includes a policy of decentralized health. These maternal deaths are found primarily among campesinas, women in the countryside, in the poor neighborhoods.

This is one of the proposals, and then [there is] the entire theme of political participation because we see Lugo practically surrounded by men so we, from the women's table, began to propose the need for women to occupy public posts, not only because they're women, but also for their abilities, the suitability that occupying a public post implies. We want to see this installed as a policy of the state and that the institution that is in charge of women's affairs function as such. This ministry hardly has a budget so we want to establish a relationship with the new secretary of women to give more political support.

Another big issue for women is that of violence. Here it's a massive and generalized [problem]. There are cases of women being killed by their partners. This is another issue we want to see taken up for policy of the state, the violence within families and murder of women.

We can't move backward on the issue of women. Now there's an entire discussion on the decriminalization of abortion, but it's very polarized. Sectors of the Church and the churches are up against women's and feminist organizations. We think that this has to be publicly debated to generate new thinking around the issue of abortion. It's a difficult struggle but we think that one of the proposals we in the women's sector [of the FSP] want to make is that the state be secular precisely to avoid it being taken over by religious fundamentalism. That's why we propose public policies with a focus on rights because with the fall of the dictatorship we were able, at a minimum, to secularize the state and create conditions for that, so this is our struggle. And even though Lugo comes from the Catholic Church, for us the struggle is more complicated. We have to make some advances at a minimum and can't allow for steps backward. Even the last Colorado government put many women in the most relevant posts and began big discussions on the issue of abortion. We have to keep moving forward on these issues.

Francisco Estigarribia. Photo by Clifton Ross.

Francisco Estigarribia, member of National Coordination of Adolescent and Child Workers (CONNATs)
"We understood work as something natural, but also something that lent dignity to one's personal life, from childhood all the way to old age"

Interview and translation by Clifton Ross, August 2008

I've taken the bus through Asunción to meet Francisco at his office. The bus winds through the streets of the city, past colorful markets that nevertheless look poorer than anything I've seen in Argentina. An itinerant salesman is trying to sell passengers a Spanish-Guaraní dictionary and I'm trying to pay attention to the street signs for some clue as to where I am and where I'm going in a city that is completely unfamiliar to me. Between blocks I steal glances at the book I'm reading, Genocidio Americano: La Guerra del Paraguay *by Julio José Chiavenato. The book details the War of the Triple Alliance when Brazil, Uruguay, and Argentina, financed by the Bank of London, attacked Paraguay and destroyed the country.*

The most moving passage of Chiavenato's history describes the final battles of Paraguay. After six years of forging its own weapons, making its own ammunition to defend the country against three invaders that were financed by the world's greatest empire of the time, Paraguay no longer had men left to defend it. And so the children went into battle. In the section titled "The Most

Heroic American Battle: Twenty thousand soldiers against thirty five hundred Paraguayan children," Chiavenato describes the Battle of Acosta Ñu. The children were between the ages of nine and fifteen, though there were also children of six, seven, and eight years. The children, some of whom had pasted straw on their faces to look like men, were quickly surrounded by the Brazilians. Some, grabbing the legs of the Brazilian soldiers, begged for their lives, only to have their throats cut. The mothers of the children were in the woods watching the slaughter, and a few ran into the battlefields to take up lances and lead the children, only to die with them. In the evening after the battle, the mothers went to find and bury their children, only to have the Brazilians set the field on fire, killing the mothers and the last surviving children.

I read the passage of the Battle of Acosta Ñu some time after the interview with Francisco. I couldn't help thinking of Francisco and the other youth and children I met in his office, and how much their current struggle with the ILO and UNICEF, even if less bloody or dramatic, is in continuity with that earlier battle of the heroic children of Paraguay. The difference today, at least in Latin America, is the difference between the neoconservatives and the neoliberals: the latter, unlike the former, recognize that "it's more efficient to 'take' a country and dominate it economically than to establish this domination by force of arms," as Chiavenato wrote. And there's another difference: whereas the children and adolescents of Paraguay were the final victims of the imperial war of the Triple Alliance, today's youth in Paraguay are on the front lines of struggle.

I'm nineteen years old. I'm part of the National Coordination of Adolescent and Child Workers, CONNATs, an organization which arose some twelve years ago to work and fight for the social recognition of youth, particularly for children and adolescents who work, and in some cases live, on the streets or who work in the communities or at home with our parents. We're an organization of children and adolescents who identify with the working class. We are a movement that believes in the organized activism of children and adolescents.

We believe that children and adolescents from the working class have a lot to offer in the different sociopolitical processes of their countries. Over time we've proven this in the experience of the movement of child workers, which started thirty years ago, with the experience of MANTHOC, (El Movimiento de Adolescentes y Niños Trabajadores Hijos de Obreros Cristianos, the Movement of Adolescent and Child Workers, Children of Christian Workers), which came out of the Catholic Worker Youth at that time. And later the experience grew throughout all of Latin America and after a long time, in Paraguay. In Paraguay the experience began eighteen years ago and just two years ago our organization consolidated and became more solid, dedicated, and committed to growth. That's the organization of which I'm a part and which I represent.

I've been active in the organization for nine years, starting at the age of ten. I started [working by] selling empanadas in the streets of my community at the age of six. My mother made the empanadas and my brothers and I went out to sell in the community to help out our family, which was in need at that time. It enabled us to offer something to the house and pay for our studies, because here [in Paraguay] school isn't free. [We were] able to feel independent, not depend on an adult or other person.

The sense and value of our work in that moment didn't have only a monetary or economic value but also an educational and political value, because we were able to contribute to our families. We learned a lot, felt free, and entered fully into life. We understood the world in different ways because our work allowed us to share with the others working in the streets, in the communities, in the workplaces and schools. We had a different vision of the world.

So at the age of nine I went to work washing windows and windshields in the Asunción [bus] terminal. I also worked as an itinerant salesperson for nearly two years and at eleven, almost twelve, I was part of an organization of shoe-shiners there in the terminal, which formed part of CONNATs. That's where I began to work in the organization with a more political educational vision and some two years later I began to work as a militant in the organization because I became aware that it was the vehicle for the working class and the poor to struggle and put forth demands. So I was moved forward in life by the work I'd done since childhood in the context of my family since everyone in my family, from the eldest to the youngest, my parents and eight children, all worked.

Just last year I finished secondary school because I had to work to survive and to be able to study. I worked in the mornings, did political work in the afternoons and studied at night. That was my routine for the time I've been in the organization. I'm not complaining. [Work] has enabled me to get to know a different world than the one I'd know by only going to school, [sitting] in front of the television or only [being] in the community. I've moved forward and possibilities have opened up. I've been lucky to get to know other activists with great formation and clarity within the political militancy of our social movement.

In 2001 we held a meeting of Latin America and the Caribbean here in Asunción and eleven countries participated, eleven delegations from organizations and groups of children and adolescents and institutions that worked with children. This was a great inspiration. In 2002 we organized a mobilization demanding free and quality education for children and adolescents where we were able to mobilize around a thousand people in the streets: parents of adolescent and children workers, friends, relatives, people from the communities, and groups and organizations of children who are fighting within this context.

In 2003 about fifteen hundred people went out to protest Article 38 of the Convention on Child Labor of the ILO (International Labor Organization) which advocated making it illegal for children under the age of fourteen to work or be part of any economically productive activity. This article was being ratified in the Paraguayan Parliament and we hadn't been consulted.

The year 2003 was important in the fight against a system that had all the tools, possibilities, and conditions at its disposal to advance its proposals. The movement of child and adolescent workers, along with the efforts of campesino, indigenous, women, and labor movements, were able to stop the free trade agreement [between Paraguay and the United States]. This was an important battle in recovering from a very low level of participation by the popular sectors in the social and political process of our country. Up to then only the campesinos were active and they remained a strong presence and the vanguard of the struggle in our country.

One morning in 2005 President Nicanor Duarte Frutos gave an order to Minister Mercedes Urites, secretary of children and adolescents, to clear the streets of the country of children and adolescent [workers]. So evidently the state, which should be a state of justice, this state considers us, the people, to be things, like trash or rubble of society, which explains the order to "clean" the streets of children and adolescents.

And starting with that order, the minister, Mercedes Urites, began making raids in the streets to take children and adolescents from their families, detain them in centers, take them to homes and, in many cases, to adoption centers. Barracks and other institutions were offered. It was a critical situation and we organized a mobilization and around two thousand children, adolescents, adults, and other movements and organizations turned out for a national march and showed strong support.

In Latin America, as in Asia and Africa, the work that we children do has always existed in the history of our continents and particular countries. Before the Industrial Revolution we children and adolescents worked with our parents in the communities and in the gardens and fields. We were a natural part of daily work and the life of our communities. We played, we worked in the fields, we watched our younger brothers and sisters, and we had a noneconomic view of work, or at least a view that wasn't exclusively economic. We understood work as something natural, but also something that lent dignity to one's personal life, from childhood all the way to old age.

This perspective on work, this understanding of the world, was enslaved to the ideology and model of the conquistador, the Europeans, who brought along a different model of childhood to that held by people of the Caribbean, Latin America, and Africa. [In the European model] children are supposed to only play and study. This is the model imposed on us, even now with the ILO, which has promoted the end of child labor. They've misinterpreted the idea of work that has been held by the indigenous people, campesino communities, and the families of Latin America and the Caribbean. They've imposed models and forms on children and adolescents that don't reflect the realities we experience in all of Latin America and, again, they're bringing the European model here to impose on us.

Forty-seven percent of Paraguayans are children under the age of eighteen, and I think in Latin America that's a fairly normal figure. Nearly half of the population is under eighteen and therefore can't vote or legally take any legal responsibility. Nevertheless, from the age of fourteen and in many cases the age of twelve, we can be imprisoned and forced to take responsibilities for crimes. But we can make no decisions in our country. That's the reality of our continent, our world.

In fact child and adolescent work isn't the main problem or the issue that we should be discussing in relation to the Latin American, Asian, or African situations. Where we need to begin with this discussion of the dangerous work situations in which children and adolescents find themselves, as defined by the ILO, is that these situations are the product of extreme necessity and a consequence of the disregard for the legitimate rights of people. So the ILO, UNICEF, and the international agencies and organizations proposed infant work as the problem, but they're wrong in their conception of work and in their way of reading the reality of children and adolescents. We believe that their reading and their position is paternalistic and adult-centered which says that children and adolescents aren't capable of being an active part of society. And they've avoided every sort of possibility to meet with us in a space of serious, responsible, and honest debate as equals.

Daily life in our country, for the majority: First, we don't have a guarantee that we'll be living in the morning. That's the reality. We aren't guaranteed that we and our families will be able to eat. Day after day, it's a permanent struggle for survival, not just for us but for our families, given the extreme poverty of our country and the continent.

We have to rise early. If we're fortunate enough to be able to study, we study in the mornings or afternoon or at night. In my case, I worked from six in the morning until noon. I directed an organization in the afternoon and worked as a militant in the organization. And at night I went to school.

For one who isn't part of an organization in our country, the choice is more likely between drug addiction and delinquency—vice, delinquency, death, or suicide—versus the struggle for survival in this world. These are the two options and here one has to decide which way to follow. Either one you take, you face an opportunistic society of inequality that doesn't believe in its children or adolescents or the youth, which it keeps in these conditions. That's the reality we face, the extreme poverty in which we live. Many children and adolescents and their families have to skip days eating: one day we eat, the next day we don't; the next day we eat, the next day we don't. Many of our compañero children and adolescents find themselves in the streets or end up on drugs. We're called "delinquents" but that's just another form of resistance to the world that falls on us. That's our reality.

Today on our continent we have President Chávez, who was a child and adolescent worker, a fact that was one of the most important elements driving him into the presidency of the republic. We have Evo Morales, indigenous, who, from his culture itself took on work as an identity from his community and his interpersonal relationships with the world. And we have here Fernando Lugo, who came to understand the experience of children and adolescent workers who arrived with serious proposals, ideas, and analysis responsibly presented to the new government. And these have been the most clear demonstrations that in reality the ILO and the dominant paternalistic and adult-centered thinking has failed in its focus and way of looking at children and adolescents.

Marielle Palau, Base Investigaciones Sociales (BASE Social Research)
"The coup was aimed at facilitating the actions of large corporations"

Interview by Clifton Ross, October 2012
Translation by Luis Ballesteros

Marielle Palau is a researcher at BASE Social Research, a Paraguayan research and education center for movements and civil society organizations, working since the 1980s on rural problems, social movements, human rights, and agribusiness. I contacted her by Skype to get her analysis of the June 2012 impeachment of President Fernando Lugo, which many people considered a coup.

Various sectors had high expectations in 2008, when Lugo took office, but he had to govern having an absolute minority in the Parliament. He was unable to bring any policies to fruition because he was boycotted by a partisan political class, mainly by the traditional parties that had the majority in the Parliament. From the very start of Lugo's term of office, this proved to be a colossal hurdle. On the other hand, Lugo had a fairly progressive electoral program, particularly on some issues that are very dear to the social movements, such as agrarian reform. However, the progress on agrarian reform was minimal, partly because of the lukewarm efforts of the government itself and also because of the stiff opposition from the national Parliament. Although Paraguay has a presidential regime, Parliament has significant political clout. In retrospect, we can even see how a parliamentary coup d'état could have been staged with a certain legal facade; this is indicative of the great power of Parliament in Paraguay.

During Lugo's term, there was a very significant rapprochement between the social movements and the government. In some ways, the social movements considered Lugo's government their friend, and stopped using their historical fighting tools or, at least, substantially reduced social struggles. The social organizations were more concerned with threats to impeach the president than with advancing their own agenda. Hence, they decreased their level of pressure, of mobilization, and of land occupation, which in turn resulted, for example, in practically nonexistent advances in terms of agrarian reform. It also emboldened the right-wing parties to exert considerable pressure on Lugo's management of the government.

Conversely, we did see some important advances under Lugo, especially in relation to agribusiness in Paraguay. The person in charge of the ministry that controlled permits for the entry of transgenic seeds into the country was quite close to all the social organizations and to the entire ecological and environmentalist milieu. Many actions were actually taken in coordination with the social movements to prevent the use of more transgenic seeds in Paraguay. Among the first moves by the coup government of [Federico] Franco was the release of transgenic cotton, and it went on to approve a new release of transgenic maize seeds.

So it's clear that there was always a contradictory situation between the social movements and Lugo's government. For example, the government did not respond to the historical claims of the peasant movement, but the latter basically felt that it should defend Lugo's government, regardless of whether or not it was fulfilling the movement's demands. In political terms, the movement understood Lugo's government as a leap forward that broke more than sixty years of uninterrupted rule by the Colorado Party, and believed that the favorable political momentum would allow continued construction of the democratic project in the country.

Overall, the Lugo years saw a major demobilization of the movements in general, basically because they did not want to put the kind of pressure on the government that the Right would use as a pretext to declare a situation of ungovernability or some such thing. So advances for the movements were negligible. Only very few advances were achieved in the area of agrarian reform.

During Lugo's government, the antiterrorist law was approved. This law directly criminalizes and persecutes the social sector, but still the movements were advocating for the continuity of Lugo's government, because it involved a qualitative leap for the country in terms of democracy.

Progressive governments and social movements

Progressive governments often institutionalize the struggles of social movements by implementing welfare policies—for example against poverty—that tend to fragment social struggles and discipline the movements. So progressive governments tend to play a role of appeasing social forces and channeling their demands and claims through the institutions of the state. The problem is that in Paraguay with an oligarchic, corrupt, and clientelist state, the institutions of the state are not in a position to really respond to the social movements, because the movements make structural demands, and progressive governments, in this case Lugo's, didn't have any type of policy, strategy, or plan to change the country's structure.

So land, the economic model, and all the other issues related to allowing real participation by the movements were not addressed, and the movements' force was used to stave off the advance of the Right but not to promote their own maturation and the advancement of their historical struggles and claims. I think that the problem lies more in the movements than in the governments, since the movements should strive to recover their autonomy and to continue to push forward the people's agenda.

There is where I place the challenge; not in the governments but, above all, on the movements. Supporting a certain presidential candidate should not be tantamount to demobilizing the social movements. In the presence of progressive governments, the appropriate action to take would be for movements to continue pressing such governments to gain ground in structural issues such as land [reform] in Paraguay or the limits that need to be set to the mercantilist logic of capital. So while progressive governments impose a degree of restraint on the movements, at the time they generate certain expectations that changes are possible at a political-electoral level.

We're now realizing that in addition to taking the presidency of the republic, it is of utmost importance to have a larger presence in the national Parliament. The presidency itself is not very useful without power in Parliament. So there is an ongoing struggle to reach a consensus on a presidential candidate, and also an intense discussion and great effort devoted to [developing] the list for Parliament and Senate. We have seen the need to combine various forms of struggle. In other words, electoral struggle is important, but [it must be] combined with the struggle on the streets.

2012 coup in Paraguay

[The 2012 impeachment of Lugo] was an outright coup d'état disguised by a legal gimmick; that is, it used an existing article of the law, but it was directly staged. It is important to take into account that there had been twenty-three attempts to impeach the president since he took office. Prior to the coup, there never were enough votes to set an impeachment in motion. However, this spectre of impeachment was always used as political blackmail against Lugo's government. Whenever Lugo wanted to introduce any measure that would have the slightest effect on the interests of the dominant class, the possibility of impeachment loomed large.

Then suddenly there was a fast-track lawsuit that lasted less than twenty-four hours and by which thirty-nine senators violated the popular will of 70 percent of the Paraguayan population. That was the actual coup d'état, because its implementation and justifying arguments were devoid of legality or legitimacy, as the entire process was flawed and clearly aimed at getting rid of the stones in the shoe, namely, those small things that Lugo's government was doing.

These included restrictions on transgenics and agribusiness in Paraguay, the demand for large soya exporters to comply with environmental regulations, discussions about land unduly awarded to large landowners who now also own large soya fields, as well as some limitations that were being imposed on the incorporation of the Rio Tinto Alcan company in Paraguay. But I'd say that the single most important element behind the coup was that Lugo's government, basically the Iguazú Front, was gaining ground as a political force with a broad basis of popular support and good chances of winning the 2013 elections.

The coup, in keeping with the U.S. "logic," was a preemptive strike. It was a strike not to curb what was being done, but to keep the Paraguay progressive and left-wing sectors from winning next year's elections.

In that context, I would add that there are many signs that the Curuguaty massacre, which took the lives of more than fifteen peasants and police officers, was something orchestrated by the same sectors of the dominant class as an excuse for the impeachment of Lugo. The vast majority of the population and social organizations believe that this was a parliamentary coup very similar to the one staged in Honduras, even if the reaction of the citizens was different.

In the short term, there is no evidence of U.S. involvement in a coup. This only comes to light later. For example, the involvement of the United States in the coup d'état against Salvador Allende wasn't evident at first but only in the course of time. Still, what happened here is very similar to the coup that took place in Honduras. Unlike the model of military-led coups of the 1960s and 1970s, these are parliamentary coups that intend to put up a façade of legality but without any legitimacy, and whose final beneficiary is the dominant class. In Paraguay, the dominant class is highly retrograde, and its political proposals are those of a troglodyte, but it is impressively adept at bringing in large corporations as staunch partisans of the right-wing parties. So the winners from this coup are the soya sector, which is closely linked to a series of global corporations and also, probably, this Canadian corporation, Rio Tinto Alcan. Above all, the coup was aimed at facilitating the actions of large corporations.

Now different types of repression are underway. An ideological persecution is on the rise. Virtually all the employees who had joined the public administration on the basis of competitive selection since 2008 were dismissed for political reasons, which is in serious violation of both national law and international treaties. I think this is an important element. Another important element is the persecution against freedom of speech. Several public media changed their news directors and space is being denied to voices that accuse the coup government from various public media. A vast part of the business press is directly in favor of the coup. The media refuses to cover many of the actions undertaken by civil society, in order to minimize their impact.

On the other hand, there is also a violation of human rights, because some demonstrations and other organized actions that have taken place to express discontent against the coup government have been repressed. Violations of human rights are occurring but unlike other coups in the past, they are much more discreet, as it were. Now they selectively hit the sectors that fight them.

Uruguay

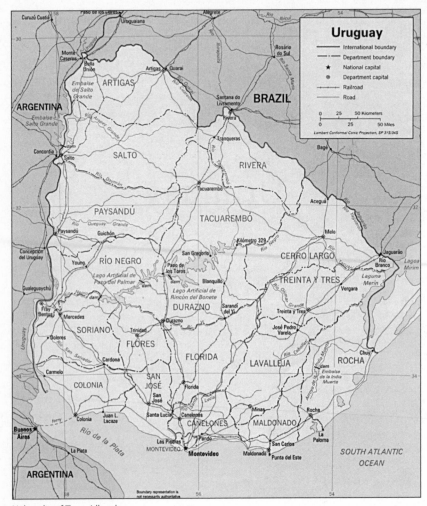

University of Texas Libraries

INTRODUCTION
Movements seek their place in the welfare state

By Raúl Zibechi

S trictly speaking, there are no social movements in Uruguay. However, there are some social movement organizations, as well as a powerful trade union movement and dozens of NGOs that work hand-in-hand with what they call "civil society" and, above all, with a state that has always regulated the life of the population and that permeates all the pores of society but, chiefly, the collective and individual imaginary of Uruguayans.

Actually, the people who live in the expanse of territory where Uruguay is now located did not want this country. The British Crown, in a geopolitical move, decided this country should emerge right at the border between two large South American nations: Argentina and Brazil. "I placed a piece of cotton between two glasses," said Lord Arthur Ponsonby, after wrapping up the treaty with those countries, under the auspices of Great Britain.

The former Banda Oriental (Eastern Bank), which now roughly covers the surface of the Eastern Republic of Uruguay, used to be a border territory. The Spanish and Portuguese Crowns tried to establish military posts there for almost three centuries so they could secure the navigation of the rivers used to ship gold and silver from Upper Peru, now Bolivia. That was the main strategic value of the area. It was practically unpopulated and devoid of natural resources. There were never mines or plantations that would warrant the exploitation of slave labor brought from Africa or uprooted from the indigenous communities.

José Artigas, who led the battles against the Spanish and the Portuguese to achieve independence, created the Federal League (or League of the Free Peoples) in 1814 with some provinces that are now a part of Argentina (Córdoba, Corrientes, Entre Ríos, Santa Fe, Misiones, and the Eastern Bank itself) to avoid becoming subordinated to the powerful oligarchy of Buenos

Aires, which controlled most of the territory that formerly constituted the Viceroyalty of Río de la Plata. When that project succumbed, first to the Portuguese and then to the Brazilian military power, Artigas preferred to flee to exile in Paraguay. He never felt represented by the country born as a British ward in 1830, and never returned. The country was born artificially with only thirty thousand inhabitants and without an economy of its own.

The second important moment in the history of Uruguay was the first third of the twentieth century, namely the period of decline of the British Empire and the rise of the global power of the United States. The political force that ruled almost the entire life of the country, the Red Party (*Partido Colorado*), represented professionals and the owners of midsized and large businesses residing in Montevideo, whereas the National Party was composed of landowners. The Partido Colorado won a short-lived civil war and took José Batlle y Ordóñez to the presidency in 1904. He modernized the country and endowed it with its main institutions, which have largely endured to this day, including nationalizations, social policies to combat poverty, and laws giving women the right to vote. Not until 2004, a century after those reforms were implemented, did the political culture inherited by the Left come together in the Frente Amplio (Broad Front), a full-fledged party that succeeded in taking the government.

Eric Hobsbawm, in his *History of the Twentieth Century*, called Uruguay the only true democracy in Latin America. For a considerable part of the century it was known as "the Switzerland of America," because of the social peace that prevailed and the cultural and racial homogeneity of its population. Some characteristics that were common to all the countries in the region were absent in Uruguay. There was never a true landowning oligarchy, for example, partly because the Banda Oriental was populated rather late, and partly because private property took a long time to consolidate itself there, as it was a territory where the border moved many times.

The armed forces were not important either. For a long time, the armed gangs of the two traditional parties predominated. Then Batlle decided to fragment them into departmental units to make sure that they would not have sufficient unity to pose a threat to his government.

The Catholic Church also arrived late in this part of Río de la Plata, perhaps because there were not as many "souls" to save as there were across the rest of the continent. Hence, in Uruguay the famous alliance between "the sword, the cross and the land"—that is, militaries, church, and landowners—was never as powerful as in other places. This society was much more open, a situation the hundreds of thousands of Spanish and Italian immigrants found when they arrived at the end of the nineteenth century and the beginning of the twentieth, which facilitated their smooth integration into their new country.

This long detour aims to explain two facts that are clearly manifested nowadays: the low level of conflict and, therefore, the weakness of social movements, and the decisive role played by the state, which is able to meet the demands of a sparse and aged population, which has hovered at around three million inhabitants for the last five decades.

A middle-class culture predominates, one that trusts state institutions as guarantors of labor stability and individual progress, while offering frameworks for negotiation that are seldom exceeded from below. The Uruguayan welfare state was very important, both materially and subjectively.

Since the great economic and financial crisis of 2002, which left 40 percent of the population poor, the marginal sectors have grown exponentially and at certain times have managed to organize themselves. However, in 2005, when the Frente Amplio took office, the new Ministry of Social Development attended to their most crucial demands and needs, making major efforts to address poverty.

The trade union movement continues to be the backbone of the popular movement in Uruguay, which is not the case in other Latin American countries, where the poorest sectors have been able to create new movements of indigenous people, landless peasants, and city dwellers.

The foregoing does not mean that there are no organized popular sectors in Uruguay outside the state-centered trade-union logic, but they are weak, consisting of garbage recyclers, housing cooperatives, community radio stations, unemployed people from the country, and people living in illegal urban settlements.

It is likely that in the coming years, when the impact of the global crisis is felt in this part of the world, that these sectors called "marginalized," because they are at the margin of the formal economy and of welfare benefits, will make their voice heard louder than that of the institutionalized trade unions.

Helios Sarthou, ex-senator, Frente Amplio
"Debt generated under a dictatorship has to be considered invalid"

Interview and translation by Clifton Ross, March 2006

The members of Frente Amplio (FA, Broad Front) constructed their party from the ground up over more than forty years by means of coalition-building and grassroots organizing. It survived a dictatorship, the hegemony of a two-party state determined to lock it out, and all the travails of a left third-party, building on victories like the referendum to prevent privatizations at the moment when neoliberalism was the "only alternative," and deft govern-ance of Montevideo, before taking national power in 2004.

The FA represents, therefore, the great power of left coalitions to win elec-toral victories, but also, once in power, the "necessity" of governing from the "center," and it transformed its identity from an opposition movement to a state power.

In the years since it has come to power, the FA, first under Tabaré Vazquez, and then under José Mujica, the latter a former Tupamaro guerrilla, has undeniably benefited the majority of Uruguayans with increased salaries, social benefits, and services. Nevertheless, it has its critics, and among them the renowned Helios Sarthou.

Sarthou is a lawyer and professor of law at the University of the Republic of Uruguay in Montevideo and one of the founders of the FA. I first came across his name when I was strolling around the stalls of the street vendors at the Mercado de los Artesanos beside the Plaza Cagancha, trying to orient myself in the city. I noticed Sarthou's picture and name in the stall of one man who was selling jewelry and with whom I'd struck up a conversation on politics. When I asked the vendor who Helios Sarthou was, he replied, "He's someone who didn't sell out." That's when I knew I would have to talk to him.

Helios Sarthou is part of the left current of the FA and when he was senator and parliamentarian, representing the Movement for Popular Participation (formed out of the National Liberation Movement or Tupamaros), he focused his energies on promoting human and labor rights and community media. He remained in government for nearly a decade when, along with more radical members like Jorge Zabalza and others, he broke relations with the Mujica faction of the FA and formed the Left Current.

Eventually I managed to get the phone number for Sarthou from another vendor and soon found myself on the bus to his apartment in a highrise just a few blocks from the ocean. We conducted the interview in his study, where his desk space was dwarfed by towering bookshelves and stacks of papers. The interview was conducted in mid-March 2006, when Tabaré Vásquez was president of the country. He has since been replaced by former guerrilla-leader José Mujica, although Sarthou's critique of the Frente Amplio remains relevant.

The Frente Amplio has made a fundamental change. It has adopted three or four positions that negate the original Frente of 1971. Back then it was anti-imperialist and anti-capitalist; it defended the organization of agrarian

Helios Sarthou. Photo by Clifton Ross.

reform; it resisted privatizations; it resisted the International Monetary Fund (IMF). You could say that all this has changed since it began to govern, October 31 [2004].

October 31 was a colossal triumph in this country. I'd never seen people that way, moving through the streets of Montevideo and in the interior. It was a real joy because the Left had won against the traditional parties for the first time in the nation's history. Then, beginning on March 1 of last year, the situation began to deteriorate. As of March 1 this year, they've been governing a year and, first off, they've completely given in to the IMF, signing a letter of intention to dismantle the Central Bank, which governs macroeconomic policy, to convert it into a technical service organization of the IMF and against the political will [of the people].

Never has there been such a firm, hard dependence; it's much worse than what existed before even under the traditional parties. The major actor there is Senator Astori, an economist who, evidently, as things go, was made minister in the United States so as to guarantee that he was really going to manage the economy of the country.[1] This letter of intention establishes the privatizations and all the rubrics and components for orientation to the IMF recipe. Beyond this, we've been tied to conditions of payment of the foreign debt and these conditions force us to imitate the economic policy of our rivals: We imitate the Colorado and Blanco Parties as we increase our dependence. This phenomenon of dependence has meant that we have no resources to pay for social expenses like Social Security, the costs of national health insurance and education, all of which has been important in our country.

So the payment on the foreign debt is going to absorb all our resources. This is going to have grave consequences. [And yet] Law 16.173 approved by the Vienna Convention establishes that debt generated under a dictatorship has to be considered invalid because there was no valid consent given by the people. We could have established that the debt generated under eleven years of dictatorship we wouldn't have to pay. The law exists, and the Convention establishes it, but Minister Astori capitulated and was named "minister of the year" or some such thing. Of course. How could they not name him "minister of the year" if he's implementing the policy of capital and international interests?

The other law is 13.751. I'm giving you the numbers so that no one will think I'm pulling this out of the air. This law was approved by the International Pact on Economic, Social and Cultural Rights of the UN, PIDESC. It's the first article, numeral two, which allows the foreign debt to be paid over time or postponed if it compromises the essential means of the country's existence, and we're in that situation. We have a tremendous problem of emigration of our people, since there's no work. There's an obvious crisis in health, all this to say that it's affecting our means of subsistence. It would have been possible to negotiate with the IMF and say, "Gentlemen, we're under protection of the Pact and the Vienna Convention. We're not going to pay the debt the dictatorship generated. Find the delinquents and make them pay yourselves."

The Left Current has stated this publicly; we continue to say that. But the government has bent because it's in a position of absolute dependence. [For the government to] maintain this would be to lose the protection of an extension on payments of the debt. Because this is worse: the Left rising to govern and continuing with the policy of extending the debt on the false economic assumption that they'll be able to attract investors. And what happened? No investors arrived because this market is very small so investors only are drawn by dirty projects, like this paper mill project that will leave us contaminated, that will ruin our land, so fit for cattle, and change it into a monoculture of eucalyptus, which will contaminate. That's the investment that's coming, that or the financial sector that caused a crisis in 2002. Yes, there was capital for perpetrating financial fraud, but not to generate good clean work because it's not worth it to come here.

Gustavo, Pablo, and Noelia, Galpón de Corrales
"The solutions have to come from the people"

Interview and translation by Clifton Ross, March 2006

I came across the newsstand of the anarchists from Barrikada as I strolled around downtown Montevideo. It looked like any other of the kiosks that dot the city, except for the selection of books. Certainly there were the usual maga-zines—Good Housekeeping, Elle, and Reader's Digest, and their equivalents in Spanish—but they also had anarchist books and zines.

One of the guys staffing the kiosk was Pablo, a clean-cut young man who offered to take me to visit the Galpón of Corrales, a community center in a working-class district of Montevideo that exemplified the DIY approach to life for which the anarchist community worldwide is known. Later, over coffee in a local café, I expressed my admiration, and my skepticism, of anarchism, and in particular the anarchists in Venezuela who were in the opposition to the Bolivarian process. "Yes," he said, "we know about that. That's why we broke with the Venezuelan anarchists." Why was that, I asked. "Precisely because they were opposing Chávez, who's played a crucial role for progressive social change and taken a strong anti-imperialist line on behalf of all Latin America. Incredulous, I tried to clarify. "Wait, you mean you broke with your fellow anarchists in defense of a head of state representing a government?" The irony wasn't lost on Pablo. "Yes," he confirmed, with a slight smile. "Because we're not anarchists in a nineteenth-century sense but anarchists of the here and now." He went on to talk about territoriality and the project of the Galpón of Corrales which he invited me to visit with him. I accepted.

We arrived early one rainy autumnal March evening at the Galpón, and after Noelia had taken me on a tour of the center, from the kitchen and dining room into the community radio station, we stopped into the library to conduct the interview.

Gustavo: We were working on a neighborhood paper. We were somewhat connected to the conflicts of FUNSA, the factory across the street with a long history of struggle, and the need arose for a food pantry in the neighborhood. We were getting to know the problems of the neighborhood and it became clear to us the need for a community café where we could bring neighbors together. Right away there was a proposal for a community radio [station] for communication. Gradually other activities were added on. This place was a bar that closed with the factory, and it then became the location where all the social projects and activities were centralized as a main social center.

Corpograf: Demonstration to protest the Frente Amplio government's jailing of workers occupying and producing at their workplace at CORPOGRAF, March 2006.
Photo by Clifton Ross.

We started with the café in Villa Española; the radio [station] started in a little place on Avenida 8 de Octubre and, along with the paper, we began putting together little collectives of neighbors and youths. That was in 1999. On March 14 the café started functioning here. Then sometime in 2000 and the beginning of 2001 all the activities were brought together here in this center as a social center to coordinate different activities functioning as commissions as well as by general assembly.

We've worked together in all the struggles of the neighborhood, participating in gatherings between neighborhoods, internal meetings, and working on health issues. In 2003, for instance, there was a big push to get health care for children, and we worked with the local neighborhood health clinic on that.

One of the strong responses of the neighborhood came in one of many struggles we've had since 1999. This one came when there was an attempt to evict us. We'd been here in this location since the bar closed, sometime around the end of 2003 or the beginning of 2004. The owners tried to evict us and a big assembly happened here, with more than three hundred people. There was a march and the street was closed down and the mayor's office intervened to keep us from being evicted.

This is also an artistic space: every Friday night there's an artistic event. Today, for instance, the jugglers are coming for a variety show of jugglers from all the neighborhoods. The Galpón de Corrales is also a meeting space for artists, and there's also open space for *candombe*[2] and a theater group called Churrinche that has come to present its work of recovering indigenous culture.

There are different artistic expressions that intersect here in the Galpón and that's the objective: to gather diverse artistic expressions, respond to the different problems of the neighborhood, and build the social center as an environment for the participation of neighbors. We've made progress in that area, and in organizing the social development of the neighborhood.

Pablo: This all arises from certain important ideas. Territoriality has been an important concept in all this. Territoriality implies the neighborhood creates its own organizational expressions to resolve its basic problems. Here no one can bring readymade solutions, be it the state or the mayor, but the solutions have to come from the people, from their own experience. Of course in the beginning a lot of work has to be done, but the important thing is that the people doing it be [living] here in the neighborhood. They're from the neighborhood, and we aren't; and so we could easily be kicked out, something that seems right to us.

This concept of territoriality is one of the ideas we're working with, and the other, which we've talked about, is the "anarchism of the here and now." Here there's not discussion or too much theory, and you won't find people talking about anarchism, but rather practicing it in essence. And also there's absolutely no divorce from the practical necessity of politics. It's true that it's a slow process, and everything happens slowly here, each thing in its time, but that's how it all happens. Whatever support that comes is a result of work and achievement of the people here. It's having a stake, and that's a stake in the territory.

Noelia: The majority of those who participate here in the Galpón live very nearby and there are compañeros who, for the work being done, travel here from farther away just to participate, but they're the minority. The majority are from here in the neighborhood. So, for instance, the radio is going to be transmitting in a little while. They transmit Thursdays, Fridays, Saturdays, and Sundays. They're here after dinner all week, and bread is baked today. The library is open every day.

We work horizontally by means of commissions that develop the tasks and promote participation, and each one opts for what it wants. We also try to promote the arts, as was already mentioned, and all this within the neighborhood. But also, since we've seen how this works here in the Galpón and we've arrived at a certain level [of organization], we've also seen the need for that organization in other neighborhoods. In 2003 we had the first meeting of autonomous neighborhood organizations here in the Galpón and we're looking forward to the fourth such meeting next month [April 2006]. What these gatherings consist of is the coordination and exchange of different neighborhood experiences here in Montevideo and other places like Canelones and Rocha Maldonado. We're interested in other experiences so as to be able to develop and strengthen people's power. We're invested in that also: not just in working here, but also together with other compañeros in other places who are doing the same thing.

In these meetings people talk about what they're doing in their locale, but also we talk about how those experiences can be strengthened. We exchange books that we don't have from libraries and support projects that are just getting started, like radio stations or libraries.

Gustavo: Community radio is one of the tools, but, in keeping with the concept of territoriality, it's important to emphasize that you can't organize a neighborhood with just one tool. That's why the social center tries to create and promote different kinds of tools for organizing a neighborhood. The idea of territoriality is an attempt to respond to a fragmented and dispersed working class that no longer exists as it did dozens of years ago. The gathering spaces of the working class, if they exist, are weakened, like the unions. They haven't lost their validity, but there are also huge pockets of unemployed throughout the neighborhoods, so new instruments need to be created.

Territoriality is a political concept that has to be included with other important libertarian ideas. We try to build horizontal relations, direct democracy, and direct action at every level. As Pablo was saying, the café is moved forward by the neighbors. This is what we advocate: that the solution to the problems involve those directly affected. So the café, the dinners, the community bakery, the community garden, the radio, all that is moved forward by the neighbors, the youth, the people themselves. There are no leaders; there's a horizontalism and so collective participation is essential to us.

A lot of kids drop out of school or don't do well in school because of other social problems. So we work in this area, strengthening the community radio, creating a recycler's cooperative and organizing other productive enterprises; encouraging self-organized projects to resolve problems of unemployment and family support; working to build and coordinate interneighborhood unity. We do all this from a libertarian perspective, but we know that we work in a society with great contradictions that we have to confront: that the dominant ideology permeates the oppressed class; that the subjectivity of our people is really regressive so that the ideological struggle is one of the struggles to be undertaken at this time and in that context there's the idea of the here and now, the daily struggle. That's where the great obstacles have to be met and overcome. The ideological struggle continues to be one of the pillars of social change. That's the instrument that we believe we have to use today, and the social centers have to be built up in all the neighborhoods.

Really, the ideological struggle has to be done in many areas. We believe that for social change to take place it's not enough to promote an existential activity. You have to respond to urgent problems but also find way to conscientize the people and develop a sense of class. The consciousness of class has to be recuperated. The subjectivity of class and the subjectivity of struggle have to be regained, the sense of belonging to a class, to work from there to dynamize the contradictions with the opposing class, with the oppressor class. And this takes place in the day-to-day struggle with the things of daily life. It's done at the round table, with collective gatherings; with the youth; in the workshops, in getting to know the experience of other neighborhoods; it's done in getting to know popular culture, and also in the community library. Those are all elements of the ideological struggle, feeding and strengthening the subjectivity of our people.

One of the issues in all the neighborhoods is daily nutrition, feeding the children. There's a lot of malnutrition and misery in the homes and a lot of social disintegration. Out of that come many other problems, like the high dropout rate in the schools and low educational levels of children, which are connected to limited access to food. The lead poisoning in children in many neighborhoods is also related to malnutrition. With few vitamins and low nutrition, children are more likely to contract illnesses and to be vulnerable to contaminants like lead. We work a lot with neighborhood health centers and now we're without a pediatric doctor in the neighborhood. So the people here went out to block a main highway here in a direct action and as a result we got a pediatric doctor on contract, sent out from the ministry of health. So health is one of the issues important to the neighborhood.

Another issue here is work. That's why we've tried to develop projects of productive enterprises like cooperatives, microenterprises that lead to larger productive projects. There's the community bakery where we bake the bread for our café, but also families get their bread there. The community garden is another project, and various families let us use their land and benefit from the garden, and it also provides vegetables for the community café.

IWD: Women playing the traditional Afro-Uruguayan candombe drums at an International Women's Day march in Montevideo, 2006. Photo by Clifton Ross.

Since last December we've been working on the Cooperative of Artisanal Production "Los Galponeros," which does homemade production of food for businesses or on demand. That cooperative is just beginning, but we're trying to push forward and include more unemployed compañeros. We started with making sweet breads, puddings for Christmas, and other holidays. Now, after the holidays, they're making sports food, sandwich trays, biscuits, and different kinds of other food.

Another productive activity, which we think is one of the most important, is the sorter's cooperative. In the neighborhood with the unemployment and the deindustrialization that happened with the factory closing, the cooperative of the garbage recyclers was formed. It's a very small project of some sorters who come here to the Galpón. It could be anything from plastic bags to office paper or cardboard or metal. Organizations in the neighborhood contact the Galpón and the Galpón talks with the workers and they go out and gather the materials, carry them away and split the profits. Right now this cooperative is very small, but they've managed to sell directly to the industrial center and bypass the intermediaries. That's what we're trying to avoid [the intermediaries] so that the cooperative sorters will have sufficient stock, have access to weighing, transport, and so forth to be able to sell directly to the factories themselves and avoid being exploited as they are these days.

Argentina

Argentina

- —— International boundary
- —·— Province boundary
- ★ National capital
- ⊙ Province capital
- ┼┼┼ Railroad
- —— Road

The city of Buenos Aires comprises a federal district.

| 0 | 100 | 200 | 300 Kilometers |
| 0 | 100 | 200 | 300 Miles |

Lambert Conformal Conic Projection, SP 25S/80S

University of Texas Libraries

INTRODUCTION
New movements show another world is possible

By Marie Trigona

Argentina's 2001 economic collapse gave birth to social movements that showed that another world is possible. Neighbors gathered in popular assemblies, workers took over their factories, and unemployed workers known as *piqueteros* staged massive road blockades, all rebelling against austerity and demanding an end to impunity for crimes against humanity, while employing horizontal and democratic organizing methods.

Crisis spurred this upsurge of activity, but it arose in a highly politicized country with a long history of struggle—rooted in the traditions of the nineteenth-century European immigrants who came to find work in the "breadbaskets" in the interior of the country and the industrial ports of the Río de la Plata.

Argentina is the second largest country in South America, bounded by the Andes on the west and the Atlantic Ocean on the east. It shares borders with Chile to the west, Bolivia and Paraguay to the north, and Brazil and Uruguay to the northeast. The country's political and cultural life developed around its urban centers; one-third of its population of forty million lives in Buenos Aires, a capital with a reputation of being the Paris of South America.

Not unlike the sixteenth-century Spaniards who landed along the Río de la Plata with dreams of a land and river of silver, nineteenth-century immigrants sought to *"hacer la América"*—to pick money off the streets of Buenos Aires. Still, it was not a river of silver or streets paved with gold but cattle, sheep, and wheat that fueled Argentina's rapid growth and prosperity.

The first recorded visit by Europeans to Argentina dates to 1516. The expedition led by Juan Díaz de Solis landed in the Río de la Plata basin to declare the territory for Spain. However, the majority of the soldiers were killed in confrontations with Indians. Juan de Garay established the second and lasting settlement in Buenos Aires in 1580.

With Spain's colonial efforts focused on the territories of the north, in the Southern Cone an independent spirit prospered among the new generation of *criollos*, Spaniards born in the new world. Severe restrictions on trade in the rest of South America created resentment, and by 1776 Buenos Aires had become a flourishing port and haven for smugglers.

Argentina abolished slavery in 1813, three years before it declared its independence from Spain. Following disputes between centrists and federalists, the country established a formal constitution in 1853, and a national unity government in 1860.

In the middle of the nineteenth century, young workers from Italy, Spain, and elsewhere in Europe began flooding the streets of Buenos Aires and other cities, seeking work in the fertile pampas—the interior plains that produced cheap wheat and meat for the European market.

The immigrants brought their political traditions, including syndicalism and anarchism. At the turn of the century, Italian, Spanish, Russian, Slavic, and German workers founded the country's first unions, which functioned as anarcho-syndicalist federations, among them the Federación Obrera Regional Argentina (FORA), established in 1901.

The social conditions the immigrant laborers encountered provided fertile ground for social discontent. Argentina had established a constitutional government but in practice, corruption, clientelistic relations, and *caudillismo* denied real representation to Argentina's residents whether they were native or not. While Argentina had the highest wages in Latin America, urban workers lived in overcrowded *conventillos* (tenements) and worked in harsh conditions for little pay. They organized not only in their workplaces, with militant strikes, but also in their communities, staging rent strikes, establishing schools, and opening libraries.

To open lands for the expanding wheat and cattle industries, General Julio Argentino Roca launched the "Campaign of the Desert" against the indigenous in the Patagonia. According to historian Osvaldo Bayer, the 1879 campaign amounted to genocide; it resulted in the mass killing of thousands, "the enslavement of indigenous along the frontlines," and the seizure of thirty million hectares of land.

Tango spanned the prosperity and struggle of the late nineteenth and early twentieth centuries, reflecting the nation's African roots. Tango emerged in the working-class neighborhoods of Buenos Aires to become the ballad of Argentina, which would convert the outrage of the years into music, as author Jorge Luis Borges wrote.[1]

Peronism shaped twentieth-century Argentine politics more than any other political movement. Juan Domingo Perón came to power in 1946, and under a populist doctrine that espoused mediating tensions between social classes.

Perón served as president three times, creating a movement based on social justice and economic independence, forging the path of corporatist capitalism over socialism. Peronism embraced policies that generated employment and narrowed the gap between the rich and the poor—a major departure from previous constitutional governments and dictatorships that had repressive relationships with Argentina's working class.

From 1946 to 1962, the government supported state-protected industrialization, and invested in the infrastructure necessary for development. Perón's second wife, Eva Perón, became an iconic figure, beloved for her advocacy on behalf of the country's poorest. She also supported a women's movement; Argentinian women finally got the right to vote in 1947.

The military overthrew democratic governments in 1962 and 1966, actively persecuting Peronism and its supporters and driving Peron himself out of the country. He spent eighteen years in exile, mostly in Franco's Spain, since Franco had been a big influence on him.

In 1966 the military took on the task of repressing the inevitable social conflict with their decision to do away with traditional politics through the institutionalization of state repression. The Left regained power during this period, with growing unrest culminating among union activists and students. A year after the French upsurge in May 1968, rebellion hit Argentina in the city of Córdoba. The 1969 alliance of workers and students produced violent resistance against the military dictatorship of General Juan Carlos Ongonía.

The political conflict created instability and opened the opportunity for the military to launch a coup to suppress the Left. In the two years preceding the 1976 coup, Isabel Perón's government launched a severely repressive campaign. The right-wing death squad "Triple A," or Argentine Anticommunist Alliance, indiscriminately attacked anyone they suspected as a dissident. The National Commission on the Disappearance of Persons (CONEDEP) reported in 1983 that the Triple A killed more than 1,500 people. The methodology of state repression climaxed on March 24, 1976, with a military junta that ushered in unimaginable tactics of terror. The dictatorship, led by General Jorge Videla, disappeared more than thirty thousand people, with the overwhelming majority being labor activists and sympathizers.

One of the most important literary records of the abuses that occurred during the Videla dictatorship came from journalist Rodolfo Walsh. His "Open Letter from a Writer to the Military Junta" continues to be read

Faces of the disappeared. Photo by Clifton Ross.

throughout the world as attestation of a writer "committed to giving testimony in difficult times."

The letter described how economists trained by the conservative Chicago School implemented the core neoliberal policies after the advent of the military government, and exposed the abuses carried out by the junta as part of a regional plan to wipe out opposition to an economic model that created widespread inequality.

"The real salary of workers has dropped 40 percent," Walsh wrote. "They are freezing salaries with the butts of rifles while prices are soaring at the point of a bayonet, destroying any form of collective bargaining, prohibiting union assemblies, making work hours longer and raising unemployment to record levels. When the workers protest, the dictatorship calls them subversive, kidnaps entire union assemblies. In some cases, the bodies turn up dead and in other cases they never turn up."[2]

Walsh was one of those who was disappeared. As he delivered the letter, he was gunned down, then taken to the ESMA (Escuela de Mecánica de la Armada, Navy Mechanics School), the most notorious of the more than 365 clandestine detention centers operated during the dictatorship. Survivors describe ESMA as Argentina's Auschwitz.

Many of the victims disappeared in this terror campaign were drugged and dropped into the sea from military planes in the death flights. Inside the ESMA and other clandestine detention centers, the military set up maternity wards for pregnant female prisoners. An estimated five hundred babies were born inside detention centers, taken from their mothers, and appropriated by military or civilians with ties to the junta.

During the dictatorship, much of the population remained silent due to the censorship and terror imposed by the military. Those who did not stay silent risked being disappeared themselves. The Mothers of the Plaza de Mayo began protesting on April 30, 1977. Having visited police stations, prisons, judicial offices, and churches but finding no answers, the Mothers began to do weekly vigils, wearing white head scarves to symbolize the diapers of their lost and disappeared children. Nothing could stop their protest, not even physical attacks or endless threats. In 1977, three of the founding Mothers and two French nuns, who supported the efforts of the Mothers, also became part of "the disappeared."

The transition to democracy was stifled by the prolonged impunity granted under the Due Obedience and Full Stop laws, which prevented members of the military from facing criminal prosecution. During the 1990s, military officials who had tortured and assassinated so-called dissidents during the junta were often spotted at nightclubs, vacation spots and high-profile restaurants.

Even with judicial roadblocks, human rights groups continued to push for investigations into the disappearance of tens of thousands. Founded in 1995, H.I.J.O.S. (Daughters and Sons for Identity and Justice against Forgetting and Silence) developed the *escrache* ("exposure") protest held at the home or workplace of an unpunished criminal as a method to deliver justice. The Grandmothers of the Plaza de Mayo continued to demand that the kidnapped children be returned to their families. The Grandmothers have recovered the true identity of 107 of the estimated 500 missing children now in their thirties.

In 2005, with the support of then-president Néstor Kirchner, the Supreme Court overturned amnesty for the military. According to the human rights NGO the Center for Legal and Social Studies (CELS), more than fifteen hundred former members of the armed and security forces are facing charges of human rights abuses during the dictatorship. While Argentina's government has taken the lead in supporting efforts to try former military and police for rights abuses carried out during the junta years, justice has been slow.

The junta needed to disappear a generation of activists to implement the neoliberal model, which the leaders of the 1990s continued to use. Carlos Menem, president from 1990 to 1999, intensified the policies implemented during the dictatorship. To solve hyperinflation in 1991, Menem, with the blessing of the international financial community, masterminded a radical economic plan. They dismantled the public sector, privatized, and liberalized the economy to free trade. They also invented the system of convertibility to strangle exports by fixing parity between dollar and peso. This process resulted in the closure of thousands of factories. Corrupt union leaders and politicians balked at the deindustrialization of the economy while the IMF touted Argentina as a South American success.[3]

By 2001, the country exploded, in a total economic collapse. Thousands of factories had closed and businesses went bankrupt. More than half of the population was living in poverty, and unemployment rates soared above 27 percent. The people took to the streets banging pots and pans. They shouted, "*Que se vayan todos!*" ("All of them must go!"), and the protests forced out four presidents in less than three weeks following December 20, 2001. Police killed thirty-one people over the course of two days of popular rebellion.

Hundreds of neighborhood assemblies came together to meet people's basic needs and create a space for mutual solidarity. Alternative media counterinformed. Unemployed workers demanded dignity. And workers in bankrupt businesses occupied their workplaces and questioned the entire logic of capitalism.

At the height of the crisis in 2001, the *piqueteros* or unemployed workers' organizations (MTDs) spread throughout the nation, especially around the crumbled suburban industrial belts of Buenos Aires, Córdoba, and Rosario. The MTDs (Unemployed Workers' Movement), not a party or a union, took direct action to put public pressure on the government to obtain provisions of food supplies, basic necessities, social policy measures, and improvements in the infrastructure. They took their name from their method, the *piquete*, or road blockade. As unemployed workers, they lacked the strike as a weapon, but the blockade offered a way to tangibly disrupt commerce.

The late 1990s became synonymous with the *corte de ruta* [cutting off or blocking the road], which emerged in areas such as Cutral Có in Southern Neuquén and Tartagal/General Mosconi in Northern Salta, where the oil industry was privatized and restructured under Menem's administration.

More than thirteen thousand people work in Argentina's occupied factories and businesses, also called "recovered enterprises." The sites, which number more than two hundred, include hotels and ceramics factories, balloon manufacturers, suit factories, printing shops, and transport companies.

Many of Argentina's recovered enterprises borrowed the slogan "Occupy, Resist, Produce" from Brazil's Landless Workers' Movement (MST). First, the workers occupied their workplace, in a number of different circumstances, widely in the context of a fraudulent bankruptcy. Then, they had to defend the occupation and resist forceful eviction attempts. Production was frequently started when the workers were resisting and fighting for legality. Often, actions such as highway blockades, street protests, and even threatening to destroy the sites of production accompanied the occupations.

Many feel that, despite political and market challenges, Argentina's recovered enterprises represent one of the most advanced strategies in defense of the working class and resistance against capitalism and neoliberalism. Worker-run businesses have battled for laws to protect workers' jobs, opened legal doors for other recovered enterprises, and supported community projects and other initiatives for social change. The three hundred or so recovered enterprises in Argentina, Venezuela, Brazil, and Uruguay have built an extensive international solidarity network.

The Kirchner governments have reversed some of the policies implemented during the '90s. The Kirchners' policies would be unthinkable if the social movements that emerged from the political vacuum of 2001 had not transformed the political landscape of Argentina. The economy has shown robust growth since Néstor Kirchner took office in 2003, and grew at an 8 percent rate in 2011. During his term, Kirchner apologized for the military's disgrace during the dictatorship and aligned his government with the regional integration efforts of the MERCOSUR South American Trade Block.

His successor and wife, Cristina Fernández de Kirchner, has promoted Evita Peron–style social reform. In her latest term, Fernández de Kirchner won with an overwhelming 54 percent of the votes. Her economic policy has included the renationalization of the oil giant YPF and Aerolineas Argentinas. Another turning point since 2003 has been the new media law to democratize media access and open up the airwaves to community media.

Abortion is still illegal in the country except in extreme cases of rape. However, as feminists continue to fight to legalize abortion, progress has been made in other areas. Argentina approved a gay marriage law in 2010, making it the first Latin American country where same-sex couples can wed.

Transgenetic soy has largely fueled Argentina's rapid economic recovery. And the environment, food sovereignty, campesinos, and indigenous are paying the consequences of a monoculture industry. The cultivation of genetically modified crops has become a regional trend, with Argentina as the world's third largest exporter of GMO soy. While the tax on soy has funded many of the nation's social programs, its production threatens to ravage the nation. Once profits from soy dry up, Argentina will be left with only the devastating impact of monoculture: displaced rural populations, nutrient-depleted soil, deforestation, and poisoned communities. Transnational mining efforts along the Andean Cordillera have also produced similar outcomes of irreversible environmental devastation.

Argentina's economic model touches on historic challenges for the nation and its legacy of Peronist style leadership. The nation's economic recovery came at the cost of co-optation of much of the spontaneous protest that emerged from the 2001 crisis. And the issue of impunity and state repression continues to challenge its road to recovery, with new disappearances, such as that of Jorge Julio López,[4] and the assassination of campesino leaders resisting the GMO soy model.

Diego Benegas Loyo, H.I.J.O.S. (Daughters and Sons for Identity and Justice Against Forgetting and Silence)
"Silence and fear seem to work together, but they also go away together"

Testimony and research by Diego Benegas Loyo, November 2012

Diego Benegas Loyo has been closely involved with H.I.J.O.S. as a researcher and frequent participant in their actions, and offered this reflection for inclusion in the book. We found it so interesting that we departed from our strict interview format.

A rich history predates H.I.J.O.S.'s *escraches*, which arose in postdictatorship Argentina.

Claiming to "reorganize" the country, Argentina's last dictatorship launched a large-scale plan of systematic extermination in 1976 that "disappeared" about thirty thousand people, mostly political dissidents. After the junta fell in 1983, the first democratic postdictatorship government tried and sentenced some members of the military regime.

But this first effort at investigation and accountability came to an early halt. Soon, Congress passed new laws granting virtual impunity, first, establishing a sixty-day deadline for starting prosecution and then limiting responsibility to only top generals, who were later forgiven by broad presidential pardon decrees. By the 1990s, this particular version of "national reconciliation" configured a situation where most agents of concentration camps continued their normal lives unknown to the public or their neighbors, and nobody was accountable for the genocide. Within this policy of "forgive and forget" torturers could even recount their deeds on mass media without fearing prosecution. In those days, Capt. Adolfo Scilingo shockingly went public with his participation in "death flights" that threw drugged prisoners from helicopters into the sea—the law had granted impunity. It was 1995, and H.I.J.O.S. was about to form.

H.I.J.O.S. was never alone; on the contrary, it built from a long legacy of human rights activism. Its familial name (literally, "daughters and sons") linked to the tradition of the "Mothers" and "Grandmothers" of Plaza de Mayo. It also continued their spirit, and the radicalism of their claims: One of H.I.J.O.S.'s first slogans was, "We don't forgive, we don't forget, we don't reconcile." H.I.J.O.S., however, innovated in substantial ways. It gradually opened its membership, thus not all H.I.J.O.S. are biologically linked to the disappeared, and significantly, it organized horizontally: using consensus instead of voting, developing weekly assemblies and yearly nationwide congresses, and avoiding hierarchies, leaders, and representatives.

The word "*escrache*" comes from the *Lunfardo* slang of Buenos Aires City found in most tango lyrics and means ruining somebody's image. Now it's widely used to name this particular type of demonstration. H.I.J.O.S. performed its first escrache on January 16, 1997, at Sanatorio Mitre, a hospital in the Buenos Aires commercial district of Once. The target was Jorge Luis Magnaco, a physician who attended disappeared women giving birth in the clandestine detention center at the Navy Mechanics School (ESMA); the mothers were later killed, their children appropriated. This escrache consisted mainly of distributing flyers in Magnaco's waiting room, letting his patients know about his involvement.

Later, escraches evolved greatly, incorporating music, theater, giant puppets, trucks, and sometimes even a large crane. H.I.J.O.S. started taking months to work in neighborhoods, often returning later for other actions. While some escraches involved hundreds of people, others did not take to the streets. In the first years, H.I.J.O.S.'s escraches changed in two essential

Poster: Announcement of an escrache action by H.I.J.O.S., 2006. Photo by Clifton Ross.

directions: their focus moved from the target person to the neighbors, and their goal evolved from denunciation to community-building.

They entered a new period in 2005, when Congress and the Supreme Court revoked and nullified the laws and decrees that had granted impunity. Since then, and perhaps in parallel with all the Left, a closer, more complex relation with the government has made the organization revise deeply its goals and methods. At the same time, other groups have taken escraches and used them in different ways, even some that H.I.J.O.S. would not approve of; escraches have expanded and diversified, even transcending their origins in H.I.J.O.S.

Escraches as a window on new ways of building power

However, it is undeniable that escraches are crucial to understand H.I.J.O.S., and H.I.J.O.S. is crucial to comprehend the emergence of new ways of building power. Escraches are a specific approach to what politics is, what it means, and what it does. As seen from the escrache, an H.I.J.O.S. way of building power centers on affective links, aims to change cultural patterns, and works with ethical values. With these three foundations, escraches put in action a theory of the effects of the genocide in the social body presenting a proposal for a way out; they work with an implicit theory of what society is, how it works, and a conception of how it could be.

Escraches worked with feelings at multiple points. Using the streets of the neighborhood for a public political event was a central part of this. Escraches defied the "untouchable" state of the agents of state terrorism, breaking walls of fear. They also worked by breaking silence on topics that were not discussed publicly at the time, for beyond the demonstration proper, its most powerful element was that it was *public*: done in a public space, in view of everyone. The public character of the escrache betrayed some invisible code of silence. Silence and fear seem to work together but, interestingly, they also go away together. "[It is incredible] when you face the assassin and you shout in his face that you know what he did, and you know who he is," an H.I.J.O.S. Mendoza member said in 2002.

Here we see another product of the genocide: the isolated individual. H.I.J.O.S. aims at rebuilding networks of solidarity, for it argues the dictatorship attacked mutual trust, isolating individuals, cutting their links, specifically horizontal links. For state terrorism is a system of terror but it is also a system of control. Its propaganda campaign completed an intervention aimed at turning social beings into individuals who would relate only vertically, up to their superiors and the state and down to their subordinates, this is, students, employees, wives, children. The Argentine dictatorship pioneered the neoliberal societal project, which requires people to envision themselves as individuals. Cutting horizontal emotional links was part of this construction. Restoring them is part of fighting both neoliberalism and the subjective effects of genocide.

Here we might stop to think how a tactic based on rejection can build solidarity, for the escrache isolates and rejects *one* individual. However, it is not the case of a community rejecting its weak members, as the media often portray. It is a small group signaling to the neighborhood community that one of its members holds special status, as he avoids legal prosecution for crimes against humanity: torture, kidnapping, and mass murder. He is untouchable and enjoys privileges granted by law and the government; the escrache invites the neighbors not to harm him or attack him. Escraches are not revenge. They invite neighbors to stop yet another privilege, this time granted by default by the neighborhood: the secrecy about his deeds. In fact, some of the speeches that close the escrache's demonstration declare, "Now the neighbors know." It is up to the neighbors to decide what to do about it. Escraches change feelings from fear, suspicion, and isolation to defiance, trust, and solidarity. They change what we think of the world and our place in it. They aim at cultural patterns.

Escraches are a counterhegemonic force. They show dissenting voices, breaking the illusion of uniform opinions. Their structure mirrors the actions of state terrorism, which attempted to homogenize society by silencing and disappearing dissent. Thus escraches assume a society composed of a multiplicity of voices and opinions; their intervention is directed at changing meanings, uses, and customs. By staging dissenting voices, escraches break the illusion that opinions are homogeneous. They make the point that not everyone agrees with the official version of "national reconciliation." As the illusion of "reconciliation" had an important role in justifying the state of impunity, the escrache's intervention aims directly at the mechanisms that legitimize the status quo. However, there is more to the escrache than just showing dissent.

Escraches also mirror (replicate in reverse) the campaign of disappearances. While state terrorism relied on demobilization, the escrache aims to mobilize. While state terror happened by the anonymous hand of secret task forces, the escrache relies on identifying and publicizing. "The neighborhood, like politics, and like justice, does not belong to them; it belongs to the neighbors, who are here and do not want to live with a genocidal [criminal]," an H.I.J.O.S. capital member shouted into a megaphone in front of the house of a dictatorship police officer. Rather than promoting silence, escraches open a forum for discussion of national politics in neighborhood streets.

In the last decade, the state has adopted a new human rights policy, restarting trials for genocide, recovering sites, instituting holidays, and including related content in school curricula. As have other human rights organizations, H.I.J.O.S. has developed a more complex relation with the government, participating in different events and spaces. This process, however, is not free of contradictions and conflicts. With these trials, for example, the police only reluctantly search for their comrades, and some judges, citing "humanitarian reasons," have commuted sentences to house imprisonments, which police have often failed to enforce. For this reason, taking part in state projects and judicial trials does not mean that H.I.J.O.S. abandons the street. Informed by neighbors of sentenced genocide criminals who were breaking their house arrest, H.I.J.O.S. has done escraches at their houses, demanding that they be sent to common prisons. In fact, beyond inviting people to attend as audiences and informing the public with online "diaries of the trials," H.I.J.O.S. continues to mobilize by "accompanying" these trials with escrache-like street events at the court door.

Fifteen years of escraches have revealed justice as a complex social process, showing us that only people organizing can push the state to start it. But they have also taught us that that is not enough: Only people in the street can ensure that justice becomes a reality.

Franco Basualdo, Prensa de Frente
"We want bottom-up change through action and not only talk among a handful of people"

Interview by Marcy Rein and Clifton Ross, September 2008
Translation by Luis Ballesteros

We did this interview in a noisy coffee shop in the train station at Plaza Once in Buenos Aires. About a week before, riders irate at the persistently poor service provided by the city's privatized commuter rail system had set fire to cars and painted graffiti at two suburban stations. The incidents were making front-page news, with politicians blaming the Left for the vandalism and left party activists denying the accusations. It seemed that something simmered under the surface, and maybe Franco could explain it to us. We were also curious to know what lasting impressions the uprising of December 19–20, 2001, had made on the country.

Most of us at the Prensa de Frente (PF, Front Press) are members of an organization called the Frente Popular Darío Santillán and our origin is the work with the unemployed workers' movement; specifically the Anibal Verón movement. Along the process, we became politically organized, going beyond the mere analysis of information behind reality. Well, the change we proposed was that "it is no longer sufficient to work with unemployed workers; we have to develop a trade union line, a student line, a press work, a work on gender." Ours is a popular front.

In the PF there are no roles assigned; there are no specific editors or writers but roles are socialized, without a vertical structure. This is a small collective where roles are alternated and there is no concentration of the decision-making role.

Subsidized capital, not services

The trains are a starting point to talk about public and social policies in Argentina. Companies continue in private hands and they render poor service, but they're still subsidized by the state with billions of pesos. That subsidy isn't reinvested since the ticket price and trains aren't subsidized but only the infrastructure of the companies engaged in providing the railroad service.

For example, the branch line that was set on fire last week is about sixty kilometers long and along 90 percent of its trajectory has only grade crossings, without tunnels or bridges. Another thing is that the frequency of trains is negatively affected because they have to stop for cars to pass. This ends up frustrating people. On top of that, the government has now accused the Left of having set fire to the train. In the last two months this line had two derailments. Two weeks ago a train caught fire on its own. So blaming left-leaning activists after a series of incidents due to lack of maintenance or because of the failure to reinvest sounds like an attempt to divert attention from the real reasons. The bottom line here is to minimize expenditure in maintenance and social benefits and maximize profit.

Six months ago, the president launched a plan to build a bullet train, a high-speed train. This decision was made at a time when the existing trains are in very bad condition. It doesn't make any sense to invest $15 billion in a bullet train that would go from Buenos Aires to Rosario and Córdoba and would be as expensive as the airplane. Freight trains are the only ones that work properly because they carry the agricultural products. This fact contradicts the argument that there's no money to finance the proper railway operation. This proves that the government isn't willing to invest because it's easier to give a subsidy than to generate control mechanisms to oversee investment plans and it's also easier to make highly profitable businesses like the bullet train. To illustrate it clearly, half of the money spent on the bullet train would suffice to revamp the entire railway system of the country.

We took the example of the railway system because the same story occurs in most public services: telephone, gas, energy, electricity. This isn't the case with the water, as it's managed by a private company. The water service was privatized and bought by a French company called Suez. This company had its concession to the radio waves revoked because of some irregularities and for reasons of national security regarding this strategic sector.

Water and some train lines were again put under state control. More accurately, these were nationalized because national groups took charge of them but they weren't under state control and thus the latter wasn't in a position to review rates and investments and give them a social orientation, as would be the case with a public service in the service of society, and not, as in this case, where society is in the service of profit. No improvement has been made and people travel like cattle, more uncomfortable than cattle being taken to the slaughterhouse.

These sorts of structural things clarify the fact that, despite surface changes in the government away from quintessential neoliberalism, it's still not the national and popular government it claims to be. A real national and popular government would be in favor of the needs of the people and not of the business sector through subsidies.

Right now we're in time when conflict in the agricultural sector has brought about an increased politicization of society, which has put on the table the role of the state and the private sectors. I don't foresee a way out in the short term, as we are still living the aftermath of the class defeat at the hands of the dictatorship.

Anyway, I think progress is being made at an organization level and in more significant infrastructure constructions that are gradually being completed. The truth is that in the past few years we've been punished, not through repression but by budget cuts for community kitchens and social security. These appear to be low-profile measures in a situation of increased employment and more trade union conflicts.

Limits of autonomy

Autonomous positions were very helpful in 2001–2002 vis-à-vis the discrediting of the political class. Autonomists claimed that they were not politicians, the state, the Church, or bureaucratic trade unions. That was useful and it also occurred as a reaction to the dogmatic Left, but its scope wasn't broad enough to reach a political projection that would permeate the masses.

This autonomist conception was present in some meetings of the 2001–2002 assembly movement and some movements of unemployed workers, somewhat in line with the logic of Holloway but in an extreme fashion, like an assimilation not of the Zapatismo of the sixth or the "Other Campaign" but only of the Zapatismo based on liberated territories. In my opinion, that's the dogmatic conception of Marxism, autonomism, or socialism, which is regressive, because I believe in dynamics and not in statics. Final definitions don't exist.

We don't propose verticalism, as our organizational premises are based on grassroots democracy, but we don't see horizontality and grassroots democracy as the same thing. Horizontality is a conception that tends to homogenize everything. When we live in a complex and fragmented society there is no homogeneity and especially after the advent of neoliberalism that fragmented all forms of work and generated, for example, domestic work, something that didn't exist before. The last standard of domestic work before neoliberalism was the first industrial revolution and artisans. So what we see now is this: you have to sharpen analysis to see what forms work will take under twenty-first-century capitalism.

We do believe that compulsive horizontality is absurd and regressive and the conception of "we're all the same" doesn't advance analysis and what we see a lot of the time are "cut and paste, one size fits all" copies of European conceptions of autonomy.

This means reproducing Eurocentrism in Latin America along with an extreme opposition to labor unions. I am not too fond of trade union bureaucracy but even so, when I had some conflicts in my work, we organized ourselves, affiliated with a trade union and elected a representative. Hence, fetishism of autonomism contends that there are no valid institutions to question, and many times autonomists end up being subsidized by NGOs and European foundations. And so what happens? We're all equal, but you're the one who takes the money.

I think it's an issue that should be raised, not only to the autonomists, but to all who are maintained by NGOs or foundations: it not only reproduces the Eurocentric logic but it's also one of the ways capital manages to keep political expressions contained.

Our origins are in the social movements and we try not to dissociate the social from the political dimension. Social action is not a charitable activity of visiting poor people to help them. Social action is based on clear politics that must accurately target the sectors with which we have to work.

In the past seven years, from 2001, we've experienced an extensive change. We changed because we have a political projection and not only action. In addition to direct action, we have a school where seventy of our comrades study revolutionary traditions in Latin America and the basic concepts of Marxism. This ensures a supply of militants with a knowledge base and not only militants that have a background as mass leaders, which is a step forward to go beyond autonomism. From 2001 to date there has been a revaluation of the political class.

In this context, it is necessary to go past the stage of "throw them all out" and become more proactive to be better poised for the next "throw them all out" situation. Now our political analysis is better structured than before. We are building another logic of power to offset the limitations of autonomism, which doesn't envisage a struggle for power. Well, we don't believe in the Marxist theory about taking power, as we don't advocate top-down change. But we do want bottom-up change through action and not only talk among a handful of people.

We aren't fighting to take the positions of politicians but to establish an organizational structure at a social level. The bottom-up approach, but with a good sense of direction.

Autonomy states that its enemy is the capitalist social relation. Our role here is to combine all the traditions of social struggle with Marxist, anarchist, and autonomist conceptions. The "throw them all out" situation in 2001 was a bit complicated because you indiscriminately condemn politics and politicians across the board. I think the problem is that in Argentina institutionalism was always, or almost always, conceived for domination. Therefore, it's difficult to trust true representation by trade unions or political parties, which were made for domination and not for allowing participation. Also, this is occurring amid the circumstance of a government claiming to have a new policy that is apparently encouraging participation but there is no opening, no room for political participation or discussion. Even the most reformist policies don't have a participatory budget. What we're seeing at a federal level is a policy to contain social outbursts. The failure by the provincial states to implement these kinds of social containment strategies leads to social eruptions and weariness, manifested in drug addiction, robberies, or setting trains on fire. This is the balance of the deficit of legitimate political organizations and their failure to put in place mechanisms to avoid this.

The way out is to continue building policies from and for the popular sectors. The Argentinian people have established natural political practices, with belligerent conceptions. Burning trains is a typical reaction of the Argentinian people that doesn't occur in other countries.

In Argentina there's a lingering link of community in all neighborhoods, despite the fragmentation of work, which gives workers a sense of identity. Organization is the only way out, independent of the institutions and parties. We think that the parties in power and the other parties, including the leftist parties, are discredited because of dogmatism and ideologism. They speak an unintelligible language not accessible to the common people. They speak with a fantasy of the industrial subject, who in Argentina is dead as an individual subject. We don't believe in diversity of the subject either, but we do believe in the different forms and labor fronts workers are now adopting. That's why we're working in areas like culture, gender, training, and education.

Ernesto "Lalo" Paret, Movement of Recovered Companies
"Hunger made us unite"

Interview by Clifton Ross and Marcy Rein, April 2012
Translation by Luis Ballesteros

Lalo Paret (left) with Cecilia Sainz.
Photo by Clifton Ross.

We first met Lalo at the Oakland premiere of Avi Lewis and Naomi Klein's movie, The Take, *presented at the Humanist Hall. Cecilia Sainz, as translator, was on tour with Lalo, who appeared as one of the protagonists in the movie. On a trip to Buenos Aires in 2006 I stayed with Cecilia and her husband Mariano Andrade and met Lalo once again. We became friends on a long night drive to Paraguay in 2008 and Marcy and I looked Lalo up when we were back in Buenos Aires again in the spring of 2012. Lalo is still working as an organizer with the recovered enterprises in Buenos Aires and the region, something he's been doing now for many years.*

I think most comrades are suffering a process of attrition and exhaustion and every day they commit all over again to try to realize what we yearned for from the first day. In the end, all that most of the workers who made it possible to recover the companies had wanted was just to live from their own work. Not all of the comrades could or can grasp what is involved in their gesture of taking the factory, putting it to work, and facing the market or being a part of it.

This model of not having a boss wasn't optional; it was just the best they could do. I think that the greatest experience this collective has gained is the possibility of knowing that despite any situation of crisis or abuse from the employers, organized workers can perform a productive process with these market rules, the rules of capitalism. At the same time workers have been able to create a market where the prevailing values are the same as those lived by the collective day after day at the factory. And that makes it possible to devise other forms of commercial organization that are currently being tested.

Maybe now we need to try an economic model that guarantees experiences such as recovered companies and community associations, which are also producers, an exchange market of their own since it's impossible to think of many cases that a recovered company has been given the lead under the rules of capitalism. Otherwise, it would seem that everything we did was not to stop being dogs but only to change collars, and here the goal is to stop being dogs. But this transition isn't easy.

The best experience that could be taken from all this by the comrades in their lifetime is the experience of collective construction which is the challenge of our era, not only for the workers but for society as a whole. Workers, the ones left behind, the underdogs, were the ones who had the possibility of lighting the fuse of this collective construction.

And it's incredible how the nobodies or the workers not only of Argentina but of Latin America have been subject to a process of destruction ever since the 1960s. So now we find workers who are not clear about where to turn, as they only know that they want to eat.

Making a decent living from their work

Somebody asked me once in Oakland that if workers had already taken the means of production then they were ready to take power. Well, poor guy, he has never been in a factory, because all any worker wants is to live from his work. He wants to complete his eight or six hours of work and make a decent living for him and his family.

That's power, and power is when everyone can live that way and nobody has to go off chasing a logic of abstract power because the end result of this would be like buying the rat race of the American dream.

I think that is the common goal of all simple men in the world: make a decent life out of their work, and that situation is far too familiar to the compañeros at the factory. Success can be defined in this case as the fact that more than two individuals get together and use the factory as the common factor through which they join their interests and create wealth to be distributed, which becomes a strong bond. This is the construction of power now, that is, the possibility to face all difficulties collectively, while looking for a common goal. Collective construction is the challenge of our time.

The other precedent underlying the experience in Argentina, Latin America, and anywhere in the world is that the organization or self-management of workers or the occupancy of factories is possible and it is here to stay. I think that is the most important fact for the working class in the world. It's possible to work collectively without a boss.

That's why it's essential to understand what workers have done by taking the factory, that they've lit a fuse that can make you realize that everything you actually learned is that this crappy capitalist system is of no use to you anymore. Because, ultimately, what's the famous security we're talking about? Security for what? That you can live decently? Well, everybody wants to live decently, the rich and the poor, even if they don't act accordingly. I mean, I think the essence of man is something else.

Back in 2006 and 2003, we said that we were certainly pregnant with something. We knew that we were going to give birth to something but we didn't know what it was going to be called. I feel that specifically here in Argentina the social transformation process is intact and it does not stem from the political forces and does not belong only to this political process. My belief is that all political processes try to use the social historical processes.

One thing is clear: the capitalist model is exhausted. Somewhere in the world the possibility to try a new kind of model will appear. I don't know what and where this new kind of model will emerge. Maybe it will happen in the United States—hopefully—and it will nurture itself from all of these experiences and maybe it will not be perfect either because no collective process is perfect, but that's because it's collective. It's what is possible and it isn't meant to please everyone.

This crisis of capitalism seems final. However, one or two times per century it's seemed final too. What is the crux of this situation? That the new generations do not only understand but also live this order as a senseless order.

And so whatever comes along is going to be fiercely resisted by the old regime, as has historically been the case. But the defense of the old regime in many cases will be pointless because this is a generational matter. And technology is going to play a key role, because it's not only a tool of capitalism but, also, technology and technological revolution will make it possible for new generations to understand that in this process the transforming power of technology will be a magical tool that will be part of what is occurring now in situations like the occupancy of recovered factories and other initiatives of workers.

We have to realize that what we did on the field by recuperating factories was tantamount to lighting a fuse that didn't go out. The new generations will have the possibility to use new technologies and come together with our actions on the field.

Chilavert: Press operator at the worker-run print shop Chilavert in Buenos Aires.
Photo © Jorge Pousa.

Need got us together and that need plus unity made it possible for us to take away anything from power. Now we're in a different situation. Now we eat but we forgot all we thought when we lit the fuse. I have no doubt that the fuse is lit up everywhere, in Latin America and in the United States as well. The crux of the matter is where will there be a sufficient degree of organization to give shape to what is to come? Will it come from the trade unions? From the structures? I don't know. There's an underground construction currently in process not only in connection with workers but also in art and culture. Everything is part of the same underground construction.

The "progressives"

The political structures try to stave off and own these processes. Rhetoric and discourse make the government appear more left-leaning than us. I am sick and tired of the discussions about being progressive. Progressive in which aspect, why? After all, all these progressive processes [in Latin America] aren't so transformative as far as social policy is concerned. This is mere *gattopardism* or political pantomime, making changes so that nothing changes.

Currently in Latin America it's very difficult to maintain the autonomy of each organization or collective because progressive politicians take ownership of the initiatives of workers. However, ultimately the issue here is not to maintain autonomy but to keep a clear view of the reason why we agreed to recover a factory or to rebuild a community. The political moment will pass and you don't strengthen your autonomy if you get too close to political interests. Maybe this strengthens the factory and the production aspect but it can be said that it's conditioned by the moment. You become a part of the progressive political process.

We have to consider that in Latin America, particularly in Argentina, the cooperative framework was the result of a legal need and not because we believed in a cooperative. Really, if we were told to "make a workers' association" we would have made a workers association. This was not due to our cooperativist spirit. Of course not.

Hunger was what made it possible. The dictum was "make me a cooperative" and we made a cooperative, but we could have been anything. Now, in this political climate all over the world, the political system is exhausted and empty. Then there's a constant quest for things that can breathe some life into politics. So any individual constituting or constructing an idea or a body or collective lays some foundation for politics because, particularly here in Argentina in 2001 we wanted to burn them all and oust them all. We wanted all politicians and the political class out. This same political class that is currently ruling, with some new faces, but the vast majority of them are the same. Now, is this a strength of politics or a weakness of society today?

In many cases I can't understand how many comrades who have a substantial background and formation consider that contributing to a political process would strengthen their collective. I don't believe in today's political moment.

I do believe that we need to construct. If one believes that the order is exhausted, why would you contribute to it? If you believe that it is exhausted and you are constructing other possibilities and alternatives, why would you contribute to that order? That comes into question because I don't know many comrades who are congressmen, senators, or officers who have strengthened the popular collective.

It is almost like being imprisoned. You don't have many alternatives. We have some proposals for this situation. If we create our own jobs we would have to be free from a whole bunch of tax burdens, etc., etc. The truth is that we didn't set the rules of capitalism. You asked me about experiences and they have to do with lighting a fuse; that the dreams we had at the first stage of the recovered company are still intact because they have to do with simple things of life and there is no telling if they concur or not with complex things like those proposed by Marx or Bebel or any of those characters. It is something much simpler and programmatic and it is essentially associated with being able to make a decent living off your work... nothing else. It seems a utopia but there is no other dream.

The lessons of 2002

Think about it, one of the claims in 2002 was not the banner of any organization. Everything proclaimed by the organizations that fought against neoliberalism was not included in the banner of struggle at the outbreak. This was a combination of interests, mainly the economic crisis that pummeled the middle class and that, obviously, later on there were very many organizations contending that they had been saying for ten years that this was going to happen, because everything was a lie, but the reaction reflects the fact that the political agenda of the organizations was not taken into account.

Should the same conditions of 2000 occur again in Argentina, it would now be much easier to get organized and accomplish a goal, much easier now than before, because at that time our will to organize was because there was no other choice. Now we know that organization is the tool that would allow us to immediately overcome a given situation. At that time, hunger made us unite and we learned a lot. Now circumstances have forced the organizations to change their objectives, probably because many objectives had to do with concrete things such as mere survival, but we learned a lot in the process. Should a situation like that of 2000 occur again, the degree of organization would be wonderful and now we'd be able to quickly discuss the reasons for organizing ourselves too, not only to eat and to find a way to survive. Now we already know what we need to do to eat, but we also learned that eating is not enough. Then maybe we would dare to think that it's not enough only to take the factories but it would also be necessary to take what some people call "power." I believe that such stage would be the maturation of a process. Now the outlook for unity would be much broader than in 2000.

Claudia Acuña, Colectivo lavaca
"We exposed how obscene and pornographic the economic model is"

Interview by Marcy Rein and Clifton Ross, April 2012
Translation by Luis Ballesteros

Born out of the storm of protest and organizing that broke in Argentina in 2001, the Buenos Aires-based lavaca collective has grown up to be many things.[5] *It publishes books, a website (www.lavaca.org), weekly radio podcasts, and a stylish two-color monthly tabloid (with yellow accents on the black-and-white) called* Mu. *(La vaca means "cow" in Spanish, and the magazine is the voice of lavaca). The collective also runs a café/bookstore/fair trade emporium where it hosts music, poetry, and workshops. "Café Mu" is located on Hipólito Yrigoyen, just two and a half blocks from the Argentine National Congress, putting it in the middle of the action for numerous protests and rallies.*

Lavaca offers communications support to the social movements and also creates actions of its own, as Claudia Acuña explains below. The collective has been particularly involved with the long-running anti-mining struggle in the remote northwest Argentina town of Famatina. Residents of the town—led by a group of women—have fought off a succession of foreign companies who wanted to dig for gold in the mountain that gives the town its name.

Acuña—who gave up a career in corporate media to help found lavaca— was hard to get in touch with, but when Lalo Paret introduced us just as we were finishing our interview with him in the café, she sat down and shared a couple of hours with us then and there.

Lavaca is a collective with a large feminine presence, but it also involves a large presence of men who adopt a feminist message in all respects. Feminism isn't a discourse for us, it's a practice. Particularly in the case of feminism, a type of wild divide is appearing in Latin America. I would venture to say that the grassroots, the popular sectors for many years have been a project of the Church so that sensitive issues in the agenda of feminism, such as abortion and free sexuality, aren't allowed. We can agree to make revolution but we cannot agree on your right to decide over your own body or whether you want to be a mother or not.

The women's issue here is related to natural resources, because the body of a Latin American woman is a body of exploitation. It is a body exploited by capitalism, as we already know, given that it turns it into flesh for prostitution or flesh for illegal work, but it is also a body exploited by the Left, sending women to the front of the picket line and then denying them their voice and their leadership. It is a body exploited by the NGO portraying her as a "poor little thing" and victimizing her, never allowing a woman to stand up and speak for herself with all her contradictions.

As a collective, in our ten years of existence we faced the most violent situations when we dealt with the subject of women, basically the area of prostitution, because this bar (Café Mu) is in the middle of twelve plazas where prostitution is rampant in the city. For us, they aren't prostitutes; they're sisters, they're women. In this context, it's not like, "This is a workshop. I have come to teach you."

We favor unsigned street actions, from which no one can accumulate power. We don't even carry out actions as lavaca. We don't carry out actions because we're lavaca. We're women and that's why we carry out actions. We're men and that is why we carry out actions against machismo. And if there is no logo, there is no chance to accumulate power.

Last year we staged an action [we called] "Neither women nor the land are merchandise." We made a link between women engaged in prostitution and mining exploitation, given that in Lunfardo a woman is called a *mina* (mine).[6] We made stickers to look like the prostitution ads posted in some public payphones, but we used the addresses and telephone numbers of multinational mining companies. Instead of calling a brothel, you ended up calling Barry Gold, Yamaha Gold, Estrata Copper, Santa Cruz Mining Company. By associating prostitution with mining exploitation, we exposed how obscene and pornographic the economic model is.

Fighting for resources

If somebody tells you there are no assemblies, I have to tell you that there many, and of a horizontal type, no less. The entire country is witnessing a battle for the natural resources, oil, soybeans, mining. These struggles centered on basic and tangible needs aren't felt or seen the same in the cities, where to get water you just need to open the faucet. But when you're in the mountain range you immediately notice the consequences of the lack of water on your crops because the mining companies are taking more and more water. If you are here in the capital you might think that nothing is happening because all the action is in the provinces and in the outlands of the country, in the mountain ranges. We're talking about places difficult to access, places that are located four to five hundred kilometers from the airport.

Five different regions did picket lines in February and March of this year (2012) and this led to the interruption of the entire mining process in Argentina. This was the result of a great deal of underground work and was carried out mostly by women. There were two events of repression; you can see from photos that they [some of the women] have dog bites on their breasts as a result of the police repression, but the day after such repression, the women returned to set up another picket line and stayed there.

But what did the companies do? All of them held a meeting at the Government House and forced the state, in some kind of mining coup against the government, to sign what we call "the Mining State," which explains the slogan of "People against the Mining State." The state became a miner and the government minister signed in a public capacity with all the mining companies that a new corporation of mining states was being born. And that's very symbolic.

Then a series of economic problems surfaced; subsidies were cut and the price of yerba maté increased. It was as if a sequence of tremors from the brutal repression that occurred in February were taking place, a repression that didn't stop anyone.

The women of Famatina

For six years there's been a permanent picket line at fifteen hundred meters of altitude, kept by three individuals via cellular phone. They call the people by tolling the bells of the church and then the entire town gathers there, at a time of leading-edge technology, no less. One girl mentions that once she was making love and as soon as she heard the bells tolling she dashed off to meet with the rest of the people. This is the level of radicalism and commitment that you can still find in places located far from the capital, which has shifted to the right, and hopelessness is high because the revolution is no longer around the corner.

Intellectuals and people from the Left come here talking about "exploitation"; I say "natural resources," but people there say, "Don't touch Famatina," or "Water is worth more than gold." Famatina is the name of that mountain. "Don't touch it" is a slogan the people there made up. They paint it everywhere. You'll notice that this is not about exploitation of natural resources. "You're not going to touch it," it's almost like you say to a child, "Don't touch, don't touch."

[The women from Famatina] are now our friends. We do not speak in terms of support and construction because many things are woven together. We went to the occupation and we slept with them in the car because there was nowhere else to go, at an altitude of two thousand meters. There we all created a great camraderie, because they saw that we didn't arrive by plane just to watch but practically on the back of a donkey because we had taken a rundown bus.

One woman is the Pilates instructor and another one is the warehouse clerk. What are their means of communication? The warehouse, the gym, the school, the teacher. They don't need the TV or the radio because they spread the word about women being hit or repressed. That way they give their support to the women's cause and their protests at the picket lines. It isn't an immediate or spectacular fact, but it is like a simmering process that resembles magma that comes out in certain situations. It's called politization. They didn't conceive a way of organization other than through assemblies, which is to say here everyone is a leader.

Famatina: Community resistance to mining at La Famatina has support all over Argentina. Pictured here, a participant at a march in Rosario in January 2012. Photo © Matías Garcia Gamra.

The means of communication that they've constructed independently has been more effective than mainstream media, because the latter made the movement and its discourse visible only if it was convenient for them. Having their own means of communication avoided any distortion in the message they wanted to get across. Even if you don't have access to TV, you still have, for instance, an Internet radio.

The fact that a mining company cannot open in this town or in Esquer sets an example. How did people find out of what occurred two thousand kilometers away? Well, we have our media and the dissemination of information is a prerequisite for a quick organization.

This process of organizing and meeting at assemblies has reconnected people. Even though the people use the Internet to find out about other experiences, they've developed their own methods and ways of communication, recovering their oral history and connecting with us to exchange information.

Chile

CHILE

Legend	
⊛	National capital
◉	Administrative region capital
○	City, town
✈	Major airport
–··–··–	National boundary
–·–·–·–	Administrative region boundary
———	Main road
———	Secondary road
———	Railroad

The boundaries and names shown and the designations used on this map do not imply official endorsement or acceptance by the United Nations.

United Nations Map No. 4395 Rev. 0, March 2010

INTRODUCTION
Chile reclaims its history of resistance

By Marcy Rein

Neoliberalism slammed Chile first and hardest of all the Latin American countries, rammed through by the September 11, 1973, military coup. Chile's 9/11 overthrew the country's elected Marxist president and installed the dictatorship of General Augusto Pinochet, whose seventeen-year reign of terror aimed to stamp out socialism and implant the "free-market" system so deeply in the country's economy, politics, and society that it could never be uprooted.

Chile still lives under the dictatorship-era constitution and suffers the greatest income inequality and poorest education quality of any country in the Organization for Economic Cooperation and Development.[1] But the country's long tradition of democracy and working-class organizing—which persisted even in the depths of the dictatorship—has begun to revive. In 2011–2012, massive protests rocked Chile like the earthquakes that so often jolt this long, narrow country, and the social movements began to shake the whole neoliberal edifice.

Geography and resource base

Chile lies like a spine along the west coast of South America, reaching four thousand miles from its shared border with Peru and Bolivia in the Atacama Desert to the glaciers of Torres del Paine and the Antarctic Ocean beyond. That long stretch spans several geographic regions, each with a resource base that feeds the export-driven economy: the arid north, rich in copper, nitrates, and lithium; the center, with the historic port of Valparaíso, the capital of Santiago and the Valle Central (Central Valley), the produce-growing region at the heart of the country's bourgeoning agribusiness, including its famous vineyards; the south-central area around the Bío-Bío River, center of the forestry industry; and spectacular Patagonia, home base for fishing and salmon-farming and a lure for tourists and the energy companies that seek to exploit its rushing rivers for hydroelectric power.

The country grew from the center out; long distances and rugged terrain contributed to the development of an internal colonialism, with the center extracting wealth from the peripheries and providing little in return. Control of this wealth, however, has been contested since the Spaniard Pedro de Valdivia arrived and established settlements in 1540. The Mapuche, Chile's most numerous indigenous people, defended their lands in the southern region of Araucania with centuries of armed resistance. They negotiated a treaty with the Spanish crown in 1641 and lived unconquered until the 1860–1883 Occupation of Araucania. That twenty-three-year war of genocide cost the Mapuche 95 percent of their territory, which the state opened to agricultural development.[2]

Chile declared independence from Spain in 1818 and established its bourgeois democracy, which held until 1973 with only two brief periods of military rule.[3] But foreign powers have controlled its mineral wealth since the rise of its mining industries. Britain dominated the country's commerce in the mid-nineteenth century, then split control of the nitrate fields with U.S. firms during the boom years of 1883–1920. U.S. domination began with the growth of copper mining in the 1920s.

Working-class resistance

The working class grew with the mining industry and began advocating for its interests through mutual aid societies (which evolved into anarchist unions) as well as direct action and participation in political parties.[4]

Urban workers and artisans made up the base of the Partido Demócrata (Democrat Party) founded in 1887. Its support boosted reform president José Manuel Balmaceda to power. Balmaceda planned to nationalize the nitrate fields, but was ousted in a coup in 1891, ushering in a government that did the bidding of the "agromineral, financial and merchant oligarchy and British economic interests."[5] It deployed violent repression against escalating union organizing among miners and dockworkers, culminating in the 1907 massacre at the Santa María de Iquique School.

Incensed by poor working conditions and the high cost of living, miners and dockers struck the port of Iquique. The walkout soon spread through the entire nitrate-mining region, with an estimated fifteen to twenty thousand workers taking part. Strikers occupied the school, army troops opened fire, and hundreds were slaughtered.[6] This massacre proved a turning point for both labor and left organizing. Workers formed the country's first national labor federation (Federación Obrera de Chile—FOCH) in 1909; Luis Emilio Recabarren founded the Socialist Workers' Party that year as well, which became the Communist Party.

Anarchists, communists, and socialists contended for influence in the workers' movement, and unions organized behind various left parties that were an organic part of politics. The Socialist Republic of Chile lasted from June 4 to September 13, 1932; the Popular Front government elected in 1938 was one of three in the world.[7]

Industrialization, urbanization, left participation

The economic strategy the Popular Front used to lift Chile out of the Great Depression shaped the country for the next thirty-five years. The government supported industrial growth to diversify the economy, adopted steep tariffs to protect homegrown industry, and participated directly in several economic sectors: electricity, petroleum, iron and steel, transportation, communications, and banking.

This "import substitution industrialization" model expanded the working class and the unions, "strengthening political parties of a popular character and developing a culture of citizenship, rights and democracy, in spite of the deep social inequalities," Emir Sader wrote.[8]

Urbanization also brought unemployment, hunger, and lack of adequate housing and health care. Some city-dwellers occupied lands and built new housing developments, under the leadership of the Movement of the Revolutionary Left (MIR). Worker, peasant, and student movements coalesced behind the Unidad Popular (UP, Popular Unity) a coalition of Communists, Socialists, and other left parties. The UP won the 1970 presidential elections, bringing Salvador Allende to power. Allende, a physician who had served as minister of health in the first Popular Front government, broadened land reform and fully nationalized the banking system and key industries, most notably the copper mines.

Chile's 9/11

Even before the election of Allende, Chile's priorities distressed transnational capital—especially U.S.-based Anaconda and Kennecott Copper, and International Telephone and Telegraph, which owned 70 percent of the Chilean telephone company. Well-documented overt and covert efforts to change the country's direction date from the mid-1950s.[9]

Washington spent millions trying to marginalize the Left and avert Allende's election. When that failed, it turned to destabilizing the UP government. It cut off the flow of capital to Chile by denying loans from the

Inter-American Development Bank, the World Bank, the Export-Import Bank and other sources. Covert U.S. operations financed opposition media and political groups and underwrote a truckers' strike.

Despite these efforts, the UP got more votes in the 1972 legislative elections than Allende garnered in 1970. Then plotting for the coup began.[10] All the branches of the Chilean military collaborated in the September 11 putsch.

The Pinochet dictatorship killed or disappeared 3,428 people[11] and detained or imprisoned another 150,000; around 200,000 fled into exile.[12] With secret police and surveillance, media censorship, bans on political activity, takeovers of universities, and even book-burnings, the regime aimed to eradicate the culture of democracy, solidarity, and resistance.

Poor and working-class communities bore the brunt of the repression; 80 percent of the political prisoners were workers and peasants.[13] Police raided houses in poor neighborhoods and dumped corpses in vacant lots.[14] The government expropriated Mapuche lands and sold them at cut-rate prices to the big forestry companies.[15]

With people stunned and society shredded, the dictatorship began to build a "free market" society from the ground up, following the radical doctrine preached by the University of Chicago economists. The regime reversed land reform and nationalizations (except copper), opened the economy to foreign investment and "free trade," suppressed unions, and privatized everything, including Social Security, education, health, transportation, and utilities. Chile's new constitution, passed in 1980 by a suspect plebiscite, institutionalized ironclad protections for private property and elite domination of the legislature.

Poverty and unemployment skyrocketed after the coup. People began organizing just to survive. They created common kitchens (*ollas comunes*) where they pooled scarce food, children's dining rooms (*comedores infantiles*), and clandestine organizations of the homeless and unemployed. Professionals fired from privatized schools and universities collaborated with grassroots activists in popular education projects.

Another economic crisis in 1982–1983 pushed people into the streets despite the risks of repression, kicking off three years of mass protests. At the same time, business interests and elements of the elite that had pressed for the coup began chafing against the international condemnation the Pinochet regime brought on the country. Switching intervention modes, in 1985 the United States began training and supporting an elite opposition that would provide a veneer of formal democracy but leave neoliberal restructuring in place.[16]

Limited democracy

The 1980 constitution provided for a plebiscite on Pinochet's leadership in 1988. A broad "Coalition of Parties for the NO" won that vote. The 1989 presidential and congressional elections brought to power the first government of the Concertación de Partidos por la Democracia (Concert of Parties for Democracy, CPD)—but this was democracy within strict limits.

Pinochet remained commander-in-chief of the armed forces until 1998, his 1980 constitution remained in force, and the Concertación agreed not to prosecute members of the junta for human rights abuses.

The social movements, so active in the previous decades, found themselves disoriented and marginalized in the early 1990s. In part this stemmed from collective trauma suffered under the dictatorship, but it also had to do with the Concertación's political and ideological alignment, and deep shifts on the left. The CPD drew in fifteen different parties, including the Socialists (who had renounced revolutionary Marxism) and the Christian Democrats, but it operated through the parties' leadership and did not address the bases. This ruptured the relationship of left parties and popular forces that had been so powerful in Chilean history.

At the same time the Left, notably the Socialist Party, moved its focus from economic justice to democratic participation. "Through privatization, decision-making on important policy questions had largely moved to private firms and therefore outside the jurisdiction of state policy," Julia Paley observed.[17]

The CPD also wove a discourse that placed the highest value on stability, and cast demands for rights and services as threats to order and national unity, even twisting the first Truth and Reconciliation Commission (the "Rettig Commission") report to this end. The document put a Cold War frame on the events of the 1970s and '80s, blaming the Left for the extreme political polarization that led to the coup and repression.

While marginalizing political activity, the CPD co-opted popular organizations. Lacking money to support human services, it recruited grassroots groups to help provide them, either as volunteers or as grantees, turning them into NGOs. Existing NGOs, which did research and organizing under the dictatorship, were frequently brought into the Concertación government, though largely in advisory roles.

Recuperated movements

Life conditions remained harsh for the majority of Chileans, exposing the gap between the rhetoric and practice of the CPD. The gap between workers and employers widened during the 1990s. The richest 10 percent "accounted for 50 percent of GDP, while poorest 10 percent represented scarcely 2.5 percent."[18] Employers capitalized on the lack of worker protections to maximize the use of temporary and subcontracted labor. In the countryside, small landowners became poorly paid seasonal workers, as the reversal of land reform begun under Pinochet accelerated with the growth of agribusiness.[19] Retirees suffered under the privatized pension system, with only about one-third receiving adequate coverage.[20] The costs of privatized services, especially education and transportation, put heavy burdens on working families.

Public workers, teachers, and students staged big mobilizations in 1997. That same year, Mapuche activists of the Coordinación Arauco-Malleco (CAM) set fire to three trucks belonging to the company Forestal Arauco.

Under Pinochet, the forestry industry had become an important arm of the export economy, expropriating and polluting Mapuche land and water resources. A new generation of activists grew up watching the destruction of their communities and militantly determined to stop it. The CAM fused anticapitalist analysis with a recuperation of Mapuche cultural identity and goal of national liberation. Its resistance to capital took form in land occupations and sabotage; the Foresta Arauco action inspired similar protests. The government, in turn, criminalized all forms of Mapuche protest and employed COINTELPRO-type tactics to fragment the movement.[21] This policy sharpened under the government of Ricardo Lagos, a socialist elected on the Concertación ticket in 2000.

Lagos's election coincided with Pinochet's return to Chile from England and the beginning of legal proceedings against the former dictator. In the years that followed, Chilean courts put other human rights abusers on trial as well.[22] Pinochet died in December 2006 before his case concluded, but the prosecutions played an important role in revitalizing the social movements.[23]

Another socialist, Michele Bachelet, succeeded Lagos in 2006. As a woman in a country that didn't allow women to vote until 1949, the daughter of an Air Force general who died in prison because he supported Allende, and a former prisoner herself, she embodied a certain kind of progress, but did not break with neoliberalism.

A rise in transit fares sparked a protest by Santiago secondary school students in April 2006 that morphed into the "Penguin Revolution," so called because the students wore dark uniforms with white shirts. Students from all over the country joined in two months of demonstrations, occupations, and walkouts. Their demands evolved to a call for a constitutional amendment to end the privatization of the educational system.

Grandparents: Two elder participants in the afternoon of culture at Santiago's Parque Almagro at the beginning of the 2012 school year. Their signs say, "We grandparents support our grandchildren." Photo by Clifton Ross.

The government offered only material concessions. The students held out for structural reforms, and came away empty-handed, disillusioned with "progressives"—but they changed the political atmosphere, leading to a new wave of social movement activity. Subcontracted workers in the copper and forestry industries struck in 2007, and won better wages.

Voters punished the CPD in 2010 by electing conservative Sebastian Piñera, the richest person in Chile. Under his leadership, the government pushed forward an ambitious hydroelectric energy program, including the construction of five dams on Patagonia's Pascua and Baker rivers to power the copper and food-processing industries.

Close to 80 percent of local residents opposed the HidroAysén project, which would threaten their livelihoods and the area's unique ecosystems by flooding twenty-three square miles and installing more than twelve hundred miles of transmission lines.[24] Opposition to the dams spread nationally and internationally, with around ninety thousand people in the streets in May 2011 following the government's approval of the project.

A month later, two hundred thousand students mobilized in Santiago against the high cost of education and the inequity it reflects and perpetuates. Their support and demands broadened as they sustained the protest throughout the school year. They occupied, struck, stayed in the streets with a full spectrum of theatrical and creative protests. Teachers, parents, and union members joined in. Unions staged a two-day general strike in August 2011 to support the students and demand new labor laws and a public pension.[25] An estimated one million people turned out for an Acto Cultural in August. The movement protested the logic of neoliberalism, calling for renationalization of copper, progressive tax reform, and a new constitution.

The Piñera government responded with minor reforms and heavy repression. Police met the demonstrations with tanks, tear gas, water cannons, provocateurs, and gunfire, killing a sixteen-year-old as he watched a demonstration in Santiago.

In February 2012 Patagonians came together in the Movimiento Social de Aysén, a broad front fighting longstanding demands for higher wages, lower prices for fuel and staples, better health and education facilities, and citizen consultation on major hydroelectric dams. The movement united small business owners, fishers, right-wing militants, and socialists.[26] The forty-day uprising included a nearly two-week-long road blockade, cutting traffic into and out of the isolated region. The government agreed to negotiate over the movement's major demands, but turned around and approved the Río Cuervo dam just weeks later, which would sit on an earthquake fault and be closer to Puerto Aysén than the proposed HidroAysén dams. Chile's Supreme Court later found the approval unconstitutional.

Similar protests broke out in the northern city of Calama, which, like Aysén, suffered under the country's internal colonialism.

The sense of interconnection among the social movements continued to deepen as these various protests progressed. Actions in April 2012, as the student movement geared up for the new school year, reflected the demands for free, quality education and Patagonia without dams, for regional equity, freedom for Mapuche political prisoners and respect for indigenous land and cultural rights. But the year proved relatively quiet. As with the Penguin Revolution, the upsurge in 2011 provided more lessons and movement-building moments than concrete victories. The movements still face a huge open question: How can they build a form to unite their efforts and contend for power? Many of today's activists express profound disillusionment with political parties, but they need, as Edmundo Jiles observes in the following interview, "a transformative political project."

"How could all this be translated not only into a social movement but also into an advance toward the generation of a political movement?" Jiles asks. "That is the challenge: Generating a political movement with transformative capacity. It has to happen eventually."

Edmundo Jiles, Agrupación de Derechos Humanos José Calderón Miranda
"Our challenge is generating a political movement with a transformative capacity"

Interview by Clifton Ross and Marcy Rein, March 2012
Translation by Luis Ballesteros

The tall slant-topped poles cast lattice-work shadows across the "Lugar de Memoria" (Place of Memory) in Paine, Chile. Between the poles on the ground lie tablecloth-sized mosaics dedicated to the town residents who were killed, disappeared or imprisoned during the dictatorship of the 1970s. Each mosaic bears a name and a few images reflecting special details about the person honored—musical instruments, or tools, or a white dove with a letter in its mouth for a man who always had a good word for everyone.

Paine (that's three syllables, Pah-ee-nay) is a small, dusty farm town famous for its watermelons, which lies about forty-five minutes south of Santiago by train. Paine lost more people to the Pinochet dictatorship, per capita, than any other place in Chile—a punishment for its strong support of agrarian reform during the Allende years.

The Agrupación de Derechos Humanos José Calderón Miranda worked for years with other groups to establish the "Memorial Paine." Edmundo Jiles has served the group in various leadership roles for nine years, four of them as president. Jiles grew up in Santiago in a highly political family. As teenager, he belonged to the youth wing of the Christian Democratic Party, then became disenchanted with it and dedicated himself to his work with a construction workers' union and the broader labor movement. After the coup he was imprisoned and tortured, he admitted reluctantly, as we stood in the memorial. "Not only did the dictatorship murder, imprison, and torture people: It killed our dreams, our sense that another world is possible," he said. In his comfortable

Edmundo Jiles. Photo by Clifton Ross.

home not far from the memorial, he talked with us about the 1970s, and shared a perspective on today's social movements, marked by having been part of the hopes and dreams of the Allende years.

I had the opportunity to live through a very interesting and, to a certain extent, privileged historical period. At that time we saw the triumph of the Cuban Revolution, the Second Vatican Council adopted the preferential option for the poor, the United States lost the Vietnam War. It was a very intense period, and only a few generations in the world have experienced periods of such agitation and so many utopias and dreams of building a better world.

From that perspective, Chile wasn't the exception. From the time of Eduardo Frei Montalba, from 1964 on, there was effervescence in, and growth of, social organizations among trade unions, women, youth and the population at large. And as the movements grew, so did their demands on the state.

Subsequently, the electoral victory of Salvador Allende in 1970 ushered in an era of social effervescence. The people were very happy with a moderate program that attempted to build socialism within the parameters allowed by the constitution and the laws. Expectations ran high among Chileans, and this also generated substantial organization that allowed for widespread citizen participation, to such an extent that capital was annoyed and resented it.

President Allende's program included the nationalization of forty companies that would be run by the state or under a scheme of mixed ownership. The Right started boycotting and the popular response was to occupy the industries, put them into production and request the state's intervention, which caused a direct financial impact on the business establishment. Their boycott of the project gave rise to the black market, hoarding, stoppage of production, road blockades, bridge and railroad blockades, etc.

They made a point of instilling discontent among citizens and polarizing the country's social atmosphere, aided, of course, by the CIA, with U.S. money that funded media businessmen to generate discontent and create the conditions for a coup d'état.

The coup and its aftermath

Finally, the coup d'état was staged in 1973. This unleashed a savage repression. All political parties were destroyed and outlawed; trade union organization, which by then was very strong, was abolished and social leaders were persecuted, etc. There are still thousands of exiles out of the country and thousands of prisoners, missing and tortured people, and people who were relocated from one extreme of the country to another.

Particularly during the initial years of the dictatorship, the intention was to engender fear, break up social organization, and tear away the social fabric to stifle any demands on the government.

Life under the dictatorship was very difficult because the leaders who were not killed had to go into exile or serve a long time in prison, which broke trade union organization. Women's organizations ceased to exist. The first two or three years our efforts were focused on saving threatened lives by helping blacklisted people hide or getting them into embassies.

New organizations arose later, particularly those centered on developing survival strategies: communal kitchens, children's dining rooms (*comedores infantiles*), small craft workshops, artisanal production of basic food such as bread, for example, bakeries. This occurred for many years, in spite of the dictatorship.

Later the same organized groups developed a complete program for the export of handicrafts they'd made. Some of these groups made handicrafts in prisons and sent them to United States, Sweden, Germany and other countries. These were sold thanks to international solidarity and the proceeds helped sustain families.

Communal kitchens were organized on the basis of joint efforts and ended up being allocated to children, because they weren't adequate to feed complete families. Many times, I could see children eating grass and people going out to hunt pigeons for food, knowing that pigeons are scavengers, almost like rats.

Social movements in Chile

Social movements in general lack ideology, although in the Chilean case they make proposals and demands to the state, but that's as far as they go. They don't have their own programs and there are no political parties at the forefront interpreting the social movements to channel the social aspirations. That doesn't exist in Chile; there are no national projects.

In the case of the students' movement last year, they had very clear proposals and well-defined demands of the state, but they're alone. There's no party to interpret that movement, and the strategy of the governments was to wait for the movement to fade away and become discredited, because there are also anarchist groups that take advantage of social mobilizations to make their own protests and commit acts of violence. Then the security forces allow and encourage damage to public and private property so they can repress—and they generally repress only the groups of people that are protesting peacefully and defending their lawful rights.

This causes discontent among citizens because a substantial part of society is sympathetic to the claims and proposals of the students' movement, but they're also unhappy with the damage, acts of violence, destruction, and the existing repression, and this is a source of discontent against the students' movement that leads to its exhaustion.

But I don't believe that it's exhausted because with the students' movement, just now at the beginning of the school year, a very interesting phenomenon is taking place, since alliances with other social movements are being forged, specifically with the social movement in Aysén. [Note: See interview with Iván Fuentes in this chapter.] This also occurred in Calama, Rancagua, Concepción, Antofagasta, etc.

As I mentioned before, social movements generally don't have a long-term historical project; political parties and the social movements are dissociated. Hence, the strategy that has been used here and in the case of Mexico, Argentina, Bolivia, and Ecuador, which has been roughly the same, is to take debates from civil society to direct them through an institutional channel.

For example, when the pseudodemocracy was recovered, there was a large and strong women's movement. What the government did was to institutionalize the issue of women and created the office of women and, therefore, the proposals, claims, and aspirations of women had to be made through that office. The same occurred with the youth and the creation of the National Office of the Youth, with a state budget, public officers—and no young people were involved with that office. Again, the debate is taking from the citizens and directing them down an institutional path.

What did they do with the students' movement last year? This movement was proposing changes to the constitution, the labor code, free education, etc. The response from the authority, the president, the ministers, and Congress was that students weren't entitled to speak about the constitution, which means that the students are citizens entitled to speak only on the subject of education. But what the students are asking is not an issue within the scope of students' organizations but one that has to be debated in Congress, where things are debated within the current institutionality.

The purpose is to steal the agenda or the points for discussion that the social organizations have to discuss and take them within four walls in the offices of Congress or of the ministries. It's a strategy that has yielded very good results [for the power structure]. This ends up weakening and undermining social organization. Then, since they can't answer the social organizations or the leaders or meet the demands because they aren't allowed to do so by the model, then what the model does is to transfer public resources to private pockets. Then, education isn't free.

The state can subsidize a part of education but it can't make it free. It has to be paid in the future by the student or his or her family. Then the state offers credits; the money goes to the banks and the latter lend the money to the students. The state provides money to the banks with a 2 percent annual interest rate, then the banks charge a 7 to 9 percent annual interest rate to the student and, finally, a child's education, if he or she succeeds in becoming a professional, is tantamount to having a twenty-to-thirty-year mortgage on a house. So the state can't provide free education because its ideology and model prevent it from doing so. In other words, if education is free, how can banks or education companies earn money?

And the social organizations, at least historically in Chile, have never undertaken to take power or dispute the control of the state in their capacity as social organizations, because social movements here amalgamate various ideologies, such as in the specific case of Aysén: There are right-wing people, small businessmen, militants of National Renewal and of UDI, the party in power itself, together with Christian Democrats, socialists, communists, etc. They unite to solve their common problems locally. Common problems are beyond ideologies but solutions can be common. The solutions aren't ideological but they still involve the social and economic area. The current political parties in Chile have also been unable to gather the social discontent to channel through a program or a proposal, and reaching power by the electoral route.

Channeling protest to produce change

So in this regard social movements are highly neglected. They're generating expectations that they've been able to translate to the vast majority of the population, with clear-cut demands and claims, but they don't have official political forces to support them, channel their demands, and cause things to truly change, because true change involves changing all those taking the seats of Congress, La Moneda (National Palace), and the municipalities.

In the government of Allende, the social movement, unlike the parties on which the government was based, strongly supported the government. This is something the president realized and admonished the parties, because there were parties that were against the social movements. There were many social claims that were not included in the program and it meant even further deepening the program that the president had at that time the existing government coalition.

For that reason, the political parties were complaining and even accusing the social movements and the social leaders at that time of developing a political parallelism. Well, they didn't realize that the fundamental force of the government resided in the social movements and not in the coalition of parties, despite the latter's unambiguous support. But now the story is very different because nowadays the social movements are almost spontaneous and even though they have specific claims and demands and question the state, they don't have the technical tools required for policy-making.

For example, to change the education law, it's necessary to have knowledge not only of economics to study the budgets, for example, but also of pedagogy, teaching methodologies, review of contents, etc. And so there should be political parties to make their professionals available to the movement, but this isn't done because it's more comfortable to retain their share of power in the state, no matter how minor or small it might be. The political parties choose to maintain the social organizations as electoral clients.

How can we generate the sufficient capacities to prepare this necessary project of a country? How can we recover the utopias that have been long lost? How could all this be translated not only into a social movement but also into an advance toward the generation of a political movement? That is the challenge: Generating a political movement with transformative capacity. It has to happen eventually.

Aysén: Mobilization on March 16, 2012, during the forty-day uprising in Aysén. Photo licensed under CreativeCommons by *El Ciudadano*.

Iván Fuentes, Social Movement for Aysén
"That the resources of Chile go to four or five families: that's the real violence"

Interview first published in the Santiago-based bimonthly *El Ciudadano*, no. 121, March 2012
Translation by Clifton Ross

Iván Fuentes became the face and the voice of Aysén, a region that exploded in February 2012 as a result of a long list of grievances that the central government refused to address. The geography of Chile aggravates the effects of the country's internal imperialism, especially for the south, which lacks road connections and relies on expensive ferries. This raises the cost of basic necessities. What Fuentes says here can be repeated by Chileans in the remote north and west and by other Patagonians, most of whom felt deep sympathy for the people of Aysén. Reading between the lines, it shows the extent to which Chileans of all stripes, conservative to far left, are entirely cynical about the political parties, and the way desire for greater representation of regional interests cuts across more superficial political divisions.

After weeks of protests that included a thirteen-day road blockade, the Social Movement for Aysén signed an agreement with the government that

addressed some of its key concerns, but since then the government has either
failed to follow through, or—as with the approval of the Río Cuervo dam—
broken its promises.

[The Concertación] had the opportunity to get things done, and it didn't.
When it came to power, the youth from the 1980s, like me (I'm now forty-
four), we had a lot of hope. Big steps were taken, but Patagonia was left
behind, and that's why they lost power. Poor people accept their suffering,
but they get even, and they do that with their vote. [Sebastian Piñera] won
as a reprimand. I didn't vote for him, but I think this was a scolding, a vote
to punish the Concertación.

The demands [of the southern region] go back before the Concertación.
There were people like Baldemar Carrasco, ex-senator, elected in Aysén in
1969. For years he fought for the demands we're making now. But these
demands were left behind. The ANEF (Agrupación Nacional de Empleados
Fiscales), the CUT (Chile's main labor federation), the small fishermen and
truck drivers couldn't maintain them over time because each group had to
do so from his or her own context and perspective. But now we've gathered
these demands together from each sector and with the backing of Patagonia
are presenting them as eleven points.

In Aysén there's a clear desire to resolve the problem, but it doesn't
seem the government feels the same way. If the Chilean state believes that
those in the streets are nothing more than violent revolutionaries who they
have to wipe off the face of the earth, they're mistaken. There are other kinds
of violence: the violence of disdain, the violence of neglect, the violence
that the resources of Chile go to four or five families: that's the real violence.

We're not asking for free health or education. We're asking for, among
other things, a hospital with specialists and a university with four or five
courses of study that would have to do with our potential, like forestry,
fishing, and farming, so our young people could become professionals
there. Each day the small fishermen are becoming poorer in Chile. We're a
region that for twenty-five years has been asking for the same things.

Ours is a movement that cuts across lines with deep criticism for the
current political scheme. The country today is demonstrating against a
system, not against politicians. People want to vote for persons, not for
certain political parties. So this is a wake-up call for politics in Chile; Chilean
politics are sick and they have to be healed.

I'm not of any particular political party, nor is this movement political.
The demands represent deep social feelings that cross lines. My compañero
Misael Ruiz is right-wing, and a militant in the Renovación Nacional. I'm

not a militant of any party, but my work is social. We want people to regain
their faith in politics, in our way of doing politics, valuing people dedicated
to doing the things they were born to do. These people have no wage nor
title, but they work from their hearts and they're able to give, to leave something for their children and work for their community. Those are the leaders.

[Our decision to lift our blockade] wasn't an expression of our weakness
but a show of our generosity of spirit, of will and humility. We're not trying
to weaken the hand of the government, but we just want our demands recognized. The government said it resolved everything but it couldn't show us
the resolution because we were blockading the roads. It took a lot of work
to convince the people in the streets that they had to open them up, but
we managed and we could say to the government, "There they are. All the
roads are open and functioning and the gas, the flour, all the supplies were
passing through and businesses were operating. So now, sirs, show me the
solutions that you were holding back and couldn't show us?"

From then until now it's been a week, more than a week. The lie continues until the truth comes, and we've always spoken the truth.

We don't regret [lifting the blockade] because humility is always greater
than arrogance: Arrogance has never led to anything good. We'll never come
to an understanding by fighting it out with the Special Forces, throwing
rocks in the streets. I don't want two or three more people being blinded.[27]
It's going to haunt me that they've been blinded. Imagine if someone were to
die. It would be terrible. I don't feel responsible but I do feel pain for it. Still,
we had to act, because if we hadn't, we would never have had the opportunity to let Chile know that Patagonia exists.

There's been a centralism [in Chile] for a long time. The great city is the
city of opportunities but we have to leave and go out to find [opportunity].
We want the regions to participate more. Punta Arenas wants to be more
independent. Fine. Each region has its formula and the state can continue
receiving all the goods the regions produce. But Santiago can't be all of
Chile. It has to be the capital of Chile, a capital of brothers that share better.

My own life goes hand in hand with the eleven demands of the movement. I have five little boys and I want to see them go to the university, but
they'll have to go to Temuco or Valparaíso. If someone gets sick, he or she
has to be taken off the island of Puerto Aguirre in an airplane. If it's during
the day, that's fine, but if it's night, you'll have to be lucky because we're
talking about a minimum six-hour trip. It makes me very sad to see people
who are sixty-five or seventy years old, living on seventy-five lucas a month,
and water costs thirty-five. We pay the highest water bills in all of Chile
and everywhere you look it's a cascade. We pay the highest electric bills

in Chile in a region where it rains nine months a year. A kilo of fish costs eight hundred pesos. Benzene costs 1,130 pesos a liter. All these things are continually hitting you.

The Chilean state has to divide things up better. How is it that in the far north [of Chile] people can't take water out of a well with a bucket because there's so little water left in the well that they have to use a pitcher to fill the bucket and take out water to drink? This is because kilometers further up there's a big capitalist who has taken over the water. And what are we to do about our campesinos? They have to leave [the countryside]. Where to? To the big city. They head to the world of concrete with their little children and they're lost in the margins because the poor who go to the city can't live in the center. And that campesino was the one who made the goat cheese and planted grain, and this grain was what arrived in the city.

When we step on the capitalists' toes, the whole world is moved. Before the protest, [the capitalists] were the first to call the government to tell them, "Hey, get rid of these guys who are rising up." They weren't thinking of solutions; they were thinking of power. We respond in all humility and say, "If you're making money, invest in your surroundings." We don't trample the dignity of the people but rather we gather into a great flock for mutual protection and that way we have power equal to theirs. They have the power of money. We have the power of unity and solidarity.

It's all cost us a lot. If it were just up to me, to Iván Fuentes, I'd cut a piece of wood from a tree and sit down to wait. But it's not up to me. I'm the spokesperson for a group of people who are hungering, thirsting, and waiting for justice. We're not worn out, but we are tired. Still, I have faith. I hope the government at some moment will want to change. We can make history together. President Piñera still has the chance to do things the others haven't done.

La Negra, on women and the violence of the state
"Do what you have to do at a micropolitical level"

Interview by Marcy Rein and Clifton Ross, March 2012
Translation by Christy Rodgers

La Negra is a young radical feminist activist. She and a friend talked with us at length over a pot of tea in their apartment but asked to remain anonymous because of the political work they do. Members of the postdictatorship generation, they regard the established Left and Right with equal skepticism, disdain the government, and advocate a "DIY" approach. They see the legal restrictions on Chilean women as expressions of deep cultural violence and misogyny.

Chile is one of only five countries in the world to completely ban abortion, even when a woman's life is in danger. Women needing abortions work through extralegal channels, such as the national hotline run by Lesbians and Feminists for the Right to Know. The all-volunteer project, open 24/7 every day of the year, counsels women on safe use of the abortion drug "misoprostol," as well as their legal rights.[28] Women choosing to have children fare better: Chile has a lower infant mortality rate than the United States, thanks in part to reforms in the health-care system since 2002 that improve access to services.[29]

Negra: It's like a seed of insurrection. The whole student movement came along, and you see Magallanes,[30] that the people also shut down around the gas issue, and now we're seeing Aysén shutting down in the same way. It's part of a chain of insurrection in Chile.

There are people who really have been beaten down these last twenty years and that's also getting a response. So if it's not the students now, something else will come: They're selling off the water, there's the GMOs. There's enough issues for a good while. That's clear. The looting's going on all over the place, what they're trying to sell you. There's issues.

If it's not education it's the right to water; if it's not Hidroaysén, it's the Pascualama mine, so it's a little of everything. And there's almost always women in all that, their rights and abortion and all those things, but those seem like almost the least important thing in this whole context. You have to put yourself in that context, at least as people who are more on top of it, more aware. You have to put yourself into this context, [consider] why the state and the government want to repress. I don't know about "kill," because there have been deaths in this "democracy" that we have, in quotes, there have been killings by the cops, the police state. According to them, those are isolated cases, but there's definitely a social atmosphere that we don't [know] where it's going, either, we don't know what's happening. It's serious.

People are experiencing bluntly that the state is the repressor, but not much is known [about it], and on the other hand there are a lot of people who support it. There's a political class, a fake class that supports this type of thing, [that says,] "They're the Indians in the South, how can they not help the country's growth and development?," like that.

For me, at least, there is the type of violence experienced under the state, but there's also a cultural violence, societal violence that produces some things women know about. There's a lot of women who are super-oppressed because they are harassed for not being mothers. There are roles that are so integrated into the culture that [it's hard for] the women who want to get out of them, with this religious thing behind it. So yes, there are a lot of women who are being viewed badly. They can't do what they want because there's this very oppressive culture behind them.

Many are victims of this reproduction of hetero-patriarchal culture that doesn't question itself about a lot of things, because it's all set up to reproduce itself. I understand there are also men who are oppressed, who at the same time tell [other men] not to cry. They're also imposing a role on you, so in that way it's social and cultural repression. The structure is sick, and there's a lack of questioning of the structure, of gender/sexuality. They tell you it's a given, it's something totally natural, when really it's something super artificial, super ideological.

I'd like to add some thoughts from the political class on references to gender. Senator-elect Ena Von Baer in a [talk she gave] around the right to abortion said, "A woman who gives her body is basically making a home for a life that's going to develop, and she has no right to terminate that life. We can't know at what moment the fetus is not viable." Where women have this almost sacred responsibility to interrupt our lives so that the fetus can grow, they never talk about a woman's right to have a life with fewer children or without any.

This also supposes that if the pregnancy isn't viable, women should carry the dying fetus in their womb until it dies outside. We're subjected to the power of Opus Dei women, who see reality only through their social class and their religiosity.[31]

Means of resistance

"Well I'm a musician, and I work for the government." No. Try not to do it, not just be underground inside it. Maybe other people went underground with masks, went to the jungle. Here in the city you have to do it a different way, like refusing to pay taxes to the government, since you'll get them back afterward in tear gas, gases, repression.

So instead, [figure out] how to be self-sufficient, try not to sell out. Apart from that, I'm not able to see it at a systemic level or as a social movement, because it's complicated to analyze.

I think you can develop a practice. It's about uneducating yourself from this way of thinking that depends on the government, [for example] because the government has to provide housing for you. You can scavenge your stuff, go up to the top of the hill, and build your house. You can do these things. There are things that I talk about at a personal level, because at the collective level it's different.

If you work at a micropolitical level, you can find a way not to depend on the government. If that was done massively the guys in power wouldn't have anybody to dominate, the people to use their credit cards, those businesses they set up just to get rich themselves.

But what do they have to do with health care, with work? You have to look for ways not to depend on that. If it's done at a massive level, that's good.

Knowing that the Right and Left are the same, who do you trust? Who do you trust to represent you, after twenty years of this shit that we've had since the dictatorship? The only thing I see is do what you have to do at a micropolitical level. I see it like that right now. Maybe later it'll change into something else, but now you can think about why you can think like that.

You can think about it at the level of education too. There's experience in Argentina, where they use barter a lot to educate a community. There are people who are saying so long to their doctors, they're treating their cancer in another way. There are practices that make you think, "Hey I don't depend so much on this." Instead you can live perfectly well without feeling I [have to] depend on something else, something bigger than me to survive, or to live.

Just [do] civil disobedience and don't validate their laws and we're outta here—but you have to have a subversive mind to be able to subvert that sucker. Same way, from the little body you have, your little insignificant life, there still has to be some way, even if it means resisting with all your life, there has to be something, because if not, let 'em kill me, let 'em crush me.

Friend: That's why it's difficult how to make an organized mass resistance [out of] this.

Negra: Because it's very deeply entrenched in the body of the culture of subjectivity.

Friend: But at the same time, people were thinking about the issue of abortion, of [women and legal abortion]. What Negra was saying at the beginning is that now we're not asking the state and the government to legalize abortion or to guarantee it for you in some way, because they're not going to do it, because it's their way of controlling bodies, too.

Negra: But you talk to somebody, to a woman without much learning, much education, but speaking from her life experience she says, "Sure, this woman says that I'm the vessel of the child to come. She has twenty kids, but of course she's Opus Dei and she has a nanny for every kid, and this is my reality that I have to work with: My husband almost rapes me. I don't know if I've ever had an orgasm in my life. I have five kids to feed, and I'm going to have an abortion however I can. I have to." And that's the Chilean woman's reality.

You start talking to Chilean women and they've all had abortions. Abortion exists. Now, making it legal or not is another issue. It exists and it's everywhere. So from where we stand, we say, "Okay, let's help this, let's educate or let's try to have support networks for women so that they can do it in the best way possible." But not asking the state to make a law legalizing abortion. You're wasting energy instead of channeling it to your organization, your life.

José Ancalao, Federation of Mapuche Students (FMS)
"What unites us should be the deep-rooted feeling of being Mapuches and wanting to reclaim our rights, language, identity"

Interview by Marcy Rein and Clifton Ross, April 2012
Translation by Christy Rodgers

José Ancalao was hard to track down, perhaps because he seems to always be on the move. He has a very steady but intense energy that seems to be extraordinarily focused. In addition to studying full time and working as a leader of the FMS, he sits on the directing body of the Chilean Confederation of Students (known as CONFECH in Chile), and works with a group of people in his home community who are putting together a Mapuche cultural center. He's suffered deeply for his work on behalf of his people—physical beatings from police, imprisonment, and harassment—but he doesn't seem to consider that important to talk about. We did the interview in Santiago's Parque Forestal on a warm early fall day, with the sounds of traffic whooshing by in the background.

I belong to a Mapuche community called Ignacio Solquemilla de Puren. It's located between the two little towns of Puren and Lumaco, three hours northwest of Temuco. Well, this community lost much of its land in 1881 when Mapuche territory officially became part of Chile. So my family was decimated, more than half of them were killed. (The occupation of Araucanía took place from 1879 to 1893 and 1894, when eight hundred fifty thousand Mapuches were killed by the Chilean army. It was an attempted genocide of the time.)

There is a lot of poverty in the community. Actually very few Mapuche communities have [many] comforts; most of them are very poor, which is why we Mapuche students have less access to education, because we are poorer than the average poor Chilean, so we have less access and the system is more weighted against us when we want to get higher education or to go to a good university.

José Ancalao. Photo by Clifton Ross.

Today people in the rural areas have no water because the forestry plantations have dried up all the ground water, the aquifers. They have to send trucks with hoses to deliver water to the countryside. People are leaving the rural areas for the city because it's very bad in the countryside. It's full of tree plantations, the water is polluted with pine pollen and it's very sad to see. And people are being uprooted more and more because there's no opportunity. There's no way to keep being a Mapuche peacefully under these conditions, so people look for a better life and that's how the Mapuches have ended up in the big cities.

Mapuche women went to work in the houses of rich people. Many Mapuches come to work in construction and that's been happening since the 1980s. A large percentage of the population live in the outskirts of Santiago—I'd venture to guess that as much as 80 percent of the population in the outer areas is indigenous: Mapuche or Aymara or Atacameño. And the same thing happens in Temuco, and in many cities. So today it isn't like it was forty years ago. Today 60 percent of Mapuches live in cities, according to the last census.

Thus there is a great deal of discrimination against the Mapuche. A lot of racism. Today there's a stereotype of the weak Mapuche, the drunk, and the terrorist, because the government wants to decrease the number of indigenous people, and especially Mapuche, the largest indigenous group in Chile.

This is basically a silent form of extermination, through denial of education, denial of participation in decision-making, and a whole series of things that keep us locked into a complex reality, but [also] with many young people rising up today in the Mapuche communities, city or country, in Santiago, Temuco, Valdivia, or Concepción.

Basically, many young people are rising up to support rescuing our language, identity, culture and land, some more radical than others, some not very radical, but that is part of the diversity of the Mapuche people.

The Federation of Mapuche Students sought to include in [the statement of] CONFECH that Chile is a diverse country with several indigenous peoples. We wanted to join this movement but from our specific situation as Mapuche, so we had to fight a tremendous struggle to get into CONFECH, and finally we did. We wanted to be part of decision-making in the student movement, and that's why we joined CONFECH and today we are members and participants in the student movement. In 2012 we've been following up on the work we did last year.

Theft of resources

When Mapuche land became part of Chile, the Mapuche were clustered on small parcels of land, and the government confiscated all the large landholdings, expropriated them, took them away, and sold the lands at a very low price and gave them away to French, English, Swiss, and Italian settlers, and members of the army who had taken part in the War of the Pacific against Peru and Bolivia. The lands were given to them.

So the conflict today is that the Mapuche communities want back the land that belonged to their grandparents, but this is not the settlers' fault or the Mapuches'; it's the responsibility of the government.

The government thinks it's a poverty problem. It thinks the problem is poverty, alcoholism, violence—but not politics. It doesn't believe that it's a political, historical, and cultural problem from years back that no government has been capable of solving. Not the Left, Right, or center. No government of Chile has been capable of solving this problem. Not one. Not even Allende. Not even Allende who is a great figurehead, much respected, but no real advances were made then because the land that was redistributed under Allende was given to peasant farmers, not the Mapuches. They were never dealt with as Mapuches by the Popular Unity government.

Origins of the struggle

The first Mapuche movement protest happened in 1910 in the southern territory of the Bío-Bío, with the Caupolicán Society, who were the sons of the

Mapuche leaders who survived the war. They wanted some kind of plat-form to unite the Mapuche movement and begin to politically demand the return of lands, recovery of language and identity to become rooted again in the land as we are.

After that, the Caupolicán Society became the Araucana Corporation, when they had already been working for a long time, since 1950; after twenty years of movement work it succeeded in electing the first Mapuche con-gressmen. They had about seven Mapuche congressmen. They had a sec-retary of state, the Mapuche Venancio Coñuepán, but after the Pinochet dictatorship, the whole movement that had been so difficult to build col-lapsed, was destroyed, fell apart, but not just because of the military dic-tatorship but because of the closed nature of the leftist movement of that time, the 1960s.

In the 1960s there was a trend that you surely are aware of, *indigenismo*, which is like "by indigenous people, for indigenous people, but without indigenous people." Like: "We fight for you, we'll speak for you. We are moving forward through you. You stay there." Practically a colonialist form of domination. So what was a struggle for autonomy, for self-determination, became a class struggle with the other peoples.

That's how it began, and later, in 1973, it was reaffirmed with the Pinochet government, the military dictatorship, and then the indigenous movement rose again in the 1980s. Right in the middle of the dictatorship, young Mapuches began to organize. That's when they began to organize to recover their cultural roots.

But beyond preserving the culture, they did a lot of political work, and they began to set up the first Mapuche movements right in the middle of the dictatorship. One of them was Admapu, a tremendous Mapuche organiza-tion of the time. Another is the All Lands Council, and the Arauco Malleco Coordination in 1996–97. And so the Mapuche movement continued to develop in democracy, [during] the Concertación (the governing coalition after the removal of Pinochet), but without many changes between the dictatorship and the transition to democracy, instead the same policies of domination are maintained, the same repressive neocolonialism, denial of cultural differences, denial of the existence of first peoples.

Violence and police brutality
Various acts of violence have happened over the last twelve or thirteen years. Estates have been set on fire, the houses of landowners, forestry company trucks, their tree plantations have been set fire to, and the government blames the Mapuches. The Mapuches are the guilty ones, according to the

government, these are terrorist acts according Pinochet's 1980 law, which was a law to eliminate extreme left-wing armed movements in Chile in the 1980s. This is the "terrorism" there is in Chile, but it's never been proven that the Mapuches have participated in these violent acts.

Most of them have been set-ups. It's never been proven that Mapuches have participated in any of these actions. When the antiterrorist law is applied to someone, they lose all their rights: they can be tortured, many things... held incommunicado, for an unlimited time, as long as the investigation continues. That means if the investigation lasts twenty years, they can be in jail for twenty years. At the trial the prosecutor can present witnesses whose faces are masked and voices distorted. The antiterrorism law violates every constitutional protection, as well as the international human rights charter. This means there's no respect for that in the antiterrorism law. None. It's basically a terrorist law that governments have imposed here in Chile. President Lagos and President Michelle Bachelet used it, and now the right-wing government has and is using it.

The Mapuches have no freedom today in their own homes because the police shoot whenever they want to, they raid whenever they want to. There's no rule of law, as the saying goes. No equality. And there's a lot of police violence as well.

I've been arrested like ten times and they've beaten me three times. They've broken my ribs. It's something you just take for granted, but this kind of violence is not natural even though many people take it for granted. In many places in the country the children play "Cops and Mapuches." So it's something really deeply shocking to go to a Mapuche community where there's a conflict with the police, and children of three, four, and five years old are playing "Cops and Mapuches." Really shocking.

Mapuche movement today

There are many aspects to the Mapuche struggle: reclaiming our culture, language, identity, reclaiming educational and linguistic rights for indigenous peoples, having our own university that we'd share with non-Mapuches, intercultural and public, for example. Ensuring that the Mapuches who come to the city to study have a place to live. So these are the perhaps basic things today that will be just the tip of the iceberg in the future, and that's what we young people are involved in.

There are other Mapuches who are struggling through the political parties. I don't know, that's their thing, but they argue and fight for their space in the political parties. There are a number of Mapuches who are preaching in the churches. Others are Catholic priests. So there are different aspects of the Mapuche struggle today. At heart let's not be divided by the hurdles of intolerance: let's be united in our feeling, our desire and our determination to achieve our common goals: self-determination, autonomy, and political organization to achieve autonomy.

If we are get autonomy tomorrow what will the Mapuches do, if we have nothing, if we're poor? We have no economic power, we have no political power; we have nothing. So it's part of what we have to create. If our great-great grandparents and great grandparents spoke to us about the Mapuche republic in 1920, we've gone backward. We've gone backward in time in terms of political projections, but the struggle has been ongoing, but today we have look for ways to occupy [political] space.

That's what we are doing in the Federation of Mapuche Students, to raise this ideal that what unites us should be the fact that we're Mapuches, whether we're Christians or no, members of the Socialist Party or the Renovation Party on the right, but the deep-rooted feeling of being Mapuches and brothers and wanting to reclaim our rights, language, identity, and that's what we are doing now.

We haven't been working for very long. The federation is not even a year old, but we're doing a lot of work with youth, with the high school students, with Mapuche language courses, with really basic things, actually. But the main thing to begin [any] longer-term work that will be solid, is that maybe it's going to go a little slower. We participate in activities in our communities, in the New Year's ceremony we call We Xipantu, and the Nquillatún, which is a ceremony performed every two or four years depending on the place.

We participate in meetings we call *chagun*, with young people from other areas, from the mountains, the coast, from different places, and these things are done very much in our way. We call conversation "*luchambe;*" we call speeches "*guaipitún*," meaning the act of public speaking, and many things like that.

We know that this isn't a short-term effort, that it's a very long-term question. Surely when I'm no longer the director they'll see results of this work, but it's something we have to build ourselves, because we are also responsible for the lives our children and our grandchildren will live, just as our ancestors did so that we could be here today. So we young people have a heavy load to carry as part of that responsibility.

Marjory Cuello. Photo by Marcy Rein.

Marjory Cuello, Confederation of Chilean Students (Confederación de Estudiantes de Chile, CONFECH)
"Students alone will not change education"

Interview by Clifton Ross and Marcy Rein, April 2012
Translation by Christy Rodgers

Hundreds of thousands of people flooded the streets of Chile for mass student-led mobilizations during the 2011 school year, virtually shutting down many universities. Secondary-school students took over more than two hundred schools. Teachers and other union members, parents and neighbors joined the student protests.

Rich as the year was in political lessons, it fell short on concrete policy changes. Going into the new academic year in the spring of 2012, the student movement was regrouping and looking for new, creative actions. CONFECH, the Confederation of Chilean Students—the umbrella group linking the federations at different universities—decided to kick off the year by reaching out to the community with an "Acto Cultural."

The day of culture in Parque Almagro, near downtown Santiago, featured lots of music, with some bands so popular that crowds sang along; vendors

*sold crafts, posters and T-shirts; political groups passed out literature, and,
of course, some of the student leaders addressed the crowd. We got a chance
to interview Marjory Cuello before she spoke, though we had to get almost a
block away from the booming speakers to be able to hear. Cuello at that time
was general secretary of the University of Valparaiso Students' Federation
(Federación de Estudiantes de la Universidad de Valparaíso, FEUV), a post
equivalent to president. She also worked with the National Students' Union,
a grassroots group whose members study together and work in other organizations, and served on the executive board of CONFECH.*

Today we in CONFECH, the national students' movement, are trying to
establish a benchmark to begin mobilizing in 2012, knowing that things
were frozen in 2011, even though we succeeded in presenting some deeply
structural demands that directly attack the capitalist system and the neoliberal model. Today what we want to do is show the citizenry that we aren't
asleep, we didn't go away. On April 25, we'll have our first national CONFECH
march, and this means that we students don't just have demands; we also
have solutions, alternatives to the model, and we believe that a quality education can basically be public and free.

We're saying that resource distribution in Chile is highly unequal, not
only in education but also in all the other areas of society like work, health
care, and housing, and that democracy in Chile is very limited and not very
participatory. We're proposing new forms of policy-making where it's not
the leaders making the decisions but our comrades in constant discussion.

The alternative model we're planning is a progressive tax reform, so
that they thoroughly redistribute resources and address all the social needs.

In addition we're proposing renationalizing the copper industry, which
after the [Pinochet] coup was taken and sold to foreign businesses, and
today Chile doesn't get the benefits or profits from a resource that essentially
belongs to all Chileans, as do other natural resources like lithium and water,

We strongly support all the campaigns against hydroelectric dams; we
believe that sustainable development should be one of the fundamental
pillars of the political economy of [all] governments.

Our other proposal is to reduce military spending in Chile, which is
disproportionately high. Too much money is spent on the armed forces
today. That money should be designated for social needs.

Building unity to fight for solutions

We understand that students alone will not change education. We aren't
going to get free tuition alone, nor will the rest of the social changes be

created by all the [different] sectors working in isolation. We believe that connection is essential for that; we have to unify the social movement to obtain the profound changes Chile needs. Today it's not just students but workers, all the different unions, workers, and political associations that have to join the struggle to fundamentally change the Chilean social model.

We also know that Chile is not the only one suffering the consequences of this model. We know that many countries in Latin America and the whole world are suffering the consequences and are entering into crisis, like Greece, even the United States, where there have been many demonstrations. We believe that worldwide awakening and above all worldwide social power is what should create the change in the model today.

We're in a stage of beginning to get to know the other actors, make contact with the unions, other workers' organizations. Now we're officially coordinating with CUT (Central Unitaria de Trabajadores de Chile), which is one of the main workers' organizations. We've also sought contacts with other unions that may not be part of CUT, but that can be worked with, and also with the Teachers' College, and with the parents' association and its representatives. Bit by bit we're trying to build our work in coordination together with everyone for the demonstration and also on the proposed alternative model, so that our proposal isn't just about education but other social concerns as well.

CONFECH is the national organization for university students; high school students are organized in different coordinating bodies like Coordinating Assembly for Secondary Students (ACES), and National Coordination of Secondary Students (CONES). Yes, nationally there's a new awareness among students that we experienced in 2011 and that we now hope will continue, but yes, we're coordinating nationally as student and as social [movements].

In Chile, both the right wing and the moderates have expanded the [neoliberal] model, the state subsidized model, and personally I and part of my organization are very critical about the fact that today the Communist Party makes electoral deals with the moderates.

We believe that moving to the political center is not the answer; we believe that the Communist Party today should turn left at last, and mainly we are counting on the unity of the Left. I believe that that is something we need to learn from history: that without unity there, nothing will change. All the leftist organizations must have space in a common social and political project.

The traditional parties have distanced themselves from the masses; they've distanced themselves from the concrete problems of the citizens.

That's why there's this new awakening among young people in political organizations that count on struggling for a change in the model but from within the masses, and don't get too far away from them whether one is or isn't in an institutional position. To lose the umbilical cord with the people will always result in failure.

Today the students and one or two other social sectors are building a bottom-up structure, not a top-down one like the traditional political parties have. Mainly we make decisions in the assemblies, and there are other intermediate bodies. Afterward the higher leadership comes in, but those leaders have to answer to everything that has been discussed by the base with all of our comrades.

That is the new form that the traditional parties have forgotten, making decisions in the top party leadership, forgetting finally about the electorate that chose them and that has its own demands and that aren't reflected now by the political class, in the formal institutions. We have criticisms of the institutions, however, we believe that all forms of struggle are valid, when and if there's a direct feedback loop between base and leaderships, any type of work is valid.

We learned in 2011 that alone we will achieve nothing; that was one of the main lessons. It's necessary to link up with other sectors and actors. We also learned that mobilization, strikes, takeovers are not an end in themselves, but tools of struggle. Nonetheless, we can't discard them, but we also know that we have to be a little more creative and do these types of things that we're doing today that bring us closer to the public.

We know that free education is a long-term struggle, however we also know that we must achieve concrete gains for our comrades, and that's the discussion we're in now, trying to see what we are going to consider an advance but never lose sight of the goal of free education and really a more just society.

I belong to a political organization called the National Students' Union that was formed in 2011, and is also a result of the demonstrations, but we have been working collectively as a political organization for many years in my university and that's where we first started coming; today I'm general secretary of the federation, which is like the presidency. I study history, so my course work in my studies is quite critical of the current model, of how things have been in Chile's history.

My studies also happen through self-learning and daily learning with our comrades who know there's something wrong and together we have to change things. The National Students' Union today is a very large organiza-tion. We're in every part of Chile, and we count on all the comrades who want to organize a more just society and free education having an organizing space like the National Students' Union where they can say what they want.

"We are the grandchildren of the dictatorship"

So that brings me up to today and personally my plans are to go to Teachers' College, work in colleges, the university and help other young folks to get a political education, so that their university or college experience doesn't just give them the same thing. That's what we hope, that in their educational institutions, the kids can get all the tools they need to mobilize and politicize themselves.

My family thinks of itself as middle-class and is not involved politically. But sure, they have opinions, they always taught us to develop our own opinions, and, well, here are the consequences.

I was born in 1987, certainly that's the other thing our generation has. We didn't live through the dictatorship. We're the grandchildren of the dictatorship, so generally we know there was a great deal of suffering and persecution, and a great deal of struggle too, during the dictatorship, but we know that emotionally we shouldn't take on that fear. Instead we should get rid of it and start up something again that possibly our parents left unfinished.

Particularly with this government, we've suffered a lot of repression; in fact many people have told us that this level of repression hasn't been seen since the dictatorship, since the struggle against the dictatorship in the 1980s. In the supposed democracy we have, that brute force is called on to silence the social movements because the social movements are correct. Historically the upper class has used moments of brute force to repress the demands of the people, so we believe we're on the right track, precisely because they are repressing us so much.

There's the Federation of Mapuche Students that we've dealt with in CONFECH, to bring the theme of multiculturalism to the fore. Clearly we've lived through a maximum period of repression against students for the last two years. However, the Mapuche people have lived through it for many years now. Today the government is trying to silence their demands, to repress their culture as well, as if it went against the established order. We believe that we must build a tolerant country, one where as many cultures as possible can live together. There aren't just the Mapuches but the Aymara as well, and there are other ethnicities that have their own demands. It's necessary that we give the space to survive and persist to those cultures that are basically where we all come from.

Contributors

Interviewers and introducers:
ACOGUATE, the Coordination for International Accompaniment in Guatemala is a network of eleven autonomous committees in ten countries of North America and Europe. ACOGUATE places trained international observers as protective accompaniment alongside individuals and organizations in human rights and social movements who face threats due to their work. More information about the mandate of ACOGUATE, its network, and accompanied cases can be found at www.acoguate.org.

Marc Becker is a professor of Latin American history at Truman State University at Kirksville, Missouri, and author of several books on Ecuador, including *Pachakutik: Indigenous Movements and Electoral Politics in Ecuador* (Rowman & Littlefield Publishers, Inc., 2011) and *Indians and Leftists in the Making of Ecuador's Modern Indigenous Movements* (Duke University Press, 2008).

Diego Benegas Loyo is a psychoanalyst and researcher of subjectivity and political action. A Fulbright grantee, he writes on social movements, queer and migrant subjects, electronic action, and sociology of trauma. He is a professor at the Barceló University Institute and New York University Buenos Aires.

Ben Dangl has worked as a journalist throughout Latin America for over a decade, and is the author of *The Price of Fire: Resource Wars and* Social Movements *in Bolivia* and *Dancing with Dynamite: Social Movements and States in Latin America*, both published by AK Press. He is the founder and editor of *Upside Down World*, an online publication covering politics and social movements in Latin America, and edits *Toward Freedom*, a website offering a progressive perspective on world events. Dangl is currently in a doctoral program in Latin American history at McGill University. For more of his writing, see www.bendangl.net.

Mar Daza is a Peruvian popular educator, researcher, and feminist activist, who currently directs the Programa Democracia y Transformación Global (www.democraciaglobal.org) and has collaborated with different social organizations as well as participated in activist networks over the last years. In her work, Daza focuses on cultural change, the intersections of domination and social struggles, and the alternative discourses and social relations that emerge from social struggle. She edited *Crisis y movimientos sociales en Nuestra América: Cuerpos, territorios e imaginarios en disputa* (Lima, 2012).

Michael Fox has worked for many years as a freelance journalist, radio reporter, and documentary filmmaker covering Latin America. He is a former editor of *NACLA Report on the Americas*. He is also the coeditor of *Venezuela Speaks! Voices from the Grassroots*, and the codirector of the documentary films *Beyond Elections* and *Crossing the American Crises*, all available from PM Press. He is currently a leadership organizer with the United Workers in Baltimore, where he uses media as tool for grassroots organizing. His work can be found at blendingthelines.org.

J. Heyward is a prisoner rights advocate, solidarity activist, and community journalist based in Oakland, California, and is currently living in Washington, DC. Heyward's articles and interviews have been published in the *San Francisco Bay View Black National Newspaper*, *Z Magazine*, and at upsidedownworld.org.

Raphael Hoetmer is a Dutch researcher, popular educator and activist who has been living in Peru over the last nine years. He is associate researcher of the Programa Democracia y Transformación Global (www.democraciaglobal.org), and collaborator with different social organizations over the last years in Peru. His collaborative research focuses on social movements in Peru, with special attention for conflicts over territories, for the dialogue among different social movements, and for the processes of internal organization and strengthening within social movements. He edited *Repensar la política desde América Latina. Cultura, Estado y movimientos sociales* (Lima,

2009) and *Minería y territorio en el Perú. Conflictos, resistencias y propuestas en tiempos de globalización* (Lima, 2009) and was coeditor with Mar Daza of *Crisis y movimientos sociales en Nuestra América: Cuerpos, territorios e imaginarios en disputa* (Lima, 2012).

Hilary Klein spent six years in Chiapas, Mexico, working with women's projects in Zapatista communities. She now lives in Brooklyn and works at Make the Road New York, where she oversees the workers' rights, affordable housing, and leadership development programs. Hilary is currently working on *Compañeras*, a book about women's participation in the Zapatista movement. She is the author of the forthcoming book *Compañeras: Zapatista Women's Stories*.

Courtney Martinez, originally from South Texas, is currently based in Guatemala City, Guatemala as the Communications Coordinator for the Network in Solidarity with Guatemala (NISGUA). Before working for NISGUA, she served as an international human rights accompanier in Guatemala from 2011–2012.

Mario A. Murillo is professor and chair of the department of Radio, Television, Film in the School of Communication at Hofstra University in New York, and was a Fulbright Scholar in Colombia in 2008. Author of *Colombia and the United States: War, Unrest, and Destabilization* (Seven Stories, 2004), he is working on a book about Colombia's indigenous movement and its uses of communication in its mobilizing and organizational efforts. He is an award-winning radio journalist who has reported for NPR's *Latino USA*, Pacifica Radio, and WBAI Radio in New York.

Phil Neff was a coordinator of ACOGUATE and the Guatemala Accompaniment Project of the Network in Solidarity with the People of Guatemala from 2010 to 2012. He writes about solidarity and human rights issues for the blog Cascadia Solidaria (cascadiasolidaria.wordpress.com). He currently lives in Seattle, Washington.

NISGUA, the Network in Solidarity with the People of Guatemala, based in the United States, employs strategic, creative, and coordinated grass-roots activism and advocacy to pursue justice for war crimes, to change harmful U.S. policies, and to promote communities defending their rights in the face of natural resource extraction in Guatemala. NISGUA provides international human rights accompaniment via the ACOGUATE project in

Guatemala. To learn more about NISGUA's more than thirty years of work in Guatemala, visit www.nisgua.org.

Fabíola Ortiz dos Santos is a Brazilian journalist who lives in Rio de Janeiro and reports for the international news agency Inter Press Service (IPS), the Portuguese News Agency (LUSA), and several Brazilian outlets, including O Eco, an environmental website, Universo Online (UOL) and São Paulo–based Opera Mundi. She graduated from the School of Social Communication of the Federal University of Rio de Janeiro (UFRJ). In 2012, she was a finalist of the Journalists&Cia/HSBC Press and Sustainability Award for the story "Cacique de cocar, terno e iPhone comercializa carbono" ("With a cockade, suit and iPhone, indigenous leader commercializes carbon").

Hernán Ouviña is a professor of the Faculty of Social Sciences and a graduate of political science at the University of Buenos Aires (UBA), a researcher of the Institute for the Study of Latin America and Caribbean at UBA, a member of the editorial committee of *Revista Cuadernos del Sur*, and a visiting researcher at the Antonio Gramsci Institute in Rome. Ouviña is the author of *Zapatismo para principiantes* (Zapatismo for Beginners), coauthor of *Gramsci and Education: Pedagogy of Praxis and Cultural Politics in Latin America*, and the author of numerous articles, compilations, and interviews published in Latin America and Europe.

Adrienne Pine is a militant medical anthropologist who has worked in Honduras, Mexico, Korea, the United States, and Egypt, and is the author of *Working Hard, Drinking Hard: On Violence and Survival in Honduras*. Prior to and following the June 2009 military coup in Honduras, she has collaborated with numerous organizations and individuals to bring international attention to the Honduran struggle to halt state violence (in its multiple forms). She has also conducted extensive research on the impact of corporate health care and health-care technologies on labor practices in the United States.

Susan Spronk teaches international development at the University of Ottawa. She is a research associate with the *Municipal Services Project* and has published various articles on working-class formation and water politics in Latin America.

Marie Trigona is a writer and media-maker whose work has focused on social movements in Latin America. She has reported for *Free Speech Radio*

News, Radio France International, *Z Magazine*, the *Buenos Aires Herald*, *NACLA Report on the Americas*, and *Dollars & Sense*, among many others. She currently resides in Seattle, where she works with a union and dances tango.

Jeffery R. Webber is a lecturer in the School of Politics and International Relations at Queen Mary, University of London. He is the author of *Red October: Left-Indigenous Struggles in Modern Bolivia* and *From Rebellion to Reform in Bolivia: Class Struggle, Indigenous Liberation and the Politics of Evo Morales.* Webber sits on the editorial board of *Historical Materialism* and is coeditor of *The New Latin American Left: Cracks in the Empire.*

Raúl Zibechi is an international analyst for *Brecha*, the weekly newspaper of Montevideo, Uruguay, a lecturer and researcher on social movements at the *Multiversidad Franciscana de América Latina*, and an adviser to several social groups. He writes the monthly "Zibechi Report" for the Americas Program (www.americasprogram.org). His columns appear regularly in Lafogata.org, *NACLA Report on the Americas*, upsidedownworld.org, ZNet, Lavaca.org and counterpunch.org. He has published numerous books, including *Genealogía de la Revuelta, Argentina: la Sociedad en Movimiento* (Letra Libre, 2003) *Dispersar El Poder: Los Movimientos Como Poderes Antiestatales* (Tinta Limon Ediciones, 2006), and *Territorios en Resistencia: Cartografía Política de las Periferias Urbanas Latinoamericanas* (Lavaca Editora, 2008). Two of his books, *Territories in Resistance* and *Dispersing Power*, are available in English from AK Press.

Additional editing:

Mickey Ellinger is a longtime activist and freelance journalist in the San Francisco Bay Area. With Mrs. Alice Royal and photographer Scott Braley she wrote *Allensworth the Freedom Colony*, published by Heyday Books in 2008, and she writes regularly *for News from Native California*.

Translators:

Luis Ballesteros studied International Relations at the School of Political Science of the National Autonomous University of Mexico. He works as a court-appointed translator and a translator of diverse materials for an array of public and private entities, including the Center for Gender-Related Studies of Mexico, and he has collaborated as translator with women in the National College of Postgraduates researching gender, sociopolitical, and economic issues in indigenous regions of Mexico. He has been an observer and participant, as a member of Mexican civil society, in some of the processes mentioned in the book. His e-mail is luisreyballesteros@prodigy.net.mx.

Margi Clarke is an organizer and consultant who has worked since the 1980s on immigrant rights, international solidarity, environmental justice and cooperative economics. As a consultant and bilingual trainer, she supports community-based groups and movement-building alliances with strategic planning, leadership coaching, and organizational practices for sustainability. She is a member of RoadMap, a national consulting network serving social justice organizations, and a cancer survivor and yoga teacher. Margi lives in the San Francisco Bay Area with her husband and two teenage boys. She can be reached MargiClarke@gmail.com.

Chuck Morse is an American translator, editor, and writer. He translated Juan Suriano's *Paradoxes of Utopia: Anarchist Culture and Politics in Buenos Aires, 1890–1910* and Abel Paz's *Durruti in the Spanish Revolution* (both AK Press). He also publishes widely on urban affairs. He is currently writing about the city of Oakland, where he lives, at the Project Oakland blog (http://www.project-oakland.org/).

Margot Pepper is a Mexican-born Bay Area journalist whose work has appeared in *Utne, Monthly Review*, ZNet, *Dollars & Sense, NACLA Report on the Americas*, the *San Francisco Bay Guardian, Rethinking Schools, El Tecolote, El Andar*, Canada's *The Scoop*, on Common Dreams, counterpunch.org, and elsewhere, and can be found at http://www.margotpepper.com. She is also the author of a book of poetry, *At This Very Moment* and a memoir about her year working in Cuba, *Through the Wall: A Year in Havana*.

Christy Rodgers is a freelance editor, translator, and writer living in San Francisco, California. She is the author of an English translation of *Mejor Desaparece* (Just Disappear), a novel by Carmen Boullosa, published by VDM Press, and a cotranslator and editor of *Canto de las Moscas* (Song of the Flies), a collection of poetry by María Mercedes Carranza, published by Freedom Voices Press.

Photographers:

Thanks to all the photographers who made images available for this book. In addition to the interviewers and introducers, they include AIDESEP, Casa de America, Jp Catepillan, CONAIE, Consejo de Pueblos del Occidente, Correo del Caroní, El Ciudadano, Matías Garcia Gamra, Sean Hawkey, Kevin Hayes,

Graham Hunt, Silvia Leindecker, Elisângela Leite/Redes da Maré, MHOL, Mariana Mora, Mundo al Reves, NISGUA, and Jorge Pousa.

EDITORS

Clifton Ross has published half a dozen books of translation, fiction, and poetry in the United States and internationally. He translated and coedited, with Ben Clarke, the first book of Zapatista writings to appear in English, *Voice of Fire: Interviews and Communiques of the Zapatista National Liberation Army* (Berkeley: New Earth Publications, 1994). Since 2006 he has been visiting Latin America, documenting his experiences (in articles published at www.dissidentvoice.org, counterpunch.org, and upsidedownworld.org) and gathering material for this book. His first feature-length movie, *Venezuela: Revolution from the Inside Out*, was released on DVD in 2008 by PM Press. In 2005 Ross represented the United States in the Second World Poetry Festival of Venezuela, and his book of poetry, *Translations from Silence*, published by Freedom Voices Publications, was the recipient of PEN Oakland's 2010 Josephine Miles Award for Literary Excellence. That book was published in translation as *Traducciones del Silencio* by *Editorial Perro y Rana*, Venezuela, in 2011.

Marcy Rein is a writer, editor, and organizer who has engaged with a wide range of social movements and organizational forms over the last thirty-five years, including publication collectives, labor and community organizations, and electoral campaigns. Her articles have appeared in women's, queer, labor, and left publications including the pioneering radical feminist journal *off our backs*, the now-defunct national *Guardian*, *San Francisco Bay Times*, *Labor Notes*, *AFL-CIO Now!* (the national labor federation's blog), and *Race, Poverty & the Environment*. In the 1990s she edited the Northern California progressive monthly *News for a People's World* and the National Writers Union quarterly, *American Writer*. She then spent twelve years with the International Longshore and Warehouse Union as a writer and sometimes editor on its newspaper and as the communications specialist for its organizing department.

Acknowledgments

This book wouldn't have been possible without the international solidarity and support of dozens of people, some of whom ran great risks to trust a dusty gringo or two arriving by bus from god-knows-where. Special thanks to Briseyda Escalona, who did much of the transcription work. She can be contacted through her website at http://www.virtual-arts.blogspot.com/. Thanks also to Courtney Martinez for transcriptions in the Guatemala chapter.

Argentina
Special thanks to Cecilia Sainz and Mariano Andrade who opened their home to us and helped connect us to the right people, not to mention orienting us to the changing politics of their country. Ernesto "Lalo" Paret, besides giving us a great interview, offered us a ride to Paraguay, which not only enabled us to be part of the final act of the inauguration of President Fernando Lugo but also sealed a lifelong friendship.

Bolivia
Thanks to Keith Richards, whose guidance, friendship, and company on a trip to Isla del Sol not only opened up vistas on Bolivian politics but also were a great comfort. Thanks to Israel Quispe who took us to remote areas of the country so we could watch the educational process of bringing the new constitution to Bolivians who had long been neglected.

Chile
Thanks to Claudia Guerra, for sharing such a wealth of information and contacts; to Edmundo Jiles for introducing us to Paine and welcoming us

into his home; to the compañero/as of Editorial Quimantú (http://www.quimantu.cl) for sharing their history and hospitality; to Fernando Pairican for in-depth background on the Mapuche; to Karina Garcia Albadiz and the poets of *Plano Inclinado*; to Rodrigo Suarez of El Puñal; Christian of Restaurant El Pimentón in Valparaiso; to Katy Fox-Hodess, and to Ana Fox-Hodess and Francisco Nunez Capriles for orientation and contacts.

Colombia
Special thanks to "la profe" Martha Henriquez for all her instruction on Colombian politics and for great leads to exceptional people in the country. Thanks also to CRIC, who opened up archives and films for our use.

Ecuador
Special thanks to Armando López and Amanda Trujillo of Minga Social for working in "minga" on this project, never knowing if it would come to fruition. (Minga Social is a grassroots organization that organizes information and media for social movement groups. They aim to bridge the interstices between movements and heal the divisions that tend to emerge between left and revolutionary organizations.) Also to Dioyenes Lucio at FENOCIN and to Soledad Ortega of Píllaro, who opened up her home to us.

El Salvador
Thanks to CISPES in El Salvador and New York, particularly Alexis Stoumbelis and Laura, for great help and support, and to Patricia Dubon in San Salvador for befriending her gringo lodger and offering helpful suggestions.

Guatemala
Many thanks to Courtney Martinez and Phil Neff at the Network in Solidarity with the People of Guatemala (NISGUA) for coming through at the last minute with great ideas, energy, and materials.

Honduras
Thanks to Nery Augusto and Suyapa Rodríguez for guidance and protection in dangerous moments and to the guides who brought us safely through the jungle into Nicaragua when we were trapped on the border.

Mexico
Thanks to the Luna Vicencio family for putting us up and putting up with us. Especially thanks to Patricia Luna and her sister Luz María.

Nicaragua

Thanks to the Sandinista border police who managed to keep us out of trouble for our illegal entry to the country from Honduras without a visa in July 2009. They demonstrated that revolutionary values and heart still exist among the people in Nicaragua. Thanks to Daniel Alegría and the taxista Mario, who, on another occasion, went beyond the fare toll to help us get around Managua.

Paraguay

Thanks to people at P-Mas and to Juan de Dios, Raúl Gonzalez at Ecocultura. tv, to people in the Frente Social y Popular, and to others who gave a warm welcome, but especially to the official who let us enter without a visa, on the basis of our José Martí T-shirt, so we could be present at the inauguration of Lugo.

Peru

Thanks to Raphael Hoetmer of the Program for Democracy and Global Transformation (PDGT) for coordinating and directing the gathering of materials for the chapter on Peru. The PGDT was founded at the San Marcos University in Lima as a transdisciplinary space for the analysis of power, democracy, and social movements in the contemporary globalizing world. During its ten years of existence, the PDTG has developed into an autonomous center for action-research, emancipatory popular education, and critical popular communication, which combines theoretical and political reflection with the direct work with social organizations. The dialogues among different social movements and different forms of knowledge (academic, popular, etc.) are central to its work. As such the Program aims to contribute to the struggles for autonomy and self-determination, radical democracy, and ecological, gender, and social justice within Peru, *Nuestra América* ("Our America"), and the world. For more information, see www. democraciaglobal.org.

United States

Thanks to Jesse Clarke, Mickey Ellinger, Garrett Lambrev, Alberta Maged, Kevin Rath, and Margaret Randall for critical reading and helpful suggestions on our introductions. Thanks to Jon Platania, for support and friendship through this process.

Uruguay

Thanks to the street vendors who told us who we needed to interview and gave us contact information; to the people at Barrikada and the Galpón like

Pablo Salomon who educated us about anarchism *a la uruguaya*. Thanks also to the late Rubén Prieto, who welcomed us at Comunidad del Sur. And special thanks to Raúl Zibechi for being so generous with his knowledge and contacts.

Venezuela

Too many people to thank individually, but some come to mind as really significant friends: José Sant Roz, Betty Osorio, and her husband Humberto Martinez, who opened their home to me as did my dear friend Juan Veroes. Thanks also to Arturo Albarrán, to Luis Paz, and Ramon Ramírez. And Malacara, Diego Sequera, Juan Canelones, Emilio Gúzman, Marc Villá, Iraima Mogollón, Franco Munini, Otto Gonzalez, and everyone in Maturín who so warmly welcomed us. Finally, thanks to Tamara Pearson who gave critical feedback on an early draft of the introduction to the Venezuela chapter and helped improve and correct it.

Resources

Visit our companion website for links, updates, and clips from some of those interviewed here: www.latinamericansocialmovements.org. You can contact the editors of this book at untiltherulersobey@gmail.com

Also, keep informed with the good folks at www.upsidedownworld.org and www.nacla.org.

Notes

FOREWORD

1   The closely linked concepts of "formation" and "conscientization" appear through-out this book. "Formation" refers to political education, developing an analyti-cal framework and tools that help us understand the world in order to change it. "Conscientization" is consciousness-raising, or, as the Friere Institute puts it, "The process of developing a critical awareness of one's social reality through reflection and action" (Concepts Used by Paulo Friere, http://www.freire.org/paulo-freire/concepts-used-by-paulo-freire).

INTRODUCTION

1   Eduardo Galeano, *Open Veins of Latin America* (New York: Monthly Review Press, 1973), 18.

2   See Greg Grandin, *Empire's Workshop: Latin America, the United States, and the Rise of the New Imperialism* (New York: Holt Paperbacks, 2006).

3   Francisco Dominguez, "The Latin Americanization of the Politics of Emancipation" in Geraldine Lievesley and Steve Ludlam, eds., *Reclaiming Latin America: Experiments in Radical Social Democracy* (New York: Zed Books, 2009), 46. See also Naomi Klein, *The Shock Doctrine: The Rise of Disaster Capitalism* (New York: Metropolitan Books, 2007).

4   Operation Condor was a coordinated intelligence operation in the 1970s and '80s of the military dictatorships of the Southern Cone, aided and, to some degree, directed by the CIA. It was responsible for the murder, torture, and disappearance of tens of thousands of left and human-rights activists.

5   Xavier Albo, "Making the Leap from Local Mobilization to National Politics," *NACLA Report on the Americas* 29, no. 5 (March–April 1996): 15.

6   William I. Robinson, *Promoting Polyarchy: Globalization, US Intervention and Hegemony* (New York: Cambridge University Press, 1996), 2.

7   Nora Lustig, Luis F. Lopez-Calva, and Eduardo Ortiz-Juarez, "Declining Inequality in Latin America in the 2000s: The Cases of Argentina, Brazil and Mexico," (ECINEQ working paper 2012-266, September 2012), http://www.ecineq.org/milano/WP/ECINEQ2012-266.pdf.

8   Albo, "Making the Leap."

9   Patrick Barrett, Daniel Chávez, and César Rodríguez-Garavito, eds., *The New Latin American Left: Utopia Reborn* (London: Pluto Press, 2008), 37.

10 William I. Robinson, *Latin America and Global Capitalism* (Baltimore, MD: Johns Hopkins Press, 2008), 342.

11 James Petras and Henry Veltmeyer are in a minority of those who maintain that "All of the social movements . . . are engaged in a struggle for state power." We feel the relations between states and movements is more complex and few, if any, social movements represented here are even interested in "taking state power." Petras and Veltmeyer, *Social Movements and State Power: Argentina, Brazil, Bolivia, Ecuador* (Ann Arbor, MI: Pluto Press, 2005), 3.

12 Even inside Venezuela, the question of whether or not the Bolivarian process is "revolutionary" or "reformist" continues to be hotly debated. Whatever the outcome, the process has clearly been one built from reforms, some coming quickly, others slowly, but the Bolivarians have yet to gain complete "hegemony" or total control of the state and its institutions, even if they eventually "reform" their way there.

13 See Barrett, Chávez, and Rodríguez-Garavito, *The New Latin American Left*, 33–37. They conclude their discussion on this complex topic by saying that "the distinct logics driving movements, parties and governments can thus give rise to diverse relationships of collaboration or confrontation."

14 Raúl Zibechi, *Progre-Sismo: La domesticación de los conflictos sociales* (Santiago: Editorial Quimantú, 2010), in particular "Introducción a la edición Chilena" and chap. 1, "La 'lucha contra la pobreza' como contrainsurgencia."

15 Robinson, *Latin America and Global Capitalism*, 292.

16 Ibid.

17 Ibid, 346.

18 For more on the TCC, see "Exposing the Financial Core of the Transnational Capitalist Class," Project Censored, http://www.projectcensored.org/exposing- financial-core-transnational-%E2%80%A8capitalist-class/.

19 Raul Zibechi, *Política y Miseria* (Buenos Aires: La Vaca Editora, 2011), 7.

20 Ibid.

21 Raúl Zibechi, *Territories in Resistance* (Oakland: AK Press, 2012), 276–78; Robinson, *Latin America and Global Capitalism*, 344–45.

22 For an insightful, book-length treatment of the relationships between social movements and governments in the region, see Benjamin Dangl, *Dancing with Dynamite: States and Social Movements in Latin America* (Oakland: AK Press, 2010).

23 Robinson, *Latin America and Global Capitalism*, 343.

MEXICO

1 The death toll at the time of this writing was 101,199 with more than 10,000 people missing during Calderón's six-year presidential term—higher than the wars in Iraq and Bosnia, according to *Mexico Evalua*, based on official figures. See www.mexicoevalua.org.

2 David Bacon, "Building a Culture of Cross-Border Solidarity," Institute for Transnational Social Change, UCLA, 2011, http://www.labor.ucla.edu/programs/pdf/CrossborderSolidarity.pdf.

3 Zapatistas often refer to the EZLN simply as "the organization."

4 From an interview with the author, originally published in an article by the author by CIEPAC in 2001.

5 From an interview with the author and originally published in ¡*Viva Nuestra Historia! Libro de Historia de la Organización de Mujeres Zapatistas "Compañera Lucha"* (San Cristóbal de las Casas: Ediciones Autónomas en Rebeldía, 2003), 24.

6   Ibid., 36

7   See p.455 n.4.

GUATEMALA

1   Andrés Cabanas, "El Proyecto Patriota: Neoliberalismo militarista," Memorial de Guatemala. http://memorialguatemala.blogspot.com/p/neoliberalismo-militarista.html.

2   International Work Group for Indigenous Affairs, "Indigenous peoples in Guatemala." http://www.iwgia.org/regions/latin-america/guatemala.

3   See Severo Martínez Peláez, *La Patria del Criollo, An Interpretation of Colonial Guatemala,* trans. Susan M. Neve and W. George Lowell (Durham, NC: Duke University Press, 2009); and Marta Elena Casaús Arzú, "La metamorfosis del racismo en la élite del poder en Guatemala," *Revista Nueva Antropología* 17, no. 58 (December 2000): 27–72, http://www.redalyc.org/articulo.oa?id=15905803. Martínez Peláez's influential analysis centers the role of class struggle and ideology in determining Guatemala's colonial history. Casaús Arzú offers incisive, empirically rigorous analysis of the nature of racism from within Guatemala's ruling class.

4   Omar Lucas Monteflores, *El anarquismo en Guatemala: El anarco sindicalismo en la ciudad de Guatemala 1920–1932* (Guatemala: Universidad de San Carlos, 2011), https://docs.google.com/file/d/0BxolbZDtPTaWXzBjTWkyRjNST28/edit. Focusing on anarchist organizing, the smallest current in the country's nascent workers' movement, Monteflores also presents a detailed panorama of labor generally.

5   Stephen C. Schlesinger and Stephen Kinzer, *Bitter Fruit: The Story of the American Coup in Guatemala* (Cambridge, MA: Harvard University, 2005). This influential book offers a detailed history of Guatemala from the Ubico regime through the 1954 coup and its aftermath, with a close analysis of the role of the U.S. in orchestrating the counterrevolution.

6   Kate Doyle and Peter Kornbluh, eds, "CIA and Assassinations: The Guatemala 1954 Documents," *National Security Archive Online Briefing Book No. 4,* http://www.gwu.edu/~nsarchiv/NSAEBB/NSAEBB4/index.html.

7   Mario López Larrave, *Historia del movimiento obrero en Guatemala* (Guatemala, 1976), 34: https://docs.google.com/file/d/0BxolbZDtPTaWOUotVnZXbGF4YUU/edit.

8   For an overview of the cooperative movement, see Beatriz Manz, *Paradise in Ashes: A Guatemalan Journey of Terror, Courage, and Hope* (Berkeley: University of California Press, 2004)

9   NISGUA, "Dam-Affected Communities Speak Out for Free, Prior, Informed Consent," November 2, 2010, http://nisgua.blogspot.com/2010/11/dam-affected-communities-speak-out-for.html.

10 See Fundación Paz y Solidaridad, CCOO, *Operation Sofía: Taking the Fish's Water Away* (Madrid, 2011): http://www.pazysolidaridad.ccoo.es/ficheros/documentos/3_Taking%20the%20Fish.pdf/; and Ricardo Falla, *Massacres in the Jungle: Ixcán, Guatemala, 1975–1982,* trans. Julia Howland (Boulder, CO: Westview Press, 1994).

11 For a very detailed history of transformations within the Guatemalan military, drawing on interviews with high-ranking officials, see Jennifer Schirmer, *The Guatemalan Military Project: A Violence Called Democracy* (Philadelphia: University of Pennsylvania Press, 1999). President Otto Pérez Molina's marriage into a powerful sugar industry family is just one example of the phenomenon of military-oligarchy alliances.

12 For stunning photography and reflections on the CPRs by Guatemalan and international voices, see Jonathan Moller, *Our Culture Is Our Resistance: Repression, Refuge, and Healing in Guatemala* (New York: powerHouse Books, 2004).

13 See Francisco Goldman, *The Art of Political Murder: Who Killed the Bishop?* (New York: Grove Press, 2008); and Susan C. Peacock and Adriana Beltrán, *Hidden Powers in Post-conflict Guatemala: Illegal Armed Groups and the Forces Behind Them* (Washington, DC: Washington Office on Latin America, 2003). Goldman's novelistic and investigative treatment of the Gerardi case is one of the best illustrations of the mechanisms of impunity and military intelligence, while WOLA's report offers documentation of military ties to organized crime and clandestine "hidden power" pressure groups.

14 See NISGUA's blog for updates on progress in the genocide trials and other cases: http://nisgua.blogspot.com/2012/01/efrain-rios-montt-to-stand-trial-for.html; http://nisgua.blogspot.com/2012/02/general-on-trial.html; http://nisgua.blogspot.com/2012/03/eternal-life-to-our-loved-ones.html.

15 See William I. Robinson, *Transnational Conflicts: Central America, Social Change, and Globalization* (New York: Verso, 2003) for a description of this process of neo-liberalization. See also the Guatemalan alternative political economy journals *El Observador* and *Enfoque*, which have rigorously documented the family and corporate ties between business, military, and state actors, as well as offering detailed agricultural and economic policy analysis.

16 Examples of high-profile territorial defense movements include the Western Maya People's Council (CPO), http://consejodepueblosdeoccidente.blogspot.com/; the Departmental Assembly of Huehuetenango (ADH), http://adh-huehue.blogspot.com/; and Resistencia de los Pueblos, http://resistenciadlp.webcindario.com/. For a detailed analysis of territorial defense processes see Caren Weisbart, "Beyond Recognition: Alternative Rights-Realizing Strategies in the Northern Quiche Region of Guatemala" (CERLAC, 2012): www.yorku.ca/cerlac/Weisbart.pdf.

17 For recent unionization statistics see ACOGUATE, "Fallo de la Corte de Constitucionalidad en caso laboral de SITRAPETEN," http://acoguate.org/2011/06/30/fallo-de-la-corte-de-constitucionalidad-en-caso-laboral-de-sitrapeten/; for historical stats Larrave, *Movimiento obrero en Guatemala*, 45.

18 Among the most infamous recent violent evictions are the Nueva Linda massacre in 2004 and a series of evictions in the Polochic Valley during 2011.

19 For analysis of land concentration, see FAO, *Dinámicas del mercado de la tierra en América Latina y el Caribe: concentración y extranjerización* (2012), 253–84. For an overview of union and campesino movements, see Solidarity Center, *Justice for All: The Struggle for Worker Rights in Guatemala*, 2008, http://www.solidaritycenter.org/files/pubs_guatemala_wr.pdf.

20 Systematic rape of women detained by the police continues, with a 2005 study showing up to 75 percent of women sexually assaulted by state agents in prison; despite 43 percent of these cases being denounced, only one has gone to trial. See ACOGUATE, "Caso Juana Mendez Rodríguez," March 29, 2008, http://acoguate.org/2008/03/29/caso-juana-mendez-rodriguez/.

21 See Patrick Ball, Paul Kobrak, and Herbert S. Spirer, "State Violence in Guatemala, 1960–1996: A Quantitative Reflection," Washington, DC, American Association for the Advancement of Science (AAAS) Science and Human Rights Program and International Center for Human Rights Research, 1999, 81–82, http://shr.aaas.org/projects/human_rights/guatemala/report/Guatemala_en.pdf.

22 Oswaldo J. Hernández, "Sepur Zarco: el recreo de los soldados," PlazaPública, October 1, 2012, http://www.plazapublica.com.gt/content/sepur-zarco-el-recreo-de-los-soldados; G. Ortiz, J. Ramos, "Los Testimonios de las mujeres de Sepur Zarco," El Periódico, September 30, 2012, http://www.elperiodico.com.gt/es/20120930/pais/218583.

23 For more on H.I.J.O.S., CPR Urbana, and Radio Guerrilla, see http://hijosguate. blogspot.com; http://cpr-urbana.blogspot.com; https://www.facebook.com/pages/ Radio-Guerrilla/146817538771419.

24 In the process of "accompaniment," outsiders offer their protective presence, witness and advocacy to communities whose rights and survival are threatened by political violence. Optimally, the relationship is one of mutual respect and the accompaniers take leadership from the communities they support. H.I.J.O.S. sees accompaniment as a useful tool for defending communities fighting dispossession by land development projects and for people fighting for justice and restitution of their losses from the genocide of the 1980s.

25 See ACOGUATE article cited in n17 above, and "Dos entrevistas sobre sentencia en el caso de SITRAPETEN," June 30, 2011, http://acoguate.org/2011/06/30/ dos-entrevistas-sobre-sentencia-en-el-caso-de-sitrapeten/.

HONDURAS

1 Jefferson Boyer, "Food Security, Food Sovereignty, and Local Challenges for Transnational Agrarian Movements: The Honduras Case," *Journal of Peasant Studies* 37, no. 2 (2010): 319–51.

2 Ibid.

3 Ibid.

4 In his most recent book, *El golpe de Estado del 28 de junio de 2009, el Patrimonio Cultural y la Identidad Nacional*, Euraque details the efforts made by the Ministry of Culture and the Honduran Institute of Anthropology and History (of which he was director) under the Zelaya administration to begin to reverse the damage done to indigenous peoples and the nation by Mayanization. Darío Euraque, *El Golpe De Estado Del 28 De Junio De 2009, el Patrimonio Cultural y La Identidad Nacional* (San Pedro Sula, Honduras: Central Impresora, S.A., 2010).

5 See Daniel Aaron Graham, "Ghosts and Warriors: Cultural-Political Dynamics of Indigenous Reource Struggles in Western Honduras" (PhD diss., University of California, Berkeley, 2009), http://danielgrahamphd.files.wordpress.com/2011/10/ graham-super-dissertation.pdf.

6 U.S. readers may be more familiar with the acronym "LGBTQ," for lesbian, gay, bisexual, transgender, queer. Activists in other places, including some Latin American countries, sometimes refer to themselves as "LGBTTI," for lesbian, gay, bisexual, transgender, transvestite, intersex. (See, for example, Suyapa Portillo Villeda, "'Outing' Honduras: A Human Rights Catastrophe in the Making," in NACLA *Report on the Americas* 45, no. 3 (Fall 2012), accessed at https://nacla.org/article/ outing-honduras-human-rights-catastrophe-making.)

7 Tim Russo, "Hondurans Continue Protests in Bajo Aguán Region," *NACLA*, March 5, 2012, http://nacla.org/news/2012/3/9/hondurans-continue-protests-bajo-agu%C3%A1n-region.

8 Accessed at http://quotha.net/node/948.

EL SALVADOR

1 See the Coordinadora's website: http://cepaebajolempa.wordpress.com/hacemos/ la-coordinadora-asociacion-mangle/.

NICARAGUA

1 See Gary Webb, *Dark Alliance: The CIA, Contras, and the Crack Cocaine Explosion* (New York: Seven Stories Press, 1999); and Alexander Cockburn and Jeffrey St. Clair, *Whiteout: The CIA, Drugs, and the Press* (London: Verso, 1999).

2   See Kenneth E. Morris, *Unfinished Revolution: Daniel Ortega and Nicaragua's Struggle for Liberation* (Chicago: Lawrence Hill Books, 2010), 161. According to Morris, "The Bush administration pumped more money per vote into [Violeta Chamorro's] election than it had spent on its own 1988 presidential campaign."

3   From an unpublished interview with Fernando Cardenal conducted by Clifton Ross and Marcy Rein, July 2004.

4   For an excellent analysis of the post-electoral divisions and transformation of the FSLN from 1990 to 1995 see Gary Prevost's essay, "The FSLN" in *Nicaragua Without Illusions: Regime Transition and Structural Adjustment in the 1990s*, Thomas W. Walker, ed. (Wilmington, DE: SR Books, 1997).

5   In Latin America the rule by *caudillo,* or a strong, charismatic political and military leader, is generally traced back to the early nineteenth century and figures like Simón Bolívar. *Caudillismo* appears under many names around the world and has been ubiquitous in South and Central America.

6   See Morris, *Unfinished Revolution,* 186–92. For more on the transformation of the FSLN from a revolutionary party to a traditional populist party under the "caudillo" Daniel Ortega, the Pact, and the Zoilamérica Narvaez affair, see Karen Kampwirth, ed., *Gender and Populism in Latin America: Passionate Politics* (University Park: Pennsylvania State University, 2010), in particular Kampwirth's essay, "Populism and the Feminist Challenge in Nicaragua: The Return of Daniel Ortega," 162–79.

7   Kampwirth, *Gender and Populism in Latin America.*

8   Alejandro Bendana, "Democratizing the FSLN—and Nicaragua," *NACLA Report on the Americas* 39, no. 1 (July–August 2005): 4.

9   Morris, *Unfinished Revolution,* 202

10 See Envio, "Nicaragua Is the Municipal Elections' Big Loser," http://www.envio.org.ni/articulo/3907; and "Elections 2011: Nicaragua Lost Again," http://www.envio.org.ni/articulo/4448.

11 See the interview with Victor Hugo Tinoco, 133–38 in this volume. See also Morris, *Unfinished Revolution,* 207–10, and a detailed analysis by Gloria María Carrión Fonseca at *Envio*, http://www.envio.org.ni/articulo/4607.

12 It remains an open question whether the U.S. government ever "feared" the Sandinistas, but they certainly attempted to instill fear in the North American public of the "threat" of the "Sandino-communists." But it appears that the U.S. government now has ceased to consider Nicaragua any sort of concern. See Kirsten Weld, "A Workshop Abandoned: WikiLeaks, U.S. Empire, and Central America," *NACLA Report on the Americas* 45, no. 1, (Spring 2012): 73.

13 Richard Feinberg and Daniel Kurtz-Phelan, "Nicaragua between Caudillismo and modernity: the Sandinistas Redux?" *World Policy Journal* 23, no. 2 (Summer 2006): 76.

14 Morris, *Unfinished Revolution,* 193.

15 Dennis Rodgers, "Nicaragua's Gangs: Historical Legacy or Contemporary Symptom?," *NACLA Report on the Americas* 45, no. 1, (Spring 2012): 66.

16 Rein and Ross interview, 2004.

17 International Federation for Human Rights, FIDH, http://www.fidh.org/-Nicaragua,672-?id_mot=813.

COLOMBIA

1   The National Front was a mutually agreed-upon powersharing agreement between the Liberal and Conservative Parties that began in 1958 in the wake of the tragic moment in Colombian history known as La Violencia. La Violencia was a brutal period of extreme interparty political violence that was sparked by the assassination of the charismatic Liberal Party leader Jorge Eliécer Gaitán on April 19, 1948, the most

dramatic episode of an escalating assault against Liberals by Conservatives in the countryside. Under the National Front, the two parties rotated control of the presidency every four years from 1958 to 1978, and shared the spoils of local and departmental political offices. While the National Front is often referred to as the official end of La Violencia, the undemocratic nature of the arrangement, which closed out alternative political or social movements from the national landscape, eventually led to the emergence of FARC in 1964 as an armed opposition to this cozy yet undemocratic political system. See Gonzalo Sánchez and Donny Meertens, *Bandits, Peasants, and Politics: The Case of "La Violencia" in Colombia* (Austin: University of Texas Press, 2001).

2   It is clear that many factors beyond the drug trade played a role in the relative stability of the Colombian economy, prior to and during the regional debt crisis of the 1980s, including the diversification of the economy and the increased levels of industrialization that began in the 1960s. Colombia was the only Latin American country in the 1980s that did not see one year of declining GDP in the entire decade. For a comprehensive look at the Colombian economy in the late twentieth century, see Alvin Cohen and Frank R. Gunter, eds., *The Colombian Economy: Issues of Trade and Development* (San Francisco: Westview Press, 1992).

3   For a thorough examination of the long history of violence in Colombia's history, see Charles W. Bergquist, Ricardo Peñaranda, Gonzalo Sánchez, eds., *Violence in Colombia: The Contemporary Crisis in Historical Perspective* (Wilmington, DE: SR Books, 1992) and *Violence in Colombia: Waging War and Negotiating Peace* (Wilmington, DE: SR Books, 2001).

4   See World Bank estimates, http://data.worldbank.org/country/colombia.

5   For a concise historical overview of the complex evolution of FARC, from a popular yet small peasant army rooted in the struggles of the Colombian Communist Party and radical elements of the Liberal Party, to a unified political and military force in the 1980s that brought the government to the negotiating table, and eventually to the large armed insurgency with fronts operating in every department of the country, fueled by profits from kidnapping and the drug trade, see Mario Murillo, *Colombia and the United States: War, Unrest and Destabilization* (New York, Seven Stories, 2004).

6   For a compelling look at the origins of the Patriotic Union and their eventual demise at the hands of the Colombian right-wing, see Steven S. Dudley, *Walking Ghosts: Murder and Guerrilla Politics in Colombia* (New York: Routledge, 2004).

7   See Forrest Hylton, *Evil Hour in Colombia* (Verso: New York, 2006).

VENEZUELA

1   For a more complete analysis of social policy in Venezuela from 1960 to 2007, see Lissette González and Tito Lacruz, "Política Social en Venezuela," http://biblioteca2.ucab.edu.ve/iies/bases/iies/texto/GONZALES_Y_LACRUZ_2007.PDF

2   Javier Corrales and Michael Penfold, *Dragon in the Tropics: Hugo Chávez and the Political Economy of Revolution in Venezuela* (Washington, DC: Brookings Institution Press, 2011) 16–20. See also Alan R. Brewer-Carías, *Dismantling Democracy in Venezuela: The Chávez Authoritarian Experiment* (New York, NY: Cambridge University Press, 2010).

3   Cristina Marcano and Alberto Barrera Tyszka, *Hugo Chávez: The Definitive Biography of Venezuela's Controversial President* (New York: Random House, 2007), 270

4   Damián Prat, *Guayana: el milagro al revés, El fin de la soberanía productiva* (Caracas: Editorial Alfa, 2012). The phenomenon of doubling the workforce as production dropped was discussed in an interview by the author with Emilio Campos, Secretary General of Sutracarbonorca, in Ciudad Guayana, Venezuela, May 2, 2013.

5   Jose Gil "De Cada 100 dólares que ingresan a PDVSA apenas 4 son ganancia neta real," *El Comercio* April 23, 2013.

6   Corrales and Penfold, *Dragon in the Tropics*, 79

7   Interview with economist Orlando Ochoa, http://www.noticierodigital.com/2013/06/orlando-ochoa-en-la-razon-la-deuda-de-pdvsa-supera-los-153-mil-millones/.

8   Human Rights Watch, "Punishment before Trial: Prison Conditions in Venezuela," http://www.unhcr.org/refworld/publisher,HRW,,VEN,3ae6a7df0,0.html.

9   "Impunity in Venezuela: The Price of Justice," *The Economist*, January 26, 2013, http://www.economist.com/news/americas/21570705-family-case-against-government-faces-extermination-price-justice.

10 Corrales and Penfold, *Dragon in the Tropics*, 140.

11 Examples include General Raul Baduel (ret.), former minister of defense, charged, convicted, and imprisoned for "corruption" after challenging the Referendum of 2007; Judge María Lourdes Afiuni, recently released after having been held without trial for three years, and others. See also the interview in this volume with Orlando Chirino, in particular, the reference to Rubén González, union activist imprisoned for leading a strike. The inner workings of this process are also considered in Marcano and Tyszka, *Hugo Chávez*, 135–37. The authors describe Chávez's attempts to exact revenge on a former ally, Jesús Urdaneta, with trumped-up charges of "human rights violations."

12 When the PSUV was initiated in 2007 Chávez proclaimed that it would be "the most democratic party in Latin America." Many grassroots-level activists, however, complain of its top-down command structure, saying that there are few channels of communication from the base to the top.

13 Juan Carlos Triviño Salazar, "The Promise of Transformation through Participation: an Analysis of Communal Councils in Caracas" online at http://www.iss.nl/news_events/iss_news/detail/article/48404-wp-558-the-promise-of-transformation-through-participation-an-analysis-of-communal-councils/.

14 Steve Ellner, "A New Model with Rough Edges: Venezuela's Community Councils," VenezuelAnalysis, June 11, 2009, http://venezuelanalysis.com/analysis/4512.

15 The iron industry, including Orinoco Iron (Ferrominera Orinoco) was nationalized by Carlos Andrés Pérez in 1975. Union leader and then–PSUV militant González got a seven-year sentence for leading a peaceful strike in 2009. He was released when massive demonstrations shook the country, but at the time of this writing he continues to face harassment by the Maduro government.

16 February 4, 1992, was the date of the failed military coup led by Lieutenant Colonel Hugo Chávez and others and directed against then-president Carlos Andrés Pérez.

ECUADOR

1   Luis Macas attended the same high school that produced the renowned Marxist sociologist Agustín Cueva. Thanks to Forrest Hylton for pointing this out.

BRAZIL

1   The definition of the solidarity economy is broad, but it generally refers to any activity—co-ops, fair trade, local currencies, barter markets, socially responsible businesses—that is rooted in cooperation, participation, and solidarity over profit.

2   Solidarity businesses are companies that trade within the solidarity economy, subordinating profit to cooperation and solidarity. In southern South America the term often refers to tiny businesses run by an individual or a group of artisans selling their arts and crafts.

3   Erik German, "Running Out of Real Estate in Rio's Slums," Global Post, April 12, 2011, http://www.globalpost.com/dispatch/news/regions/americas/brazil/110408/housing-real-estate-favelas.

PERU

1   These are community-based grassroots peasant organizations that deal with security, communitarian justice, and the defense of the common goods of the communities in the north of the country.

2   Originally grassroots organizations that collectively organize the preparation of low-cost food in the popular neighborhoods of the bigger cities. Nowadays they have been incorporated in state facilities but still integrate thousands of women around the country.

3   AIDESEP is the representative organization of the Amazonian indigenous people with social bases throughout the Peruvian Amazon.

4   President Alberto Fujimori was sentenced to twenty-five years in prison for crimes against humanity in April 2009. Vladimir Montesinos, his intelligence chief, is in an ongoing trial for charges ranging from drug and arms trafficking to murder.

5   These are peasant organizations, with majoritarian female participation, that seek to control violence within the communities that is directed primarily at women and children. The interesting thing is that they seek solutions to the issue of violence and machismo from within the community, and, only when there are no other options, through the state's legal system.

6   Agricultural Corporations of Social Interest, created as a result of the agrarian reform commenced in 1969, during the progressive military government of Juan Velasco Alvarado.

7   Peasant Confederation of Peru, the main rural organization, hegemonized in that period by the Unified Mariateguista Party, a revolutionary party that was a member of Izquierda Unida.

8   Patria Roja Communist Party, an offshoot of the Socialist Party founded by José Mariátegui.

9   Coup d'état by President Alberto Fujimori through which on April 5, 1992, Parliament was closed and the Judicial Power was suspended.

10   Uprising of the people in Arequipa against the privatization of the state power company by the government of Alejandro Toledo, in June 2002, which forced the government to reverse the measure.

11   See Inter-American Commission on Human Rights, Report No. 69/04: "Petition 504/03. Admissibility, Community of San Mateo de Huchanor and its Members, Peru," Oct. 15, 2004, accessed at http://www.cidh.oas.org/annualrep/2004eng/Peru.504.03eng.htm

12   The lack of identification cards means transsexuals can't fill out even simple paperwork, such as an application for school or a job. This presents a real barrier to their living decent lives.

BOLIVIA

1   See Sinclair Thomson, *We Alone Will Rule: Native Andean Politics in the Age of Insurgency* (Madison: University of Wisconsin Press, 2002).

2   In Benjamin Dangl, "New Politics in Old Bolivia: Public Opinion and Evo Morales," Upside Down World, November 28, 2007, http://upsidedownworld.org/main/bolivia-archives-31/1021-new-politics-in-oldbolivia-public-opinion-and-evo-morales.

3   For an overview of recent Bolivian social movement and political history see Benjamin Dangl, *The Price of Fire: Resource Wars and Social Movements in Bolivia* (Oakland: AK Press, 2007).

4   Benjamin Kohl and Linda Farthing, *Impasse in Bolivia: Neoliberal Hegemony and Popular Resistance* (London: Zed Books, 2006).

5   For more information on the U.S. war on drugs in Bolivia, see the Andean Information Network, http://ain-bolivia.org/.

6   See Oscar Olivera and Tom Lewis, ¡*Cochabamba! Water War in Bolivia* (Cambridge, MA: South End Press, 2008).

7   Raúl Zibechi, *Dispersing Power: Social Movements as Anti-State Forces* (Oakland: AK Press, 2010).

8   For more information the relationship between social movements and leftist governments in contemporary Latin America, see Benjamin Dangl, *Dancing with Dynamite: Social Movements and States in Latin America*, (Oakland: AK Press, 2010). For information specifically relating to Bolivia, see pp. 13–39.

9   For broad coverage of the TIPNIS issue, see Emily Achtenberg's articles for *NACLA Report on the Americas*: https://nacla.org/category/tags/tipnis.

10 The leftist Tupak Katari guerrilla movement was active in Bolivia in the 1970s. Rivera and the current vice president of Bolivia, Álvaro García Linera, were active in this movement.

11 The Agenda of October is a radical set of demands put forth by social movements that participated in the 2003 Gas War in Bolivia, a social protest against the privatization and export of the country's gas reserves, and against the repressive, neoliberal government of Gonzalo Sánchez de Lozada, who was overthrown in the protests.

12 Leftist critics of Morales's nationalization of gas reserves have pointed out that this was not an all-out expropriation of the industry but more of a renegotiation of contracts with private companies that simply gave the government more control in the industry.

13 At the time of this interview, doctors had been on strike for two months in protest of a policy by the Morales government that stipulated that doctors had to work eight hours per day instead of six.

PARAGUAY

1   John Gimlette, *At The Tomb of the Inflatable Pig* (New York: Knopf, 2004)

2   See "Opposition Parties" in *Paraguay: A Country Study*, eds. Dannin M. Hanratty and Sandra W. Meditz (Washington, D.C.: Library of Congress, 1990), http://lcweb2.loc.gov/frd/cs/pytoc.html.

3   See "The Twin Pillars of the Stroessner Regime" in ibid.

4   Raúl Zibechi, "Paraguay's Hour of Change," IRC Americas Program, September 24, 2007, http://www.cipamericas.org/archives/935.

5   "Represor regresa a Paraguay por enfermedad," http://www.telesurtv.net/noticias/secciones/nota/48894-NN/represor-regresa-a-paraguay-por-enfermedad/.

6   Peter Lambert and Ricardo Medina, "Contested Discourse, Contested Power: Nationalism and the Left in Paraguay," *Bulletin of Latin American Research* 26, no. 3 (2007): 349–50.

7   Adolfo Gimenez, "Reorganizacion syndical no debe repetir los errores" in *Movimientos Sociales y Expresion politica*, eds. Marielle Palau and Aristides Ortiz (Asuncion: Centro de Estudios Paraguayos Antonio Grausch, 2005), 33–35.

8   Juan Carlos Yuste "Actores sociales emergentes en la transición paraguaya" in *Movimientos Sociales y Expresion politica*, eds. Marielle Palau and Aristides Ortiz (Asuncion: Centro de Estudios Paraguayos Antonio Grausch, 2005), 72–73.

9   González, "Lugo's Dilemmas." See also Pablo Stefanoni "¿Fin de época en Paraguay?" *Le Monde Diplomatique* South American edition, July 2007, http://www.lemondediplomatique.cl/article583,583.html.

10 Javiera Rulli and Grupo de Reflexión Rural (Argentina), *Paraguay Sojero*, 2006. See http://www.nwrage.org/content/human-and-environmental-rights-violations-due-gm-soy-expansion-paraguay

11 Zibechi, "Paraguay's Hour of Change"; Hanratty and Meditz, "The Twin Pillars of the Stroessner Regime."

12 Elizabeth Bravo Velásquez, Javiera Rulli, et al., *Repúblicas unidas de la soja: realidades sobre la producción de soja en América del Sur* (Buenos Aires: Grupo Reflexión Rural, 2007), 221–34.

13 Discussion with Galeano, *La Soja Mata*, http://www.lasojamata.org/en/node/235.

14 Raúl Zibechi, "Militarism in Paraguay: The Other Side of the Economic Model," CIP Americas Program, October 17, 2011, http://www.cipamericas.org/archives/5581.

15 Michael Fox, "Paraguay Celebrates Lugo's Historic Victory" Upside Down World, April 19, 2008, http://upsidedownworld.org/main/content/view/1243/44/.

16 See April Howard and Benjamin Dangl, "Dissecting the Politics of Paraguay's Next President," Toward Freedom, April 10, 2008, http://towardfreedom.com/home/content/view/1280/1/.

17 Diego González, "Lugo's Dilemmas," CIP Americas Program, September 24, 2009, http://www.cipamericas.org/archives/1861.

18 http://news.bbc.co.uk/2/hi/americas/country_profiles/1222081.stm.

19 Discussion with Galeano, *La Soja Mata*, http://www.lasojamata.org/en/node/235.

20 For more details on the Curuguaty land conflict, see "Tragic Week in Paraguay," by Javiera Manuela Rulli and Reto Sonderegger, Upside Down World, June 24, 2012, http://upsidedownworld.org/main/paraguay-archives-44/3705-tragic-week-in-paraguay.

21 For more on the right-wing, corporate agenda of Franco, see Benjamin Dangl, "Paraguay's Bitter Harvest," Toward Freedom, July 26, 2012, http://www.towardfreedom.com/americas/2909-paraguays-bitter-harvest-multinational-corporations-reap-benefits-from-coup-government.

22 For more information, see Benjamin Dangl, "In the Shadow of the Coup," Upside Down World, August 7, 2012, http://upsidedownworld.org/main/paraguay-archives-44/3801-in-the-shadow-of-the-coup-social-movements-for-democracy-mobilize-in-paraguay.

URUGUAY

1 Danilo Astori became minister of finance in 2005, then vice president in 2010. He favors free trade agreements and is generally seen as very "pro-market."

2 Drumming and dance originating in Uruguay among the African population, candombe often has political overtones and was sometimes used by African slaves to satirize dominant white society.

ARGENTINA

1 Jorge Luis Borges, "A History of the Tango," in *Selected Non-fictions* (New York: Viking, 1999), 394–404.

2 The letter can be found in Spanish at http://www.ciudadseva.com/textos/otros/carta.htm.

3 Labor organizations like the CTA (Central de Trabajadores de la Argentina) resisted the privatization of industry but corrupt unionists with ties to Peronism sold out, were paid off, or literally became business partners in the newly founded conglomerates that took control of the industries. A good example of this corruption is the murder of Mariano Ferreyra. José Pedraza, a union leader, was also owner of a cooperative that outsourced along the train lines. When contracted workers protested "tercerización," or outsourcing, Pedraza and his thugs attacked the protest killing

Ferreyra. The CGT is full of thugs and did little to resist the reversal of labor protections that were passed in the 1990s. Now workers are fighting to gain democratic representation and often have to fight the bureaucratic leaders.

4   Jorge Julio López was disappeared in September 2006 after testifying in the first trial of war criminals from the military dictatorship.

5   The collective never capitalizes its name.

6   Lunfardo is a dialect spoken in working-class neighborhoods of Buenos Aires and is used often in tango lyrics.

CHILE

1   MercoPress/South Atlantic News Agency, "Chilean Municipal Elections are Anticipating a Return of the Left-Wing Coalition," Oct. 31, 2012, http://en.mercopress.com/2012/10/31/chilean-municipal-elections-are-anticipating-a-return-of-the-left-wing-coalition.

2   Mapuche historian Fernando Pairicán Padilla, interview with Clifton Ross and Marcy Rein, Santiago de Chile, April 18, 2012.

3   Emir Sader, *The New Mole: Paths of the Latin American Left* (London and New York: Verso, 2011), 9–10.

4   L. Gambone, "The Libertarian Movement in Chile: 1840–the Present," http://dwardmac.pitzer.edu/Anarchist_Archives/worldwidemovements/chilemovement.html.

5   Harry E. Vanden and Gary Prevost, *Politics of Latin America: The Power Game,* 2nd ed. (New York and Oxford: Oxford University Press, 2006), 437.

6   Memoria Chilena: Biblioteca Nacional Digital de Chile, "Masacre de la Escuela Santa María de Iquique," http://www.memoriachilena.cl/temas/index.asp?id_ut=masacre delaescuelasantamariadeiquique; also Jaime Ramón Olivares, "Longshoremen and Miners Strike," St. James Encyclopedia of Labor History Worldwide. Ed. Neil Schlager. Vol. 1. (Detroit: St. James Press, 2004), 560–62.

7   The other two Popular Front governments ruled Spain and France; following the strategy of the Comintern, the popular fronts united Communists, Socialists, and other forces to oppose fascism. Chile's Popular Front drew in the Radical Party, which actually was a party of the center.

8   Sader, *The New Mole,* 30.

9   Naomi Klein, *The Shock Doctrine: The Rise of Disaster Capitalism* (New York: Henry Holt and Company, 2007), 72–77. The radical free-market economists from the University of Chicago, in cahoots with the agency that would become the U.S. Agency for International Development (USAID), trained a hundred Chilean students between 1957 and 1970 and established a local base at Santiago's Catholic University.

10 Klein, *The Shock Doctrine,* 601n63.

11 This figure comes from Chile's 1990–1991 National Commission for Truth and Reconciliation (the "Rettig Commission"), as reported at Truth Commission: Chile 90, in Truth Commissions Digital Collections, http://www.usip.org/publications/truth-commission-chile-90.

12 Alfredo Riquelme Segovia, "Chile: The Twentieth Century," in *Encyclopedia of Latin American History and Culture* 2nd ed., Vol. 2., eds. Jay Kinsbruner and Erick D. Langer (Detroit: Charles Scribner's Sons, 2008), 337–50.

13 Klein, *The Shock Doctrine,* 132.

14 Julia Paley, *Marketing Democracy: Power and Social Movements in Post-Dictatorship Chile* (Berkeley and Los Angeles, California: University of California Press, 2001), 61.

15 Fernando Pairicán Padilla interview, April 2012.

16 William I. Robinson, "Promoting Polyarchy in Latin America," in *Latin America After Neoliberalism: Turning the Tide in the 21st Century,* eds. Eric Hershberg and Fred

Rosen (New York: The New Press and North American Congress on Latin America, 2006), 109

17 Julia Paley, *Marketing Democracy*, 99–100

18 Segovia, *Chile: The Twentieth Century*, 349.

19 William I. Robinson, *Latin America and Global Capitalism: A Critical Globalization Perspective* (Baltimore, Maryland: The Johns Hopkins University Press, 2008), 79

20 Roger Burbach, "Bachelet Victory in Chile," ZNet, Jan. 16, 2006, http://www.zcommunications.org/bachelet-victory-in-chile-by-roger-burbach.

21 Fernando Pairicán Padilla and Rolando Álvarez Vallejos, "*La Nueva Guerra de Arauco: La Coordinadora Arauco-Malleco y Los Nuevos Movimientos de Resistencia Mapuche en El Chile de la Concertación (1997–2009),*" in Un década en movimiento: Luchas populares en América Latina en el amanecer del siglo XXI, ed. Massimo Modonesi and Julián Rebón (Buenos Aires: CLACSO, 2011)

22 According to the Human Rights Watch World Report 2012, "Most recorded cases of extrajudicial executions and enforced disappearances committed during military rule (1973–1990) have been heard in court or are now under judicial investigation. Judges continue to convict former military personnel for these crimes. However, given the seriousness of the crimes, final sentences are often unacceptably lenient." http://www.hrw.org/world-report-2012/chile.

23 Roger Burbach, "Pinochet's Trial and Tribulations," *Z Magazine*, May 2000, http://www.zcommunications.org/pinochets-trial-and-tribulations-by-roger-burbach.

24 International Rivers, "Patagonia's Rivers at Risk," June 2011, http://www.internationalrivers.org/resources/patagonia-s-rivers-at-risk-2630.

25 J. Patrice McSherry and Raúl Molina Mejía, "Chile's Students Challenge Pinochet's Legacy," *NACLA Report on the Americas* 46, no. 6 (November 2011): 29–39.

26 One protagonist in the Aysén movement drew a parallel between that struggle and the 1918 "Guerra de Chile Chico," in which white homesteaders along the banks of Lago General Carrera successfully defended their land and livelihoods against Chilean army soldiers brought in to protect developers' interests. After three years of fighting, the developers abandoned their claims. (Andres Gillmore, "HidroAysén: Un Caso Parecido al de la Guerra de Chile Chico," *Viento Patagon,* August 2011, http://www.vientopatagon.cl/2011/08/hidroaysen-un-caso-parecido-al-de-la.html).

27 Teófilo Haro, a mechanic who was participating in one of the numerous marches in Aysén, lost an eye after being shot in the face by soldiers. See Mauricio Becerra Rebolledo, "El carabinero que me disparó me dijo: 'Aquí te remato, hueón,'" *El Ciudadano* 121, March 7, 2012, http://www.elciudadano.cl/2012/03/07/49301/teofilo-haro-"el-carabinero-que-me-disparo-me-dice-'aqui-te-remato-huevon'"/.

28 Emily Anne, "The Chilean Safe Abortion Hotline: Assisting Women With Illegal, But Safe, Misoprostol Abortion," October 23, 2012, accessed at: http://upsidedownworld.org/main/chile-archives-34/3933-the-chilean-safe-abortion-hotline-assisting-women-with-illegal-but-safe-misoprostol-abortion.

29 Rogelio Gonzalez et al., "Tackling Health Inequities in Chile: Maternal, Newborn, Infant, and Child Mortality Between 1990 and 2004," *American Journal of Public Health* 99, no. 7 (July 2009): 1220–26, accessed at: http://www.ncbi.nlm.nih.gov/pmc/articles/PMC2696659/.

30 Fierce protests against hikes in the price of gasoline around the southern city of Punto Arenas forced the government to negotiate with the Citizens Assembly of Magallanes and lower the prices. See Raúl Zibechi, "A New Chile Is Possible," January 25, 2012, Americas Program, accessed at: http://www.cipamericas.org/archives/6256.

31 Opus Dei is a Roman Catholic organization, ordinarily associated with secretive, right-wing politics.

Index

Page numbers in *italics* refer to illustrations. "Passim" (literally "scattered") indicates intermittent discussion of a topic over a cluster of pages.

abduction. *See* kidnapping

abortion: Argentina, 388; Bolivia, 323; Chile, 404, 429–32 passim; Nicaragua, 119, 143, 144, 145, 147; Paraguay, 353–54; Peru, 281

academia. *See* universities and colleges

ACAR. *See* Asociación de Coordinadores de Ambiente por los Agricultores de Rangel (ACAR)

Acevei, Hipólito, 342–47

ACOGUATE, 38–43, 50–56, 443

Acuña, Claudia, xxv, 403–7

ADISMI (Association for the Integral Development of San Miguel Ixtahuacán, Guatemala), 53

adolescents, 355–60 passim, 422–23

ADP. *See* Alternative Democratic Pole (ADP)

AFL-CIO, 35, 60

Afro-Latin Americans, 170; Brazil, 245, 249, 252, 263, 265; Colombia, 152, *157*, 169, 170; Ecuador, 211, 226, 233, 234, 235; Honduras, 60, 61, 63, 71; Peru, 275, 278, 301. *See also* Garifuna people

Agrarian Campesino Leagues. *See* Christian Agrarian Leagues

agrarian reform, 169; Bolivia, 307, 308; Brazil, 246, 248, 250–56 passim; Chile, 413, 414, 416, 419, 434; Ecuador,

213; Honduras, 60–61; Paraguay, 331, 349–50, 362; Peru, 282; Uruguay, 370–71

agribusiness, xvi, xix–xxv; Brazil, 248; Chile, 411, 415; Ecuador, 228, 240; El Salvador, 86, 99; Guatemala, 34, 38; Honduras, 59–61 passim, 73; Paraguay, 334–36, 348–49, 353, 361, 363

agriculture: Argentina, 382, 394, 395; Brazil, 250–55 passim, 258; Chile, 412; Colombia, 159; El Salvador, 111; Honduras, 60; Paraguay, 348–51 passim; Peru, 278, 287–91 passim; urban, 319; Venezuela, 191–98 passim. *See also* agribusiness; agroecology; agrotoxins; coca growers (*cocaleros*); corn; genetically modified (GMO) crops; monoculture (agriculture); pesticides; seeds; soy; sugar industry

agroecology, 191–96, 226–29 passim

agrotoxins, 260, 335, 353

Agrupación de Derechos Humanos José Calderón Miranda (Chile), 419–25

AIDESEP (Peru), 279, 463n3

AIDS. *See* HIV/AIDS

ALBA. *See* Bolivarian Alternative for the Americas (ALBA)

Albarrán, J. Arturo, xxv, 186, 191–96, *191*

Albo, Xavier, xviii

Alemán, Arnoldo, 118–19, 126, 134, 136, 143, 144

Alexis Lives Foundation (Venezuela), 187

Alianza Patriótica por el Cambio. *See* Patriotic Alliance for Change (APC)

Alianza Republicana Nacionalista. *See* ARENA (Nationalist Republican Alliance)

Allende, Salvador, 364, 411, 413–14, 419, 420–21, 424, 434

Alternativa Boliviariana para las Américas. *See* Bolivarian Alternative for the Americas (ALBA)

Alternative Democratic Pole (ADP, Colombia), 164–65, 167, 168

alternative media, 44–48 passim, 188, 216, 373–78 passim, 386, 403–7 passim

alternative press, 20, 23–24, 282, 285, 311

Amaral, João, 251–52

Amazonian peoples, 279, 281, 286, 296–98, 297

Amazon rainforest conservation, 268–71

American Federation of Labor-Congress of Industrial Organizations. *See* AFL-CIO

amnesia and memory, collective. *See* historical memory

anarchists and anarchism, 213; Argentina, 382, 397; Bolivia, 316, 319; Chile, 412, 413, 422; Mexico, 25; Nicaragua, 115; Uruguay, 373–78; Venezuela, 373

Ancalao, José, 342–37, 433

Andean cosmology/ideology, xv, 314–16

anticommunism: Argentina, 383; Colombia, 154; Guatemala, 34, 35, 49; Honduras, 60, 61, 67, 78; Nicaragua, 117, 119, 460n12; Paraguay, 352

antihunger programs, xxiii, 90, 119, 145, 248

antimilitary movements, 334

antimining activism. *See* resistance to mining

APPO (Asamblea Popular de los Pueblos de Oaxaca, Mexico), xxvii, 6, 14–20 passim

April 19th Movement (M-19, Colombia), 153, 166–65, 167, 169

aquaculture, 100, 192, 198, 289, 412

Árbenz, Jacobo, xvii, 34

ARENA (Nationalist Republican Alliance, El Salvador), xvii, 85–89 passim, 93–96 passim, 101, 102, 106, 110, 111

Argentina, xxiv–xxvi passim, 247, 281, 286, 367–68, 381–407, 466n3; Paraguay relations, 333; War of the Triple Alliance, 332

armed struggle, xvii–xviii, 221; Brazil, 246–47; Colombia, 153–54, 156, 164–67 passim, 171, 173–74, 214; El Salvador, 85; Guatemala, 35; Mexico, 4; Nicaragua, 115–16, 117–18, 120, 133; Paraguay, 333; Peru, 282, 276–77, 281–82. *See also* ex-guerrillas; Zapatistas

arrogance, 294, 325, 427

arson as protest, 393, 394, 397, 416, 435

art, 45, 47, *106*, 110, *139*, 375, 419. *See also* murals and muralists

Artigas, José, 367–68

Asamblea Popular de los Pueblos de Oaxaca. *See* APPO (Asamblea Popular de los Pueblos de Oaxaca)

Asociación de Coordinadores de Ambiente por los Agricultores de Rangel (ACAR, Venezuela), 192, 193

Asociación Interétnica de Desarrollo de la Selva Peruana. *See* AIDESEP

assassination, 86; Argentina, 385, 388; Brazil, 250, 269; Colombia, 171, 460n1; El Salvador, 89, 91–96 passim, 106; Guatemala, 33, 34–35, 38, 41, 48, 53; Honduras, 64, 77, 78, 80; Paraguay, 336. *See also* death threats

Astori, Danilo, 371, 372, 465n1

AUC (United Self-Defense Forces of Colombia), 154–55, 156

autonomism, 395–97 passim

Autonomous Movement of Women (Nicaragua), 145, 147

autonomous spaces, xxvi–xxvii; Brazil, 249; El Salvador, 96–100; Mexico, 10–12, *11*; Nicaragua, 138–43; Uruguay, 373–78; Venezuela, 186–90. *See also* encampments (protest)

Aymara people and culture, xv, xix, xxiv, 275, 315, 316, 321, 433, 442

Aysén, Chile, 418, 422, 423, 425–28, *425*, 429

Bachelet, Michele, 416, 436

Ballesteros, Luis, 3–8, 447

banana industry, 59–60, 125–29 passim, 171, 212, 215, 263
Bancosur (Banco del Sur), 183
banks and banking, 183, 223, 355, 414; Brazil, 248; Chile, 413, 423; Ecuador, 217, 223, 240; Mexico, 5, 22; Paraguay, 335, 344; Uruguay, 367, 371; Venezuela, 197–98. *See also* Inter-American Development Bank; World Bank
Barrett, Rafael, 341
Barrios, Paula, 38–44
Barzón Movement (Mexico), 5–6
Basualdo, Franco, xxv, 393–98
Batlle y Ordóñez, José, 368
Battle of Acosta Ñu, 356
Bechtel, 306, 323
Becker, Liz, 351–54
Becker, Marc, 211–15, 443
Belmiro Dos Santos, Raimundo, 268–71
Benegas Loyo, Diego, 388–93, 443
biodiesel industry, 335
black Latin Americans. *See* Afro-Latin Americans
Blanco, Hugo, 281–86, *282*
blockades: Argentina, 381, 386–87; Bolivia, 306, 307; Chile, 418, 421, 425, 427; Ecuador, 220; El Salvador, 90; Guatemala, 37; Mexico, 14, 19; right-wing, 421
blogs, 45–47 passim
Bolívar, Simón, 180, 182, 187, 246, 460n5
Bolivarian Alternative for the Americas (ALBA), xxvii, 66, 73, 88, 132, 182
"Bolivarian Revolution," 179–84 passim, 192, 194, 456n12
Bolivia, xi–xxv passim, 183, 212, 229, 286, 305–28, 422, 464nn10–13; Chaco War, 332; map, 304
Bolsa Familia, xxiii, 248, 262
Brazil, xx, xxiii–xxv, 241, 245–71, 310, 327, 336; map, 244; Uruguay relations, 368; worker-run businesses in, 387
Britain. *See* Great Britain
Buchanan, Juana, 72–73
Buenos Aires, 367–68, 381, 382, 386, 389, 398, 403–7 passim; dialect/slang, 389, 466n6; Plaza del Mayo, 385, 389; rapid transit, 394; worker-run print shops, *401*
Bustamante, Oscar, 26–29

Caballero, Santiago, 16–17
Caceres, Oscar, 338–42
cafés, 373–77 passim, 404
CAFTA, 110
Calderón, Felipe, 6, 456n1
Campesino Confederation of Peru (CCP), 282–85 passim
Canada, 194; industry in Latin America, 22, 53, 90, 91, 364
Capriles, Henrique, 207, 208
Caracazo, 1989, xix, 181, 187
Cardenal, Ernesto, 116, 118
Cardenal, Fernando, 116, 118, 120
Cardoso, Pedro, 261–65
Carrión, Magdiel, 290–96, *291*
Catholic Church, xviii; Bolivia, 323; Chile, 404; Colombia, 161; Ecuador, 213, 226, 231; Guatemala, 35, 36, 37; Nicaragua, 119, 144; Paraguay, 333, 336, 341, 354; Peru, 293, 299, 301; Uruguay, 368. *See also* Opus Dei; theology of liberation
Catholic Worker Youth, 356
caudillos and caudillismo, 118, 140, 141, 237, 326, 331, 382; definition, 460n5
CCURA. *See* United Revolutionary Autonomous Class Current
CELAC (Community of Latin American and Caribbean States), xxvii, 182
Center for Popular Education, Mixteque. *See* Centro de Educación Popular de Mixteque (CEP)
Central America Free Trade Agreement (CAFTA). *See* CAFTA
Central American Forum of the Peoples. *See* Foro Mesoamericano de los Pueblos
Central American Parliament, 101, 104
Central Intelligence Agency. *See* CIA
Central Sandinista de Trabajadores (CST, Nicaragua), 120–25
Centro de Investigación de la Comunicación (CINCO, Nicaragua), 145
Centro de Educación Popular de Mixteque (CEP, Venezuela), 196–99 passim
Centro de Educación Popular para el Desarrollo Integral de la Familia. *See* CEPDIF
CEP de Mixteque. *See* Centro de Educación Popular de Mixteque (CEP)

CEPDIF (Venezuela), 192, 193
CEPZONAL Rangel (Venezuela), 198
Chaco War, 332
Chamorro, Milton, 216–20, 216
Chamorro, Violeta, 118, 460n2
Chávez, Angélica Domínguez, 17–18
Chávez, Hugo, xxiii–xxvii passim, 179–90
passim, 194–208 passim, 214, 360, 373,
462nn11–12, 462n16; Bolivia relations,
390; elections, xiv, xx, 181; Nicaragua
relations, 119, 137; Zelaya connection,
66
Chiapas, Mexico, xix, 5, 8–13
Chiavenato, Julio José, 331, 355–56
Chilavert, 401
child and adolescent workers, 355–60
passim
children: Argentina, 407; Honduras, 67,
68, 69, 70–71; Paraguay, 355–60; sexual
orientation, 301; UN rights convention,
143; Uruguay, 377; Venezuela, 185
child soldiers, 356
Chile, 318, 328, 364, 411–42, 467n22;
Bolivia relations, 307; "Guerra de Chile
Chico," 467n26; map, 410; Paraguay
relations, 333
Chilean Confederation of Students
(CONFECH). See CONFECH
China, 60, 290, 314, 327
Chiricente, Luzmila, 296–97
Chirino, Orlando, xxv, 186, 204–8, 205
Cholango, Humberto, xxv–xxvi, 220,
221–25, 221
Christian Agrarian Leagues (Paraguay),
333, 340–42
Chuji, Monica, xxv, 230–36, 231
churches. See Catholic Church;
Evangelical churches
CIA, 34, 60, 61, 117, 118, 421, 457n7
CINCO. See Centro de Investigación de la
Comunicación (CINCO)
City of Plastic (Cidade de Plástico, Brazil),
261–64 passim
civil disobedience, 17, 431
class consciousness, 377
class struggle, 44, 239, 253, 255, 435
clientelism, xx, 168; Argentina, 382;
Chile, 424; Mexico, 3; Nicaragua, 140;
Paraguay, 332, 352–53, 362; Peru, 277;
Venezuela, 179
clothing industry. See garment industry

coca growers (cocaleros), 277, 305, 306, 320
Cochabamba Water War, 306, 309–10
COFADEH (Honduras), 80, 81
coffee, 10, 34, 86, 117, 194
coffee shops. See cafés
Colectivo lavaca (Argentina), 403
collective bargaining and contracts, 124,
205–8 passim, 239, 384
collective memory (and amnesia). See
historical memory
collectives and collectivity, xii, xiii, 284;
Argentina, xxvi, 393–94, 398–407
passim; Brazil, 251, 253, 262; Chile, 441;
Colombia, 157, 158, 162, 164, 170, 174;
Ecuador, 237, 239; El Salvador, 96;
Guatemala, 36, 42, 45, 47, 52; Honduras,
61; Mexico, 9, 11, 13, 14, 18, 19, 26–29;
Nicaragua, 118, 121, 124, 141, 143;
Paraguay, 331, 341, 342, 346–50 passim;
Peru, 279, 295, 296; Uruguay, 373–78
passim; Venezuela, 188–89, 192, 196,
205–9 passim. See also minga (concept)
colleges. See universities and colleges
Colombia, xviii, 151–75, 460–61nn1–2;
map, 150
colonialism, xv, xxiv, 239, 241–42, 248;
Bolivia, 308, 316, 319; Chile, 412, 418,
435
Colorado Party (Paraguay), 332–33, 337,
341, 351–54 passim, 361
Comité de Familiares de Detenidos
Desaparecidos en Honduras. See
COFADEH
commissions for truth and reconciliation.
See truth commissions
"communes": Venezuela, 179, 186–90
passim, 194, 205
communism, repression of. See
anticommunism
Communist Party, xxi; Chile, 413, 440;
China, 314; Colombia, 167, 461n5;
Ecuador, 226; Peru, 276
communitarian work, indigenous. See
minga (concept)
communities of peace. See peace
communities
Communities of Population in Resistance
(CPRs, Guatemala), 36, 45
community building and organizing:
Ecuador, 216–20 passim, 237–38; El

Salvador, 96–100; Uruguay, 375–76; Venezuela, 185, 188–90 passim, 198

community centers, 373–78

"community councils": Peru, 288, 292; Venezuela, 179, 185, 194, 198–200, 205

community media, 188, 216, 369–76 passim, 387

commuter trains, 393–97 passim

compensation to victims. *See* reparations

Comunidades de Población en Resistencia. *See* CPR Urbana

CONACAMI (Peru), 285, 288

CONAIE (Ecuador), xxii, xxvi, 213–18 passim, 225, 230, 232, 236, 286

CONAMAQ (Bolivia), 313, 385

CONFECH (Chile), 432, 434, 438–42 passim

Confederación Campesina del Perú. *See* Campesino Confederation of Peru (CCP)

Confederación de Estudiantes de Chile. *See* CONFECH

Confederación de Nacionalidades Indígenas del Ecuador (CONAIE). *See* CONAIE

Confederación Kichwa del Ecuador. *See* ECUARUNARI

Confederación Nacional de Comunidades del Perú Afectadas por la Minería (CONACAMI). *See* CONACAMI

Confederation of Indigenous Nationalities of Ecuador. *See* CONAIE

CONNATs (Paraguay), 355–60 passim

Consejo Cívico de Organizaciones Populares e Indígenas de Honduras. *See* COPINH (Civic Council of Popular and Indigenous Organizations of Honduras)

Consejo Nacional de Ayllus y Markas del Qullsuyu (CONAMAQ). *See* CONAMAQ

Consejo Regional Indígena del Cauca (CRIC, Colombia). *See* CRIC

Consejo Socialista Nacional de Agroecología. *See* COSONA

conservation of natural resources, 268–71, 296–98, 324

consumer costs, 206, 372, 416, 425, 427–28

constitutions, xv, xvii; Bolivia, 307, 313, 320, 323–24; Brazil, 246; Chile, 411,

414–20 passim, 423; Colombia, 155, 164, 167; Ecuador, 222, 230; Guatemala, 55; Honduras, 63, 64, 72, 77, 79; Mexico, 15, 25; Nicaragua, 138, 147; Paraguay, 334; Venezuela, 181, 190, 201, 204, 206

Contras, 117, 119, 128, 133

Convention on Child Labor, 358

cooperative land ownership, 170

cooperatives, xii; Argentina, 402; Brazil, 250, 251, 252, 257–63 passim; Ecuador, 216–19 passim; Guatemala, 35, 40; Nicaragua, 116, 138; Paraguay, 340, 349; Uruguay, 376–78 passim; Venezuela, 195, 198

Coordinadora Civil (CC, Nicaragua), 132, 138–45 passim

Coordinadora del Bajo Lempa y Bahía de Jiquilisco (El Salvador), xxvii, 96–100

Coordinación Nacional de Niños, Niñas y Adolescentes Trabajadores. *See* CONNATs

Coordination for the Self-Determination of Indigenous Peoples (CAPI, Paraguay), 342–48

COPINH (Civic Council of Popular and Indigenous Organizations of Honduras), 61–62

copper, 290–96 passim, 411–18 passim, 439

corn, 60, 98, 99, 258, 361

coronelismo, 246, 248

corporations, multinational. *See* multinational corporations

Correa, Rafael, xx–xxv passim, 66, 215, 222–34 passim, 239–40, 326

corruption: Argentina, 382, 386, 466n3; Bolivia, 309, 318; Brazil, 247, 250; Colombia, 156; Guatemala, 41, 55; El Salvador, 86, 90; Nicaragua, 119, 120, 136, 137; Paraguay, 332, 333, 351, 352, 362; Peru, 277; Venezuela, 180, 184, 200, 203, 205

cosmology, Andean. *See* Andean cosmology/ideology

COSONA (Consejo Socialista Nacional de Agroecología, Venezuela), 195

Coto de Cuellar, Lilian, 101–5

cotton, 258, 338, 361

coups, xvii; Brazil, 246; Ecuador, 214; Chile, 364, 411, 414, 421; fear and rumors of, 87, 338; Guatemala, 34;

Honduras, 49, 59, 63, 73, 364; Paraguay, 333, 337–38, 360, 363–64

CPR Urbana (Guatemala), 44–47 passim

CRIC (Regional Indigenous Council of Cauca, Colombia), 160, 162, 163, 170, 314

crime: Brazil, 249; El Salvador, 97, 99, 108, 109; Guatemala, 40; Nicaragua, 119, 145; prevention, 99; Venezuela, 184. *See also* drug trafficking; impunity; kidnapping; murder of women; organized crime; rape

criminalization: of abortion, 147, 354; of protest, 37, 53, 56, 89, 201, 208, 240, 277, 351–54 passim, 362, 416

CST. *See* Central Sandinista de Trabajadores (CST)

Cuba, xvii, 116, 246, 333, 420

Cuello, Marjory, 438–42

Curuguaty massacre, 2012, 337, 363–64

Dalton, Roque, *106*

dams, xvi, xxiv, 87, 98, 328; Bolivia, 318; Brazil, 269; Chile, 417, 426, 439; El Salvador, 110; Guatemala, 35, *43*; Honduras, 61. *See also* resistance to dam building

Dangl, Ben, 305–10, 316–23, 331–38, 443–44

Daza, Mar, 275–81, 444

death squads, 61, 88, 383

death threats, 38, 53, 80, 268–71 passim

debt, 162–63; Brazil, 247–48; Paraguayan lack of, 331; Uruguay, 372; Venezuela, 208

deforestation, 282, 335, 388

de Francia, José Gaspar Rodríguez. *See* Francia, José Gaspar Rodríguez de

de León, Javier, 53–56

del Socorro Solís, Altagracia, 125–28

demonstrations. *See* protests

denunciation campaigns, 388–93 passim

detention centers. *See* prisons and prisoners

development, sustainable. *See* sustainable development

dictatorships, xvi–xviii passim; Argentina, 383–95 passim; Brazil, 245–51 passim; Chile, 411–22 passim, 435, 442; Colombia, 151; Ecuador, 212; El Salvador, 86; Honduras, 60; Mexico, 25; Nicaragua, 115, 116, 138, 146;

Paraguay, 331–38 passim, 352; Uruguay, 372; Venezuela, 180, 206

disappearances and disappeared people, xvii, 457n7; Argentina, 383–93 passim, *384*, 466n4; Brazil, 249; Chile, 414, 419, 421, 467n22; Colombia, 153, 171; El Salvador, 89, 91, 95–96; Guatemala, 33–46 passim, 56, 62; Honduras, 78, 81; Mexico, 4, 17, 23; Paraguay, 333, 340; Peru, 277

doctors, 317–18, 320, 321–22, 389, 429, 464n13

drug trafficking, 264–68 passim, 318, 325. *See also* war on drugs

Duarte Frutos, Nicanor, 358

ecology, agricultural. *See* agroecology

economic growth, 242, 275–76; Argentina, 381, 387; Chile, 413, 416

Ecuador, xix–xxvi passim, 211–42, 286, 422; map, 210

Ecuadorian Federation of Agricultural Workers (FETEP), 226

Ecuadorian Federation of Evangelical Indians (FEINE), 213, 215

Ecuadorian Federation of Indians (FEI), 213

ECUARUNARI, xxii, 213, 218, 220, 221–22, 285

education, xiii; Chile, 411, 416, 418, 423, 424, 432, 434, 439–43 passim; Colombia, 161; of indigenous people, 236, 238, 239; Mexico, 17, 19; Nicaragua, 122, 124; Uruguay, 377; Venezuela, 190; Zapatistas, 13. *See also* teachers; universities and colleges

Egypt, 326

Ejército de Liberación Nacional (Colombia). *See* ELN (National Liberation Army)

Ejército Guerrillero de los Pobres (EGP). *See* Guerrilla Army of the Poor (EGP)

Ejército Popular de Liberación (Colombia). *See* EPL (Popular Liberation Army)

El Alto, Bolivia, 305–10 passim, 316, 317

elections, 224, 327; Brazil, 247; Chile, 413–14, 417, 420, 426; Colombia, 167; Ecuador, 212, 214, 215; El Salvador, 85, 93–95, 109; Honduras, 64, 73, 87; Mexico, 6, 20, 23; Nicaragua, 118, 119,

135, 136, 137, 460n2; Paraguay, 336; Peru, 280; Venezuela, xiv, xx, 179, 181, 184, 190, 208

electoral fraud: Colombia, 169; El Salvador, 85, 94–95; Honduras, 63, 64, 73, 87; Mexico, 6, 22, 23; Nicaragua, 119, 136–37; Venezuela, 179, 184, 207

ELN (National Liberation Army, Colombia), xviii, 166

El Observador (Guatemala), 53

El Salvador, xvii, xxvii, 78, 85–111; map, 84

emigration, Latin American, 4, 86

encampments, 50–53 passim, 125–28, *251*, 252, 253, 261–65

energy privatization, 74–75, 277, 463n10

energy programs, hydroelectric. *See* hydroelectric programs

environment, xxii, xxvi, xxvii, xxx, 242, 260; Argentina, 388; Bolivia, 309, 310, 324; Brazil, 258, 260, 267, 269; Colombia, 164; Ecuador, 232, 234; Guatemala, 37, 53; Honduras, 86, 88, 92, 93, 96–97, 103; Nicaragua, 129, 131; Paraguay, 335, 337, 338, 344, 346, 349, 361, 363; Peru, 280, 282, 286–98 passim; Venezuela, 192, 193, 203–4. *See also* deforestation; pollution

EPL (Popular Liberation Army, Colombia), 153, 166, 167

escrache actions, 388–93 passim

Escuela de Mecánica de la Armada (ESMA), 385, 389

Estigarriba, Francisco, 355–60

eucalyptus, xviii, 322

Euraque, Darió, 61, 459n4

Eurocentrism, xv, 242, 396

European immigrants. *See* immigrants, European

European Union, xxvii, 130, 164

Evangelical churches, 62, 299–300

evictions, 97, 335, 374; of protesters and occupiers, 14, 16, 38, 51, 218, 220, 387

ex-guerrillas, xxviii, 90, 96, 101, 164–70, 370, 464n10

exhumation of graves, 37, 42, 43

exiles and refugees. *See* refugees and exiles

exports, xiv; Argentina, xxiv, 386, 388; Bolivia, 307, 327, 328, 464n11; Brazil, xxiv, 254; Chile, 411, 416, 421; Ecuador, 228; Guatemala, 34, 48; Honduras, 59;

Paraguay, xxiv, 331, 335, 363; Peru, 276, 277, 278

expulsions from political parties. *See* political purges

extractive reserves (Brazil), 268–71

EZLN. *See* Zapatistas

factories, maquiladora. *See* maquiladoras

factory closures, 38, 378, 386

factory takeovers, 387, 398–403 passim, *401*

FARC (Revolutionary Armed Forces of Colombia), xvii–xviii, 153–57 passim, 166, 168, 256, 461n1

Farabundo Martí National Liberation Front. *See* FMLN (Farabundo Martí National Liberation Front)

farming. *See* agriculture; aquaculture; worm farming

favelas, 245, 266–68

Federación Nacional de Organizaciones Campesinas e Indígenas (FENOCIN). *See* FENOCIN

Federation of Mapuche Students (FMS, Chile), 432, 437

FEI. *See* Ecuadorian Federation of Indians (FEI)

FEINE. *See* Ecuadorian Federation of Evangelical Indians (FEINE)

femicide. *See* murder of women

feminists and feminism, 404; Argentina, 388; Bolivia, 319–23 passim; Brazil, 255; Chile, 404, 428–32; Guatemala, 39, 412; Honduras, 62–63; Nicaragua, 143–47; Paraguay, 354

FENOCIN (Ecuador), xxvi, 213, 226–30 passim

Fernández de Kirchner, Cristina, 387

Ferrari, Veronica, 298–302

fish farming. *See* aquaculture

fishing, 99, 100, 412, 426

Flores, Cilia, 195

Flores Magón, Ricardo, xxi, 20–21, 25, 115

FMLN (Farabundo Martí National Liberation Front, El Salvador), xvii, xxvii, 85–97 passim, 101–11 passim

FNRP (National People's Resistance Front, Honduras), 59, 63, 64

food: costs, 109, 206, 428; production and distribution, 357, 373, 378, 414, 421; self-sufficiency, 252; sovereignty, 229,

230, 388. *See also* gardens; hunger; nutrition and malnutrition

foreign trade. *See* exports; imports

forests, 286–87, 290, 318. *See also* deforestation; logging industry; rainforest conservation

former guerrillas. *See* ex-guerrillas

Foro Mesoamericano de los Pueblos, 129, 130

Fox, Michael, 245–61, 336, 444

France, 246, 259, 394, 466n7; emigrants, 434

Francia, José Gaspar Rodríguez de, 331, 332, 341

Francis of Assisi, Saint, 341–42

Franco, Federico, 337–38, 361

fraud, 38, 372, 387. *See also* electoral fraud

free trade agreements, 110, 129, 130, 229, 358, 387. *See also* NAFTA

Free Trade Zones, Nicaraguan, 122, 123, 130

Freire, Paulo, 116, 193, 199, 246

Frente Amplio (Uruguay), xx, 368–74 passim

Frente de Resistencia Urbana (FRU, Brazil), 265

Frente Farabundo Martí para la Liberación Nacional. *See* FMLN (Farabundo Martí National Liberation Front)

Frente Nacional de Resistencia Popular. *See* FNRP (National People's Resistance Front)

Frente Social y Popular (FSP, Paraguay), 338, 340, 348, 351, 352, 354

Front for the Development of the Northern Border (Peru), 294–95

FRU. *See* Frente de Resistencia Urbana (FRU)

FSLN (Sandinista National Liberation Front, Nicaragua), xvii, 115–47 passim, 460n12; purges, 133, 135, 144, 146–47

FSP. *See* Frente Social y Popular (FSP)

Fuentes, Iván, 425–28

Fuerzas Armadas Revolucionarias de Colombia. *See* FARC (Revolutionary Armed Forces of Colombia)

Fujimori, Alberto, 277, 280, 284, 300, 463n4, 463n9

Funes, Mauricio, 86–89 passim, 93, 110

FURD. *See* University Front of Roque Dalton (FURD)

Galeano, Eduardo, xv, 341

Galeano, Jorge, xxviii, 348–51, *348*

Galeano, Leticia, 337

Galpón de Corrales (community center, Uruguay), xxi, 373–78

gangs, 106, 109–10, 266, 368

garbage gleaning, 378

García Linera, Álvaro, 313, 464n10

García Pérez, Alan, 224, 277

gardens, *11*, 226, 289, 298, 319, 376, 377

Garifuna people, 34, 59, 61

garment industry, 257–61

gas, natural. *See* natural gas

Gas War, 2003, 307, 309–10, 464n11

gay, lesbian, bisexual, and transgender people. *See* LGBTTI (LGBTQ) people

gay marriage, 388

general strikes, 34, 59–60, 213, 333, 418

genetically modified (GMO) crops, xvii, xxiv, 248, 254, 349, 388

genetically modified (GMO) seeds, 227, 361

genocide: Argentina, 382, 389–93 passim; Chile, 412, 432; Guatemala, 33, 36, 37, *44*, 45, 46, 48, 458n20; Peru, 276

genocide trials (Argentina), 392–93

gold, xxiv, xxvii, 87, 90, 93, 202–4, 215, 367, 404, 406

González, César Alejandro, 195–96, 462n15

Goulart, João, xvii, 246

government subsidies. *See* subsidies

government unions, 204–5, 207

graffiti, 44, *44*, 47, *123*, 393

Grandmothers of the Plaza de Mayo (Argentina), 385, 389

Gran Polo Patriótico (GPP, Venezuela), 186–90 passim

Great Britain, 48, 332, 367, 368, 412

Green, Sharyl, 323–28

Guaraní people, 249–50, 331, 340–41, 350

Guatemala, xvi, xxiii, 33–56, 75, 85, 458–59nn20–21; map, 32

Guatemalan National Revolutionary Unity. *See* URNG (Guatemalan National Revolutionary Unity)

Guerrilla Army of the Poor (EGP, Guatemala), 35, 46

guerrilla warfare. *See* armed struggle

Guevara, Edwin Enrique Álvarez, 50–53

Gutiérrez, Lucio, xxvi, 214, 215, 223, 229

Gutiérrez Hernández, Rufino, 14–16

Guyana, 206

Hanauer, Ana, 250–56

health: Nicaragua banana workers', 126–28 passim; Paraguay, 353, 354; Uruguay, 374, 377. *See also* medical care; mental health

Hemispheric Social Alliance, 129, 130

Hernández, Jordi, 16

Hernández, Sara, 73–77

heterosexuality, 301–2

Heyward, J., 85–90, 106–11, 444

HidroAysén project (Chile), 418, 429

highway blockades. *See* road blockades

highway construction, 241, 310, 318–28 passim; Bolivia xxiv; El Salvador, 110; Guatemala, 35; Venezuela, 180

H.I.J.O.S. (Daughters and Sons for Identity and Justice against Forgetting and Silence): Guatemala, 44–48; Argentina, 385, 388–93

historical memory. *See* long memory (concept)

HIV/AIDS, 63, 78, 79, 300

Hoetmer, Raphael, 275–81, 444–45

Homeless Movement of Bahia (Brazil). *See* Movimento Sem Teto Bahia (MSTB)

Homosexual Movement of Lima, 298–302, *299*

Honduras, xxi, 49, 59–81, 85, 92; map, *58*

Honeycomb 2021 (El Panal 2021, Venezuela), 186–90

horizontal organization, xxii, 396; Argentina, 381, 389, 391, 405; Brazil, 265; Guatemala, 45; Honduras, 61, 63, 64; Mexico, xxvii, 6, 21, 26; Nicaragua, 121; Paraguay, 340; Uruguay, 375, 376; Venezuela, 194, 199. *See also* collectives and collectivity; cooperatives

housing, xiii; Argentina, 382; Brazil, 261–67 passim; Ecuador, 216–20 passim; evictions, 97, 335; Venezuela, 200

Howard, April, 319–23

Humala, Ollanta, 225, 277, 278

hunger, 9, 60, 142, 173, 413, 421–22. *See also* antihunger programs

hunger strikes, 101

hydroelectric programs, xvi, xxiv, 87; Bolivia, 318–19; Brazil, 269; Chile, 412, 417–18, 439; Ecuador, 240; El Salvador, 98, 103; Guatemala, *43*; Honduras, 61

Ibero-American University, 7, 26, 27, 28, 29

IIRSA (Integration of South American Regional Infrastructure), 241

ILO. *See* International Labour Organization (ILO)

IMF, xvi, 183, 221; Argentina relations, 386; Bolivia relations, 306–7; Brazil relations, 247; El Salvador relations, 86, 87; Nicaragua relations, 115, 141; Uruguay relations, 371, 372; Venezuela relations, 187

immigrants, European, 245, 252, 368, 381, 382, 434

impeachment, 337–38, 360, 363–64

imports, 179, 194

imprisonment, 167, 201, 436; of children, 359; Chile, 414, 416, 419, 421, 432; El Salvador, 110; of ex-presidents, 463n4; Guatemala, 34–35; Honduras, 70; Mexico, 6, 17; Venezuela, 181, 205, 207, 462n11. *See also* prisons and prisoners

impunity, 458n20; Argentina, 381, 385, 388, 389, 390, 392; Brazil, 248, 249; Chile, 415; Guatemala, 36–42 passim; Nicaragua, 119; Venezuela, 184

Indian theology, 341–42

indigenous languages, 161, 164, 331, 350, 437

indigenous peoples: Argentina, 382; Bolivia, 235, 305, 308–24 passim, *322*; Brazil, 245, 249–50; Chile, 412–18 passim, 432–37, 442; Colombia, 156–64 passim, *157*; Ecuador, 211–15 passim, 220–23 passim, 230–36 passim; El Salvador, 85–86; Guatemala, 33–43 passim, 53, 54; Honduras, 59, 60, 74; Mexico, xix, 18; Nicaragua, 142, 314; Paraguay, 331, 335, 348, 350; Peru, 275, 276, 281–86 passim, 290, 291; Venezuela, 186, 201–4. *See also* Amazonian peoples; Indian theology

inequality, 352; Brazil, 248; Chile, 411, 415–16; Honduras, 67; Mexico, 23; Paraguay, 335, 352–53
insurrection. *See* uprisings
Inter-American Development Bank, 344, 413–14
International Labour Organization (ILO): child labor stand, 356–60 passim; Convention 169, 55–56, 296–97
international law, 37, 55–56
International Monetary Fund. *See* IMF
international solidarity. *See* solidarity, international
Internet, xix, 7, 43, 407. *See also* blogs
iron, 327, 413, 462n15
Isiboro-Sécure Indigenous Territory and National Park (TIPNIS). *See* TIPNIS
Italy, 259; emigrants, 245, 268–69, 382, 434

Japan: industry in Latin America, 324
Jiles, Edmundo, 419–24, *420*
juntas: Argentina, 333, 383–89 passim; Brazil, 247; Chile, 415; Guatemala, 34; Nicaragua, 120
Justa Trama (Brazil), 258–59

Kichwa people, 213, 230–42, 276, 281
kidnapping, 80, 81, 153, 154, 171, 293, 333, 385, 392
Kirchner, Néstor, 386, 387
Klein, Hilary, 8–13, 445

labor unions. *See* unions
Lackowski, Peter, 323–28
Lagos, Ricardo, 416, 436
Landless Workers' Movement (MST, Brazil), xi, xii, xx, xxvi, xxvii, 225, 248–56 passim, 333; influence in Argentina, 387
land reform. *See* agrarian reform
land rights, 73, 79, 169, 213, 288
land takeovers: Brazil, 246, 248, 249, 269; Chile, 434, 435; Ecuador, 216–20; Guatemala, 37; Mexico, 8, 10–12; Peru, 284
languages. *See* indigenous languages; Portuguese language; Spanish language
La Paz, Bolivia, xv, 305–11 passim, 316, 319
lavaca collective (Argentina), 403–7
law, international. *See* international law

lawsuits, 42, 51, 295, 363
lead, 324, 377
leadership, xxi, 19–20, 99, 107, 237, 296. *See also* caudillos and caudillismo
Lenca people, 59–62 passim, 85
Lenin, Vladimir, 119–20, 285
lesbian, gay, bisexual, and transgender people. *See* LGBTQ people
Lewites, Herty, 119, 133, 135
LGBTQ people, 62–64 passim, 77–81, 298–302, 299, 388. *See also* transsexuals
liberation theology, xviii, xxi; Brazil, 250; Guatemala, 35; Ecuador, 213, 221; Honduras, 60, 62; Nicaragua, 116; Paraguay, 333, 340
libraries, 92, 373, 375–77 passim, 382
lithium, xvi, 411, 439
Lobo, Pepe, 64, 73, 87
"Local Peace Zone" (El Salvador), 96–100
lockouts, 181
logging industry, 297, 412, 414, 416, 417
long memory (concept), 316, 317
López Obrador, Andrés Manuel, 6, 7, 20, 21, 25, 225
Lucas García, Romeo, 35, 37
Lucha Indígena (*Indigenous Struggle*), 282, 285
Lucio, Dioyenes, xxv–xxvi, 226–30
Lugo, Fernando, xx, 336–39 passim, 342, 350, 351, 354, 361–62; impeachment, 337–38, 360, 363–64
Lula da Silva, Luiz Inácio, xx, xxiii, xxiv, 247–48, 256
Luna, Patricia, 13–20

Macas, Luis, 215, 236–42, 237
Maduro, Nicolás, 179, 184, 195, 203, 208, 462n15
MAQL. *See* Quintín Lame Armed Movement (MAQL)
Majaz (mining company), 290, 293, 296
malnutrition. *See* nutrition and malnutrition
Mam people, 53–56 passim
Maoism, xix, 25, 167, 212
MAP. *See* Popular and Agrarian Movement (MAP)
Mapuche people, 412–18 passim, 432–37, 442

Mapuche Students' Federation. *See* Federation of Mapuche Students (FMS)

maquiladoras, 122–23, 334

marches: Argentina, 407; Bolivia, xix, 310, 321, 322; Chile, 439, 467n27; Ecuador, xix, 231, 233; Honduras, 70, 71, 72, 80; Mexico, *15*, 16, 27; Nicaragua, 126, 127, 128, 131, 132; Paraguay, 358; Peru, 279, 280, *291*, 293, 294, 295, *299*; Uruguay, 374, *378*

Marcos, Subcomandante, xix, xxi, 5

Martinez, Courtney, 44–49, 445

Marx, Karl, 315

Marxism and Marxists, 25, 116, 187, 220, 395–97 passim, 415

MAS. *See* Movimiento al Socialismo (MAS)

Maya people, 33–36 passim, 39, 61. *See also* Lenca people; Mam people

media: Argentina, 387, 406, *407*; El Salvador, 108; Honduras, 85; Mexico, 7, 24; Paraguay, 364; Peru, 294, 300. *See also* alternative media; Internet; radio; television

medical care, 106, 317–18, 353, 426, 429, 430. *See also* doctors

medicine, 317–18. *See also* traditional medicine

Mejía, Yamilet, xxviii–xxx, 143–47

memory, historical. *See* long memory (concept)

Mendes, Chico, 250, 269

Mendez, Roberto, 44–49

Menem, Carlos, 386, 387

mental health, 106

MERCOSUR, 387

Mesa de Unidad Democrática (MUD, Venezuela), 182

mestizos: Ecuador, 211, 215, 218, 226, 235; Guatemala, 34, 46; Honduras, 59, 60; Nicaragua, 115

Mexico, xxvii, 3–29, 35–36, 422; map, 2. *See also* Zapatistas

micropolitics, 319, 431

military juntas. *See* juntas

minga (concept), xviii, 158–59, 237, 350

Minga Social (Ecuador), 216, 226

mining, xvi, xxv, xxvii, 87; Argentina, 405–7 passim; Bolivia, 306, 309, 317, 318, 321, 324; Chile, 412–18 passim, 429, 439; Ecuador, 215, 223; El Salvador, 90–96 passim, 110; Guatemala, 35, 37, 48, 53–56 passim; Mexico, 22; Paraguay, 338; Peru, 277–78, 280, 281, 286–96 passim; Uruguay, 367; Venezuela, 202–4. *See also* copper; gold; silver

Miskitu people, 59, 314

MLN-T. *See* Tupamaros

M-19. *See* April 19th Movement (M-19)

Molina, Luisa, 138–43, *139*, 144

monoculture (agriculture), xvi, 42, 98, 335, 349, 372, 388

monopolies, 24, 26, 29, 34

Monsanto, 335, 338

Montenegro, Sofia, 145, 147

Montesinos, Vladimir, 463n4

Morales, Evo, xx, xxiii, 66, 225, 305–14 passim, 318–28 passim, 360

MORENA (Movement for National Renewal, Mexico), 7, 20–26 passim

Morris, Kenneth E., 460n2

Mothers of the Plaza de Mayo, xi, 385, 389

Movement of Recovered Companies, 398–403

Movimento dos Trabalhadores Rurais Sem Terra. *See* Landless Workers' Movement (MST)

Movimento Sem Teto Bahia (MSTB), 262

Movimiento Agrario y Popular (MAP). *See* Popular and Agrarian Movement (MAP)

Movimiento al Socialismo (MAS, Bolivia), xxv, 306–13 passim

Movimiento Armado Quintín Lame. *See* Quintín Lame Armed Movement (MAQL)

Movimiento Campesino Paraguayo (MCP), 333

Movimiento de Liberación Nacional-Tupamaros. *See* Tupamaros

Movimiento de Renovación Sandinista. *See* Sandinista Renewal Movement (MRS)

Movimiento Pachakutik. *See* Pachakutik Movement

Movimiento Revolucionario Tupac Amaru (MRTA). *See* Tupac Amaru Revolutionary Movement (MRTA)

Movimiento Unificado Campesino del Aguán (MUCA), 73–77

MUD. *See* Mesa de Unidad Democrática (MUD)
Mujeres Creando (Bolivia), 319, 322–23
Mujeres Transformando el Mundo (MTM, Guatemala), 38–44
Mújica, José, 370
multinational corporations, xiii–xiv, 335–36; Bolivia, 306, 317, 323–28 passim; Brazil, 254; Guatemala, 34, 42, 48–56 passim; Nicaragua, 125–28 passim; Paraguay, 349; Peru, 286, 293
Muñoz, Gabriela Schvartzman. *See* Schvartzman Muñoz, Gabriela
murals and muralists, 9, 44, *44*, 47, 91, 110
murder, political. *See* assassination; disappearances and disappeared people
murder of prisoners, 385, 389
murder of women, 38–39, 354, 389, 458n20
murder rates, Venezuelan, 184
Murillo, Mario A., 151–58, 445
music, 44, 350, 382, 389, 404, 438

NAFTA, xix, 6
narcotrafficking. *See* drug trafficking
Narvaez Murillo, Zoilamérica, 118, 143, 144
Natarén, Oswaldo, 106–11
National Coordination of Adolescent and Child Workers (CONNATs). *See* CONNATs
national debt. *See* debt
National Federation of Peasant, Indigenous, and Black Organizations (FENOCIN). *See* FENOCIN
nationalization: Argentina, 387, 395; Bolivia, 307, 309, 317, 464n12; Chile, 412, 413, 414, 418, 421, 439; Guyana, 206; Uruguay, 368; Venezuela, xxiv, 181, 183, 204, 208, 462n15
National Liberation Army (Colombia). *See* ELN (National Liberation Army)
national parks, 197, 203, 310
National Students' Union (Chile), 439, 441–42
National Workers' Union (Venezuela). *See* UNT (Unión Nacional Trabajadores de Venezuela)
natural gas, 307, 309–10, 324, 328, 464nn11–12

nature, 341–42. *See also* conservation of natural resources; forests
Navy Mechanics School, Argentina. *See* Escuela de Mecánica de la Armada (ESMA)
Neff, Phil, 33–38, 445
Nespolo, Nelsa Inês Fabian, 257–61
Network of Women against Violence (Nicaragua), 143, 147
Nicaragua, xvii, xxi, 78, 85, 115–47; Honduras border, 65, 70; map, *114*; Sandinista revolution, 117–24 passim, 133–40 passim, 146, 221
nitrate fields, 411, 412
nongovernmental organizations (NGOs), 287–88; activist opinions of, 285, 396, 404; Brazil, 266; Chile, 415; Colombia, 153; Guatemala, 37; Nicaragua, 120, 130, 147; Peru, 279, 287–88; Uruguay, 367
nonhierarchical organization. *See* horizontal organization
North American Free Trade Agreement (NAFTA). *See* NAFTA
Nurses in Resistance (Honduras), 69–73
nutrition and malnutrition, 60, 164, 248, 377

Oaxaca, Mexico, xxvii, 6, 13–30
Obed, Isis, 68–69, 71
occupation of territory, xii–xiii; Brazil, *251*, 261–65; Guatemala, 38, 50–53 passim; Mexico, 14; Nicaragua, 131; Paraguay, 353. *See also* encampments; land takeovers
occupation of workplaces, 386, 387, 398–403 passim, *401*
OFRANEH (Honduras), 61–62
oil and oil industry: Argentina, 387, 405; Bolivia, 309, 324, 332; Ecuador, 212, 215, 223; Guatemala, 35, 49; Paraguay, 332; Peru, 297; Venezuela, 180, 181, 183–84, 206; Venezuela–Nicaragua deals, 119, 142
Ojeda, Julieta, xxv, 319–23
oligarchy, xxiii; Argentina, 367–68; Brazil, 246, 248; Chile, 412; Ecuador, 212, 214, 240–41; El Salvador, 87; Guatemala, 33, 35, 36, 37, 50, 457n11; Honduras, 60; Mexico, 23, 24; Nicaragua, 120, 129; Paraguay, 337, 362; Venezuela, 183
Olivera, Oscar, 323–28, *325*

Open Veins of Latin America (Galeano), 341, 455n1
Operation Condor, xviii, 23, 247, 455n4, 457n7
Oppressed but Not Defeated (Rivera Cusicanqui), 316
Opus Dei, 284, 430, 431, 468n31
Organización Fraternal Negra Hondureña. *See* OFRANEH
organized crime, 35, 36, 109, 458n13
Orozco, Rosangela, 186–90
Ortega, Daniel, 117–20 passim, 125, 126, 130, 133–46 passim
Ortega, Zoilamérica. *See* Narvaez Murillo, Zoilamérica
Ortiz dos Santos, Fabíola, 266–71, 445–46
Otro Mundo Es Posible, 128–33
Ouviña, Hernán, 18–20, 446

Pachakutik Movement (Ecuador), 214, 218, 237
Pacific Rim Mining Corporation, xxvii, 90, 91, 92, 93
Pagoada, Marina, 70–73
Palau, Marielle, 360–64
Paley, Julia, 415
PAN (National Action Party, Mexico), 3, 6, 22, 24
Panama, 118, 163, 342
Pando massacre, 2008, *308*, 309, *322*
Paniagua, Gloria, 128–33
Paraguay, xxiv–xxviii passim, 331–64; map, 330
paramilitary operations: Bolivia, *308*; Colombia, 154–55, 165, 171; El Salvador, 88; Guatemala, 35; Paraguay, 337. *See also* death squads
Paret, Ernesto "Lalo," 398–403, *398*, 404
parks, national. *See* national parks
Partido Acción Nacional. *See* PAN (National Action Party)
Partido de la Revolución Democrática. *See* PRD (Party of the Democratic Revolution)
Partido dos Trabalhadores. *See* Workers' Party (PT)
Partido Revolucionario Institucional. *See* PRI (Institutional Revolutionary Party)
Partido Socialista Unido de Venezuela. *See* PSUV
party purges. *See* political purges

paternalism, 28, 168, 198, 283, 359, 360
Patriotic Alliance for Change (Paraguay), 337, 340
Patriotic Union (UP, Colombia), 154, 167
pay. *See* wages and salaries
Paz, Octavio, 3
PDVSA (Petróleos de Venezuela Sociedad Anónima), 181, 183, 204
peace communities, 170–75
Pemón people, 201–4
Peña Nieto, Enrique, 26
"Penguin Revolution," 416, 418
Pérez, Andrea Morales, 120–25
Pérez Anchiraico, Margarita, 286–90
Pérez Molina, Otto, 33, 48, 457n11
permaculture, 99–100
Perón, Eva, 383
Perón, Juan Domingo, 383
Peru, xxi, 224, 275–302; map, 274
pesticide use, 335, 337, 353
Petras, James, 456n11
Petróleos de Venezuela Sociedad Anónima. *See* PDVSA (Petróleos de Venezuela Sociedad Anónima)
petroleum. *See* oil and oil industry
physicians. *See* doctors
Pine, Adrienne, 59–64, 69–77, 446
Piñera, Sebastian, 417, 418, 426, 428
"Pink Tide," xvi, xx–xxiv passim
Pinochet, Augusto, xvii, 333, 411–19 passim, 435, 436, 439
piqueteros, 381, 386, 393, 395
Plan Mesoamerica, 87
Plaza de Mayo, Buenos Aires, 385, 389
plebiscites, 215, 219, 414, 415
Police Pacification Units (UPPs): Rio de Janeiro, 266–68
political parties, socialist. *See* socialist parties
political prisoners: Chile, 414, 416, 418, 421; Mexico, 6, 17; United States, 25; Venezuela, 201, 207, 462n11
political purges, 133, 135, 144, 146–47
pollution, 267, 289, 293, 416, 433. *See also* toxic waste dumping
Polo Patriótico (Venezuela), xx, 186. *See also* Gran Polo Patriótico
Popular and Agrarian Movement (MAP, Paraguay), 348–51
Popular Education Center for Integrated Family Development. *See* CEPDIF

Popular Education Center of Mixteque. *See* Centro de Educación Popular de Mixteque (CEP)

Popular Education Centers of Rangel Municipality. *See* CEPZONAL Rangel

Popular Front governments, 413, 466n7

popular uprisings. *See* uprisings

Portugal, 246, 249–50, 367, 368

Portugal Mollinedo, Pedro, xv, 311–16

Portuguese language, 245

poverty, xiii, 235–36, 351; Bolivia, 235–36; Brazil, 248, 261–65 passim; Chile, 414, 432; Colombia, 152; Ecuador, 236; Honduras, 66; Mexico, 9–10; Nicaragua, 115, 120, 132; Paraguay, 335, 352–53, 360; Venezuela, 184

PRD (Party of the Democratic Revolution, Mexico), 4, 6, 20, 28

Prensa de Frente (PF, Argentina), 393–94

Prestes, Luís Carlos, 250

PRI (Institutional Revolutionary Party, Mexico), 3–4, 7, 16, 22–28 passim

prisons and prisoners, 165, 184, 249, 421; murder of, 385, 389. *See also* imprisonment; political prisoners; women prisoners

privatization, xviii, 15, 37, 110, 334, 349, 370, 386, 414–16 passim, 466n3; of aid, 136; of education, 74, 416; of energy, 74–75, 277, 463n10; of hospitals, 90; of mines, 286, 306; of oil and gas, 387, 464n11; of pension systems, 416; protests against, *297*; of transportation, 393; of water, 15, 74, 90, 240, 306, 323, 394

prostitution, 300, 404, 405

protests: Argentina, 385, 388–97 passim, 405, 406; Bolivia, 306–10 passim, *308*, *322*; Chile, 411–18 passim, *417*, 425–28 passim, 438, 439; Colombia, 156; Ecuador, 211; El Salvador, 88–89, 90; Guatemala, *43*, *55*; Honduras, 68; Mexico, 26; Nicaragua, 125–28, 131, 146; Paraguay, 333, *334*; Peru, 277, 280, 300, 301; Uruguay, *374*; Venezuela, 187, 201, 202, *202*. *See also* encampments; marches

PSUV (United Socialist Party of Venezuela), 179, 184–89 passim, 195, 207, 462n12

PT. *See* Workers' Party (PT)

public shaming campaigns. *See* shaming campaigns

public transportation, 393–97 passim, 416

Pukara (Bolivia), xv, 311

purges. *See* political purges

Quichua people. *See* Kichwa people

quilombos, 249, 250, 263–64

Quintín Lame Armed Movement (MAQL, Colombia), 153, 166, 167

Quito, Ecuador, 216–20 passim

radio, 85, 216, 294, 373–76 passim, 394, 403, 407

railways, 393–97 passim

rainforest conservation, 268–71, 296–98

Ramírez Cuevas, Jesús, 20–26

ranching, 171, 287–91 passim, 295, 343, 345, 349, 352, 382

rape, 16, 39–41 passim, 118–19, 143, 144, 171, 388, 431

Reagan, Ronald, xviii, 117, 134

reconciliation and truth commissions. *See* truth commissions

recovered enterprises, 387, 398–403 passim, *401*

recycling and recyclers, 319, 369, 376, 378

refugees and exiles, 45, 46, 96, 336, 368; from Chile, 383, 414, 421; gay, 77–81; from Guatemala, 35–36; from Honduras, 65

Regeneración (Mexico), 20, 23–24

Rein, Marcy, xiv–xxx; Nicaragua interviews, 120–25, 143–47; Venezuela interviews, 191–201; Argentina interviews, 393–410; Chile interviews, 411–24, 428–42

religion, 131, 140, 175, 212, 284, 326–27, 341–42. *See also* Catholic Church; Christian Agrarian Leagues; Evangelical churches

reparations, 36, 40, 41, 156–57, 277, 278, 289, 459n24

repression: Argentina, 382–93 passim, 405, 406; Brazil, 248–49, 251, 255, 256; Chile, 412–16 passim, 421, 429, 436, 442, 467n22; Colombia, 152–55 passim, 171; Ecuador, 213; El Salvador, 88–89, 94–95; Guatemala, 33–38 passim, 44–45, 48; Honduras, 62, 65–71 passim, 75–81 passim; Mexico,

4, 6, 13–18 passim, 26, 28; Nicaragua,
117; Paraguay, 333, 340, 364; Peru,
276–83 passim, 293, 295, 300, 301;
Venezuela, xix, 184, 187, 189. *See also*
anticommunism; disappearances and
disappeared people; imprisonment;
state terrorism; torture
reproductive rights, 143–46 passim
resistance to dam building, *43*, 61, 418,
439
resistance to highway construction, 310,
318, 321, 322, 324, 327
resistance to mining, 53–56 passim, 91–96
passim, 280–82 passim, 286–96 passim,
318, 404, *407*
revolts. *See* uprisings
revolutions, 62; Bolivia, 316; Cuba, 116,
246, 333, 420; Guatemala, 34; Mexico,
xxi, 3, 9, 25, 115; Nicaragua, 117–24
passim, 133–40 passim, 146, 221;
Venezuela, 179–84 passim, 192, 194,
456n12
Rio de Janeiro, 266–68
Ríos Montt, Efraín, 35, 37, 48
Rio Tinto Alcan, 338, 363, 364
Riozinho do Anfrísio Extractive Reserve
Association (Brazil), 268–71
Rivera, Marcelo, 91–96 passim
Rivera, Miguel, 91–96, *91*
Rivera Cusicanqui, Sylvia, xxiv, 316–19,
464n10
road blockades: Argentina, 381, 386–87;
Bolivia, 306, 307; Chile, 418, 421, 425,
427; Ecuador, 220; Mexico, 14, 19; Peru,
279; Uruguay, 377
Robinson, William, xxii, xxiv
Rodríguez, Nery, 65–69, *65*
Roman Catholic Church. *See* Catholic
Church
Romero, Alexis, xxiv, 201–4
Roque Dalton Revolutionary Front
(FURD, El Salvador). *See* University
Front of Roque Dalton (FURD)
Ross, Clifton, xiv–xxix; Argentina
interviews, 393–407; Bolivia interviews,
311–23; Colombia interviews, 158–75;
Ecuador interviews, 216–36; El
Salvador interviews, 91–105; Honduras
interviews, 65–69; Mexico interviews,
13–29 passim; on Nicaragua, 115–20;
Nicaragua interviews, 120–47;

Paraguay interviews, 338–64; Uruguay
interviews, 369–78; on Venezuela,
179–86; Venezuela interviews, 191–201,
204–8
rubber bullets, 68
rubber tappers, 250, 268–71
Ruiz, Manuela, 158–59
Ruíz Ortíz, Ulises, 13–18 passim

Sader, Emir, 413
Saint Francis of Assisi. *See* Francis of
Assisi, Saint
Sainz, Cecilia, 398, *398*
salaries. *See* wages and salaries
Salinas, Carlos, 23
Salinas Ponce, Sari, 296–98 passim
same-sex marriage, 388
Sánchez, Leda, 69–73
Sánchez de Lozada, Gonzalo, 307, 464n11
Sandinista National Liberation Front. *See*
FSLN (Sandinista National Liberation
Front)
Sandinista Renewal Movement (MRS,
Nicaragua), 118, 119, 128, 133–38 passim,
147
Sandinista Revolution, 117–24 passim,
133–40 passim, 146, 221
Sandino, Augusto, xxi, 115–16, 121, 138, *139*
Sanford, Victoria, 458n20
San Isiboro Sécure National Park
(TIPNIS). *See* TIPNIS
Santos, Juan Manuel, 152, 153, 156
Sarthou, Helios, 369–72, *371*
school takeovers, xxvi, 438
schoolteachers. *See* teachers
Schvartzman Muñoz, Gabriela, 338
Scilingo, Adolfo, 389
seamstress cooperatives. *See* women
garment workers' cooperatives
secrecy, 118–19, 136, 392
Secretariat of Information and
Communication (SICOM), 338
seeds, 159, 194, 227, 335, 338, 361
self-management, 45, 188, 340, 399. *See
also* cooperatives; occupation of
workplaces
Sendero Luminoso (Shining Path, Peru),
276, 282–83, 286, 300
sexual slavery, 39, 40
shaming campaigns, 388–93
shantytowns, 261–67 passim

Shining Path. *See* Sendero Luminoso (Shining Path)
Shuar people, 213, 230–36
Sicilia, Javier, 8
silence, 39, 46, 391
Silva, Eliana Sousa. *See* Sousa Silva, Eliana
silver, xvi, 48, 305, 324, 367, 381
SITRAPETEN (Guatemala), 50–53
slavery, xvi, 42, 211, 246; Argentina, 382; Bolivia, 305; Brazil, 249; Guatemala, 33; Paraguay, 341; Peru, 301; Uruguay, 465n2. *See also* sexual slavery
SNTE (Sindicato Nacional de Trabajadores de la Educación, Mexico), 14, *15*
social centers. *See* community centers
Social Movements of Aysén (Chile), 425
socialism, 168–69, 186–90 passim, 208, 247, 254, 285, 315
socialist parties: Brazil, 265; Chile, 415; Ecuador, 213, 218, 228; Venezuela, 179, 184–89 passim, 195, 207, 462n12
Socorro Solís, Altagracia del. *See* del Socorro Solís, Altagracia
solidarity, 314–15, 350, 391, 441; international, 8, 43, 73, 75, 92, 129, 131, 187, 221, 222, 296, 421
solidarity economy, 192, 257–59 passim, 462–63nn1–2
Solidarity with Honduras (UK), 77–81
Solís, Fernando, 53–56
Somoza, Anastasio, xvii, 116, 120, 125, 138, 146
Sosa, Flavio, 18–20
Sousa Silva, Eliana, 266–68
Soviet Union, xvii, 60, 183
soy, xvi, xvii, xxiv; Argentina, 388, 405; Paraguay, 335–37 passim, 348–53 passim, 363, 364
Spain, 162, 383; emigrants, 368–69; industry in Latin America, *43*, 48; influence, 152, 211; invasion and colonies, xvi, 85, 162, 180, 249, 305, 367, 381–82, 412
Spanish language, xv, 161, 236
Spronk, Susan, 186–90, 446
state subsidies. *See* subsidies
state terrorism, 35, 36, 39, 391, 392
stencil art, *106*
street gangs. *See* gangs

strikes: Argentina, 382; Bolivia, 306, 307, 320, 464n13; Brazil, 247, 248; Chile, 412, 414, 418; Ecuador, 213; El Salvador, 101; Guatemala, 34; Mexico, 14; Venezuela, 207. *See also* general strikes; hunger strikes
Stroessner, Alfredo, 332–40 passim
student movements: Brazil, 246; Chile, 413, 416–17, 422, 423, 438–42; El Salvador, 106–11; Guatemala, 34; Honduras, 62; Mexico, 7, 26–29
Subcomandante Marcos. *See* Marcos, Subcomandante
subsidies: Argentina, 394, 395, 406; Chile, 423, 440; Colombia, 168; El Salvador, 87; Mexico, 6; Venezuela, 180
sugar industry, xiii, xvi, xxiv, 34, 35, 129, 188, 249, 263, 457n11
superhighways, 241, 310, 318–28 passim
sustainable development, 54, 158, 294–95, 321, 439

takeovers. *See* factory takeovers; occupation of territory; school takeovers
tango, 382, 389
taxation, 22; Argentina, 388; Bolivia, 307, 324; Chile, 418, 439; resistance to, 17; Venezuela, 206, 208
teachers: Brazil, 262; Chile, 416; Guatemala, 38, 44; Ecuador, 236, 238; El Salvador, 85, 101; Honduras, 65–69 passim, 74, 79; Mexico, 6, 14–18 passim; Peru, 277, 278, 283; Venezuela, 190
teachers' unions, 6, 14–18 passim, *15*, 38, 101, 248, 277
teenagers. *See* adolescents
Tekojojá Popular Movement (Paraguay), 338, 339, 340
television, 7, 22–29 passim, 182
terrorism, state. *See* state terrorism
theology, Indian. *See* Indian theology
theology of liberation. *See* liberation theology
Tinoco, Victor Hugo, xxviii–xxix, 133–38
TIPNIS, xxiv, 310, 317–27 passim
Toledo, Alejandro, 277, 463n10
torture, xvii; Argentina, 385, 389; Chile, 419, 436; El Salvador, 91; Honduras, 76, 80; Peru, 293, 295
toxic waste dumping, 286–90

toxins, agricultural. *See* agrotoxins
trade, foreign. *See* exports; imports
trade unions. *See* unions
traditional medicine, 235, 297, 318, 331
trains, 393–97 passim
transgenic crops and seeds. *See* genetically modified (GMO) crops; genetically modified (GMO) seeds
transnational corporations. *See* multinational corporations
transportation, public. *See* public transportation
transsexuals, 300, 301, 459n6, 463n12
trials, 41, 56; Chile, 416, 436; Argentina, 389, 392–93, 466n4. *See also* impeachment
tribunals, 39, 129; electoral, 102, 103, 219
Trigona, Marie, 381–88, 446
Tróchez, Walter, 63–64, 78, 80
truth commissions, 36, 37, 276, 280, 415
Tuberquía, Jesús, 170–75, *172*
Tupac Amaru, xxi, 276
Tupac Amaru Revolutionary Movement (MRTA, Peru), 276, 300
Tupak Katari guerrilla movement (1970s, Bolivia), xxi, 305, 310, 316, 317, 464n10
Tupamaros (Uruguay), 370

UN. *See* United Nations
UNASUR (Union of South American Nations), xxvii, 182–83
unemployed workers' organizations, Argentinean. See *piqueteros*
unemployment: Argentina, 385, 386; Brazil, 248; Chile, 414; Nicaragua, 120; Paraguay, 332; Venezuela, 206
UNESCO, 116
UNICEF, 356, 359
Unidad Revolucionaria Nacional Guatemalteca. *See* URNG (Guatemalan National Revolutionary Unity)
Unión Nacional de Trabajadores de Venezuela. *See* UNT (Unión Nacional de Trabajadores de Venezuela)
Union of South American Nations (UNASUR). *See* UNASUR (Union of South American Nations)
Unión Patriótica. *See* Patriotic Union (UP)
unions, xviii, 8; Argentina, 382–86 passim, 395, 396, 466n3; Bolivia, 317; Brazil, 265; Chile, 412–14 passim, 421, 426, 440;

Ecuador, 239–40; Guatemala, 34, 35, 38, 50–53; Honduras, 60; Nicaragua, 120–25; Paraguay, 333, 348; Peru, 277, 285; Uruguay, 367, 369; Venezuela, 204–8 *See also* government unions; strikes; teachers' unions
Unisol Brasil, 257, 258
United Fruit Company, 34, 59–60
United Kingdom. *See* Great Britain
United Nations, 39, 133, 219, 336, 372; Convention on the Rights of the Child, 143; FAO, 229. *See also* UNESCO; UNICEF
United Self-Defense Forces of Colombia. *See* AUC (United Self-Defense Forces of Colombia)
United Socialist Party of Venezuela (PSUV). *See* PSUV
United States, xvi–xvii, 246, 247; in Brazil, 246, 248; in Chile, 364, 412, 413–14, 421, 466–67n9; in Colombia, 151–52, 155, 157, 162–63, 165, 214; in Ecuador, 214; in El Salvador, 86–90 passim; Guatemala relations, 34; in Honduras, 60–64 passim, 364; Latin America immigration, 4, 86; Latin American opinion, 128; in Mexico, 22, 23; military bases, 214, 225; natural gas import plan, 307; in Nicaragua, 115–18 passim, 127, 134, 460n2; Nicaragua abandonment of concern, 460n12; in Panama, 118, 163; Paraguay relations, 335–36, 358; solidarity movements, 8, 120–21; Uruguay relations, 371; Venezuela meddling, 181
Univens (Brazil), 257–61, *259*
universities and colleges: El Salvador, 106, 107; Guatemala, 34; indigenous views, 162; Mexico, 19, 26–29 passim; Venezuela, 181
University Front of Roque Dalton (FURD), 106–11
UNT (Unión Nacional de Trabajadores de Venezuela), 204, 208
uprisings, xii, xix; Argentina, 383, 386–87; Bolivia, 305–10 passim, 323, 324; Chile, 418, 425–29 passim, *425*, 434; Ecuador, 211, 221; Peru, 276, 279; worldwide, 326. *See also* Caracazo, 1989; revolutions; Zapatistas

Urban Resistance Front. *See* Frente de Resistencia Urbana (FRU)

Uribe Vélez, Álvaro, 151–52, 155–56, 168

URNG (Guatemalan National Revolutionary Unity), 35, 36

Uruguay, xx, xxiv, 247, 332, 367–78, 387; map, 366

USAID, 61, 466–67n9

USSR. *See* Soviet Union

La Vaca (collective). *See* lavaca collective

Vallejo, Camila, 27, 29

vandalism, 393, 394, 397, 422

Vanesca, Ana, 261–65

Vargas, Antonio, 214, 215

Vazquez, Tabaré, xx, 370

Velasco Alvarado, Juan, 276, 282, 463n6

Velasco Ibarra, José María, 212, 214

Veltmeyer, Henry, 456n11

Venezuela, xiv, xix–xxiv passim, 179–208, 373, 387, 462nn11–15 passim; Bolivia relations, 309; map, 178; Nicaragua relations, 119, 136, 137, 142

Vera, Emiliano, 342–47

Via Campesina, xix, 229, 255, 256

Vicenta Dávila, María, xxv, 186, 192, 196–201, *197*

victim reparations. *See* reparations

Videla, Jorge, 383

Villarán, Susana, 299, 300

La Violencia (Colombia), 460n1

violence against women, 38–43 passim, 71, 145, 147, 281, 354. *See also* murder of women

wages and salaries, 161; Argentina, 382, 384; Bolivia, 306–7; Brazil, 248, 262; Chile, 417; El Salvador, 103; Mexico, 22; Venezuela, 206, 208

Walsh, Rodolfo, 383–85

warfare, guerrilla. *See* armed struggle

War of the Triple Alliance, 332, 355–56

war on drugs, 22, 86, 151, 214, 306

waste. *See* garbage gleaning; toxic waste dumping

water, 405, 406, 428, 429, 433; bottling plant unions, 50–53; contamination, 90; costs, 427; democratization, 228; pollution, 433; privatization, 15, 74, 90, 240, 306, 323, 428, 429; recovery of

springs, 192–93. *See also* hydroelectric programs

watersheds, threats to, 292

Water War, Cochabamba, 2000, 306, 309–10

weavers, 192, 193

Webber, Jeffery R., 186–90, 236–42, 446

welfare, xxiii–xxiv, 132, 168, 242, 248, 262, 362, 369. *See also* "Zero Hunger" programs

Wolff, Antonio Navarro, xxviii–xxix, 164–70

women: Argentina, 383, 404–7 passim; Bolivia, 319, 322–23; Brazil, 255, 263; Chile, 422, 428–32 passim; Ecuador, 212, 219–20; El Salvador, 101–5 passim; in EZLN, 5, 8–13; Guatemala, 38–43; Honduras, 73–77 passim; in MST, 255; Nicaragua, 120–25, 143–47; Peru, 288, 296–98; Uruguay, *378*; Venezuela, 192–93, 196–97. *See also* reproductive rights; violence against women

women garment workers' cooperatives, 257–61, *259*

women prisoners, 385, 416, 458n20

"Women Transforming the World" (MTM, Guatemala) 38–44

worker bargaining and contracts. *See* collective bargaining and contracts

"worker control" (government-created), 206–8

worker cooperatives, 252, 257–61, *259*

worker lockouts, 181

worker-run businesses, 377–78, 387, 398–403 passim

worker self-management. *See* self-management

workers, child and adolescent. *See* child and adolescent workers

workers' movements. *See* Landless Workers' Movement (MST); occupation of workplaces; *piqueteros*; unions

Workers' Party (PT, Brazil), 247, 248

workers' pay. *See* wages and salaries

workplace occupation. *See* occupation of workplaces

World Bank, xvi, xx, xxiii, 115, 221, 326; alternative to, 183; Chile relations; 413–14; El Salvador relations, 86, 87; Guatemala relations, 35

World Social Forum, xix, 143, 257, 258

worm farming, 191, 192, 198

yerba maté, 341, 342, 406
Yonda, Luis, 160–64
#YoSoy132 (Mexico), 7, 26–29
youth. *See* adolescents

Zapatistas, xix–xx, 5, 225; influence
    outside Mexico, 63, 129, 395; on
    leadership, xxi; women, 8–13, *9, 11*
Zelaya Rosales, José Manuel, 49, 59, 65–73
    passim, 77, 79, 459n4
"Zero Hunger" programs, xxiii, 90, 119,
    145, 248
Zibechi, Raúl, xi–xiv, xxiii, 261–65,
    281–86, 367–69, 447

Venezuela: Revolution from the Inside Out (DVD)

Directed by Clifton Ross

ISBN: 978-1-60486-017-7
$19.95   Length: 85 minutes

Venezuela: Revolution from the Inside Out is a voyage into Latin America's most exciting experiment of the new millennium, exploring the history and projects of the Bolivarian Revolution through interviews with a range of its participants, from academics to farm workers and those living in the margins of Caracas. This introduction to the "revolución bonita" ("pretty revolution") offers in-depth interviews, unforgettable images and a lively soundtrack that will open new vistas onto this hopeful human project.

As he totes his camera on bus and car trips all over Venezuela, director Clifton Ross becomes our tour guide through the Bolivarian Revolution. He sweeps us through its history and takes us to its works-in-progress on the ground. These schools, rural lending banks and cooperatives weave the fabric of Venezuela's "Socialism of the 21st Century." They show its failures and successes, its warp and woof. Through it all runs the frayed but unbreakable thread of a people in struggle.

Extras Include: *Meeting Chavez* (10 minutes) and *Message to the North American People* (12 minutes).

Featuring: Dr. Steve Ellner, Universidad de Oriente, Puerto La Cruz; José Sant Roz, Universidad Socialista del Pueblo, Mérida; Jutta Schmitt, Universidad de los Andes, Mérida; Christene DeJong, Center for Latin American Studies, University of California, Berkeley; Roger Burbach, Director of the Center for the Study of the Americas, Berkeley, CA.

Venezuela Speaks!
Voices from the Grassroots

Edited by Carlos Martinez, Michael Fox, and JoJo Farrell

ISBN: 978-1-60486-108-2
$22.95   320 pages

For the last decade, Venezuela's "Bolivarian Revolution" has captured international attention. Poverty, inequality, and unemployment have all dropped, while health, education, and living standards have seen a commensurate rise. The international mainstream media has focused predominantly on Venezuela's controversial leader, President Hugo Chavez, who has routinely been in the headlines. But without the active participation of large and diverse sectors of society, Chavez's moment on the scene would have ended long ago.

Venezuela Speaks!: Voices from the Grassroots is a collection of interviews with activists and participants from across Venezuela's social movements. From community media to land reform; cooperatives to communal councils, from the labor movement to the Afro-Venezuelan network, *Venezuela Speaks!* sheds light on the complex realities within the Bolivarian Revolution. These interviews offer a compelling oral history of Venezuela's democratic revolution, from the bottom up.

"Venezuela Speaks! *is a very important book in the growing literature of books on Venezuela's Bolivarian Revolution. Almost all of the books written on this topic so far take a 'top-down' perspective on what is happening in contemporary Venezuela. This book, though, provides an unfiltered participant's perspective on Venezuela's incredibly diverse social movements and, in the process, dispels the notion that President Chavez is the only one who counts when trying to understand Venezuela.*"
— Gregory Wilpert, author of *Changing Venezuela by Taking Power: The History and Policies of the Chávez Government* and editor of Venezuelanalysis.com

"*Michael Fox, Carlos Martinez, and JoJo Farrell cut through the mist that usually surrounds discussions of Venezuela to enter a world of impressive political and cultural diversity.* Venezuela Speaks! *is a geography of struggle, a sociology of passion, and an ethnography of hope, of the unrelenting insistence that people have a right to control their own lives, and that in doing so, a better world will be made.*"
— Greg Grandin, author of *Empire's Workshop: Latin America, the United States, and the Rise of the New Imperialism*

"*The authors of this book are not starry-eyed ideologues; they are experienced activists who have traveled the world observing diverse efforts at ending poverty and injustice. They portray a Venezuela in struggle that we can all learn lessons from in our efforts to save humanity from itself.*"
— Kevin Danaher, cofounder of Global Exchange and Green Festivals

Beyond Elections: Redefining Democracy in the Americas (DVD)

Directed by Sílvia Leindecker
and Michael Fox

UPC: 760137481799
$19.95   Length: 104 minutes

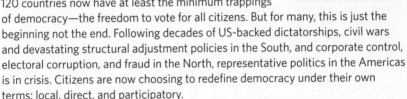

What is democracy? Freedom, equality, participation? Everyone has his or her own definition. Across the world, 120 countries now have at least the minimum trappings of democracy—the freedom to vote for all citizens. But for many, this is just the beginning not the end. Following decades of US-backed dictatorships, civil wars and devastating structural adjustment policies in the South, and corporate control, electoral corruption, and fraud in the North, representative politics in the Americas is in crisis. Citizens are now choosing to redefine democracy under their own terms: local, direct, and participatory.

In 1989, the Brazilian Worker's Party altered the concept of local government when they installed participatory budgeting in Porto Alegre, allowing residents to participate directly in the allocation of city funds. Ten years later, Venezuelan President Hugo Chavez was swept into power with the promise of granting direct participation to the Venezuelan people; who have now formed tens of thousands of self-organized communal councils. In the Southern Cone, cooperative and recuperated factory numbers have grown, and across the Americas social movements and constitutional assemblies are taking authority away from the ruling elites and putting power into the hands of their members and citizens.

Featuring interviews with: Eduardo Galeano, Amy Goodman, Emir Sader, Martha Harnecker, Ward Churchill, and Leonardo Avritzer as well as cooperative and community members, elected representatives, academics, and activists from Brazil, Canada, Venezuela, Argentina, United States, Uruguay, Chile, Colombia, and more. *Beyond Elections* is a journey that takes us across the Americas to attempt to answer one of the most important questions of our time: What is democracy? Extras include video, audio, and resource materials on participatory democracy.

"Beyond Elections proves that democracy can and should be more than casting a ballot every four years. This empowering documentary gives hopeful and concrete examples from around the Americas of people taking back the reins of power and governing their own communities. Beyond Elections is a road map for social change, drawing from communal councils in Venezuela and social movements in Bolivia to participatory budgeting in Brazil and worker cooperatives in Argentina. The film gracefully succeeds in demonstrating that these grassroots examples of people's power can be applied anywhere. Particularly as activists in the US face the challenges of a Obama administration and an economic crisis, this timely documentary shows that the revolution can start today right in your own living room or neighborhood."
— Ben Dangl, author of *The Price of Fire* and editor of the websites Upside Down World and Toward Freedom

Teaching Rebellion: Stories from the Grassroots Mobilization in Oaxaca

Edited by Diana Denham
and the C.A.S.A. Collective

ISBN: 978-1-60486-032-0
$21.99   384 pages

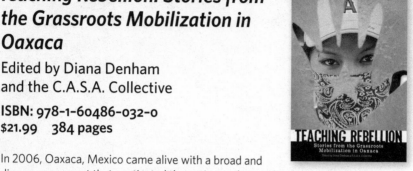

In 2006, Oaxaca, Mexico came alive with a broad and
diverse movement that captivated the nation and earned
the admiration of communities organizing for social justice around the world.
What began as a teachers' strike demanding more resources for education quickly
turned into a massive movement that demanded direct, participatory democracy.
Hundreds of thousands of Oaxacans raised their voices against the abuses of
the state government. They participated in marches of up to 800,000 people,
occupied government buildings, took over radio stations, called for statewide labor
and hunger strikes, held sit-ins, reclaimed spaces for public art and created altars
for assassinated activists in public spaces. Despite the fierce repression that the
movement faced—with hundreds arbitrarily detained, tortured, forced into hiding,
or murdered by the state and federal forces and paramilitary death squads—people
were determined to make their voices heard. Accompanied by photography and
political art, *Teaching Rebellion* is a compilation of testimonies from longtime
organizers, teachers, students, housewives, religious leaders, union members,
schoolchildren, indigenous community activists, artists, journalists, and many
others who participated in what became the Popular Assembly of the Peoples of
Oaxaca. This is a chance to listen directly to those invested in and affected by what
quickly became one of the most important social uprisings of the 21st century.

*"Teaching Rebellion presents an inspiring tapestry of voices from the recent popular
uprisings in Oaxaca. The reader is embraced with the cries of anguish and triumph,
indignation and overwhelming joy, from the heart of this living rebellion."*
— Peter Gelderloos, author of *How Nonviolence Protects the State*

*"These remarkable people tell us of the historic teachers' struggle for justice in Oaxaca,
Mexico, and of the larger, hemispheric battle of all Indigenous people to end five
hundred years of racism and repression."*
— Jennifer Harbury, author of *Truth, Torture, and the American Way*

*" During their marches and protests, whenever the Oaxaca rebels sighted a reporter,
they would chant: 'Press, if you have any dignity, the people of Oaxaca demand
that you tell the truth.' Teaching Rebellion answers that demand, with ample
dignity, providing excellent context to understand the 2006 uprising and extensive
and eloquent interviews with the participants themselves; an amazing read and an
important contribution to the literature of contemporary rebellion."*
— John Gibler, author of *Mexico Unconquered: Chronicles of Power and Revolt*

Diario De Oaxaca: A Sketchbook Journal of Two Years in Mexico

Peter Kuper, with an introduction
by Martín Solares

ISBN: 978-1-60486-071-9
$29.95   208 pages

Painting a vivid, personal portrait of social and political
upheaval in Oaxaca, Mexico, this unique memoir
employs comics, bilingual essays, photos, and sketches
to chronicle the events that unfolded around a teachers' strike and led to a seven-
month siege.

When award-winning cartoonist Peter Kuper and his wife and daughter moved
to the beautiful 16th-century colonial town of Oaxaca in 2006, they planned to
spend a quiet year or two enjoying a different culture and taking a break from the
U.S. political climate under the Bush administration. What they hadn't counted on
was landing in the epicenter of Mexico's biggest political struggle in recent years.
Timely and compelling, this extraordinary firsthand account presents a distinct
artistic vision of Oaxacan life, from explorations of the beauty of the environment
to graphic portrayals of the fight between strikers and government troops that left
more than 20 people dead, including American journalist Brad Will.

*"Kuper is a colossus; I have been in awe of him for over 20 years. Teachers and students
everywhere take heart: Kuper has in these pages born witness to our seemingly endless
struggle to educate and to be educated in the face of institutions that really don't give
a damn. In this ruined age we need Kuper's unsparing compassionate visionary artistry
like we need hope."*
— Junot Díaz, Pulitzer Prize winning author of *The Brief Wondrous Life of Oscar Wao*

*"Peter Kuper is undoubtedly the modern master whose work has refined the socially
relevant comic to the highest point yet achieved."*
— *Newsarama*

"An artist at the top of his form."
— *Publisher's Weekly*

*"Oaxaca Diary reveals to us how so many aspects of a city can be combined on the
same page by an adept artist; poetry, magic, beauty, mystery, fear, as well as the
different faces that protest can assume when politicians hold a city hostage… "*
— Martín Solares from his introduction

Maria's Story: A Documentary Portrait of Love and Survival in El Salvador's Civil War (DVD)

Directed by Monona Wali and
Pamela Cohen

ISBN: 978-1-60486-322-2
$19.95   Length: 60 minutes

It is El Salvador, 1989, three years before the end of a brutal civil war that took 75,000 lives. Maria Serrano, wife, mother, and guerrilla leader is on the frontlines of the battle for her people and her country. With unprecedented access to FMLN guerrilla camps, the filmmakers dramatically chronicle Maria's daily life in the war as she travels from village to village organizing the peasant population, and helps plan a major nationwide offensive that led the FMLN into the historic peace pact of 1992. Skirting bullets and mortar attacks, recounting a childhood of poverty and abuse by government troops, suffering the tragic loss of her daughter to enemy fire, and spending precious moments with her husband and surviving daughters, Maria brings viewers to the heart of the fight for a more just society.

This critically acclaimed and award-winning film first aired on the PBS Documentary Series, *P.O.V.* in 1991. Revolutionary in its making, *Maria's Story* broke ground as one of the first documentaries to use small format video. Traveling with only backpacks and solar powered batteries and living on the run with the guerrillas for two months, the filmmakers were able to capture otherwise unattainable footage. The resulting intimate portrait of Maria and her compatriots reveals a universal tale of love and survival in times of war.

Celebrating its 20th anniversary, the film is available for the first time on DVD. Included is an update of Maria Serrano and her family twenty years after the end of the civil war.

DVD contains both English and Spanish versions

"Documentary at its most illuminating and succinct"
— Los Angeles Times

"As the camera jiggles and the bullets fly one comes as close to combat as one will ever get in the movie theater."
— San Francisco Examiner

"An emotionally powerful film which communicates from the heart."
— San Francisco Bay Times

Capital and Its Discontents: Conversations with Radical Thinkers in a Time of Tumult

Sasha Lilley

ISBN: 978-1-60486-334-5
$20.00   320 pages

Capitalism is stumbling, empire is faltering, and the
planet is thawing. Yet many people are still grasping
to understand these multiple crises and to find a way
forward to a just future. Into the breach come the essential insights of *Capital
and Its Discontents*, which cut through the gristle to get to the heart of the matter
about the nature of capitalism and imperialism, capitalism's vulnerabilities at
this conjuncture—and what can we do to hasten its demise. Through a series
of incisive conversations with some of the most eminent thinkers and political
economists on the Left—including David Harvey, Ellen Meiksins Wood, Mike Davis,
Leo Panitch, Tariq Ali, and Noam Chomsky—*Capital and Its Discontents* illuminates
the dynamic contradictions undergirding capitalism and the potential for its
dethroning. At a moment when capitalism as a system is more reviled than ever,
here is an indispensable toolbox of ideas for action by some of the most brilliant
thinkers of our times.

"*These conversations illuminate the current world situation in ways that are very useful
for those hoping to orient themselves and find a way forward to effective individual and
collective action. Highly recommended.*"
— Kim Stanley Robinson, *New York Times* bestselling author of the *Mars Trilogy* and
The Years of Rice and Salt

"*In this fine set of interviews, an A-list of radical political economists demonstrate
why their skills are indispensable to understanding today's multiple economic and
ecological crises.*"
— Raj Patel, author of *Stuffed and Starved* and *The Value of Nothing*

"*This is an extremely important book. It is the most detailed, comprehensive, and best
study yet published on the most recent capitalist crisis and its discontents. Sasha Lilley
sets each interview in its context, writing with style, scholarship, and wit about ideas and
philosophies.*"
— Andrej Grubačić, radical sociologist and social critic, co-author of *Wobblies and
Zapatistas*

Moments of Excess: Movements, Protest and Everyday Life

The Free Association

ISBN: 978-1-60486-113-6

$14.95   144 pages

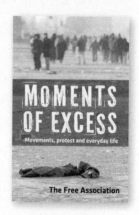

The first decade of the twenty-first century was marked by a series of global summits which seemed to assume ever-greater importance—from the WTO ministerial meeting in Seattle at the end of 1999, through the G8 summits at Genoa, Evian and Gleneagles, up to the United Nations Climate Change Conference (COP15) at Copenhagen in 2009. But these global summits did not pass uncontested. Alongside and against them, there unfolded a different version of globalization. *Moments of Excess* is a collection of texts which offer an insider analysis of this cycle of counter-summit mobilisations. It weaves lucid descriptions of the intensity of collective action into a more sober reflection on the developing problematics of the 'movement of movements'. The collection examines essential questions concerning the character of anti-capitalist movements, and the very meaning of movement; the relationship between intensive collective experiences—'moments of excess'—and 'everyday life'; and the tensions between open, all-inclusive, 'constitutive' practices, on the one hand, and the necessity of closure, limits and antagonism, on the other. *Moments of Excess* includes a new introduction explaining the origin of the texts and their relation to event-based politics, and a postscript which explores new possibilities for anti-capitalist movements in the midst of crisis.

"More than a book, Moments of Excess *is a tool for 'worlding' . . . it speaks to questions that are crucial in creating a better world, all the while asking and opening more questions . . . Reading this book, I felt like a part of a conversation, a conversation that I didn't want to end."*
— Marina Sitrin, editor of *Horizontalism: Voices of Popular Power in Argentina* and (with Clifton Ross) *Insurgent Democracies: Latin America's New Powers*

"Reading this collection you are reminded that there is so much life at the front-line, and that there is no alternative to capitalism without living this life to the full. The message is clear: enjoy the struggle, participate in it with your creative energies, be flexible and self-critical of your approach, throw away static ideologies, and reach out to the other."
— Massimo De Angelis, author of *The Beginning of History: Value Struggles and Global Capital* and editor of *The Commoner*

"Wonderful. Fabulous. The Free Association's work have been writing some of the most stimulating reflections on the constantly shifting movement against capitalism—always fresh, always engaging, always pushing us beyond where we were . . . exciting stuff."
— John Holloway, author of *Change the World Without Taking Power* and *Crack Capitalism*

Portugal: The Impossible Revolution?

Phil Mailer, with an afterword
by Maurice Brinton

ISBN: 978-1-60486-336-9
$24.95   288 pages

After the military coup in Portugal on April 25, 1974,
the overthrow of almost fifty years of Fascist rule, and
the end of three colonial wars, there followed eighteen
months of intense, democratic social transformation
which challenged every aspect of Portuguese society. What started as a military
coup turned into a profound attempt at social change from the bottom up and
became headlines on a daily basis in the world media. This was due to the intensity
of the struggle as well as the fact that in 1974-75 the moribund, right-wing
Francoist regime was still in power in neighboring Spain and there was huge
uncertainty as to how these struggles might affect Spain and Europe at large.

This is the story of what happened in Portugal between April 25, 1974, and
November 25, 1975, as seen and felt by a deeply committed participant. It
depicts the hopes, the tremendous enthusiasm, the boundless energy, the total
commitment, the released power, even the revolutionary innocence of thousands
of ordinary people taking a hand in the remolding of their lives. And it does so
against the background of an economic and social reality which placed limits on
what could be done.

*"An evocative, bitterly partisan diary of the Portuguese revolution, written from a
radical-utopian perspective. The enemy is any type of organization or presumption of
leadership. The book affords a good view of the mood of the time, of the multiplicity of
leftist factions, and of the social problems that bedeviled the revolution."*
— Fritz Stern, *Foreign Affairs*

*"Mailer portrays history with the enthusiasm of a cheerleader, the 'home team' in
this case being libertarian communism. Official documents, position papers and
the pronouncements of the protagonists of this drama are mostly relegated to the
appendices. The text itself recounts the activities of a host of worker, tenant, soldier
and student committees as well as the author's personal experiences."*
— Ian Wallace, *Library Journal*

*"A thorough delight as it moves from first person accounts of street demonstrations
through intricate analyses of political movements. Mailer has handled masterfully the
enormous cast of politicians, officers of the military peasant and workers councils, and
a myriad of splinter parties, movements and caucuses."*
— *Choice*

Wobblies and Zapatistas: Conversations on Anarchism, Marxism and Radical History

Staughton Lynd and Andrej Grubačić

ISBN: 978-1-60486-041-2
$20.00   300 pages

Wobblies and Zapatistas offers the reader an encounter between two generations and two traditions. Andrej Grubačić is an anarchist from the Balkans. Staughton Lynd is a lifelong pacifist, influenced by Marxism. They meet in dialogue in an effort to bring together the anarchist and Marxist traditions, to discuss the writing of history by those who make it, and to remind us of the idea that "my country is the world." Encompassing a Left libertarian perspective and an emphatically activist standpoint, these conversations are meant to be read in the clubs and affinity groups of the new Movement.

The authors accompany us on a journey through modern revolutions, direct actions, anti-globalist counter summits, Freedom Schools, Zapatista cooperatives, Haymarket and Petrograd, Hanoi and Belgrade, 'intentional' communities, wildcat strikes, early Protestant communities, Native American democratic practices, the Workers' Solidarity Club of Youngstown, occupied factories, self-organized councils and soviets, the lives of forgotten revolutionaries, Quaker meetings, antiwar movements, and prison rebellions. Neglected and forgotten moments of interracial self-activity are brought to light. The book invites the attention of readers who believe that a better world, on the other side of capitalism and state bureaucracy, may indeed be possible.

"There's no doubt that we've lost much of our history. It's also very clear that those in power in this country like it that way. Here's a book that shows us why. It demonstrates not only that another world is possible, but that it already exists, has existed, and shows an endless potential to burst through the artificial walls and divisions that currently imprison us. An exquisite contribution to the literature of human freedom, and coming not a moment too soon."
— David Graeber, author of *Fragments of an Anarchist Anthropology* and *Direct Action: An Ethnography*

"I have been in regular contact with Andrej Grubačić for many years, and have been most impressed by his searching intelligence, broad knowledge, lucid judgment, and penetrating commentary on contemporary affairs and their historical roots. He is an original thinker and dedicated activist, who brings deep understanding and outstanding personal qualities to everything he does."
— Noam Chomsky